**Association for
Computing Machinery**

Advancing Computing as a Science & Profession

ANCS'14

The Tenth 2014 ACM/IEEE Symposium on
Architectures for Networking
and Communications Systems

Sponsored by:

ACM SIGARCH, ACM SIGCOMM and IEEE Computer Society

Association for
Computing Machinery

Advancing Computing as a Science & Profession

The Association for Computing Machinery
2 Penn Plaza, Suite 701
New York, New York 10121-0701

ISBN: 978-1-4503-2839-5 (Digital)

ISBN: 978-1-4503-3381-8 (Print)

Additional copies may be ordered prepaid from:

ACM Order Department
PO Box 30777
New York, NY 10087-0777, USA

Phone: 1-800-342-6626 (USA and Canada)
+1-212-626-0500 (Global)
Fax: +1-212-944-1318
E-mail: acmhelp@acm.org
Hours of Operation: 8:30 am – 4:30 pm ET

Printed in the USA

Message from General Chair

It is my pleasure to welcome you to the Tenth ACM/IEEE Symposium on Architectures for Networking and Communications Systems (ANCS 2014).

First of all, I would like to thank Bill Lin, steering chair of ANCS, for inviting me to be the General Chair. He has offered me guidance in continuing this meeting series, often sharing best practices from the previous events. Indeed, it has been a pleasure working with him.

I want to thank many volunteers who have worked over the past year to organize the meeting. Gordon Brebner and Isaac Keslassy, our Program Co-Chairs, have done an outstanding job in putting together an excellent technical program. I am indebted to them for their technical leadership in organizing this meeting.

I would like to thank Young Cho for handling the local arrangements, Weirong Jiang for interfacing with ACM and IEEE and handling the budget, Yi-Hua Edward Yang for overseeing the publicity, and Hoang Le for producing these proceedings. My student Yun (Rock) Qu maintained the website. Danai Chasaki administered the student travel awards. Won So handled the posters.

Farrah Khan at ACM offered me assistance in obtaining approvals and provided logistical support.

I would like to thank all our volunteers for their tireless efforts. The meeting would not be possible without the enthusiastic effort and commitment of these individuals.

I hope you enjoy the meeting and the touristic sites around the Marina.

Viktor K. Prasanna
University of Southern California
General Chair

Message from the Program Co-Chairs

Welcome to the Tenth ACM/IEEE Symposium on Architectures for Networking and Communications Systems (ANCS 2014). It is our pleasure to present an excellent conference program for the meeting, consisting of 19 technical papers. The papers cover a wide range of networking disciplines, including software defined networking, data center networking, low-energy networking, and packet processing. There is also a poster session including 15 posters. Last, but not least, we are very pleased to include two keynote addresses on hot networking topics.

Each submitted paper was assigned to at least five reviewers, selected from the 42 members of the Technical Program Committee (TPC). The program committee members subsequently participated in an active teleconference to select the final set of papers to be accepted to the conference. A tremendous amount of dedicated hard work was done by the TPC, and we are most fortunate to have had an outstanding team that helped to run the technical program selection process in a professional, responsive, and friendly, manner. We thank the TPC members greatly.

These are exciting times for networking research. We are delighted to bring you groundbreaking research that explores the relationship between the algorithms and architectures of networks and the hardware and software elements from which these networks are built. We hope that you enjoy the exciting technical program.

Gordon Brebner and Isaac Keslassy
ANCS 2014 Program Co-Chairs

Table of Contents

Poster Session 2

2014 ACM/IEEE Symposium on Architectures for Networking and Communications Systems Organization

General Chair : Viktor K. Prasanna *(University of Southern California, USA)*

Program Chairs : Gordon Brebner *(Xilinx, USA)*
Isaac Keslassy *(Technion, Israel)*

Poster Chair : Won So *(NetApp, USA)*

Proceedings Chair : Hoang Le *(Sandia National Laboratories, USA)*

Local Arrangements Chair : Young Cho *(USC/ISI, USA)*

Publicity Chair : Yi-Hua Edward Yang *(Xilinx, USA)*

Finance Chair : Weirong Jiang *(Xilinx, USA)*

Student Travel Grant Chair : Danai Chasaki *(Villanova University, USA)*

Web Chair : Yun Rock Qu *(University of Southern California, USA)*

Steering Chair : Bill Lin *(University of California, San Diego, USA)*

Steering Committee : H. Jonathan Chao *(Polytechnic Institute of New York University, USA)*
Patrick Crowley *(Washington University in St. Louis, USA)*
Bill Lin *(University of California, San Diego, USA)*
Andrew W. Moore *(University of Cambridge, UK)*
Walid Najjar *(University of California, Riverside, USA)*
Viktor Prasanna *(University of Southern California, USA)*
Scott Rixner *(Rice University, USA)*
Tilman Wolf *(University of Massachusetts Amherst, USA)*

Program Committee: Yehuda Afek *(Tel-Aviv University, Israel)*
Mohammad Alizadeh *(Cisco, USA)*
Alex Bachmutsky *(Ericsson, USA)*
Theophilus Benson *(Duke University, USA)*
Greg Byrd *(North Carolina State University, USA)*
Danai Chasaki *(Villanova University, USA)*
Nikolaos Chrysos *(IBM Research, Switzerland)*
Paolo Costa *(Microsoft Research, UK)*
Chita Das *(Penn State University, USA)*
Colin Dixon *(IBM Research, USA)*
Qunfeng Dong *(Huawei, China)*
Ilija Hadzic *(Bell Labs, Alcatel Lucent, USA)*

Poster Selection Committee :   Won So *(NetApp, USA)*
Yukuen Lai *(Chung-Yuan Christian University, Taiwan)*
Haowei Yuan *(Washington University in St. Louis, USA)*
Taejoong Chung *(Seoul National University, Korea)*
Christopher Fletcher *(Massachusetts Institute of Technology, USA)*

ANCS 2014 Sponsors

The ACM/IEEE Symposium on Architectures for Networking and Communications Systems (ANCS 2014) is sponsored by the ACM Special Interest Group on Computer Architecture (SIGARCH), the ACM Special Interest Group on Communications (SIGCOMM), and IEEE Computer Society Technical Committee on Computer Architecture (TCCA).

Sponsors:

Future Networking: Reconfiguration Heartland, Challenge and Revolution

Andrew Moore
University of Cambridge
andrew.moore@cl.cam.ac.uk

ABSTRACT

In the context of network systems I will discuss the limits of reconfigurable systems. To this end, I will draw on examples from architectural trends, the silicon roadmap in a post Moore's law era, along with recent directions in future networking. I will then set out to map the current and future edges of reconfigurable systems in networking.

In this talk I will discuss the state and future of SDN, showing how reconfiguration is an essential function of all networks. The role of reconfiguration has evolved from a prototyping technology to incorporate control technologies, and beyond this to hybrid host systems, adaptive interface design and use in the control of future network-transmission systems.

As network reconfiguration must, by necessity, match the needs of both user and implementer, the emergence of SDN has, for reconfigurable systems, led to a new class of domain specific languages, a renewed interest in functional languages, and an ever-wider user base.

I conclude with a discussion of current systems and ideas as future predictors for technologies beyond 100Gb/s. In particular I will talk to the opportunities enabled by tighter photonic integration. This is alongside a forecast of how technologies, limitations, and usage will impacts the future of networking reconfiguration.

Categories and Subject Descriptors

Primary: C.5.0 General
Secondary: C.2.1 Network Architecture and Design

Keywords

Interconnect; reconfigurable systems; FPGA; Optical-integration; SDN

Bio

Andrew W. Moore is a Senior Lecturer at the University of Cambridge Computer Laboratory in England, where he is part of the Systems Research Group working on issues of network and computer architecture. His research interests include enabling open-network research and education using theNetFPGA platform, other research pursuits include software-hardware co-design, low-power energy-aware networking, and novel network and systems data-center architectures. Andrew jointly leads theNetFPGA project providing an Open-Source reconfigurable hardware/software platform for networking research and teaching, he has been principal investigator on research grants from the EPSRC (part of the UK research council), DARPA, and NSF as well as collaborations with industry partners Cisco, Xilinx, Netronome, and Solarflare. Andrew is a member of the IEEE, ACM, USENIX and a Chartered Engineer by the IET (formerly the IEE).

ANCS'14, October 20–21, 2014, Los Angeles, CA, USA.
ACM 978-1-4503-2839-5/14/10.
http://dx.doi.org/10.1145/2658260.2661779

Programmable Measurement Architecture

Minlan Yu
University of Southern California
minlanyu@usc.edu

ABSTRACT

Measurement is at least half of network management. Many data centers require huge capital investments to build larger networks with higher link speeds; yet provide surprisingly little visibility into the network and traffic. Switch vendors often treat measurement as a second-class citizen, devoting most resources to control functions. Operators have limited control over what (not) to measure, and thus have to integrate incomplete measurement data from individual devices. Inspired by software-defined networking, we propose to design and build a new programmable measurement architecture that bridges the gap between operator's measurement requirements and device capabilities. We allow operators to flexibly program queries about the network state they need, provide generic and efficient primitives at many devices (hosts, switches, and reconfigurable devices), and automatically match the queries with the primitives. Our solutions have gained significant interests from both production data center operators and programmable switch vendors.

Categories and Subject Descriptors

C.2.1 [Network Architecture and Design]; C.2.3 [Network Operations]

Keywords

Software-defined networking; network management; programmable measurement architecture

Bio

Minlan Yu is an assistant professor in the computer science department of University of Southern California. She received her B.A. in computer science and mathematics from Peking University in 2006 and her M.A. and Ph.D in computer science from Princeton University in 2008 and 2011. After that she was a postdoctoral scholar in UC Berkeley for one year. She has actively collaborated with companies such as Google, AT&T, Microsoft, and Bell Labs. Her research interest includes data networking, distributed systems, enterprise and data center networks, network virtualization, and software-defined networking. She received ACM SIGCOMM doctoral dissertation award in 2012 and Google research award in 2013

ANCS'14, October 20–21, 2014, Los Angeles, CA, USA.
ACM 978-1-4503-2839-5/14/10.
http://dx.doi.org/10.1145/2658260.2661778

WASP: A Software-Defined Communication Layer for Hybrid Wireless Networks

Murad Kaplan, Chenyu Zheng, Matthew Monaco, Eric Keller, and Douglas Sicker
Dept. of Computer Science, University of Colorado
Boulder, Colorado, USA
murad.kaplan@colorado.edu, chenyu.zheng@colorado.edu,
matthew.monaco@colorado.edu, eric.keller@colorado.edu,
douglas.sicker@colorado.edu

ABSTRACT

In this paper we introduce WASP, a general communication layer for hybrid wireless networks where multiple networks are used to complement each other. In our system, we capitalize on an infrastructure with a ubiquitous, wide-area network to help enable the creation of a local mobile ad-hoc network in an efficient, scalable, evolvable, and manageable way. In particular, in an architecture inspired by software-defined networking, we decouple the control plane and data plane in the mobile devices and shift the control plane to a centralized controller. The controller, reachable via the wide-area network, manages a collection of mobile devices by informing each device how to handle traffic based on neighbor information provided by the mobile devices. With this, a mobile ad-hoc network can help reduce the data burden on the ubiquitous network, and the ubiquitous network can help reduce the burden on the mobile devices. WASP can be used in different networks with different applications such as cellular and military networks. In this paper, we based our implementation on Android and tested on a collection of Google Nexus-4 devices to measure metrics such as battery consumption. We evaluate on an extended ns-3 simulation platform which we added the ability to run unmodified Android applications on the nodes within ns-3. Our experiments show that WASP scales better than traditional ad-hoc networks with only a minimal trade off of energy. Additionally, we show that a content distribution scheme using WASP on smartphones with cellular data plans significantly offloads bandwidth from the cellular infrastructure, and in turn reduces expensive data usage and energy usage.

Categories and Subject Descriptors

C.2.1 [**Network Architecture and Design**]: subject—
centralized networks, wireless networking

Keywords

ad hoc networking; wireless networking; software-defined networking

1. INTRODUCTION

Mobile ad-hoc networks (MANETs) are traditionally designed for environments with no pre-existing infrastructure. The need to self-organize leads to the need to exchange and process a high volume of control messages to manage its communication network and recover from changes in the network, such as through mobility. This leads to overwhelming the wireless channels which, in turn, causes packet loss. It also puts an extra overhead on mobile devices to process and forward these control packets. With these challenges, MANETs become unscalable and suffer high packet loss and error rates as the number of nodes increases.

In this paper, we explore a scenario where ubiquitous network connection exists but is expensive to use. We note that many of today's mobile devices routinely equipped with multiple interfaces. Examples of such hybrid networks can be seen in cellular infrastructures where smartphones have multiple interfaces (*e.g.*, Wi-Fi, Bluetooth, 3G/4G), and military setting where satellite or a unmanned aerial vehicle(UAV) provides ubiquitous network connection to soldiers' mobile devices that also are equipped with UHF/VHF radios. We take advantage of the existence of a long-range, ubiquitous wireless interface to offload network control and management from the wireless nodes to a centralized, general purpose server.

With this, a mobile ad-hoc network can help reduce the burden on the ubiquitous network (*e.g.*, by reducing the data downloaded through it), and the ubiquitous network can help enable the creation of a local mobile ad-hoc network (*e.g.*, by removing the burden of running complex routing protocols from the mobile devices).

We present the design, implementation, and evaluation of WASP [1], a communication layer within a mobile device for hybrid networks. In contrast to mobile ad-hoc networks, with WASP, the devices themselves do not run any routing protocols. Instead, we are guided by software-defined networking (SDN) [,]. By capitalizing on a 'one-hop' connection to a centralized controller, we transfer the duty of network management calculations from battery constrained

---

[1]WASP is named for the technologies our prototype encompasses (Wi-Fi, Ad-Hoc, Software-Defined Networking, and Personal-Mobile)

devices to a powerful server (or elastic collection of servers). When topology changes occur, we do not need to flood the network with information and wait for convergence as in a distributed protocol (such as OLSR [ ]). At the same time, we do not have to revert to such approaches as being exclusively reactive (as in AODV [ ]) where, to be more scalable, paths are calculated when two nodes attempt to communicate. Importantly, as we will show, this shift does not introduce a lot of control overhead on the expensive wide-area radio interface – our solution uses an on-demand network control protocol which is very efficient.

It is important to highlight that WASP is a general purpose communication layer for hybrid networks, not a special purpose architecture. In this paper, we evaluate with a hybrid cellular/Wi-Fi network, but can envision this easily extending to a military setting where satellite or a unmanned aerial vehicle (UAV) provides the ubiquitous, expensive coverage and another radio technology provides the local connectivity. Further, we are not limited in scope of application. To demonstrate this, layered on top of the communication layer, we provides services for aiding applications with different content distribution requirements. For example, the *web content service* uses peer-to-peer content serving of cached content similar to Firecoral [ ], but as a general service not tied to the browser. In this case, the controller also acts as a look up mechanism to track which mobile devices are caching content, make suggestions as to which device to request the content from, and enable direct communication to fetch that content.

In this paper, we make the following contributions:

- *Design* of the WASP communication layer which provides a lightweight control protocol between a central server and mobile devices, efficiently forwards traffic, and reacts quickly to failure or mobility.

- *Implementation* of WASP and associated layered services on Android, and tested in a small collection of five Google Nexus S phones.

- *Evaluation* of WASP where we demonstrate that (i) the amount of control traffic per node remains relatively small and constant with an increasing number of nodes in the network, whereas ad-hoc protocols grow exponentially and quickly become unusable, (ii) in streaming data among 100 nodes, WASP delivers up to 95% of the packets while OLSR and AODV barely deliver 10%, and (iii) a content distribution scheme using WASP significantly reduces load on the cellular infrastructure.

- *Extension to ns-3* which provides the ability to efficiently run Android application unmodified within ns-3. This capability allows us to test WASP within the context of large networks while still being able to measure the impact on a real Android device, and use the same code base for each.

2. RELATED WORK

Industrial solutions to the cellular load problems have revolved around heterogeneous networks (HetNets), a combination of cellular base stations with large and small cells, and Wi-Fi access points. While this can provide relief, it is an expensive solution and leads to significant management complexity. Others have shown the benefits of offloading from an 'expensive' (in some definition) ubiquitous / wide-area network to a local network which is less 'expensive'. For example, using a cellular radio for transmission not only has the high cost of bandwidth, but is also extremely inefficient in terms of battery usage – *e.g.*, for normal use, LTE is 23 times less power efficient when compared to Wi-Fi, and 3G is 14.6 less power efficient [ ]. This has led to a number of solutions that: (i) use Wi-Fi access points instead of cellular when available [ ], (ii) multi-cast video over Wi-Fi between a small collection of smartphones [ ], or even (iii) tether to a friend's phone to share bandwidth caps [ ]. Generalizing, these 'mobile ad-hoc networks' don't scale as the number of mobile devices is limited (*e.g.*, [ ] can only handle 7-10 mobile devices). Further, to date the resulting systems have placed a great deal of responsibility on the mobile devices themselves and in many cases, limit the generality of the local network. With WASP, we extend the heterogeneous network to any wireless devices and provide a centralized network-wide management. That is, we do not believe that additional access points are a bad thing, we simply do not treat these as special boxes, but as nodes in the system that we can leverage when they are available, each with a different set of costs.

At the other end of the spectrum, Mobile Ad-hoc Networks (MANETs) or mesh networks use routing protocols (e.g., AODV [ ], ROMA [ ], Serval [ ], and Roofnet [ ]) among nodes to determine connectivity. With WASP, we look to gain benefits of MANETs for data traffic, but do so targeting a different environment and with different goals. Rather than designed for environments with no pre-existing infrastructure, in which case the network is to be created ad-hoc, WASP is designed for an environment where there is overall connectivity that we can leverage, but wish to limit its use.

We do this with a centralized management scheme. Algorithms have been developed to centrally determine scheduling transmission slots for each radio [ ], and channel assignment in wireless mesh networks [ ]. With WASP, we designed, built, and evaluated a real hybrid wireless communication system and added a service layer on top of the communication layer. Further, systems such as Meraki's [ ], enable the central management of Wireless access points over the web, but are targeted at fixed nodes. Whereas with WASP, we go further and organize mobile nodes (in addition to fixed nodes, which can also run WASP).

Additionally, with WASP we capitalize on different interfaces, one better suited for management traffic (*e.g.*, 3G/4G cellular) and one better suited for data traffic (*e.g.*, Wi-Fi). This is similar in spirit to the separation of the VoIP wakeup notification over the cellular connection, and the VoIP data transmission over Wi-Fi [ ].

Finally, we apply techniques from software-defined networking [,] with WASP. The idea of using SDN to offload network control functions in heterogeneous networks which also takes advantage of device-to-device communication is fairly new. There have been some papers which propose similar ideas of leveraging SDN for heterogeneous networks [,], but none had a concrete architecture, implementation, or evaluation as we have with WASP. Further, while there has been a port of OpenVSwitch [ ] (which is widely used in software-defined networking) to Android [ ], it was only used to enable an application to switch between,

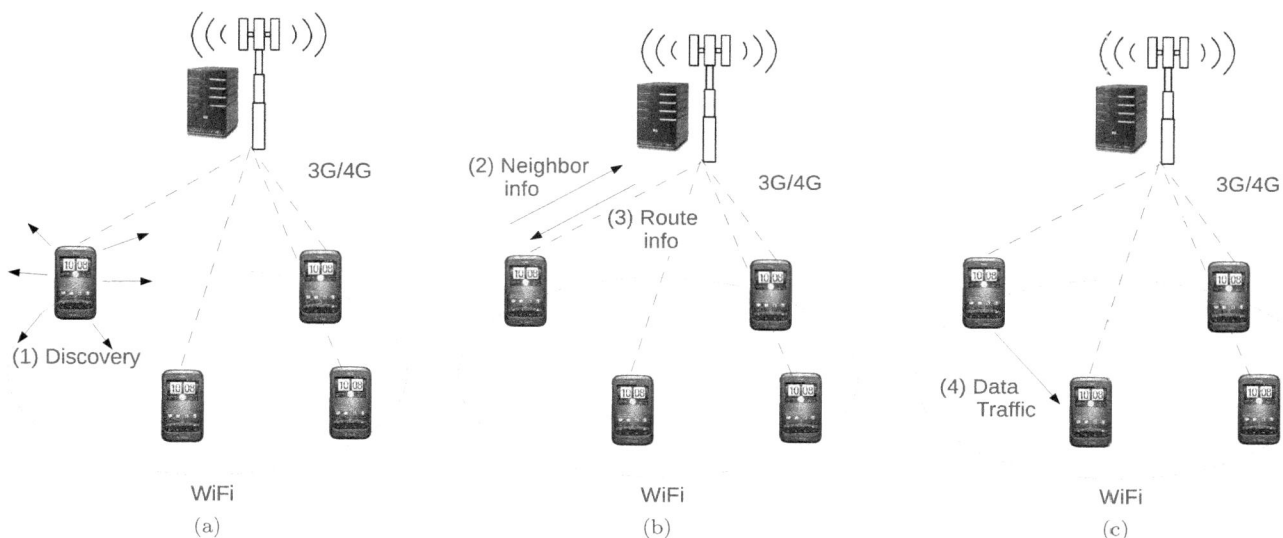

Figure 1: WASP network architecture, showing the controller and mobile devices, and the communication for (a) discovery, (b) control traffic between mobile device and controller, and (c) data traffic between mobile devices.

or use in parallel to maximize bandwidth, multiple interfaces (3G, Wi-Fi). This is more akin to MultiNet [ ] or FatVAP [ ] than WASP, as there is no network wide control.

3. ARCHITECTURE

Applying software-defined networking (SDN) [, ,] concepts to a network of mobile devices allows us to leverage ubiquitous wide-area network connectivity for low-rate management traffic, while leveraging ad-hoc connectivity for data traffic where possible. In doing so, it relieves the mobile devices from having to run the typically expensive routing protocols and enables more complex management toward network-wide optimization. As illustrated in Figure 1, WASP consists of a central controller, mobile devices, and a communication protocol among them.

Our architecture might look similar to existing SDN protocol architectures (e.g., OpenFlow [ ]), however these protocols were built to primarily target wired networks such as datacenters. As presented in this paper, OpenFlow would probably be sufficient, but we believe going forward, our design will begin to deviate from OpenFlow (e.g., adding support for channels).

3.1 Controller

A distinguishing aspect of WASP is the use of a centralized controller. Rather than intelligence in the nodes themselves, we push functionality into a centralized server as much as possible. The controller can technically reside and be accessed by any means. For example, with the current architecture, WASP relies on a direct connection (via 3G/4G) between a node and the controller. This matches our targeted operation environment where an existing cellular infrastructure has good coverage, but usage needs to be reduced.

Figure 2 shows the main components of WASP controller. The essential goal of the controller is to have a network wide view. This is accomplished by communicating and collecting

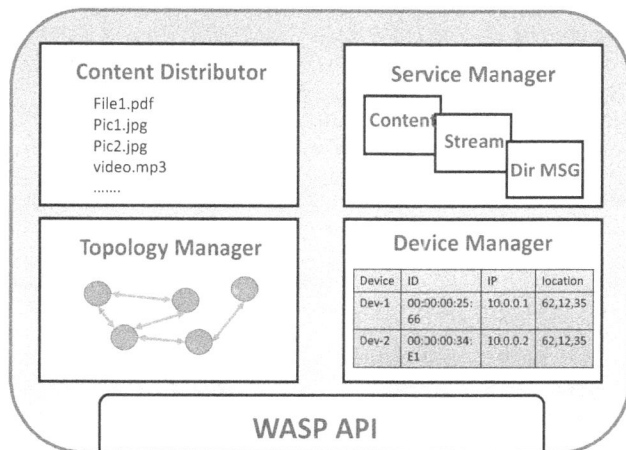

Figure 2: Overview of WASP controller's components.

information from each node through **WASP-API** . This information is managed by **Device Manager** and includes a node's ID, neighbors, data to share, available Internet connections, and any other information we can easily add in the future (e.g., location, battery). The controller uses this information to calculate the routes among nodes, through **Topology Manager** , and sends the routing tables back to the nodes to indicate what the next hop is for each destination. Importantly, with this architecture, the controller can evolve to calculate routes differently without requiring software updates to each mobile device. We can continuously add more complexity into the algorithms within the controller, and if, for example, we find a more optimal assignment of paths, we can notify the mobile devices of the change. The controller can also be used as a **Content Distributor** between the Internet and the mobile devices. As we will see in the evaluation in Section 6, if one of the nodes

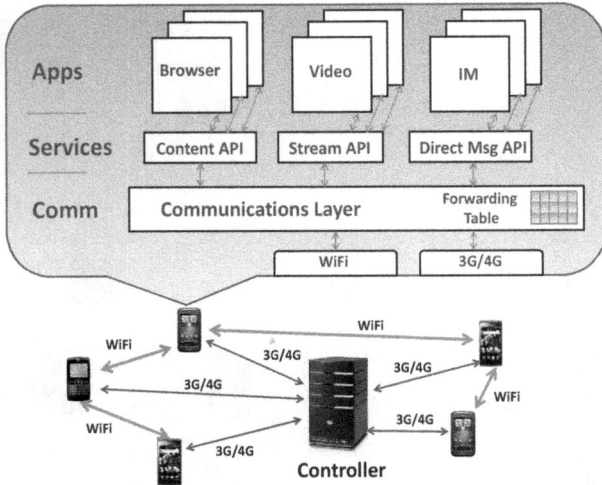

Figure 3: Overview of WASP device architecture.

Table 1: WASP Control Messages

Type (from-to)	Name	Description
Node-Controller	Node-ID	Node sends its ID to request an IP address in first time registration or reconnecting
Node-Controller	Neighbor-Update	Sent when node's neighbor table is updated
Node-Controller	Find-Data	Sent when node requests data and needs to know if any other node in the network has it (*e.g.,* file)
Node-Controller	Keep-Alive	Sent periodically (default 5sec) unless node is sending any of the previous messages
Controller-Node	Assigned-IP	Reply with IP address to Node-ID message
Controller-Node	Routing-Table	Sent to nodes that are affected by any change in network topology
Controller-Node	Data-Node	Node-ID that host the requested data in Find-Data message, or Data itself if no node hosts the data requested
Node-Node	Hello	Sent periodically (default 1sec) unless node is sending or forwarding data packets

in WASP's network requests data (*e.g.,* picture, video) and this data is not cached by other nodes in the network, the WASP controller can provide the requested data directly to the node. Another feature of WASP is that controller can manage and add more services, through **Service Manager** , and easily push them to all nodes in the network. We discuss WASP's service in more details in Section 4.

We assume that all nodes in the WASP network are registered in the controller with some unique identity. In our current implementation we use nodes' MAC addresses and can easily change it in the future for any better identification method. This helps the controller to assign unique IP addresses to the nodes and manage sub-nets to create node clusters in the network if needed. The controller keeps track of the nodes through the neighbor list messages and keep-alive messages sent from each node. If a node does not contact the controller in a specified (configurable) amount of time, and it is not reported to be a neighbor of another node, the controller will assume that this node is unreachable and delete it from network, recalculate the route, and send the updates to the other reachable nodes.

3.2 Nodes

In WASP, we take advantage of nodes equipped with multiple interfaces. We use the interface connected to the ubiquitous network to send information to the controller such as the node's ID, neighbor updates, and keep-alive messages. In return, the same interface is used to receive information from the controller, such as IP assigned and routing tables. The other interface is used for local communications among the nodes to send and receive periodic Hello messages. It is also used to send, receive, and forward data packets.

As we can see in Figure 3, at the lowest layer, the WASP communication layer provides low-level functions such as sending a message to a given node, receiving a message from another node, sending a message or query to the controller, and receiving a message from the controller. The WASP communication layer then uses the underlying socket interface to communicate with controller and each next-hop neighbor.

The WASP services are additional packages that use interfaces provided by the communication layer. Each WASP service provides an inter-process communication API, which allows bound mobile device applications to utilize its functionality. APIs are specific to services, such as: *get_content(URI)* for the web content service. Multiple applications can bind to one or more WASP service simultaneously. One example service is the web content distribution service which allows web interfaces (*e.g.,* a browser) to exchange content within the WASP mobile-to-mobile network. We discuss WASP services in more details in Section 4.

Each node in the WASP network maintains two tables. The first one is the neighbor list table. The table contains neighbor's ID and IP(assigned by the controller) and its time stamp. Every time the node receives a hello message from another node, it updates the table by either adding the neighbor, if it not existed already, or refreshing the neighbor's time-stamp. If a timer of one of the neighbors timeouts, the node deletes the neighbor from its list. In case of adding or deleting neighbor, the node updates the controller with such information. The second table is the forwarding table. It contains next-hop(neighbor ID) and destination ID fields. The forwarding table is updated whenever the controller sends route update to the node. Once the node receives a data packet to be forwarded, it looks at the packet's header and match the destination ID with the corresponding next-hop in the routing table. The node then uses the neighbor list to lookup the next-hop IP and forward the packet to it through the local communication channel.

3.3 Communication

As we mentioned in the previous two subsections, WASP manages the network through two types of control messages. One is between controller and nodes (controller-messages) and the other type is among nodes (hello-messages). Table 1 shows WASP control messages with brief description.

To reduce the number of messages sent from nodes, the node does not need to send keep-alive messages if it has recently sent the controller a neighbor update messages. Once the controller receives any message from the node, it updates its timer and considers the node reachable. At the same time, after the controller calculates the routes, rather than sending the entire routing table of the network to all nodes, it only sends routing table updates (diffs) to the nodes affected by the topology change. This approach considerably reduces the number and the size of messages sent by the controller.

4. LAYERED SERVICES

The ability to communicate within a network of mobile devices only has benefit if applications can and do use it. As such, with WASP we layer services on top of the communication layer as a mechanism to optimize the specific communication pattern.

In general, we have completed the direct communication and web services, and are in the process of adding a streaming service, and can and will expand as future work. In each case, there are alternate, probably better, implementations, but we do not go into an in-depth exploration here. These are merely meant to demonstrate the possibilities.

4.1 Direct Communication

More and more, mobile devices are already directly communicating between mobile devices. Of course, that was the original functionality of mobile devices before data plans became popular – to make calls to other mobile devices, and then later on to send text messages to other mobile devices. With data traffic, this direct communication has evolved to -include voice, video, or text chat (instant messaging). Further, services such as Samsung AllShare Play [ ], are pushing applications in the direction of mobile device-to-mobile device communication.

Extending an application to use the WASP communication layer is trivial as the communication is direct already. However, we need the application to know whether the other mobile device is within local (multi-hop) range or not, transparent to the user. To do this, a lookup (much like DNS) to the controller, will indicate whether a given user ID is currently in the same network as the inquiring mobile device, and if so, what the node identifier is.

4.2 Web Content

Web content has been shown to follow a Zipf distribution where a relatively few pieces of content are accessed most of the time [ ]. Even more, studies have shown that the popular content is getting even more popular [ ]. This has provided the basis for in-network content caching [ ] and peer-to-peer content distribution networks [ ]. We extend this concept into a mobile device-to-mobile device content distribution network with the WASP Web content service.

With the WASP Web content service, each mobile device maintains a cache of content recently accessed and can act as a server to serve up that content – capitalizing on the caching of popular content to alleviate cellular use and to help with flash crowds (the Slashdot effect). This has been explored with FireCoral [ ], but with WASP the cache is not tied to the web browser. In fact, we would not be surprised if the locality of access in a network of mobile devices is greater than found in a p2p network of computers connected over the Internet. Off course, this needs to be further studied, but our belief is based on the fact that the mobile device network has physical locality, which may introduce a bias of like individuals (*e.g.*, college students on a campus). The logically central controller (or for future exploration, other tracking mechanism) maintains a tracker to track which mobile device has cached which content. This means that the mobile devices should (and eventually must) notify the central controller of any changes to the cache.

The general flow of an access is an application uses the WASP content service (running on the same mobile device) to request a URI. The WASP content service contacts the central tracking server to find which mobile devices have cached that URI, the server responds with a list of mobile devices that are within some hop-count radius, the requesting mobile device's WASP content service then requests the URI from one of the mobile devices in the list, and if that mobile device still has the content (*i.e.*, the tracker was up-to-date), the mobile device will return the content (and if it doesn't have the content, the requesting mobile device will try the next mobile device, and eventually can fall back on the Internet over the cellular connection). At this point, the requesting mobile device caches the content, possibly evicts some other cached item, and notifies the central tracking server.

We acknowledge that there may be some privacy issues in this scheme such as other users knowing what sites a given user is visiting. However, this is not the main focus of this paper and used as an example to illustrate how an underlying mobile-to-mobile network can benefit content distribution.

4.3 Streaming Service

While the WASP streaming service is still in development phase and we leave its evaluation as future work, we discuss it here not to indicate that it is in itself a contribution, but to provide further understanding of the potential of WASP.

The streaming service provides an efficient distribution means for an emerging communication pattern. As smart mobile devices become a more integral part of our lives and as connectivity and processing power of the devices increases, so to will our consumption of streaming media such as live sports. In many cases, multiple mobile devices will be receiving the same stream. With WASP, rather than each mobile device getting the stream over the cellular connection, a single stream can be transferred over cellular and then the mobile devices collectively distribute the stream over the Wi-Fi direct mobile device-to-mobile device network. As an aside, a special case of this is where one of the mobile devices is generating the stream, in which case we can limit the cellular traffic to zero.

An effective mechanism is a multicast tree to distribute the stream. The challenge in this case is fairness – *e.g.*, the node that downloads the stream over the cellular connection is at a disadvantage from a cost and power consumption standpoint. Here, we can leverage the approach taken with SplitStream [ ] which divides the stream into multiple substreams and distribute each with a different multicast tree. In fact, there has been further research which extends this (each of which could be incorporated into WASP as future work) – SV-BCMCS [ ] leverages proximity to the basestation as an additional consideration, and Microcast [ ] capitalizes on the broadcast nature of Wi-Fi.

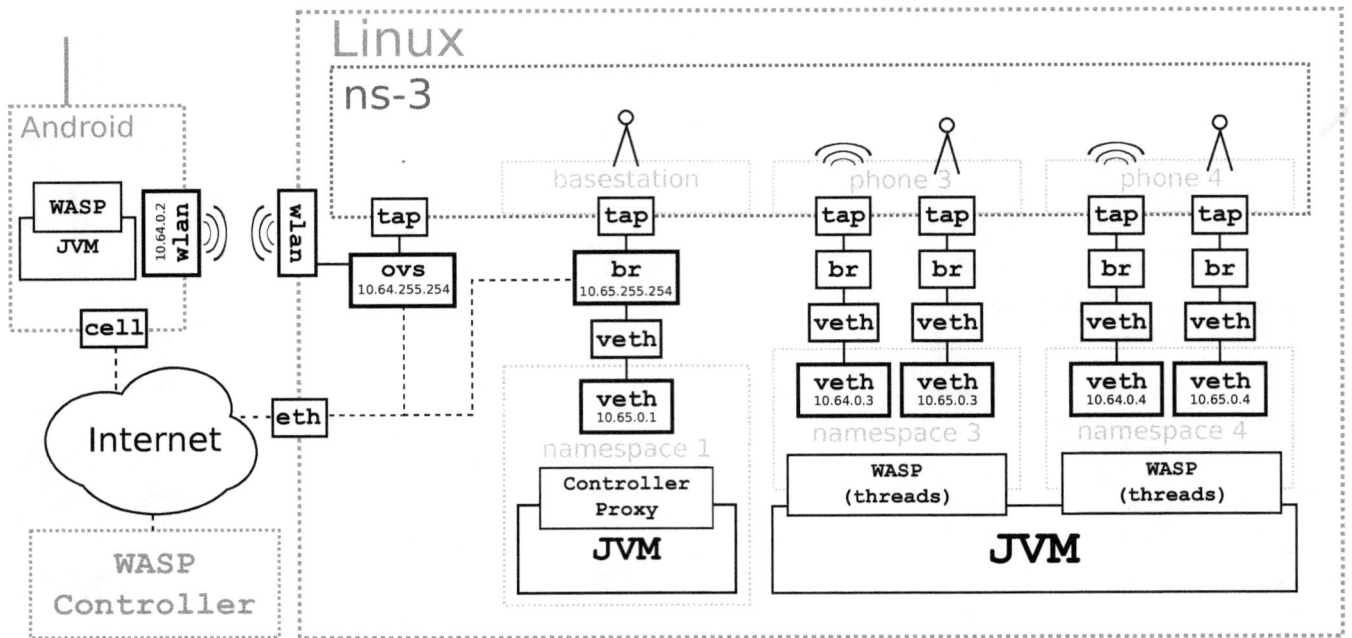

Figure 4: WASP simulation with real Android application and phone-in-the-loop.

5. IMPLEMENTATION

In this paper, we focused on the scenario of hybrid cellular networks to implement WASP. We believe WASP can be implemented on any type of hybrid networks as long as mobile devices equipped with multiple interfaces.

5.1 Controller Implementation

While WASP's architecture is flexible, for the case of a cellular network, we envision the logically centralized controller being run as a service by the cellular company in order to optimize the network (likely coupled with a hot-swappable backup server). However, a 3rd party could also assume this role since we can communicate with any server on the Internet over the cellular connection. The controller resides in the Department of Computer Science at the University of Colorado main campus with a public IP address. The controller is a server machine running Ubuntu OS with Intel-Core-i7X2GHz CPU and 8GB of RAM. We wrote 3000 lines of Java code to implement WASP's Controller prototype. Currently, the controller implementation calculates the all-pairs shortest path – a solution which does not scale well due to the algorithm complexity. We believe better approaches can be used such as clustering the network to smaller groups and manage them individually, or incremental shortest path algorithms.

5.2 Node Implementation

We built an initial prototype of WASP on top of the Android platform. WASP is implemented as a service within Android such that it runs in the background and has higher priority. For communication with the controller, each phone opens a TCP connection (through the 3G/4G interface) with the controller. The connection is used to send and receive messages and can stay in idle mode without disconnecting for up to 30 minutes depending on the cellular company [ ]. Neighbor discovery and data packet forwarding

are performed with the Wi-Fi interface and controlled by the WASP communication layer as well. We verified the operation of WASP and associated test applications on a small collection of five Google Nexus 4 devices.

5.3 Extended ns-3 Testbed

To perform evaluations beyond a small collection of phones we made use of the ns-3 simulation environment [ ]. We implemented an extension to ns-3 which provides the ability to efficiently run Android application unmodified within ns-3. Doing so allows us to test and evaluate WASP on real devices as well as within the context of large networks, while being able to use a consistent code base. This includes the WASP communication layer, WASP service layer, and an application which uses a WASP service. For the application, we are only referring to the logic of the application. The user interface is not intended to run in both ns-3 and on the phone as we do not intend to support graphical interfaces. We implemented the same extension to AODV and OLSR to compare their performance to WASP. We refrained from using the ns-3 implementation of AODV and OLSR for two reasons. First, we wanted the code of WASP in ns-3 to be the same as the Android application, and for the most direct comparison with WASP we leveraged an Android implementation of AODV and OLSR. Second, ns-3's current implementation of AODV has an implementation issue that limits the protocol's scalability and performance (as discussed in various support forums, such as [ ]). With our AODV extension to ns-3, AODV performance is greatly increased. We used the existing open source Java implementation of AODV and OLSR in our testbed and comparison to WASP [,].

Each simulation includes four types of nodes which are shown in Figure 4.

The **basestation** is the LTE access point. It mediates the LTE network and is the Internet gateway. The basestation is not part of the Wi-Fi network.

The **controller** is an application running at an arbitrary location on the Internet. For our testbed this location is a nearby virtual machine, however deployments can place this anywhere from a datacenter to the basestation.

The bulk of the testbed consists of a configurable number of **emulated nodes** with both LTE and Wi-Fi interfaces. To achieve the ability to run unmodified Android applications, each node combines an ns-3 `Node` class with the WASP client running in a Linux network namespace. The network namespaces isolate each network stack. Within each network namespace are the WASP threads representing the different parts of WASP. For efficiency, we run a single JVM for all WASP nodes, but are able to assign a collection of threads representing a single WASP node into its own network namespace. To provide the connectivity between ns-3 and the WASP client code, each interface is implemented as a chain including an ns-3 `NetDevice` class, layer 2 tap device, Linux bridge, and a virtual Ethernet pair.

In extending ns-3, we opened up a new possibility that we are currently working on – **phone-in-the-loop** (shown in the left side of Figure 1). Hardware-in-the-loop has been used extensively in testing of embedded systems. We are replicating this with the ns-3 environment with a *phone-in-the-loop* extension to verify that WASP works on a phone at larger network scales. The phone uses Wi-Fi to connect to the testbed server, but is additionally on the ns-3 emulated Wi-Fi network. The phone-in-the-loop uses our carrier's actual LTE basestation and connects to the controller over the Internet. (Note that in Figure 1 we use Open vSwitch [ ] for bridging because many wireless chipsets are not supported on Linux bridging). With this, the logic for a given node (or set of nodes) within ns-3 is being run across a real wireless channel on a real phone. As it is still early stage, we leave the evaluation and discussion of phone-in-the-loop for future work, but mention it here to provide a view into the possibility of the extended ns-3 platform.

The testbed is configured by two programs. There is an ns-3 `C++` program for creating the Phy and MAC layers of the Wi-Fi and LTE networks. Additionally a shell script creates all of the necessary devices and assigns IP addresses within each namespace (in real life, the controller will be the one assigning IP addresses to the nodes). The script also sets up Internet access by assigning IP addresses to the appropriate bridges and establishes NAT rules in `iptables`.

6. EVALUATION

In this section we evaluate the performance of WASP implementation, the benefit of our centralized approach, and compare WASP to AODV and OLSR protocols under different network settings. We start by presenting experiment setup in ns-3, evaluate packet delivery ratio and number of control packets of WASP, AODV, and OLSR. We then show the amount of traffic WASP's used through LTE. Further, we show the benefit of using WASP in interesting applications such as content distribution and flash crowd event. Finally, we describe and evaluate power consumption in WASP, AODV, and OLSR.

6.1 WASP's Performance vs. AODV and OLSR

In the following experiments we measure packet delivery ratio and total number of control packets from all nodes generated in each protocol. We designed two sets of network setups – one for fixed density and another one for fixed radius. In fixed density experiments, the density of the nodes in the simulation grid is fixed by increasing the radius as the number of nodes increases – allowing us to understand the effect the number of nodes has on performance. In fixed radius experiments, the number of nodes increases while the grid area is constant – allowing us to understand the effect increased density has on performance. With this, we can understand the performance of WASP in various scenarios. Table 2 shows number of nodes and corresponding grid radius and mobility of nodes. For each experiment we pick 10% of the nodes to be senders and 10% to be receivers. The rest of nodes simply serve to forward packets (if the controller selects a given node as part of a path). The senders simultaneously send 300 packets at the rate of 1 packet every 100ms. We ran each experiment 5 times and took the average.

Table 2: WASP vs. AODV and OLSR Experiment Parameters

	Fixed Radius	Fixed Density
Radius (meter)	250	250, 356, 437, 504, 564
Number of nodes	20, 40, 60, 80, 100	20, 40, 60, 80, 100
Mobility (m/s)	medium(1m/s)	station(0m/s), medium(1m/s), high(5m/s)
Broadcast Interval (s)	1 (WASP, AODV, OLSR)	1 (WASP, AODV, OLSR)
Neighbor Timeout (s)	3 (WASP, AODV, OLSR)	3 (WASP, AODV, OLSR)

As we see in Figures 5a, 5b, and 5c, WASP achieves higher packet delivery rate than OLSR and AODV under the same network topology, mobility and load setup. We believe this is because scalability of MANETs is limited by the fact that high volume of control messages must be exchanged and processed (e.g, in the case of OLSR) and the high packet processing overhead which causes the node to drop packets (e.g, in the case of AODV). A distinguishing feature of WASP is that we apply software-defined networking (SDN) principles and shift all the control overhead to the controller. In this way, WASP's nodes avoid exchanging large number of control packets for topology changes and the number of control packets increases linearly and proportionally to the number of nodes and their mobility as seen in Figures 5d, 5e, and 5f.

In fixed radius networks, we wanted to see the impact of making the network as dense as possible. As expected, AODV and OLSR overwhelm the network with high volume of control packets as seen in Figure 6b. This causes both data packets and many control packets to be dropped since every node is waiting for the medium to be free to send its packets. With WASP, our control traffic is significantly lower. This stems from the fact that the amount of routing control messages in OLSR and AODV grow non-linearly with the network size, as compared to WASP for which there is a linear increase. This is in contrast to discovery control messages (hello messages) which grows proportional to the network size (since each node sends at a fixed rate) in each approach (WASP, AODV, OLSR). In reducing local control messages, the network is freed for more data packets to be delivered – leading us to a considerable high packet delivery ratio, as seen in Figure 6a.

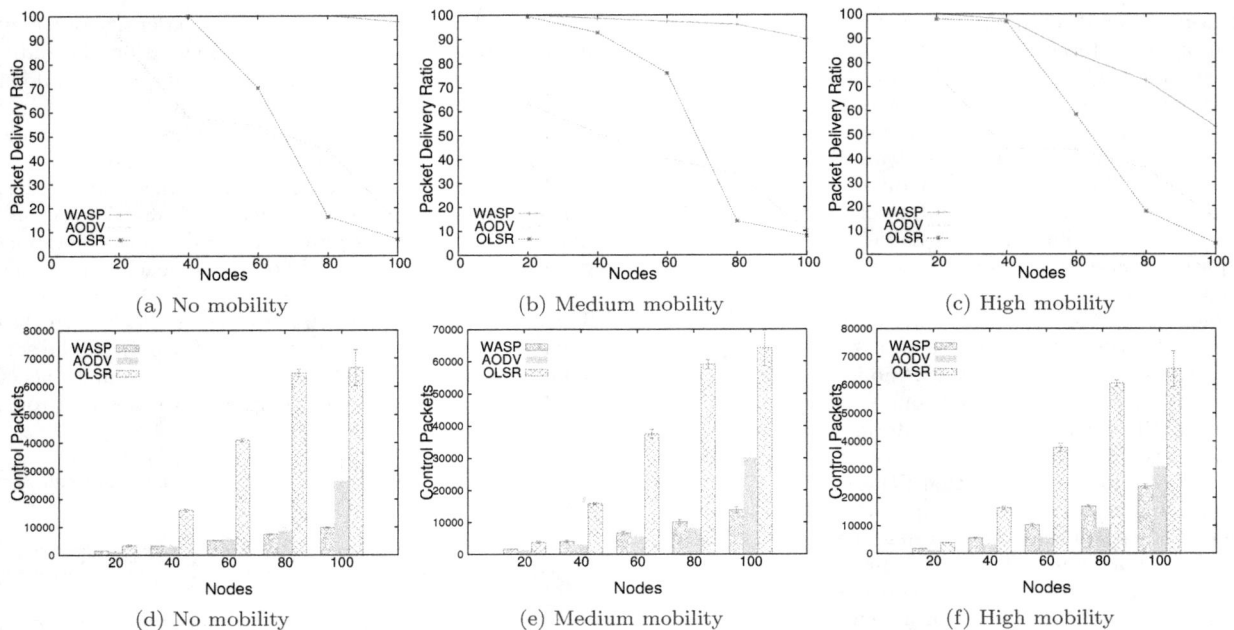

(a) No mobility   (b) Medium mobility   (c) High mobility

(d) No mobility   (e) Medium mobility   (f) High mobility

Figure 5: Performance of WASP, AODV, and OLSR under fixed density networks. (a), (b), and (c) show packet delivery ratio. (d), (e), (f) show total number of control packets generated from all nodes.

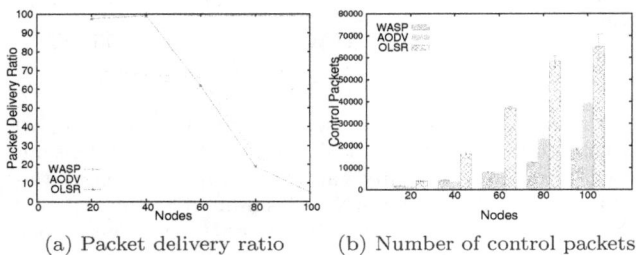

(a) Packet delivery ratio   (b) Number of control packets

Figure 6: Performance of WASP, AOVD and OLSR under fixed radius networks (a) shows packet delivery ratio. (b) shows total number of control packets generated from all nodes.

In addition to delivery performance, the amount of control traffic is important in WASP. We measured the aggregate control traffic sent over LTE over time for a network with 100 nodes within a radius of 1000m. In this experiment, each node will move at high mobility. As seen in Figure 7, the aggregate control traffic over LTE for all 100 nodes is minimal.

6.2 Throughput and Latency

As WASP is based around the ability for participating phones to relay traffic among phones via the Wi-Fi connection, an important metric is the throughput and latency of this forwarding. To determine this, we used three phones (Google Nexus-4 labeled A, B, and C) arranged in a line (*i.e.,* phone B has a Wi-Fi link to both A and C, but A and C do not have a link between them). In this setup, B will forward traffic between A and C. We used the iperf for Android application to measure throughput [ ], and our own custom application to measure latency between A and C. The mea-

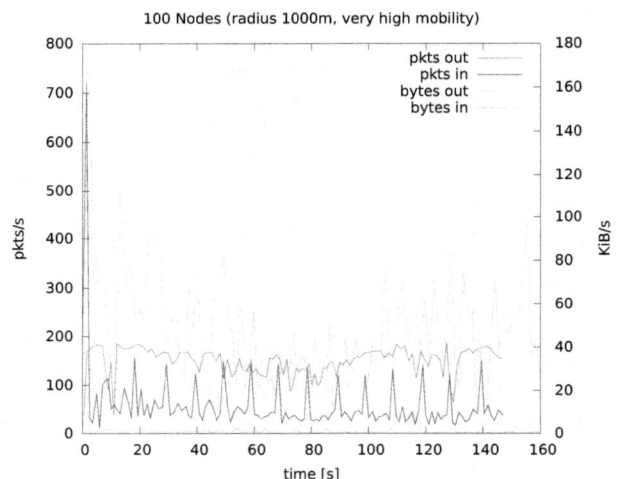

Figure 7: Control traffic over LTE over time for 100 nodes with high mobility.

sured throughput was 7.096 Mbps and the round-trip time was 11.668 ms. This compares to the direct communication between two phones measured at 12.753 Mbps throughput and 10.559 ms round-trip time. The decrease in throughput and increase in latency is to be expected with an extra hop, but the numbers are fairly reasonable given our application level forwarding in an unoptimized implementation.

6.3 Battery Consumption

While it may appear that using a cellular channel for control may lead to a design which is significantly less power efficient – *e.g.,* for normal use, LTE is 23 times less power efficient when compared to Wi-Fi, and 3G is 14.6 less power efficient [ ]. Fortunately, we show that this is not the case. A brief analysis of network and computation cost on mobile device for running WASP protocol will be given, followed by experiment setup for measuring power consumption and the experiment results on WASP, AODV and OLSR. The activities of mobile devices running WASP protocol include: (i) periodically sending and receiving "Hello" message and data packets via Wi-Fi, and (ii) sending and receiving control packets as needed to and from controller via LTE. The computation cost is small as generating the neighbor list and performing routing table lookups are $O(n)$. The major power consumption is the network load – sending and receiving control and data packets.

To learn the scalability of WASP and power consumption characteristics when the network size increases, data needs to be collected for a large network. As the major power consumption is network traffic on mobile device, we took a log file for each device sending and receiving packets via Wi-Fi and LTE in the previous ns-3 experiments, and then simulated the sending and receiving behavior on real phone (this removed any computation, which AODV and OLSR have significantly more than WASP). The simulation on the phone exactly follows the log, *i.e.*, the time interval, packet size, and network. During simulation, the screen is off and all other apps on phone are disabled.

Figure 8 shows the battery trace for a phone running WASP, AODV, OLSR, LTE (Where the phone is receiving all the data through the LTE interface), and IDLE (where the phone is not transferring any data) under fixed density and medium mobility experiment with 100 nodes. WASP is 7% less energy efficient than AODV and OLSR. This is the trade off for performance as in this size of 100 nodes and type of mobility, WASP is delivering 95% of the packets while AODV and OLSR are delivering less than 10%.

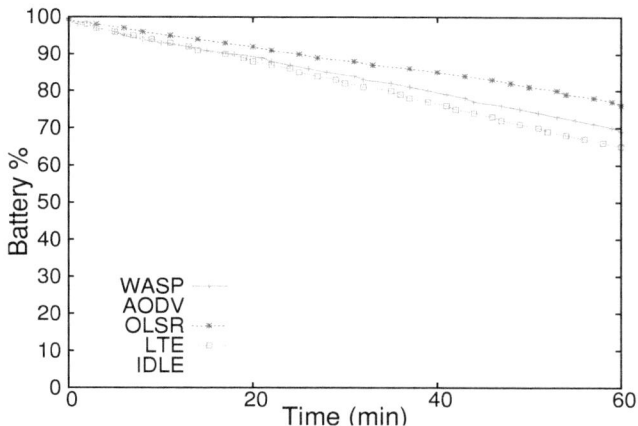

Figure 8: Battery log under fixed density and medium mobility for 60 minutes.

6.4 Content Distribution

From the applications perspective, the usefulness of WASP depends on the ability to capitalize on the phone-to-phone network for data traffic. To evaluate this, we explored the web content service to show amount of LTE bandwidth saved for different parameters – namely the network size, cache size, and acceptable number of hops.

In this experiment, each application will be continuously fetching content according to the following model (as described in [ ]): 1) Content size varies according to a Weibull distribution. We use a total of 10,000 objects (effectively cutting off the long tail). Each of these objects is assigned a URI and a size based on the distribution. 2) Content popularity follows a Zipf distribution. When fetching content, each node will select a URI based on this distribution. 3) Content is continuously fetched with the interval between each request being chosen at random between 0 and 3,000 milliseconds. 4) Content is cached with a fixed size cache with a least recently used eviction scheme.

Shown in Figure 9 is the amount of savings as a function of the network size. Interestingly, the network size seems to have little effect as we can get roughly a 35% saving in the amount of cellular traffic.

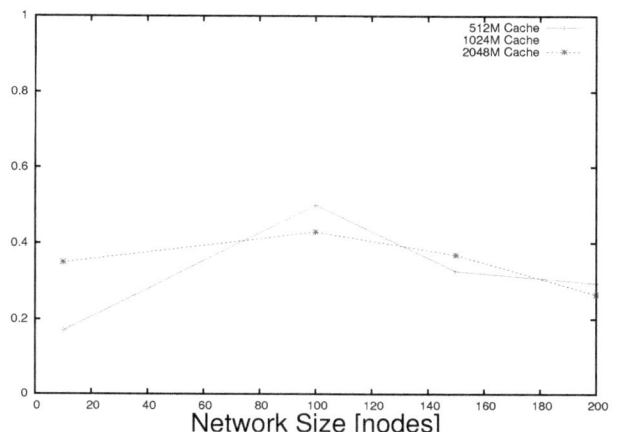

Figure 9: Fraction of traffic serviced locally as a function of network size.

In addition to providing benefits for average-case (Zipf) distribution of web requests, WASP can be a great fit in supporting a flash crowd (also known as the the Slashdot effect), where there is a single, or small set, of content that is fetched by many at roughly the same time. To evaluate this, we provided a similar setup to what was used to evaluate the Coral CDN's relief on the web server during a flash crowd [ ] In our setup within ns-3 we use 200 nodes, each mobile with using `RandomWaypointMobilityModel`. Each node is configured to access the same 3 objects starting at a randomly distributed start time between 0 and 180 seconds. We limit the number of hops away that a node can request the content from to be 3 hops. Shown in Figure 10, we can see that an initial spike of requests over LTE, as more phones access the content, the traffic over LTE quickly drops.

7. DISCUSSION

In this section we discuss WASP's possible limitations and how to overcome them in our future work.

7.1 Incentives to use WASP

One challenge WASP faces is the incentive for users to participate in the network as it requires users to forward traffic (consuming battery) on behalf of others. While a setting such as the military can force the use as the overall benefit to the collective network is greater with WASP than

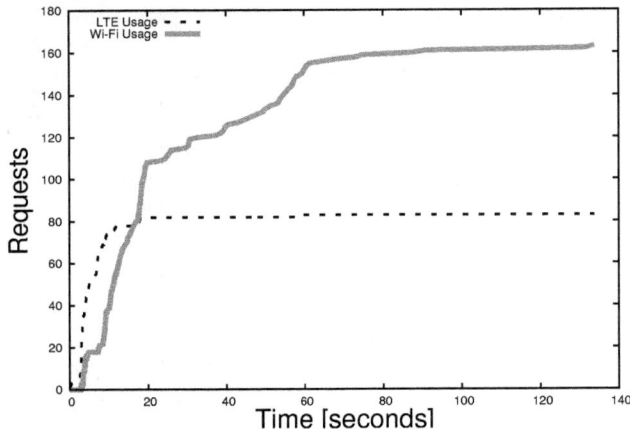

Figure 10: WASP handling a flash crowd.

without, we understand this might be a barrier for commercial networks such as cellular networks where each user is independent. We believe that overtime, everyone benefits. Even so, a barrier still remains as it is human nature to want to see evidence they are benefiting. To overcome this challenge, we envision a credit based system applied to WASP and managed by the controller. The credits can be monetary or better service for nodes participating. The controller will add/subtract credits based on node's role in the network (*e.g.*, nodes requesting data will use some credits while nodes sending or forwarding traffic earn credits). This type of scheme may fit well within the new pricing structures being explored [ ].

7.2 Wi-Fi Access Points

A push by industry is to offload data from the cellular infrastructure to Wi-Fi access points, when they are available. Unfortunately, finding Wi-Fi access points can be challenging (Even in highly dense environments such as stadiums [ ]) and accessing shared Wi-Fi access points often results in poor performance (due to many users accessing it). In an attempt to overcome these issues, node-to-node tethering apps are appearing to allow sharing of cellular data plans [ ], leading to different management for when Wi-Fi access points are available and for when they are not. Since WASP is generally targeting any hybrid network, we don't only focus on mobile devices to build our network. We view Wi-Fi access points as simply another node in the network that also has two interfaces – wired Ethernet for the 'one hop' connection (via the Internet) to the controller (optimized for long distance), and the Wi-Fi interface for communicating locally (optimized for local area). Each link simply has a cost associated with it (not just in terms of dollars) – *e.g.*, LTE might be higher cost than using Ethernet. The cost, by design, is flexible and can dynamically change. In current open Wi-Fi access points, the link from the access point to the controller might be considered free, but our model is more flexible and supports future business models and can incorporate additional costs such as where the access point is overloaded.

7.3 Energy Consumption

Although WASP considerably outperforms AODV and OLSR, it is (slightly) less energy efficient than AODV and OLSR. We believe this is because WASP uses the ubiquitous expensive channel to communicate with the controller. We believe we can reduce WASP's energy consumption by reducing the number of packets sent and received between the node and the controller. From the node's prospective, this can be done by allowing the node to wait for a little amount of time before updating the controller of any neighbor missing. With the nature of wireless networks, hello packets might be dropped or not reached easily.

7.4 Deployment on Android Today

One of the challenges we had in order to deploy WASP on Android phones was the Wi-Fi Direct interface. Wi-Fi ad-hoc mode is not accessible to unrooted phones, and Wi-Fi Direct requires user interaction to establish connections between phones which we find unpractical to our system. (WASP, using Wi-Fi ad-hoc, could authenticate connections automatically, eliminating the need for the interaction). In either case, a simple update to Android would make WASP instantly deployable.

8. CONCLUSIONS AND FUTURE WORK

In this paper we presented the design, implementation, and evaluation of WASP. WASP is built on the idea that by leveraging different interfaces which are optimized for different needs, we can provide a more efficient and scalable network for mobile devices. We show through our extended ns-3 simulation environment that WASP is more scalable than existing ad-hoc protocols, at only a small energy penalty (due to control messages going over LTE), Further, through the network WASP manages, we are able to save about 35% of traffic that would otherwise be served over cellular.

As future work we are looking to roll WASP out to real users once we overcome the Wi-Fi direct limitation. Beyond live user testing, WASP opens up much future work in evolving the control of the network and services run on the phones. Optimizing the services for the various trade-offs involved will require an in depth study of each. Further, we experimented with certain design decisions but the design space has much more to explore.

9. REFERENCES

[1] Adhoc-on-android.
    https://code.google.com/p/adhoc-on-android/.
[2] iperf for android. https://play.google.com/store/apps/details?id=com.magicandroidapps.iperf.
[3] Meraki. http://www.meraki.com/.
[4] Nicira Networks. http://nicira.com/.
[5] ns-3: A discrete-event network simulator for internet systems. http://www.nsnam.org.
[6] Open garden. http://opengarden.com/.
[7] Open vswitch: Production quality, multilayer open virtual switch. http://www.openvswitch.org.
[8] Running olsr on android phones.
    http://www.olsr.org/?q=olsr_on_android.
[9] Samsung AllShare Play.
    http://www.samsung.com/us/2012-allshare-play/.
[10] Serval: communicate anywhere, anytime.
    http://www.servalproject.org/.

[11] Serval demo: Client migration. http://www.serval-arch.org/demos/client-migration/.

[12] rfc 3626: Optimized link state routing protocol (olsr). http://www.ietf.org/rfc/rfc3626.txt, 2003.

[13] ns-3-users Google Groups: routing performance problem in large scale MANET. https://groups.google.com/d/msg/ns-3-users/1tq8kFuoy1Y/cjnlh9LDdJwJ, Nov. 2012.

[14] Y. Agarwal, R. Chandra, A. Wolman, P. Bahl, K. Chin, and R. Gupta. Wireless wakeups revisited: energy management for VoIP over Wi-Fi smartphones. In *Proc. conference on Mobile systems, applications and services (MobiSys)*, 2007.

[15] H. Ali-Ahmad, C. Cicconetti, A. de la Oliva, M. Draxler, R. Gupta, V. Mancuso, L. Roullet, and V. Sciancalepore. Crowd: An sdn approach for densenets. *2013 Second European Workshop on Software Defined Networks*, 0:25–31, 2013.

[16] J. Bicket, D. Aguayo, S. Biswas, and R. Morris. Architecture and evaluation of an unplanned 802.11b mesh network. In *Proceedings of the 11th annual international conference on Mobile computing and networking*, MobiCom '05, pages 31–42, New York, NY, USA, 2005. ACM.

[17] L. Breslau, P. Cao, L. Fan, G. Phillips, , and S. Shenker. Web caching and zipf-like distributions: Evidence and implications. In *Proc. IEEE INFOCOM*, Mar. 1999.

[18] M. Casado, M. J. Freedman, J. Pettit, J. Luo, N. Gude, N. McKeown, and S. Shenker. Rethinking enterprise network control. *IEEE/ACM Transactions on Networking*, 17(4), Aug. 2009.

[19] M. Castro, P. Druschel, A.-M. Kermarrec, A. Nandi, A. Rowstron, and A. Singh. Splitstream: high-bandwidth multicast in cooperative environments. In *SOSP*, 2003.

[20] R. Chandra, P. Bahl, and P. Bahl. MultiNet: Connecting to Multiple IEEE 802.11 Networks Using a Single Wireless Card. In *Proc. IEEE Infocom*, Mar. 2004.

[21] S.-M. Cheng, P. Lin, D.-W. Huang, and S.-R. Yang. A study on distributed/centralized scheduling for wireless mesh network. In *Proc. conference on Wireless communications and mobile computing (IWCMC)*, 2006.

[22] A. Dhananjay, H. Zhang, J. Li, and L. Subramanian. Practical, distributed channel assignment and routing in dual-radio mesh networks. In *Proc. SIGCOMM*, 2009.

[23] M. J. Freedman, E. Freudenthal, and D. Mazières. Democratizing content publication with coral. In *Proc. Symposium on Networked Systems Design and Implementation (NSDI)*, Mar. 2004.

[24] A. Greenberg, G. Hjalmtysson, D. A. Maltz, A. Myers, J. Rexford, G. Xie, H. Yan, J. Zhan, and H. Zhang. A clean slate 4d approach to network control and management. *SIGCOMM Comput. Commun. Rev.*, 35(5):41–54, Oct. 2005.

[25] S. Ha, S. Sen, C. Joe-Wong, Y. Im, and M. Chiang. TUBE: Time-dependent Pricing for Mobile Data. In *Proc. SIGCOMM*, 2012.

[26] S. Hua, Y. Guo, Y. Liu, H. Liu, and S. S. Panwar. Scalable video multicast in hybrid 3g/ad-hoc networks. *Trans. Multi.*, 13(2):402–413, Apr. 2011.

[27] J. Huang, F. Qian, A. Gerber, Z. M. Mao, S. Sen, and O. Spatscheck. A close examination of performance and power characteristics of 4g lte networks. In *Proc. conference on Mobile systems, applications, and services (MobiSys)*, 2012.

[28] S. Ihm and V. S. Pai. Towards understanding modern web traffic. In *Proc. conference on Internet measurement conference (IMC)*, IMC '11, 2011.

[29] S. Kandula, K. C.-J. Lin, T. Badirkhanli, and D. Katabi. FatVAP: aggregating AP backhaul capacity to maximize throughput. In *Proc. Symposium on Networked Systems Design and Implementation (NSDI)*, 2008.

[30] P. Kapustka. NL West Leads MLB Stadium Wi-Fi Scorecard, with 4 out of 5 Teams Offering Network Service to Fans. http://www.mobilesportsreport.com/2013/03/nl-west-leads-mlb-stadium-wi-fi-scorecard-with-4-out-of-5-teams-offering-network-service-to-fans/.

[31] L. Keller, A. Le, B. Cici, H. Seferoglu, C. Fragouli, and A. Markopoulou. MicroCast: cooperative video streaming on smartphones. In *Proc. conference on Mobile systems, applications, and services (MobiSys)*, 2012.

[32] K. O. Marc Mendonça, Bruno Astuto A. Nunes and T. Turletti. Software defined networking for heterogeneous networks. *IEEE COMSOC MMTC E-Letter*, 8:36–39, May 2013.

[33] N. McKeown, T. Anderson, H. Balakrishnan, G. Parulkar, L. Peterson, J. Rexford, S. Shenker, and J. Turner. Openflow: enabling innovation in campus networks. *SIGCOMM Comput. Commun. Rev.*, 38(2):69–74, Mar. 2008.

[34] C. Perkins, E. Belding-Royer, and S. Das. Ad hoc On-Demand Distance Vector (AODV) Routing. IETF RFC 3561, July 2003.

[35] B. Pfaff, J. Pettit, K. Amidon, M. Casado, T. Koponen, and S. Shenker. Extending networking into the virtualization layer. In *Workshop on Hot Topics in Networks (HotNets)*, Oct. 2009.

[36] A. Raniwala, K. Gopalan, and T.-c. Chiueh. Centralized channel assignment and routing algorithms for multi-channel wireless mesh networks. *SIGMOBILE Mob. Comput. Commun. Rev.*, 8(2):50–65, Apr 2004.

[37] E. J. Rosensweig and J. Kurose. Breadcrumbs: Efficient, best-effort content location in cache networks. In *IEEE INFOCOM*, 2009.

[38] J. Terrace, H. Laidlaw, H. E. Liu, S. Stern, and M. J. Freedman. Bringing P2P to the Web: Security and Privacy in the Firecoral Network. In *IPTPS*, 2009.

[39] Z. Wang, Z. Qian, Q. Xu, Z. Mao, and M. Zhang. An untold story of middleboxes in cellular networks. In *Proc. SIGCOMM*, 2011.

[40] K.-K. Yap, T.-Y. Huang, M. Kobayashi, Y. Yiakoumis, N. McKeown, S. Katti, and G. Parulkar. Making use of all the networks around us: a case study in android. In *Proc. workshop on Cellular networks (CellNet)*, 2012.

ElastiCon: An Elastic Distributed SDN Controller

†Advait Dixit, ‡Fang Hao, ‡Sarit Mukherjee, ‡T. V. Lakshman, †Ramana Rao Kompella
†Dept. of Computer Science, Purdue University, West Lafayette, IN, USA
{dixit0, kompella}@cs.purdue.edu
‡Bell Labs, Alcatel-Lucent, Holmdel, NJ, USA
{fang.hao, sarit.mukherjee, t.v.lakshman}@alcatel-lucent.com

ABSTRACT

Software Defined Networking (SDN) has become a popular paradigm for centralized control in many modern networking scenarios such as data centers and cloud. For large data centers hosting many hundreds of thousands of servers, there are few thousands of switches that need to be managed in a centralized fashion, which cannot be done using a single controller node. Previous works have proposed distributed controller architectures to address scalability issues. A key limitation of these works, however, is that the mapping between a switch and a controller is *statically configured*, which may result in uneven load distribution among the controllers as traffic conditions change dynamically.

To address this problem, we propose ElastiCon, an *elastic distributed controller architecture* in which the controller pool is dynamically grown or shrunk according to traffic conditions. To address the load imbalance caused due to spatial and temporal variations in the traffic conditions, ElastiCon automatically balances the load across controllers thus ensuring good performance at all times irrespective of the traffic dynamics. We propose a novel switch migration protocol for enabling such load shifting, which conforms with the Openflow standard. We further design the algorithms for controller load balancing and elasticity. We also build a prototype of ElastiCon and evaluate it extensively to demonstrate the efficacy of our design.

Categories and Subject Descriptors

C.2.4 [**Computer-Communication Networks**]: Distributed Systems

Keywords

Data center networks; software-defined networks

1. INTRODUCTION

Software Defined Networking (SDN) has emerged as a popular paradigm for managing large-scale networks including data centers and cloud. The key tenet of SDN is the centralized control plane

architecture, which allows the network to be programmed by applications running on one central entity, enabling easier management and faster innovation [13, 9, 5, 16]. However, many of these large-scale data center networks consist of several hundreds of thousands of servers interconnected with few thousands of switches in tree-like topologies (e.g., fat tree), that cannot easily be controlled by a single centralized controller. Hence the next logical step is to build a logically centralized, but physically distributed control plane, which can benefit from the scalability and reliability of the distributed architecture while preserving the simplicity of a logically centralized system.

A few recent papers have explored architectures for building distributed SDN controllers [12, 20, 15]. While these have focused on building the components necessary to implement a distributed SDN controller, one key limitation of these systems is that the mapping between a switch and a controller is *statically configured*, making it difficult for the control plane to adapt to traffic load variations. Real networks (e.g., data center networks, enterprise networks) exhibit significant variations in both temporal and spatial traffic characteristics. First, along the temporal dimension, it is generally well-known that traffic conditions can depend on the time of day (e.g., less traffic during night), but there are variations even in shorter time scales (e.g., minutes to hours) depending on the applications running in the network. For instance, based on measurements over real data centers in [3], we estimate that the peak-to-median ratio of flow arrival rates is almost 1-2 orders of magnitude[1] (more details in Section 2). Second, there are often spatial traffic variations; depending on where applications are generating flows, some switches observe a larger number of flows compared to other portions of the network.

Now, if the switch to controller mapping is static, a controller may become overloaded if the switches mapped to this controller suddenly observe a large number of flows, while other controllers remain underutilized. Furthermore, the load may shift across controllers over time, depending on the temporal and spatial variations in traffic conditions. Hence static mapping can result in sub-optimal performance. One way to improve performance is to over-provision controllers for an expected peak load, but this approach is clearly inefficient due to its high cost and energy consumption, especially considering load variations can be up to two orders of magnitude.

To address this problem, in this paper, we propose ElastiCon, an *elastic distributed controller architecture* in which the controller pool expands or shrinks dynamically as the aggregate load changes over time. While such an elastic architecture can ensure there are always enough controller resources to manage the traffic load, per-

---

[1]This analysis is based on the reactive flow installation although our design supports proactive mode as well.

formance can still be bad if the load is not distributed among these different controllers evenly. For example, if the set of switches that are connected to one controller are generating most of the traffic while the others are not, this can cause the performance to dip significantly even though there are enough controller resources in the overall system. To address this problem, ElastiCon periodically monitors the load on each controller, detects imbalances, and *automatically* balances the load across controllers by migrating some switches from the overloaded controller to a lightly-loaded one. This way, ElastiCon ensures predictable performance even under highly dynamic workloads.

Migrating a switch from one controller to another in a naive fashion can cause disruption to ongoing flows, which can severely impact the various applications running in the data center. Unfortunately, the current de facto SDN standard, OpenFlow does not provide a disruption-free migration operation natively. To address this shortcoming, we propose a new *4-phase migration protocol* that ensures minimal disruption to ongoing flows. Our protocol makes minimal assumptions about the switch architecture and is Open-Flow standard compliant. The basic idea in our protocol involves creating a single trigger event that can help determine the exact moment of handoff between the first controller and second controller. We exploit OpenFlow's "equal mode" semantics to ensure such a single trigger event to be sent to both the controllers that can allow the controllers to perform the handoff in a disruption-free manner without safety or liveness concerns.

Armed with this disruption-free migration primitive, ElastiCon supports the following three main load adaptation operations: First, it monitors the load on all controllers and periodically *load balances* the controllers by optimizing the switch-to-controller mapping. Second, if the aggregate load exceeds the maximum capacity of existing controllers, it *grows* the resource pool by adding new controllers, triggering switch migrations to utilize the new controller resource. Similarly, when the load falls below a particular level, it *shrinks* the resource pool accordingly to consolidate switches onto fewer controllers. For all these actions, ElastiCon uses simple algorithms to decide when and what switches to migrate.

We have described a preliminary version of ElastiCon in [7] where we focused mainly on the migration protocol. Additional contributions of this paper are as follows:

- We enhance the migration protocol to guarantee serializability. We show how these guarantees simplify application-specific modifications for moving state between controllers during switch migration. The serializability guarantee requires buffering messages from the switch during migration. This impacts worst-case message processing delay. Hence, we also explore the trade-off between performance and consistency.
- We propose new algorithms for deciding when to grow or shrink the controller resource pool, and trigger load balancing actions.
- We demonstrate the feasibility of ElastiCon by implementing the enhanced migration protocol and proposed algorithms. We address a practical concern of redirecting switch connections to new controllers when the controller pool is grown or away from controllers when the controller pool needs to be shrunk.
- We show that ElastiCon can ensure that performance remains stable and predictable even under highly dynamic traffic conditions.

2. BACKGROUND AND MOTIVATION

The OpenFlow network consists of both switches and a central controller. A switch forwards packets according to *rules* stored in its flow table. The central controller controls each switch by setting up the rules. Multiple application modules can run on top of the core controller module to implement different control logics and network functions. Packet processing rules can be installed in switches either reactively (when a new flow is arrived) or proactively (controller installs rules beforehand). We focus on the performance of the reactive mode in this paper. Although proactive rule setup (e.g., DevoFlow [6]) can reduce controller load and flow setup time, it is not often sufficient by itself as only a small number of rules can be cached at switches, because TCAM table sizes in commodity switches tend to be small for cost and power reasons. Reactive mode allows the controller to be aware of the lifetime of each flow from setup to teardown, and hence can potentially offer better visibility than proactive mode. For low-end switches, TCAM space is a major constraint. It may be difficult to install all fine-grained microflow policies proactively. Reactive rule insertion allows such rules to be installed selectively and hence may reduce the TCAM size requirement. Thus, it is important to design the controller for predictable performance irrespective of the traffic dynamics.

Switch–controller communication. The OpenFlow protocol defines the interface and message format between a controller and a switch. When a flow arrives at a switch and does not match any rule in the flow table, the switch buffers the packet and sends a `Packet-In` message to the controller. The `Packet-In` message contains the incoming port number, packet headers and the buffer ID where the packet is stored. The controller may respond with a `Packet-Out` message which contains the buffer ID of the corresponding `Packet-In` message and a set of actions (drop, forward, etc.). For handling subsequent packets of the same flow, the controller may send a `Flow-Mod` message with an add command to instruct the switch to insert rules into its flow table. The rules match the subsequent packets of the same flow and hence allow the packets to be processed at line speed. Controller can also delete rules at a switch by using `Flow-Mod` with delete command. When a rule is deleted either explicitly or due to timeout, the switch sends a `Flow-Removed` message to the controller if the "notification" flag for the flow is set. In general, there is no guarantee on the order of processing of controller messages at a switch. Barrier messages are used to solve the synchronization problem. When the switch receives a `Barrier-Request` message from the controller, it sends a `Barrier-Reply` message back to the controller only after it has finished processing all the messages that it received before the `Barrier-Request`.

Controller architecture. The controller architecture has evolved from the original single-threaded design [10] to the more advanced multi-threaded design [21, 2, 4, 8] in recent years. Despite the significant performance improvement over time, the single-controller systems still have limits on scalability and vulnerability. Some research papers have also explored the implementation of distributed controllers across multiple hosts [12, 20, 15]. The main focus of these papers is to address the state consistency issues across distributed controller instances, while preserving good performance. Onix, for instance, uses a transactional database for persistent but less dynamic data, and memory-only DHT for data that changes quickly but does not require consistency [12]. Hyperflow replicates the events at all distributed nodes, so that each node can process such events and update their local state [20]. [15] has further elaborated the state distribution trade-offs in SDNs. OpenDaylight [17] is a recent open source distributed SDN controller. Like ElastiCon, it uses a distributed data store for storing state information.

All existing distributed controller designs implicitly assume static mapping between switches and controllers, and hence lack the ca-

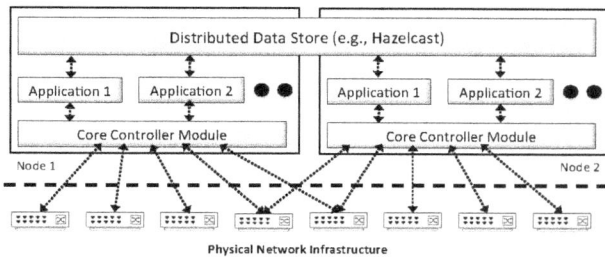

Figure 1: Basic distributed controller architecture.

pability of dynamic load adaptation and elasticity. However, the following back-of-the-envelope calculation using real measurement data shows that there is 1-2 orders of magnitude difference between peak and median flow arrival rates at a switch. In [3], Benson *et al.* show that the minimum inter flow arrival gap is $10\mu s$, while the median ranges roughly from $300\mu s$ to $2ms$ across different data centers that they have measured. Assuming a data center with $100K$ hosts and 32 hosts/rack, peak flow arrival rate can be up to $300M$ with the median rate between 1.5M and 10M. Assuming 2M packets/sec throughput[2] for one controller [21], it requires only 1-5 controllers to process the median load, but 150 for peak load. If we use static mapping between switches and controllers and install all flow table entries reactively, it requires significant over-provisioning of resources which is inefficient in hardware and power; an elastic controller that can dynamically adapt to traffic load is clearly more desirable.

3. ELASTIC CONTROLLER DESIGN

We present the design and architecture of ElastiCon, an elastic distributed SDN controller in this section. We describe the architecture of ElastiCon in three phases: First, we start with a basic distributed controller design that spreads functionality across several nodes by extending Floodlight, a Java-based open source controller [8]. We then describe the 4-phase protocol for disruption-free switch migration, which is one of the core primitives needed for implementing an elastic controller. Finally, we discuss the algorithms we use for elasticity and load adaptation in our design.

3.1 Basic Distributed Controller

The key components in our distributed controller design are shown in Figure 1. It consists of a cluster of autonomous *controller nodes* that coordinate amongst themselves to provide a consistent control logic for the entire network. The *physical network infrastructure* refers to the switches and links that carry data and control plane traffic. Note that, for simplicity, we have omitted showing the physical topology of the network that includes the hosts and their interconnections with the switches in the network.

Typically, each switch connects to one controller. However, for fault-tolerance purposes, it may be connected to more than one controller with one master and the rest as slaves. We assume the control plane is logically isolated from the data plane, and the control plane traffic is not affected by data plane traffic. Each controller node has a *core controller module* that executes all the functions of a centralized controller (i.e., connecting to a switch, event management between a switch and an application). In addition, it coordinates with other controllers to elect a master node for a newly connected

---

[2]This is based on the learning switch application. Throughput is lower for more complex applications, as shown in our experiments.

switch and orchestrates the migration of a switch to a different controller.

The *distributed data store* provides the glue across the cluster of controllers to enable a logically centralized controller. It stores all switch-specific information that is shared among the controllers. Each controller node also maintains a TCP connection with every other controller node in the form of a full mesh. This full-mesh topology is mainly for simplicity, but as the number of controllers become exceedingly large, one may consider adding a point of indirection, similar to the route-reflector idea in scaling BGP connections in ISP networks. For today's data centers, maintaining a full mesh across a few 100 controllers does not pose any scaling concerns. A controller node uses this TCP connection for various controller-to-controller messages, such as when sending messages to a switch controlled by another node or coordinating actions during switch migration. The *application* module implements the control logic of network applications, responsible for controlling the switches for which its controller is the master. The fact that state is maintained distributed data store makes switch migration easier and also helps fast recovery from controller failures.

3.2 4-Phase Switch Migration Protocol

If we use a single SDN controller, since all switches are always connected to this controller, there is no break in the control plane processing. Moving to a distributed controller architecture does not necessarily pose a problem so long as the switch-to-controller mapping stays static. However, such an architecture, which is employed by previously proposed distributed controllers, cannot adapt to the load imbalances caused by spatial and temporal variations in traffic conditions. Once a controller becomes overloaded, the response time for control plane messages becomes too high, thus impacting flows and applications running in the data center. We can mitigate such imbalances by dynamically shifting load between existing controllers or by adding new nodes to the controller pool. The basic granularity at which one can shift load is at a switch-level; simply migrate a switch from an overloaded controller to a lightly loaded one.

Unfortunately, there is no native support for safely migrating switches in existing de facto SDN standard, OpenFlow, without which one cannot guarantee that there is no impact to traffic during migration. In particular, there are three standard properties any migration protocol needs to provide—*liveness*, *safety* and *serializability*.

- **Liveness.** At least one controller is active for a switch at all times. Otherwise, a new flow that arrives at a switch cannot be properly routed causing disruption to that application. In addition, if a controller has issued a command to a switch, it needs to remain active until the switch finishes processing that command.
- **Safety.** Exactly one controller processes every asynchronous message from the switch; duplicate processing of asynchronous messages such as Packet-In could result in duplicate entries in the flow table, or even worse, inconsistency in the distributed data store.
- **Serializability.** The controller processes events in the order in which they are transmitted by the switch; if events are processed in a different order, the controller's view of the network may be inconsistent with the state of the network. For instance, if a link goes down and comes back up, the switch will generate a port status down message followed by a port status up. However, if these events are processed in the wrong order, the controller may assume that the link is permanently down.

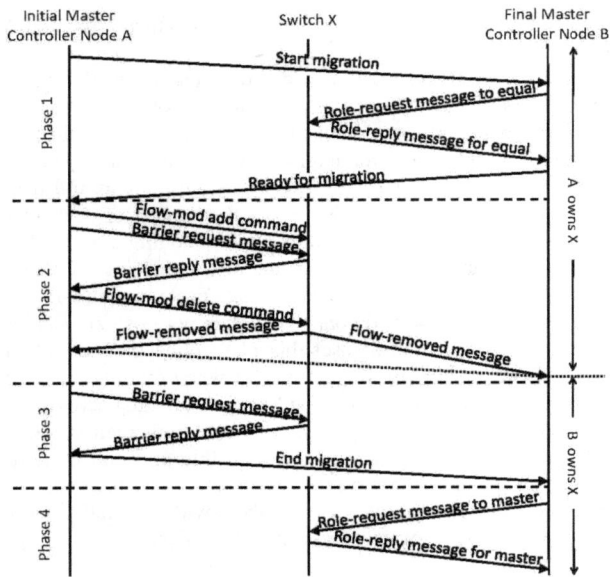

Figure 2: Message exchanges for switch migration.

Now, consider the following naive protocol that OpenFlow readily provides: The target controller can be first put in the slave mode for the switch (see Section 4 for implementation details). The target controller then simply sends a `Role-Request` message to the switch indicating that it wants to become the master. The switch would set that controller as the master and the previous master as slave. Such a naive and intuitive protocol can cause serious disruption to traffic since it can violate the liveness property. Assume that the switch had sent a `Packet-In` message to the initial master. If the switch receives the `Role-Request` message from the slave before the `Packet-Out` message from the initial master, then the switch will ignore the `Packet-Out` message since it is designed to ignore messages from any controller which is not the master/equal. Ideally, the switch can buffer all these `Packet-In` requests and try retransmitting the `Packet-In` message to the new master, but that makes the switch design complicated, which is not desirable.

In our protocol design, we assume we cannot modify the switch. There are two additional issues: First, the OpenFlow standard clearly states that a switch may process messages not necessarily in the order they are received, mainly to allow multi-threaded implementations. We need to factor this in our protocol design. Second, the standard does not specify explicitly whether the ordering of messages transmitted by the switch remains consistent across two controllers that are in master/equal mode. This assumption, which is clearly logical, is required for our protocol to work; allowing arbitrary reordering of messages across two controllers will make an already hard problem significantly harder. For ease of exposition, we use X to denote the switch, which is being migrated from initial controller A to target controller B. We first outline the key ideas that provide the desired guarantees and then describe the protocol in detail.

Liveness. To guarantee liveness, we first transition the target controller B to equal mode. After that, we transition initial controller A from master to slave mode and then transition controller B to master mode. This ensures guarantees liveness since at least one controller is active (master or equal mode) at a time.

Safety. Using an intermediate equal mode for the controller B solves the liveness problem but it may violate the safety property since both controllers may process messages from the switch causing inconsistencies and duplicate messages. To guarantee safety, we create a *single trigger event* to stop message processing in the first controller and start the same in the second one. Fortunately, we can exploit the fact that `Flow-Removed` messages are transmitted to all controllers operating in the equal mode. We therefore simply insert a dummy flow entry into the switch and then remove the flow entry, which will provide a single `Flow-Removed` event to both the controllers to signal handoff.

Serializability. To guarantee serializability, the controller A should complete processing its last message before the controller B can process its first message. However, the first message for the B may arrive before A completes processing its last message. So, we cache messages at B until the A has finished processing its last message and committed it to the switch.

Our protocol operates in four phases described below (shown in Figure 2). We now describe each phase in detail and highlight a trade-off between performance and serializability.

Phase 1: Change role of the target to equal. In the first phase, target B's role is first changed to equal mode for the switch X. Initial master A initiates this phase by sending a start migration message to B using a proprietary message on the controller-to-controller channel. B sends `Role-Request` message to the switch informing that it is an equal. After B receives a `Role-Reply` message from the switch, it informs the initial master A that its role change is completed. After B changes its role to equal, it receives control messages (e.g., `Packet-In`) from the switch, but ignores them and does not respond.

Phase 2: Insert and remove a dummy flow. To determine an exact instant for the migration, A sends a dummy (but well-known) `Flow-Mod` command to X to add a new flow table entry that does not match any incoming packet. Then, it sends another `Flow-Mod` command to delete this flow table entry; in response, the switch sends a `Flow-Removed` message to both controllers since B is in the equal mode. This `Flow-Removed` event signals a handoff of switch X from A to B, and henceforth, only B will process all messages transmitted by switch. Here, our assumption that both controllers in equal mode receive messages from the switch in the same order is needed to guarantee the safety property. An additional barrier message is required after the insertion of the dummy flow and before the dummy flow is deleted to prevent any chance of processing the delete message before the insert.

Although B processes all messages after the `Flow-Removed` message, it does not do so immediately. It caches all the messages after the `Flow-Removed` message and begins processing them in the next phase. This is needed to guarantee the serializability property. Processing of messages from the north-bound interface can continue uninterrupted.

Phase 3: Flush pending requests with a barrier. Now, B has taken over responsibility of switch X, but A has not detached from X yet. However, it cannot just detach immediately from the switch since there may be pending requests at A that arrived before the `Flow-Removed` message, for which A is still the owner. Controller A processes all messages that arrived before `Flow-Removed` and transmits their responses. Then, it transmits a `Barrier-Request` and waits for the `Barrier-Reply`. Receiving a `Barrier-Reply` from switch X indicates that X has finished processing all messages that it received before the `Barrier-Request` messages. So, only after receiving the `Barrier-Reply` message, controller A signals "end migration" to the final master B. The "end migration" message is a signal to B that A has finished processing all its messages and committed them to the switch. Once B receives the "end migration" message, it processes all the cached messages in the order that they were received. Note that delay in end migration message can potentially cause message processing latency at B. This delay can be avoided if we do not need to guarantee serializability. In that case B can start processing `Packet-In` messages right after receiving `Flow-Removed`.

Phase 4: Make target controller final master. Here, A would have already detached from X and has signaled to B to become the new master, which it does by by sending a `Role-Request` message to the switch. It also updates the distributed data store to indicate this. The switch sets A to slave when it receives the `Role-Request` message from the final master B after which it processes all messages from the switch.

Performance-Serializability Trade-off. Buffering messages from the switch at the end of phase 2 is needed to guarantee serializability. It ensures that B begins processing messages only after A has completed processing messages before the `Flow-Removed` message. The duration for buffering messages will depend on the network latencies, message loss ratio, controller processing times, etc. In our experiments, we observed that messages were never buffered for more than 50msec. However, the worst case will depend on many network characteristics and may be larger. While buffering is needed to guarantee serializability, it has two undesirable side-effects. First, the controller will be unable to respond to events from the switch while messages are being buffered. Second, buffered messages will be processed late and may be irrelevant by the time they are processed. So, the network operator should choose between two configurations of the migration protocol depending on network characteristics and application requirements. The "consistency configuration" buffers messages as described above and provides all three guarantees. The "performance configuration" does not buffer messages. It does not provide serializability but responds faster to switch events during migration.

3.3 Application State Migration

Safety, liveness and serializability guarantees of the migration protocol simplify controller application changes to support switch migration. The three guarantees together ensure that applications do not miss any asynchronous events and do not have to check for duplicate or reordered asynchronous messages from the switch before processing them. We describe the modifications to the applications and their interface with the core controller module below. We have implemented them for the routing applications in ElastiCon.

We added two methods to the interface between the core controller module and each application module. The first method, named "switch_emigrate", is invoked at the initial master controller (controller A in the above example). The core controller module invokes this method for each application after it has finished processing all messages before the `Flow-Removed` message from the switch. The method returns after the application has flushed all switch-specific state to the distributed data store. Applications also stop any switch-specific execution (like timers). The controller sends the "end migration" message only after all applications execute their "switch_emigrate" method. The second method, "switch_immigrate", is invoked at the target master controller (controller B in the above example) for each application. It is invoked after the controller receives the "end migration" message. Each application reads switch-specific state from the distributed data store to populate local data structures and starts switch-specific execution. The distributed data store should guarantee that the controller reads the state written in the "switch_emigrate" method earlier. The

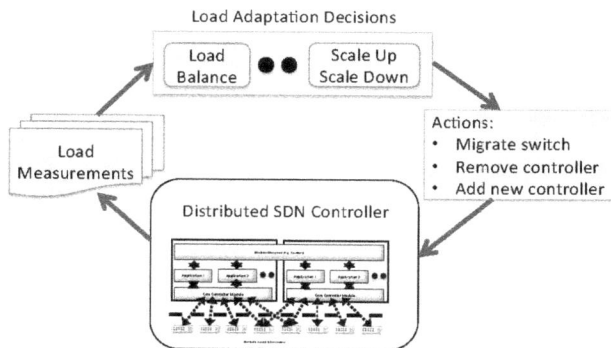

Figure 3: Load adaptation in ElastiCon.

controller starts processing cached asynchronous messages after all applications have executed their "switch_immigrate" methods.

State-transfer between applications can also be performed over TCP connections between applications instead of using the distributed data store. The above design simplified our implementation since we reused the interface between the application and the distributed data store. Using this disruption-free migration protocol as a basic primitive, we now look at load adaptation aspects of ElastiCon.

3.4 Load Adaptation

There are three key operations we envision for load adaptation in ElastiCon. If the aggregate traffic load is greater (smaller) than aggregate controller capacity, we need to *scale up (down)* the controller pool. In addition, we need to periodically *load balance* the controllers by migrating switches to newer controllers to adapt to traffic load imbalances. We show our basic approach to achieve this in Figure 3. It consists of three steps:

• Periodically collect load measurements at each controller node.

• Determine if the current number of controller nodes is sufficient to handle the current load. If not, add or remove controller nodes. In addition, if any controller is getting overloaded, but aggregate load is within the capacity, we need to trigger load balancing actions.

• Finally, adjust the switch to controller mapping by adding or removing the controllers and triggering switch migrations as needed.

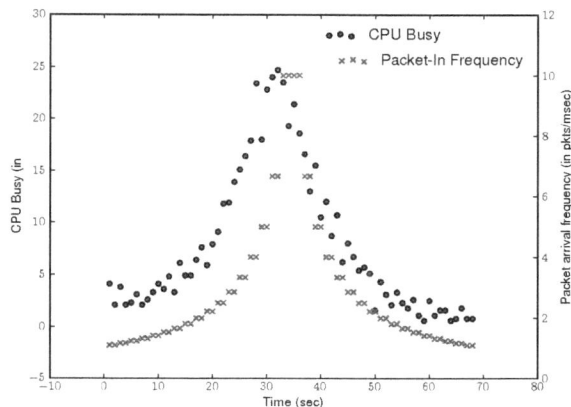

Figure 4: CPU vs. packet frequency.

3.4.1 Load Measurement

The most direct way to measure the load on a controller is by sampling response time of the controller at the switches. This response time will include both computation and network latency. However, switches may not support response time measurements, since that requires maintaining some amount of extra state at the switches that may or may not be feasible. Since the controller is more programmable, ElastiCon maintains a load measurement module on each controller to periodically report the CPU utilization and network I/O rates at the controller. Our experiments show that the CPU is typically the throughput bottleneck and CPU load is roughly in proportion to the message rate (see Figure 4). The module also reports the average message arrival rate from each switch connected to the controller. This aids the load balancer in first dissecting the contribution of each switch to the overall CPU utilization, and helps making optimal switch to controller mapping decisions. We assume that the fraction of controller resources used by a switch is proportional to its fraction of the total messages received at the controller, which is typically true due to the almost linear relationship between throughput and messages. The load measurement module averages load estimates over small time intervals (we use three seconds) to avoid triggering switch migrations due to short-term load spikes.

Algorithm 1 Load Adaptation Algorithm

---

while True **do**
    GET_INPUTS()
    $migration\_set \leftarrow$ DOREBALANCING()
    if $migration\_set == NULL$ **then**
        if DORESIZING() **then**
            if CHECKRESIZING() **then**
                $migration\_set \leftarrow$ DOREBALANCING()
            else
                REVERTRESIZING()
            end if
        end if
    end if
    EXECUTE_POWER_ON_CONTROLLER()
    EXECUTE_MIGRATIONS($migration\_set$)
    EXECUTE_POWER_OFF_CONTROLLER()
    SLEEP(3)
end while

3.4.2 Adaptation Decision Computation

The load adaptation algorithm determines if the current distributed controller pool is sufficient to handle the current network load. It sets a high and low thresholds to determine whether the distributed controller needs to be scaled up or down. Difference between these thresholds should be large enough to prevent frequent scale changes. Then, the algorithm finds an optimal switch to controller mapping constrained by the controller capacity while minimizing the number of switch migrations. Some CPU cycles and network bandwidth should also be reserved for switches connected to a controller in slave mode. Switches in slave mode impose very little load on the controller typically, but some headroom should be reserved to allow switch migrations.

While one can formulate and solve an optimization problem (e.g., linear program) that can generate an optimal assignment of switch-to-controller mappings, it is not clear such formulations are useful for our setting in practice. First, optimal balancing is not the primary objective as much as performance (e.g., in the form of response time). Usually, as long as a controller is not too overloaded, there is not much performance difference between different CPU utilization values. For example, 10% and 20% CPU utilization re-

sults in almost similar controller response time. Thus, fine-grained optimization is not critical in practice. Second, optimal balancing may result in too many migrations that is not desirable. Of course, one can factor this in the cost function, but then it requires another (artificial) weighting of these two functions, which then becomes somewhat arbitrary. Finally, optimization problems are also computationally intensive and since the traffic changes quickly, the benefits of the optimized switch-controller mapping are short-lived. So, a computationally light-weight algorithm that can be run frequently is likely to have at least similar if not better performance than optimization. Perhaps, this is the main reason why distributed resource management (DRM) algorithms used in real world for load balancing cluster workloads by migrating virtual machines (VMs) do not solve any such optimization problems and rely on a more simpler feedback loop [11]. We adopt a similar approach in our setting.

Our load-adaptation decision process proceeds in two phases, as shown in Algorithm 1. First, during the rebalancing step the load adaptation module evenly distributes the current load across all available controllers. After rebalancing, if the load on one or more controllers exceeds the upper (or lower) threshold, the load adaptation module grows (or shrinks) the controller pool.

Input to the Algorithm. A load adaptation module within ElastiCon periodically receives inputs from the load measurement module on each controller. The input contains the total CPU usage by the controller process in MHz. It also contains a count of the number of packets received from each switch of which that controller is the master. The packet count is used to estimate the fraction of the load on the controller due to a particular switch. The load adaptation module stores a moving window of the past inputs for each controller. We define utilization of a controller as the sum of the mean and standard deviation of CPU usage over the stored values for that controller. The rebalancing and resizing algorithms never use instantaneous CPU load. Instead they use CPU utilization to ensure that they always leave some headroom for temporal spikes in instantaneous CPU load. Also, the amount of headroom at a controller will be correlated to the variation in CPU load for that controller.

Output of the Algorithm. After processing the inputs, the load adaptation module may perform one or more of the following actions: powering off a controller, powering on a controller, or migrating a switch from one controller to another.

Main Loop of the Algorithm. First, the load adaptation module receives the inputs from all controllers and augments them to its stored state. All functions except the EXECUTE_* functions only modify this stored state and they do not affect the state of the controllers. After that, the EXECUTE_* functions determine the changes to the stored state and send migration and power on/off commands to the appropriate controllers.

There are two main subroutines in the rebalancing algorithm: DOREBALANCING and DORESIZING. DOREBALANCING distributes the current load evenly among the controllers. DORESIZING adds or removes controllers accordingly to the current load. DORESIZING is invoked after DOREBALANCING since resizing the controller pool is a more intrusive operation than rebalancing the controller load, and hence should be avoided when possible. Although one can estimate average load per controller without actually doing rebalancing and then determine whether resizing is needed or not, this often suffers from estimation errors.

If the first invocation of DOREBALANCING generates any migrations, we execute those migrations and iterate over the main loop again after 3 seconds. If there are no migrations (indicating that the controllers are evenly loaded), ElastiCon generates resizing (i.e., controller power on/off) decisions by invoking DoRESIZING. The power off decision needs to be verified to ensure that the switches connected to the powered off controller can be redistributed among the remaining controllers without overloading any one of them. This is done in the CHECKRESIZING function. This function uses a simple first-fit algorithm to redistribute the switches. While other more sophisticated functions can be used, our experience indicates first-fit is quite effective most of the time. If this function fails, the (stored) network state is reverted. Otherwise, ElastiCon calls DoREBALANCING to evenly distribute the switch load. Finally, the EXECUTE_* functions implement the state changes made to the network by the previous function calls. Since a migration changes the load of two controllers, all stored inputs for the controllers involved in a migration are discarded. The main loop is executed every 3 seconds to allow for decisions from the previous iteration to take effect.

Algorithm 2 The rebalancing algorithm

---

procedure DoREBALANCING()
    $migration\_set \leftarrow NULL$
    while True **do**
        $best\_migration \leftarrow$ GET_BEST_MIGRATION()
        if $best\_migration.std\_dev\_improvement \geq THRESHOLD$ **then**
            $migration\_set$.INSERT($best\_migration$)
        else
            return $migration\_set$
        end if
    end while
end procedure

Rebalancing. The rebalancing algorithm, described in Algorithm 2, tries to balance the average utilization of all controllers. We use the standard deviation of utilization across all the controllers as a balancing metric. In each iteration, it calls the GET_BEST_MIGRATION function to identify the migration that leads to the most reduction in standard deviation of utilization across controllers. The GET_BEST_MIGRATION function tries every possible migration in the network and estimates the standard deviation of utilization for each scenario. It returns the migration which has the smallest estimated standard deviation. To estimate the standard deviation, this function needs to know the load imposed by every switch on its master controller. Within each scenario, after a hypothetical migration, the function calculates the utilization of each controller by adding the fractional utilizations due to the switches connected to it. It then finds the standard deviation across the utilization of all the controllers. If reduction in standard deviation by the best migration it finds exceeds the minimum reduction threshold, ElastiCon adds that migration to the set of migrations. If no such migration is found or the best migration does not lead to sufficient reduction in standard deviation, it exits.

Resizing. The resizing algorithm, shown in Algorithm 3, tries to keep the utilization of every controller between two preset high and low thresholds. Each invocation of the resizing algorithm generates either a power on, or power off, or no decision at all. The resizing algorithm is conservative in generating decisions to prevent oscillations. Also, it is more aggressive in power on decisions than power off. This is because when the utilization exceeds the high threshold, the network performance may suffer unless additional controllers are put in place quickly. However, when the utilization goes below the low threshold, network performance does not suffer. Removing controllers only consolidates the workload over fewer controllers sufficient to handle existing traffic conditions, mainly for power

---

Algorithm 3 The resizing algorithm

---

procedure DoRESIZING()
    for all c in $controller\_list$ **do**
        if $c.util \geq HIGH\_UTIL\_THRESH$ **then**
            SWITCH_ON_CONTROLLER()
            return True
        end if
    end for
    $counter \leftarrow 0$
    for all c in $controller\_list$ **do**
        if $c.util \leq LOW\_UTIL\_THRESH$ **then**
            $counter \leftarrow counter + 1$
        end if
    end for
    if $counter \geq 2$ **then**
        SWITCH_OFF_CONTROLLER()
        return True
    else
        return False
    end if
end procedure

---

and other secondary concerns than network performance. Thus, we generate a power on decision when any controller exceeds the high threshold while requiring at least two controllers to fall below the low threshold for generating a power off decision. Triggering a decision when just one or two controllers cross the threshold might seem like we aggressively add or remove controller. But, our decisions are quite conservative because the resizing algorithm is executed only when the load is evenly distributed across all controllers. So, if a controller crosses the threshold, it indicates that all controllers are close to the threshold.

3.4.3 Extending Load Adaptation Algorithms

The load adaptation algorithms described above can be easily extended to satisfy additional requirements or constraints. Here we describe two such potential extensions to show the broad applicability and flexibility of the algorithm.

Controller Location. To reduce control plane latency, it may be better to assign a switch to a closeby controller. We can accommodate this requirement in ElastiCon by contraining migrations and controller additions and removals. To do so, in every iteration of the rebalancing algorithm (Algorithm 2), we consider only migrations to controllers close to the switch. This distance can be estimated based on topology information or controller to switch latency measurements. If the operator wants to set switch-controller mapping based on physical distance (in number of hops), he/she can use the network topology. The operator should use latency measurements when he/she wants to set switch-controller mapping based on logical distance (in milliseconds). Similarly, in the resizing algorithm (Algorithm 3), the new controllers added should be close to the overloaded controllers so that switches can migrate away from the overloaded controller. The first-fit algorithm used in CHECKRESIZING function should also be modified such that a switch can only "fit" in a closeby controller.

Switch Grouping. Assigning neighboring switches to the same controller may reduce inter-controller communication during flow setup and hence improve control plane efficiency. Graph partitioning algorithms can be used to partition the network into switch groups; and the result can be fed into ElastiCon. ElastiCon can be modified to treat each group as a single entity during migration and resizing, so that the switches of the same group are always controlled by the same controller except for short intervals during migration. The load measurements module should be modified to combine load readings of switches of a group and present it as a single entity to the load adaptation algorithm. When the rebalancing algorithm determines that the entity needs to be migrated, the EXECUTE_* functions should migrate all the switches of the group.

3.4.4 Adaptation Action

Following the adaptation decision, adaptation actions are executed to transform the network configuration (i.e., switch to controller mapping). A switch is migrated to a former slave by following the steps in our 4-phase migration protocol described before. In case of controller addition or removal, one or more switches may need to be reassigned to new master controllers that they are not currently connected to. This can be done by replacing one of the existing slave controllers' IP address of the switch with that of the new controller using the edit-config operation of OpenFlow Management and Configuration Protocol [1]. Once the connection between the new controller and the switch is established, we then invoke the migration procedure to swap the old master with the new slave controller. If a switch does not support updating controller IP addresses at runtime, other workarounds based on controller IP address virtualization are also possible (discussed in Section 4).

4. IMPLEMENTATION

In this section, we present further details on how we implement ElastiCon by modifying and adding components to the centralized Floodlight controller.

Distributed Data Store. We use Hazelcast to implement the distributed data store. Although other NoSql databases may have also worked here, we find Hazelcast a good choice due to its performance and flexibility. Hazelcast provides strong consistency, transaction support, and event notifications. Its in-memory data storage and distributed architecture ensures both low latency data access and high availability. Persistent data can be configured to write to disk. It is written in Java, which makes it easy for integration with Floodlight. We include the Hazelcast libraries in the Floodlight executable. The first Hazelcast node forms a new distributed data store. Subsequently, each Hazelcast node is configured with the IP addresses and ports of several peers. At least one of the peers needs to be active for the new node to join the distributed data store.

Controller. When a controller boots up, it publishes its own local data and retrieves data of other controllers by accessing Hazelcast. One such data is the IP address and TCP port of each controller needed for inter-controller communication. This allows the controllers to set up direct TCP connections with each other, so that they can invoke each other to set up paths for flows.

The switch to master controller mapping is also stored in Hazelcast using the unique switch datapath-id as the key. We have modified the core controller in Floodlight to allow a controller to act in different roles for different switches. The initial switch to master mapping can be determined in one of two ways. In the first method, the load adapter module running in the controller (described later) reads in the mapping from a configuration file and stores the information in Hazelcast. We also implement an ad hoc strategy by letting the controllers try to acquire a lock in Hazelcast when a switch connects to them. Only one controller can succeed in acquiring the lock; it then declares itself as the master for the switch.

Load Adaptation Module. The load measurement module is integrated into the controller. We use SIGAR API [19] to retrieve the CPU usage of the controller process. We enhanced the REST API of the controller to include CPU usage queries. The adaptation decision algorithm run on a separate host. It communicates with all controllers over the REST API. It requires the REST port and IP address of one of the controllers. Using that, it queries the controller for the IP address and REST port of all other controllers

and switch-to-controller mappings of all switches in the network. In each iteration, the program queries the CPU usage information from each controller and sends migration requests to the master controller of a switch when the switch needs to be migrated.

Adding and Removing Controllers. Migration of a switch to a newly connected controller is done in two steps. First, we replace the IP address and TCP port number of one of the slave controllers of the switch with those of the new controller. This can be done by using the edit-config operation of OpenFlow Management and Configuration Protocol [1]. Once the connection between the new controller and the switch is established, we then invoke the migration procedure to swap the old master with the new slave controller.

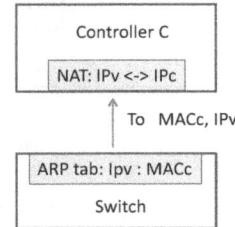

Figure 5: Controller virtual IP address binding

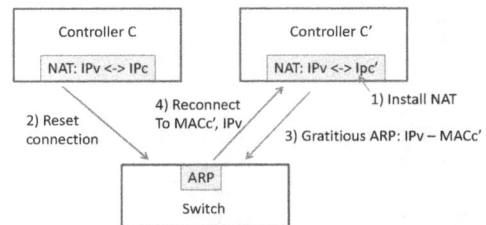

Figure 6: Controller binding change

If a switch does not support updating controller IP addresses at runtime, we can use the following procedure as a workaround, which is suitable when the control plane is configured to use the same layer 2 network (e.g., on the same VLAN). All switches are configured to use a set of virtual controller IP addresses, which will be mapped to the real controller IP addresses at runtime according to load condition. Such mapping can be realized by using ARP and Network Address Translation (NAT), as shown in Figure 5. When the virtual controller IP address ip_v for a switch is mapped to controller C's IP address ip_c, we use gratuitous ARP to bind the MAC address of the controller C with ip_v, so that the packets to ip_v can reach controller C. At controller C, we do NAT from ip_v to ip_c, so that the packets can be handled by the controller transparently.

Figure 6 shows how such binding can be changed when we need to replace controller C with controller C'. We first send a TCP reset message from C to disconnect the switch from the controller, and then use gratuitous ARP to bind MAC address of C' with ip_v. Note that connection reset to C is only done when C is not a master controller to avoid disruption in normal switch operation. When the switch tries to reconnect to ip_v, the message will reach C' instead of C. We then do a NAT from ip_v to $ip_{c'}$ at controller C' as before. Note that if the gratuitous ARP does not reach the switch before the reconnection request is sent, controller C simply rejects the reconnection request and the switch ultimately gets connected to controller C'.

5. EVALUATION

In this section, we evaluate the performance of our ElastiCon prototype using an emulated SDN-based data center network testbed. We first describe the enhanced Mininet testbed that we used to carry out the evaluation, and then present our experimental results.

5.1 Enhanced Mininet Testbed

Our experimental testbed is built on top of Mininet [14], which emulates a network of Open vSwitches [18]. Open vSwitch is a software-based virtual Openflow switch. It implements the data plane in kernel and the control plane as a user space process. Mininet has been widely used to demonstrate the functionalities, but not the performance, of a controller because of the overhead of emulating data flows. First, actual packets need to be exchanged between the vSwitch instances to emulate packet flows. Second, a flow arrival resulting in sending a `Packet-In` to the controller incurs kernel to user space context switch overhead in the Open vSwitch. From our initial experiments we observe that these overheads significantly reduce the maximum flow arrival rate that Mininet can emulate, which in turn slows down the control plane traffic generation capability of the testbed. Note that for the evaluation of ElastiCon, we are primarily concerned with the control plane traffic load and need not emulate the high overhead data plane. We achieve this by modifying Open vSwitch to inject `Packet-In` messages to the controller without actually transmitting packets on the data plane. We also log and drop `Flow-Mod` messages to avoid the additional overhead of inserting them in the flow table. Although we do not use the data plane during our experiments, we do not disable it. So, the controller generated messages (like LLDPs, ARPs) are still transmitted on the emulated network.

In order to experiment with larger networks we deployed multiple hosts to emulate the testbed. We modified Mininet to run the Open vSwitch instances on different hosts. We created GRE tunnels between the hosts running Open vSwitch instances to emulate links of the data center network. Since we do not actually transmit packets in the emulated network, the latency/bandwidth characteristics of these GRE tunnels do not impact our results. They are used only to transmit link-discovery messages to enable the controllers to construct a network topology. To isolate the switch to controller traffic from the emulated data plane of the network, we run Open vSwitch on hosts with two Ethernet ports. One port of each host is connected to a gigabit Ethernet switch and is used to carry the emulated data plane traffic. The other port of each host is connected to the hosts that run the controller. We isolated the inter-controller traffic from the controller-switch traffic too by running the controller on dual-port hosts.

5.2 Experimental Results

We report on the performance of ElastiCon using the routing application. All experiments are conducted on k=4 fat tree emulated on the testbed. We use 4 hosts to emulate the entire network. Each host emulates a pod and a core switch. Before starting the experiment, the emulated end hosts ping each other so that the routing application can learn the location of all end hosts in the emulated network.

Throughput. We send 10,000 back-to-back `Packet-In` messages and plot the throughput of ElastiCon with varying number of controller nodes (Figure 7(a)). We repeat the experiment while pinning the controllers to two cores of the quad-core server. We observe two trends in the results. First, adding controller nodes increases the throughput almost linearly. This is because there is no data sharing between controllers while responding to `Packet-In` messages.

Second, the throughput reduces when we restrict the controllers to two cores indicating that CPU is indeed the bottleneck.

Response time. We plot the response time behavior for `Packet-In` messages with changing flow arrival rate (see Figure 7(b)). We repeat the experiment while changing the number of controller nodes. As expected, we observe that response time increases marginally up to a certain point. Once the packet generation rate exceeds the capacity of the processor, queuing causes response time to shoot up. This point is reached at a higher packet-generation rate when ElastiCon has more nodes.

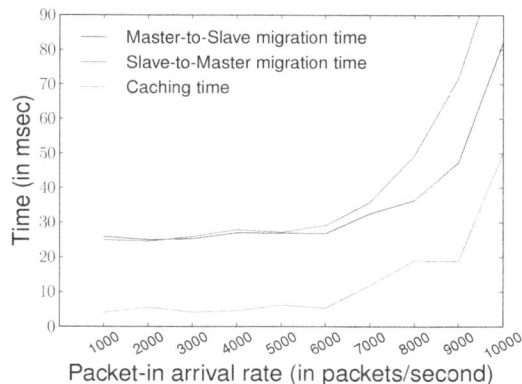

Figure 8: Migration time

Migration time. The time taken to migrate a switch is critical for the load balancing protocol to work efficiently. We define migration time for controller A as the time between sending the "start migration" message and "end migration" message. We define migration time for controller B as the time between receiving the "start migration" and sending the `Role-Request` to change to master. In a network with 3 controllers, we perform 200 migrations and observe the migration time for each migration at both controllers. We also observe the time for which controller B caches messages from the switch. We plot the 95th percentile of the migration and caching times in Figure 8. The plot shows that the migration time is minimal (few tens of milliseconds) and increases marginally as the load on the controller increases. The caching time is even smaller (around 5ms). This keeps memory usage of the message cache small (few KBs).

Automatic rebalancing under hot-spot traffic. We use a N=4 fat tree to evaluate the effect of the automatic load balancing algorithm. Three of the four pods of the fat tree are evenly loaded, while the flow arrival rate in the fourth pod is higher than that in the other three. We configure ElastiCon with four controllers, one assigned to all the switches of each pod. The master controller of the fourth pod is obviously more heavily loaded than the other three. Figure 9(a) shows the 95th percentile of the response time of all `Packet-In` messages before and after rebalancing. The `Packet-In` message rate in the fourth pod is varied on the X-axis. We truncate the y-axis at 20ms, so a bar at 20ms is actually much higher.

We observe that as traffic gets more skewed (i.e., the `Packet-In` rate in the fourth pod increases), we see a larger benefit by doing rebalancing corresponding to the 65-75% bars. At 70-80% hotspot, the system is unstable. The 95th percentile can be arbitrarily high depending on the amount of time the experiment is run before rebalancing, since the one of the controllers is overloaded (i.e., the `Packet-In` rate exceeds the saturation throughput). At 80% hot-

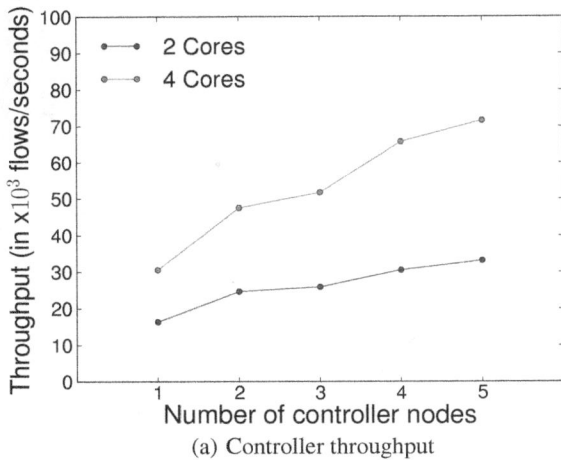

(a) Controller throughput

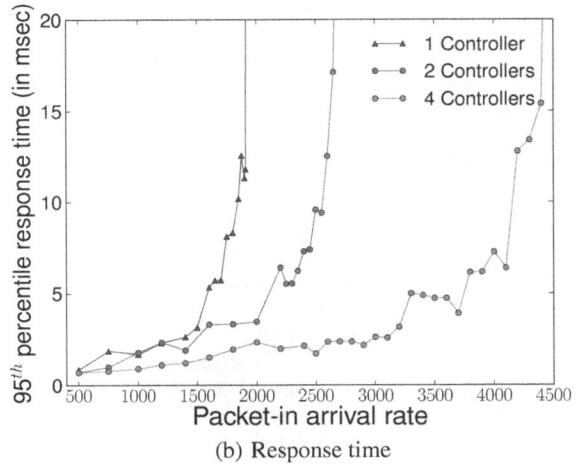

(b) Response time

Figure 7: Performance with varying number of controller nodes.

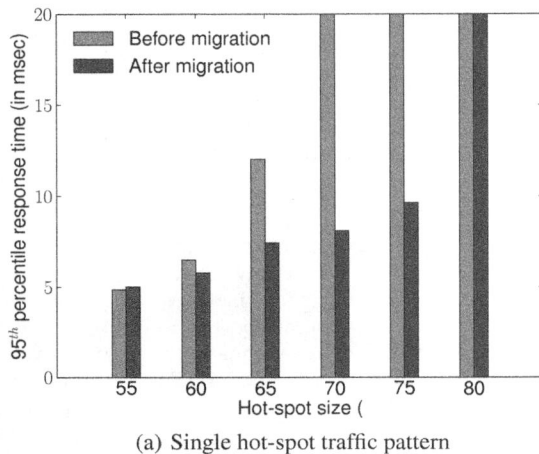

(a) Single hot-spot traffic pattern

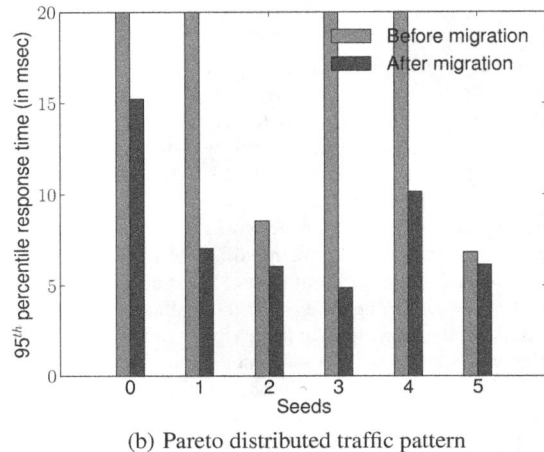

(b) Pareto distributed traffic pattern

Figure 9: Benefit of automatic rebalancing. We truncate the y-axis at 20ms. So a bar at 20ms is actually much higher.

spot, rebalancing by itself does not help as seen by the blue bar exceeding 20ms since there is no way to fit the workload among existing controllers.

Automatic rebalancing under Pareto distribution. We also evaluate the benefit of the rebalancing algorithm in the case where multiple hot spots may appear randomly following a Pareto distribution. As before, we use a N=4 fat tree with 4 controllers. The network generates 24,000 `Packet-In` messages per second. The message arrival rate is distributed across all the switches in the network using a Pareto distribution. We repeat the traffic pattern with 6 different seeds. We start with a random assignment of switches to controllers and apply the rebalancing algorithm. Figure 9(b) shows the 95th percentile response time with random assignment and with rebalancing.

Since a Pareto distribution is highly skewed, the improvement varies widely depending on the seed. If the distribution generated by a seed is more skewed, rebalancing is likely to deliver better response times over a random switch to controller assignment. But, if the Pareto distribution evenly distributes traffic across switches (see

seeds #2 and #5), random assignment does almost as well as rebalancing. In the Figure 9(b), we can observe that for all cases, rebalancing at least ensures that there is no controller that is severely overloaded while at least in four cases, random load balancing led to significant overload as evidenced by the high red bar.

Effect of resizing. We demonstrate how the resizing algorithm adapts the controllers as the number of `Packet-In` messages increases and decreases. We begin with a network with 2 controllers and an aggregate `Packet-In` rate of 8,000 packets per second. We increase the `Packet-In` rate in steps of 1,000 packets per second every 3 minutes until it reaches 12,000 packets per second. We then reduce it in steps of 1,000 packets per second every 3 minutes until it comes down to 6,000 packets per second. At all times, the `Packet-In` messages are equally distributed across switches, just for simplicity. We observe 95th percentile of the response time at each minute for the duration of the experiment. We also note the times at which ElastiCon adds and removes controllers to adapt to changes in load. The results are shown in Figure 10.

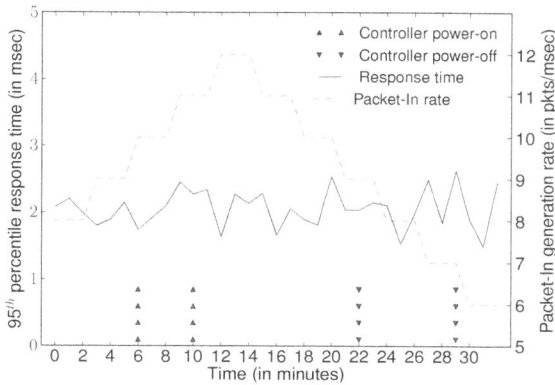

Figure 10: Growing and shrinking ElastiCon

We observe that ElastiCon adds a controller at the 6th and 10th minute of the experiment as the `Packet-In` rate rises. It removes controllers at the 22nd and 29th minute as the traffic falls. Also, we observe that the response time remains around 2ms for the entire duration of the experiment although the `Packet-In` rate rises and falls. Also, ElastiCon adds the controllers at 10,000 and 11,000 `Packet-In` messages per second and removes them at 9,000 and 7,000 `Packet-In` messages per second. As described earlier, this is because ElastiCon aggressively adds controllers and conservatively removes them.

6. CONCLUSION AND FUTURE WORK

In this paper, we presented our design of ElastiCon, a distributed elastic SDN controller. We designed and implemented algorithms for switch migration, controller load balancing and elasticity which form the core of the controller. We enhanced Mininet and used it to demonstrate the efficacy of those algorithms. Our current design does not address issues caused by failures, although we believe fault tolerance mechanisms can easily fit into this architecture. This may require running three or more controllers in equal role for each switch and using a consensus protocol between them to ensure there is always at least one master even if the new master crashes. We also plan to study the impact of application data sharing patterns on switch migration and elasticity. In addition, we plan to consider other factors like controller placement and controller performance isolation in a multi-tenant data center.

7. ACKNOWLEDGEMENTS

We thank the anonymous reviewers and Alex Bachmutsky, our shepherd, for their comments that helped improve the paper. This work was supported in part by NSF grants CNS-1054788, IIS-1017898.

8. REFERENCES

[1] OpenFlow Management and Configuration Protocol (OF-Config 1.1).
[2] Beacon. openflow.stanford.edu/display/Beacon/Home.
[3] BENSON, T., AKELLA, A., AND MALTZ, D. Network traffic characteristics of data centers in the wild. In *IMC* (2010).
[4] CAI, Z., COX, A. L., AND NG, T. S. E. Maestro: A system for scalable OpenFlow control. Tech. rep., CS Department, Rice University, 2010.
[5] CASADO, M., FREEDMAN, M. J., AND SHENKER, S. Ethane: Taking Control of the Enterprise. In *ACM SIGCOMM* (2007).
[6] CURTIS, A., MOGUL, J., TOURRILHES, J., YALAGANDULA, P., SHARMA, P., AND BANERJEE, S. DevoFlow: Scaling Flow Management for High-Performance Networks. In *ACM SIGCOMM* (2011).
[7] DIXIT, A., HAO, F., MUKHERJEE, S., LAKSHMAN, T., AND KOMPELLA, R. Towards an Elastic Distributed SDN Controller. In *HotSDN* (2013).
[8] Floodlight. floodlight.openflowhub.org.
[9] GREENBERG, A., HJALMTYSSON, G., MALTZ, D., MYERS, A., REXFORD, J., XIE, G., YAN, H., ZHAN, J., AND ZHANG, H. A clean slate 4D approach to network control and management. In *SIGCOMM CCR* (2005).
[10] GUDE, N., KOPONEN, T., PETTIT, J., PFAFF, B., CASADO, M., MCKEOWN, N., AND SHENKER, S. NOX: Towards an Operating System for Networks. In *SIGCOMM CCR* (2008).
[11] GULATI, A., ANNE HOLLER, A. M. J., SHANMUGANATHAN, G., WALDSPURGER, C., AND ZHU, X. VMware Distributed Resource Management: Design, Implementation and Lessons Learned.
[12] KOPONEN, T., CASADO, M., GUDE, N., STRIBLING, J., POUTIEVSKI, L., ZHU, M., RAMANATHAN, R., IWATA, Y., INOUE, H., HAMA, T., AND SHENKER, S. Onix: A Distributed Control Platform for Large-scale Production Networks. In *OSDI* (2010).
[13] LAKSHMAN, T., NANDAGOPAL, T., RAMJEE, R., SABNANI, K., AND WOO, T. The SoftRouter Architecture. In *ACM HOTNETS* (2004).
[14] LANTZ, B., HELLER, B., AND MCKEOWN, N. A Network in a Laptop: Rapid Prototyping for Software-Defined Networks. In *HotNets* (2010).
[15] LEVIN, D., WUNDSAM, A., HELLER, B., HANDIGOL, N., AND FELDMANN, A. Logically Centralized? State Distribution Trade-offs in Software Defined Networks. In *HotSDN* (2012).
[16] MCKEOWN, N., ANDERSON, T., BALAKRISHNAN, H., PARULKAR, G., PETERSON, L., REXFORD, J., SHENKER, S., AND TURNER, J. OpenFlow: Enabling Innovation in Campus Networks. *SIGCOMM CCR* (2008).
[17] OpenDaylight. http://www.opendaylight.org/.
[18] Open vswitch. openvswitch.org.
[19] Hyperic SIGAR API. http://www.hyperic.com/products/sigar.
[20] TOOTOONCHIAN, A., AND GANJALI, Y. HyperFlow: A Distributed Control Plane for OpenFlow. In *INM/WREN* (2010).
[21] TOOTOONCHIAN, A., GORBUNOV, S., GANJALI, Y., CASADO, M., AND SHERWOOD, R. On Controller Performance in Software-Defined Networks. In *HotICE* (2012).

A Packet-In Message Filtering Mechanism for Protection of Control Plane in OpenFlow Networks

Daisuke Kotani
Kyoto University
Yoshida-Honmachi, Sakyo, Kyoto, Japan
kotani@net.ist.i.kyoto-u.ac.jp

Yasuo Okabe
Kyoto University
Yoshida-Honmachi, Sakyo, Kyoto, Japan
okabe@i.kyoto-u.ac.jp

ABSTRACT

Protecting control planes in networking hardware from high rate packets is a critical issue for networks under operation. One common approach for conventional networking hardware is to offload expensive functions onto hard-wired offload engines as ASICs. OpenFlow networks are expected to provide greater network control flexibility by an open interface to the packet-forwarding plane and by centralized controllers. In OpenFlow networks, the approach for conventional networking hardware alone is inadequate because it restricts a certain amount of flexibility that OpenFlow is expected to provide. Therefore, we need a generic control plane protection mechanism in OpenFlow switches as a last resort. In this paper, we propose a mechanism to filter out Packet-In messages without dropping important ones for network control. Our proposed mechanism works simply. Switches record the values of packet header fields before sending Packet-In messages, which are specified by the controllers in advance, and filter out packets that have the same values as the recorded ones. We implemented and evaluated the proposed mechanism on a prototype software switch, concluding that it dramatically reduces CPU loads in the switches and passes important Packet-In messages for network control.

Categories and Subject Descriptors

C.2 [**Computer-Communication Networks**]: Miscellaneous

General Terms

Design

Keywords

Network Security; Software-defined Networking

1. INTRODUCTION

Such networking hardware as Ethernet switches commonly forwards most packets in high performance by ASICs, and its control software runs on low performance CPUs. The software and the CPUs are called a control plane. Some functions in networking hardware, which are designed under the assumption that they will rarely used, are implemented in software and executed by the control plane; however, in many cases these functions are executed frequently. Hosts connected to networks sometimes send an unexpected amount of traffic, and some of such traffic may use these functions. Some networks need to use these functions to meet requirements for the networks, and many hosts use them at the same time. In these cases, the control plane in the networking hardware becomes overloaded, operation becomes unwieldy, and networking hardware and operators often suffer from the high loads caused by such traffic. To overcome this problem, networking hardware is trying to offload the execution of these functions onto hard-wired offload engines like ASICs, Network Processors and FPGAs[1][8].

Recent advances in Software-Defined Networking(SDN)[9] based on OpenFlow[10] allow users other than networking hardware vendors to program how networking hardware with an OpenFlow support feature (switches hereafter) forwards packets by software on external computers. The software is called a controller, which centrally manages all the switches. The control plane in OpenFlow networks includes the software that handles OpenFlow messages in the switches and the control networks between the switches and the controller in addition to the controller itself.

In OpenFlow, packet-forwarding rules are defined per flow and the rules are called flow entries, which we can set for a group of flows using wildcard fields. Packets that match flow entries are processed at high speed by ASICs or other hard-wired offload engines, and these engines are called the datapath. Packets that do not match any flow entry are processed in a pre-configured way, such as sending them to the controller through the control plane as Packet-In messages or discarding them on the datapath. When the controller receives Packet-In messages, it installs new flow entries into the switches as soon as possible and forwards the packets included in the Packet-In messages. Although installing most of the flow entries before receiving the packets is recommended, the controller needs some Packet-In messages to learn the network statuses from packets, such as the MAC address learning, the multicast source detection, the ARP and the broadcast handling, etc.

This SDN trend based on OpenFlow introduces a new

problem: protecting the control plane from too many packets that bring high loads in the control plane, especially in switches, while preserving the flexibility provided by OpenFlow. In switches, there is a time lag between sending a Packet-In message and adding new flow entries that correspond to the Packet-In message. When some hosts suddenly start to send too many packets without advance notice and the switches are configured to send the packets that match no flow entry to the controller as the Packet-In messages, the switches receive too many packets and send many Packet-In messages before the controller installs the new flow entries. In this situation, the switches are overloaded by creating and sending many Packet-In messages, delaying the handling of OpenFlow messages from the controller. As a result, the control plane becomes overloaded and unstable.

A conventional way mitigates this problem by offloading more packet processing to hard-wired offload engines. However, this choice is inappropriate because programming these engines is very different from developing software, and this difference restricts the flexibility provided by OpenFlow. Many OpenFlow extension proposals use OpenFlow in various use cases [2][11][13][14][17][18][19]. These proposals process more packets in the datapath and reduce the load on the control plane, but implementing all the extensions in the datapath is almost impossible to support all the potential cases. For this reason, we assume that some functions are only provided by the controllers, and the switches need a generic control plane protection mechanism as a last resort. Limiting the total Packet-In message rate in the switches seems to be a simple solution, but this approach has a drawback; many important Packet-In messages for network control are dropped because this approach downplays their importance. As a result, the controllers may have difficulty n learning the network statuses that are necessary for network control.

In this paper, we propose a mechanism where the switches pass important Packet-In messages for network control and apply restrictions that are selected by the network operators or controller developers on less important Packet-In messages, like filtering out the Packet-In messages or greatly limiting the Packet-In message rate. The most important work of the controllers is continuing to control the networks. This work includes learning the necessary statuses for network control, and inserting and deleting flow entries quickly, etc. To continue this work, the switches should drop packets that bring overloads in the control plane, especially in the switches with low CPU performance. At the same time, the switches must not drop important packets for network control from which the controller learns the necessary statuses.

The controllers parse packets based on protocol specifications like Ethernet, IP, TCP, UDP, or other protocols and store the necessary data extracted from the packets. The header fields whose values the controllers need to get vary among the controller designs, and packets that include the same values in their header fields provide the same data for the controllers. Therefore, the controllers only need one packet of them, and the others are filtered out.

The proposed mechanism consists of two parts: Pending Flow Rules and Pending Flow Tables. The pending flow rules are entries to specify the header fields to which the controllers refers. We assume that the controllers set the pending flow rules to the switches before the switches start to process packets. The pending flow tables are lists of en-

tries where the switches record the values of the header fields in packets that are included in Packet-In messages. One pending flow table per pending flow rule is created.

When a switch receives a packet and no flow entry matches it, the switch looks up the pending flow rules that match the packet. If a matched rule is found and an entry in the pending flow table for the matched rule also matches the packet, it is regarded as less important for network control. The packet is processed by actions selected by the network operators or controller developers that specify how to process packets for less important packets for network control, such as the rate limitation for such Packet-In messages or packet flooding on the network. If a matched rule is found but the switch cannot find any entry in the pending flow table of the matched rule, a switch creates and installs a new entry in the rule's pending flow table by copying the values in the header fields specified by the rule from the packet. Then it sends the packet to the controller as a Packet-In message without any restriction. If no rule is found, the packet is discarded.

We implemented our proposed mechanism on Open vSwitch by extending OpenFlow's standard mechanisms. We discussed how our proposed mechanism can be used in various cases and showed that it introduces little inflexibility. We also experimentally showed that it dramatically reduced the CPU usage in the switches while forwarding important packets to controllers.

This paper is organized as follows. Section 2 introduces related work. We explain our proposed mechanism in Sec. 3, and its implementation to Open vSwitch in Sec. 4. In Sec. 5, we show how it can be used in various cases, and describe experiments where it reduced CPU usage in switches. Section 6 discusses our proposed mechanism, and Section 7 concludes this paper.

2. RELATED WORK

2.1 OpenFlow

OpenFlow[10], which was originally designed to give researchers and engineers an opportunity to easily test their new ideas in the networks that they usually use, defines an API of the datapath in switches for external control programs called controllers. Currently OpenFlow is considered an important protocol between the control plane and the datapath in Software-Defined Networking (SDN) [9].

In OpenFlow, packet-forwarding rules are stored in flow tables, where entries are called flow entries. The controllers manage the flow tables by the OpenFlow protocol. One flow entry consists of three elements: a condition, actions, and statistics. The condition is used to match packets and consists of a priority value and the match fields, including an input port number and such values of packet header fields as source and destination Ethernet addresses, IP addresses, and TCP/UDP/SCTP port numbers. A wildcard is allowed in each header field. The actions list those applied to the matched packets, for example, outputting to specified ports, rewriting packet header fields, sending the packets to the controller as Packet-In messages, and discarding them. The statistics include packet counters that count the matched packets in bytes, the duration until the entry's expiration, etc.

When a switch receives a packet, first it looks up its flow tables to find the flow entries that match it. If some entries are found, the packet is processed based on the entries. If no entry is found, the switch handles the packet by a pre-configured table-miss entry, such as discarding it or sending it to the controller as a Packet-In message.

Flow entries are installed in two methods: proactive and reactive[5]. In the proactive method, the controllers set as many flow entries as possible to the switches before the hosts are connected so that the switches need not to send so many Packet-In messages. In this case, most flow entries are generated using information provided by external systems, like a cloud management system. In the reactive method, the controllers create and install flow entries corresponding to the Packet-In messages when they receive the Packet-In messages from the switches. The controllers set no flow entry in advance. If the controllers know the network statuses that the controllers cannot learn in advance, such as where the hosts are connected, they need the Packet-In messages to learn the network statuses regardless of the methods used by the controllers for the flow entry setup.

OpenFlow Switch Specification 1.3 [12] and subsequent versions have a mechanism called a Meter that limits the rate of the packets in a group of flows by the number of packets or bytes. We can use a Meter to limit the rate of a group of Packet-In messages.

2.2 Increasing Scalability for OpenFlow Networks

OpenFlow networks are centrally managed by controllers, who are a bottleneck in large OpenFlow networks because they generally process more OpenFlow messages as a network becomes larger. There are two research directions to use OpenFlow in large networks.

One approach increases the message processing performance in the controllers. To achieve this, distributed controller platforms create logically centralized but physically distributed controllers. ONIX[6] and HyperFlow[15] are examples of such platforms. In them, the controllers share data by distributed databases or storage for logically centralized control, and every switch in the network communicates with one of the controllers. When the controllers need more message processing performance, an operator just adds servers that are running the control programs. This approach works well if each switch sends a few messages per second; it cannot alleviate the problem when the switches become overloaded, which is what we address.

The other approach enhances switch functionality so that the switches can process more packets by themselves. DI-FANE[19] added a topology discovery function and another function that distributes the flow entry cache to neighbor switches to easily enforce network access policies. DevoFlow[3] shows that the switches have meager flow setup performance and proposed a flow entry clone flag in the flow entries. The flow entry clone flag shows that, when a packet matches the flow entry, the switch creates and installs a new flow entry by copying the same actions as the matched flow entry and the values of all the header fields in the packet to the match fields of the new entry. This extension is mainly used for elephant flow detection. Other examples of extensions include Information-Centric Networking support[2][17], flexible sampling actions[14][18], and multiple output ports in one action[11]. These extensions are often designed for such specific use cases as access policy enforcement and elephant flow detection, but they are impractical to design, imple-

ment, and deploy new switch functions every time a new use case and a new extension emerge. The controllers are forced to execute new functions by themselves using Packet-In messages until the switches support these functions and need a generic control plane protection mechanism from many Packet-In messages.

Our previous work[7] filtered out Packet-In messages including packets that have the same values in all the header fields as the values in the previously transmitted packets. The switches create an entry by cloning the values of all the header fields in the packet to the match fields of new entries like DevoFlow[3]. The switches limit the rate of the Packet-In messages that match the entries created by this mechanism. Our previous work resembles DevoFlow[3] in terms of creating the match fields of entries, and the main difference is the actions in the newly created entries.

A serious limitation both in our previous work[7] and in the DevoFlow[3] approach is that the number of entries generated by these mechanisms is rapidly increased, as defined by a pair of IP addresses and TCP/UDP/SCTP port numbers. The entries are usually stored in TCAM or RAM of the switches, and such spaces overflow easily in many cases where this problem occurs, for example, TCP SYN flooding and ARP flooding.

AVANT-GUARD[13], which is a work for control plane protection whose motivation resembles ours, mainly protects the control plane from TCP SYN flooding attacks by a SYN cookies approach[4]. In real networks, hosts often send such packets other than TCP as UDP and ARP, and such protocols can also be used for overloading the control plane. Therefore, we need a new mechanism that can prevent the control plane from overloads regardless of the protocols used by packets.

3. PROPOSED MECHANISM

3.1 Which Packet-In Messages are Important for Network Control and Controllers?

To versatilely reduce the loads both on switches and on controllers that are caused by too many Packet-In messages, we discuss which Packet-In messages are candidates for being filtered out by the switches. This classification must be done without asking the controllers per packet.

The most important role of the controllers is to control the networks, such as the insertion and the deletion of flow entries, and packets should not be dropped that contain important data for control, including data used for the flow entries. From this point of view, if the controllers extract and store the same data from several packets, the controllers only need one such packet, and the switches can drop the others. The switches can also drop other packets that include only unnecessary header fields. When designing a mechanism to enable the switches to process Packet-In messages in this way, we need to consider the following points that current OpenFlow specifications do not handle.

The first is that the switches must forward the packet that arrived first from the packets that have the same values in their header fields to the controllers so that they can get the necessary data as soon as possible. OpenFlow expects that the controllers set the flow entries as quickly as possible if a packet matches no flow entry so that subsequent packets can be processed at the datapath. If the modification of new flow entries is delayed, subsequent packets are also for-

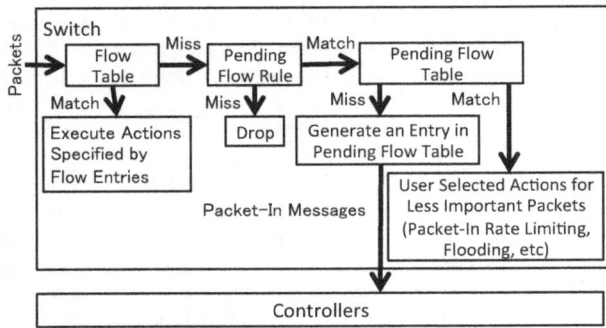

Figure 1: Conceptual diagram for the proposed mechanism. Flow tables have highest priority. Packets are discarded that match no pending flow rule. Pending flow tables determine whether the switch executes the user selected actions.

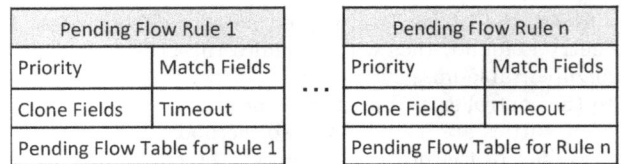

Figure 2: Relationship of concept between Pending Flow Rules and Tables. Statistics are omitted from Rules for simplicity.

warded to the controllers, or hosts cannot start to quickly communicate. This is unexpected behavior.

The second one is that different controllers must refer to different sets of header fields in packets, and the set of header fields depends on the controller design. This means that many controllers use only part of all of the header fields. For example, if a controller correlates an Ethernet address with a switch and a port, it needs to learn a source Ethernet address in the packets and only needs one packet with the same source Ethernet address. Similarly, mapping an IP address and a port only requires a source IP address in the packets, and the source and the destination IP addresses are adequate for a load balancing function using IP addresses.

In the following section, we explain our proposed mechanism that filters out Packet-In messages including packets whose header filed values are the same as the packets that have already been sent as Packet-In messages, while considering the header fields to which the controllers refers.

3.2 Overview of Proposed Mechanism

Figure 1 shows a conceptual diagram of the overview of our proposed mechanism. We added two components to the switches: Pending Flow Table and Pending Flow Rule. First, the switches look up entries that match a packet in the flow table, then in the pending flow rule, and finally in the matched rule's pending flow table. The packets are discarded that do not match any entry in these three.

The switches record the header field values in the packets into the pending flow table when they send them to the controller as Packet-In messages. The switches regard packets that match the entries in the pending flow tables as less important for network control and execute the user selected actions to filter out them.

The pending flow rules specify the header fields whose values are recorded in the pending flow tables. One pending flow rule includes a list of the header fields whose values are recorded and a pending flow table with entries generated by the rule. The header fields in the list include those to which the controller refers, and the controller sets the pending flow rules before the switches start to process the packets. If a pending flow rule matches a packet but the switch cannot find any matched entry in the associated pending flow table, the switch creates an entry for the pending flow table from

the matched rule and the packet and installs it into the table.

The user selected actions, which are applied to less important packets, must be executed at the datapath to reduce the amount of packets handled by the OpenFlow agents in the switches, and the network operators or controller developers select the actions based on their policies. If they want to minimize packet loss, for example, they select a packet flooding actions or actions to severely limit the rate of Packet-In messages. If they are not concerned with a small amount of packet loss, they select an action that discards a packet.

3.3 Pending Flow Rules

With the pending flow rules, the controllers inform the switches which header fields are important for network control. Using this information, the switches avoid recording values in less important header fields, and we can prevent the switches from explosively increasing the entries in the pending flow tables.

Each rule consists of the match fields and the clone fields, all of which list the header fields whose values should be recorded in the switch, the timeout values, a priority value, the statistics and the pending flow table associated with the rule (Fig. 2).

The match fields and priority values closely resemble the flow entries in OpenFlow. The match fields include the values of the header fields that the matched packets have, and a wildcard is allowed in each header field. If more than one rule matches the packets, the one with the highest priority value is applied.

The clone fields are header fields whose values must be recorded in switches. The clone fields include all the header fields with specific values in the match fields of the rule in addition to some header fields that are wildcards in the match fields. When the switches create a new entry in the pending flow table associated with the matched rule, the values of the header fields that are listed in the clone fields are copied from the matched packet to the match fields of the new entry. The other header fields are set to the wildcards in the new entry.

There are two timeout values in the pending flow rules. One is a hard timeout for the entries in the pending flow table that are generated by the rule, and the other is a hard timeout for the rule itself. We assume that the match fields and the clone fields in the rules should be static because their contents are determined only by the controller design. Therefore, a timeout for the rules must be long or they will not expire.

The statistics are the same as the flow entries and include the number of packets or the sum of the packet length that matches the rule, the duration from the installation, etc. They are useful to determine whether the controller should temporarily evict the pending flow rules from the switches when the spaces for storing the entries used for matching packets, such as RAM and TCAM, become full in the switches.

3.4 Pending Flow Table

A pending flow table is a list of entries that include the values in the header fields of the packets that the switch has already sent to the controller as Packet-In messages. Since we regard the packets that match the entries in the pending flow tables as less important ones for network control, we pre-configure actions for these packets, called User Selected Actions in Fig. 1, so that the switch sends fewer of them to the controller so much. The following are examples of user selected actions: limiting the rate of Packet-In messages including these packets, flooding these packets to the network, discarding them, etc. We assume that these actions are executed at the datapath to prevent the OpenFlow agents from overloading the switches.

An entry in the pending flow tables consists of the match fields, a hard timeout value and the statistics and resembles the flow entries. The match fields include an input port number and the values of the header fields in the matched packets; a wildcard is allowed in each header field. The clone fields in the parent pending flow rule specify the header fields whose values are recorded in the pending flow table, and the header fields, which are not listed in the clone fields, are wildcards in the match fields of the entries in the pending flow table.

A hard timeout value in the entries is duration until the entry's removal after the entry's insertion to the pending flow table. We assume that a hard timeout is a small value for the following reason. Packet-In messages including important packets may be lost due to other reasons than we are trying to solve, such as queue overflow, even when the datapath filters out less important packets by the proposed mechanism. In general, hosts resend lost packets at intervals of one or a few seconds if necessary. To avoid situations where the controllers do not receive important packets for a long time and hosts cannot communicate by datapaths, we need to assure that the controllers can receive important packets that are retransmitted by the hosts without being filtered out by the pending flow tables. In addition, when the controllers successfully install the new flow entries generated by the Packet-In messages, the entries in the pending flow tables corresponding to the new flow entries are not used again. Therefore, the entries of the pending flow tables must be deleted before the packets are retransmitted and need a hard timeout value within one or a few seconds.

The statistics are the same as the flow entries and include the number of packets and the packet length that matches the entry, etc. These statistics are used for deleting entries from the pending flow tables when the memory in a switch is full, for example.

Entries are added when a packet matches a pending flow rule but does not match any entry in the matched rule's pending flow table, and entries are removed when they are timed out.

3.5 An Example of Pending Flow Rule and Table

Table 1 shows an example of the pending flow rules, the pending flow tables, and the generated entries in the pending flow tables from the packets and the rules in a switch.

We assume that a controller is designed to manage hosts by IP addresses, and the switches forward IPv4 packets by IPv4 addresses and other packets by Ethernet addresses. In this context, the controller learns the hosts' IP addresses, the Ethernet addresses, and the connected port numbers and sets the flow entries using the source, destination IP, and Ethernet addresses. Rule 1 in Tab. 1 shows that a switch records an input port number, an Ethernet Frame Type (0x0800, IPv4), as well as source and destination Ethernet, and IP addresses in its pending flow table for the IPv4 packets. Rule 2 is for other packets and does not record the values of the IPv4 related header fields (Ethernet Frame Type and IP addresses). These rules do not automatically expire, and the entries in the pending flow tables have a short hard timeout value of 1 second (Timeout of Rule-Clone in Tab. 1). The switches limit the rate of the Packet-In messages including the packets that match the entries in the pending flow table.

When Packet 1 in Tab. 1 arrives at the switch and no flow entry matches it, the switch looks up the pending flow rules, and both the Rules 1 and 2 match Packet 1. The switch applies Rule 1 to Packet 1 because of a higher priority value than Rule 2 and creates an entry in the pending flow table for Rule 1 by copying the input port number, the Ethernet Frame Type, the source and destination Ethernet and IP addresses from Packet 1, and a hard timeout value in the pending flow table from Rule 1. When the switch receives subsequent packets that have the same Ethernet and IP addresses as Packet 1 within one second after the entry's insertion in Rule 1's pending flow table, the switch limits the rate of creating and sending Packet-In messages (including such packets) and does not add any new entries to the pending flow tables.

When Packet 2 in Tab. 1 arrives at the switch and no flow entry matches Packet 2, only Rule 2 matches Packet 2, and a new entry is added to Rule 2's pending flow table. In the new entry, only the input port and the source and destination Ethernet addresses are copied from Packet 2 to the match fields of the new entry. The Ethernet Frame Type and the source and destination IP addresses are set to wildcards because the clone fields in the Rule 2 do not include these fields. The subsequent packets with the same source and destination Ethernet addresses except the IPv4 packets match the new entry, and the rate of Packet-In messages (including these packets) is limited.

If an IPv4 packet with different source or destination IP addresses arrives at the switch, a new entry is created in the pending flow table for Rule 1, and the Packet-In message including this packet is sent to the controller. In the same way, if a packet other than IPv4 arrives at the switch, a new entry is created in the pending flow table for the Rule 2, and the packet is sent to the controller as a Packet-In message without any limitations.

4. PROTOTYPE SWITCH IMPLEMENTATION

We implemented our proposed mechanism in Open vSwitch[1].

Before explaining the design of our prototype switch, we explain the architecture of Open vSwitch (Fig. 3), which consists of two parts: a datapath module and a userspace

---

[1]We used a version of commit 4ca808d.

Table 1: Example of Pending Flow Rules, Packets, and Pending Flow Tables (in part). Rules 1 and 2 match Packet 1, and Rule 1 is selected because of higher priority value. Only Rule 2 matches Packet 2.

		Priority	Input Port	Ethernet Frame Type	Source Ethernet Address	Destination Ethernet Address	Source IP Address	Destination IP Address	Actions	Time-out	
Packet 1		-	1	0x0800	00:00:5e:00:53:01	00:00:5e:00:53:02	192.0.2.1	203.0.113.1	-	-	
Packet 2		-	1	0x809b	00:00:5e:00:53:03	00:00:5e:00:53:04	-	-	-	-	
Rule 1	Match	2	*	0x0800	*	*	*	*	-	∞	
	Clone	-	Yes	Yes	Yes	Yes	Yes	Yes	-	1 sec	
	Table	-	1	0x0800	00:00:5e:00:53:01	00:00:5e:00:53:02	192.0.2.1	203.0.113.1	Send as Packet-In through Rate Limit	1 sec	from Packet 1
Rule 2	Match	1	*	*	*	*	*	*	-	∞	
	Clone	-	Yes	No	Yes	Yes	No	No	-	1 sec	
	Table	-	1	*	00:00:5e:00:53:03	00:00:5e:00:53:04	*	*	Send as Packet-In through Rate Limit	1 sec	from Packet 2

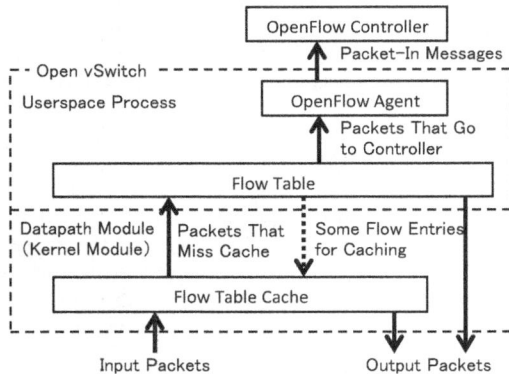

Figure 3: Open vSwitch Architecture

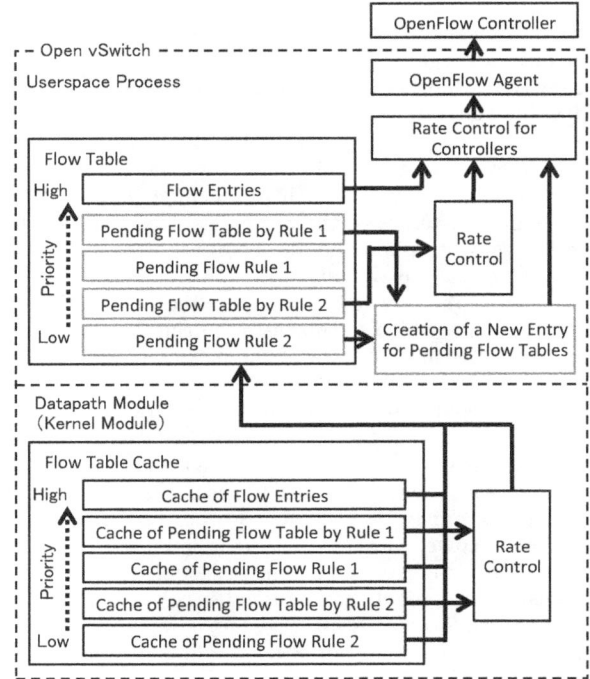

Figure 4: Overview of design of our prototype switch implementation based on Open vSwitch

process. The former is a kernel module that forwards packets in the kernel using the flow table cache. The packets that are not matched by the flow table cache are passed to the userspace process by an Inter-Process Communication mechanism. The userspace process looks up the flow entries that match the packets in the flow table, processes them, and sets the matched entry to the flow table cache in the kernel module. The packets that go to the controller are always processed at the OpenFlow agent in the userspace process, like the conventional hardware switches. In this way, most packets are processed at the kernel module; some are processed in the userspace process.

Figure 4 shows an overview of our prototype switch's design. The elements shown in red boxes are the components that we added for the proposed mechanism. In our prototype switch, we selected the actions that send packets to the controller as Packet-In messages with a very limited rate for the packets that match the entries in the pending flow tables.

We translated the two components we added in Fig. 1, Pending Flow Rules and Pending Flow Tables, into one flow table to avoid increasing the matching overhead introduced by the pending flow rules and tables. Each flow entry corresponds to an entry in the pending flow rules or tables. The flow entries for the pending flow tables have an action to limit the rate of the packets and an action to send a packet to the controller. The flow entries for the pending flow rules have a new action that we added for new entries in the pending flow table and an action to send Packet-In messages to the controller.

To get the same results as the switches that search for the flow tables, the pending flow rules, and the pending flow tables in the order (indicated by arrows in Fig. 1 for the matched entry, we assign different priority values to each component (Fig. 4). We set the highest priority value to the flow entries by the standard OpenFlow and assign the lower priority values to the pending flow table and rule sets. The pending flow table and rule sets are arranged in the order of the priority values in the pending flow rules, and within a table and a rule that comprise a set, a higher priority value is assigned to the table. The rule has a lower priority value.

In the situation of Fig. 4, Pending Flow Rule 1 has a higher priority value than Pending Flow Rule 2. In the flow table, the flow entries for the pending flow table for Rule 1 have a higher priority value than the flow entry for Rule 1. The priority values are assigned to the flow entries related to Rule 2 in the same way.

The new action's role we added is for a new flow entry in

the pending flow tables associated to the rule that matches a packet. The new action has the following parameters: the clone fields explained in Sec. 3.3, timeout and priority values for the new flow entries, and a Meter ID for limiting the rate of the packets that match the new flow entries. When this action is executed, the switches set a new flow entry for the pending flow table with the priority value in the action, a timeout value in the action, the match fields whose values are copied from the packets according to the clone fields, and user selected actions, which is to packets that match the new entry to the controller through a Meter specified by the Meter ID in our case. Although the new action is designed to limit the rate of packets that match an entry in the pending flow tables, it is easy to modify how a switch processes the packets that match the entry, such as flooding such packets to networks by replacing the actions.

Controllers can set the pending flow rules like the flow entries. A flow entry works as a pending flow rule if it has the new action that we added, a lower priority value than the flow entries for the pending flow table for the rule, and a higher priority value than the pending flow tables for the rules with lower priority.

The prototype switch uses a rate limiting mechanism in two ways. One limits the total rate of the Packet-In messages to a controller, which is shown as Rate Control for Controllers in Fig. 4. Any Packet-In message sent by a switch passes through this mechanism. In the original Open vSwitch, this mechanism has a queue of Packet-In messages per port to prevent the overflow of packets from a specific port into the queue of Packet-In messages to the controller and to avoid dropping many packets from other ports. We modified it to use only one queue because the proposed mechanism can provide a very similar function in a more generic way. The other limits the rate of packets that match the entries in the pending flow tables; this is shown as the Rate Control in Fig. 4. There are two Rate Controls for the pending flow tables: one in the kernel module and another in the userspace process. The Rate Control in the kernel module reduces the packets that are processed at the userspace process, and packets go through it if they match the flow entry cache of the pending flow tables. Packets that do not match the flow entry cache are processed at the userspace process and go through the Rate Control in the userspace process if necessary.

We implemented our own simple rate limiting mechanism for Rate Control. The Meter mechanism was not implemented in Open vSwitch when we implemented the prototype switch, although the OpenFlow specification defines it to limit the rate of the packets. Our simple rate limiting mechanism can be replaced with Meter.

5. EVALUATION

5.1 Use Cases and Pending Flow Rules

The controllers determine how the OpenFlow networks forward packets, but they often see Ethernet addresses to emulate Ethernet switches, IP addresses to emulate routers, and TCP and UDP port numbers for server and link load balancing. We can use our proposed mechanism in these scenarios as follows, and the number of required pending flow rules is summarized in Tab. 2.

Ethernet Switching: A controller emulating Ethernet switches must know the ports to which the hosts are connected and

their Ethernet addresses to create an Ethernet address table. It sets the flow entries that have a specific input port number and the source and destination Ethernet addresses in the match fields to forward packets between known hosts in the datapath. In this case, we use only one pending flow rule; the controller sets a pending flow rule to the switches to record an input port number and the source and destination Ethernet addresses.

IP Routing: A controller emulating routers must see the IP addresses in packets to associate the IP addresses with Ethernet addresses and handle the ARP packets in the IPv4 and the Neighbor Discovery in IPv6. The controller must also provide an Ethernet switching function to forward packets other than IPs between hosts in the same broadcast domain. This example represents cases where the switches see the header fields of the protocols in multiple layers, and we use the priority values in these cases. We set two pending flow rules with the highest priority values, which match the ARP and Neighbor Discovery related packets. These rules copy the values in the ARP headers and Neighbor Discovery related headers including ICMPv6 to the match fields of the new entries in the pending flow tables. The second highest priority value is assigned to the two pending flow rules that match the other IPv4 and IPv6 packets. These rules set both the source and destination IP and Ethernet addresses to the match fields in the new entries in the pending flow tables for these rules. The lowest priority value is assigned to one pending flow rule that matches the other Ethernet frames, and the rule is the same as the case of Ethernet switching. In total, five pending flow rules are used in this case.

Load Balancing: We use the proposed mechanism for controllers that also see the header fields in transport protocols like TCP and UDP. Server load balancing is one example of such functions. When a controller has the server load balancing function, it sets one pending flow rule with the highest priority value whose match fields include an IP protocol number, a destination IP address, and a destination port. The clone fields of the rule include source, destination IP, and Ethernet addresses in addition to an IP protocol number and a destination port. In this case, one pending flow rule per (destination IP address and destination port) pair is required as well as the IP routing rules. For link load balancing with flow entries, a single pending flow rule alone is necessary, and the rule matches all the packets other than those outputted to ports that are not included in the link load balancing.

Network Address and Port Translation (NAPT): Network Address and Port Translation (NAPT) is another example of functions where the controllers see the header fields in the transport protocols. The controllers with the NAPT function set one pending flow rule with the highest priority value per source IP address prefix to which the NAPT function is applied. The rule matches all the packets whose source IP addresses are in the range to apply the NAPT function, and the clone fields of the rule include an IP protocol number, source and destination ports, and IP and Ethernet addresses. Lower priority values are assigned to the rules that handle IP and Ethernet packets, as explained for IP routing.

5.2 Loads in Switches

With our prototype switch, we evaluated how much the proposed mechanism reduces the load on the switches and

Table 2: Number of Pending Flow Rules in Typical Use Cases

	# of Rules
Ethernet Switching	1
IP Routing	4 + 1 (Ethernet Switching)
Load Balancing	1 per destination (IP address, port) pair + 5 (IP Routing)
NAPT	1 per source IP prefix + 5 (IP Routing)

how many important Packet-In messages for network control a switch sends to a controller using our proposed mechanism.

To measure the above two points, we simultaneously sent two kinds of packets to the switch. One emulated where many packets were sent from a host without any advance notice, and called High Rate Packets. The other emulated where a small number of packets were sent from several hosts as usual called Low Rate Packets. Since the switch has no flow entry, it tried to send all the packets to the controller as Packet-In messages. The controller did not install any flow entries, so that the switch continued to send Packet-In messages to the controller. We measured the CPU and memory usage every second in the switch and the traffic between the switch and the controller. We also counted the number of Packet-In messages, including both the High and Low Rate Packets per second at the controller. We compared them in two cases: with and without our proposed mechanism.

We set the pending flow rules to the switch whose clone fields include the input port number, the Ethernet type, and the source and destination Ethernet and IP addresses. This emulates where the controller forwards packets by IP addresses. We limited the total rate of the Packet-In messages to 100 messages per second and limit the rate of the Packet-In messages, which include packets that match entries in the pending flow tables, to 50 packets per second by the user selected actions in the proposed mechanism. The timeout value in the entries in the pending flow tables was one second, and the pending flow rules did not expire.

High Rate Packets consisted of packets with the same source and destination IP addresses and different source and destination UDP ports, and almost all of these packets were less important for network control because we assumed that the controller could not see the UDP port numbers. To observe the effects on the loads on the switch by packet rates, we changed the High Rate Packets rates to 1000, 2000, 3000, 4000, and 5000 packets per second. These rates exceeded the rate limitation of the Packet-In messages to the controller in the switch. Each packet in the Low Rate Packets had the same source IP address but a different destination IP address; these packets were considered important for network control. We sent five Low Rate Packets per second. Both High and Low Rate Packets were sent for 30 seconds, and each packet had 128 bytes. We monitored the loads on the switch and the Packet-In messages received at the controller for 31 seconds including the start and end times for sending the packets. We omitted the first and last seconds from the measurement logs. The results below are the averages of 29 seconds.

Figure 5 shows our evaluation environment, and Table 3 shows its PC specifications. The Packet Generator PCs, the Open vSwitch PC, and the Controller PC were connected by separate 1Gbps link each. High and Low Rate Packets were sent from different Packet Generator PCs. The maximum

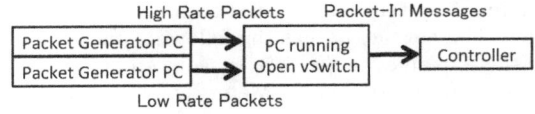

Figure 5: Evaluation setup

Table 3: PC specifications for experiment

	Packet Generation	Open vSwitch
CPU	Core 2 Duo 2.16 GHz	Xeon X5255 2.66 GHz (running at 1.99 GHz, use only 1 Core)
RAM	512 MB	8 GB
OS	Ubuntu 12.04	CentOS 6.2

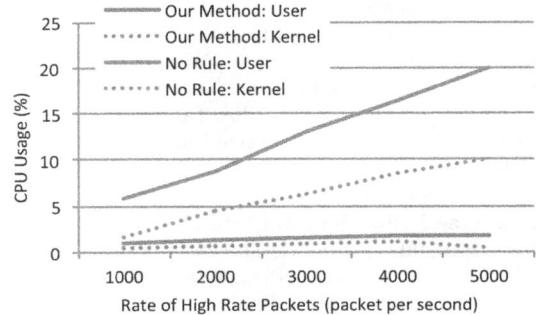

Figure 6: CPU loads in the switch

length of the queue from the kernel module to the userspace process was 1024 packets. We used Trema[16] and C to implement a controller to monitor the Packet-In messages.

5.2.1 Results

Figure 6 shows the average CPU usage in the switch. The x-axis shows the rate of the packets in the High Rate Packets, and the y-axis shows the average CPU usage by percentage. *Our Method* shows that the switch used the proposed mechanism, and *No Rule* shows that it processed packets without the proposed mechanism. *User* denotes the CPU usage in the userspace process, and *Kernel* means the CPU usage in the kernel module.

The CPU usage and its increase ratio to the packet rate are much lower in the switch with the proposed mechanism than without it. We can see this trend in both the userspace process and the kernel module. The memory usage averaged 336.9 MB and did not differ among the rates of the High Rate Packets.

Table 4 shows the average number of Packet-In messages per second received by the controller. *Our Method* means the switch using the proposed mechanism, and *No Rule* means the switch without it. *High* and *Low Rates* show that the packets included in the Packet-In messages were from High or Low Rate Packets.

Without the proposed mechanism, the packets from the High Rate Packets fill the queue of the Packet-In messages to the controller in the switch, which drops most of the packets in the Low Rate Packets that are important for network control.

Table 5 shows the average traffic in the management interface of the switch, which was mainly used for communica-

Table 4: Number of Packet-In Messages per second on average

Rate of High Rate Packets		1000	2000	3000	4000	5000
Our Method	High Rate	35.3	35.1	35.3	35.6	34.8
	Low Rate	5	5	5	5	5
	Total	40.3	40.1	40.3	40.6	39.8
No Rule	High Rate	98.0	99.8	99.1	99.3	100
	Low Rate	2.0	0.2	0.9	0.7	0.0
	Total	100	100	100	100	100

Table 5: Management traffic (in kbps) measured at switch

Rate of High Rate Packets		1000	2000	3000	4000	5000
Our Method	Sent	11.8	11.8	11.3	12.0	11.5
	Recv	1.1	1.2	1.2	1.3	1.2
No Rule	Sent	25.0	25.3	25.1	24.7	27.4
	Recv	3.7	3.7	3.7	3.6	4.0

tion with the controller. *Our Method* and *No Rule* mean the same in Tab. 4. *Sent* means the traffic that left the switch, including the Packet-In messages to the controller. *Recv* is the traffic in the opposite direction: from the controller to the switch.

If we consider the link speeds of the current servers and switches, these values are relatively small. This is due to the rate limitation of the Packet-In messages in the switch.

5.3 Processing Time of Actions in Switches

We also measured the execution time of each action in the switches to evaluate the overhead introduced by our proposed mechanism. Its major modifications included an entry in the pending flow tables when a packet arrives at the switch and limiting the rate of the packets that match the entries. To evaluate how these modifications affected the packet processing time, we measured the execution times related to the limit of the rate of the packets and sending the Packet-In messages.

In the datapath, we measured and compared the time to queue a packet to the userspace process (Queue to the Userspace Process), the rate limitation time (Rate Limit), and the time to output a packet to a port (Output Port). When the proposed mechanism was used, the packets that match the entries in the pending flow tables were processed by the Rate Limit and the Queue to the Userspace Process. Without the proposed mechanism, the packets were just processed by the Queue to the Userspace Process.

In the userspace process, we measured the time to create a flow entry for the pending flow tables (Set Filter) and to send a Packet-In message. The processing time to send a Packet-In message consists of the execution times by three components. First, all the packets that a switch tried to send as Packet-In messages are queued (Enqueue Packet-In messages). Second, the packets are dequeued and sent immediately to the controller if they get tokens for the rate limitation of all the Packet-In messages; otherwise the packets are queued in another line (Dequeue Packet-In Messages and Send). Finally, the packets are sent when they get tokens or are dropped if they fail to get tokens (Dequeue waiting Packet-In Messages and Send).

We used the same PCs in Tab. 3. We modified the code of the prototype switch to measure the execution times per component. We executed each component 1000 times and

Table 6: Execution times by components in switches

Component in Datapath	Execution Time in nsec
Queue to Userspace Process	3578.8
Rate Limitation	124.2
Output to Physical Port	485.7
Component in Userspace Process	Execution Time in nsec
Enqueue Packet-In Messages	2402.4
Dequeue Packet-In Messages and Send	8910.6
Dequeue Waiting Packet-In Messages and Send	30665.7
Set Flow Entry for Pending Flow Table	11529.0

calculated the average execution times (Tab. 6). The execution times for other components are not included in the results, such as flow table matching.

6. DISCUSSION

6.1 Effects of Our Proposed Mechanism

As we expected, our experiment results shows that switches using our proposed mechanism dramatically reduced the CPU loads in the userspace process of the switches, and its benefits rose as the rate of the High Rate Packets was increased. This is because most of the High Rate Packets are filtered out at the kernel module, and the userspace process with our proposed mechanism handles many fewer packets than in the switches without the proposed mechanism. The packet rates used in our experiment are much smaller than the maximum rate in the Gigabit Ethernet, which is about 1.5 million pps, but we infer from the results that these trends are the same because more packets are dropped by the kernel module if the packet rate is increased. In addition, the switches use the proposed mechanism for a short time, until the installation of new flow entries from sending the first Packet-In messages. Therefore, the packet rate handled by the proposed method is much smaller than the maximum packet rate in the line speed.

Regarding the ratio of the Packet-In messages received by the controller, all the Packet-In messages from the Low Rate Packets were successfully forwarded to the controller when the switches use the proposed mechanism; without it the controller sees almost no Packet-In messages by Low Rate Packets. The proposed mechanism effectively filters out only the packets in the High Rate Packets, and there is room for the switches to pass through the packets in the Low Rate Packets.

6.2 Overhead by Our Proposed Mechanism

Regarding the execution time overhead in the datapath, the rate limitation mechanism introduces small overhead, but the time for queuing packets to the userspace process is much larger than the overhead by the rate limitation mechanism and the execution time to send a packet to another port. If we drop packets by the rate limitation mechanism or send them to other ports, such packets are not queued to the userspace process. Therefore we can reduce the CPU usage in the datapath by limiting the rate of packets that are passed to the userspace process that is executed by the pending flow tables.

In the userspace process, the execution time to create and set a flow entry for the pending flow table, which includes installing a new flow entry to the flow tables, is almost the same as the time to immediately send a Packet-In messages. In addition, it requires additional large execution time if the packets that go to the controller arrive at a rate higher than the limited rate. Although the execution time by the proposed mechanism for the first packet is twice or more than the time without it, it can drop many packets at the datapath and reduce the execution rate of the process to send Packet-In messages. As a result, the total execution time is much smaller with the proposed mechanism than without it when the rate of Packet-In messages is large.

Even though the overhead evaluation is very specific to the Open vSwitch, we believe that a comparison of the execution times in the userspace process can be applied to other switches like hardware switches because they send Packet-In messages from their software OpenFlow agents.

Another overhead introduced by the proposed mechanism is the number of entries in the pending flow tables. If they are big, large memory and TCAM spaces will be occupied by the pending flow tables. We do not believe that this concern is significant. The size of the pending flow tables is determined by the number of connected hosts, the flows sent by the hosts, and the design of the controllers; these factors also determine the size of the flow tables in OpenFlow and the flow entries are assumed to be used for a long time. In addition, the pending flow rules set the header fields used for the pending flow tables based on the header fields that the controllers see, and at worst the number of entries in the pending flow tables will be almost the same as that in the flow tables. The entries in the pending flow tables will also soon expire. Therefore, the TCAM or memory space required by the pending flow tables is very small compared to the flow tables unless the controllers use some flow entry compression algorithms. We can ignore this overhead.

Another important point is the flexibility of the programs that control the networks. We showed that the controllers can use the proposed mechanism in typical use cases, Ethernet switching, IP routing, load balancing, etc. with a few pending flow rules. Using examples of the pending flow rules, we also showed that constructing pending flow rules is a similar process as discussing how controllers use the match fields in the flow tables. Considering the use cases, our proposed mechanism provides enough flexibility to determine whether packets are important for controlling OpenFlow networks.

6.3 Similarity with OpenFlow Mechanisms and Possibility for Hardware Implementation

Our proposed mechanism must also be implemented not only in software switches but also in hardware switches. Our proposed mechanism's design, which has high affinity with the flow tables in OpenFlow, simplifies its implementation in hardware switches.

The matching procedures in the pending flow rules and tables are almost the same with that in the flow table. Both use priority values, input port numbers, and the match fields for looking up their entries. In addition, we implement our proposed mechanism into one flow table by translating the pending flow rules and tables to flow entries. Therefore, both hardware and software switches can look up entries in the pending flow rules and tables without introducing additional processing overhead by reusing the flow table lookup mechanism in the OpenFlow switches.

We do not propose any specific mechanism to process packets that match the entries in the pending flow tables. Since the responsibility for this mechanism, which is called the User Selected Actions in Sec. 3.4, falls on the network operators and controller developers, we can reuse the existing OpenFlow actions and instructions for the user selected actions. If they select the actions and instructions from the existing OpenFlow mechanisms, OpenFlow switches including both hardware and software switches would be able to execute User Selected Actions in the datapath. The prototype switch implementation uses a combination of limiting the rate of matched packets and sending packets to the controller as Packet-In messages. We can replace this with Meter instruction in OpenFlow and the Output action whose output port is the controller, and OpenFlow switches that support these instructions and actions can execute them in the datapath. In Sec. 3.4, we gave another example where packets are flooded in the network. We can use a list of Output to port actions, or the Group action and a group entry whose type is All, which executes all the actions in the group entry except the output action to the input port. Both follow the OpenFlow standard, and the OpenFlow switches that support these actions can execute them in the datapath. Network operators and controller developers may prefer other actions for the user selected actions, but such selection is not assumed as with OpenFlow, which assumes that most packets are processed at the datapath.

Implementation of the pending flow rules is slightly complicated. The pending flow rules require switches to create and install a new entry in the pending flow tables, which are translated into part of the flow tables in the prototype switch. This process includes copying the values of the header fields specified by the clone fields from the packets that match the rules. Executing this process is difficult by reusing the existing OpenFlow mechanisms in the datapath, but conventional networking hardware has similar functions that create a new forwarding entry using the values in the packet header fields, such as MAC address learning and stateful firewalls. By modifying these mechanisms, we can implement action for the pending flow rules.

The proposed mechanism is still beneficial if the switches need to process the action for the pending flow rules by OpenFlow agents in the switches. After the action for the pending flow rules is executed, the subsequent packets that match the new entry in the pending flow table are filtered out in the datapath to reduce the load on the OpenFlow agents unless many packets that execute the action for the pending flow rules arrive at the switches.

6.4 Drawbacks of Our Proposed Mechanism

The proposed mechanism works well when the datapath in the switches can also extract the values of the packet header fields used in the match fields of the pending flow rules and tables and when the datapath can apply the user selected actions to the packets that match the entries in the pending flow tables. In other words, there might be some cases where the controllers use header fields in a protocol, but the datapath cannot parse the packets of the protocol and extract the values. Some OpenFlow switches support part of the header fields in the OpenFlow specifications because supporting all the header fields for matching is not mandatory in the specifications, for example, the VLAN ID in 802.1Q headers, payloads in ARP, and the ICMPv6 type and codes do not have to be parsed. We can add code to support protocols if we can write it for the switches, but most hardware switches do not allow users to modify their firmware. They can only program the behavior of the switches by the

OpenFlow protocol.

Although OpenFlow and the proposed mechanism do not define how to handle the packets that include header fields that the switches cannot parse, in some cases the switches should send such packets to the controllers without dropping them, for example, ARP packets and IPv6 Neighbor Discovery related packets. In this case, since we cannot mitigate the overloads in the switches by the proposed mechanism, we have no choice but to set the switches to send all the Packet-In messages including the packets of such protocols or to limit the total rate of Packet-In messages in total.

From the users' view, networks using the proposed mechanism may drop some packets in the beginning of such operations as connecting a new host to the networks or sending a new flow. On the network side, these operations generate a new entry in the pending flow tables. For example, when a controller sets the flow entries per host and the pending flow rules whose clone fields include source and destination Ethernet and IP addresses, and a host starts to establish several TCP sessions to the same host at the same time; the second or later TCP SYN packets may be lost because of a filtering mechanism by the pending flow tables. This should not be a big problem because Ethernet and IP networks do not assure that the networks deliver packets to destinations, and hosts retransmit packets at intervals of a few seconds if necessary until the hosts receive reply packets. If a certain kind of packet should not be dropped, we can use other mechanisms, like AVANT-GUARD[13] with our proposed mechanism, to provide special care for such packets.

6.5 Attacks and Mitigations

A malicious host can attack the networks using OpenFlow and our proposed mechanism by exploiting it. If such attackers know the header fields used by the controllers who manage a target network to forward packets, they can send packets that have different values in the header fields used by the controllers. In this case, the processes for the pending flow rules are executed frequently. As a result, the CPU load in the switches is increased if the switches are implemented to execute the actions for the pending flow rules in their CPUs, and the number of entries in the pending flow tables is explosively increased.

It is hard to distinguish these packets from others and to drop them without additional detection systems, but some mitigation exists for such attacks. Regarding the CPU load by processing the pending flow rules, controlling resources consumed by processing the rules helps keep the load low in the switches at the cost of dropping packets without processing by the pending flow rules. Temporarily disabling the proposed mechanism might be better when the switches handle packets that very frequently match entries in the pending flow rules.

To keep the number of entries in the pending flow tables low, the switches may have to evict some entries by cache algorithms. Since only the entries in the pending flow table generated by the Low Rate Packets are used, it might not be necessary to protect the switches from the overload; the Least Recently Used (LRU) algorithm may work well to evict the entries. When switches receive attacks that explosively increase the number of entries in the pending flow tables, attackers send packets whose header fields have different values for efficient attacks, and such packets do not match any entry in the pending flow tables. The simple First In First Out (FIFO) algorithm may adequately mitigate these situations.

Finally, we discuss the relationship between our proposed mechanism and existing attacks, especially DDoS and TCP SYN floods. In these attacks, hosts send many packets to a certain network without any advance notice, and preventing switches from such packets is one of our motivations if the switches are configured to send such packets to the controllers as Packet-In messages.

Whether DDoS or TCP SYN flood packets can be filtered out by the proposed mechanism depends on the controllers. When they see the port numbers in the packets, the clone fields in the pending flow rules include port numbers as well as IP and Ethernet addresses in the packets. In this case, the same situations happen with attacks that exploit the pending flow rules and tables, and we cannot completely exploit our proposed mechanism to protect the switches. When controllers are designed to use wildcards in the flow entries and the packets used by the attacks only have different values in the header fields that are set to wildcards in the flow entries, the clone fields in the pending flow rules do include such header fields. We can effectively filter out such packets with our proposed mechanism and wildcards.

7. CONCLUSION

In this paper, we proposed a new mechanism to protect the control plane, especially the software part in switches, from packets that bring excessive loads to it. In terms of the control plane protection, we need a mechanism to filter out less important packets for network control to keep the loads on the switches low in addition to extend the variety of actions that OpenFlow switches can execute. Based on the classification whether packets are important for network control, we proposed a mechanism to filter out packets that are less important for network control when controllers only see the header fields of the packets that the switches can parse. A key idea of our proposed mechanism is that the controllers set the pending flow rules to the switches, which inform the switches which header fields the controllers see. The switches record the values of the header fields specified by the controllers as the pending flow rules to the pending flow tables and use them to determine whether the switches send Packet-In messages (including packets) to the controller. By describing typical use cases and how to construct the pending flow rules in these use cases, we show that our proposed mechanism can be used in various OpenFlow use cases with a small number of pending flow rules. An evaluation experiment using our prototype switch shows that the proposed mechanism reduced the loads on switches and confirmed that the important Packet-In messages were allowed to pass through. With the proposed mechanism, we can control how packets that do not match any entry in the flow tables should be handled to maintain low loads in the switches, like OpenFlow uses flow tables for offloading packet forwarding to hard-wired offload engines such as ASICs.

Future work will provide efficient mitigation mechanisms for the explosion of the number of entries in the pending flow tables and excessive loads by attacking the pending flow rules. We only provided experimental results using a software switch, Open vSwitch. An implementation and an evaluation using hardware switches is another future work. Another future work is a way to provide flexibility of the user selected actions in the pending flow tables, such as flooding packets.

8. ACKNOWLEDGMENTS

We thank Hoang Le who shepherded our paper and the anonymous reviewers for their valuable comments. This work was supported in part by JSPS KAKENHI (No. 13J04479).

9. REFERENCES

[1] W. Bux, W. E. Denzel, T. Engbersen, A. Herkersdorf, and R. P. Luijten. Technologies and Building Blocks for Fast Packet Forwarding. *IEEE Communications Magazine*, 39(1):70–77, 2001.

[2] D. Chang, M. Kwak, N. Choi, T. Kwon, and Y. Choi. C-flow: An efficient content delivery framework with OpenFlow. In *2014 International Conference on Information Networking (ICOIN)*, pages 270–275, Feb 2014.

[3] A. R. Curtis, J. C. Mogul, J. Tourrilhes, P. Yalagandula, P. Sharma, and S. Banerjee. DevoFlow: Scaling Flow Management for High-Performance Networks. *SIGCOMM Comput. Commun. Rev.*, 41(4):254–265, Aug. 2011.

[4] D. J. Bernstein. SYN cookies.

[5] M. Fernandez. Comparing OpenFlow Controller Paradigms Scalability: Reactive and Proactive. In *Proceedings of 2013 IEEE 27th International Conference on Advanced Information Networking and Applications (AINA)*, pages 1009–1016, Mar. 2013.

[6] T. Koponen, M. Casado, N. Gude, J. Stribling, L. Poutievski, M. Zhu, R. Ramanathan, Y. Iwata, H. Inoue, T. Hama, and S. Shenker. Onix: A Distributed Control Platform for Large-scale Production Networks. In *Proceedings of the 9th USENIX Symposium on Operating Systems Design and Implementation (OSDI)*, pages 1–6, Berkeley, CA, USA, 2010. USENIX Association.

[7] D. Kotani and Y. Okabe. Packet-In Message Control for Reducing CPU Load and Control Traffic in OpenFlow Switches. *European Workshop on Software Defined Networks*, pages 42–47, 2012.

[8] J. W. Lockwood, N. McKeown, G. Watson, G. Gibb, P. Hartke, J. Naous, R. Raghuraman, and J. Luo. NetFPGA–An Open Platform for Gigabit-Rate Network Switching and Routing. In *IEEE International Conference on Microelectronic Systems Education 2007 (MSE'07)*, pages 160–161. IEEE, 2007.

[9] N. McKeown. Software-defined networking. *INFOCOM keynote talk*, 2009.

[10] N. McKeown, T. Anderson, H. Balakrishnan, G. Parulkar, L. Peterson, J. Rexford, S. Shenker, and J. Turner. OpenFlow: Enabling Innovation in Campus Networks. *SIGCOMM Comput. Commun. Rev.*, 38:69–74, March 2008.

[11] Y. Nakagawa, K. Hyoudou, and T. Shimizu. A Management Method of IP Multicast in Overlay Networks Using Openflow. In *Proceedings of the First Workshop on Hot Topics in Software Defined Networks (HotSDN)*, pages 91–96, New York, NY, USA, 2012. ACM.

[12] Open Networking Foundation. OpenFlow Switch Specification 1.3.4, Mar 2014.

[13] S. Shin, V. Yegneswaran, P. Porras, and G. Gu. AVANT-GUARD: Scalable and Vigilant Switch Flow Management in Software-defined Networks. In *Proceedings of the 2013 ACM SIGSAC Conference on Computer and Communications Security (CCS)*, pages 413–424, New York, NY, USA, 2013. ACM.

[14] S. Shirali-Shahreza and Y. Ganjali. FleXam: Flexible Sampling Extension for Monitoring and Security Applications in Openflow. In *Proceedings of the Second ACM SIGCOMM Workshop on Hot Topics in Software Defined Networking (HotSDN)*, pages 167–168, New York, NY, USA, 2013. ACM.

[15] A. Tootoonchian and Y. Ganjali. HyperFlow: A Distributed Control Plane for OpenFlow. In *Proceedings of the 2010 Internet Network Management Conference on Research on Enterprise Networking (INM/WREN)*, pages 3–3, Berkeley, CA, USA, 2010. USENIX Association.

[16] Trema Project. Trema: Full-stack openflow framework for ruby/c.

[17] L. Veltri, G. Morabito, S. Salsano, N. Blefari-Melazzi, and A. Detti. Supporting Information-Centric Functionality in Software Defined Networks. In *2012 IEEE International Conference on Communications (ICC)*, pages 6645–6650, June 2012.

[18] P. Wette and H. Karl. Which Flows Are Hiding Behind My Wildcard Rule?: Adding Packet Sampling to Openflow. *SIGCOMM Comput. Commun. Rev.*, 43(4):541–542, Aug. 2013.

[19] M. Yu, J. Rexford, M. J. Freedman, and J. Wang. Scalable Flow-Based Networking with DIFANE. In *Proceedings of the ACM SIGCOMM 2010 conference*, pages 351–362, New York, NY, USA, 2010. ACM.

Faithful Reproduction of Network Experiments

Dimosthenis Pediaditakis   Charalampos Rotsos   Andrew W. Moore

Computer Laboratory, University of Cambridge
{firstname.lastname}@cl.cam.ac.uk

ABSTRACT

The proliferation of cloud computing has compelled the research community to rethink fundamental design aspects of networked systems. However, the tools commonly used to evaluate new ideas have not kept abreast of the latest developments. Common simulation and emulation frameworks fail to provide scalability, fidelity, reproducibility and execute unmodified code, all at the same time.

We present SELENA, a Xen-based network emulation framework that offers fully reproducible experiments via its automation interface and supports the use of unmodified guest operating systems. This allows out-of-the-box compatibility with common applications and OS components, such as network stacks and filesystems. In order to faithfully emulate faster and larger networks, SELENA adopts the technique of *time dilation* and transparently slows down the passage of time for guest operating systems. This technique effectively virtualizes the availability of host's hardware resources and allows the replication of scenarios with increased I/O and computational demands. Users can directly control the trade-off between fidelity and running-times via intuitive tuning knobs. We evaluate the ability of SELENA to faithfully replicate the behavior of real systems and compare it against existing popular experimentation platforms. Our results suggest that SELENA can accurately model networks with aggregate link speeds of 44 Gbps or more, while improving by four times the execution time in comparison to ns3 and exhibits near-linear scaling properties.

Categories and Subject Descriptors

C.2.5 [**Computer-Communication Networks**]: Local and Wide-Area Networks—*Internet, Ethernet*; D.4.8 [**Operating Systems**]: Performance—*Measurements, Simulation*

Keywords

network experimentation; emulation; virtualization; time-dilation

1. INTRODUCTION

The adoption of networking technologies by a widening spectrum of applications and environments has highlighted a series of limitations in the design of the predominant protocols and architectures. In order to support the growing requirement for scalable network performance, a significant effort is put towards the development of network experimentation tools.

We identify three key properties in the realm of network modeling and experimentation: fidelity, reproducibility and scalability. *Fidelity* characterizes the ability of the experiment to replicate specific system behavior with high precision and accuracy. Examples of network experimentation fidelity can be characterized by the requirement for functional realism in terms of network hosts and network topology, the ability to reuse realistic applications and traffic models and the accurate recreation of the timing properties of the real system.

Scalability is an equally important property for experimentation platforms, defined by the ability to support and gracefully manage network experiments of growing size. This requirement is extremely difficult to meet with respect to current network architectures, primarily due to the exponential increase in their size, link speed and complexity. Experimental scalability can be further decomposed in three functional aspects: *execution time scalability*, which describes the required wall-clock time to replicate an experiment, *resource scalability*, which characterizes the ability of the platform to minimize hardware requirements, and *fidelity at scale*, which reflects the ability to maintain high fidelity as the size of the experiment increases. The three scalability aspects exhibit *Pareto efficiency*: a platform cannot improve one of them without affecting negatively the remaining two aspects.

Reproducibility is a third key property for network experimentation which has gained significant interest in the recent years [13, 32]. Reproducibility describes the ability of the platform to export and replicate experimental scenarios and its results. It requires a rich automation abstraction for the configuration of all experimental details, but must also provide guarantees on fidelity across heterogeneous hardware platforms (e.g. control the impact of host's available processing capacity on the results obtained from an experiment execution).

This paper presents SELENA, an holistic network experimentation tool supporting reproducibility and exposing explicit control on the trade-off between scalability and fidelity. The tool runs *in-a-box* and can faithfully emulate complex network architectures with high-speed links. We argue that emulation provides the optimal approach to maximize the fidelity of an experiment, due to its support for unmodified real-world software and OS. The design of SELENA combines a variety of network experimentation optimizations (e.g. VM-based emulation, link modeling, time dilation, automation API etc.) under a common framework. Unlike the popular container-based Mininet platform [13], SELENA employs OS

Tool Name	Readily available	Reproducible Experiments	Hardware requirements	Real Stacks	Unmodified applications	SDN support	Fidelity at scale Node	Link speed	Execution Speed
Simulation									
NS2 [16]	✓	✓	Low	×	×	×	●●●	●●○	●○○
NS3 [15]/ OMNeT++ [34]	✓	✓	Low	×	×	partially	●●○	●○○	●○○
FS-SDN [12]	✓	✓	Low	×	×	✓	●●●	●●○	●●○
NS Cradle [17] / DCE [32]	✓	✓	Low	✓	no full POSIX	partially	●●○	●○○	●○○
Simulation-Emulation Hybrid									
OpenVZ-S3F [37]	✓ (outdated)	×	Low	✓	✓	✓	●○○	●○○	●○○
SliceTime [35]	✓ (outdated)	×	Low	✓	✓	×	●○○	●○○	●○○
Emulation									
ModelNet [33]	✓ (outdated)	×	Average	✓	✓	×	●●○	●○○	●●● (RT)
DummyNet [5]	✓	×	Average	✓	✓	×	●●○	●○○	●●● (RT)
MiniNet [13]	✓	✓	Low	✓	✓	✓	●●○	●○○	●●● (RT)
Time-controlled Emulation									
DieCast [10]	×	×	Low	✓	✓	×	●●○	●●●	●●○
TimeJails (TVEE) [8]	×	×	Low	✓	✓	×	●●○	●●○	●●○
SELENA (this work)	✓	✓	Low	✓	✓	✓	●●○	●●●	●●○
Testbeds									
Planetlab [26]	✓	n/a	High	✓	✓	custom OVS	●●○	●○○	●●● (RT)
Ofelia [21]	✓	n/a	High	✓	✓	✓	●●○	●○○	●●● (RT)

Table 1: Comparison of popular network experimentation platforms across different dimensions

virtualization achieving better resource control and isolation and wider support for network stacks and OSes [36].

In order to overcome the inherent scalability limitations of network emulation, SELENA revisits the idea of *Time Dilation* [11]: controlling resource availability per unit of time, by virtualizing time progression in the guests of the experiment. This approach fundamentally provides users with direct control on the scalability trade-offs of an experiment. For example, time dilation opens an opportunity for near-real time execution of a large number of low-fidelity experiments to explore a variable-space, whereas when precise behavior details are sought, an experimenter can run a higher-fidelity experiment (or set of experiments) by increasing respectively the time dilation factor (TDF). Our approach improves earlier approaches in time-controlled emulation in two ways: first, it provides support for recent Xen versions and requires zero guest modifications (if it works on Xen, it works on SELENA) and second, it offers better experimental automation and reproducibility. In addition, due to the varying performance profiles of existing SDN forwarding devices [30], SELENA supports high precision switch emulation models, which further improve the fidelity of OpenFlow-based experiments.

In summary, SELENA provides the following key features:

- **Reproducibility**: A Python API can be used by experimenters to describe custom experiments, automating their creation, deployment and execution.
- **Fidelity**: Time dilation functionality [11] scales guests' view of physical resources helping to accurately model complex networks. We successfully patched the latest version of Xen and tested it against recent Linux and FreeBSD kernels. SELENA supports any paravirtualized (PV) guest, requires zero modifications and provides full POSIX compatibility. Real-world applications and network stacks can be directly tested on our platform.
- **Scalability**: Slowing down the progression of time at guests enables support for high link speeds (40 Gbps or higher) and larger networks, within a single host. In section 4.4 we describe a methodology for exploring the scalability and accuracy limits that a given TDF value can provide, helping users to better understand how to efficiently use SELENA.
- **Software Defined Networking (SDN)**: Apart from supporting all popular software switch and controller implementations, we also incorporate a flexible OpenFlow switch emulation model which offers better realism in terms of control plane behavior.

To the best of our knowledge, SELENA is the only open-source network emulation tool[1] which provides all the above features. The rest of this paper is organized as follows. Section 2 provides an overview of related network experimentation platforms. Section 3 describes the architecture and implementation details of SELENA. Section 4 evaluates the fidelity and scalability of SELENA against a real-world deployment, and compare it against the Mininet emulation framework and the ns-3 simulation platform. We also evaluate the accuracy of our switch model and the ability of SELENA to replicate real network applications. Finally, we discuss the limitations of our work in Section 5, point out future work directions and conclude in Section 6.

2. BACKGROUND AND RELATED WORK

This section presents a survey of network experimentation practices, focusing on aspects of fidelity, reproducibility and scalability. We categorize relevant approaches into four broad categories.

Simulation is a popular experimentation method, employing simplified models to replicate network functionality. ns-2 [16], ns-3 [15] and OMNET++ [34] are some of the most popular event-driven network simulators, supporting a plethora of models (e.g. for link properties, network protocols etc.). These platforms aim to provide good resource scalability, deterministic reproducibility and simplify the early-stage evaluation of new ideas by masking the complexity of system-level details. However, their fidelity is typically sacrificed in favor of scalability, influenced by the simplistic assumptions of the network and system models.

Many users consider simulation a weak method for testing new ideas because it does not incorporate real-world network stacks and it does not support execution of unmodified applications. This weakness has motivated recent efforts like DCE [32] and NSC [18], which attempt to extend ns-3 and bridge the API mismatch between real-world applications and simulation. While these attempts are a big leap forward, they compromise scalability and offer partial POSIX compatibility. Simulation platforms have also added support for recent approaches to network control. For example, FS-SDN [12] seeks to help study the macroscopic impact of network control applications on data plane performance using lightweight flow-level models.

Emulation aims to improve experimentation fidelity by enabling the reuse of real world protocols and applications within a vir-

---
[1] Available at http://selena-project.github.io

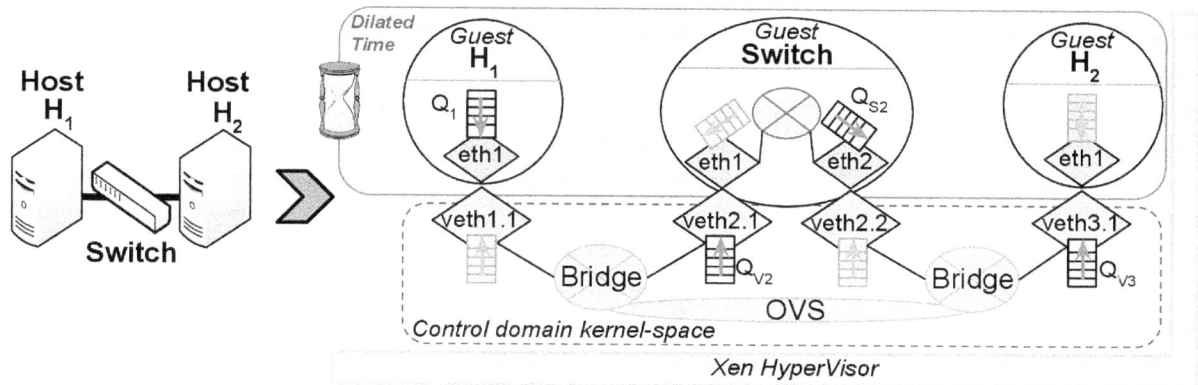

Figure 1: SELENA emulation architecture builds on Xen. Emulated hosts run in dilated time. Control domain perceives real time.

tual network. The majority of relevant platforms replace the network layers below the data-link with simplified models which replicate their functionality. The ModelNet [33] project established a pioneering approach in scalable emulation of Internet topologies. Its architecture fuses edge hosts running unmodified applications, with nodes emulating virtual network topologies using DummyNet [5]. ModelNet improved scalability by increasing hardware requirements and could only parallelize execution at the extent which a particular application and topology allows it.

Recent efforts in emulation frameworks aim to scale-down resource requirements and fit large network experiments in a single host, without significant precision losses. The improvement in computer resource virtualization allowed emulation platforms to isolate instances of virtual network components and improved control on resources usage [4, 27]. *Mininet* [13] is the most popular framework of this category, highlighting a reproducibility requirement in network experimentation. Mininet automates the testing workflow, so that a particular high-level scenario description consistently recreates the same network topologies, configurations, traffic patterns and application behaviors across different host architectures. In order to improve further the fidelity in replicating SDN architectures, Gupta *el al.* [12] developed a control plane proxy service for Mininet, enabling users to integrate switch models into network experiments.

Nonetheless, the increasing complexity of emulated systems limits their scalability and restricts the support for large network sizes and link speeds in real time. This limitation has precipitated the development of **time-controlled emulation**, where experimental time is virtualized. By executing scenarios at a slower pace, available hardware resources are scaled and therefore the accuracy of results is improved. Of particular note is *DieCast* [11] which, like SELENA, employs full-system emulation using Xen and scales CPU, disk and network I/O resources by dilating the time progression in guests. Unfortunately, DieCast's patches for time dilation are incompatible with modern versions of Xen, it requires guest modifications, it does not offer automation mechanisms for reproducible experimentation and, finally, it does not support realistic OpenFlow switch models. Similarly, TimeJails (TVEE) [8] is a VM-based solution with time virtualization support which combines multiple virtual routing instances in a single virtual machine to improve resource scalability. TVEE employs dynamic hardware resource allocation to maximize utilization and is able to emulate large numbers of virtual nodes per host.

Testbed infrastructures like Ofelia [21] and Planetlab [26], are large virtualized computer infrastructures, used for the deployment

of experiments. Such platforms achieve high fidelity, similar to multi-host emulation at the cost of increased hardware requirements. Kim *et al.* [19] highlighted potential measurement noise and biases in network measurements on Planetlab nodes, due to the shared nature of network testbeds and the limited control on resources.

Hybrid approaches like OpenVZ-based S3F [37] and Slice-Time [35] provide an alternative to experimental resource scalability and fidelity, by combining emulation with simulation. Typically, such systems enforce weak virtual time synchronization between emulated nodes, using a centralized simulation engine. SliceTime, for example, uses ns-3 to coordinate the execution of Xen guests by controlling the hypervisor's scheduling policy. Guests run independently for a quantum of time and a global service synchronizes them periodically with the ns-3 clock.

Table 1 presents a comparison of the presented network experimentation frameworks. Each entry categorizes a platform with respect to its fidelity (Real Stacks, Unmodified applications, SDN support), scalability (Hardware requirements, Fidelity at scale, Execution Speed) and reproducibility. SELENA falls under the category of "*time-controlled emulation*" and aims to combine the competitive advantages of Mininet and DieCast. It supports reproducible experimentation, it presents good scalability properties and furthermore, its functionality can be extended with custom OpenFlow switch models.

3. SELENA DESIGN

This section presents the design of SELENA. Using as reference a simple experiment scenario, we provide a high level description of its execution model (§ 3.1), followed by a presentation on how a user can construct experiments over the platform via its automation API (§ 3.2). Furthermore, we elaborate on the details of the underlying mechanisms which improves resource scalability (§ 3.3), data plane fidelity (§ 3.4), and control plane realism (§ 3.5).

3.1 Overall architecture

SELENA revisits the idea of network emulation using OS-level virtualization. Recent efforts in network experimentation [13] use lightweight approaches, like container-based virtualization. We argue that hypervisor-based virtualization provides better *heterogeneity support* (e.g. supports a wide OS range[2]) and improves *resource control granularity* [36]. SELENA uses Xen [3], a mature open-source hypervisor which exhibits good performance and

---

[2]http://wiki.xen.org/wiki/DomU_Support_for_Xen

scalability properties [22]. Furthermore, the Xen Cloud Platform (XCP) provides a rich API (xen-api), supporting remote Virtual Machine (VM) configuration and resource control. Using *xen-api*, SELENA automates the deployment and execution of virtual network topologies and experimental scenarios.

Figure 1 presents a trivial network experiment topology; two hosts interconnected through a switch. SELENA uses a simple mapping mechanism: each host or network device is mapped to a VM, while each link maps to a pair of virtual network interfaces (one for each guest) bridged in the Dom0. With respect to Figure 1, the hosts (H_1 and H_2) and the switch (*SW*) are mapped to separate VMs. Host *SW* is configured with two network interfaces, each bridged in the Dom0 using a separate bridge with an interface from hosts H_1 and H_2. The interfaces, colored pink (e.g. *veth*1.1), are Xen-specific *netback* devices, transparent to the guests of the experiment. The resulting virtual machine configuration is a precise representation of the emulated network scenario, replicating both topological and functional properties, like queue sizes, link speeds and host resource limitations. SELENA also virtualizes time for all participating guests (blue sandbox), allowing experimenters to control the trade-off between resource and time scalability and fidelity.

3.2 Reproducible experiments

SELENA exposes a programming API to specify, deploy and execute network experiments. We share the same views with the authors of Mininet [13] on experimental reproducibility and automation. We believe that both requirements are fundamental for a network experimentation platform, improving repeatability of results and simplifying the frequent trial-and-error cycles of applied research. The mechanism outlined in this section makes experimentation with SELENA simple and user-friendly. Experimenters can effortlessly re-run experiments with varying parameters, like queue sizes, link speeds, topologies and application or even host configurations. An experiment can be repeated on different platforms and hosts, requiring only the installation of SELENA and the script defining its network topology and functionality. The process of defining and executing a network experiment in SELENA consists of four steps.

Step 1 - *Network description*

SELENA provides a Python API for the definition of the network hosts and their topology, as well as their configuration parameters. Listing 1 presents the topology definition of the experiment in Figure 1. A network definition is typically composed by the user and contains two types of objects: nodes and links. A node object contains several fields defining Xen-specific guest resource configurations (e.g. memory size, virtual CPUs and affinity), the template of the VM and the node network interfaces along with their initial configuration (e.g. IP and MAC address, queue sizes). The link object is simpler and specifies the link end-points (node and interface IDs) along with the link capacity and latency characteristics.

Step 2 - *Experiment deployment*

During deployment, SELENA parses the network description, checks for common syntax or semantic errors (e.g. malformed IP addresses, duplicate links, platform resources availability) and invokes the relevant *xen-api* callbacks to create the VMs of the experiment and the required network bridges of the topology in Dom0.

Step 3 - *Experiment initialization*

SELENA uses a distributed control and monitor framework to synchronize host configuration and scenario execution, which consists of a low overhead daemon running on each host and a central coordination service running on Dom0. The guest daemon is responsible to report host status information to the coordination

```
# Node-0 (H1)
newNode(
    0, "H1"                    # unique ID, name label
    NodeType.LINUX_HOST,       # guest template
    [ (1000,                   # 1st interface, queue len
      "RANDOM",                # MAC address
      "10.0.1.2",              # IP address
      "255.255.255.0",         # NetMask
      "10.0.1.1"),             # Gateway
      (..), (..) ],            # additional interfaces
    1,                         # number of VCPUs
    "4,5,6,7",                 # VCPU Mask
    "512M"   )                 # Guest RAM
# Node-1 (H2)
newNode(1, "H2", NodeType.LINUX_HOST, .....)
# Node-2 (Switch)
newNode(2, "Switch", NodeType.LINUX_OVS, .....)
# Link: H1<--->Switch
newLink(
    (0, 0),                    # Node-0, 1st interface
    (2, 0),                    # Node-2, 1st interface
    1000,                      # Link speed in Mbps
    0.2   )                    # Latency (NetEm params)
# Link: H2<--->Switch
newLink( (1, 0), (2, 1), 1000, 0.2) )
```

Listing 1: A simple network topology: 2x hosts 1x switch

```
# Prevent arp broadcasts
setArp(0,"eth1","10.0.1.3","fe:ff:ff:00:01:03"))
setArp(1,"eth1","10.0.1.2","fe:ff:ff:00:01:02"))
# Configure the switch
pushCmd(2,["ovs-vsctl set-fail-mode br0 secure"])
pushCmd(2,["ovs-vsctl add-port br0 eth1"])
pushCmd(2,["ovs-vsctl add-port br0 eth2"])
pushOFRule(2,
    "br0", "add-flow","in_port=1,action=output:2")
pushOFRule(2,
    "br0", "add-flow","in_port=2,action=output:1")
# Run netperf for 10 seconds
pushCmd(0,
    ["netperf -H 10.0.1.3 -t TCP_STREAM -l10 -D1"])
```

Listing 2: A sample execution scenario description

service and to execute the commands of the experiment in a timely manner. The daemon communicates with the coordination service using a signaling protocol over the Xenstore service, thus minimizing the interference with the emulated network's resource. During initialization, SELENA boots sequentially all the VMs which have been created in the previous step and configures the network interfaces using the coordination service.

Step 4 - *Scenario execution*

In the final step, SELENA executes the experimental functionality. This is defined through a separate user-composed Python script, describing a sequence of time-controlled commands to run on each guest. When the scenario is executed, each command is transmitted to the guests through the coordination service (via *Xenstore*).

Listing 2 presents a simple scenario, applied on the network topology in Listing 1. The scenario installs a static datapath between the two ports of the switch and creates static ARP entries to avoid unnecessary broadcast traffic. Then it instructs *H1* to initiate a netperf session and fill the pipe of the emulated path to *H2*. Experiments in SELENA run in dilated virtual time and therefore, scenario commands are also executed in virtual time. For example, a 10 seconds *netperf* session will last multiple times longer in real-time for TDF values higher than 1.

In order to minimize the time it takes to install, configure and start large experiments, we implement a series of optimizations. Firstly, SELENA provides a set of guest templates containing the minimum required software for network experimentation. Our Linux-based guests contain a minimal 3.13 kernel and a stripped-down set of applications and tools, resulting in low memory guest footprint (20 MB) and fast boot times (2-4 seconds). Secondly, SE-LENA uses the copy-on-write disk cloning functionality of Xen, to decrease the time it takes to replicate a VM's disk image from our templates. Finally, after the completion of an experiment, guests are cached in a guest pool. During *Step 3*, the deployment script checks initially in the pool to find any matching guest VMs created from the same template and reuses it. Nonetheless, the virtual interfaces of guests and the respective bridges in Dom0 are always clean-installed. Using these techniques SELENA can cold-boot, for example, a 52 node topology in approximately 130 seconds.

3.3 Scaling resources via elastic time

An inherent limitation of real-time emulation is resource scalability for high throughput or node-count experiments. For example, emulating the packet-level behavior of a 40 GbE link in real time generates a high event rate and a potentially unmanageable CPU load. Effectively, fidelity is upper-bounded by the ability of the platform to scale the experiment computation and match the emulated system's performance properties. SELENA overcomes this limitation by virtualizing time. In order to achieve this, we implement a time virtualization mechanism in the hypervisor, which allows an experimenter to slow down time progression on guests and effectively scale network, disk I/O and CPU resources. Our approach is similar to the *bullet time* video effect: augmented per-frame time enables the viewer to perceive more details from a scene.

With respect to Figure 1, emulated nodes (H_1, H_2, SW) run inside a sandbox using a common time dilation factor (*TDF*), while Dom0 and the hypervisor operate in real-time. SELENA adjusts all guest time sources by the TDF parameter, *controlling* effectively the perception of time-progression both at the kernel and the user-space of the guest VM. Each guest continues to receive a fair fraction of available hardware resources, unaffected by time virtualization. For an experiment with TDF = 2, a virtual time of 1 second lasts 2 seconds of real time and the perceived network, disk I/O rates and CPU appear doubled within the virtual time domain.

Having created the necessary "computational headroom" to emulate faster network links, the users may choose to further adjust the speed of individual resources for guests. The amount of CPU time that a guest receives can be adjusted via the *weight* and *cap* parameters of the Xen *credit2* scheduler [2] (in non work-conserving mode). Dilating time by a large factor, however, can occasionally introduce transient scheduling inaccuracies. This effect can be minimized by scaling the *time-slice* parameter and increasing the *ratelimit* parameter (to control the minimum non-preemptive VM scheduling duration) of the Xen scheduler. In addition, disk I/O rates can be limited from within the guests through the *cgroups* mechanism and the *blkio controller*.

Implementation details

SELENA supports time dilation functionality without requiring modifications in guest OSes. Our approach takes advantage of the Linux PVOPS drivers, which provides out-of-the-box in-kernel support for Xen para-virtualized drivers. The implementation of time virtualization required limited modifications in the Xen hypervisor source code ($\approx$ 400 LoC). We have successfully patched a recent version of the Xen hypervisor (v4.3). In order to avoid xen-api toolstack modifications, we expose TDF control through the sysfs filesystem, using a modified domain creation hypercall (*XEN_DOMCTL_createdomain*).

In order to present how SELENA implements time virtualization, we initially describe guest time management in Xen. During boot, the Linux kernel selects the appropriate drivers and clock-sources.

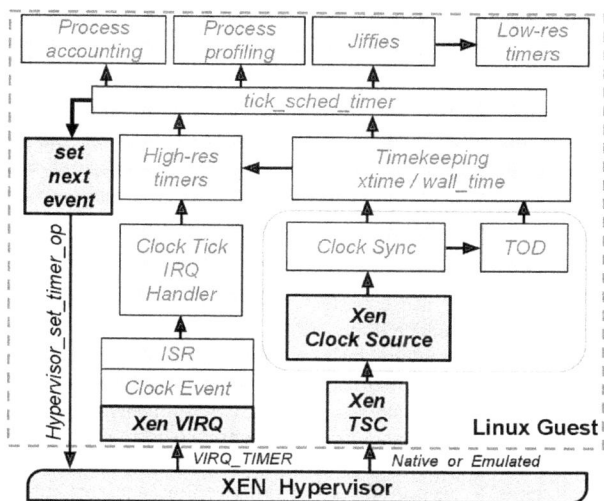

Figure 2: Architecture of the various timekeeping facilities of a Linux PVOPS kernel

Fortunately, the generic time-of-day (GTOD) framework handles transparently a variety of clock sources[3]. Figure 2 shows the Xen-specific components of the timekeeping subsystem. At the bottom reside the low-level bits of the Xen clocksource, a place which typically plays the role of the "bridge" to real hardware. An OS typically requires two elementary clock operations, *time-keeping* and *time event scheduling*, and therefore, our solution needs to support both.

In terms of time-keeping, Xen exposes to guests two timestamp values, the *system-time* (time since guest boot or resume) and the *wall-clock time* (time since epoch when system-time was zero), through a shared memory structure (`shared_info_page`). *System-time* is updated by Xen every time the guest is being scheduled. In between updates, the guest keeps accounting of wall-clock and system time by extrapolating the current values based on the value of TSC register (an x86 register counting CPU clock cycles). TSC values in Xen are obtained through the `rtdsc` instruction. They are either *native*, accessed directly from the CPU register, or *emulated*, intercepted through a trap by Xen. In order to effectively virtualize time-keeping, the hypervisor multiplies with the TDF parameter all the wall-clock, system and emulated TSC time values provided to the guest. Additionally, because native TSC values are unmodifiable, our approach multiples with the TDF value the TSC scaling factor (*tsc_to_system_mul*), a constant used by the guests to convert TSC cycles to system time.

In terms of time event scheduling, the guest PVOPS driver intercepts and translates such requests to equivalent Xen hypercalls (*HYPERVISOR_set_timer_op*). When the timer expires, the hypervisor delivers a software timer interrupt (*VIRQ_TIMER*) back to the guest and triggers the associated timekeeping interrupt handlers. Time event virtualization in SELENA is achieved in the hypervisor by intercepting timer-setup hypercalls and scaling their timeout values with the TDF parameter. Our approach also covers the case of periodic timer events used by older Linux versions. Recent Linux kernels also employ loop-based delays for timeout values lower than 10 usec. These types of events are not directly managed by the hypervisor, but our approach ensures accurate event execution.

---

[3]FreeBSD also follows a similar approach

3.4 Network emulation

SELENA emulates network links by creating pairs of guest network interface devices bridged in Dom0. The Xen architecture uses two virtual interfaces (VIFs), the *netfront driver*, exposed to the guest, and the *netback driver*, exposed to Dom0. Netfront and netback interconnect using shared memory rings. This separation of network devices into multiple VIFs introduces a challenge for SELENA to provide good guarantees for network resources, like latency and throughput. Effectively, a link in SELENA must manage at least four independent network queues (see Figure 1), running at different rates, and ensure lossless resource allocation. Ultimately, networking performance effects (e.g. queueing) must occur in the boundaries of the emulated hosts and not in Dom0.

Time virtualization in SELENA provides a useful mechanism to experiment with low latency network environments. High TDF values provide sufficient head-room to minimize packet processing delays and test high-bandwidth setups. For instance, for TDF = 1, the average RTT over an idle guest-to-guest link is approximately 300 *usec*, a value which drops to 30-50 usec for TDF = 10. SELENA uses the Linux *netem* qdisc [14] and the FreeBSD *DummyNet* [5] pipe to support constant or stochastic latency in network links. Each qdisc is configured on the egress queues of the guests, in order to maintain a common time reference between experimental nodes. In recent Linux kernels with high resolution timer support, the netem choice of SELENA provides sub-millisecond precision in latency control.

In terms of throughput, the process to ensure fidelity is more complex, as throughput can be either CPU or I/O bound. SELENA follows a two step empirical method, presented in greater detail in Section 4.4. Firstly, the user tries different TDF values to discover the minimum value which can effectively support the required throughput. Secondly, SELENA applies rate limiting at individual VIFs to match the link speed specifications of the experiment. Rate limiting uses the QoS primitive of the Xen network driver (*qos_algorithm_type:ratelimit*). To ensure accurate network resource scaling, the rate limit of a link is divided by the TDF value of the experiment. For example, a 1 Gbps link translates into a rate limit of 100 Mbps for TDF = 10. Earlier attempts to use the *HTB* qdisc primitive in guest OSes proved to be complex in terms of configuration. Specifically, the time virtualization mechanism and the scheduling effects introduced fluctuations in performance and required tuning of MTU, burst, peakrate and scheduling quanta.

The Xen network driver provides additional control on the trade-off between fidelity and resource scalability. Currently the driver provides multiple network offloading functions which can improve link throughput (e.g. TSO, UFO, TX/RX checksum offload) both on the guests and Dom0 VIFs. When these settings are enabled, we observe that guests can use very large packet sizes (64KB packets), thus improving DomU-to-DomU throughput. Nonetheless, such large packet MTU reduces the packet-level and queue multiplexing fidelity. In the experiments of section 4 we have disabled all these optimization features. Finally, in order for SELENA to support large port-count hosts/switches, we modified the Xen hypervisor source code to increase the size of the page grant table, enabling support up to 48-ports. While raw-throughput is sufficient in this first version of SELENA, opportunities for improvement by bypassing Dom0 constraints are made clear by related work such as VALE [28].

3.5 Control plane emulation

Control planes with programmatic interfaces have redefined the role of network functionalities. The SDN paradigm and its predominant realization, the OpenFlow protocol, define a set of flow-level abstraction primitives, exposed to external entities via a unified programming interface. This has made possible the instantiation of previously complex or impractical network-control ideas.

The growing interest in the SDN paradigm has been a core motivation in recent experimentation platform efforts like Mininet [13]. SELENA supports any software switch implementation which can run in a guest domain. This includes kernel-level bridges, Open vSwitch and other popular software switches (e.g. Click [20]). Nonetheless, recent measurement studies of switch devices [12,30] have highlighted a significant variability on the performance of the control plane, especially in available hardware OpenFlow switch implementations. This performance variability can be explained by a number of design choices, like the scalability of the communication channel between the switch silicon, the switch co-processor and the firmware architecture. However, existing solutions exhibit limited capabilities to reflect these performance properties and can only replicate simplified network device models, considering only per-packet processing latency and buffer sizes.

SELENA provides a tunable switch model that takes account of the tight coupling between the flow and management timescales of the network [24]. This allows users to study how traditional and new control plane performance characteristics affect the overall network performance. More specifically, we include a customizable switch implementation which supports OpenFlow [29] and builds on the Mirage framework [23]. This switch emulation model provides a simple and extensible packet processing pipeline, to which we add a rate adjustment mechanism for the different control plane functionalities. Our model exposes currently performance emulation primitives for the flow table management mechanism, the packet interception and injection mechanism and the counters extraction functionality of the switch. Section 4.5 describes a methodology used to calibrate a switch model in a SELENA experiment in order to match the performance characteristics of a production switch.

4. EVALUATION

In this section we present an in-depth evaluation of SELENA's performance and scalability. Initially, we introduce the reader to the measurement apparatus of our evaluation (§ 4.1). We compare the experimental fidelity provided by SELENA against a real system and two established experimentation platforms, Mininet and ns-3. Our evaluation considers fidelity both in terms of high-throughput links (§ 4.2), as well as larger networks (§ 4.3). Finally, we present a limit analysis of our time virtualization technique (§ 4.4) and evaluate real application performance realism in SELENA (§ 4.5).

4.1 Experimental Setup

In order to evaluate the performance of SELENA, we use two popular network topologies: a *star topology* (Figure 3(a)) and a

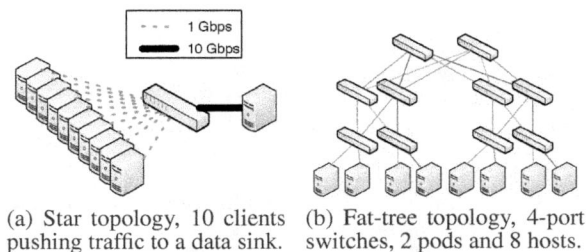

(a) Star topology, 10 clients pushing traffic to a data sink.   (b) Fat-tree topology, 4-port switches, 2 pods and 8 hosts.

Figure 3: Experimental topologies.

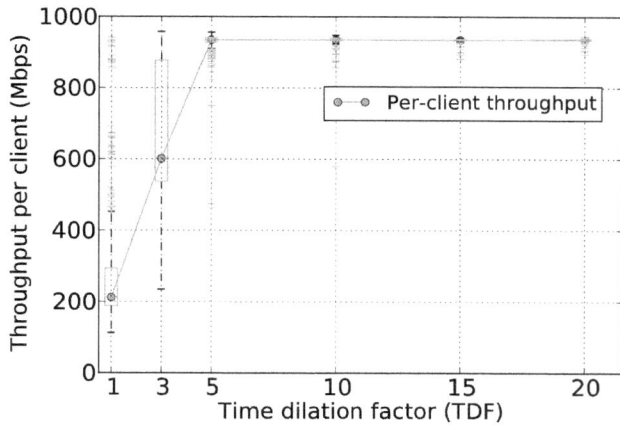

Figure 4: Per-host throughput samples for various TDF values

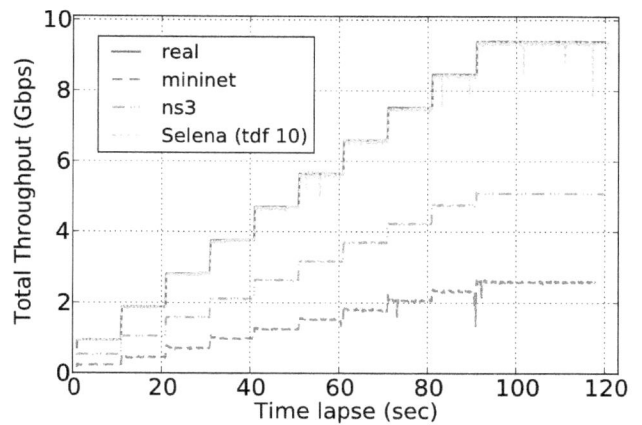

Figure 5: Aggregate achieved throughput between real, SE-LENA, Mininet and ns-3 (star topology).

special case of a CLOS, a *fat-tree topology* with 4-port switches and 2 pods (Figure 3(b))[4]. We employ these two distinct topologies as they provide a simple mechanism to test both throughput and scalability of the system for high-density setups. We replicate the experiments of each topology four times: in SELENA, in a real setup, in Mininet and in ns-3.

In the real setup, the star topology consists of a quad-core server (Intel Xeon E5-2643, 128GB RAM), 10 data generating hosts (Intel Core 2 Q6600, 4GB) and a network switch (Pica8 P-3290). The server is equipped with a 10 GbE card (Solarflare SFC9020) and acts as the data-sink. The clients are equipped with 1 GbE cards (Intel 82571EB) and the switch offers both 1 and 10 GbE interfaces. We monitor the link to the data sink using a DAG card and an optical splitter. For the fat-tree topology we run the end-host logic on the clients of the previous setup, and use 10 hosts equipped with a NetFPGA-1G card running the OpenFlow switch design [25], to replicate the switching fabric. For ns-3 we use the `CSMA` link model and develop a custom application to replicate switch functionality. For the equivalent SELENA experimental setups we use Linux VMs with stock 3.13 kernel and Open vSwitch (v1.11) for switch emulation. SELENA, Mininet and ns-3 experiments were executed on the same server (Intel Xeon E5-2643, 128GB RAM) for fair comparison.

4.2 Data plane fidelity

In this section we use the star topology to evaluate the capability of the tested experimentation platforms to support 10 Gbps traffic. For this scenario we use steady-state long-running TCP flows, generated by the netperf application in the real, SELENA and Mininet experiments and a TCP `BulkSendTraffic` application in ns-3. Starting at t=0, a new full-rate TCP-flow is initiated every 10 seconds from a previously idle host, resulting in 10 Gbps throughput at time t=90 sec.

Firstly, we analyse the impact of TDF on the per-client throughput. Figure 4 presents boxplots of the network throughput measurements from all clients, using a monitoring window of 100 msec. We notice that TDF = 5 provides a median throughput of 940Mbps, the maximum achievable TCP rate for a host in this setup. However, this TDF value exhibits a non-negligible variance with a few outliers (grey-colored marks), occurring due to Xen scheduling effects and the inability of the CPU to handle the offered load. This effect

---

[4]we employ half of the nodes in a k=4 fat-tree topology, due to lack of physical resources to replicate the complete topology in the real experiment.

is more evident for lower values of TDF (e.g. TDF = 1 achieves a median throughput of 210 Mbps). We conclude that TDF = 10 provides sufficient accuracy and throughput stability for the complete duration of the experiment.

Figure 5 presents the achievable throughput on the 10 Gbps link for the duration of the experiment, using 100 msec observation window. We used TDF = 10 for SELENA which, based on the previous findings, is sufficient to emulate accurately the throughput of the real system. Mininet is able to achieve a maximum of 2.3 Gbps throughput, with non-negligible variance, primarily due to poor scalability of CPU resources. Despite the extensive optimization of Mininet, the platform cannot mitigate CPU and memory bottlenecks in high throughput emulations. ns-3 exhibits higher performance than Mininet achieving a maximum throughput of 4-5 Gbps, but still significantly lower than the real. After analyzing the source code of the ns-3 platform, we concluded that the low aggregate performance is due to poor scalability of the `CSMA` link model at high rate, which does not support full-duplex links. Furthermore, ns-3 provides an MPI-based distributed event engine, which however, supports only point-to-point links and the achieved scalability is restricted by the clock synchronization overheads.

4.3 Flow-level fidelity

This section evaluates the flow-level fidelity of SELENA using the fat-tree topology. For this experiment we use short-lived TCP flow completion times to assess the accuracy of our platform, a metric which is widely used to characterize both the performance and fairness of TCP in the context of datacenter networks [7]. On each host we run both a data-generation and data-sink service and traffic is flowing in both directions between four pre-defined client pairs (8 Gbps aggregate bandwidth). The data-sink service on each client receives data from 10 concurrent TCP flows from the same source. When a flow transfers 10 MB worth of data it is terminated and a new transfer request is initiated immediately, thus maintaing constantly 10 concurrent flows per host. We implemented this traffic generation model in C using the async epoll-based `libev` library. The generator application is used in SELENA, real and Mininet experiments, while for ns-3 we build a similar application using the TCP abstraction.

Figure 6 presents the empirical cumulative distribution (CDF) of the flow completion times for a wide range of TDF values using SELENA, and from the real, Mininet and ns-3 platforms for 2 min-

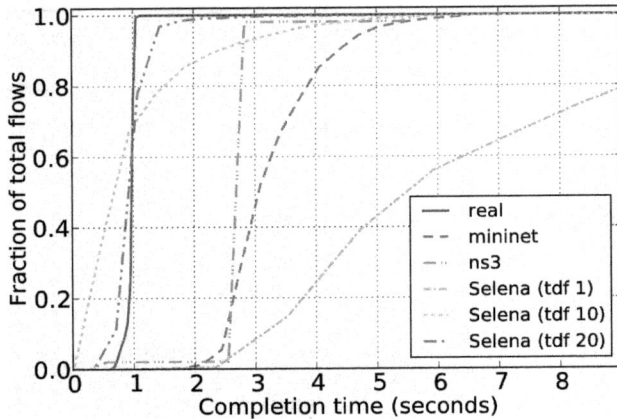

Figure 6: Comparison of flow completion time CDF between SELENA, real, Mininet and ns-3 (fat-tree topology).

utes of execution time. Additionally, Table 2 presents the number of completed flows for the duration of the experiment and the mean and variance of flow completion times for each experiment. For SELENA, we notice that TDF = 1 is highly unrealistic, introducing 6 times higher delay than the real system and significant variance. Nonetheless, as we increase TDF values, the distribution of completion times starts to approximate the behavior of the real system. A TDF = 5 reduces 4.8 times the mean latency, while higher TDF values improve further the experimental fidelity. For TDF = 20 the mean completion time is only 10 msec different from the real system, while the variance is equally reduced.

Mininet increases the mean flow completion times by a factor of 3 and exhibits significant variance, also visible by the longer tail of the cumulative distribution. Note that the majority of the flows in Mininet exhibit completion times between 2.5 and 4.5 seconds. There are also many outliers with a maximum delay of 7 seconds. Mininet clearly cannot support the required aggregate throughput of 8 Gbps using the fat-tree topology and therefore with a lower available bisection capacity flows require more time to complete. ns-3 on the other hand, has an extremely low variance with a median completion time of 2.5 seconds.

Table 3 presents the time scalability properties of the tested platforms, by comparing the wall-clock execution duration of Mininet,

Platform	Flows	Mean	std
Real	10071	0.956	0.074
Mininet	2957	3.271	0.787
SELENA TDF = 1	1512	6.469	3.236
SELENA TDF = 5	7161	1.344	1.144
SELENA TDF = 10	9285	1.036	1.035
SELENA TDF = 20	9935	0.966	0.16

Table 2: Comparison of flow-completion time statistics.

Platform	Star Topology	Fat-tree Topology
Mininet	120s	120s
ns-3	175m 24s	172m 51s
SELENA TDF = 1	120s	120s
SELENA TDF = 20	40m	40m

Table 3: Comparison of wall-clock execution times.

SELENA and ns-3 for both experiments. Mininet runs in real-time and the execution duration of an experiment is not affected by the complexity of the scenario; it simply sacrifices accuracy. In contrast, ns-3 was considerably slower than SELENA ($\approx$ 4.4x times), despite its poor scaling. This slow-down in execution time stems primarily from its single threaded design and the requirement for total ordering of events. Effectively, the execution speed of an ns-3 experiment is defined by the rate of network events.

4.4   Time dilation limit analysis

The use of Xen by SELENA, provides high scalability, supporting hundreds of guests [22]. Nonetheless, resource virtualization in Xen uses complex mechanisms to schedule guest vCPUs, manage memory, process event channel interrupts, control access to physical hardware (e.g. disk I/O), all of which can significantly affect the accuracy of an experiment. Depending on the emulated network topology and the employed workloads, the impact of system-level effects can vary.

In the star topology (Figure 3(a)), although Dom0 is allocated with 4-cores to relay packets between guests, it can use a maximum of 2.5 cores. To explain this behavior, we need to look into the implementation details of Xen's control domain which maps one kernel-thread per Dom0 core. The 10 Gbps virtual link between the switch and the server has the highest processing demands but its workload cannot be parallelized as it is served from a single netback kernel thread (for each direction) and therefore can utilize only one core. The traffic from the client-nodes to the switch (via Dom0) consumes roughly the same aggregate CPU resources with the 10 Gbps link. Some extra processing takes place also in the network stack and software bridges of the control domain.

In order to present the scalability limits of our time virtualization mechanism, we revisit the star topology experiment (Figure 3(a)) and study the limits of aggregate throughput using TDF = 20. We generate two variations of the experiment: i) 4 clients with variable link speeds and ii) an increasing number of clients each connected through a 1 Gbps link. Figure 7 uses boxplots with outliers (cyan crosses) to present the measured client throughput (1 second monitoring window) as we increase the capacity of the client links. This figure also illustrates the aggregate CPU utilization for the Dom0 and the nodes of the experiment. We observe that SELENA copes well with client link speeds up to 10 Gbps (aggregate sink-server link speed of 40Gbps), evident by the low number of outliers. For client link speeds higher than 10 Gbps, the fidelity degrades as hardware resources do not suffice to serve the offered load. As discussed, the bottleneck of this topology is the sink-server link.

Figure 8, presents a throughput analysis, similar to the previous example, but in this scenario we vary the number of client hosts, keeping link capacity limited to 1 Gbps. For this experiment, SELENA can faithfully emulate network of up to 40 clients with low variance, using TDF = 20. Beyond this number of nodes, per-client median throughput is reduced and the variance increases. Similarly to the previous example, the aggregate throughput for 40 clients is 40 Gbps, but we observe more outliers; 2.5% of client throughput observations drop below 750Mbps. This effect can be attributed to Xen's scheduling effects which increases buffering during the time a guest is not scheduled and therefore more packet losses occur.

In order to provide further evidence on the scalability of SELENA, we evaluate the star topology in terms of throughput and node count for a variety of TDF values. We present the results in Figures 9 and 10, respectively. Each data point represents the maximum throughput or node count which can be reliably supported by a specific TDF value. We consider an experimental result as reli-

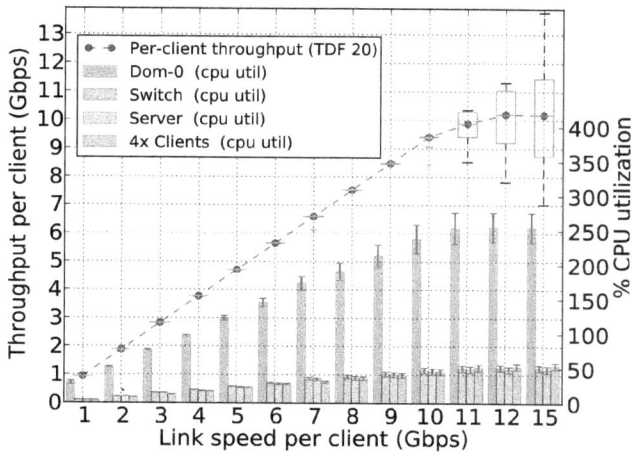

Figure 7: Link speed scalability analysis: per-client throughput and CPU utilization (star topology, 4x clients)

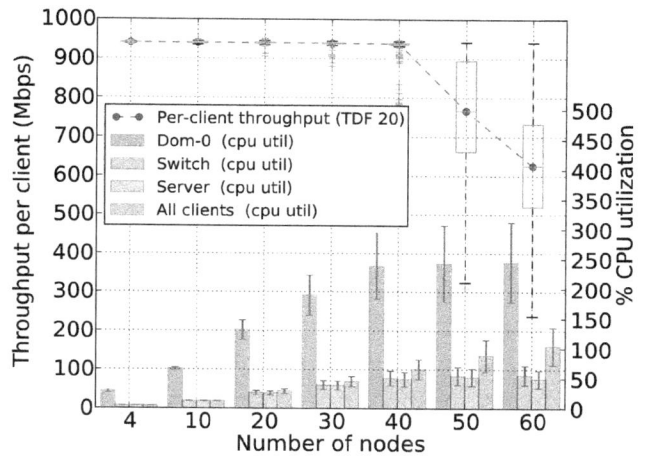

Figure 8: Node-count scalability analysis: per-client throughput and CPU utilization (star topology, 1 Gbps links)

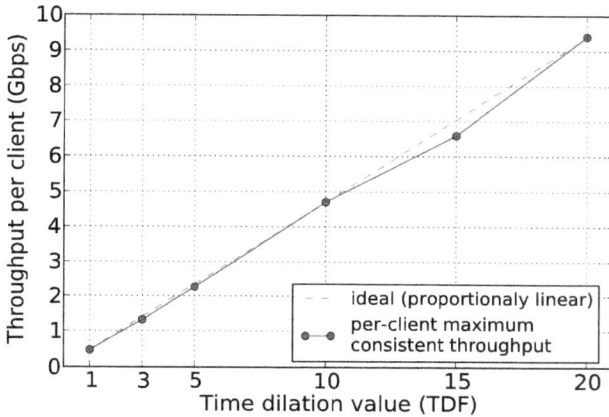

Figure 9: Overall link speed scalability vs TDF

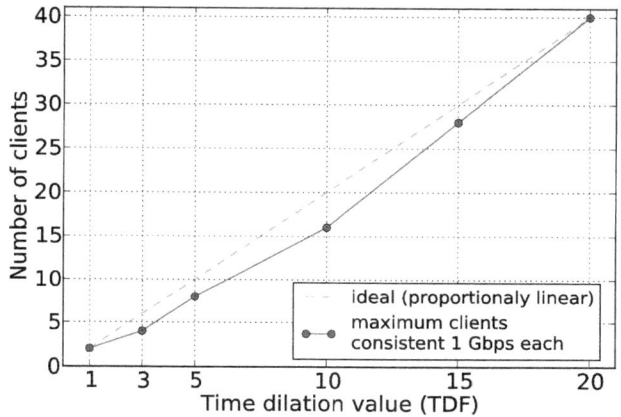

Figure 10: Overall network size scalability vs TDF

able, when the per-host throughput observation achieves the target value for the majority of measurement samples (97.5% of all samples). In both cases we observe that the experiment can achieve close to linear scalability. We should clarify that while we expect SELENA to exhibit a near-linear scalability trend for a wide range of experiments, the user is strongly encouraged to verify this assumption for different virtual topologies individually.

4.5 SELENA applications

In this section we evaluate the ability of SELENA to emulate data plane network behaviors and run real unmodified applications, using a web server deployment.

Control plane fidelity

In order to evaluate the data plane fidelity of our switch model, we assess its precision in replicating the performance characteristics of a real OpenFlow switch. We calibrate our switch emulation model by measuring the data and control plane performance profile of a production switch (Pica8 P-3290 switch[5]) using the OFLOPS [30] OpenFlow switch evaluation framework. OFLOPS runs on a Quad Core Intel PC (Q6600) equipped with a NetFPGA-

[5]http://www.pica8.com/

1G card directly connected to 4 switch ports and uses the high-precision NetFPGA-1G traffic generation backend.

Our characterization effort focuses on the behavior of a reactive control scheme. In this approach, the controller exercises per-flow forwarding decisions, thus achieving fine level of control. In detail, each newly arriving flow generates a packet exception which is propagated to the controller using a `Pkt_in` message. The controller then is responsible to install an appropriate entry in the flow table, which defines a forwarding policy for all matching packets. In order to measure each elementary interaction in this control architecture, we use the OFLOPS measurement modules to evaluate: i) the delay to install a new flow in the flow table, and ii) the delay and loss rate of `Pkt_in` messages.

Based on the OFLOPS results we observed a median flow insertion delay of 6 msec, a `Pkt_in` processing delay of 2 msec and a maximum rate of 50 `Pkt_in` messages per second. Using these settings, we configure our switch model and compare its performance with the Pica8 switch and Mininet. We setup a simple topology with two hosts, a data-sink and data generation host replicating the application behavior described in Section 4.3, interconnected through an OpenFlow switch. The data-sink host generates flow requests to the data generator host following an exponential distribution with $\lambda = 0.02$ and a constant request size of 1 MB resulting

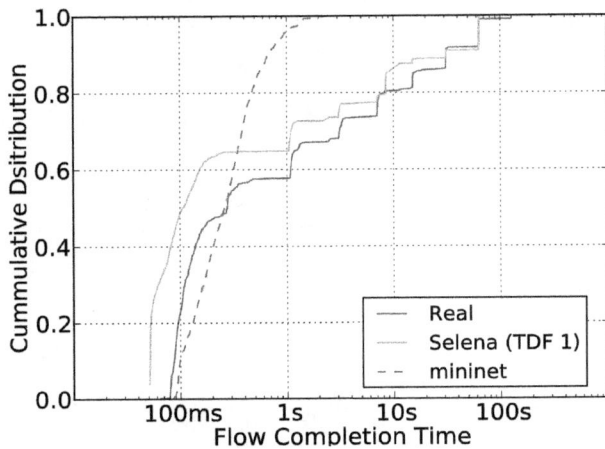

Figure 11: Comparing flow completion times between a real system, Mininet and SELENA

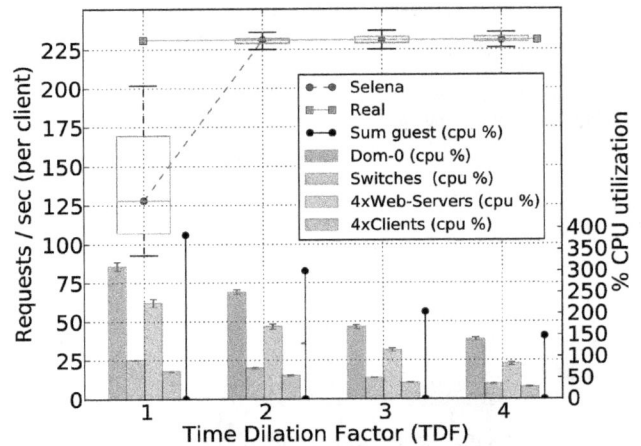

(a) Requests throughput: Real vs Selena for various TDF values

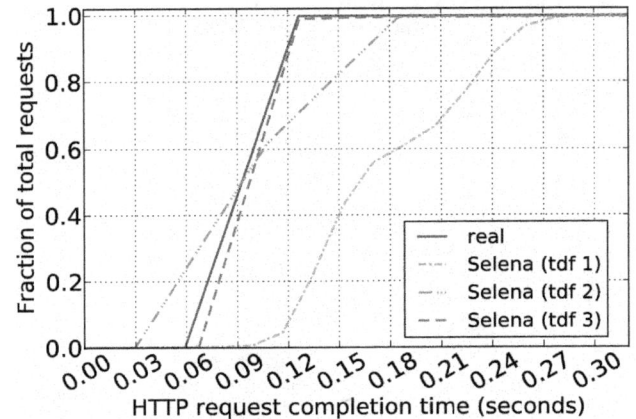

(b) Requests completion times:Real vs Selena for various TDF values .

Figure 12: Web application benchmarks: 4x clients, 4x Apache/PHP/Redis (fat-tree)

to an average 400 Mbps traffic rate. We run our experiment for 120 seconds, ensuring that the resulting number of flows is below the flow table size limits. For all experiments we used the learning switch application of NOX [9] to control the switch.

In Figure 11 we present the cumulative distribution of flow completion times for the real, SELENA and Mininet experiments. The performance observed with the real switch highlights the impact of the switch control plane design on network performance. In the real experiment, 20% of flows have a completion time higher than 10 sec. The predominant cause of this effect is the rate-limiting behavior of the switch in `pkt_in` messages transmissions. This introduces TCP SYN and SYNACK packet drop during bursty periods. As a result, the completion time distribution exhibits a stepping behavior, aligned with the back-off delay mechanism of TCP in the SYN_SENT SYN_RCVD states[6]. The adoption of Open vSwitch by Mininet, allows optimized data plane performance but it can not express such device-specific behaviors and thus over-estimates the overall performance of this experiment. Our choice to introduce a customizable model in SELENA enables higher fidelity in Open-Flow experimentation. Our model is able to capture the macro-scopic behavior of the switch. Nonetheless, our switch model exhibits a minor over-estimation in completion times. We attribute this behavior to the high load that the reactive control scheme introduces to the communication channel between the co-processor of the switch and the ASIC, which skews the obtained model.

Web server benchmarking

In this section, we evaluate the ability of SELENA to faithfully emulate network examples using a widely-used web application and compare its fidelity against an identical real-world deployment. In this experiment, we reuse the fat-tree topology (Figure 3(b), Section 4.3) and configure the four hosts of the second pod as web-servers, serving a popular dynamic web-application (Word-press 3.6). Each web service node hosts an Apache web-server (v2.4.6) and a key-value cache (REDIS 2.6.13). We also run a single MySQL (v5.5) database for all Wordpress instances on one of the four hosts. The Wordpress application uses Redis as a temporary cache for generated pages (through the *WP-Redis-Cache* plugin) in order to reduce the processing load on the web-servers. On

---

[6]We use Linux hosts with kernel 3.13, which supports TCP Fast Open [6].

the first pod, we used the four hosts as clients, each generating 25 parallel web-page requests to a specific web-server, picking a hosted page uniformly at random (approx. size 430-530KB each). The experiment recreation in Selena was identical, precisely replicating application configuration, network topology, link speeds, RAM sizes and OS version.

Figure 12(a) presents the rate of successfully completed HTTP requests per-client, measured on a per-second basis. The total duration of our experiment is 30 seconds, and for the real deployment, each client manages to achieve a near-uniform rate of ≈ 230 requests/sec (red-colored line). This is close to the theoretical limit of the network speed, implying that our experiment is network-bound. All web-server hosts handled effortlessly the offered load, filling the 1 Gbps pipe (with less than 40% CPU utilization). When running in real-time (TDF = 1), SELENA could not match the observed throughput behavior of the real testbed. In this particular example, Dom0 was not the bottleneck as the allocated cores were not fully utilized ($\approx 325\%$) and the packet-forwarding load could be fully parallelized between the four *netback* kernel threads (one per core). The aggregate processing load of guests, however, fully utilized the four allocated to them cores (we run SELENA on an 8-core Intel Xeon server). Once we used higher TDF values, we start observing almost identical throughput results with the real deployment. Higher TDF values reduced resource utilization on the execution platform, but increased the execution time of the experiment.

Figure 12(b) illustrates a latency-related aspect of SELENA's fidelity against the real deployment, for various TDF values. In reality, the application performance is bounded by the capacity of the network link, and therefore, the CDF of HTTP request completion times follows a deterministic trend, adhering to the properties of fair bandwidth-sharing. Using TDF = 1 we observe a significant latency deviation from the real system. This was due to the lack of computational resources to cope with the high event rate and due to system-level effects introduced by Xen (e.g. non-uniform scheduling at a micro-scale), common under high loads. Another interesting observation is that while a value of TDF = 2 provides sufficient throughput fidelity, it can not perfectly replicate latency properties, similar to a value of TDF = 3.

5. DISCUSSION

In the previous section, we highlighted the achievable fidelity and scalability of the SELENA platform. We now cover a number of important concerns, that we have not discussed.

Choosing the time dilation factor

SELENA, like most network emulation platforms, provides fidelity guaranteed on a statistical level. The design of an experiment must answer two questions: *"which are the metrics that better characterize the system's resulting behavior"* and *"what is the desired degree of similarity with a reference system"*. Once the first question is answered, a network emulation experiment is considered more accurate when the statistical properties of the selected performance metrics exhibit high similarity with those of a real system[7]. For instance, our evaluation considers network latency, throughput and CPU resource availability as the main aspects that define the overall system behavior. Furthermore, regarding reproducibility, users typically expect to obtain the same level of fidelity when an experiment is executed multiple times on the same or on heterogeneous platforms.

Our approach uses the technique of time dilation as the means i) to improve the fidelity of network emulation experiments, and ii) to ensure it across different execution environments. Choosing, however, an appropriate TDF value for a given experiment is not a trivial task, especially when ground truth is not known a-priori. From a practical point of view, users must choose a TDF value which provides the desired level of fidelity and also minimizes execution time. A useful rule of thumb is to choose a TDF that minimizes the maximum per-CPU utilization. Effectively, experimental fidelity degrades significantly when the experimenter under-provisions computational resources. For example, when the topology in Figure 3(a) (10x clients, 1 GbE links) is emulated using TDF = 5, the vast majority of throughput samples are very close (with a few outliers) to the theoretical maximum of 1 GbE per client. However, achieving 99.9% of throughput measurements to be within a 0.5% error margin ($\approx \pm 4.7 Mbps$), requires higher TDF values (15 or more).

We currently explore Xen's capabilities, in an effort to automate the process of resource usage monitoring. This will allow SELENA to automatically identify bottlenecks occurring spontaneously by bursty workloads. Handigol *el al.* [13] propose a different approach towards fidelity characterization, monitoring during run-time a set of invariants for network link properties (e.g. inter-packet spacing for non-empty queues). We believe that such an approach is ef-fective for high fidelity biases, capable to detect persistent long-running resource starvation, but it is not clear how it relates to the resulting overall system behavior.

Beyond network emulation

SELENA provides a scalable emulation framework to test network architectures, protocols and modern SDN applications and is best suited for experimental scenarios where the system behavior is mandated by network resources. Nonetheless, replicating the behavior of real systems can be quite convoluted, especially when it is significantly affected by the particular hardware architecture properties of the host. Disk throughput and latency, CPU cache policies, per-core lock contention and hardware features, like Intel DDIO [1] are only a few examples which are not easily reproducible in software. Effectively, the design of SELENA is primarily concerned to maximize network fidelity and may not be optimal for experiments that heavily rely on platform-specific characteristics. Furthermore, it is important to highlight that time dilation is not a panacea for high throughput experiments. For example, in order for applications to exploit high capacity links, the experimenter must optimize their configuration (e.g. increase TCP buffers and employ TCP window scaling), while in certain cases the architecture of a service may not be possible to scale for high throughput.

Scaling SELENA

SELENA is based on the Xen Cloud Platform, which can currently scale to a few hundreds of nodes on a server-grade machine [22]. Driven by the observation of the poor performing VIF bridging via Dom0, we explore zero-copy inter-guest network connectivity, similar to [28]. Furthermore, SELENA's design can support high density network experiments by distributing the experiment across multiple execution hosts. There are two main challenges for multi-host SELENA execution. Firstly, the experiment must reduce measurement noise incurred by inter-host links and the variable drifts between multiple and potentially heterogeneous hardware clock sources. Nonetheless, such biases can be minimized using high TDF values. Secondly, the deployment of experimental nodes across a set of physical hosts must be optimized based on the topology and workload of the experiment, in order to improve resource usage and avoid starvation effects. Roy *el al.* [31] presented an effective algorithm for the problem, targeting multi-host Mininet execution environments.

6. CONCLUSIONS

Despite the plethora of available network experimentation tools, the research community still requires solutions which can simplify the testing of new ideas and yet provide the necessary level of realism. Common simulation frameworks use simplifying abstraction models, trading accuracy for scalability, and network emulation tools support execution of unmodified code, at the cost of scalability. Motivated by this gap, we have designed and implemented SELENA, a network emulation platform which simplifies experimentation and allows users to trade execution speed for better fidelity as the scale of the experiment increases. Our solution builds on the Xen Cloud Platform and fully-automates the process of deploying and running experiments through an easy to use script-based interface. We have experimentally evaluated the ability of SELENA to accurately recreate large and fast network scenarios and compared its fidelity against real deployments and similar experimentation tools. SELENA is open-source and freely available (http://selena-project.github.io), in the hope that the research community will benefit from our work.

---

[7]assessed using similarity tests like the Kolmogorov - Smirnov test which compare an ECDF with a reference CDF

Acknowledgements

This work was jointly supported by the EPSRC INTERNET Project EP/H040536/1 and the Defense Advanced Research Projects Agency (DARPA) and the Air Force Research Laboratory (AFRL), under contract FA8750-11-C-0249. The views, opinions, and/or findings contained in this article/presentation are those of the author/ presenter and should not be interpreted as representing the official views or policies, either expressed or implied, of the Defense Advanced Research Projects Agency or the Department of Defense.

We thank Ilias Marinos for his useful comments and his critical views that helped us improve our work. We also thank Nik Sultana and Toby Moncaster for proof-reading the text.

7. REFERENCES

[1] Intel Data Direct I/O Technology. http://www.intel.co.uk/content/www/uk/en/io/direct-data-i-o.html.

[2] XEN Credit Scheduler. http://wiki.xen.org/wiki/Credit_Scheduler, 2013.

[3] P. Barham, B. Dragovic, K. Fraser, S. Hand, T. Harris, A. Ho, R. Neugebauer, I. Pratt, and A. Warfield. Xen and the art of virtualization. *ACM SIGOPS Oper. Syst. Rev.*, 37(5), 2003.

[4] S. Bhatia, M. Motiwala, W. Muhlbauer, Y. Mundada, V. Valancius, A. Bavier, N. Feamster, L. Peterson, and J. Rexford. Trellis: A Platform for Building Flexible, Fast Virtual Networks on Commodity Hardware. In *CoNEXT*. ACM, 2008.

[5] M. Carbone and L. Rizzo. Dummynet Revisited. *ACM SIGCOMM Comput. Commun. Rev.*, 40(2), Apr. 2010.

[6] Y. Cheng, J. Chu, S. Radhakrishnan, and A. Jain. TCP Fast Open. Internet-Draft draft-ietf-tcpm-fastopen-05.txt, IETF, Oct. 2013.

[7] N. Dukkipati and N. McKeown. Why Flow-completion Time is the Right Metric for Congestion Control. *ACM SIGCOMM Comput. Commun. Rev.*, 36(1), Jan. 2006.

[8] A. Grau, S. Maier, K. Herrmann, and K. Rothermel. Time Jails:A Hybrid Approach to Scalable Network Emulation. In *PADS*. IEEE, 2008.

[9] N. Gude, T. Koponen, J. Pettit, B. Pfaff, M. Casado, N. McKeown, and S. Shenker. NOX: Towards an Operating System for Networks. *ACM SIGCOMM Comput. Commun. Rev.*, 38(3), July 2008.

[10] D. Gupta, K. V. Vishwanath, M. McNett, A. Vahdat, K. Yocum, A. Snoeren, and G. M. Voelker. DieCast: Testing Distributed Systems with an Accurate Scale Model. *ACM Transactions on Computer Systems*, 29(2), 2011.

[11] D. Gupta, K. Yocum, M. McNett, A. C. Snoeren, A. Vahdat, and G. M. Voelker. To infinity and beyond: time-warped network emulation. In *NSDI*. USENIX, 2006.

[12] M. Gupta, J. Sommers, and P. Barford. Fast, accurate simulation for SDN prototyping. In *HotSDN*. ACM, 2013.

[13] N. Handigol, B. Heller, V. Jeyakumar, B. Lantz, and N. McKeown. Reproducible network experiments using container-based emulation. In *CoNEXT*. ACM, 2012.

[14] S. Hemminger. Netem-emulating real networks in the lab. In *LCA*, Canberra, Australia, 2005.

[15] T. R. Henderson, S. Roy, S. Floyd, and G. F. Riley. Ns-3 Project Goals. In *WNS2*. ACM, 2006.

[16] T. Issariyakul and E. Hossain. *Introduction to network simulator NS2*. Springer, 2011.

[17] S. Jansen and A. McGregor. Simulation with real world network stacks. In *Simulation Conference, 2005 Winter Proc.* IEEE, 2005.

[18] S. Jansen and A. McGregor. Validation of Simulated Real World TCP Stacks. In *WSC*. IEEE, 2007.

[19] W. Kim, A. Roopakalu, K. Y. Li, and V. S. Pai. Understanding and Characterizing PlanetLab Resource Usage for Federated Network Testbeds. In *IMC*. ACM, 2011.

[20] E. Kohler, R. Morris, B. Chen, J. Jannotti, and M. F. Kaashoek. The Click modular router. *ACM Transactions on Computer Systems*, 18(3), 2000.

[21] A. Köpsel and H. Woesner. OFELIA: Pan-european Test Facility for Openflow Experimentation. In *ServiceWave*. Springer, 2011.

[22] W. Liu. Improving Scalability of Xen: The 3000 Domains Experiment. http://goo.gl/Bt0Gz5, Apr. 2013.

[23] A. Madhavapeddy, R. Mortier, C. Rotsos, D. Scott, B. Singh, T. Gazagnaire, S. Smith, S. Hand, and J. Crowcroft. Unikernels: Library operating systems for the cloud. In *ASPLOS*. ACM, 2013.

[24] R. M. Mortier. Multi-timescale Internet Traffic Engineering. *IEEE Comm. Mag.*, 40(10), Oct. 2002.

[25] J. Naous, D. Erickson, G. A. Covington, G. Appenzeller, and N. McKeown. Implementing an OpenFlow Switch on the NetFPGA Platform. In *ANCS*. ACM, 2008.

[26] L. Peterson, T. Anderson, D. Culler, and T. Roscoe. A blueprint for introducing disruptive technology into the Internet. *ACM SIGCOMM Comput. Commun. Rev.*, 33(1), 2003.

[27] Z. Puljiz and M. Mikuc. IMUNES Based Distributed Network Emulator. In *SoftCOM*. IEEE, 2006.

[28] L. Rizzo and G. Lettieri. VALE, a Switched Ethernet for Virtual Machines. In *CoNEXT*. ACM, 2012.

[29] C. Rotsos, R. Mortier, A. Madhavapeddy, B. Singh, and A. W. Moore. Cost, performance & flexibility in OpenFlow: Pick three. In *ICC*. IEEE, 2012.

[30] C. Rotsos, N. Sarrar, S. Uhlig, R. Sherwood, and A. W. Moore. OFLOPS: An Open Framework for OpenFlow Switch Evaluation. In *PAM*, volume 7192. Springer, 2012.

[31] A. R. Roy, M. F. Bari, M. F. Zhani, R. Ahmed, and R. Boutaba. Design and Management of DOT: A Distributed OpenFlow Testbed. In *NOMS*. IEEE/IFIP, 2014.

[32] H. Tazaki, F. Urbani, E. Mancini, M. Lacage, D. Câmara, T. Turletti, W. Dabbous, et al. Direct code execution: revisiting library OS architecture for reproducible network experiments. In *CoNEXT*. ACM, 2013.

[33] A. Vahdat, K. Yocum, K. Walsh, P. Mahadevan, D. Kostić, J. Chase, and D. Becker. Scalability and accuracy in a large-scale network emulator. *ACM SIGOPS Oper. Syst. Rev.*, 36(SI), Dec. 2002.

[34] A. Varga and R. Hornig. An Overview of the OMNeT++ Simulation Environment. In *Simutools*. ICST, 2008.

[35] E. Weingärtner, F. Schmidt, H. V. Lehn, T. Heer, and K. Wehrle. SliceTime: a platform for scalable and accurate network emulation. In *NSDI*. USENIX, 2011.

[36] N. Willis. Seven problems with Linux Containers. http://lwn.net/Articles/588309/, Feb. 2014.

[37] Y. Zheng and D. M. Nicol. A Virtual Time System for OpenVZ-Based Network Emulations. In *PADS*. IEEE, 2011.

DiFS: Distributed Flow Scheduling for Adaptive Routing in Hierarchical Data Center Networks

Wenzhi Cui
Department of Computer Science
The University of Texas at Austin
Austin, Texas, 78712
wc8348@cs.utexas.edu

Chen Qian
Department of Computer Science
University of Kentucky
Lexington, Kentucky, 40506
qian@cs.uky.edu

ABSTRACT

Data center networks leverage multiple parallel paths connecting end host pairs to offer high bisection bandwidth for cluster computing applications. However, state of the art routing protocols such as Equal Cost Multipath (ECMP) is load-oblivious due to static flow-to-link assignments. They may cause bandwidth loss due to flow collisions. Recently proposed centralized scheduling algorithm or host based adaptive routing that require network-wide condition information may suffer from scalability problems.

In this paper, we present Distributed Flow Scheduling (DiFS) based Adaptive Routing for hierarchical data center networks, which is a *localized and switch-only solution*. DiFS allows switches to cooperate to avoid over-utilized links and find available paths without centralized control. DiFS is scalable and can react quickly to dynamic traffic, because it is independently executed on switches and requires no synchronization. DiFS provides global bounds of flow balance based on local optimization. Extensive experiments show that the aggregate throughput of DiFS using various traffic patterns is much better than that of ECMP, and is similar to or higher than those of two representative protocols that use network-wide optimization.

Categories and Subject Descriptors

C.2.2 [**Computer Communication Networks**]: Network Protocols—*Routing Protocols*

Keywords

Adaptive Routing; Data Center Networks

1. INTRODUCTION

The growing importance of cloud-based applications and big data processing has led to the deployment of large-scale data center networks that carry tremendous amount of traffic. Recently proposed data center network architectures primarily focus on using commodity Ethernet switches to build hierarchical trees such as fat-tree [1] [20] [25] and Clos [11] [28]. These topologies provide multiple equal-cost paths for any pair of end hosts and hence significantly increase bisection bandwidth. To fully utilize the path diversity, an ideal routing protocol should allow flows to avoid over-utilized links and take alternative paths, called adaptive routing. In this work, we focus on the investigation of throughput improvement by *routing protocols*.

Most state of the art data center networks rely on layer-3 Equal Cost Multipath (ECMP) protocol [15] to assign flows to available links using static flow hashing. Being simple and efficient, however, ECMP is load-oblivious, because the flow-to-path assignment does not account current network utilization. As a result, ECMP may cause flow collisions on particular links and create hot spots.

Recently proposed methods to improve the bandwidth utilization in data center networks can be classified in three categories: *centralized, host-based, and switch-only*.

- *Centralized* solutions utilize the recent advances in Software Defined Networking (SDN), which allows a central controller to perform control plane tasks and install forwarding entries to switches via a special protocol such as Open-Flow [19]. A typical centralized solution Hedera [2] relies on a central controller to find a path for each flow or assign a single core switch to deal with all flows to each destination host. Centralized solutions may face scalability problems [21], because traffic in today's data center networks requires parallel and fast path selection according to recent measurement studies [5, 17].

- *Host-based* methods, such as DARD [25], can be run without a central control. These methods enable end systems to monitor the network bandwidth utilization and then select desired paths for flows based on network conditions. One major limitation of host-based approaches is that every host needs to monitor the states of all paths to other hosts. In a large network such as production data centers, great amounts of control messages would occur. For many applications such as Shuffle (described in Section 4.3), each DARD host may have to monitor the entire network, which also limits its scalability. In addition, all legacy systems and applications running these protocols need to be upgraded, which incurs a lot management cost. There are also a number of host-based solutions in the transport layer such as Data Center TCP (DCTCP) [3] and multipath TCP (MPTCP) [24]. These methods are out of the scope of this work because we only focus on routing protocols.

- The last type is *switch-only* protocols which is efficient and fully compatible to current systems and applications on end hosts. It has been argued that switch-only solutions hold the best promise for dealing with large-scale and dynamic data center traffic patterns [21]. ECMP is a typical switch-only routing protocol for load balance. Many existing switch-only protocols allow a flow take multiple paths at the same time (called flow splitting) to achieve high throughput [10,21,28]. Flow splitting may cause a high level of TCP packet reordering, resulting in throughput drop [18].

In this paper, we propose Distributed Flow Scheduling (DiFS), a switch-only routing protocol that is executed independently on the control unit of each switch. DiFS aims to balance flows among different links and improves bandwidth utilization for data center networks. DiFS does not need centralized control or changes on end hosts. In addition DiFS does not allow flow splitting and hence limits packet reordering.

Based on our observations, we categorize flow collisions in a hierarchical data center networks in two types, local and remote flow collisions. DiFS achieves load balancing by taking efforts in two directions. First, each switch uses the *Path Allocation* algorithm that assigns flows evenly to all outgoing links to avoid *local flow collisions*. Second, each switch also monitors its incoming links by running the Imbalance Detection algorithm. If a collision is detected, the switch will send an Explicit Adaption Request (EAR) message that suggests the sending switch of a flow to change its path. Upon receiving the EAR, the sending switch will run the *Explicit Adaption* algorithm to avoid *remote flow collisions*. Previous solutions such as Hedera [2] try to maximize the total achieved throughput across all elephant flows using global knowledge by balancing traffic load among core switches. However we show that load balance among core switches is not enough to achieve load balance among different links. DiFS effectively solves this problem using the control messages called Explicit Adaptation Requests.

We conduct extensive simulations to compare DiFS with three representative methods from different categories: ECMP (switch-only) [15], Hedera (centralized) [2], and Dard (host-based) [25]. Experimental results show that DiFS outperforms ECMP significantly in aggregate bisection bandwidth. Compared with the centralized solution Hedera and the host-based solution Dard, DiFS achieves comparable or even higher throughput and less out-of-order packets, for both small and large data center network topologies.

The rest of this paper is organized as follows. Section 2 introduces background knowledge of flow scheduling in data center networks. Section 3 presents the detailed architecture and algorithm design of DiFS. We evaluate the performance of DiFS and compare it with other solutions in Section 4. We conclude our work in Section 6.

2. BACKGROUND AND OVERVIEW OF DIFS

2.1 Data center topologies

Today's data center networks often use *multi-rooted hierarchical tree* topologies (e.g., fat-tree [1] and Clos [11] topologies) to provide multiple parallel paths between any pair of hosts to enhance the network bisection bandwidth, instead of using expensive high speed routers/switches. Our protocol *DiFS is designed for an arbitrary hierarchical tree topology* as long as the switch organization in every pod is the same. However for the ease of exposition and comparison

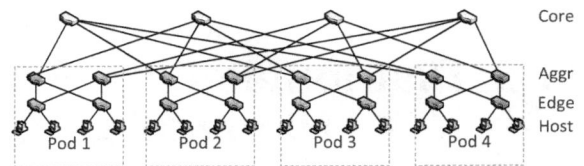

Figure 1: A fat tree topology for a datacenter network

with existing protocols, we will use the fat-tree topology for our protocol description and experimental evaluation.

A multi-rooted hierarchical tree topology has three vertical layers: edge layer, aggregate layer, and core layer. A *pod* is a management unit down from the core layer, which consists of a set of interconnected end hosts and a set of edge and aggregate switches that connect these hosts. As illustrated in Figure 1, a *fat-tree network* is built from a large number of k-port switches and end hosts. There are k pods, interconnected by $(k/2)^2$ core switches. Every pod consists of $(k/2)$ edge switches and $(k/2)$ aggregate switches. Each edge switch also connects $(k/2)$ end hosts. In the example of Figure 1, $k = 4$, and thus there are four pods, each of which consists of four switches.

A path are a set of links that connect two end hosts. There are two kinds of paths in a fat-tree network: inter-pod path and intra-pod path. An intra-pod path interconnects two hosts within the same pod while an inter-pod path is a path that connects two end host in different pods. Between any pair of end hosts in different pods, there are $(k/2)^2$ equal-cost paths, each of which corresponds to a core switch. An end-to-end path can be split into two flow segments [26]: the *uphill segment* refers to the part of the path connecting source host to the switch in the highest layer (e.g., the core switch for an inter-pod path), and the *downhill segment* refers to the part connecting the switch in the highest layer to the destination host. Similar to existing work, we mainly focus our discussion on inter-pod flows, because intra-pod flows can be handled by a simpler version of the routing protocol.

2.2 Examples of flow collision and DiFS's solutions

We define a flow collision as too many flows being transmitted to a same link, which may cause potential congestion. We show three types of flow collisions in Figure 2, where in each example some parts of the network are not shown for simplicity. If a switch experiences a flow collision on one of its links and can locally adjust the flow assignment to resolve the collision, such collision is called a *local collision*. Figure 2(a) shows an example of a local collision, where switch $Aggr_{11}$ forwards two flows to a same link. Local collisions may be caused by a bad flow assignment of static multi-pathing algorithms such as ECMP. Otherwise, the collision is called a *remote collision*. Figure 2(b) shows an example of Type 1 remote collision, where two flows take a same link from $Core_2$ to Pod_2. Type 1 remote collision may be caused by over-utilizing a core switch ($Core_2$ in this example). Hence some existing solutions propose to balance traffic among cores [2]. However balancing core utilization may not be enough. Another example of remote collision (Type 2) is shown in Figure 2(c), where core utilization is

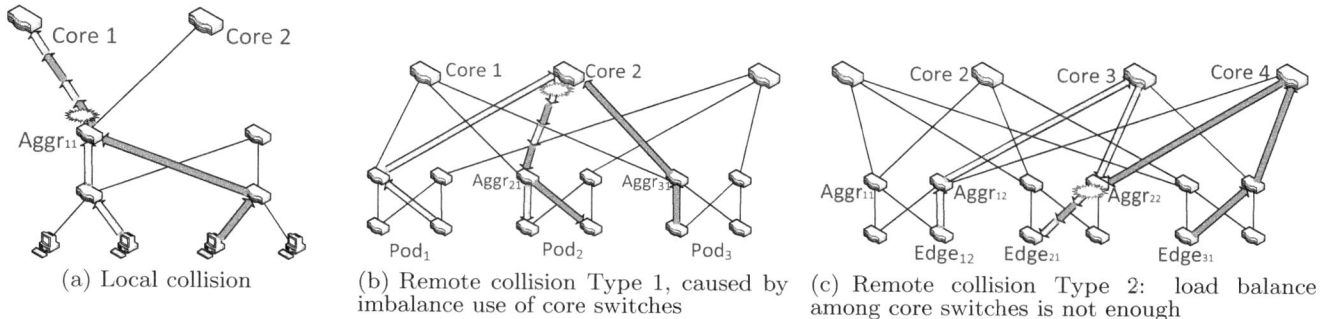

(a) Local collision   (b) Remote collision Type 1, caused by imbalance use of core switches   (c) Remote collision Type 2: load balance among core switches is not enough

Figure 2: Three types of collisions. For simplicity we use two flows to indicate a collision. In practice, a collision may be caused by many flows.

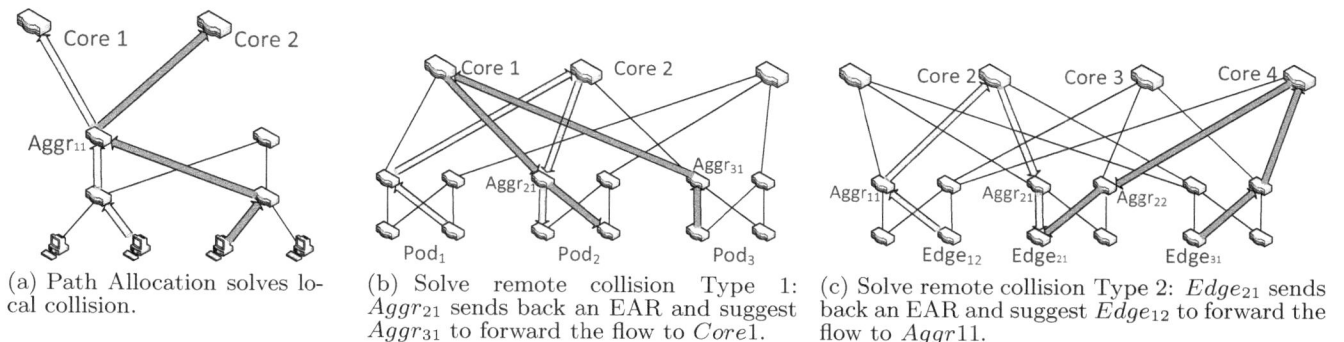

(a) Path Allocation solves local collision.   (b) Solve remote collision Type 1: $Aggr_{21}$ sends back an EAR and suggest $Aggr_{31}$ to forward the flow to $Core1$.   (c) Solve remote collision Type 2: $Edge_{21}$ sends back an EAR and suggest $Edge_{12}$ to forward the flow to $Aggr11$.

Figure 3: Resolving collisions by Path Allocation and Explicit Adaption

balanced but flows still collide on the link from $Aggr_{22}$ to $Edge_{21}$. We also observe that location collisions happen in uphill segments and remote collisions happen in downhill segments.

Local collisions can be detected and resolved by local algorithms in a relatively easy way. DiFS uses the Path Allocation algorithm to detect flow-to-link imbalance and remove one of the flows to an under-utilized link, as shown in Figure 3(a). The key insight of DiFS to resolve remote collisions is to allow the switch in the downhill segment that detected flow imbalance to send an Explicit Adaption Request (EAR) message to the uphill segment. For the example of Figure 2(b), $Aggr_{21}$ can detect flow imbalance among the incoming links. It then sends an EAR to $Aggr_{31}$ in Pod_3 (randomly chosen between two sending pods), suggesting the flow to take the path through $Core_1$. $Aggr_{31}$ runs the Explicit Adaption algorithm and changes the flow path. That flow will eventually take another incoming link of $Aggr_{21}$ as shown in Figure 3(b). To resolve the collision in Figure 2(c), $Edge_{21}$ that detects flow imbalance sends back an EAR and suggest $Edge_{12}$ to forward the flow to $Aggr_{11}$. That flow will eventually go from $Aggr_{21}$ to $Edge_{21}$, as shown in Figure 3(c).

From the examples, the key observation is that *the incoming links of the aggregate (edge) switch in the downhill segment have one-to-one correspondence to the outgoing links of the aggregate (edge) switch in the uphill segment* in a multi-rooted tree. Therefore when an aggregate (edge) switch in

the downhill segment detects imbalance and finds an under-utilized link, it can suggest the aggregate (edge) switch in the uphill segment to change the path to the "mirror" of the under-utilized link. In the example of Type 1 remote collision, $Aggr_{21}$ controls the flow to income from $Core_1$ by suggesting $Aggr_{31}$ to forward the flow to $Core_1$. In the example of Type 2 remote collision, $Edge_{21}$ controls the flow to income from $Aggr_{21}$ by suggesting $Edge_{12}$ to forward the flow to $Aggr_{11}$.

2.3 Classification of flows

In this paper, a flow is defined as a sequence of packets sent from a source host to a destination host using TCP. In our flow scheduling protocol, a flow can have only one path at any time. Allowing a flow to use multiple paths simultaneously may cause packet reordering and hence reduce the throughput. However, a flow is allowed to take multiple paths at different times in its life cycle.

Elephant and mice flows: Elephants are large, long-lived flows whose traffic amount is higher than a threshold. The other flows are called mice flows. Similar to many other work [2, 25], *our protocol focuses on elephant flows and intends to spread them as evenly as possible among all links.* All mice flows will be processed by ECMP, because recent work has shown that ECMP forwarding can perform load-balancing efficiently and effectively for mice flows [11]. Note that elephant flows do not necessarily require high demand of sending rates.

Let f_{ab} be a flow whose source is a and destination is b. A flow f_{ab} may be classified into four types for a particular switch s that runs DiFS: f_{ab} is a single-in-single-out (SISO) flow for switch s if and only if there are only one possible incoming link of s from a and one possible outgoing link of s to b. f_{ab} is a single-in-multi-out (SIMO) flow for switch s if and only if there are one incoming link of s from a and multiple outgoing links of s to b. f_{ab} is a multi-in-single-out (MISO) flow for switch s if and only if there are multiple incoming links of s from a and one outgoing link of s to b. A close look at fat-tree networks reveals that all inter-pod flows are SIMO for the edge and aggregate switches on the uphill segments, and are MISO for the edge and aggregate switches on the downhill segments. All inter-pod flows for core switches are SISO. Multi-in-multi-out (MIMO) flows may be defined similarly. However, there is no MIMO flow for any switch in a fat-tree network. They may appear in general topologies.

3. DIFS DESIGN

3.1 Components and Deployment

Typical switch architecture usually consists of two components: data plane and control plane. The data plane includes multiple network ports, as well as a flow/forwarding table and an output queue for each port. The control plane can perform general-purpose processing like collecting measurement results and install/modify the rules in the flow/forwarding tables of the data plane. As result, DiFS should be installed in the control plane of each switch. DiFS is also compatible to software defined networking such as Open-Flow [19]. The control logic of DiFS can be implemented in OpenFlow controllers which exchange control messages and update flow tables in OpenFlow switches accordingly. Compared with centralized algorithms that require a single controller responsible to the entire network, distributed and localized decision-making of DiFS offers tremendous scalability to SDN control. For example, OpenFlow switches in the same pod can be connected to one controller, which is physically close to these switches and able to handle the scheduling tasks. Controllers in different pods exchange control information that is much less than condition of the whole network.

3.2 Optimization goals

As a high-level description, DiFS intends to balance *the number of elephant flows* among all links in the network to utilize the bisection bandwidth and take the advantage of path diversity. We use the number of flows as the optimization metric instead of flow bandwidth consumption based on the following reasons:

1. A flow's maximum bandwidth consumption[1] can hardly be estimated. As shown in [2], a flow's current sending rate tells very little about its maximum bandwidth consumption. Hedera [2] uses global knowledge to perform flow bandwidth demand estimation. However, such method is not possible to be applied in distributed algorithms such as DiFS.

---

[1] A flow's maximum bandwidth consumption, also called as flow demand, is the rate the flow would grow to in a fully non-blocking network.

2. Using flow count only requires a switch to maintain a counter for each outgoing link. However, measurement of flow bandwidth consumption requires complicated traffic monitoring tools installed on each switch. Our method simplifies switch structure.

3. Using flow count as the metric, DiFS can achieve similar or even better performance compared with Hedera [2] and a variant of DiFS implementation that uses estimated bandwidth consumption as the metric. The results will be shown in Section 4.6.

Two optimization goals for load-balancing scenarios are desired:

Balanced Output (BO): For an edge switch s_e, let $o(s_a)$ be the number of SIMO flows on an outgoing link connecting the aggregate switch s_a. BO of edge switch s_e is achieved if and only if $o(s_{a1}) - o(s_{a2}) \leq \delta$, for any two aggregate switches s_{a1} and s_{a2}, where δ is a constant. Similarly we may define BO of an aggregate switch to cores. BO can be achieved by the Path allocation algorithm of DiFS with the smallest possible value of δ being 1.

Balanced Input (BI): For an aggregate switch s_a, let $i(c)$ be the number of MISO flows on an incoming link connecting the core c. BI of edge switch s is achieved if and only if $i(c_1) - i(c_2) \leq \delta$, for any two cores c_1 and c_2, where δ is a constant. Similarly we may define BI of an edge switch from aggregate switches. BI can be achieved by Explicit Adaptation of DiFS with the smallest possible value of δ being 1.

BO and BI do not interfere with each other, and hence a switch can achieve them at a same time. Although BO and BI of a switch are two kinds of optimization in a local view, we have proved that they provide global performance bounds of load balancing, as presented in Section 3.7. In Section 4 we further demonstrate that they can achieve high aggregate throughput via experiments.

3.3 Protocol Structure

DiFS uses a threshold to eliminate mice flows. Such threshold-based module can be installed on edge switches. It maintains the number of transmitted bytes of each flow. This monitoring task can be cost-efficient in switch resources using recent proposed techniques such as OpenSketch [27]. If the byte number of a flow is larger than a threshold value, the edge switch will label this flow as an elephant flow and mark the packet header to notify other switches on its path.

Each switch has a flow list which maintains three variables for every flow f: the incoming link identifier, denoted as L_i, the outgoing link identifier, denoted as L_o, and the last time this flow appeared, denoted as t. A switch also maintains two Port State Vectors (PSVs), V_i and V_o. The ith element in vector V_i is the number of flows coming from the ith incoming link. Likewise the ith element in vector V_o is the number of flows forwarded to the ith outgoing link.

There are three flow control modules in aggregate and edge switches: control loop unit, explicit adaptation unit, and path allocation unit. Control loops are run periodically by switches. The main objectives of the control loop unit are to detect imbalance of MISO flows among incoming links and send an Explicit Adaptation Request (EAR) if necessary. An EAR is a notification message sent along the *reverse flow path* to recommend switches in the flow's sending pod to choose a different path. An EAR also in-

---
Algorithm 1: Imbalance Detection in Control Loop

S = the set of all MISO flows forwarded by this switch
for $f \in S$ **do**
    L_i = incoming link of f
    min = minimum value among elements in V_i of f
    δ = imbalance threshold
    if $V_i[L_i] - min > T$ **then**
        compute a path recommendation p
        send a EAR(f, p) to L_i
        Return
    end
end

---

cludes a path recommendation. When a switch receives an EAR, it runs the explicit adaptation unit and changes the output link of the designated flow in the EAR to that on the recommended path, if possible. Path Allocation Request (PAR) is another message to request flow scheduling. PAR includes a flow identifier and requires switches to allocate an available link for this flow. Switches treat a packet with a new flow identifier as a PAR. The sender needs to explicitly send a PAR only if path reservation is allowed to achieve a certain level of performance guarantee for upper-layer applications [4]. For a SIMO flow, the path allocation unit will assign an outgoing port for this flow based on link utilization. Detailed algorithms for these modules will be presented in the following subsections.

The time period between two control loops has limited impact to the convergence time of the whole protocol execution. We will show that DiFS converges quickly under a wide range of control loop period time in Section 4.5.

3.4 Control loop

Each DiFS switch continuously runs a control loop. At each iteration, the switch executes the following:

1. Remove disappeared flows. A flow may disappear from a switch due to several reasons. For example, the flow may have finished transmission or taken another path. In each iteration, the switch will delete a flow if the difference between current time and its last-appeared time t is larger than a threshold, which may be set to a multiple of the average round-trip time of flows.

2. Re-balance SIMO flows among all outgoing links. Removing disappeared flows may cause the change of flow numbers on links. Thus flow re-balancing is necessary.

3. Send an EAR if necessary. If the switch finds a MISO flow comes in a over-utilized link, the switch will recommend other switches to change the flow path by sending an EAR. In order to avoid TCP performance degrade caused by too many EARs, DiFS forces every switch to send at most one EAR at each iteration.

We detail the steps 2) and 3) as the follows.
Re-balance SIMO flows. The purpose of re-balancing SIMO flows is to achieve BO, i.e., let the flow count difference of any two outgoing links be smaller than the pre-defined threshold δ. The solution seems to be trivial: a switch can simply move flows on overloaded links to under-loaded ones. However this simple method could cause oscillations of network status. Consider a switch s moves a

random flow f from link l_1 to l_2 for load balance. Later by receiving an EAR from another switch, s will be suggested to move f from l_2 to l_1 to avoid remote collisions. During the next control loop, s will again move f to l_1 to l_2 and so on. Such oscillation will never stop. One obvious downside of oscillations is that they will incur packet reordering and hurt TCP performance. To resolve this problem, we maintain a priority value for each flow in the flow list. When the link assignment of a flow is changed based upon the suggestion from an EAR, the priority of the flow is increased by one. When a switch re-balances SIMO flows, it should first move flows that have less priority values. This strategy intends to let flows whose assignments are changed by EARs be more stable and avoid oscillations.

Imbalance detection and path recommendation for EAR. For fairness concern, at each iteration the switch will scan each MISO flows in a random order. The imbalance detection is also in a threshold basis, which is presented in Algorithm 1.

Due to lack of global view of flow distribution, the EAR receiver should be told how to change the flow's path. Therefore the EAR sender should include a path recommendation, *which does not necessarily need to be a complete path*. In a fat-tree, both aggregate and edge switches are able to detect load imbalance and recommend an alternative path *only based on local link status*.

For the flow collision example of Figure 2(b), $Aggr_{21}$ will notice the load imbalance among incoming links and send an EAR to $Aggr_{31}$ (randomly selected between senders of the two collided flows). The path recommendation in this EAR is just $Core_1$. $Aggr_{31}$ will receive the EAR and change the flow to the output link connected with $Core_1$, and this flow will eventually come from another incoming link of $Aggr_{21}$ that was under-utilized, as shown in Figure 3(b).

For the flow collision example of Figure 2(c), $Edge_{21}$ can detect it by comparing two incoming links and then send an EAR to $Edge_{12}$ in the uphill segment. The path recommendation here is just $Aggr_{11}$. When $Edge_{12}$ let the flow take $Aggr_{11}$, the flow will eventually take another incoming link to $Edge_{21}$ and hence resolves the collision as shown in Figure 3(c).

As a matter of fact, in a fat-tree network a path recommendation can be specified by either a recommended core or a recommended aggregate switch in the uphill segment. For other topologies, more detailed path specification might be needed.

For an intra-pod flow, the path consists of two edge switches and one aggregate switch. If the aggregate switch detects load imbalance, it can also send an EAR to the edge switch in the previous hop and suggest the edge switch to send the flow to another aggregate switch. In fact, this is the one difference in our protocol when it treats intra-pod and inter-pod flows.

3.5 Operations upon receiving a PAR

In order to keep all links output balanced, we use a distributed greedy algorithm to select an outgoing link for each flow requested by a PAR. When a switch received a PAR, it first check how many outgoing links can lead to the destination. If there is only one link, then the switch will simply use this link. If there are multiple links to which this flow can be forwarded, the switch will select an local optimal link for this flow. The algorithm first find the set of links with

Algorithm 2: Path Allocation

Input: Path Allocation Request PAR
Output: None
f = flow identifier in PAR
S = set of links that can reach f's destination
if $|S| > 1$ **then**
    min = minimal value among all $V_o[l]$, $l \in S$
    for $l \in S$ **do**
        if $V_o[l] > min$ **then**
            $S = S - \{l\}$
        end
    end
    L_o = a random element in S
    increase $V_o[L_o]$ by 1
else
    L_o = the first element of S
end
record the incoming link L_i of f
record the outgoing link L_o of f
update the access time t of f

Algorithm 3: Explicit Adaptation of switch s

Input: Explicit Adaptation Request EAR
Output: None
f = flow identifier in EAR
r = recommended core or aggregate switch in EAR
L_i = current incoming link of f
L_o = current outgoing link of f
if r and s are connected **and** sending f to r can lead to the destination of f **then**
    L = the outgoing link connecting r
    if $V_o[L] >= V_o[L_o]$ **then**
        move a flow currently on L to L_o
    move f to the outgoing link L
    update the link variables of changed links
else
    forward EAR to L_i
end

---

the minimum number of outgoing flows. If there are more than one links in this set, the algorithm will randomly select a link from the set.

3.6 Operations upon receiving an EAR

An EAR includes a flow identifier and a path recommendation. As mentioned, for a fat-tree network a path recommendation can be specified by either a recommended core or a recommended uphill aggregate switch. When a switch received an EAR, it first checks if it can move the requested flow f to the recommended core or aggregate switch. If not, it will forward this EAR further towards the reverse path of f. If moving f will cause imbalance among outgoing links, the switch swaps f with another flow on the recommended link. The complete algorithm is described in Algorithm 3.

EARs may also cause network status oscillations. Consider the following scenario in Fig 4, where only part of the network is shown. $flow_1$ and $flow_2$ collide on the same link from SW_4 to SW_1 but the link from SW_5 to SW_1 is free. SW_1 may send an EAR to SW_2 and suggest SW_2 to send $flow_1$ to SW_5, in the purpose of resolving the remote colli-

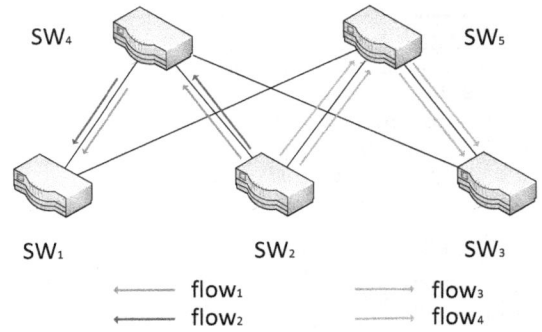

Figure 4: Oscillation problem caused by EARs

sion at SW_1. After receiving the EAR, SW_2 swaps the outgoing links of $flow_1$ and $flow_3$. However at the same time SW_3 may send an EAR to SW_2 and suggest SW_2 to send $flow_4$ to SW_4. SW_2 should then swap the outgoing links of $flow_2$ and $flow_4$. As a result the collisions still exist. By keeping executing the protocol, oscillations happen and the network status cannot converge. To deal with the problem, we allow random spans in control loops. There is some non-negligible time difference between the control loops of SW_1 and SW_3. In this way, SW_3 may notice that its collision has already been solved after SW_2 swaps the outgoing links of $flow_1$ and $flow_3$ and will not send another EAR.

3.7 Bounds on global flow balance

The local optimization on switches can lead to global performance bounds as introduced in this section.

We provide a bound on flow balance among aggregate switches in a same pod by the following theorem:

THEOREM 3.1. *In a k-pod fat-tree, suppose every edge switch achieves BO with δ. Let $n(s_a)$ be the number of flows that are sending to aggregate switch s_a. Then we have $MAX_a - MIN_a \leq \delta \cdot k/2$, where MAX_a is the maximum $n(s_a)$ value among all aggregate switches in the pod, MIN_c is the minimum $n(s_a)$ value among all aggregate switches in the pod.*

We further prove a bound on flow balance among core switches by the following theorem:

THEOREM 3.2. *In a k-pod fat-tree, suppose every edge and aggregate switch achieves BO with $\delta = 1$. Let $n(c)$ be the number of flows that are sending to core c. Then we have $MAX_{all} - MIN_{all} \leq 3k$, where MAX_{all} is the maximum $n(c)$ value among all cores and MIN_{all} is the minimum $n(c)$ value among all cores.*

Similarly we have a bound of flow balance in the receiving side.

THEOREM 3.3. *In a k-pod fat-tree, suppose all aggregate switches in a same pod achieve BI with $\delta = 1$. Let $n(s_e)$ be the number of flows that are sending to edge switch s_e. Then we have $MAX_e - MIN_e \leq k/2$, where MAX_e is the maximum $n(s_e)$ value among all edge switches in the pod and MIN_e is the minimum $n(s_e)$ value among all edge switches in the pod.*

The proof is similar to that of Theorem 3.1. Proofs in this section can be found in the appendix.

Note that the values we provide in the theorems are only bounds of the difference between the maximum and minimum flow numbers. In practice, however, *the actual differences are much lower than these bounds.*

3.8 Failures Recovery

Switches must take network failures into consideration in performing flow assignments. A network failure may be a switch failure, a link failure, or a host failure. Failures may also be classified into reachability failures and partial failures. Reachability failures refer to those failures that can cause one or more end hosts unreachable. For example, crash of an edge switch can make $(k/2)$ hosts unreachable. DiFS can tolerate such kind of failures because our algorithm relies on local, soft state collected at run time. Only flows towards the unreachable hosts are affected.

Partial failures, i.e., individual link or port failures on edge and aggregate switches, can cause performance degradation due to loss of equal-cost paths. However, DiFS can cope with such kind of failures with a simple modification. When a link or switch experiences such failure, other switches connected to the switch/link can learn the loss of capacity from underlying link state protocols. These switches then move the flows on the failed link to other available links, or send EARs to notify the other switches. We do not present the details of failure recovery due to space limit, but they are implemented in our experiments.

Loss or delay of EARs on congested link may make DiFS degrade into local link balanced algorithm like ECMP. To avoid additional cost, control messages are delivered using UDP. However, a switch will keep sending control messages at each control loop if previous flow collisions have not been resolved. In the experiments, we also take the loss and delay of control messages into consideration. Experiments show that DiFS still converges in short time under congestion. Therefore the loss or delay of control messages has limited impact to network convergence. Besides, in order to avoid the oscillation problem caused by EARs arrived in the same time, we add a random time slot to the interval between two adjacent control loop.

4. EXPERIMENTAL RESULTS

In this section, we evaluate the performance of DiFS by comparing it with three representative adaptive routing solutions from different categories: ECMP (switch-only) [15], Hedera (centralized) [2], and Dard (host-based) [25]. *Note that both Hedera and Dard use global network information which is not available to switch-only methods.*

4.1 Methodology

Most existing studies use custom-built simulators to evaluate data center networks at large scale [2] [24] [22] [21]. Simulation is able to show the scalability of the protocols for large networks with dynamic traffic patterns, while testbed experiments can only scale to up to tens of hosts. We find many of them use a certain level of abstraction for TCP, which may result in inaccurate throughput results. [2] To perform experiments with accurate results, we developed a

packet-level stand-alone simulator in which DiFS as well as other protocols are implemented in detail.[3] *Our simulator models individual packets, hence we believe it can better demonstrate real network performance.* TCP New Reno is implemented in detail as the transportation layer protocol. Our simulator models each link as a queue whose size is the delay-bandwidth product. A link's bandwidth is 1 Gbps and its average delay is 0.01 ms. Our switch abstraction maintains finite shared buffers and forwarding tables. In our experiments, we simulate multi-rooted tree topologies in different sizes. We use 16-host networks as small topologies and 1024-host networks for bulk analysis.

DiFS is compared with ECMP, Hedera, and Dard. For ECMP we implemented a simple hash function which uses the flow identifier of each tcp packet as the key. We implemented the Simulated Annealing scheduler of Hedera, which achieves the best performance among all schedulers proposed in Hedera [2]. We set the control loop period of Hedera to 0.01 seconds and Simulated Annealing iteration to 1000, both of which are exactly the same as their implementation. We also set the period of distributed control loop to 0.01 second for DiFS. As mentioned in Section 3.2, we focus on balancing the number of elephant flows among links. We use 100KB as the elephant threshold, same to the value used by other work [25].

Performance criteria. We evaluate the following performance criteria.

Aggregate throughput is the measured throughput of various traffic patterns using proposed routing protocols on the corresponding data center topology. It reflects how a routing protocol can utilize the topology bandwidth.

Flow completion time characterizes the time to deliver a flow, which is important because many data center applications are latency-aware. Besides the comparison of flow completion time among different protocols, we also care about the fairness of flow completion time of different flows routed by a same protocol.

Packet out-of-order ratio. Although all protocols in our experiments do not split flows, dynamic routing will still cause some out-of-order packets. The out-of-order ratio is measured to see whether a protocol will hurt TCP performance.

Convergence time is important to measure the stability of a dynamic routing protocol.

Control overhead. We measure the control message overhead in bytes.

Traffic patterns. Similar to [2] and [25], we created a group of traffic patterns as our benchmark communication suite. These patterns are considered typical for cluster computing applications and can be either static or dynamic. For static traffic patterns, all flows are permanent. Dynamic traffic patterns refer to those in which flows start at different times. In this paper, we evaluate the performance of DiFS against dynamic patterns similar to data shuffle in cluster computing applications such as MapReduce [8]. The static patterns used by our experiments are described as follows:

---

[2] For example, the simulator developed in [2] only simulates each flow without performing per-packet computation, and uses predicted sending rate instead of implementing TCP. The simulator that implements MPTCP [24] has been used for performance evaluation by many other projects [22] [21].

---

[3] However, it does not implement TCP ACKs and assume ACKs can all be successfully delivered.

[3] We have also implemented DiFS on NS2, but experienced very slow speed when using NS2 for data center networks. We guess the existing studies do not use NS2 due to the same reason.

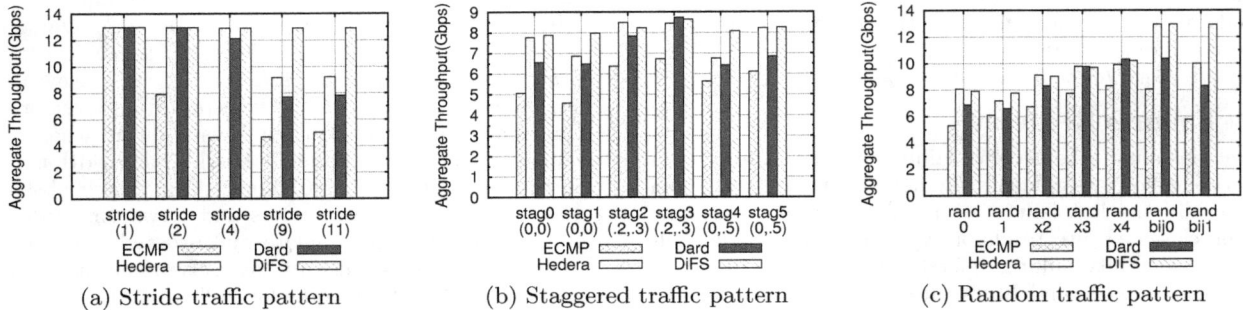

(a) Stride traffic pattern   (b) Staggered traffic pattern   (c) Random traffic pattern

Figure 5: Aggregate throughput comparison on small topologies

1. *Stride(i)*: A host with index x sends data to a host with index $(x + i) mod(num\_hosts)$, where num_hosts is the number of all hosts in the network. This traffic pattern stresses out the links between the core and the aggregation layers with a large i.

2. *Staggered(P_e, P_p)*: A host sends data to another host in the same edge layer with probability P_e, and to host in the same pod (but in the different edge layer) with probability P_p, and to hosts in different pods with probability $1 - P_e - P_p$.

3. *Random*: A host sends one elephant flow to some other end host in the same network with a uniform probability. This is a special case of *Randx(x)* where $x = 1$.

4. *Randx(x)*: A host sends x elephant flows to any other end host in the same topology with a uniform probability.

5. *Randbij*: A host sends one elephant flow to some other host according to a bijective mapping of all hosts. This is a special case of *Random* pattern which may be created by certain cluster computing applications.

4.2 Small Topology Simulation Results

In this set of experiments, 16 hosts (acting as clients) first establish TCP connections with some designated peers (acting as servers) according to the specified traffic pattern. After that, these clients begin to send elephant flows to their peers constantly. Each experiment lasts 60 seconds and each host measures the incoming throughput during the whole process. We use the results for all hosts in the middle 40 seconds as the aggregate throughput.

Figure 5(a) shows the average aggregate throughput for a variety of Stride traffic patterns with different parameters. For stride parameter $i = 1$, all three methods have good performance. DiFS achieves highest throughput for all i values and outperforms ECMP significantly when i is greater than 2. DiFS has significant lead over Hedera and Dard when $i = 9$ and 11. Note a larger value of i indicates less traffic locality. Hence DiFS is more robust than the other methods for traffic locality.

Figure 5(b) shows the average aggregate throughput for Staggered patterns. Similar to the Stride results, DiFS has the highest throughput for most cases. In two cases (stag2(.2,.3) and stag3(.2,.3)), DiFS's throughput is marginally less than that of Hedera and Dard respectively. We might find that

	ECMP	Hedera	Dard	DiFS
Shuffle time (s)	249.82	204.87	210.83	179.48
Aver. completion time (s)	224.78	178.53	191.25	157.20
Aver. throughput (Gbps)	4.31	5.30	4.61	6.10
Aver. out-of-order to in-order ratio	0.006	0.006	0.006	0.006
Max. out-of-order to in-order ratio	0.643	0.750	0.750	0.4
Aver. out-of-order window size	0.00	14.75	13.72	28.66
Max. out-of-order window size	0.00	69.00	68.00	123.00

Table 1: results of shuffle experiments

the absolute bandwidth values of all three methods in this set of experiments are less than those in the Stride experiments. According to our results on non-blocking switches and links (not shown in the figure), the average throughput for Staggered is also limited to 10-12 Gbps due to the hotspots created by the traffic pattern. DiFS results are actually very close to the limit.

Figure 5(c) depicts the throughput for Random patterns. For all cases except one, DiFS outperforms the other three protocols. In Random experiments, DiFS outperforms ECMP in the average throughput by at least 33% for most traffic patterns. For particular patterns, this value can be higher than 100%. Compared to Hedera and Dard that uses global information, DiFS achieves higher throughput for the Randbij1 pattern and similar throughput for the others. We suspect there are two major reasons why Hedera achieves less bandwidth compared to DiFS: First, Hedera ignores intra pod flows and degrades to ECMP when intra pod flows are dominant. Second, Hedera with Simulated Annealing does not assign an explicit path for each flow. Instead Hedera assigns a core switch for every single host, which may result in bottlenecks on the links connecting aggregate switches and edge switches.

4.3 MapReduce Traffic: Data Shuffle

We conduct experiments of all-to-all Data Shuffle in the 16-host multi-rooted tree topology to evaluate the performance of DiFS under dynamic traffic patterns. Data Shuffle

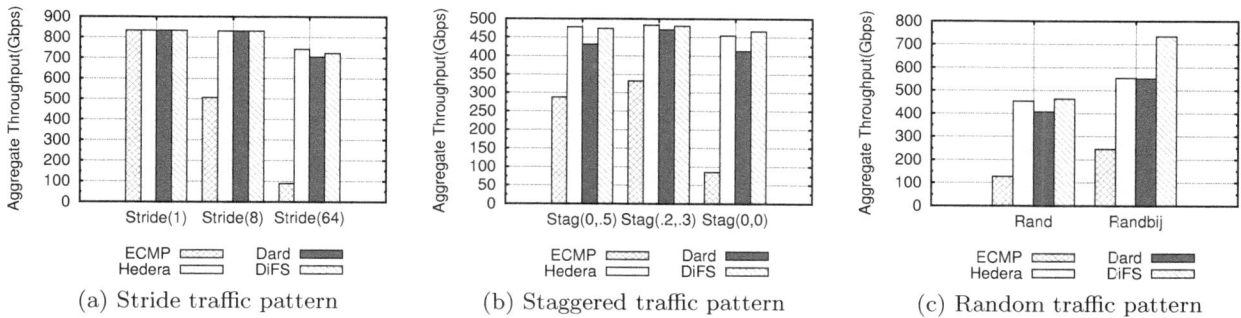

(a) Stride traffic pattern   (b) Staggered traffic pattern   (c) Random traffic pattern

Figure 6: Aggregate throughput comparison for bulk analysis

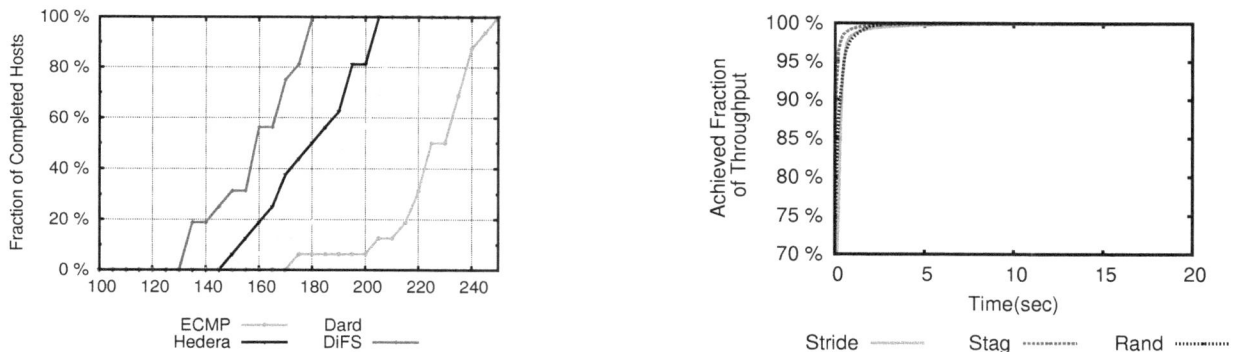

Figure 7: CDF of host completion time for data shuffle

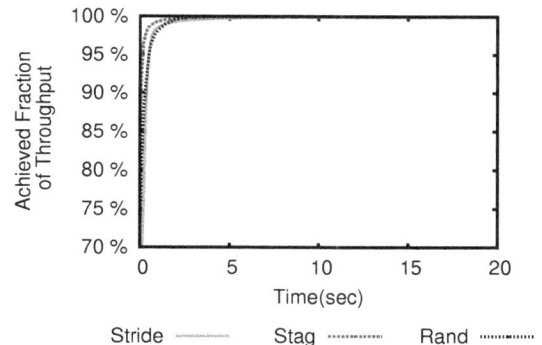

Figure 8: Convergence time of DiFS in the 1024-host network

is an important operation for MapReduce-like applications. Each host (acting as reducer) in the network will sequentially receive a large amount of data (500MB in our simulation) from all other hosts (acting as mapper) using TCP. Therefore in total it is a 120 GB Data Shuffle. In order to avoid unnecessary hotspots, each host will access other hosts in a random order. We also assume there is no disk operation during the whole process. We measure the shuffle time, average completion time, and average throughput of the three methods. The shuffle time is the total time for the 120 GB Shuffle operation. The average completion time is the average value of the completion time of every host in the network. The average aggregate throughput refers to the sum of average throughput of every host.

We also measure two variables described in [28] during the Shuffle period in order to reflect the packet reordering problem. The first variable is the ratio of the number of packets delivered out-of-order to the number of packets provided in-order in TCP by the senders. The second variable is the out-of-order packet window size, defined as the average gap in the packet sequence numbers observed by the receivers.

Table 1 shows that our algorithm outperforms ECMP by 28%, Hedera by around 13%, and Dard by 15%, in aggregate throughput. DiFS achieves the least shuffle time and average completion time per flow. In addition DiFS causes less packet reordering compared to Hedera. ECMP has the least out-of-order packets because it is a static scheduling algorithm.

Figure 7 depicts the cumulative distribution function (CDF) of host completion time of the three methods. As observed from this figure, by the time DiFS finishes Shuffle operations, around 50% hosts of Hedera have completed their jobs and only 20% hosts of Dard and 5% hosts of ECMP have finished their jobs. In general DiFS fishes flows much faster than all other protocols. All four methods have obvious variation in completion time of different flows.

4.4 Large Topology Simulation Results

Figure 6 shows the aggregate throughput comparison using a 1024-host fat-tree network ($k = 16$). We can find that ECMP performs worse in a large topology, compared with its performance in the 16-host network using the same traffic patterns. We suspect this is because the chances of collisions in path assignment for static hash functions increase when topology gets larger. We also noticed that the performance gap between Hedera and DiFS shrinks in the 1024-host network compared to that in the 16-host network due to the decreased portion of intra pod flows. However, DiFS still has the highest aggregate throughput in general except for two traffic patterns among the three figures.

4.5 Convergence speed and control overhead

Convergence speed.

Convergence speed is a critical performance metric for DiFS, because DiFS is a distributed solution rather than a centralized algorithm. We measure the convergence speed

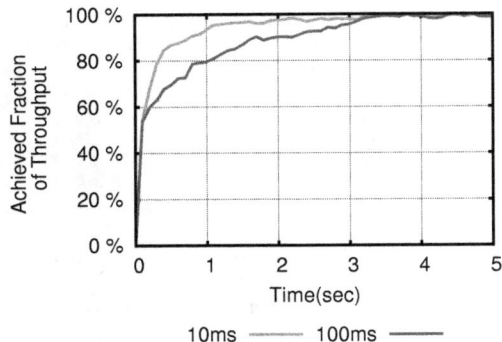

Figure 9: **Convergence time of DiFS with different control loops**

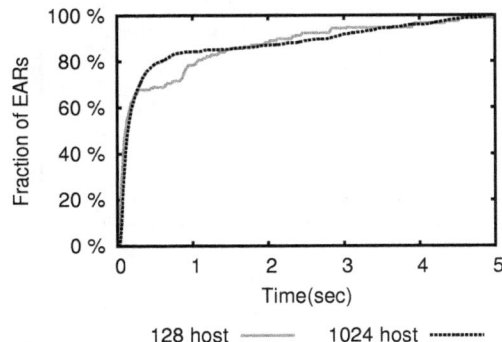

Figure 10: **Cumulative distribution of EAR-receiving times**

of DiFS for different traffic patterns using fat-tree topologies. In Figure 8 we show the achieved fraction of throughput of DiFS versus time for different traffic patterns in the 1024-host network. Even with Random traffic our algorithm may still converge to a steady state within 5 seconds. We also compare the convergence speed against the frequency of control loops in 1024 host networks using Randbij patterns. Figure 9 compares the convergence speed of DiFS with 10 ms control loops to 100 ms control loops. Although smaller frequency yields longer converge time, the throughput still converge to relatively stable state in three seconds and achieves more than 80% throughput in the first second. We may conclude that our protocol is robust under different frequencies of control loops.

Control Overhead.

As a distributed solution, the computation cost of DiFS is very low because switch only needs to consider its local flows. Hence we mainly focus on the communication overhead of DiFS, which is measured by the number of EAR messages. Aside from communication overhead, too many EAR messages may cause performance degradation because flows may be requested to change their paths back and forth.

Table 2 shows the number of EARs sent by switches under random traffic patterns in fat-tree networks with different sizes. In the measurement, we assume the size of each message is 26 Bytes, which includes the size of flow identifier and the address of recommended core or aggregate switch in an

k	Host	EAR	Control Overhead (KB)
4	16	4	0
8	128	304	7.72
16	1024	4113	104.43
32	8192	45183	1147.22

Table 2: **control overhead of DiFS for random traffic patterns**

EAR. As shown in the table, for an 8192-host fat-tree network, DiFS only generates control messages in a total size of around 1 MB. Figure 10 shows the CDF of EAR-receiving times. Within 5 seconds, all EARs have sent and received, and around 80% EARs are received in the first second.

4.6 Flow count versus flow bandwidth consumption

DiFS use the number of elephant flows as the metric for load balancing. Obviously not all elephant flows have equal bandwidth consumptions, i.e., sending rates. As discussed in Section 3.2, DiFS cannot estimate the flow bandwidth consumption due to lack of global information. A substitution for bandwidth consumption estimation is to measure the sending rate of each flow on the current path. Unfortunately, a flow's current sending rate doest not reflect its maximum bandwidth consumption [2]. We also implemented a variant of DiFS which uses measured flow sending rate as the metric for load balancing, denoted as DiFS-FM. We compare both algorithms in Figure 11(a) and Figure 11(b). The results tell that DiFS-FM has similar performance compared to DiFS that uses flow count. Therefore there is no need to deploy a particular module to keep measuring sending rates in switches.

4.7 Summary of results

To summarize the performance evaluation, we compare the important properties of adaptive routing protocols in Table 3. Our results has shown that DiFS can achieve similar or even higher throughput than Hedera and Dard that require network-wide information for routing decisions. As a local, switch-only solution, DiFS does not have the limitations of central and host-based methods such as bottleneck of a single controller and massive monitoring messages. Compared to the state-of-art networking techniques, DiFS only requires either the SDN support or simple special switch logic.

5. RELATED WORKS

Recently there have been a great number of proposals for data center network topologies that provide high bisection bandwidth [11–14, 20]. However, current routing protocols like ECMP [15] usually suffer from elephant flow collisions and bandwidth loss. Application layer scheduling like Orchestra [7] usually focuses on higher level scheduling policies such as transfer prioritizing and ignores multipathing issues in data center networks. Transport layer solutions like DCTCP [3] and MPTCP [24] optimize the resource share on fixed paths among flows. This work focuses on adaptive routing solutions.

Centralized flow routing [2, 6] usually relies on a central controller and schedules flow path at every control interval. Aside from the additional hardware and software support for

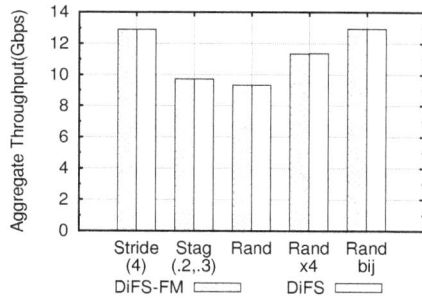

(a) 16-host network   (b) 1024-host network

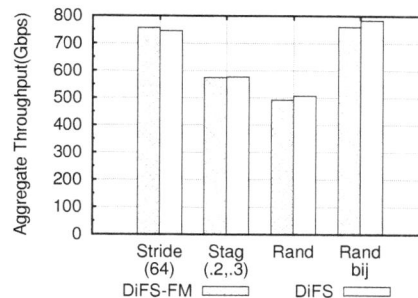

Figure 11: Flow bandwidth measurement vs flow counting

Table 3: Important properties of adaptive routing protocols.

	ECMP [15]	Hedera [2]	Dard [25]	DiFS (this work)
Network throughput	Benchmark	Higher than ECMP	High than ECMP	≈ Hedera and Dard
Flow completion	Benchmark	faster than ECMP and Dard	faster than ECMP	faster than other three
Decision making	Local info.	Network-wide info.	Network-wide info.	Local info.
Scalability problem?	Scalable	Bottleneck of a single controller	Massive monitoring msgs	Scalable
Compatibility	Standard	SDN support & monitoring tools	Changes on hosts	SDN support or switch logic

communication and computation, centralized solutions may be hard to scale out due to the single point of the controller. Recent research [5,17] shows that centralized solutions must employ parallelism and fast route computation heuristics to support observed traffic patterns.

Host-based solutions [25] enable end hosts select flow path simultaneously to enhance parallelism. Dard [25] allows each host to select flow path based on network conditions. However, Dard has potential scalability issues due to massive monitoring messages to every host. Besides, deployment of host-based solutions requires updates on legacy systems and applications.

Switch-only protocols [9,16,21,28] are also proposed. However most of them require flow splitting which may cause significant packet reordering. TeXCP [16], as an online distributed Traffic Engineering protocols, performs packet-level load balancing by using splitting schemes like FLARE [23]. Localflow [21] refines a naive link balancing solution and minimizes the number of flows that are split. Zahavi *et al.* [28] also describes a general distributed adaptive routing architecture for Clos networks [11]. Dixit *et al.* [9] uses random packet spraying to split flows to multiple paths to minimize the hurts to TCP. DiFS does not split a flow in order to avoid packet reordering.

6. CONCLUSION

This paper proposes DiFS, a local, lightweight, and switch-only protocol for adaptive flow routing in data center networks. Switches running DiFS cooperate to achieve flow-to-link balance by avoiding both local and remote collisions. Experimental results show that our algorithm can outperform the well-known distributed solution ECMP, a centralized scheduling algorithm Hedera, and a host-based protocol Dard. We will investigate flow scheduling for general network topologies in future work.

7. ACKNOWLEDGMENTS

This research is supported by University of Kentucky Faculty Startup funding. We thank the anonymous reviewers of ANCS'14 for their constructive comments.

8. REFERENCES

[1] M. Al-Fares, A. Loukissas, and A. Vahdat. A scalable, commodity data center network architecture. In *Proc. of ACM SIGCOMM*, 2008.

[2] M. Al-Fares, S. Radhakrishnan, B. Raghavan, N. Huang, and A. Vahdat. Hedera: dynamic flow scheduling for data center networks. In *Proceedings of USENIX NSDI*, 2010.

[3] M. Alizadeh, A. Greenberg, D. A. Maltz, J. Padhye, P. Patel, B. Prabhakar, S. Sengupta, and M. Sridharan. Dctcp: Efficient packet transport for the commoditized data center. In *Proceedings of ACM SIGCOMM*, 2010.

[4] H. Ballani, P. Costa, T. Karagiannis, and A. Rowstron. Towards predictable datacenter networks. In *Proc. of SIGCOMM*, 2011.

[5] T. Benson, A. Akella, and D. A. Maltz. Network traffic characteristics of data centers in the wild. In *Proceedings of ACM IMC*, 2010.

[6] T. Benson, A. Anand, A. Akella, and M. Zhang. Microte: fine grained traffic engineering for data centers. In *Proc. of ACM CoNEXT*, 2011.

[7] M. Chowdhury, M. Zaharia, J. Ma, M. I. Jordan, and I. Stoica. Managing data transfers in computer clusters with orchestra. In *Proc. of ACM SIGCOMM*, 2011.

[8] J. Dean and S. Ghemawat. Mapreduce: simplified data processing on large clusters. *Communications of the ACM*, 2008.

[9] A. Dixit, P. Prakash, Y. C. Hu, and R. R. Kompella. On the impact of packet spraying in data center networks. In *Proc. of IEEE INFOCOM*, 2013.

[10] A. Dixit, P. Prakash, and R. R. Kompella. On the efficacy of fine-grained traffic splitting protocols in data center networks. In *Proceedings of ACM SIGCOMM*, 2011.

[11] A. Greenberg, J. R. Hamilton, N. Jain, S. Kandula, C. Kim, P. Lahiri, D. A. Maltz, P. Patel, and S. Sengupta. Vl2: a scalable and flexible data center network. In *Proceedings of ACM SIGCOMM*, 2009.

[12] A. Greenberg, P. Lahiri, D. A. Maltz, P. Patel, and S. Sengupta. Towards a next generation data center architecture: Scalability and commoditization. In *Proc. of ACM PRESTO*, 2008.

[13] C. Guo et al. Dcell: a scalable and fault-tolerant network structure for data centers. In *Proc. of ACM SIGCOMM*, 2008.

[14] C. Guo et al. Bcube: a high performance, server-centric network architecture for modular data centers. In *Proc. of ACM SIGCOMM*, 2009.

[15] C. Hopps. Analysis of an equal-cost multi-path algorithm. *RFC 2992*, 2000.

[16] S. Kandula, D. Katabi, B. Davie, and A. Charny. Walking the tightrope: responsive yet stable traffic engineering. In *Proceedings of ACM SIGCOMM*, 2005.

[17] S. Kandula, S. Sengupta, A. Greenberg, P. Patel, and R. Chaiken. The nature of data center traffic: measurements & analysis. In *Proceedings of ACM IMC*, 2009.

[18] K. C. Leung, V. Li, and D. Yang. An overview of packet reordering in transmission control protocol (tcp): Problems, solutions, and challenges. *IEEE Transactions on Parallel and Distributed Systems*, 2007.

[19] N. McKeown, T. Anderson, H. Balakrishnan, G. Parulkar, L. Peterson, J. Rexford, S. Shenker, and J. Turner. Openflow: Enabling innovation in campus networks. *SIGCOMM Comput. Commun. Rev.*, 2008.

[20] R. N. Mysore et al. Portland: a scalable fault-tolerant layer 2 data center network fabric. In *Proceedings of ACM SIGCOMM*, 2009.

[21] S. Sen, D. Shue, S. Ihm, and M. J. Freedman. Scalable, opitmal flow routing in datacenters via local link balancing. In *Proceedings of ACM CoNEXT*, 2013.

[22] A. Singla, C.-Y. Hong, L. Popa, and P. B. Godfrey. Jellyfish: Networking data centers randomly. In *Proc. of USENIX NSDI*, 2012.

[23] S. Sinha, S. Kandula, and D. Katabi. Harnessing tcps burstiness using flowlet switching. In *Proc. of ACM HotNets*, 2004.

[24] D. Wischik, C. Raiciu, A. Greenhalgh, and M. Handley. Design, implementation and evaluation of congestion control for multipath tcp. In *Proceedings of USENIX NSDI*, 2011.

[25] X. Wu and X. Yang. Dard: Distributed adaptive routing for datacenter networks. In *Proceedings of IEEE ICDCS*, 2012.

[26] X. Yang, D. Clark, and A. Berger. Nira: A new inter-domain routing architecture. *IEEE/ACM Transactions on Networking*, 2007.

[27] M. Yu, L. Jose, and R. Miao. Software defined traffic measurement with opensketch. In *Proc. of USENIX NSDI*, 2013.

[28] E. Zahavi, I. Keslassy, and A. Kolodny. Distributed adaptive routing for big-data applications running on data center networks. In *Proceedings of ACM/IEEE ANCS*, 2012.

Appendix

Proof of Theorem 3.1:

PROOF. Let x and y be arbitrary two aggregate switches. Let n_{ae} be the number of flows from edge switch e to aggregate switch a.

$$n(x) = \sum n_{xe}$$

$$n(y) = \sum n_{ye}$$

Since $|n_{xe} - n_{ye}| \leq \delta$ for every edge switches e and there are $k/2$ edge switches in a pod,

$$|n(x) - n(y)| \leq \sum |n_{xe} - n_{ye}| \leq \delta \cdot k/2$$

Hence $MAX_a - MIN_a \leq \delta \cdot k/2$. $\square$

Proof of Theorem 3.2:

PROOF. The $(k/2)^2$ cores can be divided into $k/2$ groups $g_1, g_2, ..., g_{k/2}$, each of which contains $k/2$ cores that receive flows from a same group of aggregate switches.

Suppose x and y are two cores. If they belong to a same group, we can prove $n_x - n_y \leq k/2$ using a way similar to the proof of Theorem 3.1. Consider that they belong to different groups. For a pod p, x and y connect to two different switches in p, because they are in different core groups. Let s_{a1} and s_{a2} denote the switches connecting to x and y respectively. We have $n(s_{a1}) - n(s_{a2}) \leq k/2$ according to Theorem 3.1. Hence the average numbers of flows from s_{a1} and s_{a2} to each core are $\frac{n(s_{a1})}{k/2}$ and $n(s_{a2})/2$ respectively.

$$\frac{n(s_{a1})}{k/2} - \frac{n(s_{a2})}{k/2} \leq 1$$

Let n_{pc} denote the number of flows from pod p to core c. We have $n_{px} - \frac{n(s_{a1})}{k/2} \leq 1$ (BO of s_{a1}), and $\frac{n(s_{a2})}{k/2} - n_{py} \leq 1$ (BO of s_{a2}). Hence

$$n_{px} - n_{py} \leq 1 + \frac{n(s_{a1})}{k/2} - \frac{n(s_{a2})}{k/2} + 1 \leq 3$$

$$n_x - n_y = \sum_p n_{px} - \sum_p n_{py} = \sum_p (n_{px} - n_{py}) \leq 3k$$

$\square$

Blender: Upgrading Tenant-based Data Center Networking

Kevin C. Webb
kwebb@cs.swarthmore.edu
Swarthmore College

Arjun Roy, Kenneth Yocum, and Alex C. Snoeren
{arroy, kyocum, snoeren}@cs.ucsd.edu
University of California, San Diego

ABSTRACT

This paper presents Blender, a framework that enables network operators to improve tenant performance by tailoring the network's behavior to tenant needs. Tenants may upgrade their provisioned portion of the network with specific features, such as multi-path routing, isolation, and failure recovery, without modifying hosted application code. Network operators may differentiate themselves based on upgrades they offer, creating new upgrades via a lightweight programming interface. Blender safely executes multiple tenants' selections simultaneously across a shared network infrastructure. We show that the Blender model can express and extend recently proposed network functionality on existing SDN networks. We use an OpenFlow-based prototype to quantify Blender's performance and potential for deployment at scale.

Categories and Subject Descriptors

C.2.1 [**Network Architecture**]: Network topology; C.2.3 [**Network Operations**]: Network management

Keywords

network isolation; multiple tenants; SDN

1. INTRODUCTION

Data centers are rapidly evolving to accommodate the performance demands of the cloud computing model, in which raw computing resources are provisioned for users on demand. However, despite the recent explosion in the popularity of cloud computing services, the underlying data center network remains difficult to virtualize. While all users expect the network to provide basic packet forwarding, they have contradictory preferences regarding the behavior of supplemental functionality like performance isolation, latency management, multi-path route selection, failure recovery, and so on. Despite many strong proposals to augment existing networks with such features, each tackles one part of the problem in a disparate way, with no prevailing unifying approach.

This work presents Blender, a framework that supports tenants mixing desired network functionality. Regardless of whether a data

center is public, i.e., its resources are rented out to anyone willing to pay, or private, supporting only the services of the data center's owner, we make a distinction between the infrastructure provider and their tenants. Each actor holds a vested interest, from a different perspective, in the network provisioning process. The *tenants*, who use their allotted resources to support Web, corporate, social media, or other user-facing services, desire a mechanism to tailor the network's behavior to their specific needs, ideally without modifying their applications. The data center *providers*, who own and manage data center resources, wish to cater to tenants' requirements to differentiate themselves from competition, attract new customers, and increase revenue. However, since network design and ensuring tenant privacy provide competitive advantages, providers often prefer to limit tenant visibility into their networks, opting instead to supply tenants with a choice of pre-approved components. In Blender, providers can create network *upgrades* that each export functionality and network visibility in accordance with their business model.

On one hand, operators wish to support a wide variety of tenants with different performance and reliability demands [7]. On the other hand, they want to reason about network bandwidth and latency in a manner consistent with the isolated, chargeable units of CPU, disk, and memory that server virtualization provides. A consequence is that cloud providers today, such as Amazon, only make qualitative (e.g., low, moderate, high) assurances for network performance. With unpredictable network loads, today's data center operators must accept hot spots (i.e. tenants pay to wait [35]) or monitor and dynamically adjust VM placement [20], application components [39], or network flows [2] to improve utilization.

Using Blender, tenants augment their network environment by selecting and applying only the upgrades that best meet their needs. As an example, consider three tenants that share the physical data center network of a public cloud computing platform: a tenant managing a three-tiered Web service, a tenant executing a bulk data processing job (e.g., MapReduce or Hadoop), and a tenant hosting back-end business logic. Each tenant might prefer a different form of performance isolation, ranging from fully opportunistic work conservation [33] for the bulk processing tenant to reserved, predictable performance [5] for the business logic tenant. Furthermore, each tenant would benefit from a different set of supplemental upgrades to support their execution: the Web service may require bounded latency [38] to meet customer performance objectives, while the bulk processing service may fare better with support for performance-aware flow placement [2]. Such flexibility allows operators to better support tenant needs while differentiating their cloud offerings through custom resource management and charging models.

In designing such a system, we face two key challenges. First, we must ensure that the programming model used by network providers to build upgrades balances simplicity with the ability to express complex functionality. To do so, Blender defines a concise set of abstractions that capture a range of upgrades, while also enabling the run time to check and ensure that the underlying network can support the co-existence of multiple upgrades. The second primary challenge is scale. Blender must account for the finite resources available in switching hardware for managing traffic and storing forwarding entries. We overcome these hardware capacity limitations by combining a specialized tenant model with optimization techniques to prevent resource exhaustion.

This paper makes the following contributions:

- **Blender framework:** Blender supports multiple network tenants, each of whom may simultaneously deploy many upgrades on a shared physical network. Network providers use a programming model that exposes eight high-level network attributes, such as routes and rate limits, to create upgrades. Ultimately upgrades compile into a set of resource reservations across the physical network. Many upgrades use few attributes, maybe 3-4, and this is sufficient to provide upgrade modules that provide fixed or proportional network isolation. In addition, upgrades may work in concert with one another, providing work conservation, deadline-aware flow scheduling, dynamic flow placement, and other services.

- **Blender network architecture:** Blender provides this flexibility while ensuring a consistent and scalable forwarding infrastructure. It multiplexes network resources at the granularity of network tenants, which can represent an entire service or distinct applications with specific network demands. Transactional tenant allocation ensures atomic and isolated changes to network forwarding state.

- **Implementation and evaluation:** We illustrate these concepts through an OpenFlow-based [19] prototype. We demonstrate the ability to author, compose, and execute multiple network upgrades, including functionality found in recent work [2, 5, 26, 33, 38]. Blender leverages switch-based traffic policers to simplify resource allocation and dynamic traffic control; we describe the resource requirements for tenant allocations and show that for realistic resource allocation strategies, per-switch rule and policer counts are bounded by $O(numTenants * portCount)$. Even without those assumptions, our tenant-churn experiments on a 50-node, 200-VM, fat-tree testbed easily fit within the resource constraints of HP's prototype OpenFlow switches.

2. RELATED WORK

Multi-tenant SDNs. Blender is one of several systems that provision shared network infrastructure in support of multiple tenants and applications. FlowVisor [32] provides strict tenant separation by dividing the network into independent "slices", each of which maintains management routines in the form of a private SDN controller. Each tenant is free to choose, and is responsible for providing and managing, custom SDN software within their assigned slice. At the other end of the spectrum, Onix [17] provides an all-purpose controller framework designed to be shared by simultaneously executing applications. Akin to Blender, Onix provides a graph-based model of the physical network for applications to manipulate, but it requires that tenant applications mediate their own interactions.

CloudNaaS [6] allows tenants to select their desired functionality similarly to Blender, though it emphasizes end-host naming and addressing, accepting verbose network specifications in a rich language. In contrast, Blender focuses on developing a model for combining network features based on short, high-level tenant requests.

In Participatory Networking (PANE) [10], a centralized controller provides an API with which modified tenant applications can obtain network visibility and reserve link capacity. Like Blender, PANE hierarchically subdivides network resources and resolves conflicting requests with resource-specific routines. PANE exposes network information to tenant applications and requires them to engage in custom resource provisioning. With Blender, tenants make brief requests prior to executing unmodified applications in a fashion similar to a tenant's virtual machine requests from PaaS cloud providers.

Network performance isolation. Multi-tenant data centers balance the need to run the network at maximum efficiency with the desire to provide performance guarantees for individual tenants. Some schemes provide predictability via fixed performance guarantees [5, 14], but limit the number of concurrent tenants placed on the network. Others maintain proportional network shares, allowing tenants to receive performance relative to tenant demand [18, 28, 33]. These are fundamental trade-offs that any isolation model must make—no single network allocation strategy can provide every isolation property desired by a tenant or network operator [24].

Blender resolves this situation by allowing network operators to create and deploy multiple isolation models across a shared infrastructure. As opposed to monolithic approaches, tenants are free to choose the model that best represents their needs. We demonstrate this flexibility in our prototype by implementing two performance isolation upgrades, inspired by Oktopus [5] and Seawall [33] using Blender's upgrade programming model in Section 4.

Augmenting network functionality. In addition to performance isolation, Blender allows operators to offer supplemental feature upgrades to tenants. Recent proposals have demonstrated the benefits of supplying cloud tenants with functionality like latency control [3, 38], flow placement [2], load balancing [4, 36], middleboxes [25, 30, 31], and other services. Blender allows tenants to request such services via a unified resource request model, and we describe several examples upgrades based on D3 [38], Hedera [2], and DRL [26].

Network programming. Blender is far from the first system to empower applications with explicit control over the behavior of the network fabric. For example, active networking [37] provides differentiated network behavior in response to user-supplied forwarding directives. In Blender, however, tenants make concise, high-level resource requests—as opposed to active networks' per-packet model. Contemporary to active networks, Tempest [29] allows users to create virtual private networks over an ATM substrate. Tempest partitions switches into "switchlets", on which users may execute forwarding programs.

More recent projects address the need for higher-level languages for constructing and maintaining SDN controller software. Nettle [34] is a domain-specific, functional language embedded in Haskell that allows network operators to write declarative programs for reacting to OpenFlow network events. Frenetic [11] combines a declarative query language for classifying and aggregating network traffic with a functional library for describing reactive packet-forwarding policies. Like Blender, Frenetic enables the network to compose reusable software modules, however it does not provide explicit support for multi-tenancy or performance isolation. Pyretic [21] extends the ideas of Frenetic with an imperative Python-like language for sequentially composing modules that can process packets with virtual traffic headers. These efforts enable the composition of applications from the parallel and sequential execution of modular components, but efficiently compiling their directives into forwarding hardware remains challenging.

Table 1: Blender's programming attributes.

Attribute name	Conflicts	Allows upgrade to . . .
Create zones	Static	Sub-divide network regions.
Choose routes	Static	Establish VM reachability.
Create rate limits	Dynamic	Add or remove rate limits.
Modify rate limits	Dynamic	Change the enforced rate limit.
Read statistics	N/A (r/o)	Receive network traffic information.
Assign flow paths	Static	Bind a flow to a set of hops.
Intercept traffic	Static	Inspect packet content.
Modify traffic	Static	Re-write packet content.

Table 2: Upgrade allocators manipulate graphs G that contain the following logical elements. Here links and switches are given unique identifiers: l_{id} and s_{id}.

Name	Item Definition
Graphs	$G := \{\text{Switches,Links}\}$
Links	$l := \{l_{id}, \texttt{capacity, weight, state dict}\}$
Switches	$s := \{s_{id}, \texttt{state dict}\}$
Assignments	$res := \{\text{AsnType}, l_{id}, \text{Traffic,args}\}$
AsnType	$rt := \{\texttt{<upgradeID>}\}$
Traffic	$tc := \{\text{pattern}\}$

3. THE BLENDER FRAMEWORK

Blender allows network providers to specify network functionality using a small number of high-level abstractions that we call *upgrades*. A logically centralized controller executes upgrades at the request of tenants and ultimately translates their directives into forwarding and rate limiting state within a configurable subset of the network, allowing multiple upgrades to compose and execute across the same physical infrastructure. We require that the cloud provider—rather than the tenants—author and supply upgrades to ensure that they are not malicious or otherwise abusive to the network.

From the provider perspective, Blender's programming model abstracts the features and functionality of the network forwarding hardware, for example, rate limiting, providing traffic statistics, selecting flow paths, modifying packets, etc. Despite many devices implementing and exposing these features differently (e.g., in switch hardware vs. at end-host hypervisors), Blender exports a single interface for each resource; the runtime translates these calls for the particular underlying device(s) in a given network. Blender requires the network provider to enumerate the set of available features and their interface definitions. While providers are free to define their own attributes to match their hardware, environment, and goals, Table 1 summarizes the abstract attributes in Blender's programming model (API).

When providers develop an upgrade, they must label the upgrade with the required attributes to inform Blender of how the upgrade will be using network resources. Labeling an upgrade as 'using an attribute' provides two primary benefits. First, it provides the upgrade with access to the attribute's programming interface, expanding the set of events or network state updates for the upgrade to utilize (Section 3.2). Additionally, labeling assists in conflict detection (Section 3.3).

To tenants, the implementation details of upgrades are hidden. Instead, a tenant specifies a list of desired upgrades by submitting a small, high-level request to Blender's centralized controller. The request includes the number of hosts in the virtual network and the list of upgrades the tenant wishes to use (along with their parameters). Blender applies the upgrades without intervention from the tenant's application. In general, tenant applications need not be modified, except in the case of upgrades that explicitly interact with tenant code as a part of their design (e.g., deadline-aware scheduling, Section 4.3). Note that a default virtual network (one with no upgrades) provides best-effort connectivity over a spanning tree.

3.1 Tenant allocation

Before a tenant can begin using the network, Blender must initialize each of the tenant's selected upgrades. The instantiation of each upgrade begins with a static allocation phase followed by an optional runtime component. Allocation determines the structure of, reserves capacity for, and instantiates a tenant's virtual network.

If the upgrade must react to tenant's traffic in real time, Blender allows it to subscribe to event notifications exposed by specific network attributes in the programming model (Table 1).

Thus for a new tenant request, each upgrade analyzes how to meet the tenant's objectives and generates a proposed set of network changes. Blender then determines whether the changes are allowed and feasible, and if so, admits the tenant, configuring the underlying network to enforce the directives. Note that this might result in reconfiguration of the rate limits for other tenants' virtual networks, e.g., to enforce proportional bandwidth shares[1].

Blender represents resources as a logical *graph* of switches/hosts (vertices) and links (edges). Blender and its upgrades use these graphs to maintain state on behalf of the tenant's virtual network. The top half of Table 2 describes the graph, link, and traffic assignment elements to which upgrades have access. Links and switches contain a `state` annotation, a provider-defined dictionary that allows upgrades to maintain bookkeeping information across tenant arrivals and departures.

Capacity reservations. While all upgrades go through static allocation, reserving link capacity will typically be the responsibility of only one *isolation* upgrade, selected from a set of mutually exclusive upgrades that provide inter-tenant performance isolation. When a tenant submits a request, its isolation upgrade computes paths to connect the tenant's endpoints and creates capacity reservations via the API's rate limiting attribute to describe how to treat the tenant's flows.

The API's rate limiting attribute supports fixed-rate and proportionally weighted bandwidth reservations. By default, such reservations are not work conserving, however work conservation can easily be introduced by the inclusion of an additional upgrade.

The tenant's selected isolation upgrade claims resources by modifying the state of its input graph according to the type, link, and any additional arguments the reservation may require (e.g., capacity or weight). For example, for an upgrade to create a proportional reservation with a weight of w and associate it with link l the rate limiting attribute increments l's weight in the input graph by w and later installs policers to rate limit traffic over l to $l.\texttt{capacity} * \frac{w}{l.\texttt{weight}+w}$.

The isolation upgrade takes a tenant t and a network graph G as input. The upgrade is restricted to using only the resources described in G, even if additional resources may be physically available[2]. The upgrade analyzes the graph and computes a new graph representing the tenant's desired resources: $allocate(G, t, \ldots) \rightarrow G'$. If Blender admits the tenant, it *removes* the resources in G' from G. Subsequent allocations may either use the remaining re-

---

[1]This work considers Blender in the context of a trusted environment; providers install upgrades that do not sabotage other tenants.
[2]This mechanism may be combined with ACLs or other high-level resource management policies to control resource access.

Table 3: The Blender upgrade API for managing event subscriptions and performing network state updates.

Function	Description
subscribe(event, location, cb func)	Registers for event callbacks.
unsubscribe(event, location)	Unsubscribes from a callback.
update(attribute, location, [args])	Updates attribute network state.

sources in $G\backslash G'$ or subdivide those allocated to G'. This ability to pass modified graphs through successive allocations supports on-line allocation of sub-tenants. Thus, the sequence of tenant arrivals and departures forms a logical hierarchy of network graphs.

When hierarchically composing capacity reservations, we impose a simple restriction: We allow fixed allocations to sub-divide a fixed allocation, and proportional allocations may also sub-divide a fixed allocation, but never the opposite. Thus, a proportional allocation can be used to sub-divide a fixed allocation, but any future allocation after the transition to proportional must also be proportional.

Assigning upgrades to traffic. When a tenant's virtual network has been provisioned by the isolation upgrade, the remaining upgrades apply their functionality to tenant traffic and subscribe to attribute events by annotating the tenant's network graph with traffic assignments as shown in the bottom half of Table 2. Note that each link on a given network graph may have multiple traffic assignments, one for each upgrade, and those assignments are not required to be exclusive. This supports combining a fixed capacity allocation with features like work conservation and traffic-aware flow assignment. Upgrades record their assignments by annotating the state dictionaries associated with the tenant's graph. The annotations are later used to compile the tenant into hardware directives (Section 5).

3.2 Runtime upgrade execution

After allocation, the tenant may start using the virtual network, and upgrades may begin their runtime execution. While some upgrades use only static API attributes (e.g., those that reserve only fixed capacity), many upgrades wish to adapt to dynamic network conditions. Blender supports such functionality by allowing upgrades to subscribe to network events (e.g., link failures or new flows starting) and to define a control loop that continues to execute for the lifetime of a tenant. Table 3 describes the API available to upgrades for subscribing to events and updating network state.

Unlike the static allocation stage, upgrade control loops do not manipulate tenant network graphs. Instead, they interact directly with the underlying network equipment to monitor and modify the state of the network. Upgrades receive notifications when their events are triggered. An upgrade may execute an arbitrary callback function in response to an event notification, where the upgrade may choose to change its event subscriptions or update network state. We describe example upgrades that take advantage of dynamic events in Section 4.

3.3 Network attribute conflicts

In Blender, a conflict occurs when two or more upgrades attempt to modify the network, using the same network attribute, in a manner that is unsafe without external coordination. To account for the differences in attribute behavior, the specific conditions that represent a conflict are attribute-dependant. Blender uses spatial *zone* separation to reduce the likelihood of conflicts and performs attribute-specific resolution for conflicts that cannot be avoided. Zones are defined hierarchically, as subsets of the graph representing the tenant's network devices and links. Blender expects tenants to specify in which zone each of their upgrades will execute. We provide a special zone creation attribute that allows for the definition of new zones. By convention, our implementation restricts this attribute to isolation upgrades.

Even with zones scoping the use of attributes, multiple upgrades may wish to share a particular attribute within a single zone. When such a conflict is discovered, Blender executes a provider-defined, attribute-specific resolution routine[3]. The conflict resolution routine is free to take any information about the state of the network or the tenant's upgrade set into account. Depending on the cloud provider's policies and the attribute in question, resolution strategies may involve prioritizing one upgrade over another, processing each upgrade sequentially, coordinating the upgrades such that they safely share network resources, or rejecting the request. For upgrades that require coordination, the requirement is enforced in the attribute API they use.

The Blender model makes a distinction between two forms of conflicts, static and runtime conflicts, which correspond to the two stages of upgrade execution. To ensure safe execution, a static conflict is one that must be detected and resolved during the upgrade allocation stage. Consider an example in which a tenant requests multiple upgrades that assign flows to routes. We leverage attribute labeling to detect this condition, and for this example, resolve the conflict by rejecting this (nonsensical) tenant request. With a different attribute, for example modifying traffic, Blender may choose to resolve a conflict by ensuring a sequential ordering on the flow of traffic through the set of conflicting upgrades.

For some attributes, the presence of a conflict may depend not only on upgrades sharing a zone, but how the network is managed by the upgrades within that zone. For example, if multiple co-located upgrades declare that they modify rate limits, whether or not they conflict depends on their traffic assignments. For network attributes whose API have additional parameters, like traffic assignment, the network provider may opt to resolve their conflicts at runtime. These runtime conflicts are detected and resolved by the network provider's implementation of attribute `update` calls.

4. SAMPLE UPGRADES

This section demonstrates Blender's flexibility in expressing a variety of upgrades. We take inspiration from recent proposals and create two network performance isolation upgrades along with upgrades for flow path assignment, work conservation, deadline-aware scheduling, failure recovery, and distributed rate limiting.

4.1 Performance isolation upgrades

Our prototype includes a pair of performance isolation upgrades: Squid and Jetty. Squid creates fixed-capacity, predictable allocations in the spirit of Oktopus [5] and FairCloud's PS-P [24] models, allocating over-subscribed virtual network topologies. Jetty creates proportional allocations in the fashion of Seawall [33] and PS-L [24], providing isolation at the link level. Our descriptions of these upgrades focuses on our adaptation of the models and their interaction with the Blender framework. We refer the reader to the original proposals of these models for additional details of their operation.

Squid: predictable virtual networks. Squid mimics the data center isolation model provided by Oktopus [5] and PS-P [24],

---

[3]Blender's per-attribute conflict resolution routines are similar to those of PANE [10], which handles conflicts on a per-'atom' basis.

which allows tenants to request virtual networks that emulate non-blocking switches. Each switch i connects n_i VMs with bisection bandwidth b_i. The switch may be further connected to other virtual switches, forming clusters, based on an over-subscription factor O. Thus, a virtual switch must have uplink capacity $(b_i \cdot n_i)/O$ to each other switch. Like Oktopus, we assume the input graph is a singly-rooted, multi-level tree. A complete Squid request is specified as $(G, \mathtt{squid}, C_{VMs}, j, n, b, O)$.

This request will cause the Squid upgrade to embed j virtual switches, each connecting n VMs with links of capacity b, in the input network graph G. Squid will arrange the virtual switches to have an over-subscription ratio of O. The upgrade is free to choose the $n \cdot j$ endpoints from the provided $C_{VMs} \in G$ candidates.

Squid uses a first-fit strategy to find feasible virtual switch (cluster) placements. It uses a depth-first recursive algorithm that attempts to place each cluster as low in the topology as possible, minimizing the number of links traffic crosses. For each switch in the topology, Squid records the number of clusters that can be placed beneath it. To determine if a given cluster of size n_i can be placed under a switch, Squid first checks the links l in G for sufficient capacity b to connect a cluster. It then ensures that each found cluster has capacity $\frac{b_i * n_i}{O}$ to every other feasible cluster. If sufficient capacity does not exist (or if too few candidate endpoints were supplied), the Squid upgrade rejects the tenant.

If successful, this process returns a subtree under which all clusters fit, and each cluster is considered a separate zone. Squid then traverses this subgraph from the top down, creating a fixed bandwidth reservation and assigning additional upgrades to each link. The capacity it reserves is the sum of the connectivity requirements of all clusters under this link.

Jetty: proportional tenant allocations. Jetty provides proportional link capacity sharing similar to PS-L [24] at the granularity of tenants (in contrast to Seawall's entity-based proportional shares [33]). For each tenant, Jetty ensures a proportional share of capacity on each physical network link the entity uses. While we simplify our discussion of Jetty by assuming a singly-rooted, multi-level tree topology, it may be trivially extended to multi-rooted topologies. A Jetty request consists of $(G, \mathtt{jetty}, C_{VMs}, n, w)$.

Jetty begins by finding the n endpoints in C_{VMs} that are best connected to the network core. It calculates the bottleneck bandwidth on the shortest path from the top-level core switch to each endpoint and then chooses the top-n highest-capacity endpoints. Unlike Squid, Jetty never rejects requests (assuming $C_{VMs} \in G$ contains at least n endpoints). Like Squid, Jetty notes the lowest level root switch under which all VMs connect, and it creates reservations in a similar top-down process. Each reservation is proportional and uses the same weight w.

4.2 Performance isolation discussion

It is instructive to discuss how Squid and Jetty differ from their inspirations, which install traffic policers only on sending VMs. Our upgrades use in-network traffic policers in addition to end-host rate limiting. This decision allows Squid and Jetty to collapse the collection of tenant traffic across each reservation and eliminates the need for the tightly coupled VM sending rate coordination found in Oktopus. Under our scheme, the upgrades create at most one reservation per link per tenant, meaning a 48-port switch connecting hosts with 8 VMs would require at most $2 * 8 * 48 = 768$ rate policers (assuming the worst case scenario in which every VM is in a different tenant). This is well within the hardware policer count of modern top-of-rack switches; for example Cisco's 4948 E/F top-of-rack switch supports as many as 8K policers [9]. Rule

optimization (Section 6) often also allows Blender to combine the policers for multiple tenants, further reducing the hardware requirement.

4.3 Functionality-enhancing upgrades

We leverage Blender's modularity to design a variety of upgrades that improve the performance and capabilities of tenant virtual networks. At the tenant's request, Blender mixes these upgrades with the reservations applied by the isolation upgrade. For instance, a work-conserving version of Squid simply pairs a work conservation upgrade with each fixed reservation.

Flow path selection. When multiple paths connect a pair of communicating endpoints, Blender selects only one route for any individual flow that passes between them to avoid TCP reordering problems. Here, we describe two upgrades we have built for assigning flows to paths. The first upgrade, random assignment (RA), randomly maps each flow to an available route, which closely approximates conventional ECMP [16]. The second, bandwidth-maximizing assignment (BMA), is inspired by the global first-fit algorithm of Hedera [2]. BMA assigns a flow to the route with the largest available capacity.

Both flow assignment upgrades are similarly structured, and we label each with the 'assign flow paths' attribute. This label enables upgrade subscription to a 'new flow' event notification, which is triggered by the end host hypervisor when a flow begins at one of its VMs. RA simply chooses a random path in response, whereas BMA additionally utilizes the 'read statistics' attribute to read and compare path utilizations before returning a decision. While they currently perform placement for all new flows, either could easily be extended to selectively optimize only long-running or high-volume flows for bandwidth maximization.

Work conservation. Work conservation allows a tenant to contribute the unused portion of a bandwidth reservation on a link to an excess capacity pool. If other tenants on the same link are operating below their reserved capacities, capacity-hungry tenants can draw capacity from this pool. Note that the work conservation upgrade described here is implemented by querying for traffic demands and modifying the rate limits of the hardware policers that are already associated with the tenants' reservations. It does not require weighted fair queueing or any other explicitly work-conserving hardware mechanisms. This design also illustrates the flexibility of upgrades, as the excess capacity pool may be shared among all reservations on the link, regardless of their upgrade, or it may be scoped to a subset of the link's reservations.

Deadline-aware flow scheduling. While the conventional performance metric for data center applications has been bandwidth, several recent projects [3, 38] have begun to focus on latency. This work is largely motivated by reports from industry [15], which indicate that even small increases in latency can lead to a significant reduction in customer satisfaction.

For the Blender prototype, we constructed a deadline-aware upgrade that was inspired by D3 [38], which uses deadlines to schedule flow completions. Similar to D3, making use of the upgrade requires explicit interaction from the tenant application, possibly requiring application modifications. The tenant application informs its local shim of the size and deadline for each new flow that it starts. The shim then periodically computes the rate necessary for the flow to complete on time and issues a request for that capacity to the upgrade. At the same interval, the upgrade reviews its requests and produces a schedule of flow rates, which it uses to update switch rate policers.

Like D3, our flow scheduling upgrade would ideally execute directly within the network's devices. Unfortunately, our experimental switch platform was not optimized for fast rate policer updates and could not keep up with the upgrade's proposed changes. The poor performance is an issue of software (fast rate policer updating is not a frequently requested feature) and not a fundamental limitation of the hardware. To stand-in for programmable switches, we substitute the controller to execute the upgrade, which reduces the responsiveness.

Failure recovery. As the size of a network increases, so does the likelihood of a component failure. We recognize that different tenants may wish to respond to such failures in numerous ways, and the Blender model allows for such diversity. For example, one tenant may want to minimize the service interruption by automatically routing around the failure, a second tenant might want to allocate a new virtual network in a different physical location, and a third may wish to halt execution until the failure is resolved.

For our Blender prototype, we construct a failure recovery upgrade that executes at the controller and operates like the first of the three examples described above. When a link failure occurs, the upgrade determines which of a tenant's routes crossed that link and searches for an alternative path, among the network's free resources, whose annotated characteristics indicate that it could serve as an equivalent replacement. Upon finding such a link, it then applies the reservations from the failed link to the replacement and informs the appropriate end hosts to mark their future packets to use the replacement (Section 6.2).

Distributed rate limiting. DRL [26] provides a mechanism whereby multiple senders coordinate their sending rates to ensure that their aggregate traffic rate is below a maximum global rate limit, without statically limiting their rates. The DRL upgrade periodically checks the rates, across multiple links, of a coordinated set of traffic and adjusts link-local rate limits in proportion to the traffic's demand across those links. The application of DRL is useful in a situation in which a tenant would like to control the aggregate sending rate across paths that may not share any common hops. For example, in a multi-tiered, distributed service, a tenant may want to limit the global rate at which one tier can transmit to another.

5. ARCHITECTURE

This section describes Blender's architecture that compiles, installs, and monitors upgrades for multiple tenants. This design builds on a software-defined network (SDN) substrate whose switches accept rules that dictate how packets move through the network [8, 19]. In addition to the standard rule primitive that matches header fields and dictates output ports, we utilize traffic rate limiting primitives.

Unlike other SDN architectures that allocate at the granularity of flows [2, 8], Blender allocates resources to tenants as a whole. Thus, Blender needs to ensure two important forms of concurrency control. First, upgrades must receive a consistent view of the input network graph. A tenant should not observe other tenants' allocations and should execute only if it can receive all its resources. Second, a tenant's rules must be fully installed before sending traffic. This provides *per-tenant* forwarding consistency; all packets of a given tenant obey one set of forwarding and rate limiting rules at a time.

Blender provides these semantics by processing a tenant request as a transaction. Each allocation involves creating reservations, generating switch rules, optimizing the rule count (Section 6.3), and installing rules into the network. We call the first three steps

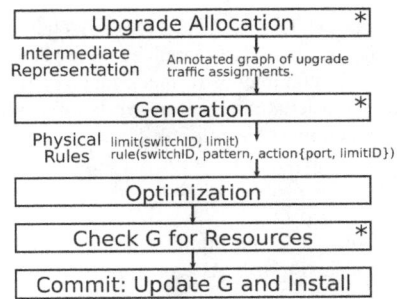

Figure 1: After allocation, compilation converts an intermediate representation of abstract limits and routes into a concrete set of rules. *'d stages can reject the tenant before it commits.

compilation as a tenant's routes and resource reservations must be converted into SDN-compatible forwarding rules. Figure 1 shows this sequence of events as Blender handles a tenant request.

Stages marked with an asterisk may abort the transaction before any changes are made to the physical network. For instance, SDN switches have limited storage capacity in their forwarding tables, and the Blender controller ensures that all network elements have sufficient space for the tenant's optimized rules. At this point Blender commits updated annotations to the tenant's input graph to reflect the tenant's resource claims. Blender commits tenants in the order it receives them. If two tenants attempt to allocate the same resources, one will ultimately commit before the other, causing the second to roll-back and either try again or be rejected, thus preventing tenants from executing without receiving their full set of resources.

Finally, after successfully committing updates to the available network resources, Blender pushes the tenant's rules into the network. To avoid the consistency issues described in [27], we wait until the tenant's network state is fully installed in all devices (i.e., consistent) before notifying the requesting tenant that the network is available and ready for use.

6. IMPLEMENTATION

This section describes an OpenFlow-based implementation of Blender. In the OpenFlow model [19], switches are simple forwarding elements whose forwarding tables are populated by an intelligent, logically-centralized controller. While we have not modified our OpenFlow switches, we are leveraging HP Labs extensions to our HP ProCurve switches. These allow an OpenFlow controller to define limiters on a switch and add a rate limiting `action` to OpenFlow rules that reference those limiters. This provides the necessary statistics and fine-grained control over switch packet forwarding and rate limiting.

6.1 Blender controller and rule installation

We implement the Blender controller in Python as a component for NOX [13], an open-source OpenFlow controller. It maintains Blender's state, including the physical network representation, allocated network graphs, connections to end-hosts, and the limiters and rules installed in the network devices. The remaining components of the system are implemented as modules within the controller, including the library of operator-installed upgrades. Useful upgrades may be written in a few hundred lines of code.

After Blender compiles and commits a tenant's virtual network, it installs routing rules and limiters on the switches. For performance, it must ensure that all rules reside in fast-path hardware lookup tables. Our switches can only install a limited number of rules into their TCAM in a short period of time, and additional rules are silently added to a slower software table. To prevent these slow software rules, we rate limit our rule installation and periodically check for and move any rules that are found to be in the software table. We have empirically determined that issuing eight rules per second works well for our switches.

6.2 End-system shim layer

Tenants interact with Blender by submitting resource requests. They do so by communicating with a local Blender shim that is running in user-space on each VM. Shims maintain a communication channel with the Blender controller. Upon connecting to the controller, the shim transmits a unique identifier on behalf of the host it represents. The controller considers this the endpoint identifier and associates it with the physical location of the VM. While this binds the VM to a physical host in our prototype, it would be straightforward to move the shim into a hypervisor or adopt recent proposals for data center address virtualization [22].

Tenants submit their requests to the local shim, which relays them to the Blender task controller. After the controller installs rules and limiters at the switches, the controller replies to each shim in the resulting virtual network. The reply contains a set of type of service (TOS) bits and an optional rate limit for each destination in the tenant's network. Upon receiving this information, the shim manipulates `iptables` to mark outgoing packets with TOS bits and `tc` to rate limit flows. For destinations with multiple paths, the shim installs TOS marking rules according to the directives of the active flow path selection upgrade (Section 4.3), where the default is random assignment. If a tenant is rejected during the allocation phase, the shim will receive a callback to indicate this failure.

6.3 Rule optimization

OpenFlow rules eventually reside in switch memory, a limited resource. Our testbed switches store rules in a TCAM, which allows wildcard matching via "don't care" entries. TCAM sizes are limited due to cost and power requirements, and Blender's rule optimization phase tries to conserve space in these switch tables by combining rules into a single wildcarded TCAM entry, when appropriate. This improves the scalability of the system by allowing more (or larger) tenant networks to be installed.

Blender's optimizer leverages two abstractions to combine forwarding rules: our tenant-based allocation strategy and a hierarchical network identifier space, as enabled by several recently proposed virtualization systems [12, 22, 23]. For each switch port in use by a tenant, it uses wildcarding to collapse all of the port's rules into a match on the longest-prefix destination and TOS field of the rule set. The optimizer is space-efficient and produces only one forwarding rule per switch port per tenant. Unfortunately, our switches do not respect OpenFlow rule priorities, making longest prefix matching, and the use of this optimizer in our testbed, impossible.

We implemented a second optimizer that is simpler and less space efficient, but does not require rule priorities, making it deployable on our switches. It uses a simple heuristic that attempts to wildcard the source address of rules at each switch. The algorithm finds the set of rules that share the same destination, TOS field, limiter, and output port. If the source address is identical for the entire set, the optimizer will collapse them into one rule with a wild card for the source address. Once this optimization occurs, the Blender controller must not admit any future rules that match this wildcard. We use this optimizer in our evaluation.

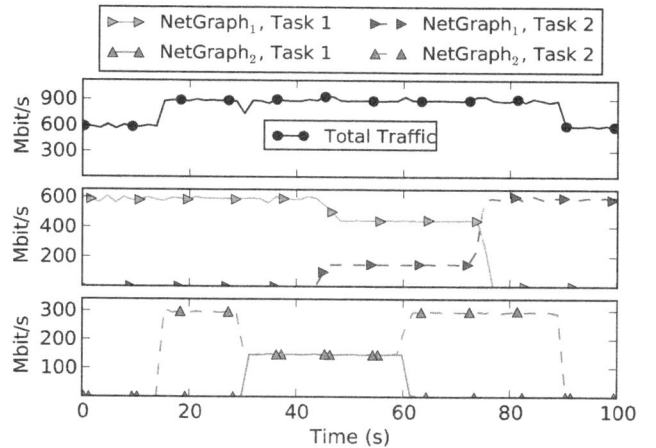

Figure 2: A composition of multiple isolation upgrades over a shared physical path. The three figures show total utilization, traffic for a 600-Mbps network slice, and traffic for a 300-Mbps network slice, from top to bottom, respectively. Each slice's events do not impact the tenant tasks operating in the other.

7. EVALUATION

Our evaluation explores Blender's ability to mix multiple upgrades across a shared network. These experiments demonstrate the functionality of the sample upgrades described in Section 4 and allow us to quantify Blender's network resource requirements.

7.1 Physical testbed

We explore Blender using a three-level, $k = 6$ fat tree [1] built from six 48-port HP ProCurve 6600-series switches running the K.14.87o OpenFlow firmware. The switches can store 1500 rules and contain 256 hardware rate policers. We use VLANs to divide each physical switch into eight six-port mini-switches. Note that while our prototype runs across a fat tree topology, we limit our topology to a single core mini-switch to reproduce topologies used by Oktopus [5] and Seawall [33].

The switching fabric carries traffic for 50 hosts, each of which contains an Intel Xeon X3210 and 4 GB of main memory. Every host uses two gigabit Ethernet interfaces; the first connects to a control network for system administration and interfacing with the Blender controller, and the second interface connects to one of the edge-level, Blender-enabled mini-switches. The hosts each house four Linux-KVM virtual machines, totaling 200 VMs.

7.2 Performance isolation

Hierarchical tenant allocation. We demonstrate Blender's ability to combine multiple isolation models on a shared physical network by hierarchically composing upgrades, as described in Section 3.1. This experiment uses the Squid upgrade to isolate pairs of Jetty-allocated tenants from one another. We first use Squid to create two virtual networks of fixed capacity: 600 Mbps (NetGraph$_1$) and 300 Mbps (NetGraph$_2$). Within each virtual network, we allocate two tenants using the Jetty upgrade. We have engineered the tenant requests to ensure that all six share a common path in the core of the physical network[4]. We then start traffic flows within the four Jetty-allocated tenants at various times.

Figure 2 shows the rate utilization across the shared physical path. The three sub-figures show total utilization, traffic for

---

[4]This was done by setting C_{VMs} to control the placement of VMs.

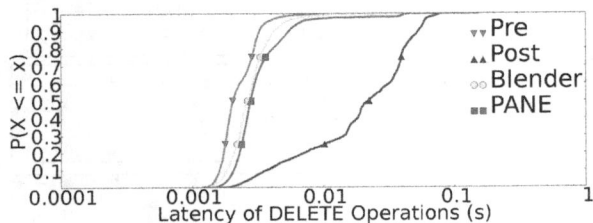

Figure 3: A comparison of performance isolation while running Zookeeper as provided by Blender and PANE [10]. Blender similarly achieves low latency without requiring modifications to Zookeeper.

NetGraph$_1$, and traffic for NetGraph$_2$, from top to bottom, respectively. Initially, a single tenant, operating within a Jetty virtual network with a weight 3, is executing a task on NetGraph$_1$. At time 15, a tenant operating within a Jetty virtual network with weight 1 begins executing a task on NetGraph$_2$. Fifteen seconds later, a second Jetty-allocated tenant with weight 1 arrives on NetGraph$_2$, causing them to each share 50% of NetGraph$_2$'s 300 Mbps capacity. At time 45, a final Jetty-allocated tenant with weight 1 starts a task on NetGraph$_1$, triggering NetGraph$_1$'s capacity to be reallocated in a 3:1 ratio. At subsequent 15-second intervals, one of the remaining tenants departs.

Notice that each pair of Jetty tenant tasks performs as if they were on their own network, responding only to new tenant arrivals on their Squid virtual network. Moreover, the combined traffic never exceeds the sum of the capacities of the Squid virtual networks.

PANE comparison. To measure the effect of Blender's performance isolation upgrades on latency, we reproduce an experiment performed by PANE [10] in which a client makes repeated DELETE requests to five Apache Zookeeper servers in the presence of heavy background traffic (iperf). The experiment runs four scenarios, and Figure 3 displays the results. The baseline, *Pre*, executes Zookeeper without background traffic, while *Post* represents the worst-case scenario with no isolation. The remaining two scenarios employ either PANE or Blender to isolate Zookeeper operations.

PANE requires modifications to Zookeeper for it to take advantage of their participatory APIs. For the details of PANE's behavior see [10]. For Blender, we represent Zookeeper and the background traffic as separate tenants, using the Squid upgrade to reserve 100 Mbps per host for Zookeeper. The background traffic receives the remaining network capacity. Using Blender, Zookeeper achieves comparable latency without application modifications.

7.3 Tenant throughput

Next, we evaluate the time for Blender to complete a set of 100 tenant tasks, using both Jetty and Squid, in a similar fashion to the evaluation in [5]. Each of the 100 tenants request a number of VMs drawn from an exponential distribution with a mean of 18. Each VM in the tenant's virtual network chooses one destination among the other VMs and sends 1500 MB to it. The tenant's task is considered complete when every VM has completed its transfer. A tenant dispatcher issues tenant requests Blender, and each requested tenant network is either accepted, in which case the tenant's task begins running, or it is rejected due to insufficient resources (lack of capacity or available VMs). The dispatcher continues to request

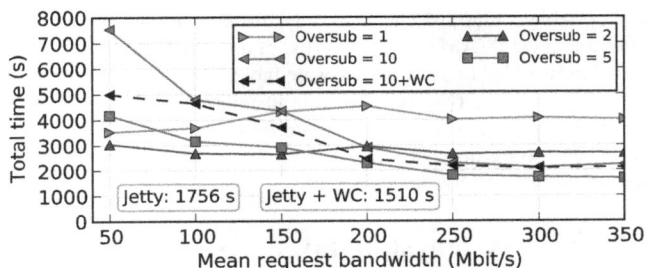

Figure 4: The time it takes Jetty and Squid to complete a set of 100 tenant tasks as we vary the tenant request parameters.

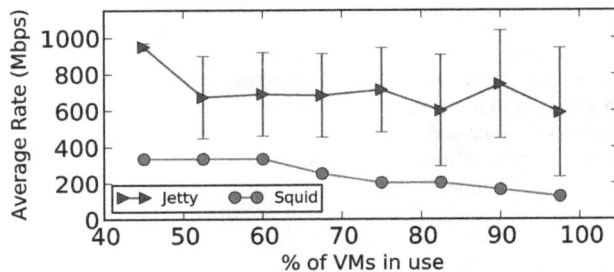

Figure 5: The mean and standard deviation (bars) of the bandwidth between the VMs of a 15-node experimental task with a varying number of background tasks.

any rejected tenants until they are all completed. We measure the time between the first tenant beginning and the final tenant ending.

For Jetty, each VM is equally likely to send to any other VM, and all tenants request equal weights for their paths. For Squid, the parameter selection process is similar to that in the evaluation of Oktopus [5]. Because Squid sub-divides its virtual networks into clusters, we assign VM destinations according to the oversubscription factor O such that the likelihood of a VM choosing an intercluster destination is $\frac{1}{O}$ for $O > 1$ and uniform likelihood for $O = 1$. Finally, Squid-allocated tenants draw their bandwidth request value from an exponential distribution whose mean we vary.

Figure 4 shows the time each configuration takes to complete the set of tenant tasks. We plot the completion time for Squid oversubscription factors of 1, 2, 5, 10, and 10 with work conservation enabled. We also show Jetty with and without work conservation. Jetty has no notion of bandwidth or oversubscription, so we present Jetty's completion times separately on the plotted results. Note that Blender allowed us to seamlessly add work conservation to improve performance, even for an isolation model that did not originally include such functionality. Without a system like Blender, such a comparison would be difficult to perform.

7.4 Allocator bandwidth and variability

In the previous experiment, Jetty achieves a higher overall throughput than Squid. However, the increase in throughput comes at a cost with respect to Squid in the form of variance. To illustrate this effect, we adjust the load on the network by installing a varying number of background Jetty tasks. Next, we install one experimental task and measure the capacity between all pairs of its VMs. Figure 5 plots the mean and standard deviation of the experimental task as we vary the total number of VMs in use. As expected, provisioning the experimental task with the Jetty allocator yields a higher average capacity than Squid, which has a

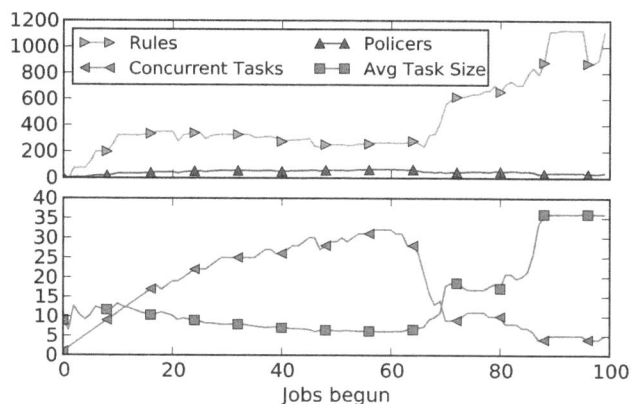

Figure 6: Rule and policer count, along with the number and average size of concurrently executing tenant tasks for a switch during the Squid $Mean = 150, Oversub = 5$ run described in Figure 4.

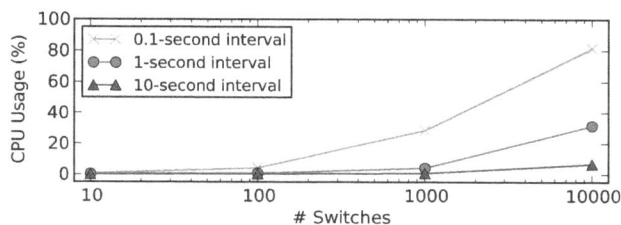

Figure 7: Work conservation's CPU utilization at the controller for a variety of switch counts and control loop intervals.

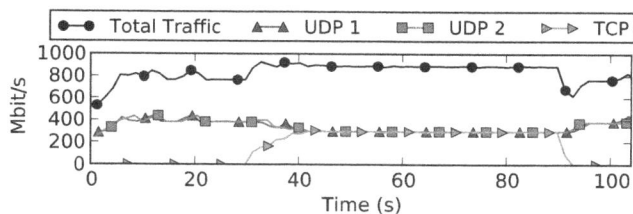

Figure 8: The work conservation upgrade controlling the traffic of three senders across a shared physical path. Each sender has a fixed-capacity reservation of 300 Mbps, which it contributes to work-conservation pool for a total of 900 Mbps. The work conservation upgrade divides the pool among the set of active senders, which varies over time.

Figure 6 illustrates the rule and policer counts for a single switch, along with the number of concurrently executing tenants and their average task size, during the execution of the Squid $Mean = 150, Oversub = 5$ run depicted in Figure 4. We selected the switch with the maximum rule count during the run. The other switches followed a similar pattern. As we described in Section 6.3, we use a sub-optimal rule optimizer due to our switches not implementing rule priority. With our better optimizer, the rule count would be equal to that of the policer count, which is a significant decrease.

Over the course of the experiment, we do not prescribe the order in which tenants execute. Our dispatcher requests tenant networks one at a time, cycling though all outstanding tenants until it finds one for which the system has sufficient resources. As the lower graph indicates, this scheme tends to initially execute smaller tenants, as they are more likely to find the resources they desire as tenants enter and leave. Around the time the 60th tenant begins executing, the switch reaches a peak of 65 allocated policers, which corresponds to the maximum concurrently-executing tenant count of 32. As the system shifts to larger task sizes, the concurrent tenant count decreases. This leads to an inflection point in the graph, beyond which policer usage decreases and rule usage increases. The trends for Jetty are similar to that of Squid, though less pronounced, due to Jetty being less constrained by available capacity.

Another important resource in any SDN is the controller. Blender allows for upgrades to execute code on the controller in response to dynamic network conditions. While this may sound like it would tax the controller, the upgrade programming model naturally enables extensions that are light-weight, with a tunable control loop interval to trade off accuracy and resource usage. As an example, our work conservation extension executes a control loop in which it periodically requests switch statistics and reassigns rate limits. Figure 7 shows the processing requirement of the work conservation extension at the controller, varying the control loop interval and the number of switches.

substantially lower variance. This experiment demonstrates that if given the opportunity to choose, different tenants would benefit from selecting an allocator that matches their applications' bandwidth and performance variability requirements. This experiment demonstrates that, if given the opportunity to choose, different tenants would benefit from choosing an allocator that best fits their applications' performance needs.

7.5 Hardware resources

Because it shares capacity evenly among concurrently executing tenants, Jetty is only constrained by the number of available VMs. As a result, it tends to keep network utilization high, and it performs relatively well, particularly with work conservation enabled. For low mean bandwidths, Squid tends to run out of VMs before it exhausts the available network capacity, leading to poor performance for larger oversubscription factors. Enabling work conservation provides a significant benefit in this region due to improved network utilization. As we increase the mean bandwidth, oversubscription becomes more beneficial due to capacity, rather than VMs, becoming the constraining resource. For the number of VMs in our network, an oversubscription factor of 5 appears to perform the best for Squid tenants.

Switches have a finite hardware capacity, which constrains their ability to store rules and police traffic. This affects the number of concurrent tenants Blender can support. This is a complex problem, as the number of rules and policers needed by a switch depends on tenant count, network size, network topology, and upgrade selection.

7.6 Dynamic upgrades

To exhibit the functionality of our sample dynamic upgrades (Section 4.3), we evaluate several upgrades:

Work conservation. To demonstrate work conservation, we configure and install virtual networks for three tenants, each of which reserves 300 Mbps across a shared path and contributes its reservation to a work-conserving pool. Figure 8 depicts the experiment's result. Initially, two of the tenants send UDP datagrams as quickly as possible across the shared path. Due to the third tenant being idle, the UDP senders draw from the excess work-conservation

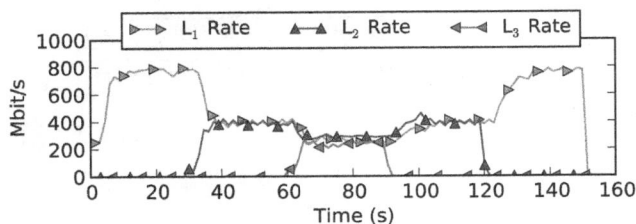

Figure 9: The Distributed Rate Limiting (DRL) upgrade enforcing an 800-Mbps global rate limit across three physically-disjoint network paths. The plot shows the outgoing rates of the three limiters, L_1, ..., L_3, that are responsible for policing the three paths. As senders begin and end their transmissions, the total traffic rate remains below the global 800-Mbps limit.

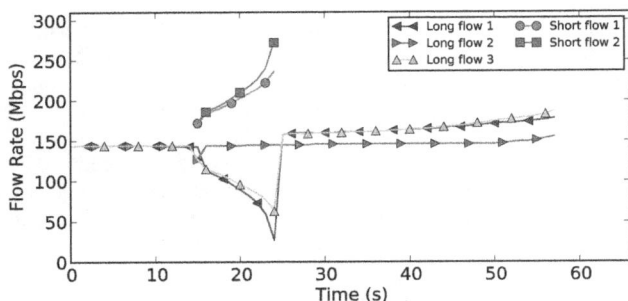

Figure 10: A combination of the BMA flow assignment upgrade and a deadline-aware flow scheduling upgrade. Long flows send one gigabyte of data with a deadline of 60 seconds, and short flows send 200 megabytes with a deadline of 10 seconds.

pool and each send at just over 400 Mbps. After 30 seconds, the third tenant begins sending TCP traffic over the shared path. Despite competing with UDP, the work conservation upgrade ensures that the third tenant's TCP traffic receives its 300-Mbps reservation. At 90 seconds, the TCP flow completes, and the UDP senders are again given the excess pool capacity.

Distributed rate limiting. To test our DRL upgrade, we construct a virtual network in which a set of three sending VMs transmit to three receiving VMs across three fully-disjoint paths. For each path, the sender creates a fixed 900-Mbps reservation along the path to its corresponding receiver. We then configure the edge-switches of all three senders to execute the DRL upgrade with a global rate limit of 800 Mbps.

Figure 9 shows the traffic departure rates from the edge-switch rate limiters associated with the traffic for each of the three senders. Every 30 seconds, one sender begins or ends its transmission, causing the DRL upgrade to reallocate the 800-Mbps budget amongst the active senders. Without DRL, we would see each sender fully utilizing its 900-Mbps reservation, however with DRL enabled, the aggregate sending rate of all three senders remains below the global limit.

Flow path selection and deadline-awareness. To evaluate the composition of these two upgrades, we configure a tenant with three paths between two VMs within a pod in our testbed. Each path is configured with a 300-Mbps reservation, and initially, the sending VM transmits three TCP flows to a receiving VM across three parallel paths. We use the BMA flow placement upgrade to

spread the flows across the available paths. Our traffic generator aims to send one gigabyte of data over each of the three flows with a deadline of 60 seconds. After 15 seconds, two additional flows begin, each with a size of 200 megabytes and a deadline of 10 seconds.

Figure 10 displays the results. Prior to the additional flows beginning, the three original flows converge to the necessary rate for on-time completion. When the two short-deadline flows start, our upgrade displaces two of the longer flows until they complete. Afterwards, the two displaced flows converge on a higher rate to make up for their displaced time. The third flow, which never shared a link with either of the short-deadline flows, continues at its original rate.

8. CONCLUSION

This work introduced Blender, a framework that enables data center operators to author and compose modular upgrades on a shared network infrastructure. Not only can Blender express many recently proposed network performance isolation models, but it allows them to easily compose with additional functionality. Data center operators can differentiate their cloud network offerings by offering tenants new upgrades, without requiring tenants to modify their deployed code base. In addition, our experiments indicate that enforcement of tenant-based resource allocation is practical given current rate limiter facilities in modern top of rack switches.

Acknowledgements

Portions of this work were funded by the UC San Diego Center for Network Systems; grants from the Broadcom Foundation, Cisco, Ericsson, and Google; and the National Science Foundation through CNS-0917339 and CSR-1018808.

9. REFERENCES

[1] M. Al-Fares, A. Loukissas, and A. Vahdat. A Scalable, Commodity Data Center Network Architecture. In *SIGCOMM*, 2008.

[2] M. Al-Fares, S. Radhakrishnan, B. Raghavan, N. Huang, and A. Vahdat. Hedera: Dynamic Flow Scheduling for Data Center Networks. In *NSDI*, 2010.

[3] M. Alizadeh, A. Kabbani, T. Edsall, B. Prabhakar, A. Vahdat, and M. Yasuda. Less is More: Trading a little Bandwidth for Ultra-Low Latency in the Data Center. In *NSDI*, 2012.

[4] Amazon. Elastic Load Balancing. http://aws.amazon.com/elasticloadbalancing.

[5] H. Ballani, P. Costa, T. Karagiannis, and A. Rowstron. Towards Predictable Datacenter Networks. In *SIGCOMM*, 2011.

[6] T. Benson and A. Akella. CloudNaaS: A Cloud Networking Platform for Enterprise Applications. In *SOCC*, 2011.

[7] T. Benson, A. Akella, and D. A. Maltz. Network Trafic Characteristics of Data Centers in the Wild. In *IMC*, 2010.

[8] M. Casado, M. Freedman, J. Pettit, J. Luo, N. McKeown, and S. Shenker. Ethane: Taking Control of the Enterprise. In *SIGCOMM*, 2007.

[9] Cisco. *Quality of Service on the Cisco Catalyst 4500 Classic Supervisor Engines*, 2006.

[10] A. D. Ferguson, A. Guha, C. Liang, R. Fonseca, and S. Krishnamurthi. Participatory Networking: An API for Application Control of SDNs. In *SIGCOMM*, 2013.

[11] N. Foster, R. Harrison, M. J. Freedman, C. Monsanto, J. Rexford, A. Story, and D. Walker. Frenetic: A Network Programming Language. In *ICFP*, 2011.

[12] A. Greenberg, J. R. Hamilton, N. Jain, S. Kandula, C. Kim, P. Lahiri, D. A. Maltz, P. Patel, and S. Sengupta. VL2: A scalable and Flexible Data Center Network. In *SIGCOMM*, 2009.

[13] N. Gude, T. Koponen, J. Pettit, B. Pfaff, M. Casado, N. McKeown, and S. Shenker. NOX: Towards an Operating System for Networks. *SIGCOMM CCR*, 2008.

[14] C. Guo, G. Lu, H. Wang, S. Yang, C. Kong, P. Sun, W. Wu, and Z. Yongguang. SecondNet: A Data Center Network Virtualization Architecture with Bandwidth Guarantees. In *CoNEXT*, 2010.

[15] T. Hoff. Latency is Everywhere and it Costs You Sales, July 2009. http://highscalability.com/blog/2009/7/25/latency-is-everywhere-and-it-costs-you-sales-how-to-crush-it.html.

[16] C. Hopps. Analysis of an Equal-Cost Multi-Path Algorithm. IETF RFC 2992, 2000.

[17] T. Koponen, M. Casado, N. Gude, J. Stribling, L. Poutievski, M. Zhu, R. Ramanathan, Y. Iwata, H. Inoue, T. Hama, and S. Shenker. Onix: A Distributed Control Platform for Large-scale Production Networks. In *OSDI*, 2010.

[18] V. T. Lam, S. Radhakrishnan, A. Vahdat, G. Varghese, and R. Pan. NetShare and Stochastic NetShare: Predictable Bandwidth Allocation for Data Centers. *SIGCOMM CCR*, 42(3), 2012.

[19] N. McKeown, T. Anderson, H. Balakrishnan, G. Parulkar, L. Peterson, J. Rexford, S. Shenker, and J. Turner. OpenFlow: Enabling Innovation in Campus Networks. *SIGCOMM CCR*, 2008.

[20] X. Meng, V. Pappas, and L. Zhang. Improving the Scalability of Data Center Networks with Traffic-aware Virtual Machine Placement. In *INFOCOM*, 2010.

[21] C. Monsanto, J. Reich, N. Foster, J. Rexford, and D. Walker. Composing Software-Defined Networks. In *NSDI*, 2013.

[22] J. Mudigonda, P. Yalagandula, B. Stiekes, J. Mogul, and Y. Pouffary. Netlord: A Scalable Multi-Tenant Network Architecture for Virtualized Datacenters. In *SIGCOMM*, 2011.

[23] R. N. Mysore, A. Pamboris, N. Farrington, N. Huang, P. Miri, S. Radhakrishnan, V. Subramanya, and A. Vahdat. Portland: A Scalable Fault-Tolerant Layer 2 Data Center Network Fabric. In *SIGCOMM*, 2009.

[24] L. Popa, G. Kumar, M. Chowdhury, A. Krishnamurthy, S. Ratnasamy, and I. Stoica. FairCloud: Sharing the Network in Cloud Computing. In *SIGCOMM*, 2012.

[25] Z. A. Qazi, C.-C. Tu, L. Chiang, R. Miao, V. Sekar, and M. Yu. SIMPLE-fying Middlebox Policy Enforcement Using SDN. In *SIGCOMM*, 2013.

[26] B. Raghavan, K. Vishwanath, S. Ramabhadran, K. Yocum, and A. C. Snoeren. Cloud Control with Distributed Rate Limiting. In *SIGCOMM*, 2007.

[27] M. Reitblatt, N. Foster, J. Rexford, C. Schlesinger, and D. Walker. Abstractions for Network Update. In *SIGCOMM*, 2012.

[28] H. Rodrigues, J. R. Santos, Y. Turner, P. Soares, and D. Guedes. Gatekeeper: Supporting Bandwidth Guarantees for Multi-tenant Datacenter Networks. In *WIOV*, 2011.

[29] S. Rooney, J. E. van der Merwe, S. A. Crosby, and I. M. Leslie. The Tempest: A Framework for Safe, Resource-Assured, Programmable Networks. *IEEE Communications*, October 1998.

[30] V. Sekar, N. Egi, S. Ratnasamy, M. K. Reiter, and G. Shi. Design and Implementation of a Consolidated Middlebox Architecture. In *NSDI*, 2012.

[31] J. Sherry, S. Hasan, C. Scott, A. Krishnamurthy, S. Ratnasamy, and V. Sekar. Making Middleboxes Someone Else's Problem: Network Processing as a Cloud Service. In *SIGCOMM*, 2012.

[32] R. Sherwood, G. Gibb, K.-K. Yap, G. Appenzeller, M. Casado, N. McKeown, and G. Parulkar. Can the Production Network Be the Testbed? In *OSDI*, 2010.

[33] A. Shieh, S. Kandula, A. Greenberg, C. Kim, and B. Saha. Sharing the Data Center Network. In *NSDI*, 2011.

[34] A. Voellmy, A. Agarwal, and P. Hudak. Nettle: Functional Reactive Programming for OpenFlow Networks. Technical Report YALEU/DCS/RR-1431, Yale University, July 2010.

[35] G. Wang and T. E. Ng. The Impact of Virtualization on Network Performance of Amazon EC2 Data Center. In *INFOCOM*, 2010.

[36] R. Wang, D. Butnariu, and J. Rexford. OpenFlow-Based Server Load Balancing Gone Wild. In *Hot-ICE*, 2011.

[37] D. Wetherall. Active Network Vision and Reality: Lessons from a Capsule-Based System. In *SOSP*, 1999.

[38] C. Wilson, H. Ballani, T. Karagiannis, and A. Rowstron. Better Never than Late: Meeting Deadlines in Datacenter Networks. In *SIGCOMM*, 2011.

[39] M. Zaharia, A. Konwinski, A. D. Joseph, R. Katz, and I. Stoica. Improving MapReduce Performance in Heterogeneous Envrionments. In *OSDI*, 2008.

BCCC: An Expandable Network for Data Centers

Zhenhua Li, Zhiyang Guo and Yuanyuan Yang
Department of Electrical and Computer Engineering
Stony Brook University
Stony Brook, NY 11794, USA
{zhenhua.li, zhiyang.guo, yuanyuan.yang@stonybrook.edu}

ABSTRACT

Designing a cost-effective network topology for data centers that can deliver sufficient bandwidth and consistent latency performance to a large number of servers has been an important and challenging problem. Many server-centric data center network topologies have been proposed recently due to their significant advantage in cost-efficiency and data center agility, such as BCube, FiConn and BCN. However, existing server-centric topologies are either not expandable or demanding prohibitive expansion cost. As the scale of data centers increases rapidly, the lack of expandability in existing server-centric data center networks imposes a severe obstacle for data center upgrade. In this paper, we present a novel server-centric data center network topology called BCube Connected Crossbars (BCCC), which can provide good network performance using inexpensive commodity off-the-shelf switches and commodity servers with only two NIC ports. A significant advantage of BCCC is its good expandability: When there is a need for expansion, we can easily add new servers and switches into the existing BCCC with little alteration of the existing structure. Meanwhile, BCCC can accommodate a large number of servers while keeping a very small network diameter, as a particular desirable property of BCCC is that its diameter increases only linearly to the network order (i.e., the number of dimensions), which is superior to most of existing server-centric networks, such as FiConn and BCN, whose diameters increase exponentially with network order. Additionally, there are a rich set of parallel paths with similar length between any pair of servers in BCCC, which enables BCCC to not only deliver sufficient bandwidth capacity and predictable latency to end hosts, but also provide graceful performance degradation in case of link failure. We conduct comprehensive comparisons between BCCC with other popular server-centric network topologies, such as FiConn and BCN. We also propose an effective addressing scheme and routing algorithms for BCCC. We show that BCCC has significant advantages over existing server-centric topologies in

many important metrics, such as expandability, server port utilization and network diameter.

Keywords

Data center networks, server-centric, dual-port server, network diameter, topology, expandability.

1. INTRODUCTION

Driven by technology advances, massive data centers consisting of tens or even hundreds of thousands servers have been built as infrastructures by large online service providers, such as Google [8], Amazon [1] and Microsoft [19], in which the performance of data center networks plays a critical role. A number of data center network structures have been proposed, which can be divided into two categories: switch-centric networks and server-centric networks. In a switch-centric network, switches are responsible for a variety of tasks such as routing and addressing, while servers are only used to send and receive packets in the network. Fat-tree [18], VL2 [10] and Portland [20] belong to this category. On the other hand, in a server-centric network, the computational intensive tasks like routing are put on the servers, which act not only as end hosts, but also as relay nodes for each other. DCell [11], BCube [12], FiConn [14] and BCN [13] belong to this category. A significant advantage of server-centric networks is that the network hardware cost can be drastically reduced, as inexpensive commodity switches are sufficient given that most complex network tasks have been shifted to servers where the computation resources are abundant. Also, because servers are much more programmable than switches, the server-centric structure can accelerate the process of network innovation.

A popular server-centric data center network is BCube [12], which is a hierarchical network with many good properties, such as low network diameter, efficient routing and so on. However, BCube is limited by its poor expandability, as expanding a BCube network, though not impossible, incurs tremendous hardware and human efforts, because the existing network structure has to undergo significant change and all the servers require more NIC ports for expansion. For this reason, BCube only fits in a limited range of applications, such as a modular data center networks within a shipping container. Another drawback of BCube is that the hardware cost increases drastically with the number of network hierarchies (or orders), because a BCube network of a large order requires each connected server to have multiple NIC ports. However, the majority of commodity servers in current market are equipped with only two NICs [6].

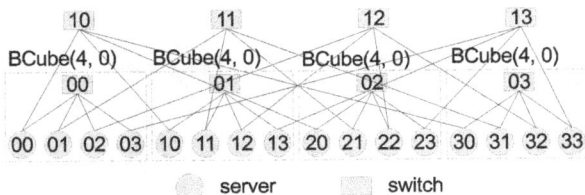

Figure 1: Structure of $BCube(4, 1)$.

In this paper, we propose a novel server-centric network topology for data center communication, called *BCube Connected Crossbars*, denoted as BCCC for short, which combines the merits of the aforementioned server-centric networks but eliminates their drawbacks. BCCC can be constructed using only dual-port commodity servers and commodity switches, which makes it a cost-effective network solution for large-scale data centers. Another very desirable feature of BCCC is that it is easily expandable, as expanding an existing BCCC network to a larger one with a higher network order requires no change to the existing network infrastructure or the number of ports of a server, which greatly facilitates data center upgrade. Unlike FiConn or BCN, the diameter of BCCC increases only linearly to the network order, which means that the communication latency between end hosts in BCCC is significantly lower than Ficonn and BCN, especially in large systems. Also, each pair of servers in BCCC is connected via a rich set of parallel paths with near-equal length, through which BCCC can not only deliver sufficient network bandwidth, but also maintain predictable network performance and robustness against link failure. To the best of our knowledge, BCCC is the first server-centric network structure so far that combines all the aforementioned desirable properties, which makes it a promising candidate for data center communication.

We also propose two efficient routing algorithms for one-to-one and one-to-all communications in BCCC respectively. In addition, we conduct a comprehensive comparison and analysis between the proposed BCCC network and existing popular server-centric networks. Finally, we use simulations to evaluate the performance of BCCC. The results show that BCCC outperforms FiConn and BCN in many aspects, such as bandwidth provisioning, average path length and performance against server/link failures.

The rest of this paper is organized as follows. Section 2 introduces the structures of BCube and Cube-Connected-Cycles [22], denoted as CCC. Section 3 describes the structure of BCCC, such as how to build it recursively and the similarities to BCube. Section 4 proposes an efficient one-to-one routing algorithm and discusses the properties of BCCC based on it. Section 5 presents an efficient routing algorithm for one-to-all routing. Section 6 provides a comprehensive comparison and analysis among typical 2-degree networks with BCube. Section 7 evaluates the performance of BCCC by simulations. Section 8 discusses expansion related issues. Finally, Section 9 concludes this paper.

2. PRELIMINARIES

BCCC is built upon two existing network topologies: BCube and Cube Connected Cycles (CCC). In this section, we introduce the background for both structures.

2.1 Structure of BCube

BCube is a recursively defined hierarchical structure. A $BCube(n, 0)$ is simply composed of an n-port switch with

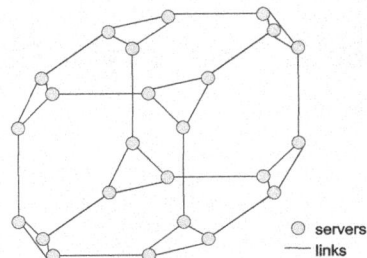

Figure 2: Structure of CCC(3).

n servers connecting to it. A $BCube(n, k)$, where $k \geq 1$, is constructed from n $BCube(n, k-1)$s and n^k n-port switches. Thus, a $BCube(n, k)$ consists of n^{k+1} $(k+1)$-port servers and $(k+1)n^k$ n-port switches. The switches are evenly divided into $k+1$ levels, and the ports of each server are indexed from 0 to k. Thus each level has n^k switches and a server connects to a switch of each level using its corresponding port. The BCube structure is closely related to the generalized Hyper-Cube [12] [7]. An example of $BCube(4, 1)$ is shown in Fig. 1 and a geometrical view of a $BCube(4, 1)$ is provided in Fig. 4(a). From Fig. 4, it can be seen that the $BCube(4, 1)$ can be treated as a 2-dimensional square and the address of each server is its coordination with this square. Servers within the same horizontal rectangle are connected by a first level switch while servers within the same vertical rectangle are connected by a second level switch.

BCube is suitable for fixed-sized modular data center networks (MDCN) inside shipping containers. It has many advantages such as large bisection bandwidth, small network diameter, as well as large aggregate data throughput. However, as mentioned earlier, expanding an existing BCube will incur high cost. Such poor expandability of BCube makes it difficult to be used in today's production data centers.

2.2 CCC: Cube Connected Cycles

CCC was proposed in [22], whose structure can be described as follows. A CCC of dimension $k(\geq 1)$, denoted as $CCC(k)$, is a graph formed by $k2^k$ nodes. Each node in this topology can be represented by a pair of numbers (x, y) where $0 \leq x < 2^k$ and $0 \leq y < k$, and is connected to three other nodes represented as $(x, (y + 1) \mod k)$, $(x, (y - 1) \mod k)$ and $(x \oplus 2^y, y)$, where $\oplus$ denotes the bitwise exclusive "or" operator [3]. The structure of CCC can also be built directly from a hypercube. First, we build a binary hypercube with order k, or a k-dimensional hypercube. In the hypercube, the degree of each node is k, that is, each node has k links, one for the connection in each order. Then replace each node with a cycle in which there are k nodes and each node can relay packets along the circle. An example of CCC(3) is shown in Fig. 2.

CCC has many good properties. First, CCC is a 3-regular network, which means that the degree of each node is always three regardless of the number of dimensions of a CCC. Such property allows us to extend a CCC network to higher dimension without changing the radix of nodes. Second, CCC has a small network diameter. Given a CCC network $CCC(k)$ with order k, its diameter is $2k + \lfloor k/2 \rfloor - 2$ for any $k \geq 4$, which is linear to the network order. CCC also shares the desirable features of a hypercube, like easy routing and addressing, as finding a route in CCC is the same as finding a route in a hypercube with each node replaced with a cycle.

3. BCCC NETWORK STRUCTURE

In this section, we present the proposed BCube-Connected-Crossbars (BCCC) structure. We describe how to build the BCCC recursively and then we discuss some similarities between BCCC and BCube.

3.1 Structure of BCCC

BCCC is a recursively defined structure built with switches and dual-port servers. First, we call the n servers connecting to a single n-port switch an *element*. Within an element, each server connects to the switch using its first port, and the second port is left for expansion purpose. We denote BCCC with order k as $BCCC(n, k)$, where n is the number of servers connected by each switch in each element. A $BCCC(n, 0)$ is simply constructed by one element and n switches, in which each server in the element connects to one of the n switches using its second port. A $BCCC(n, k)$ is constructed by n $BCCC(n, k-1)$s connected with n^k elements.

The detailed construction procedure of a $BCCC(n, k)$ network is as follows. To build $BCCC(n, k)$, first we need n $BCCC(n, k-1)$s indexed from 0 to $n-1$, in each of which the servers are denoted as $a_{k+1}a_k a_{k-1} \ldots a_0$, $a_0 \in [0, k-1], a_i \in [0, n-1], 1 \leq i \leq k+1$. Here, a_{k+1} is the most significant digit of the server with address $a_k a_{k-1} \ldots a_0$ in a $BCCC(n, k-1)$, which means that this server can be located by searching the postfix $a_k a_{k-1} \ldots a_0$ in the $(a_{k+1}+1)^{th}$ $BCCC(n, k-1)$.

Besides the n $BCCC(n, k-1)$s, the n^k elements required to build a $BCCC(n, k)$ contain n^{k+1} servers. These servers can also be denoted as $a_{k+1}a_k a_{k-1} \ldots a_0$, in which $a_0 = k, a_i \in [0, n-1], 1 \leq i \leq k+1$. We further say that two servers $A = a_{k+1}a_k a_{k-1} \ldots a_0$ and $A' = a'_{k+1}a'_k a'_{k-1} \ldots a'_0$ belong to the same element given that $a_{k+1} \neq a'_{k+1}$ and $a_i = a'_i, \forall i \ 0 \leq i \leq k$.

Overall, to build $BCCC(n, k)$, we need $(k+1)n^{k+1}$ dual-port servers, $(k+1)n^k$ n-port switches and n^{k+1} $(k+1)$-port switches. Since we need these two types of switches, we call them *type A switch* and *type B switch*, respectively. A type A switch has n ports and is used to form an element, while a type B switch has $(k+1)$ ports and is used to connect different elements. Therefore, the communication between servers within an element (i.e., intra-element communication) is conducted through the first port of each server, while the communication between servers in different elements (i.e., inter-element communication) is conducted through the second port of each server.

As aforementioned, the address of a server in the $BCCC(n, k)$ can be denoted as $a_{k+1}a_k a_{k-1} \ldots a_0$, where $a_0 \in [0, k]$, and $a_i \in [0, n-1], 1 \leq i \leq k+1$. Following a similar rule, the address of a switch can be represented as $s_k s_{k-1} \ldots s_0$, where $s_i \in [0, n-1], 1 \leq i \leq k$ and $s_0 \in [0, n+k]$. It can be observed that the address of a type B switch in a BCCC starts with $0 \leq s_0 \leq n-1$, and that of a type A switch starts with $n \leq s_0 \leq n+k$. Also, a switch with address s_i, $1 \leq i \leq k$ means that this switch belongs to the $(s_i+1)^{th}$ $BCCC(n, i-1)$.

To enable easy routing, the addresses of servers in a BCCC are determined according to the following rule: Two servers, $a_{k+1}a_k a_{k-1} \ldots a_0$ and $a'_{k+1}a'_k a'_{k-1} \ldots a'_0$, belong to the same element if there is exactly one different digit other than the least significant digit in their addresses, that is, $\exists i, 1 \leq i \leq k+1$, such that $a_i \neq a'_i$, and $a_j = a'_j, \forall j, 0 \leq j \leq k+1, j \neq i$.

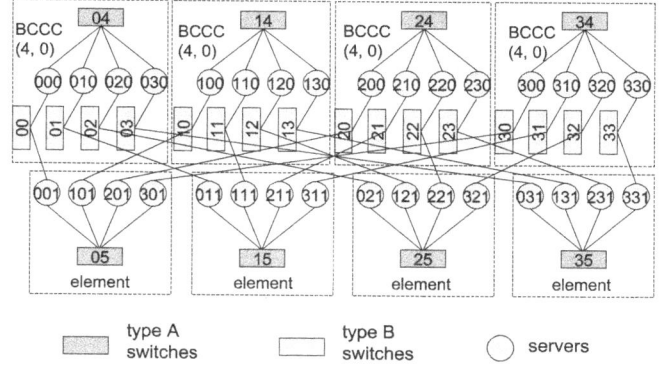

Figure 3: Topology of $BCCC(4, 1)$, which is composed of 4 $BCCC(4, 0)$s along with 4 elements.

A server is connected to a $(k+1)$-port switch via its second port, provided that it satisfies the condition that server $a_{k+1}a_k a_{k-1} \ldots a_0$ will be connected to switch $s_k s_{k-1} \ldots s_0$, with $s_i = a_{i+1}, \forall i, 0 \leq i \leq k$. Thus given the addressing scheme described above, to build $BCCC(n, k)$, we only need to connect each server in those elements, denoted as $a_{k+1}a_k a_{k-1} \ldots a_0$ where $a_0 = k$, to a switch in one of those n $BCCC(n, k-1)$'s, denoted as $s_k s_{k-1} \ldots s_0$, via its second port under the rule that $s_i = a_{i+1}$, where $0 \leq i \leq k$. This concludes the constructing procedure of a $BCCC(n, k)$.

Therefore, based on the above construction, we can see that a pair of servers $a_{k+1}a_k a_{k-1} \ldots a_0$ and $a'_{k+1}a'_k a'_{k-1} \ldots a'_0$ are neighbors, meaning that they are connected by the same switch, if and only if $\exists i, 0 \leq i \leq k+1$, such that $a_i \neq a'_i$, and $\forall j, 0 \leq j \leq k+1, i \neq j$, such that $a_j = a'_j$.

Moreover, the relationship between addresses of servers and switches can be summarized as follows: given a server $A = a_{k+1}a_k a_{k-1} \ldots a_0$ and its neighbor $A' = a'_{k+1}a'_k a'_{k-1} \ldots a'_0$, $\exists i \in [0, k+1]$ such that $a_i \neq a'_i$, and $a_j = a'_j$, where $\forall j, 0 \leq j \leq k+1$ and $j \neq i$, they are connected by a switch with address $s_k s_{k-1} \ldots s_0$ equal to

$$\begin{cases} a_{k+1}a_k a_{k-1} \ldots a_{i+1}a_{i-1} \ldots a_1 \{i-1+n\} & 0 < i \leq k+1 \\ a_{k+1}a_k a_{k-1} \ldots a_1 & i = 0 \end{cases}$$
(1)

where $\{i-1+n\}$ is the least significant digit in the address of the switch.

An example of $BCCC(4, 1)$ is shown in Fig. 3. $BCCC(4, 1)$ has 4 $BCCC(4, 0)$s and 4 elements. Servers 000, 010, 020 and 030 belong to the first $BCCC(4, 0)$, and they are connected to switch 04 via their first ports. Servers 001, 101, 201 and 301 belong to the same element, and they are connected to switch 05 via their first ports. Servers 000 and 001 are connected to switch 00, which is in the first $BCCC(4, 0)$, via their second ports. Server 011 and 211 are neighbors, which are connected by switch 15 via their first ports. Moreover, a geometrical view of $BCCC(4, 1)$ is shown in Fig. 4(b). It can be observed that servers with addresses with least significant digits equal to 0 form a 2-dimensional square and the address of each server excluding the least significant digit represents its coordination within this square. So do the servers with addresses with least significant digits equal to 1. Servers within the same horizontal rectangle form a $BCCC(4, 0)$, while servers within the same vertical rectangle form an element, and servers within the same blue rectangle are connected by a $typeB$ switch.

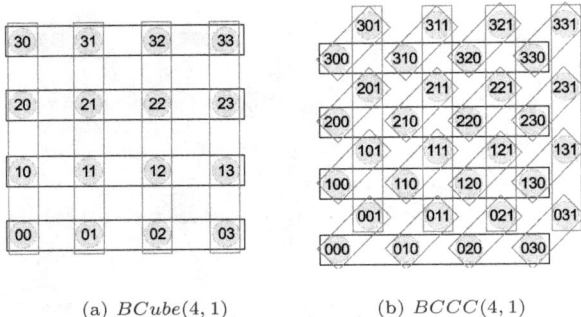

<table>
<tr><td>(a) BCube(4, 1)</td><td>(b) BCCC(4, 1)</td></tr>
</table>

Figure 4: Geometrical view of $BCube(4,1)$ and $BCCC(4,1)$. If we treat servers of $BCCC(4,1)$ within the same blue rectangle as a single node, $BCCC(4,1)$ will be reduced to a $BCube(4,1)$.

Meanwhile, for the convenience of discussing routing algorithms later, we say a server $A = a_{k+1}a_k a_{k-1} \ldots a_0$ is in the ith dimension if $a_0 = i - 1$, where $1 \leq i \leq k + 1$. By this token, servers within the same element are in the same dimension, and servers connected by a type B switch are in different dimensions.

The size of a $BCCC(n,k)$, $S_{BCCC}(n,k)$, is the number of servers within a $BCCC(n,k)$ network. We have the following property regarding $S_{BCCC}(n,k)$.

$$\begin{cases} S_{BCCC}(n,0) = S_{element}(n) = n \\ S_{BCCC}(n,k) = n \cdot S_{BCCC}(n,k-1) + n^k \cdot S_{element}(n) \end{cases}$$

$$(2)$$

Thus the size of $BCCC(n,k)$ is $(k+1)n^{k+1}$. Let $L_{BCCC}(n,k)$ be the number of linking wires required to build $BCCC(n,k)$, and d be the degree of each server. Since we know that each server is connected to switches via two wires, and there is no wire between any pair of servers, we have

$$L_{BCCC}(n,k) = d \cdot S_{BCCC}(n,k) = 2(k+1)n^{k+1} \quad (3)$$

3.2 Similarities to BCube

A $BCCC(n,k)$ can be seen as a $BCube(n,k)$ with each server replaced by $k+1$ servers connected to a crossbar switch, which is also the reason why the network is called BCCC. A $BCube(n,k)$ has $k+1$ dimensions, in which each server has $k+1$ links, each corresponding to one dimension, which is the cause for its poor expandability because increasing the network order demands servers with more ports. In comparison, each server in $BCCC(n,k)$ only needs two ports regardless of the network order, as they only need to relay packets along one dimension. If we treat the $k+1$ servers connected by a crossbar switch in a BCCC as a single server, the BCCC network can be reduced to a BCube. Therefore, a $BCCC(n,k)$ can be modified from a $BCube(n,k)$ network by replacing each server in $BCube(n,k)$ with $k+1$ dual-port servers. Each of these $k+1$ servers is connected via its first port to the original server in $BCube(n,k)$. Other ports of these $k+1$ servers are connected to an $(k+1)$-port switch. The similarities between $BCube$ and $BCCC$ can be seen from Fig. 4. We can see from this figure that if we treat servers of $BCCC(4,1)$ within the same blue rectangle as a single node, $BCCC(4,1)$ will be reduced to a $BCube(4,1)$.

Like the BCube network [12], BCCC also guarantees that switches only connect to servers and never directly connect to other switches. Similarly, servers are only connected to switches, but never directly to other servers. Since the task

of routing is shifted to servers, the switches can be treated as dummy crossbars that connect corresponding servers. Servers connected to the same switch can communicate to each other in one hop. According to the construction procedure, the radix of servers in $BCCC(n,k)$ is always 2, which is independent of the network order k. Meanwhile, to expand a $BCCC(n,k)$ to $BCCC(n,k+1)$, we only need to add new $BCCC(n,k)$s and elements into the existing structure with little alteration, except for connecting the servers in the n^{k+1} elements into the corresponding $BCCC(n,k)$s. Thus, BCCC has very good expandability, which tremendously facilitates data center update.

4. ONE-TO-ONE ROUTING

In this section, we propose an efficient one-to-one routing algorithm specifically suitable for BCCC and thereby we analyze some important properties of BCCC's structure.

4.1 One-to-One Routing

In one-to-one routing, a single source is sending packets to a single destination. Suppose two servers A and A′ want to communicate. Let $h(A, A')$ be the *hamming distance* of A and A′, defined as the number of different digits between their addresses. According to the aforementioned construction procedure, we can see that the maximum hamming distance between any pair of servers in a $BCCC(n,k)$ is $k + 2$.

Note that a server has one-hop distance to all its neighbors. Thus, a path between a source and a destination usually includes multiple hops via intermediate servers. A route between the source and the destination can be found iteratively. At each iteration, we move to some intermediate server to correct one digit a_i, $1 \leq i \leq k + 1$, in the source server's address to the corresponding digit in the destination server's address. Here, each iteration is divided into two steps. In step 1, in BCCC, in order to change a_i to a_i', a_0 must be $i - 1$, or we can say a_0 must be on the ith dimension. If not, denote the intermediate node in the current iteration as B, where $b_i = a_i$, then B must route to another server B' first, where $b_j = b_j'$, $1 \leq j \leq k + 1$ and $b_0' = i - 1$. For example, in Fig. 3, if we want to route from server 000 to server 101, where $a_2 = 0$, $a_2' = 1$ and $i = 2$. As $a_0 = 0 \neq i - 1$, we cannot directly correct a_2 to a_2' without going to another intermediate server first. Hence we need to change a_0 to 1 and route to intermediate server 001. Then we can go to step 2. Step 2 is to change digit a_i to a_i'. Like the example mentioned above, in step 2, server 001 routes to 101. It is easy to see that after at most $k + 1$ iterations, we can find a route between any source server and destination server. We give the routing algorithm in Table 1.

4.2 Structure Properties of BCCC

We now analyze some important properties of BCCC that are critical to the routing performance. The first property is on the network diameter, presented in the following theorem.

THEOREM 1. *The diameter of a $BCCC(n,k)$ is $2(k+1)$.*

PROOF. In general, a $BCCC(n,k)$ shares much similarity with a $(k+1)$-dimensional n-ary hypercube. Given a server A $= a_{k+1}a_k a_{k-1} \ldots a_0$, each digit a_i, $1 \leq i \leq k+1$, represents a coordinate in one specific dimension of the network. To eliminate difference in digit a_i between the source address and the destination address, we need to move towards the corresponding dimension by one hop. Given that a server can only relay packets along a specific dimension,

Table 1: BCCC routing algorithm to find a path from a single source to a single destination

```
Input: source A and destination A', where
    A is a_{k+1}a_k a_{k-1}...a_0 and A[i] = a_i
    A' is a'_{k+1}a'_k a'_{k-1}...a'_0 and A'[i] = a'_i, i ∈ [0, k+1]
    and Π which is the a permutation of [k+1, k, k-1, ..., 1]
Output: A list of intermediate servers of path from A to A',
    path(A, A')

BCCCRouting(A, A', Π)
    path(A, A') = {A};
    B = A;
    for (i = k+1; i > 0; i--) // k+1 iterations
        if A[π_i] ≠ A''[π_i]
            B[0] = π_i - 1;
            if A ≠ B
                append B to path(A, A'); //step 1
            B' = B;
            B'[π_i] = A'[π_i];
            append B' to path(A, A'); //step 2
    if A' ≠ B'
        append A' to path(A, A');
```

if that specific dimension is not the same as that packets need to go, then packets need to travel through a switch to arrive at the right dimension first, which adds one more hop. The packet can then move along the desired dimension afterwards. Overall, a packet needs to traverse at most 2 hops to eliminate the difference in one digit between the source address and the destination address. Since there are $(k+1)$ dimensions in total, a packet can arrive at any destination server from any source server within at most $2(k+1)$ hops. Thus, the diameter of a $BCCC(n, k)$ is $2(k+1)$. □

Take $BCCC(4, 1)$ in Fig. 3 as an example. Its diameter is 4. If we want to send a packet from server 001 to server 221, one possible path is 001, 000, 020, 021 and finally to 221. The number of hops needed for going through this path is 4. Another candidate path is from 001, to 201, 200, 220, and finally to 221. The number of hops for this path is also 4.

From this example, we can see that different permutations used in the algorithm in Table 1 lead to different paths from the source to the destination. This observation leads to the following properties.

LEMMA 1. *Given a pair of servers, $A = a_{k+1}a_k a_{k-1}...a_0$ and $A' = a'_{k+1}a'_k a'_{k-1}...a'_0$, suppose there are i different digits between their addresses excluding the least significant digit, then the length of the shortest path between them is at least $2i - 1$.*

PROOF. To reach A', we must correct every different digit in the source address. Recall that we need two hops to correct one digit for the first $i - 1$ digits of the i digits, which adds up to $2i - 2$ hops given that the packet has to arrive at the correct dimension via switches first. For the last digit to be corrected, if A' is on the correct dimension, we can directly correct the last digit in one hop without changing the order, leading to a total of $2i - 1$ hops. If not, we need to move by one more hop to A' which leads to $2i$ hops in total. □

LEMMA 2. *Given a pair of servers, $A = a_{k+1}a_k a_{k-1}...a_0$ and $A' = a'_{k+1}a'_k a'_{k-1}...a'_0$, for any intermediate server N in the path obtained by the algorithm in Table 1, the path length from A to N is at most 2 hops longer than the shortest path from A to N.*

PROOF. We denote the path from the algorithm in Table 1 as $\{A, N_1, N_2, ..., N_l, A'\}$. For any N_j, $1 \le j \le l$, the

Table 2: Building multipaths between any pair of source and destination

```
Input: source A and destination A', where
    A is a_{k+1}a_k a_{k-1}...a_0 and A[i] = a_i
    A' is a'_{k+1}a'_k a'_{k-1}...a'_0 and A'[i] = a'_i, i ∈ [0, k+1]
Output: A set of all parallel paths, PathSet

BuildingMultiPaths(A, A')
    PathSet = {};
    for i = 1; i ≤ k; i++
        if A[i] ≠ A'[i]
            P_i = DirectRouting(A, A', i);
        else
            P_i = IndirRouting(A, A', i);
        add P_i to PathSet;
    return PathSet;

DirectRouting(A, A', i)
    d = 1;
    for j = i; j ≥ i - k; j--
        π_d = j mod (k+1) + 1; // Π = π_{k+1}π_k...π_0
        d++;
    return BCCCRouting(A, A', Π);

IndirRouting(A, A', i)
    path = {A};
    B = A;
    if A[0] + 1 ≠ i
        B[0] = i - 1;
        path += B;
    set B[i] to a value different to A[i];
    path += B;
    d = 1;
    for j = i - 1; j ≥ i - 1 - k; j--
        π_d = j mod (k+1) + 1;
        d++;
    path += BCCCRouting(B, A', Π);
    return path;
```

length from A to N_j via this path is j. If j is even, i.e., $j = 2i$, we know from the algorithm that N_j has exactly i different digits from A excluding the least significant digit. By Lemma 1, we know that the length of the shortest path is at least $2i - 1 = j - 1$. If j is odd, i.e., $j = 2i + 1$, N_j has either i or $i + 1$ digits different from A excluding the least significant digit. The length of the shortest path from A to N_j is at least $2i - 1 = j - 2$. Thus, the lemma is proved. □

LEMMA 3. *For a $BCCC(n, k)$, given a pair of source and destination servers, $A = a_{k+1}a_k a_{k-1}...a_0$ and $A' = a'_{k+1}a'_k a'_{k-1}...a'_0$, that are different in every digit except for the least significant digit, i.e., $a_i \ne a'_i, \forall i \in [1, k+1]$, using the algorithm in Table 1, we can obtain two node-disjoint parallel paths between A and A' by using two different permutations $\Pi_0 = [i_0, (i_0 - 1) \bmod (k+1), ..., (i_0 - k) \bmod (k+1)]$ and $\Pi_1 = [i_1, (i_1 - 1) \bmod (k+1), ..., (i_1 - k) \bmod (k+1)]$, where $i_0 \ne i_1$ and $i_0, i_1 \in [1, k+1]$.*

The proof of this lemma is provided in Appendix A.
Given the above lemmas, we have the following theorem.

THEOREM 2. *There are $k + 1$ node-disjoint paths between any two servers in a $BCCC(n, k)$. Suppose there are i different digits between these two servers expect for the least significant digit, then the length of each path is at least $2i - 1$ and at most $2i + 5$, that is, the length difference of paths between any pair of those paths is no more than 6.*

We can build $k + 1$ paths using an algorithm based on Lemma 3 and shown in Table 2. For any pair of servers, the paths between them built by the algorithm in Table 2 fall into two categories: paths built by DirectRouting and paths built by IndirRouting. The proof that these $k+1$ paths are node-disjoint is provided in Appendix B.

Take $BCCC(4,1)$ in Fig. 3 as an example. For servers 000 and 030, there are two node-disjoint paths between them, which are $\{000, 030\}$ and $\{000, 001, 201, 200, 230, 231, 031, 030\}$, respectively, and the switches within two paths are $\{04\}$ and $\{00, 05, 20, 24, 23, 35, 03\}$, respectively. The length of the former is 1, while the later is 7. Thus, the difference of the lengths between them is 6.

4.3 Graceful Performance Degeneration upon Failures

Server or switch failure and link failure are very common phenomena in data centers today given their enormous size. One advantage of BCCC is that it has $(k+1)$ node-disjoint parallel paths between any pair of source and destination, which means that BCCC can maintain connectivity even when some servers/switches or links fail.

Once some server/switch in the routing path between the source and the destination servers fails, we need to reroute the packets to a new path. This can be easily implemented by selecting a different permutation from previous one in the proposed routing algorithm. Next, we describe a possible fault tolerant scheme. First, we set a timer for each packet sent from the source, each with a threshold c. If we have not received acknowledgments from more than c packets after the timers are up, we believe that some server/switch in the current route is down. So we send out a probing packet again using different permutation and build a new route. If we receive the acknowledgment from the destination, the new path is alive. If not, repeat the process of sending a probing packet using different permutations, until an available path is found. Finally, the routing tables in the corresponding servers and switches are updated. We can apply the same strategy to the case of link failures.

It is not difficult to find that there are also $(k+1)$ edge-disjoint parallel paths. k of these paths share the same first switch and k of them share the same last switch. Therefore, BCCC is guaranteed to be robust against single node failure, as there will be at least one path left for each server pair regardless of the location of node failure. It is also very tolerant against multiple node failures, because any pair of servers will be completely disconnected only if the two critical switches failed simultaneously.

5. ONE-TO-ALL ROUTING

In one-to-all, or broadcast communication, one specific source server sends packets to all other servers in the network. Broadcast communication is required by many common network protocols, such as ARP, hence, an efficient broadcasting algorithm is necessary.

In [12], the authors proposed a routing algorithm which speeds up one-to-all traffic by dividing the file into $(k+1)$ parts, and sending each part using one independent edge-disjoint path. This algorithm enables certain speedup, however, it does not work in the scenarios such as real-time online communication, as dividing the object into parts may result in the disorder of packets received at the destinations, yet the order of these packets is critical.

We now design a novel efficient broadcast routing algorithm for the proposed BCCC topology. This routing algorithm takes advantage of the hypercube-like structure of BCCC, and recursively broadcasts transmitted packets dimension by dimension as described in Table 3.

Table 3: BCCC broadcasting algorithm to send packets from a single source server to all other servers in the network

```
Input: source server A, A is a_{k+1}a_k a_{k-1}...a_0 and
    A[i] = a_i, i ∈ [0, k+1]
    the permutation of [k+1, k, ..., 1], Π,
    current level of and the total levels of a BCCC(n,k),
    which are d and k, respectively
Output: null

BCCCBroadcast(A, d, k, Π)
    B = A;
    if A[0] ≠ π_d − 1
        B[0] = π_d − 1;
        A sends packets to B;
    cnt = 0;
    for i = 0; i < n; i++
        C = B;
        C[π_d] = i;
        if C ≠ B
            B_neighbors[cnt] = C;
            cnt++;
    B broadcasts to all servers in B_neighbors using first port
    B_neighbors[cnt] = A;
    for each server C in B_neighbors do in parallel
        if d == 0
            cnt = 0;
            for i = 0; i ≤ k; i++
                B = C;
                B[0] = i;
                if B ≠ C
                    C_neighbors[cnt] = B;
                    cnt++;
            C broadcasts to all servers in C_neighbors using second port
            return;
        BCCCBroadcast(C, d − 1, k, Π);
```

The routing algorithm operates as follows. We first get a permutation, denoted as $\Pi = \pi_{k+1}\pi_k\pi_{k-1}\ldots\pi_1$, of array $[k+1, k, k-1, \ldots, 1]$. Π represents the sequence of the dimensions (or orders) in which the broadcast operation will be performed. The process can be treated as a broadcast tree, in which the top level, or the root, is the source. The packets are broadcast downward level by level. The servers on the ith level act as intermediate sources to the servers on the $(i-1)^{th}$ level and those intermediate sources broadcast to servers in the $(i-1)^{th}$ level in the dimension defined by π_i. Thus, if the source is in the π_i^{th} dimension, it broadcasts to all its neighbors within the same element. Or it should route to its neighbor first that is in the π_i^{th} dimension. In this way, in each level, we divide the broadcast assignment in $BCCC(n,i)$ into n sub-assignments in n $BCCC(n, i-1)$s.

This algorithm is very easy to implement in both software and hardware. One possible way to implement it is to modify the IP protocol. Each time before a server starts a broadcast, it broadcasts a probe packet first. In this probe packet, we add three fields to record the information about the current level d, the total level k of the BCCC, and the permutation Π. Each server starts to run the algorithm in Table 3 and build a routing table once they receive the probe packet. Afterwards, the packets will simply be routed by the routing tables established in each switch, and sent towards the correct servers. Though it may increase the workload for the servers and switches in software level, since the algorithm is very simple, it can be easily implemented in hardware.

We can use $BCCC(4,1)$ in Fig. 3 as an example. Suppose server 000 wants to broadcast some packets. It first broadcasts the packets to its neighbors $\{010, 020, 030\}$. For each server in this list including 000 itself, in order to change the dimension they separately send packets to their neighbors, which are 001, 011, 021, 031, respectively. Then these four servers will independently broadcast packets to their neigh-

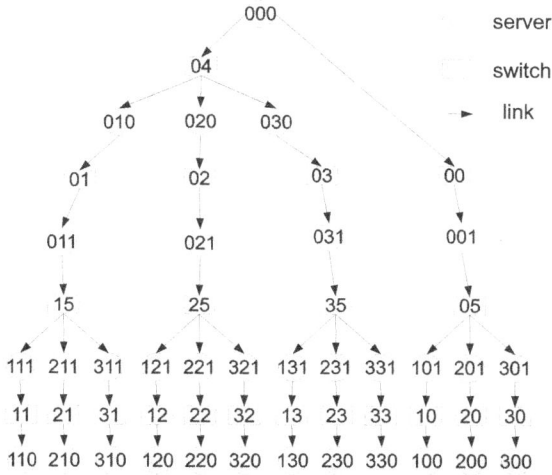

Figure 5: Broadcasting example in $BCCC(4, 1)$.

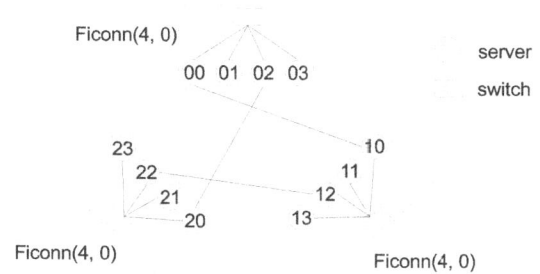

Figure 6: Structure of $FiConn(4, 1)$.

bors, which are $\{101, 201, 301\}$, $\{111, 211, 311\}$, $\{121, 221, 321\}$, $\{131, 231, 331\}$, respectively. For each server within the four list including 001, 011, 021 and 030, they independently broadcast to all their neighbors connected using their second port. Thus, every server gets the packets from server 000. The whole process is shown in Fig. 5. As can be seen from the figure, it only takes 4 hops for every server to get the packets from server 000. Notice that the diameter of $BCCC(4, 1)$ is 4. It is necessary to take 4 hops to send a packets from any source to a destination that is farthest to the source in the hamming distance.

It should be mentioned that several servers may receive the packets more than once. The redundancy occurs at the last step when every server listed in the array starts to broadcast to all its neighbor servers via its second port. In the example mentioned above, we can see that server 000 sends the packets out at the first step, and at the last step it may receive the packets back. The potential bandwidth wasting caused by such redundancy is acceptable, as there are only a few servers that will receive packets more than once. More specifically, only a few servers will receive packets twice as redundancy only occurs at the last step. As a matter of fact, the proposed algorithm can be modified to eliminate the redundancy. Based on the address of the source server A and the permutation Π, we can add one extra step to calculate which servers have gotten the packet already in the final step where $d = 0$, and if so, avoid retransmission. As the modification is very easy to implement, we skip it due to limited space.

6. COMPARISONS AMONG BCCC, BCUBE, RING, FICONN, BCN AND SWCUBE

In this section, we present a comprehensive comparison between the proposed BCCC and a set of existing network topologies including BCube, Ring, FiConn, BCN and SWCube.

6.1 Structures of FiConn, BCN and SWCube

First, we briefly review several recently proposed server-centric data center networks.

As shown in Fig. 6, FiConn [14] is also a recursively defined structure. $FiConn(n, 0)$ is the basic network unit, which is composed of n dual-port servers and an n-port switch connecting to these n servers. A $FiConn(n, k)$ is constructed as follows: if there are b servers having one port

available in a $FiConn(n, k-1)$, the number of $FiConn(n, k-1)$s in a $FiConn(n, k)$ is $b/2 + 1$. In each $FiConn(n, k-1)$, $b/2$ servers of these b servers are chosen to separately connect to one such a server in each of other $b/2$ $FiConn(n, k-1)$s.

BCN was proposed [13] as an expandable network structure using hierarchical compound graphs as shown in Fig. 7. This topology has four parameters denoted as $BCN(\alpha, \beta, k, \gamma)$, where α and β are the number of master and slave servers, respectively. The difference between a master sever and a slave one is that they are used to make expansions in different dimensions. In [13], a novel structure called HCN was also proposed and denoted as $HCN(n, k)$. In fact, $HCN(n, k)$ is a special case of $BCN(\alpha, \beta, k, \gamma)$, where $\alpha = n$, $\beta = 0$ and $\gamma > k$. $BCN(\alpha, \beta, k, \gamma)$ can expand in two dimensions separately controlled by the two parameters k and γ.

To construct $BCN(\alpha, \beta, k, \gamma)$, $BCN(\alpha, \beta, 0, \gamma)$ is used as the the building unit which consists of $\alpha + \beta$ 2-port servers and a $(\alpha + \beta)$-port switch. When $k < \gamma$, the structure is only constructed in the first dimension. A $BCN(\alpha, \beta, k, \gamma)$ is constructed using α $BCN(\alpha, \beta, k-1, \gamma)$s. Each $BCN(\alpha, \beta, k-1, \gamma)$ has α severs with one port still available, and $\alpha - 1$ of them are separately connected to the other $\alpha - 1$ $BCN(\alpha, \beta, k-1, \gamma)$s. When $k = \gamma$, $BCN(\alpha, \beta, k, \gamma)$ is constructed in the same way as in the case $k < \gamma$ first, denoted as $BCN(\alpha, \beta, \gamma)$, which consists of $\alpha^\gamma \beta$ slave servers. Then the structure is expanded in the second dimension using $\alpha^\gamma \beta + 1$ $BCN(\alpha, \beta, \gamma)$s. Each slave server in a single $BCN(\alpha, \beta, \gamma)$ is connected to another slave server in another $BCN(\alpha, \beta, \gamma)$. When $k > \gamma$, the structure is also constructed in the same way as in the case $k = \gamma$ first. Then we go back to make expansions in the first dimension, where $BCN(\alpha, \beta, \gamma, \gamma)$ is the building unit. A $BCN(\alpha, \beta, k, \gamma)$ is constructed using α $BCN(\alpha, \beta, k-1, \gamma)$s and each available master server in a single switch is connected to the corresponding slave server in another $BCN(\alpha, \beta, k-1, \gamma)$.

SWCube was proposed in [15], and the construction process of a $SWCube(n, k)$ is as follows: First, build a k dimensional generalized hypercube using n-port switches, denoted as $H_{r_1 \times r_2 \times \cdots \times r_k}^k$ where r_i represents the radix of the ith dimension. Thus a node A can be represented by a k-tuple: $A = a_1 a_2 \cdots a_k$, where $a_i \in [0, r_i - 1]$, $\forall i \in [1, k]$. Two nodes are connected directly by a link if and only if their addresses differ at only one digit, the ith digit. Thus the set of nodes whose addresses only differ at the ith digit form a complete graph. Then replace each node in this k-dimensional hypercube with a switch and insert a server into each link that connects two switches. This concludes the construction of a SWCube. Fig. 8(a) and (b) show a 1D SWCube and a 2D SWCube, respectively.

It can be seen from the construction process of a SWCube that each server has only 2 NICs and each switch has n port,

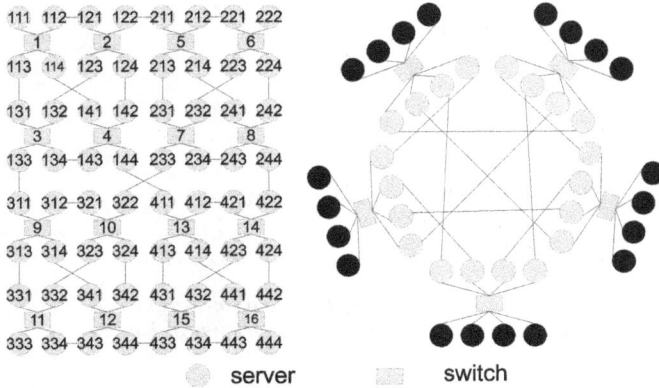

(a) An example of $BCN(4, 0, 2, \gamma)$, $\gamma > 2$. (b) An example of $BCN(4, 4, 0, 0)$.

Figure 7: Structures of BCN.

where $n = \sum_{i=1}^{k}(r_i - 1)$. The diameter of $SWCube(n, k)$ is $k + 1$. It is claimed in [15] that given the number of ports of a switch, n, with diameter less than or equal to d, $SWCube$ accommodates more servers than BCN.

6.2 Topology Comparisons

Since there is no discussion on the degrees and linking wires used by BCN in [13], for comparison purpose, we first calculate the number of linking wires used in a $BCN(\alpha, \beta, k, \gamma)$ network, where $n = \alpha + \beta$, which is expressed by the following equations.

$$\begin{cases} \frac{3}{2}\alpha^{k+1} + \alpha^k\beta - \frac{1}{2}\alpha & k < \gamma \\ \frac{3}{2}\alpha^k(\alpha + \beta)(\alpha^\gamma\beta + 1) - \frac{1}{2}\alpha(\alpha^\gamma\beta + 1) & k \geq \gamma \end{cases} \quad (4)$$

Similarly, the average degree per server in $BCN(\alpha, \beta, k, \gamma)$ is

$$\begin{cases} 1 + \frac{\alpha}{\alpha+\beta} - \frac{1}{\alpha^{k-1}(\alpha+\beta)} & k < \gamma \\ 2 - \frac{1}{\alpha^{k-1}(\alpha+\beta)} & k \geq \gamma \end{cases} \quad (5)$$

Here, we mainly focus our comparisons on the critical network metrics such as size, diameter, degree, network cost, and bisection bandwidth. For clarity, the comparisons are summarized in Table 4.

From the table, we can see that as a trade-off for good expandability, low diameter and large bisection bandwidth, BCCC requires a larger number of commodity off-the-shelf switches than other networks. Both Ficonn and BCN have links connecting servers directly, which results in fewer switches needed, however, it also causes the network diameter to increase exponentially to the network order k. In comparison, the diameter of BCCC is linear to the dimension k, which provides much better performance in terms of transmission delay.

Compared to BCube, at the first glance, it seems that $BCCC(n, k)$ requires more switches than $BCube(n, k)$. However, $BCCC(n, k)$ also accommodates many more servers than $BCube(n, k)$. Therefore, to provide a fair comparison, we use the network cost/server ratio as the criteria. The network cost mainly concentrates on the number of switches and links used, hence, we calculate the number of switches and link wires used per server. In $BCube(n, k)$, the amortized number of switches used per server is $(k+1)/n$, while in $BCCC(n, k)$ the number is $\frac{n+k+1}{n(k+1)}$. Thus, when

$$k^2 + k \geq n \quad (6)$$

the number of switches per server in BCCC is significantly lower than that in BCube. The above condition on k is gen-

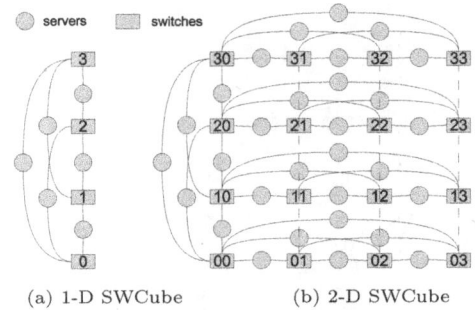

(a) 1-D SWCube   (b) 2-D SWCube

Figure 8: Structures of SWCube.

erally applicable to common data center networks, which means that BCCC is more cost-effective and scalable than BCube for data center communication. To have a more detailed comparison between BCube and BCCC, we compare the example of $BCube(8, 3)$ given in [12] with a $BCCC(8, 3)$. $BCube(8, 3)$ is constructed using 4-port servers and 8-port switches, which holds 4096 servers. A $BCCC(8, 3)$, on the other hand, can hold 16384 servers, significantly higher than BCube. Also, it meets the condition in Eq. (6), and the switch usage per server in $BCCC(8, 3)$ is better than that in $BCube(8, 3)$.

The greatest advantage of BCCC compared to BCube is that, as mentioned earlier, BCCC has a very good expandability. If we want to expand $BCube(48, 2)$ to $BCube(48, 3)$, all these 110,592 servers in this network need to be upgraded with one extra NIC. These changes incur not only the hardware cost, but also a tremendous cost of human effort. On the other hand, BCCC can be expanded without the need to change the existing components in the network, except for adding new components, which leads to significant saving in both hardware and manpower.

Given that the diameter of Ficonn and BCN increases exponentially with network order, a large network size will lead to unacceptable latency for certain pairs of servers located far away from each other. This in turn reduces data center agility, i.e., the ability to assign any task to any servers in the server pool, which is a critical metric for data centers, as it determines the server utilization, and thus operation cost and data center profitability.

Another advantage of BCCC is that all the servers have full port utilization. As we can see from Table 4, FiConn or BCN must leave some server ports idle for expansion purpose, thus cannot fully utilize all the server ports.

SWCube is another network with diameter increasing linearly to its order. In terms of diameter, both SWCube and BCCC give the best performance. SWCube is shown to accommodate more servers than BCN and FiConn under the condition that different networks are built with the same diameter and switches with the same number of ports. Under this condition, we can see BCCC can hold more servers than SWCube as the diameter increases. Table 5 shows a comparison with switches of 16 ports. Also, expandability is a problem for SWCube. From Table 5, we can observe that to increase the network size, d has to be increased. For SWCube, increasing d means adding more dimensions which in turn leads to a switch ports re-shuffle among all the existing and new added dimensions. Thus a huge rewiring cost is incurred.

In terms of network bisection bandwidth, it is difficult to tell which one is better because given the same network

Table 4: Comparisons among Ring, BCube, BCCC, FiConn, BCN and SWCube

name		# servers N	diameter	degree	# link wires	bisection bandwidth
$Ring(n)$		n	$\lfloor \frac{n}{2} \rfloor$	2	n	$\frac{2}{2}$
$BCube(n,k)$		n^{k+1}	$k+1$	$k+1$	$(k+1)n^{k-1}$	$\frac{n^{k+1}}{2}$
$BCCC(n,k)$		$(k+1)n^{k+1}$	$2k+2$	2	$2(k+1)n^{k+1}$	$\frac{n^{k+1}}{2}$
$FiConn(n,k)$		$\geq 2^{k+2}(\frac{n}{4})^{2^k}$	$\leq 2^{k+1}-1$	$2-\frac{1}{2^k}$	$(\frac{3}{2}-\frac{1}{2^{k+2}})N$	$\geq \frac{N}{2^{k+2}}$
$BCN(\alpha,\beta,k,\gamma)$	$k < \gamma$	$\alpha^k(\alpha+\beta)$	$2^{k+1}-1$	$1+\frac{\alpha}{\alpha+\beta}-\frac{1}{\alpha^{k-1}(\alpha+\beta)}$	$\frac{3}{2}\alpha^{k+1}+\alpha^k\beta-\frac{1}{2}\alpha$	$\lfloor \frac{\alpha^2}{4} \rfloor$
	$k \geq \gamma$	$\alpha^k(\alpha+\beta)(\alpha^\gamma\beta+1)$	$2^{\gamma+1}+2^{k+1}-1$	$2-\frac{1}{\alpha^{k-1}(\alpha+\beta)}$	$\frac{3}{2}N-\frac{1}{2}\alpha(\alpha^\gamma\beta+1)$	$\frac{(\alpha^\gamma\beta+2)\alpha^k\beta}{4}$
$SWCube(n,k)$		$\frac{n}{2}\prod_{i=1}^{k} r_i$	$k+1$	2	$n\prod_{i=1}^{k} r_i$	$\frac{1}{8}(\prod_{i=1}^{k} r_i)\min_{i=1}^{k} r_i$

Table 5: Size of BCCC and SWCube with different diameter d when $n = 16$

	$d=5$	$d=9$	$d=13$	$d=17$
$BCCC$	512	262144	6×16^6	8×16^8
$SWCube$	5000	52488	165888	524288

order, different networks accommodate different numbers of servers. Thus, again we use the average bandwidth allocated to each server for a fair comparison. For BCube, the bandwidth per server is 0.5, while in BCCC, it is $0.5/(k+1)$. In FiConn, it is no less than $1/(2^{k+2})$ and it is $\min_{i=1}^{k} r_i/(4n)$ for SWCube. Finally, in BCN, it is

$$\begin{cases} \lfloor \frac{\alpha^2}{4} \rfloor / \alpha^k(\alpha+\beta) & k < \gamma \\ \frac{1}{4} - \frac{\alpha}{4(\alpha+\beta)} + \frac{\beta}{4(\alpha^\gamma\beta+1)(\alpha+\beta)} & k \geq \gamma \end{cases} \quad (7)$$

Hence, we can see that BCube has the best average bandwidth per server, and FiConn has the worst one. SWCube, BCCC and BCN are in the middle. For SWCube, the best bisection bandwidth is achieved when switch ports are evenly divided into each dimension. In this case, it has similar performance to BCCC. In other words, BCCC's performance is at least no worse than SWCube. For BCN, better performance is achieved when $k \geq \gamma$. Usually, α and β are large, thus the last item in Eq. (7) is very small and can be ignored. As a result, the main contributor to the average bandwidth per server in BCN is $\frac{1}{4} - \frac{\alpha}{4(\alpha+\beta)}$. This result depends on the ratio of α to β. If β is much larger than α, the average bandwidth per server for BCN can be reduced to 0.25, while if β is far less than α the average bandwidth per server approaches 0. Thus, we cannot tell which one is better between BCCC and BCN without specifying the ratio of α to β. However, given that when β is far larger than α, the network cannot accommodate a large number of servers, while holding a large number of servers is one significant advantage for BCN manifested in [13], it is difficult for a BCN to reach 0.25 average bandwidth per server without sacrificing its large accommodation. Thus, how to make the compromise between these two considerations is a challenging problem to BCN.

To the best of our knowledge, BCCC is the only topology that combines the following merits: (1) It uses dual-port servers regardless of network order; (2) Its diameter increases linearly to the dimension; (3) No change to existing structures upon upgrade. The combination of these merits makes BCCC a promising solution for data center networks.

6.3 Cost Comparisons

Different network structures use different numbers of switches and have different sizes as well as diameters. It is difficult to allege one network structure is more cost effective than

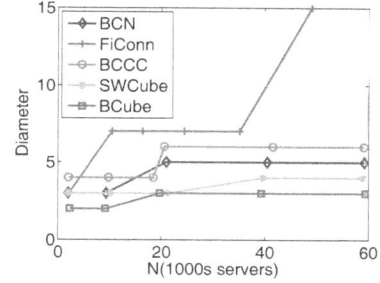

Figure 9: Diameter of each topology at different network size levels.

others. In this subsection, we use the cost model proposed in [21] to make the expenditure comparisons.

First, we equalize the network diameter of different structures at several network size levels (20000, 40000 and 60000 servers). We do so by fine tuning different topology parameters such as the number of ports of a switch. To make it feasible, we require the number of switch ports be at most 96 and the maximum number of ports per server be 6. Fig. 9 presents the resultant diameters we obtain for each of the solutions for increasing network sizes. We next arrange these structures to have a similar bisection bandwidth.

Following the cost model in [21], we consider the prices for the following three components: switches, server NICs and server cores. With regard to the fact that 40 GBE protocol has been deployed, we use the prices for 40 Gbps switches and 40 Gbps server NICs to compare. The cost model we are using assumes the prices of switches and server NICs are linear to the number of their ports and the per-port price is constant. The cost of server cores per server depends on how many cores participating in forwarding packets. Here, we assume a core is fully reserved for relaying packets. Based on the experiment data in [12], a single core can handle around 10Gbps workload. Thus to handle 40 Gbps workload, 4 cores per servers are needed. As representative of current prices, we use values of $2000 per 40 Gbps switch port, $600 per 40 Gbps NIC port and $280 per server core based on the data we gathered from Arista Networks [2], HotLava [4] and Intel [5] respectively.

Fig. 10 (a) shows the total expenditure for each topology at different network size levels, while Fig. 10 (b) presents the average cost per server of each topology at several fix network size levels. From these two figures we can see that the capital expenditure of BCube is the least competitive compared to the others. This is because in BCube, a server can own more than 2 NIC ports which incurs not only more cost of NICs but also costs of server cores as traffic load for the server to handle is also increased. SWCube and BCCC give similar cost performance. FiConn and BCN have the

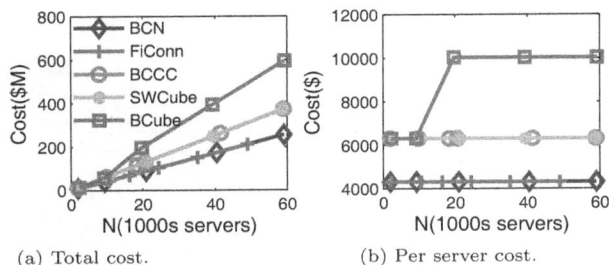

(a) Total cost. (b) Per server cost.

Figure 10: Capital expenditure of each topology at different network size levels.

most competitive capital expenditure as servers are allowed to connect to other servers without via any switches. Thus a huge cost of switch ports are saved. However, though we arrange to equalize the diameters and bisection bandwidths for all the structure, FiConn still gives the worst performance on these two aspects. On the other hand, BCN makes the best trade-off. But this advantage will vanish as the network size keeps on increasing. According to our calculation, when the size of DCN exceeds 200 thousand, BCN has to make trade-off between these two aspects. To get a better diameter, BCN has to sacrifice bisection bandwidth performance and vice versa. Moreover, in either case BCN's diameter will become exponentially larger than BCCC's.

For the cabling cost, due to Table 4, we can see that all the structures consume a similar quantity of wires. Thus the cost of cable itself for each structure will not differ so much. Besides, according to [21], the cabling cost only occupies 3-8% of the equipment cost. Thus it is not a key factor for a structure to be applied to DCNs.

7. PERFORMANCE EVALUATION

In this section, we conduct simulations to evaluate the properties of average path lengths in FiConn, BCN, SWCube and BCCC.

For simplicity, we ignore the protocol details and assume that packets are always routed along the shortest path among all the available candidate paths between the source and the destination. By saying a path is available we mean that there is no link or server failure along this path. We also assume that packets will not be dropped due to congestion control and they will always succeed in arriving at the destination as long as there is an available path.

First, we study the performance of these network structures against both server failure and link failure. For the server failure, we assume that each server fails with equal probability independently. Simulations are conducted on the average path length from a single source server to all other reachable servers in each network structure with the server failure probability ranging from 0 to 0.3. We set the network size to $BCCC(16, 2)$, $SWCube(16, 5)$, $FiConn(16, 2)$ and $BCN(6, 10, 1, 1)$, which is the same setting as [13]. From Fig. 11, we can see the average path length in SWCube increases most slowly and that in BCCC increases second most slowly. When server failure ratio increases from 0 to 0.3, the average path length in SWCube increases from 4.34 to 4.94 and that in BCCC increases from 5.06 to 6.25. However, the average path length in FiConn increases from 6.26 to 8.70, and that in BCN increases from 6.03 to 7.97.

Next, we investigate the performance against link failure. Also we assume that each link fails independently

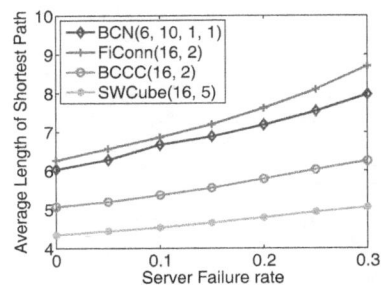

Figure 11: Average path length vs. server failure ratio.

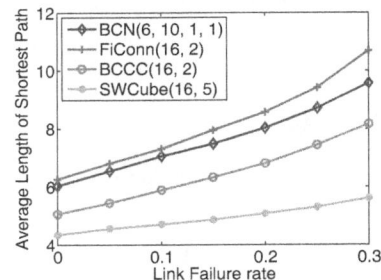

Figure 12: Average path length vs. link failure ratio.

with equal probability. We run simulations on the average path length from a single source server to all other reachable servers in each network structure with link failure rate ranging from 0 to 0.3. Again we set the network size to $BCCC(16, 2)$, $FiConn(16, 2)$, $BCN(6, 10, 1, 1)$ and $SWCube(16, 5)$ and show the performance in Fig. 12. From Fig. 12, we can also see the average path length in SWCube increases most slowly. When the link failure ratio increases from 0 to 0.3, the average path length in SWCube increases from 4.34 to 5.81. Then BCCC increases second most slowly whose average path increases from 5.06 to 8.15, while the average path length in BCN increases from 6.04 to 9.57 and that in Ficonn increases from 6.27 to 10.68.

The reason lies in the fact that both SWCube and BCCC have a plenty of parallel paths with near-equal length. If some servers/links in a path are down, we can simply choose another path without impacting performance too much. On the other hand, however, though there are also many parallel paths in BCN and FiConn, the lengths of those parallel paths vary quite significantly. If some servers/links in a path are down, choosing another path may cause a huge path length increase. Therefore, the packets delivery latency in BCN or FiConn under server/link failure is quite unpredictable. Thus we can see that BCCC and SWCube can deliver more graceful performance degradation than FiConn and BCN.

We now further evaluate the throughput performance of BCCC. We set the speed of all links, NIC ports and switch line cards to 10 Gbps. We adopt the algorithm in Table 1 to find the path between a pair of source and destination. In this evaluation, we conduct two groups of simulations for all-to-all and one-to-one communication respectively. In all-to-all communication, every server will send packets to all other servers with equal probability and the total packet sending rate for a single server can not succeed the link speed. In one-to-one mode, we choose a random permutation, thus each server will send packets to a single destination at the full rate and no two servers will send packets to the same destination. We test the performance of $BCCC(n, k)$ in combinations of n and k with different values. Then we measure the aggregate throughput for the whole network and the results are shown in Fig. 13. It can be observed that BCCC can provide high aggregate throughput especially in the all-to-all communication pattern. Thus it is very suitable for the MapReduce-like applications. According to the data we can find that the aggregate throughput of BCCC is around $N/(k+1)$ which is smaller than that of BCube, which is N [12]. However it is still significantly larger than BCN whose aggregate throughput is $N/(2^k)$ [13].

8. DISCUSSIONS

In this section, we discuss the issues of the expandability and how to enable fast routing for BCCC.

8.1 Expansion Issues

Notice that though there is no need to make changes in the existing elements of BCCC when doing expansion, it does need extra ports for type B switches. For example, when we expand a $BCCC(n,2)$ to $BCCC(n,3)$, we need to change all the type B switches from 3-port switches to 4-port ones, which incurs an extra cost. This can be solved by pre-provisioning extra ports for type B switches. Usually expanding k to 6 or 7 would provide sufficiently large network size. Thus provisioning 8-port mini switches as type B switches would meet the expansion requirement. On the other hand, it is true that BCube can also pre-provision extra NIC ports to reduce the expansion cost. However, as discussed in Section 6, so far the COTS servers are equipped with 2 NICs, which provide at most 6 ports in total. This hinders BCube from expanding to higher levels. Besides, increasing NIC ports will increase server cores needed to handle the extra incoming traffic workload, which further increases the capital expenditure of BCube. Thus it is more cost effective for BCCC to make expansions than BCube.

8.2 Routing Workload in Servers

Server centric networks transfer routing work (such as routing algorithm and routing table) from switches to servers and so does BCCC. As 40 Gbps network has been deployed, how to handle such a huge traffic workload is a big challenge for server-centric networks. One possible solution is that instead of using the software-based packet forwarding scheme, we can choose to use a hardware-based packet forward engine which frees the CPU resources and as a result reduces the core cost for server centric network significantly. Shunting NIC [9], CAFE [17] and ServerSwich [16] are some good candidates for the hardware-based packet forwarding solution. In this way, by implementing the routing algorithm and routing table in the programmable hardware, we can not only enable fast end-to-end packets forwarding but also lower the CPU resource cost in BCCC.

9. CONCLUSIONS

In this paper, we propose a novel server-centric data center network topology, called BCCC, which is a recursive network structure. BCCC can be built using only dual-port servers regardless of network size, and its expansion requires little change to the existing network structure. These properties give BCCC a very good expandability. Also, there are a rich set of near-equal-length parallel paths between any pair of servers in BCCC, which enables BCCC to provision sufficient transmission bandwidth and have graceful performance degradation upon failure. Finally, the diameter of

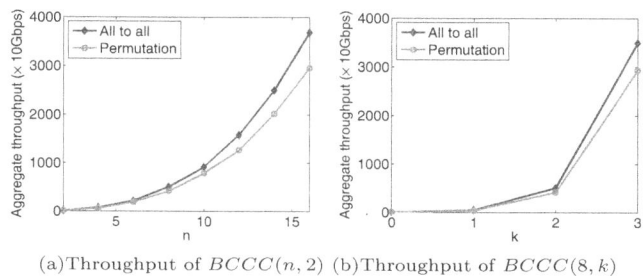

(a)Throughput of $BCCC(n,2)$ (b)Throughput of $BCCC(8,k)$

Figure 13: Throughput of all-to-all traffic pattern and one-to-one permutation pattern.

BCCC only increases linearly to the network order, which means that servers will enjoy low-latency transmission even in a large-size network. The combination of these desirable properties makes BCCC a promising networking choice for data center communication. We also present two efficient routing algorithms for one-to-one and one-to-all communications respectively. We give a comprehensive comparison between BCCC and other popular topologies, which shows that BCCC has significant advantages in many critical metrics, such as network cost, diameter, etc. over other topologies.

10. ACKNOWLEDGMENTS

This research work was supported in part by the U.S. National Science Foundation under grant number CCF-1320044.

11. REFERENCES

[1] Amazon web services. *http://aws.amazon.com/ec2*.

[2] Arista networks. *http://www.aristanetworks.com*.

[3] Cube-connected. *http://en.wikipedia.org/wiki/Cube-connected_cycles*.

[4] Hotlava systems. *http://www.hotlavasystems.com*.

[5] Intel corporation. *http://www.intel.com*.

[6] Rack servers. *http://buildprice.cisco.com/catalog/ucs/rack-server*.

[7] L. Bhuyan and D. Agrawal. Generalized hypercube and hyperbus structures for a computer network. *IEEE Trans. Computers*, c-33(4):323–333, April 1984.

[8] S. Ghemawat, H. Gobioff, and S. Leung. The google file system. *ACM SOSP'03*, October 2003.

[9] J. M. Gonzalez, V. Paxson, and N. Weaver. Shunting: A hardware/software achitecture for flexible, high-performance network intrusion prevetion. *In ACM Conference on Computer and Communication Security*, 2007.

[10] A. Greenberg and et al. Vl2: A scalable and flexible data center network. *ACM SIGCOMM*, August 2009.

[11] C. Guo and et al. Dcell: A scalable and fault-tolerant network structure for data centers. *ACM SIGCOMM'08*, August 2008.

[12] C. Guo and et al. Bcube: A high performance, server-centric network architecture for modular data centers. *ACM SIGCOMM'09*, August 2009.

[13] D. Guo and et al. Expandable and cost-effective network structures for data centers using dual-port servers. *IEEE Trans. Computers*, 62(7):1303–1317, July 2013.

[14] D. Li and et al. Ficonn: Using backup port for server interconnection in data centers. *Proc. IEEE INFOCOM*, 2009.

[15] D. Li and J. Wu. On the design and analysis of data center network architectures for interconnecting dual-port servers. *Proc. IEEE INFOCOM*, 2014.

[16] G. Lu, C. Guo, Y. Li, and Z. Zhou. Severswitch: A programmable and high performance platform for data center networks. *Proc. Eighth USENIX Conf. Networked System Design and Implementation(NSDI)*, pages 15–28, 2011.

[17] G. Lu, Y. Shi, C. Guo, and Y. Zhang. Cafe: A configurable packet forwarding engine for data center networks. *Proc. ACM SIGCOMM Workshop Programmable Routers for Extensible Services of Tomorrow(PRESTO)*, August 2009.

[18] A. L. M. Al-Fares and A. Vahdat. A scalable, commodity data center network architecture. *ACM SIGCOMM'08*, August 2008.

[19] R. Miller. Ballmer: Microsoft has 1 million servers. *http://www.datacenterknowledge.com/archives/2013/-07/15/ballmer-microsoft-has-1-million-servers*.

[20] R. Mysore and et al. Portland: A scalable fault-tolerant layer 2 data center network fabric. *ACM SIGCOMM*, August 2009.

[21] L. Popa, S. Ratnasamy, G. Iannaccone, A. Krishnamurthy, and I. Stocia. A cost comparison of data center network architectures. *In Proc. ACM CoNEXT*, December 2010.

[22] F. P. Preparata and J. Vuillemin. The cube-connected-cycles: A versatile network for parallel computation. *Commun. ACM*, 24:300–309, May 1981.

APPENDIX

A. PROOF OF LEMMA 3

PROOF. Based on the two permutations Π_0 and Π_1, we can build two paths P_0 and P_1 using the routing algorithm in Table 1. We denote them as $\{A, N_1^0, N_2^0, ..., N_i^0, ..., N_{l_0}^0, A'\}$ and $\{A, N_1^1, N_2^1, ..., N_i^1, ..., N_{l_1}^1, A'\}$, respectively, where N_i^j is the ith intermediate server in P_j. By Lemma 2 we know that $|l_1 - l_0| \leq 2$.

First, we show that N_i^0 cannot appear in P_1. On one hand, N_i^0 cannot appear in P_1 at different positions other than within the range $[i-2, i+2]$. Otherwise, by Lemma 2, the shorter path is even shorter than the shortest path. It contradicts with the definition of the shortest path. On the other hand, N_i^0 cannot appear in P_1 at the positions within the range $[i-2, i+2]$ either. It cannot be at the position $i \pm 2$ in P_1. Suppose N_i^0 has j digits different from A except for the least significant digit, but in P_1, $N_{i\pm2}^1$ has $j \pm 1$ digits different from A except the least significant digit. Then N_i^0 cannot be within the position range $[i-1, i+1]$ in P_1, as in this case, A goes to N_i^0 and N_j^1, $j \in [i-1, i+1]$, separately along P_0 and P_1 by correcting different digits. Thus, N_i^0 cannot be N_j^1. In sum, N_i^0 cannot appear in P_1. Vice versa, N_i^1 cannot appear in P_0.

Next, we show that any switch in P_0 cannot appear in P_1 except for the first and the last switches in P_0. We denote S_i^j as the ith switch in P_j. Suppose S_i^0 also appears in P_1 and in each path S_i^0 is connected with two different servers. Thus, in total, S_i^0 is connected to 4 servers, denoted separately as N_i^0, N_{i+1}^0, N_j^1 and N_{j+1}^1. If S_i^0 is the n-port switch, all the four nodes must be in the same dimension. Then due to the path finding algorithm, N_{i+1}^0 and N_{j+1}^1 must be the same, which contradicts with the fact proved earlier that N_{i+1}^0 cannot appear in P_1. If S_i^0 is the $(k+1)$-port switch, N_i^0, N_{i+1}^0, N_j^1 and N_{j+1}^1 must have the same addresses except for the least significant digit. However, since A goes separately along P_0 and P_1 to N_i^0 and N_j^1 by correcting different digits, N_i^0 and N_j^1 cannot have exactly the same addresses except for the least significant digit. This is a contradiction. Therefore, switches in P_0 cannot appear in P_1 except for the first the last switches in P_0. Similarly, switches in P_1 cannot appear in P_0 except for the first and last switches in P_1. □

B. PROOF OF THEOREM 2

PROOF. Suppose there are i digits differences between the source and the destination excluding the least significant digit, i paths are built by DirectRouting and $k+1-i$ paths are built by IndirRouting. By removing the same digits in the source and destination except for the least significant digit, we can put them into a subnetwork $BCCC(n, i)$, and due to Lemma 3, paths built by DirectRouting are parallel.

Then we show that paths built by IndirRouting are also node-disjoint parallel. To be in this case, there must be at least two digits excluding the least significant digit that are the same in the source and destination addresses. Suppose those two digits are the ith and j^{th} digits, where $i \neq 0$, $j \neq 0$ and $i \neq j$. Thus according to the algorithm in Table 2, the value in the ith digit of intermediate servers in the first path must be different from the one in the second path. For the same reason, the value in the jth digit of intermediate servers in the first path must also be different from the one in the second path. Thus, intermediate servers that appear in the first path cannot appear in the second path. Similarly, intermediate servers in the second path cannot appear in the first path either. All intermediate switches that appear in the first path cannot appear in the second path, except for the first and the last switch, as a switch connects to those servers with only one different digit. However, based on the description above, we know that there are at least two different digits. For the same reason, all intermediate switches, except for the first and the last one, in the second path cannot appear in the first path.

Finally, we show that paths from different categories are node-disjoint parallel. Due to the algorithm, the intermediate servers in the path built by DirectRouting cannot appear in the path built by IndirRouting, as for servers in the former path and the later path, there must be at least one digit different each other. Also for the same reason, the intermediate switches except for the first and the last one, which appear in the path in one category, cannot appear in the paths in the other category, as the servers the switches connect have at least one digit different from those in the path in the other category.

From Lemma 1, we know that the length of the shortest path among all the paths is at least $2i - 1$. The longest path happens when IndirRouting is used. It costs at most 2 hops for the source to route to the intermediate node B. In this case, there will be $i + 1$ digits different expect for the least significant digit between B and the destination. By Lemma 2, the path between B and the destination built by the algorithm in Table 1 is at most $2(i+1) - 1 + 2 = 2i + 3$. Plus the additional 2 hops for the source to B, in total the length of the longest path is at most $2i + 5$. □

Efficient and Programmable Ethernet Switching with a NoC-Enhanced FPGA

Andrew Bitar, Jeffrey Cassidy, Natalie Enright Jerger, Vaughn Betz
Edward S. Rogers Sr. Department of Electrical and Computer Engineering
University of Toronto, Toronto, Ontario, Canada
{andrew.bitar,jeffrey.cassidy}@mail.utoronto.ca,{enright,vaughn}@ece.utoronto.ca

ABSTRACT

Communications systems make heavy use of FPGAs; their programmability allows system designers to keep up with emerging protocols and their high-speed transceivers enable high bandwidth designs. While FPGAs are extensively used for packet parsing, inspection and classification, they have seen less use as the switch fabric between network ports. However, recent work has proposed embedding a network-on-chip (NoC) as a new "hard" resource on FPGAs and we show that by properly leveraging such a NoC one can create a very efficient yet still highly programmable network switch.

We compare a NoC-based 16×16 network switch for 10-Gigabit Ethernet traffic to a recent innovative FPGA-based switch fabric design. The NoC-based switch not only consumes $5.8 \times$ less logic area, but also reduces latency by $8.1 \times$. We also show that using the FPGA's programmable interconnect to adjust the packet injection points into the NoC leads to significant performance improvements. A routing algorithm tailored to this application is shown to further improve switch performance and scalability. Overall, we show that an FPGA with a low-cost hard 64-node mesh NoC with 64-bit links can support a 16×16 switch with up to 948 Gbps in aggregate bandwidth, roughly matching the transceiver bandwidth on the latest FPGAs.

Categories and Subject Descriptors

C.2.1 [**Computer-Communication Networks**]: Network Architecture and Design—*packet-switching networks*; C.2.6 [**Computer-Communication Networks**]: Internetworking—*routers*

General Terms

Design, Performance, Algorithms

Keywords

Switch architecture; Network-on-chip; FPGA

ANCS'14, October 20–21, 2014, Los Angeles, CA, USA.
Copyright 2014 ACM 978-1-4503-2839-5/14/10 ...$15.00.
http://dx.doi.org/10.1145/2658260.2658272.

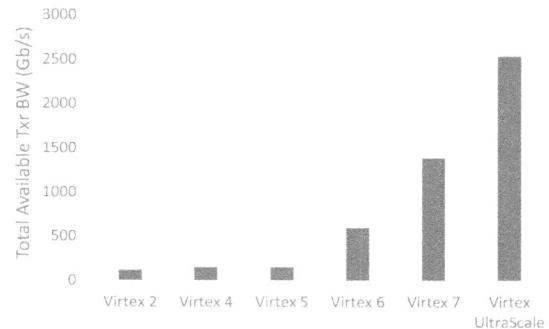

Figure 1: Growth of transceiver bandwidth in the Xilinx Virtex family from Xilinx datasheets [28]

1. INTRODUCTION

Field-programmable gate arrays (FPGAs) have seen widespread adoption in many industries thanks to their reduced engineering costs and faster time to market compared to application-specific integrated circuits (ASICs). The trade-offs that must be made when building designs on an FPGA rather than an ASIC were studied extensively in Kuon and Rose's work, where they showed a programmability overhead of $18 \times$-$35 \times$ in area and $3 \times$-$4 \times$ in critical path delay [20]. Despite this, the FPGA market has grown to approximately \$5B / year in revenue, with the communications segment accounting for approximately 45% of that revenue.[1] While FPGA vendors continue to push the total transceiver bandwidth on their devices (Figure 1), the question remains whether designers can, in fact, saturate the available bandwidth. The FPGA's soft reconfigurable fabric runs considerably slower than ASICs, forcing designers to handle high bandwidth I/O with wide, slow buses. Not only does this consume significant programmable interconnect area, it also poses design challenges for timing closure.

Despite these challenges, FPGA's have the key advantage of reconfigurability. This characteristic lends itself well to the recent advent of software-defined networking (SDN) [22]. Increasingly, computer networks need the ability to efficiently adapt to new routing and forwarding protocols as they become available. Some recent work has proposed augmenting ASIC designs with some programmability through the use of match tables [9]; the resulting chip has moderately higher hardware cost than a conventional ASIC but enables flexible packet header processing and lookup table reconfig-

---

[1]Based on revenue reported by the major FPGA vendors.

uration. Should FPGA switch designs succeed in efficiently supporting modern bandwidth demands, then they could provide even greater programmability suitable for SDN.

Recent work by Dai and Zhu presented a new 16×16 FPGA-based switch fabric design that can support an aggregate bandwidth of 160 Gbps [11]. It did so by leveraging the FPGA's hardened memory resources. Using this hard resource, rather than the general-purpose programmable logic fabric, to perform much of the switching is key to successfully handling high bandwidth I/O. Prior to Dai and Zhu's work, there was little published material that showed how a high-radix FPGA-based switch could be built that saturates the available transceiver bandwidth.

Still, Dai and Zhu's switch relies on the FPGA's soft (programmable) interconnect both to bring data from the transceivers to the memory modules and to connect the memory modules. These connections are wide, requiring both a large amount of programmable routing to make all the connections, and many pipeline registers to close timing. Such designs generally require many time-consuming compilations and iterative re-pipelining to close timing. This added design effort is a growing problem in FPGA design, especially with the ever-increasing I/O bandwidth being brought on the chip [1]. As this trend continues, FPGA architecture needs a new interconnect that raises the level of abstraction and makes it simpler to achieve timing closure.

Thanks to the work done by Dally and Towles [13], many chip multiprocessors (CMPs) have adopted Networks-on-Chip (NoCs) to cope with high on-chip bandwidth. Recent work by Abdelfattah and Betz has proposed augmenting FPGA architecture with an embedded NoC to cope with the growing FPGA design challenges [1]. Their work makes a strong case for a NoC that is hardened in the chip's silicon, as it achieves significantly better bandwidth per area than "soft" programmable NoCs while consuming a small fraction of the FPGA area. They show that such a NoC more than pays for itself even if it only handles the distribution of data from a single high-speed DDR3 interface throughout an FPGA design [1]. In this work, we seek to determine if additional gains can be realized in a complete application. Demonstrating such applications would encourage FPGA vendors to augment their chips with this new form of interconnect.

We present a new implementation of a switch fabric crossbar using a NoC-enhanced FPGA. Rather than using the hardened memory resources to perform the switching, the design instead uses the hardened NoC proposed by Abdelfattah and Betz. The NoC not only manages to replace the switching logic, but also most of the soft interconnect needed to bring data from the transceiver to the switch points. This results in significant area and latency savings compared to Dai and Zhu's memory-based switch. The design also provides a high degree of programmability suitable for SDN. Thus, we show that switch fabric design is an important FPGA application that can benefit from an embedded NoC. In doing so, we make the following contributions:

- Describe four different possible NoC-crossbar configurations that can efficiently support a 16×16 160 Gbps switch fabric;

- Develop a custom routing algorithm tailored specifically to this application and show it outperforms traditional routing algorithms;

N	16
Data Width	256 bits
Core Frequency	160 MHz
Latency	250 ns
Registers	36945 (12%)
LUTs	49537 (32%)
BRAMs	224 (27%)

Table 1: Memory-Based Switch Design on Virtex6-240T

- Compute the NoC-crossbar's hardware cost and compare it to crossbar designs by Dai and Zhu [11] and Goossens et al. [16];

- Perform detailed throughput and latency analysis and simulation to quantify the NoC-crossbar's performance; and

- Demonstrate the switch's potential to scale to higher bandwidths.

In Section 2, we give a brief overview of Dai and Zhu's memory-based switch, Abdelfattah and Betz's work on a NoC-enhanced FPGA and related work on ASIC NoC-based switch fabrics. Our NoC-based crossbar design is described in Section 3, along with various possible design configurations and routing algorithms. We prove analytically that the switch can support sixteen 10 GbE ports. The hardware cost of our design compared to Dai and Zhu's, as well as another FPGA-based NoC-switch, is presented in Section 4. Section 5 presents our performance evaluation of the design, and Section 6 describes how the design can be scaled to higher bandwidth traffic.

2. BACKGROUND

2.1 Memory-Based Switch

Dai and Zhu have proposed a new 16×16 switch fabric design on an FPGA that is able to handle 10-Gigabit Ethernet traffic (160 Gbps aggregate) [11]. The design is described as a "memory-based switch" (MBS), as it uses the FPGA's hardened SRAM to perform some of the switching function, with the remainder being handled by multiplexers built from the FPGA logic fabric to cascade the memory-based switches into a larger crossbar. Since the SRAMs are hard resources, they can run at a much higher clock frequency than the soft FPGA logic. In their design built on a Xilinx Virtex6-240T, the memory modules are set to run at four times the clock frequency of the soft fabric.

Table 1 summarizes the properties of the MBS design. In comparison, a straightforward logic-based crossbar implementation would have consumed significantly more FPGA area, likely being unable to fit on the Virtex6-240T device. The majority of the logic utilization in the MBS comes from the pipeline registers needed for the wide, long connections that bring data to and from the transceivers, as well as the multiplexers and clock crossing logic. The hardware cost and latency of the MBS are compared with the NoC-based switch in Sections 4 and 5.

90

Hard/Mixed/Soft NoC	Hard (Hard routers and links)
Number of Routers	64
Channel Width	64 bits
Core Frequency	925.9 MHz
Topology	Mesh

Table 2: Properties of the embedded NoC used in our switch design

2.2 NoC-Enhanced FPGA

Abdelfattah and Betz [1] propose the inclusion of a hardened NoC as a new FPGA resource. Their baseline architecture, as depicted in Figure 2, provides a mesh topology with routers equally spaced across the chip. Since the routers do not carry the overhead of programmability, the network can run at a higher clock frequency, approximately 1 GHz in a 65 nm process, while using significantly less area than a comparable all-soft NoC such as that of Papamichael and Hoe [25]. The NoC's routers interface with the FPGA's programmable logic through a fabric port that absorbs the clock crossing logic needed to bring data from the slow FPGA fabric to the faster NoC. The fabric port is capable of interfacing with FPGA designs of any frequency.

The links between routers may be either dedicated ("hard NoC") or use the FPGA's programmable interconnect fabric ("mixed NoC"). The hard NoC provides a fixed mesh topology and uses no programmable interconnect, thus easing the design and routing of the circuit logic and providing the fastest and most area- and power-efficient design [4]. The mixed NoC has the advantage of flexible, programmable topologies. Due to additional capacitive loading from the interconnection switches, the mixed NoC must run at a lower clock rate and/or insert additional pipeline registers.

In building our NoC-based switch, we use the "hard NoC" proposed by Abdelfattah and Betz, as it runs at a higher clock frequency, thus supporting higher throughputs. Table 2 summarizes the properties of the NoC used by our design. Details of the NoC's router architecture are described in Section 3.

2.3 NoC-Based Switch Fabric Design

NoCs have been used to design high-radix ASIC-based switches targetting supercomputer networks [6, 26]. Ahn *et al.* [6] improve the efficiency of their NoC-based switch design by exploiting properties of the traffic pattern. They focus on topological optimization to reduce area based on how global traffic patterns manifest themselves as particular local traffic patterns within a single switch. Underwood *et al.* [26] also focus on topology modifications to realize a 4 TB/s switch based on a NoC for HPC applications.

Several recent proposals show that a NoC can produce a more efficient switch design than a conventional crossbar [16, 19, 23]. There are several benefits to this approach: faster clock speed due to short wires and simple, distributed routers; improved load balancing and path diversity; and improved scalability. Goossens *et al.* [16] propose a switch design that features a mesh network, load balanced routing and a unidirectional flow from inputs on one side of the mesh to outputs on the other side. Follow-on work [23] improves upon their architecture by placing I/O on all four sides of the chip, reducing the size of the required network. They

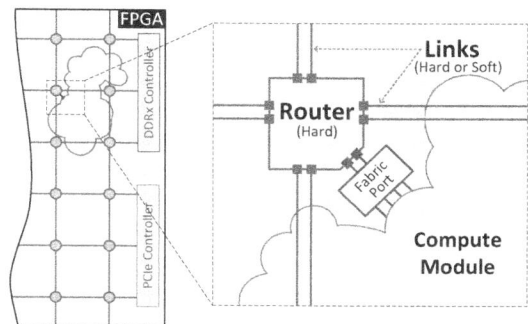

Figure 2: Depiction of the proposed hard NoC-FPGA fabric interface from Abdelfattah and Betz [1]

demonstrated a soft FPGA-based implementation of both of these designs [19].

In this work, we show that a flexible hard NoC coupled with the soft FPGA fabric greatly outperforms a logic-based NoC-switch implemented in a traditional FPGA. We also address the reality of FPGA transceivers being arranged in columns, generally on the east and west side of the chip, and the necessary overhead of bringing data from the transceivers to the NoC-crossbar. Despite using a hard NoC, we show that our design is flexible enough to implement different NoC-crossbar configurations and routing algorithms that can improve performance.

3. PROPOSED DESIGN

The relative economy of Dai and Zhu's memory-based switch was due to their careful optimization of the design to make maximal use of FPGA hard resources to avoid the programmability overhead. We propose to extend that concept by exploring use of the novel hard resource (NoC routers and links) that was proposed by Abdelfattah and Betz. Instead of "memory is the switch", we extend the concept of "the NoC is the switch" [16]. Using the 64-node embedded NoC, we design a crossbar that can support switching between 16 Ethernet ports each running at 10 Gbps. We call this design a "hard-NoC switch" (HNS).

The NoC's architecture is based on that presented by Abdelfattah and Betz [3], who used a parametrized open-source state-of-the-art virtual channel router [8]. The router has five ports, two virtual channels (VCs) per port, and an input buffer depth of ten flits per VC. The router has three pipeline stages and supports speculation which reduces the pipeline depth to two under low-load conditions. The router interfaces with the FPGA's soft logic through a programmable fabric port. Routers are connected with hard (non-programmable) links that are 64 bits wide. The NoC runs at a fixed clock frequency of 926 MHz [1]; thus, each link can support up to 59.3 Gbps.

Data arriving at the FPGA must go through some processing before being brought to the NoC to be switched to the appropriate output (Figure 3). The FPGA's transceiver performs clock recovery and determines the incoming serial data. The data is then converted from serial to parallel, with the exact parallel width chosen by the designer. For example, for 10G Ethernet, a conversion to 64-bit wide data at 160 MHz is reasonable. Once the data is brought onto the

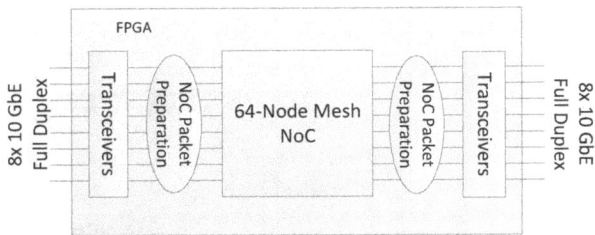

Figure 3: Conceptual overview: the NoC is the switch

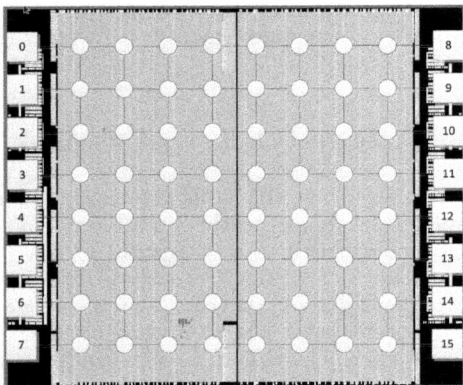

Figure 4: Stratix V floorplan showing transceiver columns at east and west sides with overlaid hard links and routers for NoC

FPGA fabric, the designer has the flexibility to do various amounts of processing before handing the data to the NoC. For example, packet header inspection and buffering can occur in the soft FPGA logic at 160 MHz. This logic examines the destination port of the Ethernet packet and inserts a NoC packet header indicating the appropriate destination router. The data is inserted into the NoC via the fabric port of the on-chip routers. Hardened clock conversion logic within the fabric port up-converts the data rate to the NoC clock rate of 926 MHz [1]; the data is then injected into the NoC. The NoC steers the data across the chip through multiple routers until it reaches the appropriate destination router, whose fabric port down-converts the data back to 160 MHz. More programmable logic can then buffer up flits until the entire Ethernet packet is ready to be sent out to the output transceiver. Note that by simply modifying the soft logic, the radix and communication protocol (e.g. 40G Ethernet or SONET) of the switch can be changed; this re-programmability is key to the success of FPGAs, making it especially suitable for SDN. In the evaluation of our design, we focus on the crossbar fabric functionality, as other aspects of a full-featured switch, such as packet processing and error checking, are included at the discretion of the designer.

The NoC has the additional flexibility of being able to implement various routing algorithms and flow control mechanisms. We describe four different possible routing algorithms in Section 3.2, and evaluate their performance in Section 5. A virtual channel (flit-buffered), credit-based flow control mechanism is used in our NoC, as it is supported by the router architecture [8] and takes advantage of the avail-

able VCs. In contrast, Goossens *et al.*'s NoC-based switch design uses store-and-forward (packet-buffered) flow control in its NoC in order to be amenable to mathematical analysis [16]. They also focus on 53B ATM cells as the unit of data transfer in their network; our proposed design can support Ethernet frames up to 1518B; supporting large packets with store and forward flow control would lead to infeasibly large buffer sizes. Virtual channel flow control outperforms store-and-forward in NoCs, as it better utilizes buffer space [14] and reduces latency [12].

3.1 NoC Injection Point Placement

As shown in Figure 4, the Altera Stratix V FPGA (28nm) has transceivers in the east and west columns of the chip, as is typical in commercial FPGAs for layout reasons. By assigning one router node per transceiver, we can connect any receiver to any transmitter and implement crossbar functionality. The FPGA's programmable interconnect allows designers to configure these connections to best suit the switch's application. Selecting the optimal transceiver injection points in the NoC is analogous to the memory controller placement problem studied by Abts *et al.* [5].

The simplest placement of injection points connects each transceiver to its nearest router, attaching only the 8 east- and west-most routers to a transceiver (Figure 5(a)). Routers in the middle of the chip do not inject or eject traffic, merely serving to connect the outer columns. We shall refer to this switch layout as "two-sided". Although the short connections have the benefit of no additional pipeline registers being consumed, the layout can result in poor utilization of the network – under certain traffic conditions, some links may be very heavily used while others carry no traffic at all, a situation explored in Section 5.

To better spread incoming traffic throughout the network, injection points can be distributed around the perimeter of the mesh, as in Figure 5(b), which we call the "four-sided" switch layout. Pipeline registers will be needed for the longer soft connections in order to close timing. One could also use the soft interconnect to set injection points in a "diamond" configuration, as in Figure 5(c). This injection point placement was inspired by the "diamond" configuration that proved to be efficient for memory controller placement [5]; however, the traffic patterns in the memory controller design and the switch design are quite distinct requiring further analysis and exploration.

Lastly, further extending the soft connections allows the 16 injection points to be configured in a conventional 4×4 mesh topology at the center of the 64-node network (Figure 5(d)). Such a switch configuration minimizes the average hop count between source-destination pairs, and thus has the most potential for latency savings. However, this comes at the cost of additional pipeline registers needed for the soft connections and reduced bisection bandwidth compared to the other configurations. We consider each of these four possible switch configurations in our evaluation.

3.2 Routing Algorithms

The NoC's routing algorithm determines the path taken by a packet from its source to its destination. An oblivious routing algorithm selects a path without considering the network's current state, such as contention along the chosen path. Algorithms that do consider the network's cur-

(a) Two–sided

(b) Four–sided

(c) Diamond

(d) Dense

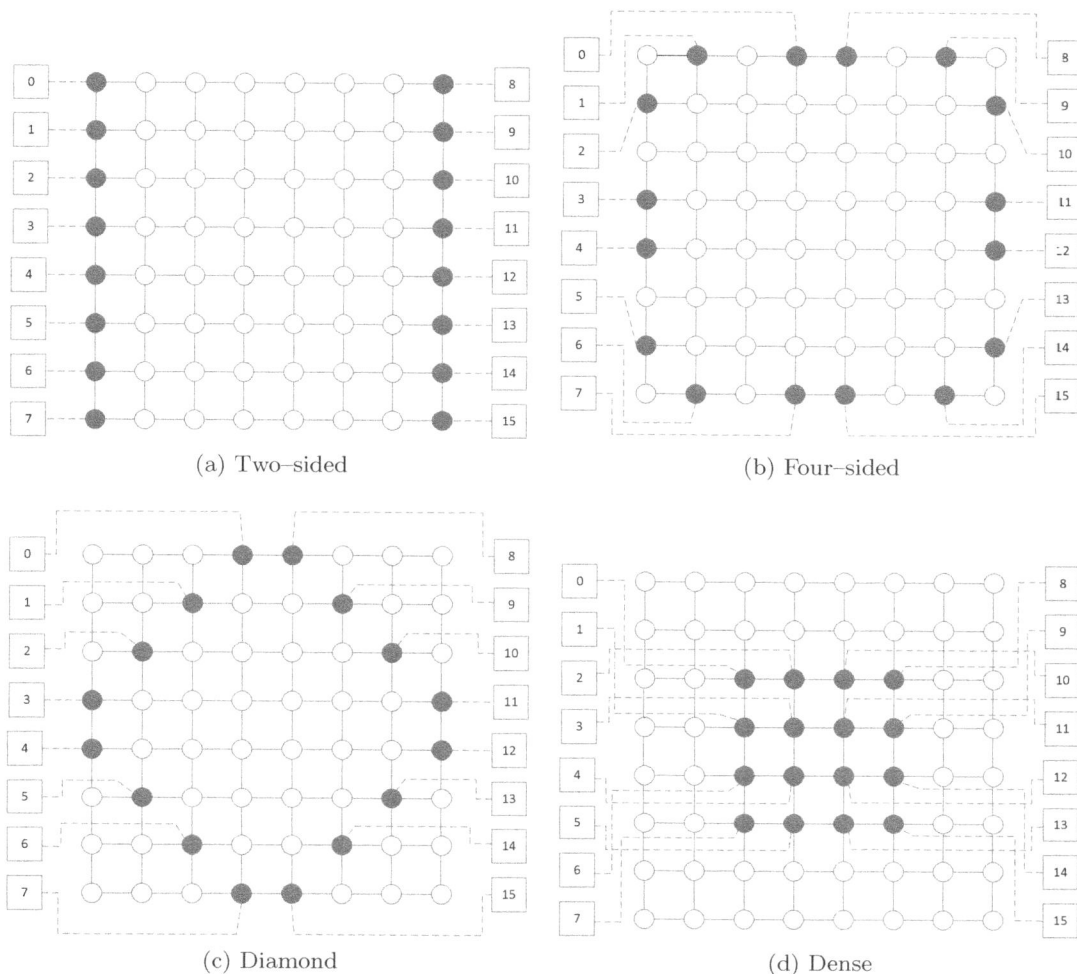

Figure 5: Switch configurations – dashed blue lines represent soft connections that use the FPGA's programmable interconnect. Solid black lines represent the hard (non-programmable) NoC inter-router links.

rent state, known as adaptive routing algorithms, attempt to steer away from paths with high contention.

The simplest routing algorithm for a mesh topology is dimension-order routing (DOR). Packets are routed to their destination along one dimension, then along the second dimension. Such an algorithm is both oblivious and deterministic; it does not consider path contention nor does it take advantage of path diversity. However, it has the benefit of being very simple, requiring very little overhead in the packets and in the routers. It also does not need VCs to break deadlock, as the algorithm is inherently deadlock free. For each of the four switch configurations described above, a YX DOR algorithm is tested, where all packets are sent to their destination first along the Y dimension (North/South), then along the X dimension (East/West).[2]

An oblivious routing algorithm such as DOR fails to adapt to stressful traffic patterns that result in high contention.

Thus, a minimal adaptive routing algorithm is also tested. Using local queue length as a metric for link contention, the minimal adaptive algorithm chooses the minimum route with the least contention at every hop. Choosing only among minimum routes ensures that packets travel from source to destination using the least amount of hops. However, this algorithm is not inherently deadlock free; two VCs are needed to break deadlock. One VC supports minimal adaptive routing while the other acts as an "escape" VC routing using DOR in case deadlock should occur [15].

As described by Dally and Towles [14], minimal adaptive routing only uses link contention data local to a router, so it can effectively balance *local* link loads, but not *global* link loads. We do not consider more complex globally adaptive algorithms because the nature of our traffic patterns can lead to much simpler traffic spreading algorithms. Since the location of the injection points in the network is known, a custom oblivious routing algorithm can be designed that spreads traffic globally across the network. A 64-node mesh with only 16 injection points can greatly reduce contention by keeping paths between source-destination pairs as disjoint

---

[2]YX routing was chosen over XY because it has a lower maximum channel load when injection points are arranged in columns.

```
int row, col;  // row and column of
               // intermediate node
row = src_row;

if (src and dest are on same side) {

  if (src and dest are <4 hops apart) {
    col = src_col;
  }
  else {
    col = rand{0,1} away from src_col;
  }

}
else {
  col = rand{1,2,3,4,5,6};
}
```

Figure 6: Algorithm for selecting intermediate node in the Column-Select routing algorithm

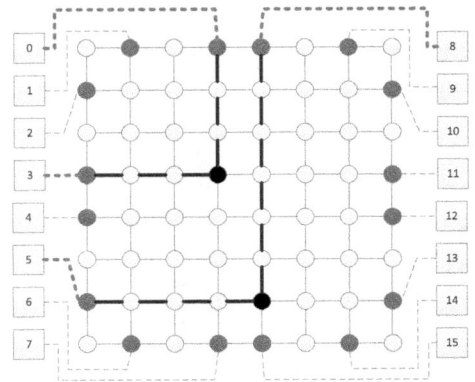

Figure 7: Illustration of the Smart DOR algorithm when routing node 5 to node 8, and node 3 to node 0. The paths between these two routes, which would have overlapped under YX routing, are separated by the algorithm. The black router represents the selected intermediate router.

as possible. We describe here two custom routing algorithms developed for the two-sided and the four-sided switch configurations. As both algorithms use two-phase routing, two VCs are sufficient to break deadlock [24]. On the other hand, a basic DOR algorithm already does a good job in keeping distinct source-destination paths separated in the diamond and dense configurations. We do not present a custom algorithm for those two configurations, since it was found that a custom oblivious routing algorithm does not improve latency much over DOR.

Two-Sided Custom Routing Algorithm: "Column-Select"

The two-sided switch layout with a DOR algorithm will result in all traffic using only the east- and west-most columns for routing in the Y dimension. Our custom routing algorithm focuses on better utilizing the middle six columns in the mesh. Similar to Valiant's algorithm [27], this is done by selecting an intermediate router in the mesh, routing all packets first to this intermediate node before routing to the destination. Routes to and from the intermediate node still follow YX routing. The algorithm for selecting the intermediate node is described in Figure 6. It aims to minimize the contention that occurs in the east- and west-most columns of the mesh, while still keeping most packets in minimal routes. To reduce contention caused by routing between nodes on the same side of the mesh, some packets are permitted to be routed one column away from the minimal route. Allowing these packets to deviate any further from the minimal route negates the latency savings from the reduction in contention. We call this algorithm "Column-Select", as it spreads traffic by selecting different columns for different routes. Unlike the other routing algorithms that we assess, Column-Select can theoretically cause packets to arrive out-of-order. Our simulations reveal that the frequency of out-of-order arrival is <0.2% for stressful permutation traffic.

Although Column-Select's non-determinism makes it more difficult to guarantee a low maximum channel load (as the same column may get picked in several consecutive instances), it does allow source-destination pairs to take advantage of path diversity. We show in Section 5 that the maximum channel load still remains low with both uniform random and permutations of stressful traffic.

Four-Sided Custom Routing Algorithm: "Smart DOR"

As with the two-sided custom algorithm, an intermediate router is analytically selected before sending the packet from the source. Since injection points are spread evenly across the perimeter of the mesh, the intermediate node selected is either the one on a XY or YX route. Of these two possible intermediate nodes, if there is one that is not on the perimeter of the mesh, then that is the one that is chosen. Otherwise, basic YX routing is used. We refer to this algorithm as "Smart DOR", as it is a deterministic algorithm that minimizes overlap of routes of distinct source-destination pairs by analytically selecting between an XY or YX route. Figure 7 illustrates how the algorithm prevents path overlap. Note that Smart DOR guarantees packets will arrive in order.

3.3 Crossbar Throughput Guarantees

To provide a crossbar functionality for the switch, the NoC must support the injection rate of the switch inputs. In other words, the NoC's maximum channel load at worst-case traffic must not exceed its link capacity. *Maximum channel load* is defined as the throughput of the channel carrying the highest throughput of all channels in the network for a given traffic pattern. Should the maximum channel load exceed the link capacity, the NoC would no longer be able to handle the injected data, resulting in packets being dropped. Of the four switch configurations described above, the two-sided configuration with YX routing is the least effective at spreading traffic across the network. Thus, by showing here that this configuration can support 16×16 switching of 10 Gbps traffic, then it can be concluded that the rest of the switch configurations and routing algorithms can support it as well. This is verified by simulation in Section 5.

A switch fabric crossbar must be able to switch traffic at the injection rate as long as every destination is only being driven by a single source at a given time. Since an output port can only sink traffic at up to the injection rate, a switch's ability to handle multiple sources sending traffic to a single destination is enabled not by its crossbar, but by its buffering and allocation mechanism. Efficient switch

Switch Implementation		LUT count	Register count	BRAM count	Tot. Equiv. LAB Area
Memory-Based Switch [11]		49537 (11.7%)	36945 (5.8%)	224 (9.7%)	**5850**
NoC-Based Switch	MDN [19]	75604 (17.8%)	52131 (8.1%)	0 (0%)	**7561**
	HNS Two-Sided	8960 (2.1%)	0 (0%)	-	**896**
	HNS Four-Sided	8960 (2.1%)	1024 (0.2%)	-	**999**
	HNS Diamond	8960 (2.1%)	1024 (0.2%)	-	**999**
	HNS Dense	8960 (2.1%)	2048 (0.3%)	-	**1101**

Table 3: Hardware cost of switch implementations. LUT count for HNS designs refers to equivalent LUT area of the hard NoC. Percentages refer to Stratix V-5SGTC5 resource budget (28 nm).

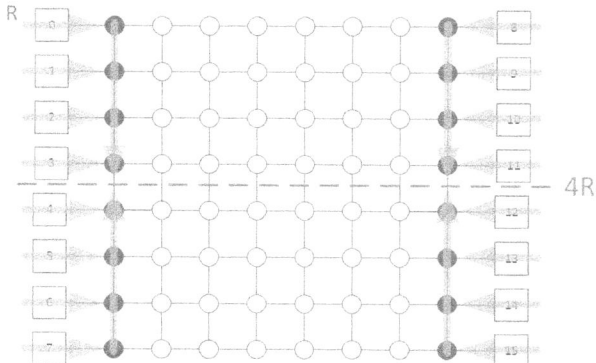

Figure 8: Worst-case maximum channel load for the two-sided crossbar configuration with YX DOR is 4R (R: injection rate)

buffering has been extensively studied in previous work, including Dai and Zhu's Combined Input and Grouped Crosspoint Queued architecture (GCQ) [11]. This paper focuses on the efficacy of using the NoC as the switch fabric's crossbar. Any necessary input or output buffering can be added to the crossbar by using the FPGA's memory resources.

Worst-case traffic for the two-sided crossbar can be derived as follows. Under YX routing, which does not allow 180° turns, the traffic across any horizontal cut (i.e. cutting vertical links) may only come from the east- and west-most columns of the mesh. Taking a horizontal cut across the middle of the mesh, the worst-case traffic occurs when all eight nodes from the bottom-half of the mesh are sending to the eight nodes at the top-half, and/or vice-versa (Figure 8). With YX routing, this results in traffic equivalent to four times the injection rate being sent across each of the east- and west-most links that are cut. Under this worst-case scenario, the maximum channel load is therefore four times the injection rate. For 10-Gigabit Ethernet traffic, the NoC's links must support 40 Gbps in order to maintain this throughput. The proposed 64-node, 64-bit wide NoC runs at 925.9 MHz [1], giving it a link capacity of 59.26 Gbps. We conclude that the 16×16 hard-NoC switch can guarantee 10 GbE throughput.

4. HARDWARE COST

Abdelfattah and Betz synthesize routers and hard links in a TSMC 65nm process [3]. Based on data provided by their web-based tool [2], the 64-node, 64-bit wide NoC con-

sumes an equivalent area of 896 Logic Array Blocks (LABs) for both its routers and links. This accounts for the area consumed by the NoC crossbar, but not for the soft links between the NoC and the transceivers. Knowing that the NoC's routers are equally spaced across the FPGA, three to four adjacent routers cover a distance of approximately 1/3 to 1/2 of the chip. Since soft links run at 160 MHz (Section 3), those that bypass three to four routers will therefore require one stage of pipeline registers to close timing. Since the soft links are bi-directional (64 bits in each direction), every soft link requiring pipelining will need 128 pipeline registers. The four-sided and diamond configurations have 8 soft links needing pipelining, while the dense configuration has 16, resulting in 1024 and 2048 pipeline registers consumed, respectively.

Dai and Zhu provided a working Verilog design targeting a Xilinx Virtex-6 FPGA (40nm), and list synthesis results by FPGA resource type (shown in Table 3). Goossens et al.'s NoC-based switch, originally designed for ASICs [16], was also implemented as a soft design in an FPGA by Karadeniz et al. [19]. Their design, called the Multidirectional NoC (MDN), was synthesized on a Xilinx Virtex-5 FPGA (65 nm). The resource consumption results from their synthesis include the resources consumed by their design's Network Interface (NI) blocks. One NI is placed at each of their switch's I/O ports to perform buffering and partitioning of packets prior to sending them into the NoC-based crossbar. As we wish to only compare the hardware cost of the crossbar, the cost of the NI is removed in the MDN results shown in Table 3.

The most advanced process for an FPGA in production is 28 nm, which is offered by both Altera (Stratix V) and Xilinx (Virtex 7). We therefore convert the memory-based and NoC-based switch designs to a 28 nm equivalent for comparison purposes. Assuming the resource consumption of each design remains approximately the same when synthesized on Altera's 28 nm device, we compute the hardware cost as a percentage of a Stratix V-5SGTC5 device (Table 3).[3] In order to compare the area cost of each switch configuration, the resource count of each resource type (look-up table (LUT), register, BRAM) is converted to a total equivalent LAB count. Block RAM (BRAM) area cost is equivalent to four times the LAB area cost on Stratix V devices [21]. To be conservative, we assume that registers used in Dai and Zhu's and Goossens et al.'s designs do not consume any additional resources by using the registers in the Logic Elements (LEs)

---

[3]Xilinx and Altera devices have very similar LUT and register architectures. Virtex devices use 18Kb BRAMs, which are nearly equivalent in size to Stratix's 20Kb BRAMs.

Flit size	64 bits
Packet Size	64-1504 bytes (mean: 580)
Injection Rate	10 Gbps
Injection Process	Bernoulli
Router Delay	3 cycles (2 w/ speculation)
Router Buffer Depth	10 flits
Flow Control	Virtual Channel
Num. VCs	2
Sim Warmup Period	30,000 cycles
Sim Data Collection Period	100,000 cycles

Table 4: Simulation Settings

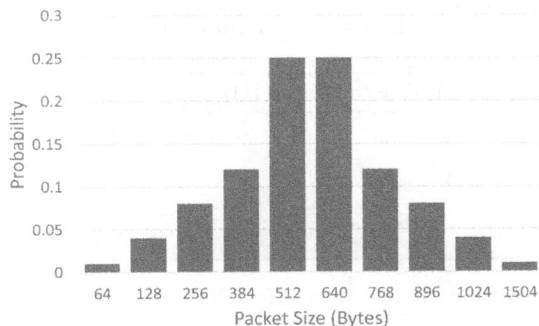

Figure 9: Distribution of packet sizes

that have already been consumed by the design's LUTs. On the other hand, we assume the registers used in the HNS designs consume their own LEs. Since 10 6-LUTs fit into Stratix LABs, we also assume that there are always exactly 10 LUTs per LAB.[4]

Our HNS switch configurations consume only 2.1% of the LUT area available, and little to no registers. When compared to the FPGA implementation of the MDN switch [19], the HNS consumes 6.9×-8.4× less area. The area savings is in large part due to the hardening of the NoC in the FPGA's silicon, as Abdelfattah and Betz showed that a hard NoC is 26× more area-efficient than an equivalent all-soft NoC [1].

Comparing to the memory-based crossbar, the HNS design consumes 5.5× less LUT area and 18× less registers. Moreover, the HNS does not use any BRAMs in the crossbar, unlike the MBS which relies on memory to perform much of the switching. Although use of the hardened SRAM resources allows the MBS to achieve better area-efficiency compared to the MDN switch, it still suffers from high amounts of pipelining for its soft connections. Additionally, while the MBS implements clock crossing logic in the FPGA's logic fabric, Abdelfattah and Betz's NoC includes a fabric port that subsumes this logic [1], leading to additional area savings. Overall, the HNS crossbar is 5.3×-6.5× more area-efficient than the MBS crossbar.

5. PERFORMANCE EVALUATION

Two key performance metrics must be evaluated for a switch: throughput and latency. The throughput supported by the NoC is dependent on its maximum channel load. This can be analytically determined based on the injection points placement and the routing algorithm used. Latency, on the other hand, is highly dependent on the applied traffic.

5.1 Evaluation Setup

In order to measure the average latency of the different proposed configurations of the HNS, the design was simulated in Booksim, a comprehensive interconnection network simulator [18]. Along with providing standard traffic generators and network topologies, the simulator also provides the ability to create custom traffic patterns and routing algorithms, which was necessary in the evaluation of the HNS. Booksim was also used by Dai and Zhu to evaluate the performance of the memory-based switch, enabling a fair comparison for the two designs.

---

[4]Note that it is possible to fit more than 10 LUTs in a single LAB if (n<6)-LUTs are used.

Table 4 summarizes the simulation settings used in the evaluation of latency. The flit size was set to match the channel width of the NoC. Dai and Zhu tested their memory-based switch only at two possible packet sizes, 32 bytes and 512 bytes. Since Ethernet frames range in size from 64 to 1,518 bytes [17], we instead test our switch with a distribution of packet sizes spanning this range, as this is both a more realistic and more difficult test scenario. Every time a source wished to inject a packet into the network, it randomly selected between ten different packet sizes based on the probability distribution shown in Figure 9. This distribution was not based on a specific application; although different applications that use Ethernet traffic have characteristic packet size distributions, we use a normal-like distribution to test our design in the most general scenario.

10-Gigabit Ethernet traffic can support data rates up to 10 Gbps. This implies that the average Ethernet data rate is below 10 Gbps. However, in order to demonstrate that the HNS can fully support 10 GbE, a Bernoulli injection process was used with an average injection rate of 10 Gbps. Although Ethernet traffic typically has bursty behaviour, the data rates of the bursts can never exceed the capacity of the Ethernet channel. Our latency measurements represent a more aggressive scenario as the injection rate may exceed 10 Gbps at certain intervals of the simulation.

The simulated router architecture is similar to the one proposed by Abdelfattah and Betz for their embedded NoC. The router operates with a 3-stage pipeline, with the possibility of being reduced to two stages given successful speculation. With 2 VCs and a buffer depth of 10 flits, the router's buffer size is far below the average size of Ethernet packets being routed. Although it is usually recommended that router buffer size be equal to a packet size for on-chip networks, that is unrealistic given the large packets in this application. The most critical factor in buffer sizing is being able to cover credit turnaround time, and our ten-flit buffers are more than sufficient for this purpose. Goossens et al. proposed splitting large packets into several smaller portions that are routed independently by the NoC and reassembled at the output [16]. However, since an Ethernet frame must be sent with no intra-packet gaps, the latency of a packet becomes at least the latency of the portion that takes the longest to reach the output.

The switch's general use case was modelled with uniform random traffic, a traffic pattern that models every transceiver being equally likely to send packets to any of the others. The same traffic pattern was used by Dai and

Zhu to test the memory-based switch, therefore providing a fair comparison point. The random nature of this traffic pattern permits cases where multiple sources are sending packets to a single destination at the same time – a case that does not need to be supported by a switch fabric's crossbar. Since our NoC-based crossbar has built-in buffering at the crosspoints (i.e. routers), it is able to support such traffic scenarios, unlike a conventional fully-connected crossbar. However, more strenuous traffic patterns with higher frequencies of multiple-sources-to-single-destination (MSSD) would need input and/or crosspoint/output buffering [11]. As mentioned previously, this can be added using the FPGA's memory resources.

Permutation traffic is typically used to stress a network [14]. To stress our crossbar, we run permutations of distinct source-destination pairs, where a single source drives a single destination for the entirety of the simulation. We use a script that searches for a traffic permutation that leads to the worst-case latency for each crossbar configuration under a single-source-to-single-destination (SSSD) traffic pattern. This traffic pattern also verifies that the HNS can support the rated aggregate bandwidth of the switch.

5.2 Throughput Results

The maximum channel load achieved by each routing algorithm for each HNS configuration can be seen in Table 5. The worst-case maximum channel load was analytically determined (Section 3.3), then verified using stressful SSSD traffic permutations in simulation. Maximum channel load under uniform random traffic (UR) was also measured in order to measure the throughput supported by the switch in the general case.

Having the injection points lined up in only two of the possible eight columns in the two-sided configuration leads to the worst maximum channel load. As shown in Section 3.3, a maximum channel load of four times the injection rate still allows the embedded 64-node NoC to handle 10-Gigabit Ethernet traffic, as the maximum supported link bandwidth is approximately six times the injection rate (~59 Gbps). By using our custom two-sided routing algorithm, Column-Select, the maximum channel load under stressful permutation traffic is reduced to twice the injection rate. The two-sided switch configuration can thus support the same throughput as the other configurations, and at the least area cost since it does not need additional pipeline registers for its soft transceiver-to-NoC connections. The Smart DOR custom four-sided routing algorithm achieves the same maximum channel load reduction.

If a designer wishes to keep the routing algorithm simple, then the results show that changing to a Diamond or Dense configuration can also reduce the maximum channel load to twice the injection rate, while keeping the routing algorithm as a simple YX DOR scheme. This flexibility highlights one of the benefits of using a FPGA; the switch designer can choose whether to use an improved routing algorithm or change the switch injection points in the NoC in order to achieve their desired throughput.

Overall, through routing algorithm and/or configuration changes, the worst-case maximum channel load of the NoC-based crossbar can be brought down to as low as twice the injection rate (Table 5). Since the maximum link capacity that can be supported by the 64-node, 64-bit wide NoC is 59.3 Gbps, the maximum injection rate that can be fully

Switch Configuration	Routing Algorithm	Max. Channel Load (R: injection rate)	
		UR	Permutation
Two-sided	YX	2R	4R
	Min Adapt	2R	4R
	Column-Select	1R	2R
Four-sided	YX	1R	4R
	Min Adapt	1R	4R
	Smart DOR	1R	2R
Diamond	YX	1R	2R
	Min Adapt	1R	2R
Dense	YX	1R	2R
	Min Adapt	1R	2R

Table 5: Maximum channel load of different switch configurations and routing algorithms

supported is 29.6 Gbps. Thus, the HNS crossbar can fully support a 16×16 switch with an aggregate bandwidth of 474 Gbps (29.6 Gbps per port). In the general case of uniform random traffic, maximum channel load can be reduced to the injection rate. Under such traffic, the crossbar can support an aggregate injection bandwidth of up to 948 Gbps (59.25 Gbps per port).

5.3 Latency Results

Packet and flit latency results for each HNS configuration are shown in Figure 10. The flit latencies are compared with the zero-load latency of each configuration. The zero-load latency is defined as the average flit latency over all source-destination pairs when there is no routing contention. This acts as the lower bound flit latency for each crossbar configuration.

When comparing the four different HNS configurations with basic YX routing, the two-sided configuration has the lowest area consumption, but worst latency. Because it connects each transceiver to its nearest router, it does not need any long connections that require pipeline registers. However, this is also its downfall; the six innermost columns of routers add unnecessary latency to the network. Using YX routing creates severe contention, as multiple source-destination pairs are routed along shared paths. Interestingly, the ability of minimal adaptive routing to adapt to network contention does not reduce latency in the two-sided configuration. This is likely because the majority of contention in the network happens when routing within the east-most or west-most columns of the mesh. Since the path choices available to minimal adaptive routing must be minimum paths, the algorithm cannot escape contention when routing within those two columns. A fully adaptive routing algorithm could better steer away from this contention, but would require a more complex router to support it [14].

In Section 3, we showed that a custom oblivious routing algorithm can be designed to make better use of the network resources, thereby reducing network contention. This is verified by Figure 10, as the Column-Select and Smart DOR algorithms lead to a packet latency reduction of 15.8% and 15.1%, respectively, under stressful permutation traffic.

The four-sided, diamond, and dense crossbar configurations take advantage of better injection point placement to

(a) Packet latency under UR traffic

(b) Packet latency under permutation traffic

(c) Flit latency under UR traffic

(d) Flit latency under permutation traffic

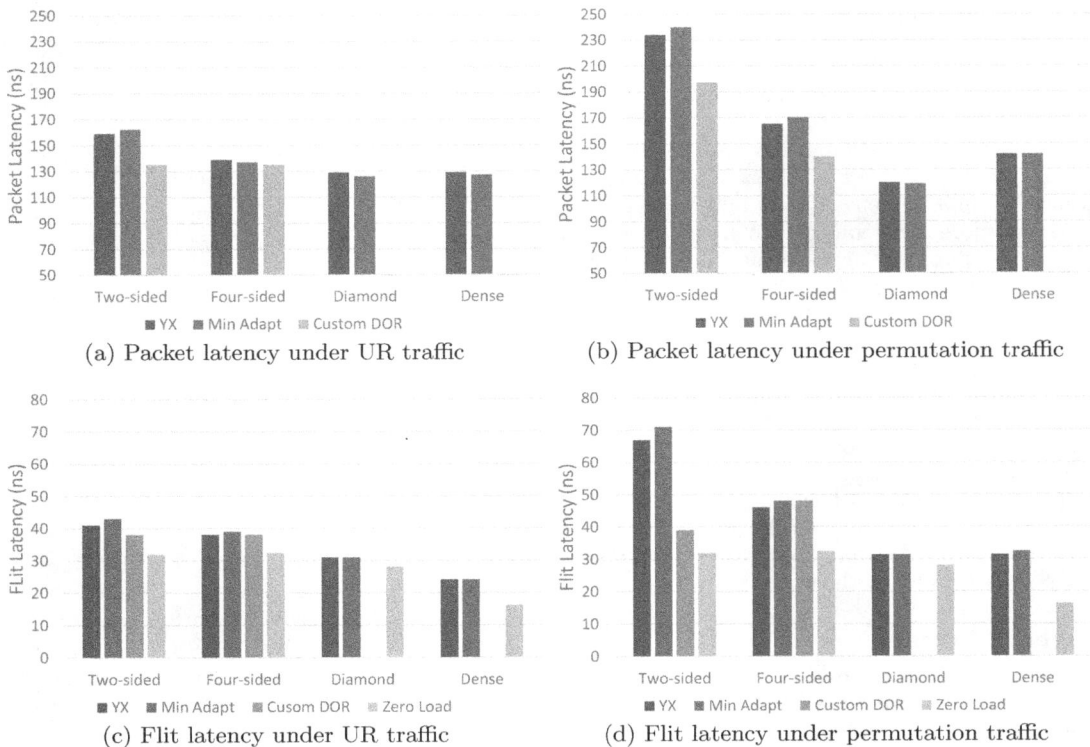

Figure 10: Packet and flit latency under uniform random (UR) and stress permutation traffic. "Custom DOR" refers to Column-Select for the two-sided configuration, and Smart DOR for the four-sided configuration.

reduce network contention. Under uniform random traffic, the dense configuration has the lowest latency results thanks, in part, to its reduced zero-load latency. However, the diamond configuration succeeds the most at spreading traffic throughout the 64-node mesh, thus achieving the best performance under stressful permutation traffic. With simple YX DOR, changing the crossbar configuration from two-sided to a diamond results in a latency reduction of 48.7%. In fact, permutations of SSSD traffic lead to better diamond performance compared to uniform random traffic where MSSD traffic is possible. This is because a diamond's injection point placement keeps most distinct source-destination routes separated, allowing it to handle SSSD traffic with minimal congestion. The fact that the diamond's flit latency approaches the zero-load latency of the configuration verifies that congestion is very low. The diamond configuration therefore performs best for the crossbar functionality of the switch fabric.

6. DISCUSSION

6.1 Area and Performance Wins

In proposing the HNS, we sought to present an important FPGA application that could benefit from an embedded NoC. The HNS yielded advantages over previous efficient FPGA-based switch designs, such as the memory-based switch, confirming that a NoC-enhanced FPGA would be a useful architecture for this application. In Section 4, we showed the hard-NoC switch was 5.3×-6.6× more area effi-

cient than the memory-based switch. In order to compare latency, we consider the fact that the crossbar traversal latency of Dai and Zhu's MBS is 250 ns (Table 1). The average crossbar traversal latency of the HNS is measured by the flit latency in Figure 10. The diamond configuration has an average flit latency of 31 ns under both uniform random and stressful permutation traffic – more than 8× better than the memory-based switch. This performance advantage can be largely attributed to the NoC's higher clock frequency (926 MHz vs. 160 MHz).

Freeing the FPGA's programmable logic in the HNS design leaves potential for other system components to run in parallel. Packet processing is a possible application, as it could perform packet manipulations necessary for a given protocol. Attig and Brebner showed that packet parsing logic that can handle up to 343 Gbps of Ethernet traffic consumes 9.2% of a Virtex-7 device [7], which can easily fit alongside the HNS.

One key feature of the embedded NoC is its ability to easily interface with all of the different FPGA I/Os. This includes the ability to communicate with DDR memory [1]. Should a certain output port on the FPGA be overloaded by a burst of traffic, packets destined for that port could be steered to the FPGA DDR controller through the NoC and temporarily buffered in DDR until the traffic burst subsides. Thus, packets could be preserved, rather than dropped, while network issues are handled elsewhere. Traffic management logic to handle such a scenario could be implemented in the FPGA's programmable logic fabric.

6.2 Preserving the FPGA's Generality

Direct network topologies, such as a mesh or torus, are not designed for high-radix switching applications. Instead, indirect networks, where a node can only act as either a terminal (injects/accepts packets) or a router (routes packets), provide better suited topologies. For example, Ahn *et al.* investigated indirect Clos and butterfly topologies for their ASIC-based NoC-switch [6]. However, the NoC-enhanced FPGA used in our design was not built specifically for a switch application; Abdelfattah and Betz sought to introduce a new communication architecture that would benefit many different FPGA applications [1]. A mesh is a low-cost topology that efficiently services the entire FPGA.

Despite using a mesh topology, the HNS design can still support high throughputs at low latencies, and scale to even higher throughputs in an area-efficient way (Section 6.3). The coupling of the FPGA programmable fabric with the hard NoC makes this possible; customizing the NoC injection points via the programmable interconnect led to 48.7% reduction in latency. Implementing application-specific routing algorithms also led to significant latency improvements. All of this was done without sacrificing the generality of the FPGA; an entirely distinct application could efficiently use the same NoC by setting up its own injection points and routing algorithm. In contrast, Karadeniz *et al.* also used the FPGA to build a NoC-based switch without sacrificing the FPGA's generality [19], but the cost of building the entire design from the FPGA fabric resulted in 6.9×-8.4× worse area consumption.

6.3 Scalability

With high bandwidth applications such as server virtualization and cloud computing becoming increasingly common, switch fabrics must be able to scale efficiently to serve growing bandwidth demands. This includes being able to support the next generation of Ethernet. Chanda of Cisco Systems described 40-Gigabit Ethernet as "the next logical step in the evolution of the data network," predicting that 40 GbE switching will completely replace 10 GbE by 2018 [10]. By using a NoC-enhanced FPGA for our switch fabric, we present a flexible design capable of being reconfigured to support new generations of traffic protocols.

We now propose scaling the HNS design to support 40-Gigabit Ethernet. If the aggregate bandwidth that needs to be supported by the switch remains 160 Gbps, then the radix of the switch reduces from 16×16 to 4×4. In this scenario, the architecture of the NoC-based crossbar does not need to change. The programmable logic bringing the data from the transceivers to the NoC can be reconfigured to split all 40-Gigabit traffic entering the chip into four different injection points into the NoC, which are independently switched to the output, then re-assembled by more programmable logic before being brought to the output transceiver. The NoC-based crossbar effectively remains 16×16, but is now supporting a 4×4 switch of higher port bandwidth through channel bonding. The FPGA's logic would need to be wide and fast enough to handle 40 Gbps, which can be done by running 128-bit wide buses at 312.5 MHz, or 256-bit wide buses at 156.25 MHz. Both of these can be supported by the latest FPGA devices.

It is more likely that the aggregate bandwidth demand on the switch will also increase with future generations of Ethernet. Let us consider a 16×16 switch fabric that must

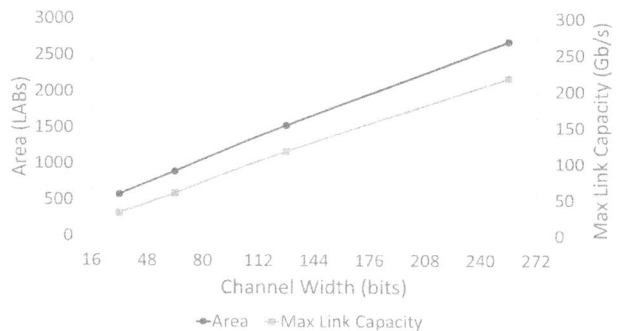

Figure 11: Hardware cost and max link capacity of varying the 64-node NoC's channel width [2]

support 40-Gigabit Ethernet at each of its ports – an aggregate bandwidth of 640 Gbps. As is shown in Section 5, the 64-node, 64-bit wide NoC-crossbar can fully support an aggregate bandwidth of 474 Gbps, while offering up to 948 Gbps in the uniform random case. To fully support a 640 Gbps switch, architectural changes to the NoC are needed.

We propose widening the NoC channel width from 64-bit to 128-bit as an efficient and feasible method of scaling the crossbar. Widening the NoC's channels increases its link capacity from 59.26 to 117.4 Gbps, at an area increase of 1.7× (Figure 11). The total logic area of the 64-node, 128-bit wide NoC still only consumes 3.6% of a Stratix V-5SGTC5 FPGA. Thus, this widened NoC can efficiently implement a 16×16 crossbar capable of fully supporting up to 939 Gbps in aggregate bandwidth (58.7 Gbps at each port).

Future generations of Ethernet will undoubtedly support bandwidths that go beyond 40 Gbps. 100-Gigabit Ethernet is already on the horizon, with talk of 1-Terabit Ethernet soon becoming a possibility. As illustrated in Figure 11, widening channel width beyond 128 bits can continue to provide even higher throughput, at the cost of more transistor consumption. We predict that as the number of transistors on a chip continues to grow in future generations of FPGAs, having an embedded NoC with wider channels will remain a small fraction of the device's area budget. Thus, widening the NoC's channel width provides a means to efficiently scale the HNS design to future generations of Ethernet.

7. CONCLUSION

As FPGAs continue to support increasingly high I/O bandwidth, there is a growing need for a new FPGA interconnect architecture that can better support such data rates. Abdelfattah and Betz propose embedding a network-on-chip in the FPGA silicon, thereby providing designers a new interconnect that raises the level of abstraction and makes it simpler to close timing for high throughput designs.

In this work, we present an important FPGA application that can benefit from an embedded NoC. A network switch fabric designed using the NoC to perform the crossbar function is shown to support 16×16 switching at 10-Gigabit Ethernet rates. Additionally, we show how a designer can use the FPGA's reconfigurable fabric to customize the switch to support different traffic protocols and different NoC injection points. Four different injection point placements are proposed. Arranging the traffic injection points in a "diamond" configuration leads to the best latency results, offering a 48.7% improvement over a "two-sided" configuration.

Customizing the NoC's routing algorithm also proved to be an effective way to improve its performance. By developing a Column-Select algorithm for the two-sided configuration, and a Smart DOR algorithm for the four-sided configuration, we achieve 15.8% and 15.1% latency reduction, respectively. Additionally, the algorithms allow the configurations to improve their maximum supported aggregate bandwidth from 237 Gbps to 474 Gbps, matching the bandwidth's of the "diamond" and "dense" configurations. Each of the configurations also managed to support up to 948 Gbps in aggregate bandwidth given uniform random traffic.

The NoC-based design is compared to another implementation of a switch done by Dai and Zhu using the traditional FPGA resources. Dai and Zhu's switch design takes advantage of the FPGA's hardened SRAM resources to saturate the transceiver bandwidth. The diamond HNS design consumes $5.8\times$ less area and achieves an $8.1\times$ latency reduction.

Finally, we show that widening the channels of the embedded NoC is an effective way to scale the switch to support future generations of Ethernet traffic, such as 40 and 100 GbE. The "hard-NoC switch" can support the high bandwidth of modern switch fabric design while preserving significant flexibility through the use of the FPGA's programmable logic. We conclude that network switch fabric designs clearly benefit from a NoC-enhanced FPGA, providing support for the inclusion of an embedded NoC in future FPGA devices.

8. ACKNOWLEDGEMENTS

The authors would like to thank Mohamed Abdelfattah and Mario Badr for their insightful discussions and opinions, David Lewis and Tim Vanderhoek for providing Stratix V relative block areas, and the anonymous reviewers for their valuable feedback. This work was supported by NSERC, Altera, and a QEII-GSST scholarship.

9. REFERENCES

[1] M. Abdelfattah and V. Betz. The case for embedded networks-on-chip on FPGAs. *IEEE Micro*, pages 80–89, 2013.

[2] M. S. Abdelfattah. NoC Designer. http://www.eecg.utoronto.ca/~mohamed/noc_designer.html, 2013. Accesed: 2014-05-07.

[3] M. S. Abdelfattah and V. Betz. Design tradeoffs for hard and soft FPGA-based Networks-on-Chip. In *FPT*, pages 95–103, 2012.

[4] M. S. Abdelfattah and V. Betz. The power of communication: Energy-efficient NOCS for FPGAS. In *FPL*, pages 1–8. IEEE, 2013.

[5] D. Abts, N. D. Enright Jerger, J. Kim, D. Gibson, and M. H. Lipasti. Achieving predictable performance through better memory controller placement in many-core CMPs. In *SIGARCH*, volume 37, pages 451–461. ACM, 2009.

[6] J. H. Ahn, S. Choo, and J. Kim. Network within a network approach to create a scalable high-radix router microarchitecture. In *HPCA*, pages 1–12. IEEE, 2012.

[7] M. Attig and G. Brebner. 400 Gb/s programmable packet parsing on a single FPGA. In *ANCS*, pages 12–23. IEEE, 2011.

[8] D. U. Becker. *Efficient microarchitecture for network-on-chip routers*. PhD thesis, Stanford University, 2012.

[9] P. Bosshart, G. Gibb, H.-S. Kim, G. Varghese, N. McKeown, M. Izzard, F. Mujica, and M. Horowitz. Forwarding metamorphosis: Fast programmable match-action processing in hardware for SDN. In *SIGCOMM*, pages 99–110. ACM, 2013.

[10] G. Chanda. The market need for 40 gigabit ethernet. Technical report, Cisco Systems, 2012.

[11] Z. Dai and J. Zhu. Saturating the transceiver bandwidth : Switch fabric design on FPGAs. In *FPGA*, pages 67–75, 2012.

[12] W. J. Dally. Virtual-channel flow control. *IEEE TPDS*, 3(2):194–205, 1992.

[13] W. J. Dally and B. Towles. Route packets, not wires: On-chip interconnection networks. In *DAC*, pages 684–689. IEEE, 2001.

[14] W. J. Dally and B. P. Towles. *Principles and practices of interconnection networks*. Elsevier, 2004.

[15] J. Duato. A new theory of deadlock-free adaptive routing in wormhole networks. *TPDS*, 4(12):1320–1331, 1993.

[16] K. Goossens, L. Mhamdi, and I. V. Senin. Internet-router buffered crossbars based on networks on chip. In *DSD*, pages 365–374, 2009.

[17] IEEE Standard 802.3 for Ethernet. Technical report, IEEE, 2012.

[18] N. Jiang, D. U. Becker, G. Michelogiannakis, J. Balfour, B. Towles, D. Shaw, J. Kim, and W. Dally. A detailed and flexible cycle-accurate network-on-chip simulator. In *ISPASS*, pages 86–96. IEEE, 2013.

[19] T. Karadeniz, L. Mhamdi, K. Goossens, and J. J. Garcia-Luna-Aceves. Hardware design and implementation of a network-on-chip based load balancing switch fabric. In *ReConFig*, pages 1–7, 2012.

[20] I. Kuon and J. Rose. Measuring the gap between FPGAs and ASICs. *TCAD*, 26(2):203–215, 2007.

[21] D. Lewis. Altera, personal communication, April 2014.

[22] N. McKeown, T. Anderson, H. Balakrishnan, G. Parulkar, L. Peterson, J. Rexford, S. Shenker, and J. Turner. OpenFlow: enabling innovation in campus networks. *SIGCOMM*, 38(2):69–74, 2008.

[23] L. Mhamdi, K. Goossens, and I. V. Senin. Buffered crossbar fabrics based on networks on chip. In *CNSR*, pages 74–79, 2010.

[24] T. Nesson and S. L. Johnsson. ROMM routing on mesh and torus networks. In *SPAA*, pages 275–287. ACM, 1995.

[25] M. K. Papamichael and J. C. Hoe. Connect: Re-examining conventional wisdom for designing NoCs in the context of FPGAs. In *FPGA*, pages 37–46. ACM, 2012.

[26] K. Underwood, E. Borch, J. Sizer, T. Stremcha, and M. Strom. Evaluating on-die interconnects for a 4TB/s router. In *ICS*, pages 203–212, 2013.

[27] L. G. Valiant and G. J. Brebner. Universal schemes for parallel communication. In *Theory of computing*, pages 263–277. ACM, 1981.

[28] Xilinx Inc. Xilinx Virtex Family Datasheets.

Laying out Interconnects on Optical Printed Circuit Boards

Apostolos Siokis, Konstantinos Christodoulopoulos, Emmanouel (Manos) Varvarigos
Computer Engineering and Informatics Department, University of Patras, Greece, and
Computer Technology Institute and Press – Diophantus, Patras, Greece
{siokis,kchristodou,manos}@ceid.upatras.gr

ABSTRACT

Short distance optical interconnections, on-printed circuit boards, on-backplanes, and even on-chip, are a promising solution for replacing copper interconnections in future Data Center and HPC systems. Since photonic technology introduces new network building blocks, topology design for all the packaging levels should be reconsidered. This paper focuses on the on-board level of the packaging hierarchy, and proposes lay-out strategies for optical interconnection networks on optical printed circuit boards (OPCBs), based on direct topology families (tori, meshes and fully connected networks). We also describe a methodology for designing OPCBs given a set of input parameters, including building blocks specifications as well as traffic demands. The on-board topology design methodology generates all the feasible designs within the topology families examined, following our proposed OPCB lay-out approach, and selects the optimal designs based on specific optimization criteria.

Categories and Subject Descriptors

C.2.1 [**Computer-Communication Networks**]: Network Architecture and Design - *Network topology*; C.5.4 [**Computer System Implementation**]: VLSI Systems

Keywords

Optical interconnects; Optical printed circuit boards; Waveguides; On-board topology lay-out; Direct networks

1. INTRODUCTION

The ever-increasing network load in Data centers (DC) and High-Performance Computing (HPC) systems pushes the electrical-copper interconnection technologies to their limits. As the need for bandwidth grows, electrical interconnects cannot keep pace due to wiring density [1,2], high power dissipation, increased signal degradation and crosstalk between neighboring channels. On the other hand, photonic technologies offer superior bandwidth-distance product at much lower energy consumption. These reasons lead to the replacement of copper based communication in a from-outside-to-the-inside manner [3]: fiber optics have already replaced copper in long-haul (MAN and WAN) telecom systems in the range of 10's to 10000's of km's, and are penetrating shorter distances (<= 100's of meters) in campus and enterprise LANs. At this point active optical cables are the norm for rack-to-rack communication in DC and HPC systems.

Even so, power consumption of data communication is still daunting. Prediction studies for performance, bandwidth requirements and power consumption, back in 2010, projected that a 10PF HPC machine in 2012 would require 5MW [24]. One of the top500 HPC systems, 2011 K-supercomputer with 10PF performance, requires more than double the predicted amount of power (~12.7 MW) [25]. The global demand for electricity from data centers was around 330bn kWh in 2007 and it is projected to rise to more than 1000bn kWh by 2020 [26]. So, to cope with both the energy and bandwidth limitations, optical technologies target to be deployed in even shorter (in-the-box) distances in the near future: board-to-board, on-board (module-to-module), and even on-chip (distances < 20 mm).

This new era brings an entirely new technology portfolio of network modules for short-distance communication. These include: Optical Printed Circuit Boards (OPCBs), printed with multi-mode (usually polymer) or single-mode (polymer or glass) waveguides, optical transceiver chips (usually VCSELs – Vertical Cavity Surface-Emitting Laser for Tx, and PDs – PhotoDiodes for Rx), optoelectronic and photonic routers, Arrayed Waveguide Gratings (AWGs), backplanes for passive board/daughtercard optical interconnection, chip-to-board coupling technologies, optical RAMs, among others. Recently completed and ongoing research efforts include IBM's "Terabus" for tranceiver optochips-on-optoboard and "C2OI" for intra-chip and off-chip communication [4], IBMs-Columbia University research on photonic networks-on-chip [5], Intel-UCSB joint initiative research on silicon laser, modulator and amplifier configurations [6]. Several European research initiatives have focused on specific optical interconnection technologies (like FP7 POLYSIS [7]).

FP7 PHOXTROT [8] investigates the development of low cost and energy efficient optical interconnects at chip-to-chip, board-to-board and rack-to-rack levels of the packaging hierarchy. Within PHOXTROT, various photonic technologies are being developed, but the research activities also examine how these can be deployed at the different packaging levels. Thus, to take advantage of the new photonic technologies we need to reconsider the architectures for HPC systems and DCs at the different hierarchical levels. Architectural issues such as on-board, on-backplane and system level topologies, number of waveguides for chip-to-board communication, number of routers on board, number of channels/waveguides for router-to-router communication, lay-out of topologies in waveguide levels, board pinout, switching paradigms (packet vs. circuit) are issues that need to be re-visited, re-addressed, and re-evaluated.

A key difference between electrical and optical interconnects is the physical layer, which constrains the interconnects that can be designed. While related constraints in electrical interconnects are well understood and subsystems and whole systems building methodologies are well established, there is no related work in optical interconnects, especially for the lower hierarchical levels. A recent survey [9] discusses the benefits of photonic technologies for next generation HPC systems and DCs, but mainly for inter-rack communication. A number of on-board optical architectures that use such "in-the-box" photonic technologies have been proposed, including a shared optical bus [18], a high-speed clock distribution tree [19], a meshed waveguide architecture for optical backplanes [20] and an optical bus for optical backplane interconnections [21].

Since the underlying technologies and the packaging constraints of the various levels of the packaging hierarchy determine the feasible system level topologies/architectures, we chose a bottom-up approach and focused on the packaging of optical modules on boards. In particular, we propose lay-out strategies for on-optical printed circuit board (OPCB) topologies, "translating" existing lay-out strategies for electrical PCBs into a form suitable for OPCBs. We mainly target HPC system designs and thus we focus on direct networks such as meshes, tori and fully connected networks. We also present a general methodology for designing interconnects on OPCB, using a set of packaging and required performance parameters as inputs. Our methodology incorporates the lay-out strategies we propose, but it can also be enriched with other strategies. To the best of our knowledge, this is the first work that presents a structured lay-out strategy for OPCBs. There are software suites for OPCB design, but, however, they focus on physical layer and propagation modeling of the waveguides and do not provide design guidelines/methodologies for topology lay-outs on OPCBs. Although we focus on OPCBs, we plan to re-apply our approach (somewhat modified) for higher packaging levels (rack, set of racks, up to the whole system). Note that methodologies for topology design have been presented in the past [10,11], but aimed for electrical/copper interconnects. Compared to that, we put more emphasis on and have a more detailed model for the lay-out strategy of the (optical) topologies.

The contributions of this paper are:

- We outline the similarities and differences between lay-out models for electrical interconnects and optical waveguided communications in order to capture the peculiarities of the latter in a lay-out model suitable for optical interconnects (Subsection 2.3).

- We propose a way to organize and lay-out an optical router chip and hosts chips in network nodes, suitable for direct network topologies (Subsection 2.4).

- We propose a lay-out strategy for optically interconnected direct topologies of nodes, suitable for OPCBs (Subsection 2.3).

- We propose an articulate methodology for on-OPCB topology design that incorporates our lay-out strategies and takes into account network performance metrics while keeping in mind that the OPCB will be part of a bigger system (Section 4). This methodology maximizes the number of hosts on-OPCB given the available board area while using the minimum number of (active) router chips, but other optimization objectives can be easily employed.

- We apply our designing OPCB methodology to highlight potential bottlenecks and to explore the benefits of technological advancements in photonic integration (Section 5).

This paper is structured as follows. In Section 2 we present lay-out strategies for interconnects on OPCBs. In Section 3 we introduce the performance metrics that we consider. In Section 4 we present our methodology for designing on-board interconnects,

and we apply it to obtain the results presented in Section 5, using PHOXTROT subsystem specifications as input. Conclusions follow in Section 6.

2. LAY-OUT STRATEGY FOR INTERCONNECTS ON OPCBs

In this section we present lay-out strategies for interconnection networks on OPCBs. These lay-out strategies are incorporated in our topology design methodology described in section 4. To determine the number of modules and the topologies (within the topology families considered) that are *feasible* in the on-board packaging level we need to calculate the required area and worst case losses of each design. So we start in Subsection 2.1 by describing the topology families (tori, meshes, fully connected) we consider, followed in Subsection 2.2 by general electronic lay-out strategies for them. Then, in Subsection 2.3 we reveal the differences between copper and waveguided interconnections and describe our strategy for laying out on OPCBs. In Subsection 2.4 we describe the way we organize optical interconnection building blocks (routers and transceiver optochips) in network nodes. Finally, in Subsection 2.5 we briefly discuss waveguide length matching.

2.1 Considered network families

Interconnects can be distinguished in two classes: (a) direct networks in which every host is directly connected to a routing element, and (b) indirect networks in which there are routing elements with no hosts connected to them. The majority of direct topologies are either configurations of or isomorphic to meshes, tori, k-ary n cubes, while popular indirect topologies are trees (including fat-trees), clos, and butterfly networks.

In this work we target mainly HPC environments and thus we focus on direct networks. More specifically, we focus on meshes, tori and fully-connected networks (FCN). Note that several HPC systems in the Top500 are built with tori/meshed networks [12,13,14].

Formally [15], a n-dimensional mesh has k_1 x k_2 x ... x k_n nodes, k_i nodes along dimension i, where $k_i \geq 2$ and $1 \leq i \leq n$. Note that since this is a direct network, the nodes correspond to a routing element and one or more hosts that are directly connected to it. A node x is logically identified by n coordinates $(x_1, x_2, ... x_n)$, where $1 \leq x_i \leq k_i$ for $1 \leq i \leq n$. Two nodes x and y are neighbours and are connected through a link if and only if $y_i = x_i$ for all i, $1 \leq i \leq n$, except for one coordinate j, where $y_j = x_j \pm 1$.

A n-dimensional torus is the equivalent mesh with added wrap-around links. Formally, in a k_1 x k_2 x ... x k_n torus, two nodes x and y are neighbours if and only if $y_i = x_i$ for all i, $1 \leq i \leq n$, except one, j, where $y_j = (x_j \pm 1)$ mod k_j.

Finally, in a fully connected network (FCN) of N_r nodes, every node is connected with the other N_r - 1 nodes.

2.2 Lay-outs for electrical interconnection networks

The authors in [27] present lay-outs for a variety of interconnection network topologies, and provide formulas for the required lay-out area and required tracks, assuming copper wiring.

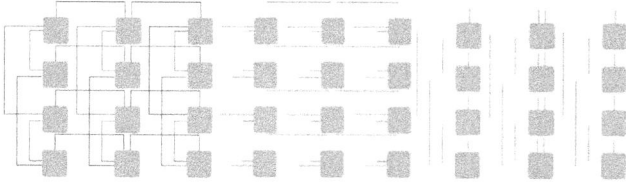

Figure 1. (a) 2-D grid array (3x4) lay-out of 3x2x2 mesh, (b) and (c) layer one and two implementing the horizontal and vertical wires.

The model used, following the well known Thomson model, assumes at least 2 layers of wiring, where odd layers include horizontal wires, while even layers the vertical ones, to avoid crossings. All connections between nodes are realized on a 2-D grid, and all bends are 90^0 (when viewing both layers), implemented using "vias" connecting the two layers. Note that as discussed above, for the indirect networks under study, nodes consist of a routing element and one or several host attached to it, while the network is build by connecting the routing elements. In the next section we will discuss how to build nodes, but here we consider them as a single block.

In this paper we examine two types of network topology lay-outs: collinear and 2-D. In the former all network nodes are placed along a line, while in the latter nodes are placed along rows and columns, forming a 2-D grid array. Figure 1(a) depicts an example of a 3x2x2 mesh, laid out in a 2-D grid of 3x4 nodes, with wires also laid out in a 2-D grid. Note that the wiring, although depicted in one layer, is done in 2 (or more) layers, and Figure 1 (b) and (c) show the related 2 level implementation. 2-D lay-outs are constructed using collinear lay-outs along the rows and columns. A single row of the 2-D lay-out in Figure 1(a) is a collinear lay-out of 3 nodes, requiring 1 wiring track. A single column of the 2-D lay-out is a collinear lay-out of 4 nodes (2x2), requiring 3 wiring tracks. In what follows we will only consider collinear lay-outs, having in mind that 2-D lay-outs are constructed by using them.

We have calculated the number of tracks for collinear lay-outs of meshes and tori of arbitrary dimensions using the strategies in [27]. For a collinear lay-out of a k_1 x k_2 x ... x k_n torus, the number Y of tracks parallel to the lay-out direction is:

$$Y = \sum_{i=0}^{n-1}(a_i \cdot \prod_{j=0}^{i} k_j), \ a_i = \begin{cases} 1, if \ k_{i+1} = 2 \\ 2, if \ k_{i+1} > 2 \end{cases}, \ k_0 = 1 \quad (1)$$

For the equivalent mesh, the number of tracks would be the same as Eq. (1) but with $a_i = 1$ in all cases. The number of tracks for a strictly optimal collinear lay-out of a fully connected network (FCN) is $\lfloor N^2/4 \rfloor$ [27]. We consider only collinear FCNs, because this topology family is difficult to be layed-out in a 2-D grid.

We have also calculated the worst case crossings for tori and meshes of arbitrary dimensions as well as FCNs, for the above discussed lay-out strategies. Both the worst-case crossings number and the number of tracks will be used for the estimation of the worst-case losses.

In the FCN, a *type-i* link connects two nodes whose addresses differ by *i*. The $N(N-1)/2$ links of the FCN can be classified into type 1, 2, 3, ..., $N-1$, and there are $N-i$ type-i links. In the FCN lay-outs of [27], all nodes meet the same number of crossings in the worst case. The largest number of crossings appears in the $\lceil \frac{N}{2} \rceil$ and $\lfloor \frac{N}{2} \rfloor$ links of every node. We calculate the

number of crossings for link $(1, 1 + N/2)$. This link will meet $\left(\lceil \frac{N}{2} \rceil - 1 \right)$ links from nodes 2, 3, ... $\lceil \frac{N}{2} \rceil$. Thus, the total number of worst case crossings is $\left(\lceil \frac{N}{2} \rceil - 1 \right) \cdot \left(\lceil \frac{N}{2} \rceil - 1 \right)$.

For k_1 x k_2 x ... x k_n meshes and tori we do not use a closed-type formula, but we calculate the number of crossings in a recursive manner. The mesh and torus collinear lay-outs of [27] are also built recursively using a bottom-up approach, starting with a single dimensional ring (or chain array for mesh) and inductively moving to higher dimensions. The worst case crossings appear in (but not necessarily only in) the highest dimension (dimension n) links: the links that connect k_n segments of the k_1 x k_2 x ... x k_{n-1} subnetworks (or a wraparound link in a torus). In brief, for every dimension i, $1 \leq i \leq n$, we create a vector of size $k_1 \cdot k_2 \cdot ... \cdot k_{n-1}$, using subvector patterns of size $k_1 \cdot k_2 \cdot ... \cdot k_{i-1}$ and repeat them $k_i \cdot ... \cdot k_{n-1}$ times. A vector in dimension i will contain the number of crossings that the highest dimension (dimension n) links will exhibit due to links of dimension i at hand. Adding elementwise the resulting n vectors we get a final $k_1 \cdot k_2 \cdot ... \cdot k_{n-1}$ vector that contains the total number of crossings for the highest dimension links. The number of the worst case crossings is the max element of this vector.

2.3 Lay-outs of interconnection networks on OPCBs

The main differences between optical waveguided communication and the copper interconnects described above, from the lay-out point of view, are:

(a) waveguide bends require a bending radius, and

(b) crossings are allowed in the same layer (a crossing angle of $90°$ is preferable due to losses and crosstalk) [22, 23].

The lay-outs of direct topologies described in Subsection 2.2 can be applied on OPCBs with the following modifications. As before, network nodes form the building blocks and are constructed by one router chip and hosts following the strategy described in the next Subsection. We assume two symmetrical layers, each for one direction of communication between nodes. Given the collinear lay-out of nodes (remember that 2-D lay-outs are constructed from row- and column-wise collinear layouts), at each layer the links are laid out in a 2-D grid, bends have a given radius, and crossings are allowed to occur.

In case where more than one link is needed between two nodes and since bends are (space and loss) expensive, we route multi-waveguide links together, as bundles, in a single "waveguide track". Waveguides distance within a track is standard pitch (250µm) – or the waveguide pitch preferred, but since bending radius and chips sizes are at least two orders of magnitude larger, we neglect tracks width in our calculations. The first track parallel to the collinear lay-out direction of nodes is placed at r_o space from the node, while the space S left between following tracks is related to the desired waveguide crossing angle θ and the bending radius r_o as follows:

$$S = (1 - cos\theta) \cdot r_o \quad (2)$$

Thus, according to Eq. (2), if $90°$ crossings are used, the tracks spacing equals the bending radius ($S=r_o$). Smaller bending radius and smaller crossing angles lead to less required area, but to higher losses. Since crossings are allowed in the same layer, even only one layer would suffice if the worst case losses (due to bends, crossing, and distance) allow that.

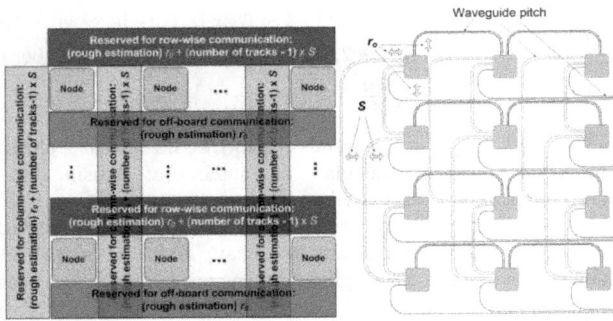

Figure 2. (a) Lay-out design rules on 2D grid for OPCBs. Space reserved for row-wise, column-wise and off-board communication. (b) Lay-out of the 3x2x2 mesh of Figure 1 on OPCB, following the strategy shown in (a).

Also note that the bends and crossings appear in a specific and deterministic order: for every waveguide, an initial bend (or bends) take place, followed by all the crossings, followed by a final bend (or bends).

To lay-out a topology on an OPCB we reserve area for row-, column-wise and off-board communication. Our generalized approach for 2-D grid lay-outs is depicted in Figure 2(a). It assumes that network nodes have pinouts from two of their sides for inter-node interconnection (North and West sides – see next Subsection for a way to construct such nodes). For the communications of the nodes in the same row, we reserve the space above the nodes. The required area depends on the number of waveguide tracks, which is determined by the row-wise collinear topology (Subsection 2.2). For the communications of the nodes in the same column, we reserve the space left to the nodes, again depending on the required tracks. Finally, for off-board communication we reserve the space beneath the nodes that has width equal to r_o, since we assume that all off-board waveguides from all nodes at the same row are routed in parallel with standard pitch (or the pitch preferred) between them, at r_o distance from the nodes. If nodes use a single side for pinout, then the required area for waveguides is the same, but more bends are required. For simple collinear lay-outs, the proposed strategy is that of a single row of a 2D, as depicted in Figure 2(a), but the required distance between nodes is r_o, because no column-wise communication takes place. Figure 2(a) also gives an estimation of the total required area. In Figure 2(b) a 2-D (3x4) lay-out of a 3x2x2 mesh is depicted (equivalent to network of Figure 1). Two waveguides form a bundle and are used within column and row tracks, while one waveguide/node is used for off-board communication.

In principle, the reduced link-to-link separation (waveguide pitch) and the allowance of crossings in the same layer (compared to electrical interconnects) allow denser integration and reduction of PCB thickness (layer count). The usage of WDM, will further increase the data density in Gbps/mm. However, a potential issue is crosstalk with respect to crossing angle, for angles less than 90°. To the best of our knowledge there is not yet a design rule/formula for crosstalk as a function of the crossing angle. Measurements for crosstalk can be found in [21], but only for the examined bus architecture. Another manufacturing issue for OPCBs is that the performance of multimode waveguide components depends on the launch conditions at the component input (see discussion in [23]). Note that we have not assumed

WDM, which would enable multiple wavelengths to be transferred within a single waveguide. So links are point-to-point, as in electrical interconnects, and we plan to explore the benefits of WDM in future work.

2.4 Node construction and lay-out

We now describe how we organize and lay-out network nodes suitable for direct network architectures that are laid out according to the previous Subsection. In our approach a network node consists of a router chip and one or several optochip (hosts) connected in a star topology. The transceiver optochips provide optical inputs/outputs to processors or memory modules. We construct nodes with 2-pinout sides (North and West), Figure 3(a), as used in network creation (see Figure 2(a)), assuming router chips with peripheral pinout (4-sides) and optochips with a single side pinout. We have also developed lay-outs with single side pinout routers, Figure 3(b), since this is considered easier to manufacture and mount on OPCBs. The predominant Tx modules for optoelectronic or photonic router chips are Vertical-Cavity Surface Emitting Lasers (VCSELs) while the Rx modules are PhotoDiodes (PD). We assume that the VCSELs and PD arrays are laid out at the peripheral of the chip, forming as many rows as the layers supported in the OPCB platform (two in our case). Else, if the chip pins are laid out in a matrix, we assume that the Tx and Rx pins can be mapped in a way that enables to view the chip as a bulding block with peripheral pinout.

In both cases, to construct the node we arrange the router chip and host chips in 2-D arrays. We assume that we have $M = N_{node} + 1$ chips of the same size, where N_{node} is the number of optochips – adding one for the router chip. We arrange these chips in a 2-D array with $D_x = \lceil \sqrt{M} \rceil$ columns and $D_y = \lceil \sqrt{M} - 0.5 \rceil$ rows, while placing the router at the top-left position. Note that placing the router in the middle and leaving space between transceiver optochips in order to save waveguide bends, would ultimately lead to more required area. Such alternative lay-outs are not ruled out and are left for future studies. Also, note that depending on M, some of the array positions maybe left blank. In both cases (2 and 1 pinout side) nodes can be constructed without waveguide crossings, by appropriate spacing and allocation of router pins. Finally, note that, to save space, we use for intra-node connections (hosts-to-router) a smaller bending radius r_i, as compared to r_o used for inter-node communication, since the traveled distances within a node are smaller and no crossings occur.

The node lay-out strategy with waveguides exiting 2 (North and West) sides using router chips with peripheral pinout (4-sides) is depicted in Figure 3(a). We show the required space between the modules to allow the waveguides to take the required turns (of r_i radius) and we also depict the allocation of the Tx router pins (for 2-D lay-outs) to make the star topology and exit the node without crossings. They are arranged in the following manner (clockwise): {pins for row communication, pins for intra-node communication for hosts: $[(1,2),(1,3),...,(1,D_x)],...,$ $[(D_y,2),(D_y,3),...,(D_y,D_x)]$, $(D_y,1)$, $(D_{y-1},1)$,..., $(3,1)$, $(2,1)$, pins for off-board communication, pins for column communication}. If more pins are needed for a specific type of connection, then more pins can be reserved from the "neighboring pin areas", maintaining however the ordering. For collinear node topologies, both pinout router areas for row and column communication will be used just for the row-wise communication.

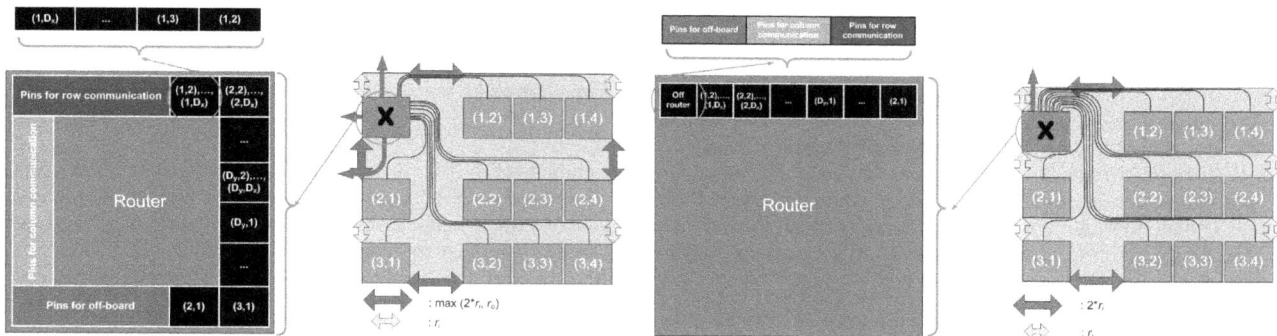

Figure 3. Node lay-out and Tx pin allocations of the router (similar for Rx) for (a) router chips with peripheral pinout, (b) router chips with North-side pinout.

A similar pin allocation pattern is followed for the Rx router pins. The node lay-out strategy with waveguides exiting a single (North) side using router chips with single-side pinout is depicted in Figure 3(b).

2.5 Waveguide length matching

An important issue for electrical PCB designers is trace/link length matching. The trace length mismatch tolerance is determined by (i) the protocols tolerance in timing skew and (ii) the propagation speed of the signals in the medium. The majority of the high-performance, high-speed protocols are serial (eg InfiniBand, Serial RapidIO, PCI-Express). In these protocols a serial lane is composed of two differential signaling pairs per direction. A single link between two devices can consist of multiple serial lanes where the data is striped across these lanes. The length matching requirements between differential pairs are usually very tight, while length matching requirements between lanes are looser. Differential signaling is used in electrical interconnects since differential signals are less susceptible to crosstalk and also tend to produce less electromagnetic interference (EMI) than single-ended signals. Optical signals do not suffer from the aforementioned problems, they have low crosstalk, allowing denser waveguide spacing [1, 3]. This is particularly important, since the much smaller pitch between parallel lanes makes the length mismatch very small. Moreover the propagation speed is higher in polymer optical waveguides than the related electrical lanes [29], relaxing the trace length mismatch tolerance even further. To provide a concrete example, we will take the lane-to-lane skew matching values for of PCI-express 3.0. In PCI-express lane-to-lane skew should be less than $2UI+500$ps which corresponds to 750ps for PCI-e 3.0 (UI=125ps, since the channel rate of a differential pair is 8Gb/s). Assuming polymer waveguides with refractive index $n \approx 1.5$, thus signal propagation speed $c/n \approx 2 \cdot 10^8$ m/s, the tolerated differences in waveguide lengths would be $(2 \cdot 10^8$ m/s$) / 750$ps = 150 mm for lane-to-lane waveguides. We can calculate the difference in the waveguide lengths (taking into account the tracks-width) between the two links: Assuming bending radius r_o, then the length of a $90°$ bend for the inmost waveguide is $S_i = 2 \cdot \pi \cdot r_o \cdot 90°/360° = \pi \cdot r_o / 2$ and the length of the equivalent $90°$ bend for the outmost waveguide is $S_o = \pi \cdot (r_o + pitch) / 2$, where $pitch$ is the waveguide pitch. The length difference for 2 bends is $\Delta S = 2 \cdot (S_o - S_i) = \pi \cdot pitch$. For standard pitch of 250μm, $\Delta S = 785$ μm << 150 mm. If we assume 32 waveguides in a single layer, for a single link (PCI-e x32), 50μm wide waveguides and standard pitch (250 μm). In this case, length difference between the inmost and the outmost waveguide would be (for 2 bends): $\Delta S = \pi \cdot [31 \cdot (250+50)] = 29.2$ mm < 150 mm. Taking all the above into account, in the following

paragraphs we will assume a single-ended signaling, serial, multi-lane protocol, tolerant to lane-to-lane mismatches.

However, for the sake of completeness, we will discuss some potential solutions for de-skewing. A design option could be to route differential signals in different waveguide layers over same paths. Another option could be to route the differential signals in the same layer, in successive waveguides, and use S-shaped bends in the shorter lane to increase its length. S-shaped waveguide bends (see [28] and references cited there) are smoother and in principle far less expensive in losses than $90°$ bends. S-bends can be generated by two circular arcs of constant radius R, sine, cosine or raised cosine functions. A waveguide S-bend structure made of two circular arcs with a constant radius of curvature R is specified as: $R = \pm \frac{L^2}{4d}\left(1 + \frac{d^2}{L^2}\right)$, where L is the transition length and d is the lateral offset. The path length of such an S-bend is $S = 2 \cdot R \cdot \theta \cdot \pi / 180$, where θ is in degrees. If S-bends are used for length matching, then the designer should pay attention where these will be placed, in order to maintain the crossing angles between (row-wise, column-wise, off-board) waveguides. To the best of our knowledge, there isn't yet a design rule/formula for S-bend losses as a function of R, L, d, θ. However, measurements for d =10 mm can be found in [28]. Finally, more aggressive waveguide pitch (such as 62.5 μm) would further reduce length mismatches.

3. PERFORMANCE METRICS FOR NETWORK DESIGN

We discuss now the performance metrics that we take into account in our OPCB design methodology described in Section 4. The layout strategies discussed in the previous section specify if a topology is feasible in terms of area and losses, while the performance metrics discussed here characterize the topology, irrespective of the actual layout. Both of these features are taken into account in the Automatic Topology Design Tool we present in the next section.

We assume that our system of N hosts (optochips) in total consists of N_r nodes, where each node consists of a single router interconnected with N_{node} hosts, and thus N_r is also the number of routers on the board. The two most representative and general metrics of performance for interconnection networks are throughput and latency [15]. Both throughput and latency are functions of topology, routing policy, flow control, interconnect characteristics, switch architecture, as well as traffic characteristics. We use two metrics that are closely related to throughput and latency, namely Speedup and Average Distance that will be described below. We design networks assuming Uniform Traffic (commonly used for topology design), that is each source is equally likely to send to each destination.

While the quality of an interconnection network should be measured by how well it satisfies the communication requirements of targeted applications, on the other hand problem-specific networks are inflexible and thus good "general purpose" networks should be opted for. This is why Uniform Traffic which is quite generic is typically chosen for the topology design phase. It is also useful for emulating global exchange traffic with no underlying data locality (such as HPC applications based on Fast Fourier Transformation - FFT). In the future we plan to evaluate the resulting designs under realistic traffic patterns using simulations.

Ideal Throughput and Speedup. Throughput is the number of bits per second the network can transport from input to output. It is a function of topology, routing policy, flow control, interconnect characteristics, switch architecture, as well as traffic characteristics. The throughput that a topology can carry can be calculated assuming ideal routing (perfect load balancing over alternative paths) and flow control (no idle cycles on the bottleneck channels), what is defined in the literature as *Ideal Throughput* λ_{ideal} [15]. It equals the input bandwidth that saturates the bottleneck channel(s) for a specific traffic pattern, assuming that the hosts have infinite injection bandwidth so as to reach the saturation point. Considering a real system where hosts have a specific maximum injection bandwidth λ_{max} limited by hosts' pinout and channel rates, then the Ideal Throughput under traffic injection constraints $\lambda_{ideal-ic}$ is defined as follows:

$$\lambda_{ideal-ic}(\lambda_{max}) = \begin{cases} \lambda_{ideal}, & if\ network\ is\ saturated\ before\ \lambda_{max} \\ \lambda_{max}, & otherwise \end{cases}$$

The *Speedup* of the network is defined as the ratio of the available bandwidth of the bottleneck channel to the amount of traffic crossing it (under ideal conditions as discussed above). As opposed to Ideal Throughput, Speedup is unitless.

$$Speedup(\lambda_{max}) = \frac{Bottleneck\_channel_{bandwidth}}{Bottleneck_{Traffic}(\lambda_{max})} \quad (3)$$

Speedup is very useful when designing networks. Speedup equals to 1 means that, under ideal conditions, the network can accommodate the injected traffic with no congestion. That is, hosts can inject their maximum bandwidth λ_{max} without reaching network saturation point. Designing a network with Speedup greater than 1, allows non-idealities in the implementation. Speedup is related to ideal throughput under traffic injection constraints as follows:

$$\lambda_{ideal-ic}(\lambda_{max}) = \begin{cases} Speedup(\lambda_{max}) \cdot \lambda_{max}, & if\ Speedup(\lambda_{max}) \le 1 \\ \lambda_{max}, & otherwise \end{cases}$$

$$\rightarrow \lambda_{ideal-ic}(\lambda_{max}) = \begin{cases} \lambda_{ideal}, & if\ Speedup(\lambda_{max}) \le 1 \\ \lambda_{max}, & otherwise \end{cases} \quad (4)$$

where we used Speedup to identify whether the network is saturated with the maximum injection bandwidth or not. In our model, we assume that data that has to be transmitted from a router to a router is distributed evenly over their connecting waveguides, and we assume infinite flow granularity. To calculate the Speedup, we must calculate the values of $Bottleneck\_channel_{bandwidth}(\lambda_{max})$ and $Bottleneck\_Traffic$.

For Uniform Traffic, the bottleneck channels are the bisection channels and the traffic that crosses the bisection width is distributed uniformly [15]. Thus, we must calculate the bisection bandwidth and the traffic that crosses the bisection channels. The bisection bandwidth B_b is calculated as follows

$$B_b = 2 \cdot B_w \cdot C \quad (5)$$

where B_w is the bisection width of the examined topology, and C is the channel rate. In this, we take into account traffic in both directions, since we assume uni-directional waveguides. Closed type formulas for B_W of tori and meshes can be found in [16], while for a FCN of N_r nodes we have $B_w = \left\lfloor \left(\frac{N_r}{2} \right)^2 \right\rfloor$. The amount of traffic that crosses bisection channels is found as follows. For N hosts, there are $N-1$ candidate destinations on board (not considering self-traffic) and N_{node}-1 candidate destinations that are connected to the same router. Let's assume that p_{on} of the host's injected traffic is destined for on-board communication. Since every host injects λ traffic, the total inter-router traffic is $N \cdot \lambda_{max} \cdot p_{on} \cdot (1 - \frac{N_{node}-1}{N-1})$. In Uniform traffic, half of that will cross bisection channels. So taking into account self-traffic as well, we have

$$Bottleneck_{Traffic}(\lambda_{max}) = \frac{N \cdot \lambda_{max} \cdot p_{on} \cdot \left(1 - \frac{N_{node}-1}{N-1}\right) \cdot \left(1 + \frac{1}{N_r - 1}\right)}{2} \quad (6)$$

Note that parameter $p_{off}=1-p_{on}$, which corresponds to the percentage of off-board traffic, is one of the key parameters considered in the methodology (Section 4). As such we examine how this parameter affects the performance, in the related Section 5.

Average distance and zero load latency. The average distance (number of hops traversed on average) for meshes, under Uniform Traffic, is calculated by adding the average distance for each dimension [17]. Following the same rationale, we can calculate the average distance for Torus. In Tori, average distance in dimension i equals to $\frac{k_i}{4} - \frac{1}{4k_i}$ if k_i is odd and $\frac{k_i}{4}$ if k_i is even [15]. Average distance in an FCN equals $\frac{(N_r-1)}{N_r}$. All the above take into account self-traffic. Zero load latency is the latency experienced by packets on average, at a load where no contention occurs. Assuming store and forward switching, the zero load latency T_0 is:

$$T_0 = h_{av} \cdot (T_r + T_{trans} + T_{prop}) \quad (7)$$

where h_{av}, T_r, T_{trans}, T_{prop} are average distance, average router delay, transmission delay, and propagation delay, respectively.

4. METHODOLOGY FOR DESIGNING INTERCONNECTS ON OPCBs

In this section, we present our methodology for designing OPCBs, which incorporates the lay-out strategies we presented in Section 2 to identify whether a design is feasible and uses the performance metrics described in Section 3 to judge its efficiency. Our methodology has been implemented in an Automatic Topology Design Tool (ATDT), to aid topology design. We assume two different schemes for off-board communication: off-board communication through waveguides, or alternatively through vertical cabling. In the second case no waveguides for off-board communication is needed and no board pinout constraint is imposed.

The OPCB design methodology in ATDT follows 2 stages. In the first stage, given physical (such as module footprints and pinouts, channel rates, losses, power budget, board pinout) and performance (required Speedup) inputs, the injected bandwidth from hosts and the probability for off-board communication per host, all the feasible designs are generated. More specifically, we examine different number of optochips on board. For every such case, we examine different number of routers on board. For every such case all feasible mesh, torus and fully connected networks are generated. A design is feasible if

(i) The performance constraints are satisfied (the resulting design offers enough bisection bandwidth and the board pinout is large enough to achieve on- and off-board Speedup at least equal to the required), and

(ii) There is at least one lay-out of the network that satisfies the board area and worst case losses (power budget related) constraints.

The second stage takes all the feasible designs and chooses the optimal one. The optimality criterion used is the maximization of the number of the transceiver optochips (hosts) on-OPCB with the minimal number of utilized router chips. Ties are solved by minimizing the on-OPCB zero load latency. Note that other optimization criteria can be applied, without having to re-execute phase 1, and this is one of the main reasons we followed such a two-phase approach.

Below, we present our methodology using pseudocode, and then we elaborate on several details.

Algorithm: OPCB design

/*__Goal:__ Maximize hosts on-board, while ensuring on- and off-board Speedup $\geq S$*/

Inputs:
s_r: side in mm of the (square shaped) router chip
s_h: side in mm of the (square shaped) host chip
A: OPCB area (as *board height* x *board width*)
r_i: bending radius for host-router waveguides
r_o: bending radius for router-router waveguides
U_R: router chip pinout (number of pairs of Tx/Rx)
U_B: board pinout – set to inf. for vertical cabling
W_h: waveguides (pairs) for host-router connection[1]
θ: waveguide crossing angle
B: power budget
L_p: propagation loss per mm
L_b: power loss due to a waveguide bend
L_c: power loss due to a crossing
N_{max}: max number of hosts to be attempted to fit on board
r: channel rates
p_{off}: percent of off-board traffic/host ($p_{on} = 1 - p_{off}$)

Outputs:
N: number of host optochips on OPCB
N_r: number of nodes (routers utilized) on board
W_b: waveguides (pairs) within a waveguide bundle
U_{off}: number of router channels for off-board communication
topology: (mesh or torus or FCN) router-router topology on OPCB

/*phase 1: find all feasible OPCB designs*/
1. **for** (increase N by 2, until N_{max})
2.   **for** (increase N_r by 1, until current value of N)
3. $N_{node} \leftarrow N/N_r$ /*number of hosts connected to a router*/
4.   **if** ($U_R - N_{node} \cdot W_h < 0$)||($N_{node}$ is not an integer)
5.   continue /*infeasible – not enough router channels*/
6.   **endif**
7.   Node_construct(s_r,s_h,r_i,r_o,N_{node}) /*node lay-out*/

8.   **for** (2 iterations:at 2nd swap node height with width)
9.   **for** (FCN, all meshes, all tori topologies of size N_r)
10. $W_b \leftarrow Rq\_waveguides(S,topology,N,N_r,N_{node},W_h,r,p_{off})$
11. $U_{off} \leftarrow U_R - N_{node} \cdot W_h - W_b \cdot topology\_degree$
12.   **if** $N_r \cdot U_{off} > U_B$
13. $U_{off} \leftarrow \lfloor U_B/N_r \rfloor$ /*nodes share the available U_B*/
14.   **endif**
15. $Speedup_{off} \leftarrow (U_{off} \cdot r)/(p_{off} \cdot W_h \cdot r \cdot N_{node})$
16.   **if** ($Speedup_{off} < S$)
17.   continue /*infeasible: not enough offboard pinout*/
18.   **endif**
19.   **for** (all possible lay-outs: collinear and 2D)^2
20.   **if** (A suffices) && ($B \geq worst case loss$)
21.   (Keep OPCB design as feasible)
22.   **endif**
23.   **endfor**
24.   **endfor**
25.   **endfor**
26. **endfor**
27. **endfor**

/*phase 2: choose optimal OPCB design*/
28. **for** (all feasible OPCB designs of phase 1)
29. (Choose as optimal the design maximizing N and solve ties by maximizing N/N_r and then minimizing latency)
30. **endfor**

A design that exhibits high Speedup would allow non idealities in the implementation (not perfect routing and flow control). Since the on-OPCB networks are small, we chose $S = 1$ as the minimum acceptable on- and off-board Speedup value. p_{on} is indirectly related with the size of the system. For uniform traffic $p_{on} = (N - 1)/(N_{total} - 1)$, where N_{total} is the total number of transceiver optochips in the system. The function in line 7 implements the node construction strategy described in Subsection 2.4. The function in line 10 calculates the number of waveguides required in a router-to-router bundle (the "fatness" of the links) for a given topology, in order to achieve on-board Speedup (equal to or) higher than S, using Eq. (3)-(6). In line 12, if the total required board pinout (from all routers) is greater than the available board pinout, then the board pins are equally distributed in all on-board routers. In the case of vertical cabling (U_B=inf), and this is not imposed. If the router pins for off-board do not suffice for its off-board communication (off-board Speedup < S: line 16), then the OPCB design is not feasible. Lay-outs generated in line 19 are based on the lay-out strategies presented in Subsection 2.3, taking into account whether vertical cabling is used. In line 20, worst case loss is identified as the maximum of the total loss of the worst row-wise and column-wise router-to-router waveguide. Loss calculations include the longest path length, the bends, and the crossings (to create the topology on the direction under study, plus meeting the vertical direction networks, plus the off-board cabling for column-wise networks), following Subsections 2.2 and 2.3.

5. APPLYING THE METHODOLOGY: PERFORMANCE RESULTS

In this section we apply our proposed methodology for OPCB design (presented in the previous Section) for specific and realistic device and module attributes. We focus on multi-mode optical

---

[1] Depends on processor computational power and communication -to-computation ratio

[2] Function of node-height-and-width, N_r, topology, W_b, θ, r_i, s_w, w_p

interconnection modules, since at this point they are more mature than single-mode modules. However, our topology lay-out strategy and methodology can be used for both multi- and single-mode OPCBs.

First, we list the specifications of the multi-mode modules used as a baseline scenario, most of them driven by Phoxtrot [8] so as to have realistic device and module attributes. Then, we examine the potential benefits of photonic technological advancements, such as smaller module footprints, smaller bending radiuses and smaller crossing angles on the required area using our lay-out approach (Subsection 5.1). In Subsection 5.2 we apply our proposed methodology for OPCB design, using the ATDT, for the specific and realistic device and module attributes described below. Finally, in Subsections 5.3, 5.4, 5.5 we examine the impact of board pinout, off-board communication schemes and router pinout respectively on-OPCB network design.

Polymer Multi-mode Waveguides. The size of the polymer waveguides assumed as baseline is 50μm x 50μm, with a minimum parallel separation (waveguide pitch) of 250μm. The propagation loss is L_p=0.05dB/cm for 850nm wavelength. We assume two optical layers of waveguides, one layer for each communication direction. Bending radius values for polymer waveguides at (around) 850nm and corresponding losses can be found in [22]. Based on that, we assume r_o=20 mm for inter-node communication with L_b=1 dB loss per bend, and r_i=10 mm for intra-node. Optical waveguides allow crossings with various crossing angles [22, 23]. As baseline we assumed θ=90° crossing with L_c=0.023dB loss, but we will however examine the impact of smaller crossing angles, on lay-out area (Subsection 5.1) – assuming that crosstalk is not an issue.

Router chip. We assume an optoelectronic packet switching router chip that provides U_R=168 Tx (VCSELs) and 168 Rx (PDs) elements at r=8Gbps channel rate. It is actually an electronic chip with embedded parallel optical interfaces. The Tx and Rx modules are arranged in two 12 x 14 matrices. The optoelectronic router chip footprint (on-board) is s_r x s_r = 52mm x 52 mm. These specifications correspond to a commercially available router chip, already used in actual network products. The state-of-the-art commercial application of the chip was realized by directly connecting fiber cables to the optical Tx and Rx interfaces (vertical cabling). Within PHOXTROT the goal is to integrate the chip on-board to realize multi-mode polymer waveguide OPCBs. The chip has electrical SerDes in 25 Gbps for the processor-to-router connections. However, in this work we will assume that the processor-to-router connections are realized optically using the Tx/Rx interfaces (see host optochip below). The router chip-to-board integration is still under active research. We will first assume that all channel pins are available, using all four sides of the router: 42 Rx and 42 Tx channels per router side (baseline scenario). We will also make more conservative assumptions (current status): 12 Tx and 12 Rx available from each side, (48 bidirectional channels in total).

Host optochip. A host optochip is an active Tx/Rx interface module on top of which the processors or memory modules will be located. For these studies, we assume that the host optochips will accommodate only processors, making the simplifying

assumption that processor-to-memory connections are realized electrically in a separate layer, not affecting the optical layer in terms of area. The channel rate is r=8Gbps. Regarding the optochip's footprint on-board, we will assume optochip footprint to be s_h x s_h =52mm x 52 mm (equal to the router). The number of channels we will assume is W_h=12 (assuming processor chips of 1 TFLOPS – as Intel Xeon Phi 3100 – and communication-to-computation ratio equal to 0.1 bps/FLOPs).

Power Budget. The transmitters assumed are VCSELs operating at 850 nm, using $P_{VCSEL} = 4.7\ dBm$ power. The receivers are PDs with sensitivity $PD_{sens} = -13dBm$. We assume that chip-to-board and board-to-chip couplings are realized with a microlens system of mirrors (MLA). Egress and input lens losses (VCSEL-to-mirror and mirror-to-PD) are 1 – 2dB, and waveguide input and egress facet losses (mirror-to-waveguide and waveguide-to-mirror) are 1 – 3 dB. Thus, assuming a total 3dB loss for chip-to-waveguide and waveguide-to-chip couplings, we have a power budget of: $B=P_{VCSEL}-P_{couplings}-PD_{sens}$=11.7dBm. This is the power budget for a single optical waveguide on-board, connecting either two router chips or a router chip with a host optochip. This budget can be *spent* on lay-out-related losses, that is, the waveguide length, the bends and crossings.

5.1 Topology lay-out strategy and required area

In this subsection we apply our lay-out approach for a single topology and we examine the benefits on the required lay-out area, varying a single technological parameter at a time. Specifically, we examine the impact of smaller chip footprints (s_h = s_r = 26 mm, and s_h = s_r = 10 mm), smaller bending radiuses (r_o = r_i = 10 mm and 1mm - for both intra- and inter-node connections), and smaller crossing angles (θ = 60°, 45°) on the required area. Note that some of these values are unrealistic and are used as the reference/extreme scenario, in an attempt to understand the effect of them on the layout area. Such small bending radius and chip sizes would make the waveguide pitch relevant if there were many waveguides within a waveguide bundle/track and many waveguide tracks – large topologies (not the case for the simulation results of sections 5.2, 5.3), but we neglect such issues here. The topology we chose is a 4 x 4 torus, laid out in a 2-D (4 x 4) fashion, where every router accommodates N_{node}=4 optochips. U_{off}=2 router channels are used for off-board and W_h=2 channels for router-to-router connection. Module footprints and sizes for the baseline scenario were described above.

The estimated node and network lay-out areas are presented in table 1. The first column contains the total area required (in mm x mm) for a single node (a single router and 4 optochips). The second column contains the total area required (mm x mm) for the 2-D lay-out of the 4 x 4 torus. The third column shows the improvement in the total-layout area as a result of the modification of the related single lay-out parameter (chip footprints, bending radiuses, crossing angles). The fourth column contains the *lay-out area efficiency* values. We define lay-out efficiency as the ratio of the total area of the chips (routers and hosts) to the total lay-out area:

$$a = \frac{chips\ area}{total\ layout\ area} \qquad (8)$$

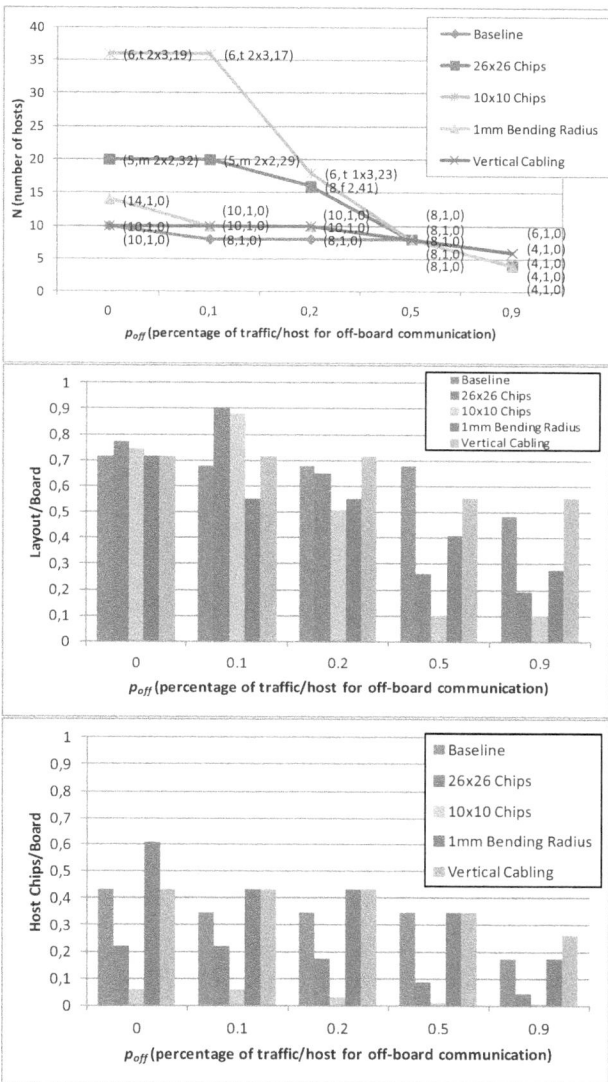

Figure 4. (a) Number of hosts on-OPCB, (b) α_b, and (c) α_h, for board pinout $U_B = 96$, varying the percentage of off-board traffic (p_{off}).

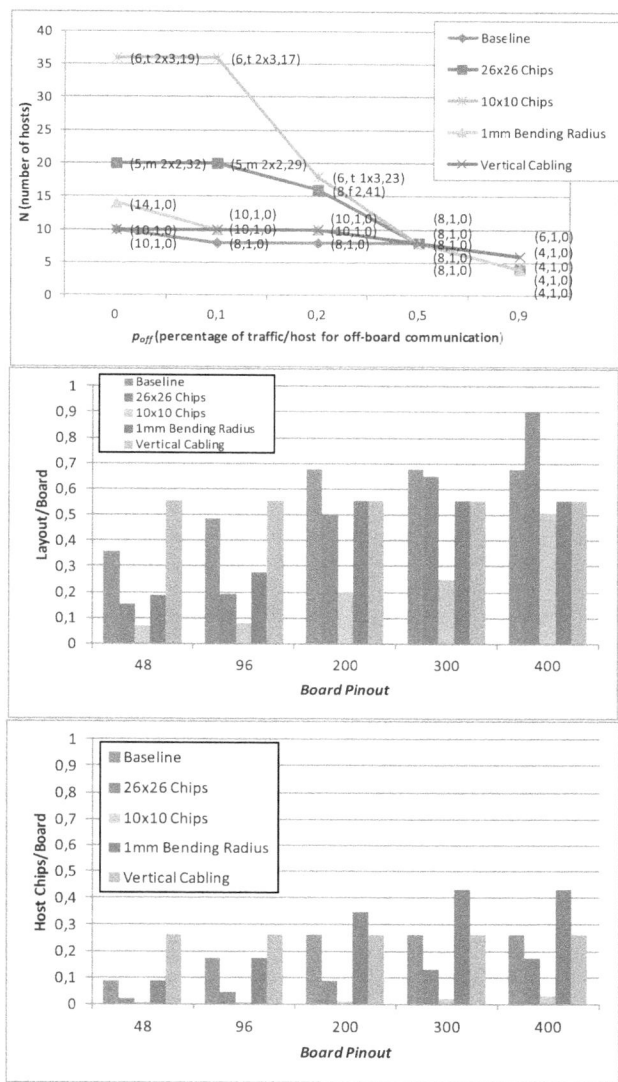

Figure 5. (a) Number of hosts on-OPCB, (b) α_b, and (c) α_h, for $p_{off} = 0.90$ off-board traffic, varying the board pinout.

Different lay-out strategies for a given topology would result in different α values. Eq. (8) would be equal to 1 in the ideal lay-out scenario where the lay-out of a topology would require the same area as the total area of the chips.

Node areas are rectangles since a node contains an odd number of chips (4 hosts and 1 router). The 50mm x 50mm square area in the 10mm x 10mm chip size case, is due to host-to-router bending radius (also 10mm). The total area in that case it is a 362mm x 442mm rectangle due to the extra waveguide tracks for off-board communication. Different crossing angles do not reduce node area since no crossings occur within nodes. Using 10mm bending radiuses also does not reduce node area, since, in the baseline scenario r_i was also set to 10mm. As it can be seen in Table I, all aforementioned improvements in OPCB technologies lead to reduced required area. However, it is clear that the greatest benefit regarding the required area can be obtained by reducing the chip footprints. The impact of the utilization of half size chips (26mm x 26mm) is somewhat similar to the impact of the (extremely aggressive) assumption of 1mm bending radius.

Having 10mm x 10mm chips (the footprint of the single-mode all-optical router developed in PHOXTROT) leads to less required area than the 1mm bending radius. The lay-out area efficiency (metric α, see Eq. (8)) increases by reducing the "layout-related" overheads, namely bending radiuses and crossing angles. On the other hand, reducing chip sizes leads to reduction of the lay-out efficiency, since although the total area is reduced, a larger portion of the layout area is the "overhead", that is, it is empty. The greatest benefits for lay-out efficiency come from reducing the bending radiuses.

5.2 On-OPCB methodology and off-board traffic

We now apply our proposed methodology for OPCB design, using the ATDT, for specific device and module attributes, to evaluate how these parameters interplay and examine their impact on on-board interconnects design.

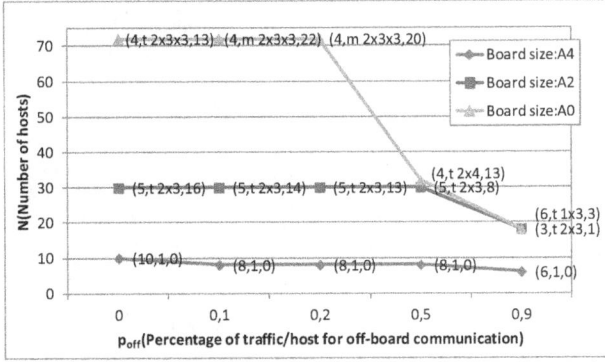

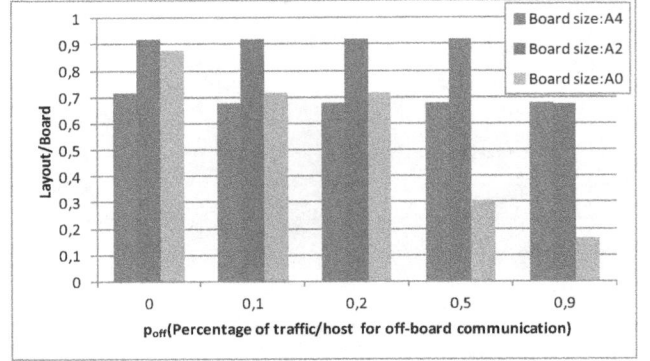

Figure 6. **(a) Impact of board size on-OPCB network design using waveguides for off-board communication. (b) Related a_b metric.**

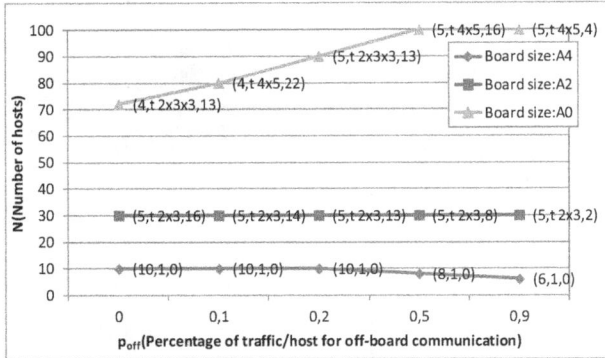

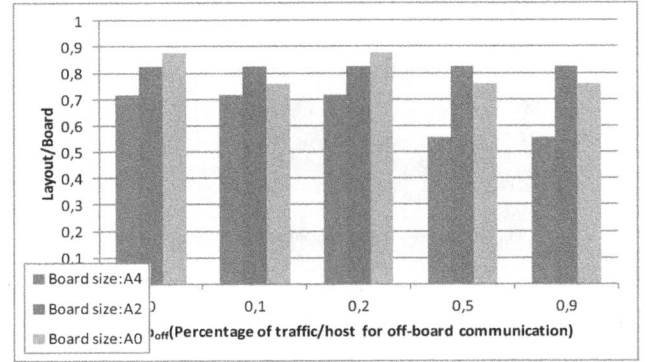

Figure 7. (a) Impact of board size on-OPCB network design using vertical cabling for off-board communication. (b) Related a_b metric.

TABLE I: Impact of smaller chip footprints, waveguide bending radiuses and crossings angles in layout area.

	Node area	Lay-out	%	α
Baseline	176x134	698x946	-	0.328
Chips with $s_h=s_r=26$	98x182	490x634	53	0.174
Chips with $s_h=s_r=10$	50x50	362x442	75.8	0.050
$r_0=r_i=10mm$	176x134	618x826	22.7	0.424
$r_0=r_i=1mm$	158x107	438x646	57.1	0.765
$\theta=60^0$	176x134	658x906	9.7	0.363
$\theta=45^0$	176x134	641x889	13.7	0.380

We assume board area equal to A4 paper size (297mm x 210mm) and board pinout $U_B=96$ (PHOXTROT's target for multi-mode OPCBs). In what follows, by board size we actually refer to the board area available for the optical layer. The rest baseline parameters were described in the beginning of this Section. The results are presented as graphs. Points in the graphs are denoted by (N_{node}, T, W_b), where N_{node} is the number of hosts (optochips)/node, W_b is the waveguides within a waveguide bundle for router-to-router communication and T represents the topology which is *"t"* for torus, *"m"* for mesh, *"f"* for fully connected, followed by the dimensions of the specific router-router networks. Networks with a single node are not classified to belong to any family. For example, in Figure 4(a), the first point (6, *t* 2x3, 19) for the 10mm x 10mm Chips scenario denotes a 2x3 torus network. A single node in this network is comprised of a router and 6 optochips. 19 bidirectional channels (19 Tx and 19 Rx waveguides) are used for router-to-router connections. The

(10, 1, 0) point for the baseline scenario denotes a single node network: 1 router with 10 hosts connected (for single node networks we skip using any of the *"t"*, *"m"* or *"f"* symbols). We also define two new metrics, the *board utilization* a_b and the *hosts' board utilization* a_h as follows:

$$a_b = \frac{layout\ area}{board\ area} \quad (9), \quad a_h = \frac{host\ chips\ area}{board\ area} \quad (10)$$

In Figure 4(a) we present the resulting designs by varying the percentage of off-board destined traffic per host p_{off}. This can be viewed as examining boards destined for systems with different total sizes. We compare the baseline scenario with scenarios utilizing: (i) and (ii) smaller chips (26mm x 26mm and 10mm x 10mm, respectively), (iii) smaller bending radiuses (1 mm for both intra- and inter-node connections) assuming 1 dB loss (equal to 20mm radius loss – an extreme assumption, but made in order to examine the impact of ideally small bending radiuses) and (iv) vertical cabling. In vertical cabling scheme, off-board communication takes place through fiber cables connected to the routers, not through waveguides, leading to fewer crossings and thus smaller losses, while board pinout U_B is neglected. Figures 4(b) and (c) depict the related a_b and a_h values, respectively.

As depicted in Figure 4(a), the highest integration of clients (hosts) on-OPCB can be achieved using smaller chips. Smaller bending radius and vertical cabling also allow more hosts on board. For off-board traffic percentage p_{off} equal and higher to 0.5, board pinout becomes the bottleneck, reducing the number of hosts that can be accommodated. The usage of smaller chips or radiuses would allow more modules on board. This is also apparent from Figure 4(b), where at $p_{off}=0.5$ the utilization drops

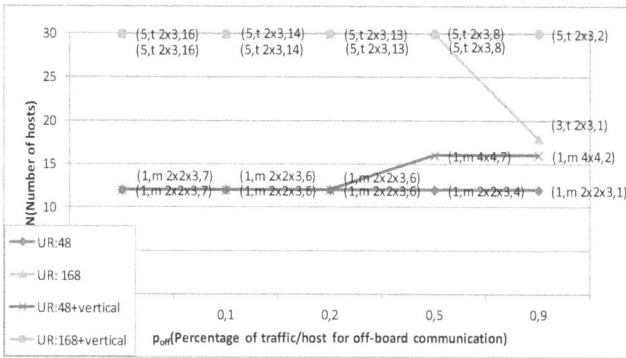

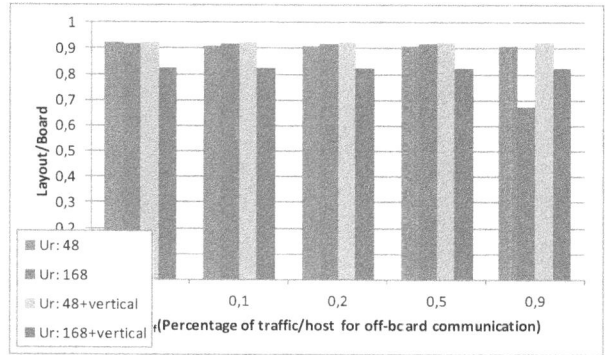

Figure 8. (a) Impact of less available router pinout on-OPCB network design (board size: A2). (b) Related a_b metric.

dramatically for scenarios (i), (ii) and (iii). This also affects a_h (Figure 4(c)) which also drops as p_{off} increases. The "spike" in Figure 4(b), at p_{off}=0.1 off-board traffic for 26mm x 26mm and 10mm x 10mm chips is due to the extra waveguide tracks required for off-board communication (not needed for at p_{off}=0 off-board traffic). For the vertical cabling case (scenario (iv)) the main bottleneck is the board area or the router chip pinout: more routers are added to accommodate the hosts' requirements for off-board traffic, which after a point is constrained by space (A4 board area). Regarding the resulting topologies, mesh and torus networks are more suitable when a large number of routers is needed (provided that there is enough available area and board pinout to be accommodated on board), since FCNs have greater connectivity degree (more demanding on router-to-router channels) and are laid-out only in collinear fashion.

5.3 Impact of board pinout

In Figure 5(a) we examine the same scenarios, but keep constant the required off-board traffic p_{off} (and in particular p_{off}=0.9) and vary the board pinout U_B. Figures 5(b) and (c) depict the related a_b and a_h values, respectively. U_B=48 pinout is the state-of-the-art for OPCBs, while U_B=96 is targeted in PHOXTROT for multi-mode boards. As explained, the board pinout does not affect vertical cabling scheme designs. Also remember that in all designs a requirement is to ensure that off-board Speedup is at least equal to 1. Results indicate that state-of-the-art 48 board pinout only allow very few hosts integrated on-OPCB, while a large portion of the board area remains unused: 144x154 is the total lay-out area for the (2, 1, 0) baseline. PHOXTROT's targeted 96-pinout board slightly improves that. A 200-pin OPCB would allow more hosts on board, allowing at the same time to harvest the area benefits that can be obtained from smaller chips and smaller bending radiuses. A far larger board pinout (400) and the use of 10mm x 10mm chips would allow denser integration (151x230) and more efficient usage of board area. This is also apparent from Figures 5(b) and (c), where a_b and a_h tend to increase as board pinout increases.

5.4 Impact of board area and off-board communication schemes

Figures 6(a), 7(a) illustrate the impact of off-board communication schemes (waveguided or vertical cabling) and board sizes on OPCB network design, while Figures 6(b), 7(b) depict the relative a_b values. The board pinout value used is U_B=400. For the waveguided off-board communication, as p_{off} grows, less hosts can be accommodated due to pinout constraints (for $p_{off} \geq 0.5$). On the contrary, in off-board communication via

cables, the board pinout constraint is not imposed. Thus, as available board area increases, the number of on-OPCB hosts tend to increase. For the baseline scenario in Figure 7(a), the constraint is the available board area: as p_{off} increases, more routers are required in order to accommodate the increasing off-board destined traffic. However, they can not be accommodated due to OPCB area constraints.

Thus, since a single router can not satisfy the increased off-board traffic requirements, fewer hosts must be connected to the single router. Board utilization (Figure 7(b)) does not necessarily increase as p_{off} increases in vertical cabling scheme: the lay-out of a topology using cabling for off-board communication is more lay-out area efficient (8) than the lay-out of the same topology using waveguided communication for off-board cabling, since the former does not introduce on-OPCB "lay-out overhead" due to off-board waveguides. Furthermore, the same router-to-router topology could accommodate a larger number of hosts with the same board utilization: eg topologies (4, t 4x5, 22) and (5, t 4x5, 16) use about the same portion of the board. This is due to blank positions in the intra-node 2D array (Subsection 2.4) that in the latter case are filled with hosts.

5.5 Impact of router pinout

Figure 8(a) illustrates the impact of available router pinout U_R on-OPCB network design, for both vertical cabling and waveguided off-board communication, while Figure 8(b) depicts the related board utilization. The board pinout value used is U_B=400 and board area is equal to A2. Apparently, larger router pinout leads to more hosts on-OPCB in all examined cases.

6. CONCLUSIONS

We proposed lay-out strategies for on-optical printed circuit board (OPCB), and we also presented a general methodology for designing optical interconnection networks/architectures, using a set of packaging and required performance parameters as inputs. Our methodology incorporates the lay-out strategies we proposed but it can also be enriched with more lay-out strategies. The topology design methodology consists of two phases. In the first phase we generate all the feasible designs (in terms of area, losses and performance) within the topology families examined, using our proposed OPCBs lay-outs. In the second phase, we select the optimal designs based on specific optimization criteria. We applied our methodology for the on-board level of packaging hierarchy using PHOXTROT subsystem specifications as input. Our results indicate that reducing the footprints of the chips and also increasing the board pinout, can allow more hosts to be accommodated on OPCBs. Our future work includes the expansion of our methodology for higher packaging layers and the incorporation of WDM, and enriching the topology families with bus like topologies. We also plan to evaluate our designs performance under realistic traffic patterns using simulations.

7. ACKNOWLEDGMENTS

This work was supported by the European Commission through the FP7 ICT-PHOXTROT (ICT 318240) project.

8. REFERENCES

[1] J. H. Collet, F. Caignet, F. Sellaye, and D. Litaize, "Performance constraints for onchip optical interconnects," *IEEE J. Sel. Topics in Quantum Electron.*, vol. 9, no. 2, pp. 425–432, Mar./Apr. 2003.

[2] G. Astfalk, "Why optical data communications and why now?," *Appl. Phys., vol. A 95*, no. 4, pp. 933–940, 2009.

[3] M. Taubenblatt, "Optical interconnects for high performance computing," *in Proc. Optical Fiber Communications (OFC/NFOEC)*, Los Angeles, CA, 2011, paper OThH3.

[4] C. L. Schow et. al., "A 24-Channel, 300 Gb/s, 8.2 pJ/bit, Full-Duplex Fiber-Coupled Optical Transceiver Module Based on a Single "Holey" CMOS IC", *IEEE/OSA J. Lightwav. Technol.*, vol. 29, no. 4, Feb. 2011

[5] http://lightwave.ee.columbia.edu/?s=partners&p=funding_agencies

[6] http://www.intel.com/content/www/us/en/research/intel-labs-hybrid-silicon-laser.html

[7] http://www.ict-polysys.eu/

[8] http://www.phoxtrot.eu/

[9] Kachris, Christoforos, and Ioannis Tomkos. "A survey on optical interconnects for data centers." *Communications Surveys & Tutorials, IEEE* 14.4 (2012): 1021-1036.

[10] Basak, Debashis, and Dhabaleswar K. Panda. "Designing clustered multiprocessor systems under packaging and technological advancements." *Parallel and Distributed Systems, IEEE Transactions on 7.9 (1996):* 962-978.

[11] Gupta, Amit K., and William J. Dally. "Topology optimization of interconnection networks." *Computer Architecture Letters* 5.1 (2006): 10-13.

[12] Chen, Dong, et al. "Looking under the hood of the ibm blue gene/q network." *Proceedings of the International Conference on High Performance Computing, Networking, Storage and Analysis.* IEEE Computer Society Press, 2012.

[13] Abts, Dennis. "Cray XT4 and Seastar 3-D Torus Interconnect." *Encyclopedia of Parallel Computing* (2011): 470-477.

[14] Ajima, Y., Takagi, Y., Inoue, T., Hiramoto, S., Shimizu, T. "The tofu interconnect." High Performance Interconnects (HOTI), 2011 *IEEE 19th Annual Symposium on*. IEEE, 2011.

[15] W. J. Dally and B. Towles. "Principles and Practices of Interconnection Networks", *Morgan Kaufmann*, 2004.

[16] Aroca, Jordi Arjona, and Antonio Fernández Anta. "Bisection (band) width of product networks with application to data centers." *Theory and Applications of Models of Computation.* Springer Berlin Heidelberg, 2012. 461-472.

[17] Grange, Matt, et al. "Optimal network architectures for minimizing average distance in k-ary n-dimensional mesh networks." *Networks on Chip (NoCS), 2011 Fifth IEEE/ACM International Symposium on.* IEEE, 2011.

[18] X. Dou et al., "Optical bus waveguide metallic hard mold fabrication with opposite 45° micro-mirrors," *in Proc. Optoelectron. Interconnects Compon. Integr. IX*, 2010, pp. 76070P-1–76070P-6.

[19] R. T. Chen et al.,, "Fully embedded board-level guided-wave optoelectronic interconnects", *Proc. IEEE*, vol. 88, no. 6, pp. 780–793, Jun. 2000.

[20] J. Beals et al., "A terabit capacity passive polymer optical backplane based on a novel meshed waveguide architecture," *Appl. Phys. A: Mater. Sci. Process.*, vol. 95, no. 4, pp. 983–988, 2009.

[21] Bamiedakis, N., Hashim, A. , Penty, R.V. , White, I.H. "A 40 Gb/s Optical Bus for Optical Backplane Interconnections", *Lightwave Technology*, vol.32 , issue: 8, Apr. 2014.

[22] Wang, Kai, et al. "Photolithographically manufactured acrylate polymer multimode optical waveguide loss design rules." *Electronics System-Integration Technology Conference, 2008. ESTC 2008. 2nd.* IEEE, 2008.

[23] A Hashim, N Bamiedakis, RV Penty, "Multimode Polymer Waveguide Components for Complex On-Board Optical Topologies." *Journal of Lightwave Technology* 31.24 (2013): 3962-3969.

[24] Pepeljugoski, Petar K., et al. "Low power and high density optical interconnects for future supercomputers." *Optical Fiber Communication Conference.* Optical Society of America, 2010.

[25] http://www.top500.org/system/177232#.U3mxKnbm5Gk

[26] Make IT Green: Cloud Computing and its Contribution to Climate Change. Greenpeace International, 2010.

[27] Yeh, C.-H., E.A. Varvarigos, and B. Parhami, "Multilayer VLSI lay-out for interconnection networks," *Proc. Int'l Conf. Parallel Processing*, 2000, pp. 33-40.

[28] Bamiedakis, Nikolaos, et al. "Cost-effective multimode polymer waveguides for high-speed on-board optical interconnects." *Quantum Electronics, IEEE Journal of* 45.4 (2009): 415-424.

[29] Haurylau, Mikhail, et al. "On-chip optical interconnect roadmap: challenges and critical directions." *Selected Topics in Quantum Electronics, IEEE Journal of* 12.6 (2006): 1699-1705.

Integration and QoS of Multicast Traffic in a Server-Rack Fabric with 640 100G Ports

Nikolaos Chrysos,
Fredy Neeser
IBM Research–Zurich
{cry,nfd}@zurich.ibm.com

Brian Vanderpool,
Mark Rudquist
IBM STG, Rochester, USA
{vanderp,rudquist}@us.ibm.com

Kenneth Valk,
Todd Greenfield,
Claude Basso
IBM STG, Rochester, USA
{kmvalk,toddg}@us.ibm.com
basso2@fr.ibm.com

ABSTRACT

Flexible datacenters rely on high-bandwidth server-rack fabrics to allocate their distributed computing and storage resources anywhere, anyhow, and anytime demanded. We describe the multicast architecture of a distributed server-rack fabric, which is arranged around a spine-leaf topology and connects 640 Ethernet ports running at 100G. To cope with the immense fabric speed, we resort to hierarchical, tree-based replication, facilitated by specially commissioned fabric-end ports. At each (port-to-port) leg of the tree, a frame copy is forwarded after a request-grant admission phase and is ACKed by the receiver. To save on bandwidth, we use a packet cache in our input-queued switching-nodes, which replicates asynchronously forwarded frames thus tolerating the variable-delay in the admission phase. Because the cache has limited size, we loosely synchronize the multicast subflows to protect the cache from thrashing. We describe our policies for lossy classes, which segregate and provide fair treatment to multicast subflows. Finally, we show that industry-standard Level2 congestion control does not adapt well to one-to-many flows, and demonstrate that the methods that we implement achieve the best performance.

Categories and Subject Descriptors

C.2.1 [**Computer-communication networks**]: Network Architecture and Design

Keywords

Datacenter fabrics; server-rack interconnects; multicast

1. INTRODUCTION

Flexible performance-optimized datacenters (PoDs) rely on high-bandwidth server-rack fabrics that expedite the on-demand allocation of the available but distributed computing and storage capacity. Such versatile systems can be dynamically tailored to the specific needs of tenants or applica-

tions. At the same time, the datacenter users can capitalize on network support for one-to-many (multicast) communication. Relevant enterprise and high-performance computing applications include provisioning of financial servers, caching of critical or popular data, n-redundant file stores, publish-subscribe services, one-to-many collectives, all of which push data to large numbers of receivers simultaneously. Efficient network-level multicast transmission tapers off the server load per message and moderates the network utilization.

In this paper, we describe the multicast architecture of a distributed server-rack fabric. The fabric connects 640, 100G Ethernet ports through a *flattened* spine-leaf topology. Internally, it provides *small buffers* and *lossless end-to-end scheduled service*, avoiding backlogs and reducing frame delay. The provision of sophisticated traffic management at the targeted scale demands prudent and intelligent architectures. Our system concentrates the frame processing, replication, and scheduling functions at the network edges (leaf switches). This decision drastically simplifies the spines, which are ultra-high-radix, shallow-buffered packet switches, enabling dense, high-bandwidth connectivity.

Multicast traffic dramatically escalates the processing and forwarding rates at fabric ports. In our implementation, a port can process and forward a new (unicast) frame every 6.6 ns (i.e., 64B at 100G). Effectively, for 512B or larger frames, a port can fanout to eight peers at full 100G speed. For system-level multicast groups, consisting of several hundreds of listeners, we do (non-router-assisted [1]) hierarchical multicasting in hardware, which seamlessly integrates multicast with unicast processing, and narrows the ACK implosion problem. The replication nodes are drawn from a pool of specially commissioned fabric-end ports (*surrogates*), thus releasing multicast destinations (user or terminal ports) from the extra load. There is one surrogate port per leaf switch, receiving frames from the fabric and forwarding copies to local multicast destination ports and to remote surrogate ports, deeper in the hierarchy. The fabric employs credit-based flow control, from ingress to egress, to prevent queue overflows. To recover from soft errors anywhere along the path, CRC, sequence numbers, and unicast retransmissions on the failing port-pair leg are utilized.

We denote the number of terminal destinations of a multicast flow (i.e., the cardinality of its fanout set, F) as $|F|$. At each source or surrogate port, x, the *local fanout set*, $f(x)$, of a multicast flow consists of a combination of destinations ($\in F$) and surrogate ports. The port forwards the multicast flow by spawning $|f(x)|$ unicast-oriented *subflows*.

To forward a unicast frame from one port to another, we use a reliable, distributed, *request-grant/credit-ACK* protocol. To transmit a frame, a port must first request and be granted credits for the egress buffer at the target leaf switch. Effectively, we forward the $|f|$ multicast copies of a frame asynchronously from one another—i.e., fanout or call splitting [2, 3, 4]. On the other hand, typical input-queued crossbars achieve line rate only when all copies are sent at the same time. In our design, we achieve line rate forwarding with a *multicast packet cache* that replicates the asynchronously forwarded copies. The packet cache is located in front of the crossbar of edge switches, and can use up to eight crossbar ports to simultaneously forward eight multicast subflows at 100G. Because the cache has limited size, it may have to evict useful packets. We loosely synchronize the *Virtual Output Queues (VOQs)* that hold the copies of a multicast flow to ward off such unwanted evictions.

A flow control action is imminent when a frame arrives at a source port or when a frame loops back from the egress to the ingress side of a surrogate port. If the frame belongs to a lossy traffic class, we may decide to drop it when we have run out of payload buffers. But besides the payload, the *multicast headers* that we maintain for frame copies consume space. To prevent a congested subflow, which makes slow progress, from consuming too many headers, we may also reject frame copies that target congested destinations, using a per-VOQ drop. We have opted for an advantageous drop-from-head policy, which overcomes the negative interactions between tail-drop and VOQ synchronization. In addition, we randomize the drops, in a random-early-detection fashion, to maintain fairness across the subflows.

If the arriving frame belongs to a lossless traffic class, the port may issue a per-priority PAUSE message to avoid losses. At ingress ports, these messages are standard Ethernet PAUSEs that hold off the upstream network interface from sending new frames from the indicated priority. At surrogate ports, PAUSEs are fabric-internal messages, that nevertheless perform a similar function: they prevent the egress side of the surrogate, which receives fabric frames, from forwarding new frames to the ingress side.

With lossless traffic classes, proper congestion management is a key enabling technology. Without it, a congested multicast flow can choke the fabric (at a given priority traffic class). First, we demonstrate that the industry-standard method, *Quantized Congestion Notifications (QCN)*, does not work properly with one-to-many multicast flows. Then we demonstrate that our congestion management architecture, first presented and evaluated for unicast traffic in [5], which *(a)* places the QCN congestion points at fabric inputs instead of fabric outputs, and *(b)* modifies the standard-QCN marking scheme, works smoothly with multicast flows.

Our contributions in this paper are the following:

- We report the (reliable) multicast architecture of a massive 100G Ethernet server-rack fabric, implemented in 32 nm, using hierarchical multicast replication in hardware.

- We *(i)* propose a packet caching scheme that extends the multicast capabilities of input-queued crossbars by replicating *delayed* frame copies, and *(ii)* describe a productive subflow synchronization scheme.

- We present efficient flow control schemes for lossy multicast classes, demonstrate that industry-standard QCN

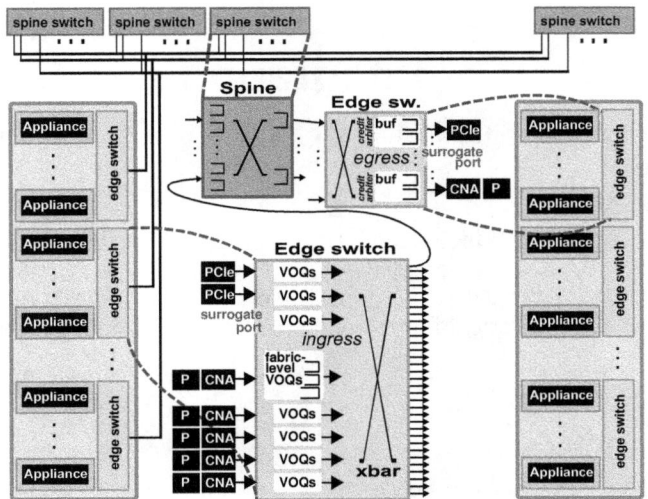

Figure 1: A distributed server-rack fabric connecting the appliances in multiple racks (two racks are shown). The fabric has small ingress and egress fabric buffers at (network-)edge switches, and shallow packet buffers at the spines. One port in every edge switch is a surrogate, used in hierarchical replication of multicast frames.

does not work well with one-to-many flows, and propose a solution that mitigates the shortcomings of QCN.

- We evaluate the performance of our implementation using several micro-benchmarks, full-system broadcasts, as well as concurrent provisioning of many servers.

The remainder is structured as follows. In Sec. 2, we present the underlying server-rack fabric, and the port-level forwarding of multicast traffic. Continuing with Sec. 3, we describe the multicast packet cache and the VOQs synchronization mechanisms. Section 4 describes our congestion management schemes for lossy and lossless traffic classes. Section 5 presents the formation of system-level replication trees using surrogate ports. Computer simulations throughout these sections evaluate the performance of the system and demonstrate important trade-offs. Finally, we discuss our design points in Sec. 6 and conclude in Sec. 7.

2. FABRIC & FRAME PROCESSING

In this section, we first present the topology of the fabric, and its unicast queuing and scheduling functions. Then, we outline how multicast processing fits in the picture.

2.1 Server-rack fabric

In this paper we set out to enable efficient multicast traffic support in the holistically-designed server-rack fabric shown in Fig. 1, which provides 640 100G Ethernet and 256 PCIe Gen3 (x8) ports. Abstractly seen, the fabric is a *large switch* built around a spine-leaf (fat-tree) topology. The main bulk of memory storage is provided at fabric-input and fabric-output (ingress and egress) buffers of leaf switches, in a similar fashion with *Combined Input-Output Queued (CIOQ)* architectures.

The leaf switches are integrated into the backplane of a cluster of server racks. Every leaf constitutes the network-edge point for five (5) servers, offering 100 Gb/s bandwidth to each on a single Ethernet link. Additionally it offers one surrogate and two PCIe ports, for a total of eight (8) main ports. Shown in Fig. 1 are also the *Converged Network Adapters (CNAs)*, which, for Ethernet traffic, constitute the interface between the servers (P) and the fabric ports.

The leaf (or edge) switches, coordinated by a central control unit, are responsible for MAC learning, frame replication and forwarding, thus collectively acting as a distributed, high-capacity bridge. Only Ethernet ports participate in multicast communications. The forwarding tables of the fabric are populated by snooping the multicast-group conversations between hosts and routers that are carried through Internet Group Management Protocol (IGMP) messages.

At its ingress side, an edge switch stores the incoming frames in fabric-level (i.e., network-level) VOQs, segments the frames into variable-size fabric-internal packets with size up to 256B, and injects them into the interconnect. The journey of a packet (or cell) inside the interconnect sets off at the crossbar of the sourcing edge switch, goes through a spine, and terminates at the crossbar of the target edge switch. The packet can use any spine (and any edge-to-spine) link, as enforced by a packet-level spraying routing mechanism that overcomes the limitations of Equal-Cost-Multi-Path (ECMP) alternatives [6]. Link-level retry is used when traveling between leaf and spine switches. The frames are reassembled at their target edge switch, in egress buffers, and are forwarded to their destination in order. (At surrogate ports, the forwarded frames are looped back to the ingress side of the surrogate.) The source ports receive an acknowledgment for each such forwarded frame to release the ingress memory occupied. If a frame experiences a soft error, its source port will retransmit it after a timeout.

Internally, the fabric uses hop-by-hop credit-based flow control, thus obviating buffer overflows. The egress buffers are flow controlled using a scheduled, port-to-port, credit protocol: to inject a frame inside the fabric, a VOQ must first request and be granted credits from the output-port arbiter located at the target edge switch. The arbiter hands out credits, which correspond to packet slots (buffer units) in its local egress memory, using a variant of deficit round-robin. The per-VOQ requests, grants, and ACKs, are 10-byte messages, using the same links as data.

As shown in Fig. 1, the crossbar inside edge switches has a dedicated 130 Gb/s interface (36 Bytes at 454 MHz) for every main port. As described in Sec. 3, an Ethernet or surrogate port can combine all these crossbar interfaces, eight in total, to fanout to eight (8) new ports at 100G. The crossbar additionally provides eight (8) 130 Gb/s interfaces, each attached to four (4) optical links that connect to the spines at 25 Gb/s—please observe the crossbar-internal speedup.

The spines are cell-based, CIOQ *switching elements*, with small input and output buffers (16 packets per port), oblivious of the higher-level protocols. They reside in separate chassis, and provide 136 bidirectional ports, at 25 Gb/s, that can be arbitrarily connected with leaf switches. In the configuration that we consider, there are 128 edge switches, with 32 links, each connected to one of the 32 available spines. Thus, for Ethernet traffic, this configuration features an over-provisioning ratio of 8:5 (=32·25:5·100), which accommodates the internal overheads, leaving some headroom to compensate for scheduling inefficiencies.

The fabric *has been implemented* using 32 nm technology, in 19.7x19.7 mm² for the leaf nodes and 18.4x18.4 mm² for

Table 1: System parameters

	Parameter	Value
Ingress terminal	shared buf. T_{th} (lossy)	185 KB
Ingress terminal	per-VL buf. (lossless)	227 KB
Ingress surrogate	shared buf. (lossy)	84 KB
Ingress surrogate	per-VL buf. (lossless)	32 KB
Egress terminal	per-VL buf.	140 KB
Egress surrogate	per-VL buf.	100 KB
PAUSE (ingress)	STOP Q_{hi} (lossless)	160 KB
PAUSE (ingress)	GO Q_{low} (lossless)	90 KB
Term. VOQ drop	V_{th} (lossy)	60 KB
Surr. VOQ drop	V_{th} (lossy)	50 KB
Header pool high	per-VL H_{hi} (lossy)	500 hdrs
Header pool low	per-VL H_{low} (lossy)	470 hdrs
Header pool	per-VL (lossless)	291 hdrs
Multicast cache	number of entries C	128 packets
VOQ sync	block threshold	18 packets
VOQ sync	resume threshold	12 packets
QCN (ingress)	Q_{eq} (queue equil.)	90 KB
QCN (egress)	Q_{eq} (queue equil.)	50 KB
QCN	w (weight for ΔQ [7])	2
QCN	I_s (sampling interval)	150 KB

the spines. The ingress and egress payload buffers in edge switches use inexpensive on-chip EDRAMs and are partitioned in buffer pools, per port and per *virtual lane (VL)*.

Note that each VL corresponds to a single Ethernet priority level, configured to provide either lossy or lossless service. Lossy VLs share their payload buffers at the ingress. For lossless traffic classes, each VL is allocated private buffers, and the ingress terminal port issues a (per priority level) PAUSE message to its upstream CNA when the aggregate occupancy of the VOQs in the corresponding VL exceeds a threshold value, Q_{hi}. Furthermore, the CNAs implement QCN rate limiters, which throttle the injections of an Ethernet flow in response to received congestion notification messages. The fabric has QCN congestion points at both fabric outputs and fabric inputs.

Although this switching fabric may look far more complicated than a standalone switch module, its port-to-port scheduled flow control, coupled with its true multi-path routing and its internal over-provisioning, make it behave as a large, fair, CIOQ switch.

Small-scale tests have been performed on real hardware. In this paper, we report performance results from clock-cycle accurate simulations. Table 1 summarizes the key simulation parameters. We consider 40-meter links between the spines and leaf switches—a full deployment of our system may use even smaller links.

2.2 Queuing and scheduling of multicast frames

Frame replication and forwarding are executed at fabric-input and surrogate ports. Surrogates look and act like other ports, but they neither send nor accept external traffic. Instead, they loopback the frames that they receive from other source or surrogate ports, replicating them for local and remote destinations. The multicast headers of these copies are stored in the VOQs at the ingress side of the surrogate.

Receiving a multicast frame, a port looks up its MAC address in a local Forwarding Database (FDB) to obtain

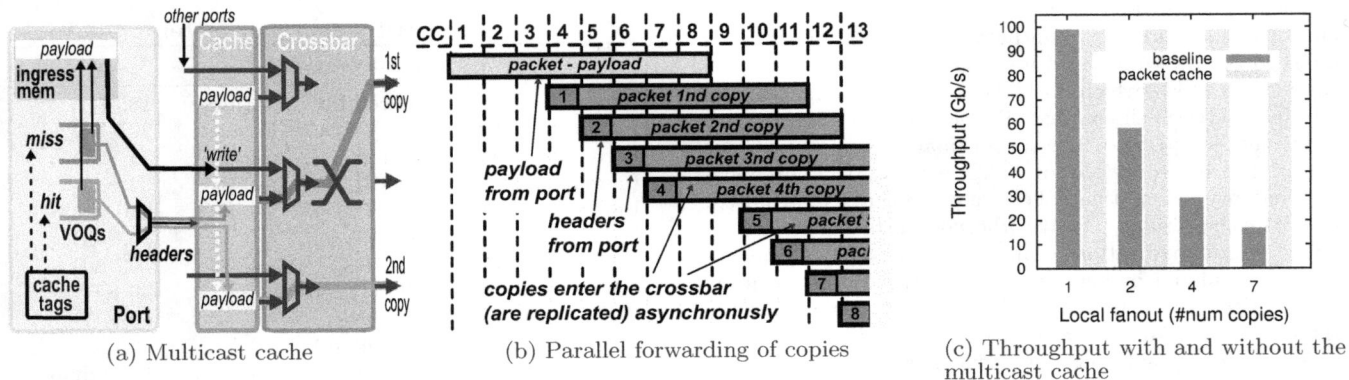

(a) Multicast cache

(b) Parallel forwarding of copies

(c) Throughput with and without the multicast cache

Figure 2: (a) Replication of packets using the multicast cache and the input-queued crossbar. The cache is first instructed to write the packet payload, and immediately receives the first header. The second copy, transmitted at an arbitrary point in time, does not use the payload interface. Instead, only its header is sent to the cache, which combines it with the stored payload and transfers the copy to the target fabric port. The cache can use multiple crossbar input ports to forward packet copies in parallel. (b) The 256B payload is transmitted from the port in 8 cycles. The header for the first copy always travels 3 clock cycles behind the payload. Additional copies are forwarded by issuing one header per cycle. Effectively, up to eight 256B packet copies can be transmitted every eight cycles. In the figure, the headers for copies 5 to 8 delay for a couple of cycles, to demonstrate the asynchronous replication of copies using the multicast cache. (c) Throughput of a 99 Gb/s multicast flow for varying local fanout $|f|$.

a Multicast ID (MID), which is then used to access a local multicast/broadcast table (MCBC). The MCBC outputs the local fanout set of the frame. Effectively, following the payload of a frame, a port additionally receives one *multicast header* per clock cycle, identifying the surrogates and destinations that are waiting for a copy. To a large extent, every incoming header is treated as a new *unicast frame* arrival. At most, 8 multicast headers per frame are received at 100G ports.

We adopt a VOQ-based queuing architecture for multicast traffic. The payload of the frame is written into the intended buffer pool, using a single linked list of available (256B) *buffer units*. Every associated multicast header, which now also points to the head buffer unit, is en-queued into the target VOQ. Each VOQ is associated with an egress fabric port and a virtual lane, and may store packet copies from different multicast flows.

After inserting a multicast header in its VOQ, the source (fabric-input or surrogate) port may issue a request to the target port, and will be able to forward a new copy after receiving a grant from the corresponding output arbiter. As with unicast traffic, the receiving port also ACKs the proper receipt of frames to their source port. After all copies of a frame have been acknowledged, the source port releases the space that the frame occupied in its ingress payload pool.

One widely used protocol for multicast in input-queued switches is *one-shot scheduling* (or non-fanout splitting), in which a port forwards all copies of a packet simultaneously, together with the full list of target destinations. In these systems, the switch interconnect is responsible for replicating the packet [8]. This strategy may minimize the bandwidth overhead, but stipulates that all copies will be granted and residing at the *Head Of Line (HOL)* position of their VOQ at the same time.

In our distributed, asynchronous system, the copies of a multicast frame experience variable arbitration latencies, and may not all be eligible for transmission at the same time.

Furthermore, one-shot scheduling may result in waiting for a grant from a congested port before delivering a frame to ports that are ready to accept it. While this blocking may be anticipated with non-selective (e.g., FIFO) queuing, our VOQ architecture can do better. Therefore, we have opted for a strict (call) fanout splitting, unicast-oriented, delivery mode, where every copy is forwarded independently.

Overall, our VOQ-based multicast queuing organization, in combination with fanout splitting scheduling, is free of HOL-blocking, providing markedly superior performance than plain FIFO [9]. In addition, it uniformly integrates unicast with multicast processing, abating the complexity of the design. At the same time, it seamlessly propagates the benefits of reliable quality-of-service, which we have in place for unicast traffic, to one-to-many flows.

3. ASYNCHRONOUS PACKET REPLICATION

The fanout splitting scheduling that we use would typically require a port-to-fabric bandwidth proportional to the number of local copies ($|f|$) of multicast frames. In our design, the interface of a port to the fabric interconnect is a port-speed line that ends at the corresponding input of the input-queued crossbar inside the edge switch (refer to Fig. 1). Thus, having to send a frame $|f|$ times over this interface, the bandwidth of a 100G flow will drop proportionally. To overcome this limitation, we use a caching mechanism inside the fabric, which stores and replicates packets— i.e., segments of frames.

As shown in Fig. 2(a), the edge switch stores the payload of the port-injected packets inside a *multicast cache*. The cache is physically located at the inputs of the crossbar, and is shared among all local Ethernet (and surrogate) ports. Only one port can write into the cache at a time. Each port maintains *cache tags* that indicate which of its previously sent packets are presently cached. When it decides to inject a new copy, the port looks up its tags. If it is a hit, the port

VOQs local stop
123 ··· h idle h+1
remote restart
idle 1 2 3
remote idle last copies
1 2 3
Time

(a) Subflows synchronization

VOQs A
1 stopped, waits 3
B
2 stopped, waits 1
C
3 stopped, waits 2
VOQ C
1 2 3
VOQ B VOQ A

(b) Freedom from deadlock

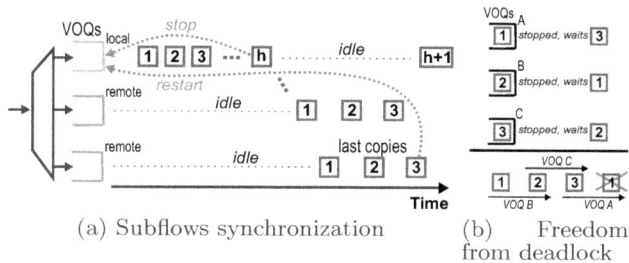

Figure 3: (a) The synchronization mechanism on a multicast flow with 3 copies, for $S_{\text{low}} = S_{\text{hi}} - 2$. The local subflow is suspended after sending the first S_{hi} packets ahead of other subflows. It is restored after the two remote subflows have sent their first 3 copies. (b) A hypothetical but impossible deadlock situation.

issues the corresponding multicast header together with a cache address, instructing the cache to replicate the cached packet. If it is a miss, the port will send the packet payload again, which can be stored in the cache for a second time if additional copies follow.

In our implementation, for tags we use the address of the payload at the ingress port memory. The cache lines, which keep the packets' payload, are 256B, and are mirrored in eight (8) SRAM blocks, one for each crossbar input attached to the local Ethernet, surrogate, and PCIe ports (refer to Fig.1). Each cache mirror can independently feed a 100 Gb/s subflow into the crossbar.

As shown in Fig.2(b), the time of a 256B packet at a crossbar input (or output) is eight (8) clock cycles. In this time period, a port can issue eight (8) multicast headers. Effectively, the cache can serve in parallel all (up to eight) subflows of a multicast flow.

Ideally, the multicast cache will evict a packet after all the copies have been forwarded. However, because the cache has limited space and it is shared among all Ethernet ports in the edge switch, we also use a least-recently-used (LRU) eviction policy. The sourcing port is informed about the premature packet eviction, updates its tags, and forwards the next copy through the payload interface.

Figure 2(c) depicts the throughput of a single multicast flow, sending 1522B frames, as a function of its fanout. As can be seen, without the multicast cache (baseline), the throughput drops linearly with the fanout. In contrast, using the cache, the throughput is at 100G for any fanout.

3.1 Approximate synchronization of subflows

Because the cache is shared among multiple ports, it is important to use it judiciously. The following scenario reveals some of the impending troubles. Consider that we launch a 100G multicast flow that targets three (3) destinations, one local, in the source edge switch, and two remote. Due to the different propagation delays in the request-grant loops of the corresponding subflows, by the time that a remote one receives a first grant, the local subflow may have already forwarded enough frames to fill up the cache.

In this scenario, the granted packets of remote subflows may result in cache misses, limiting the achievable bandwidth by a factor of two. Furthermore, these late packets will compete for cache space with packets of the running-

ahead local subflow. With the cache being such wildly thrashed, every copy may have to use the payload interface.

Our first remedy is to overprovision the cache, so that it fits the largest request-to-grant *round-trip time (rtt)* worth of packets, assuming no contention. However, in practice, when a slightly delayed subflow experiences cache misses, it can be pushed even further behind, because, for improved efficacy, the ports prioritize frames that hit in the cache. As a result, even transient contention episodes can, at times, desynchronize the subflows. In addition, instead of allocating more cache entries for a single flow, it is preferable to enable efficient operation with the least possible space.

In our system, we can loosely synchronize the VOQs that carry copies from the same multicast flow, as a measure against cache thrashing. The method is schematically shown in Fig.3(a). We use a small *VOQ sync CAM* which is searched for VOQ identifiers (13 bits), and keeps a *pkts_ahead_cnt* field. The algorithm starts when a VOQ begins forwarding a frame copy. If this is *not* the last copy of the frame, and the VOQ does not have an entry in the sync CAM already, we allocate a new entry for it. Afterward, we increase the *pkts_ahead_cnt* field in the VOQ entry by the number of packets in the frame. If the *pkts_ahead_cnt* now exceeds threshold S_{hi}, we suspend the corresponding VOQ, waiting for the ones lagging behind to catch up. When a VOQ forwards the last copy of a frame, we identify all VOQs in the sync CAM that have sent this frame already, and decrement their *pkts_ahead_cnts* by the corresponding number of packets. Suspended VOQs whose *pkts_ahead_cnt* now cross threshold S_{low} are restored. Suspended VOQs are also restored after a timeout (3 microseconds), or when their sync CAM entry is released. VOQ entries are released when they are evicted or when their *pkts_ahead_cnts* becomes zero.

Figures 4(a,b) present the receive throughput of a multicast flow, sourced at 99 Gb/s, which targets 4 local and 4 remote destinations, for varying cache sizes, C (16 to 128 packets), and frame sizes (512B to 9022B). Parameters S_{low} and S_{hi} are set to 18 and 10 packets respectively. In our system, the base request-to-grant rtt of local subflows is $\sim$100 ns, and that of remote subflows $\sim$1100 ns, which amounts to 55 256B packets at 100 Gb/s. As can be seen in the figures, without VOQ synchronization, for cache sizes smaller than 64 packets, the throughput can drop below 30 Gb/s because the local subflows fill up the cache before the remote subflows have sent their copies. In contrast, with VOQ synchronization, even a 16-packet cache delivers full throughput, with the exception of large Jumbo (9022B) frames (36 packets), which push the cache stress to the limit.

Besides the actual payload buffers in the cache, which are implemented in dense modern SRAMs [8 (cache mirrors) Cx256x8-bit arrays], a considerable cost is incurred in cache tags. These are 14-bit memory buffer-unit identifiers, stored in latches, requiring a Cx14-bit CAM at each port. As a reasonable trade-off between cost and performance, we sized the cache at $C = 128$ packet entries.

In Fig 4(c), we depict the evolution of cache occupancy in time for 1522B frames. As can be seen, with VOQ synchronization, a 128-packet cache has less than 40 occupied entries for 1522B frames, creating headroom that can be allocated to multicast flows from neighbor ports. At the other extreme, without synchronization, a 32-packet multicast cache fills up—its occupancy is around 20 packets because the cache controller selects one entry with no out-

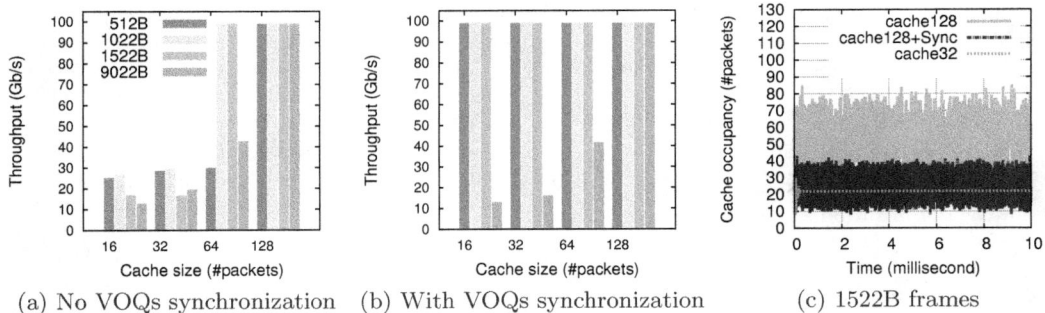

Figure 4: (a,b) Throughput of a multicast flow heading to 4 local and 4 remote destinations, for varying cache and frame sizes. (c) Time series of cache occupancy.

standing headers to evict in every clock cycle with less than 10 entries available.

Multiple concurrent flows: The synchronization mechanism introduces dependencies between VOQs: A VOQ can be blocked waiting for another one to transmit a frame. When many multicast flows are active at the same port, their subflows can be arbitrarily distributed to VOQs. Effectively, impertinent subflows may block one another. For example, a local subflow, in VOQ A, may be blocked waiting for its sibling remote subflow, thus blocking another VOQ carrying irrelevant subflows.

Nevertheless, for ports experiencing a large aggregate fanout, from multiple flows, the synchronization mechanism is automatically disabled, as discussed next. When a new VOQ that sends a frame finds the sync CAM full, we evict one busy entry using an LRU policy. An unexpected benefit comes from these evictions. Because the sync CAM is small (24 entries), at ports with many sending VOQs, it will systematically evict busy entries and unblock those that were suspended. We have verified this behavior in our experiments in Sec 5.2.

Below we further prove that the VOQ dependencies cannot form circles and therefore deadlocks. Consider the circular dependency depicted in Fig 3(b). Three frames are shown: Frames 3 and 1 are sent by VOQ A, frames 1 and 2 by VOQ B, and frames 2 and 3 by VOQ C. These three frames do not necessarily belong to the same multicast flow, and their indexes do not necessarily reflect their arrival order. All VOQs have been suspended by the synchronization mechanism. In particular, for VOQ A to send frame 1, VOQ C must first forward frame 3. Similarly, VOQs B and C are blocked waiting for VOQs A and B to forward frames 1 and 2, respectively. Effectively, a cyclical dependency is formed and the system is in deadlock. However, as shown by the inlet of Fig. 3(b), each VOQ forwards frames in FIFO order. It follows that: According to VOQ B, frame 1 has arrived before frame 2, for C, frame 2 has arrived before 3, and for A, frame 3 has arrived before 1. Because it is impossible to simultaneously satisfy all VOQs' orders, deadlocks cannot occur.

4. FLOW CONTROL AT FABRIC EDGES

So far we have described the forwarding and scheduling of multicast frames at fabric ports. In this section, we turn our attention to the flow control mechanisms, which shape the arriving traffic. Together these mechanisms determine the rates and the backlogs of the multicast subflows.

4.1 Lossy traffic

Figure 5(a) depicts a multicast frame arriving at a terminal or surrogate port. Shown are the per VL payload and multicast header pools. The payload is accompanied by a *concurrent header*, which specifies a VL, and thus the intended buffer pool. In lossy traffic classes, the payload is dropped when the occupancy of buffers that are shared by lossy VLs exceeds threshold T_{th}.

If the payload is accepted, the MCBC outputs the multicast headers which carry private VL identifiers and are stored in their corresponding header pools. No headers follow a dropped payload. The VOQ table contains one entry for every active VOQ at the port, with fields such as the outstanding requests, grants, sequence numbers,etc. Additionally every VOQ table entry has a pointer to the memory location that stores the HOL multicast header of the corresponding VOQ. The remaining multicast headers in the same VOQ are connected below, along a single linked list.

The copies of a single frame may fall at most into two different VLs: one for those targeting a final destination and one for those targeting a surrogate deeper in the hierarchy. For each arriving header, a separate drop decision is made. A header is dropped when its header pool reaches an occupancy threshold (H_{th}), or when the total available memory for multicast headers is full. If the header is accepted, a slot in the headers memory is occupied until the corresponding copy is received and ACKed by its (terminal or surrogate) target port.

In our implementation, the MCBC outputs the MC headers at a fixed sequence: if a flow heads to destinations *d1* to *d8*, the port always receives first the header for *d1* and last the one for *d8*. This fixed sequence triggers the following fairness issue. If the occupancy of the target header pool is close to its drop threshold, the "first" headers have a better chance of being accepted than the rest.

In the tests that follow, we set the header pool threshold at a low value (100 headers), to artificially induce multicast header drops. We configured a single multicast flow, at 99 Gb/s, targeting 1 local and 7 remote destinations. In this experiment, we have found that, for 99 Gb/s load, the remote copies are ACKed after approximately 3500 ns. Therefore, with 100 total headers available in the pool, there are 12.5 headers available per subflow. Each multicast header

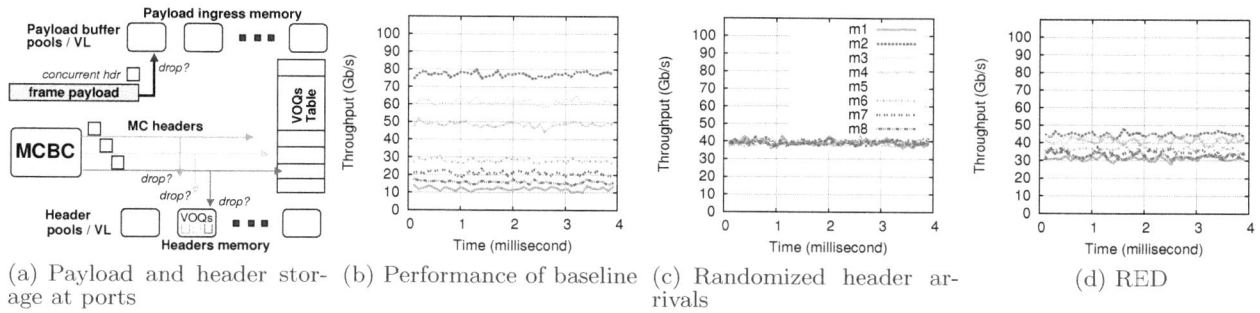

(a) Payload and header storage at ports   (b) Performance of baseline   (c) Randomized header arrivals   (d) RED

Figure 5: (a) Buffering of payload and multicast headers at fabric ports. (b-d) Per-subflow throughputs of a multicast flow heading to one local and seven remote destinations. In this scenario, we purposely reduce the header pool threshold so as to induce drops. 1522B frames.

carries one 1522B frame, which amounts to 120 ns at 100 Gb/s. Therefore, the expected throughput of the subflows is $\frac{120 \cdot 12.5}{3500} = 42.6$ Gb/s.

In reality, the subflow throughputs exhibit a wide spread, as shown in Fig. 5(b). One subflow is at 80 Gb/s, implying that it got ∼8 in 10 of its headers accepted. At the other end of the spectrum, one subflow only had ∼1 in 10 headers accepted and a throughput slightly above 10 Gb/s. The ordering of the subflows in the throughput ranking, from top to bottom, follows precisely the arrival order of subflow headers. This happens because, as the headers arrive at the port in bursts of eight, it is very likely that, in the interim between bursts, headers are released from the pool, making some space for the first headers of the next burst but not sufficient for all.

Figure 5(c) verifies that by randomizing the order of headers with every frame, the subflows receive exact fair throughputs, close to 40 Gb/s. Nevertheless, to simplify the implementation, we eventually opted for a *Random Early Detection (RED)* drop strategy. In particular, we use two thresholds, H_{hi} and H_{low}. Headers are accepted when the header pool occupancy is below H_{low}, and are dropped when it exceeds H_{hi}. For occupancies in between those thresholds, headers are dropped with probability p. Our tests have shown that optimal performance is obtained for $p = 0.5$: Too low a probability p, and the scheme is ineffective. On the other hand, too high a drop probability, and H_{low} becomes a hard drop threshold. As can be seen in Fig. 5(d), using the RED method with $H_{hi} = 100$, $H_{low} = 70$, and $p = 0.5$, we get reasonably good performance.

Optimized VOQ-drop policy: The drop functions discussed in the previous section treat all subflows equally. For lossy priority levels, we have augmented our VOQ architecture with a selective drop mechanism: Once its backlog exceeds a predefined threshold V_{th}, a VOQ starts dropping copies. Effectively, this equalizes the subflows' arrival rates with their service rates. Doing so, we prevent a congested subflow from monopolizing its header pool, and from holding off the release of shared payload buffers.

In the following experiments, we configured a multicast flow at 99 Gb/s, heading to 4 local and 4 remote destinations. Initially, the multicast flow is alone and receives full throughput. Between 1 to 2 ms, its first local destination is targeted by 7 unicast flows, by 3 unicast flows between 2-3 ms, and by 1 unicast flow between 2-4 ms. In this experiment, all unicast and multicast flows are of the same lossy

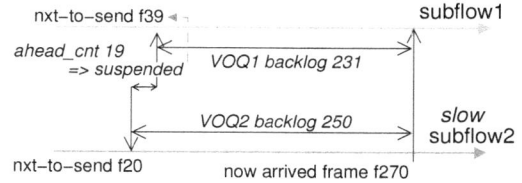

Figure 7: Illustration explaining why drop-from-head works better with VOQ synchronization than tail-drop. For clarity, consider single-packet frames and assume that the ACK arrives immediately after sending the frame copy from its source port. Furthermore, for the sake of simplicity, assume that $S_{hi} = S_{low} = 18$: Subflow 2 is congested, however due to VOQ synchronization, its distance from the fast subflow 1 is bounded. Currently, subflow 1 is suspended as its *pkts_ahead_cnt* exceeds 18. At the same time, the tail-drop function is about to reject the new frame f270 for subflow 2, because the corresponding VOQ 2 has a backlog of 250 buffer units. A first observation is that dropping frame f270 cannot unblock VOQ 1. In contrast, the drop-from-head policy will drop frame f20 instead of f270. The VOQ synchronization mechanism regards such dropped-from-head frames as having been forwarded. Effectively, after dropping f20 from VOQ 2, the *pkts_ahead_cnt* of VOQ 1 will be decremented by the number of packets in f20, and subflow 1 will be unblocked. From there on, the fast subflow sends frames at full speed, the slow one drops (from head) those that stay behind, and their "next-to-send" pointers run side-by-side.

priority level, and are fairly served at fabric-egress ports. As also shown in Table I, there are $T_{th} = 740$ shared lossy payload buffers at each ingress terminal port (185 KB).

In the first experiment, shown in Fig. 6(a), we deactivate VOQ synchronization. As can be seen, the per pool drop policies, alone, cap all subflows to the bandwidth of the most congested one. Even worse, because there is no VOQ synchronization, the fast-moving subflows fill up the cache, and when the congestive episode elapses at 4 ms, the throughput is still bounded at 60 Gb/s. This is corrected by VOQ synchronization in Fig. 6(b), but still the congested subflow dictates the rates of all.

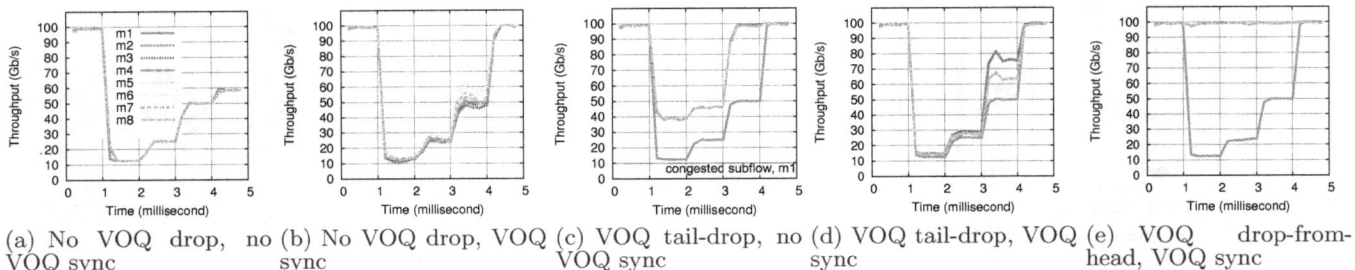

(a) No VOQ drop, no VOQ sync   (b) No VOQ drop, VOQ sync   (c) VOQ tail-drop, no VOQ sync   (d) VOQ tail-drop, VOQ sync   (e) VOQ drop-from-head, VOQ sync

Figure 6: Throughputs of the multicast subflows heading to 4 local and 4 remote destinations. In time period 1 to 2 ms, a local destination is also targeted by 7 unicast flows, in 2 to 3 ms, it is targeted by 3 unicast flows, and by 1 unicast flow in 3 to 4 ms. 1522B frames.

In Fig. 6(c), we activate VOQ tail-drop, keeping VOQ synchronization silent: VOQs with backlog $\geq V_{th} = 240$ buffer units (60 KB) don't accept new headers. As shown in the figure, between 2-3 ms, the non-congested subflows reach their fair share (99 Gb/s). Nevertheless, while the congestion is more severe in 1-3 ms, throughputs are far from optimal.

Furthermore, enabling VOQ synchronization in Fig. 6(d) actually does more bad than good, nullifying the benefits of VOQ drop. That was to be expected, since VOQ synchronization equalizes the service rates of the subflows. Hence, on one hand, the VOQ drop policy can nicely segregate the subflows. On the other hand, VOQ synchronization has to slow down the non-congested subflows, but prevents cache thrashing. Fortunately, we can reconcile the two methods, and get the best from each, by modifying the VOQ drop policy from tail-drop to drop-from-head.

Figure 6(e) verifies the excellent performance of drop-from-head. The throughputs of the fast subflows are *virtually unaffected* by the congested one. As explained in greater detail by the caption of Fig. 7, this happens because, after dropping the next-to-send frame of a slow VOQ, we can decrease the *pkts_ahead_cnt* of fast but blocked VOQs, therefore resuming their progress.

4.2 Congestion control for lossless traffic

For lossless service classes (priority levels), drops are not permitted anywhere in the fabric, including at fabric ports. To avoid drops, the ingress ports issue PAUSE messages when a pool exceeds an occupancy threshold, Q_{hi}. The PAUSE messages from fabric-ingress ports (i.e., at the source of the multicast tree) are per Ethernet priority level and are received by the CNAs. In contrast, the PAUSE messages from surrogate ports are routed to the egress side of the surrogate, forestalling the loop back of new frames at a given VL. The egress VL pools at surrogate and destination ports, of either lossy or lossless classes, are flow controlled by the port-to-port, request-grant credit protocol.

With lossless traffic, saturation trees can be created. As a response, IEEE has recently standardized a congestion control scheme for Ethernet (Layer-2) networks, called *Quantized Congestion Notification (QCN, 802.1Qau)* [7]. Standard QCN performs congestion detection at switch output (fabric-egress) queues. Each congestion point samples the arriving frames, and when it detects congestion, it issues a *congestion notification message (CNM)* for the Ethernet flow of the most recently sampled frame. In response to the received CNM, the QCN rate limiter, implemented at the CNA, decreases the flow's injection rate.

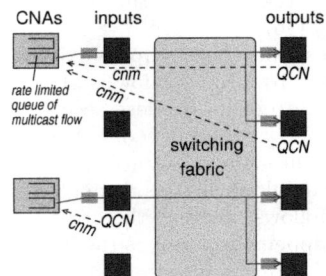

Figure 8: With QCN congestion points at outputs (industry-standard solution), a single multicast frame from the CNA may generate two CNMs, misleading QCN. In contrast, with QCN congestion points at inputs, each multicast frame yields at most one CNM.

However, as shown in Fig.8, using the standard QCN strategy, a *multicast frame* heading to two destinations can be sampled twice, and generate two ($|F|$ in general) CNMs. This multiplication of CNMs can breed unfair treatment of multicast flows. In Fig. 9(a), we have configured one such flow heading to four local destinations, and three unicast flows, from remote leaf nodes, each one targeting a distinct destination of the multicast flow. As can be seen, with QCN congestion points at the outputs (fabric-egress buffers), the unicast flows receive less CNMs and therefore get almost twice more bandwidth than the multicast flow.

In a previous publication [5], we found that, for unicast traffic, placing the congestion points at the inputs instead of outputs improves QCN's fairness and reduces the bandwidth overhead of CNMs. Furthermore, for multicast traffic, this alternative will generate at most one CNM per multicast frame, whatever the fanout of the flow may be. Indeed, as shown in Fig. 9(b), with QCN congestion points at fabric inputs (ingress buffers), the multicast flow performs equally with the unicast ones.

In our next experiment, we test two multicast flows coming from the same fabric source port. Flow T1 heads to local destinations 1 and 2, and flow T2 heads to local destinations 3 and 4. Three (3) unicast flows, from remote leaf nodes, target the first destination, 1, of multicast flow T1. Figure 10 plots the per (sub)flow throughputs. Multicast flow T1 is expected to receive a bandwidth of 25 Gb/s, because

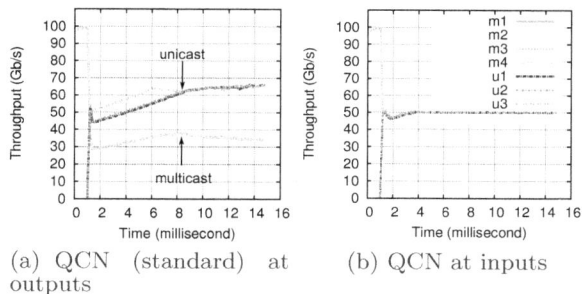

(a) QCN (standard) at outputs   (b) QCN at inputs

Figure 9: The throughputs of multicast subflows m1, m2, m3, m4, and unicast u1, u2, u3, shown separately for QCN congestion points at inputs and at outputs. Unicast flow u_i targets the same destination as subflow m_i.

that is the fair share of its most congested subflow. Without QCN (i.e., PAUSE-only in Fig.10(a)), T1 enters the fabric input at full speed, depleting its port of available buffers. In response, the port exerts PAUSE to the CNA, which indiscriminately blocks both T1 and the non-congested flow T2.

QCN can perform better than the PAUSE-only solution, by throttling T1's departures from the CNA at 25 Gb/s. However, with congestion points at the inputs, shown in Fig.10(b), QCN behaves no better than PAUSE alone. In this experiment, we used the QCN-standard flow marking scheme, which sends the CNMs to the most recently received frames. In our design, we have corrected this shortcoming with an *occupancy sampling* flow-marking scheme for QCN, which sends the CNMs to the flow with the largest occupancy in the monitored payload buffer pool [5]. Figures 10(c,d) demonstrate that our rectified flow-marking scheme, with congestion points at the inputs, performs in par with standard QCN at switch outputs. In addition, as previously verified in Fig. 9, it adapts favorably to multicast one-to-many flows.

5. MULTICAST REPLICATION TREES

Figure 11 depicts an arbitrary, multi-hop, replication tree. In this example, some copies are delivered directly from the source port (one in the source leaf and one in a remote one), other copies pass through one surrogate port, and some final copies pass through two surrogate ports.

Assignment of virtual lanes: As said before, each VL corresponds to one priority level, but two or more VLs may be used for the same priority. We use multiple VLs per priority level to separate the traffic and avoid deadlocks in replication trees. In particular, the per VL pools at the ingress side of a surrogate port can be seen as the (flow controlled for lossless VLs) extension of the corresponding (per VL) pools at the egress side of the surrogate. To avoid deadlocks, we increment the frame's VL when it is injected into the fabric from a terminal or surrogate port. Effectively, a frame with priority level P holding space in a pool of VLP_i can only wait for space in a higher VLP_j, $j > i$. By imposing this partial order on the resources, we prevent the corresponding circular dependencies and the ensuing deadlocks in replication trees [10].

Our replication trees have up to four surrogates, thus, a frame starting with VLP_0 at its source port can reach its destination port with VLP_5. However, because at the last hop in the frame's path (from a source or surrogate port to the final destination), we reuse the starting virtual lane of the frame, we need only 4 VLs per priority level.

An example is shown at the inlet of Fig.11. The payload of a frame with Ethernet priority $P = 0$ is stored in payload pool VL0 at its source port, $VL0_a$ at the 1st-level surrogate, $VL0_b$ at the 2nd-level surrogate, and VL0 again at its egress port. Not shown in the figure are the per-VL multicast header pools. At the source port, the header of the copy is stored in header pool $VL0_a$, and in header pools $VL0_b$ and VL0 at the 1st- and 2nd-level surrogate, respectively.

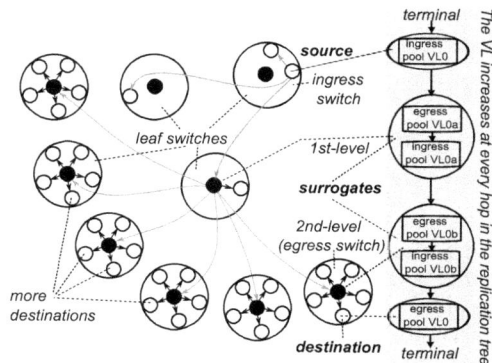

Figure 11: One possible replication tree. VL assignment for a frame at the source, 1st/2nd level surrogates, and destination. The frame belongs to priority 0 and uses the payload pool of VL0 at its source and destination ports.

Expansion speed: Each (terminal or surrogate) port can fanout to a maximum of $|f| = 8$ ports at full 100G speed. Therefore, in theory, N leaf nodes can be reached in logarithmic, $\log_{|f|} N$, time. In practice, a surrogate port will forward some copies to its local ports, offering replication at the egress switch without consuming extra leaf-spine bandwidth. This however narrows the effective fanout towards new leaf nodes. Assuming that the source and surrogate ports always replicate to all local destinations (4 at source and 5 at surrogates), a message that passes through n surrogates can reach $D(n)$ terminal destinations, where,

$$D(n) = 4 + 4 \cdot 5 \cdot \sum_{i=0}^{n-1} 3^i \qquad (1)$$

As said above, our hierarchical replication exploits up to $n = 4$ levels of surrogates, thus a multicast flow is limited to 804 terminal destinations. This is adequate for our 4-rack system, which provides a total of 640 user Ethernet ports at 100 Gb/s[1].

5.1 Bandwidth Overhead

In an ideal multicast replication scheme, each frame would travel to the spines only once, which would spawn one copy

---

[1]Wider fanouts are possible in 2x40G port configurations. However, for clarity, we consider only 100G ports.

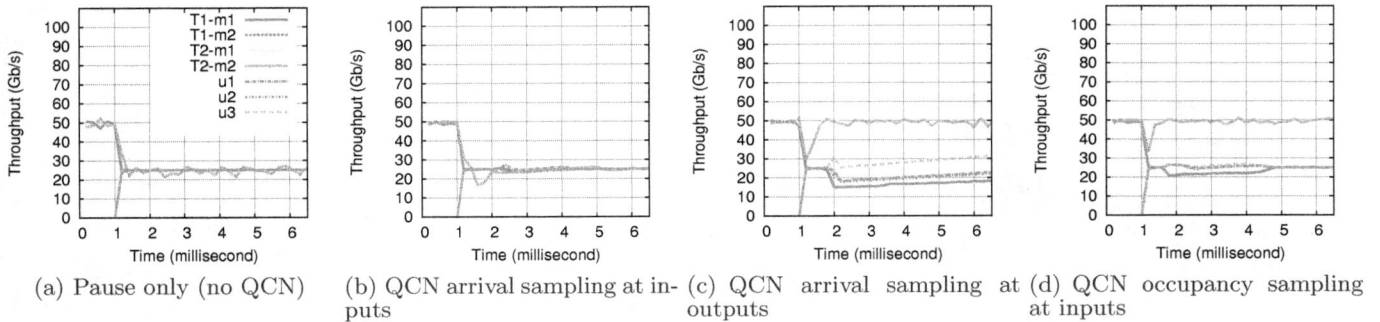

(a) Pause only (no QCN) (b) QCN arrival sampling at inputs (c) QCN arrival sampling at outputs (d) QCN occupancy sampling at inputs

Figure 10: The throughputs of multicast subflows T1-m1, T1-m2, T2-m1, and T2-m2, as well as of unicast flows u1, u2, and u3. All unicast flows target the same terminal port with subflow T1-m1.

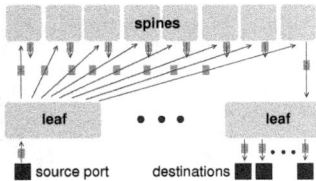

Figure 12: Bandwidth consumption of frame replication: (The diagram assumes single-path routing of frame's copies on 8 100G leaf-spine links, whereas our system actually sprays the load on 32 25G links.) The port sends the payload of the frame once to the ingress leaf switch, which outputs 8 copies to the spines. The latter send the copies to the target egress switches, which replicate them internally for all local destinations. Only 8 spines (32 in reality) and one egress switch are shown.

for every target egress (leaf) switch. Finally, the latter switches would fanout to all local destinations. Similarly, as shown in Fig.12, in our replication scheme, every egress switch receives each frame only once, replicating it internally. Therefore, we load the spine-to-leaf links as much as the ideal scheme. However, we consume extra bandwidth to send the frames to the spines as many times as we send them to the target egress switches. Therefore, the bandwidth consumption of our replication method, L, is, at most, two times the ideal L^* (we omit the full proof due to space limitations):

$$L \leq 2 \cdot L^* \qquad (2)$$

5.2 Concurrent provisioning of many servers

In our next experiment, we consider a typical application of multicast traffic. In particular, we source multicast traffic from 6 user ports in 3 leaf switches (2 sources per leaf). Every source hosts 10 multicast flows, each targeting all terminals in 20 egress leaf switches. Thus, every multicast flow has a fanout $|F| = 100$ ($20 \cdot 5$). All multicast flows are configured on the same lossy priority level and use two levels of surrogates. The 20 target switches (5 with 1st-level surrogates and the rest 15 with 2nd-level surrogates) of each flow are randomly selected from a fixed set of 40 distinct switches. It follows that, with a load of λ Gb/s at source ports, the average demand at the destinations is $6 \cdot \frac{20}{40} \cdot \lambda$ Gb/s. Therefore, the maximum feasible load is 33.3 Gb/s.

From Eq.(1), for $n = 2$, a tree can deliver a message to at most 84 destinations. The 2-level trees in the current experiment offer a larger reach, because source ports do not deliver local copies. Effectively, with a fanout of 5 at the sources being dedicated for remote surrogates, our trees can extend to $5 + 5 \cdot 5 = 30$ egress leaf switches or 150 terminals.

Figure 13(a) presents the average receive throughput at destinations against the input load. We see that the receive throughput at destinations grows linearly with the input load. However, for a source load of 30 Gb/s, the average receive throughput is 83 when it should be approximately 90 Gb/s. The last attested feasible source load is 25 Gb/s (i.e., 2.5 Gb/s per individual multicast flow), at which destinations are 76% utilized.

We conjecture that the cause for this throughput limitation is the statistical load imbalance at destinations. In simulations, we have seen that, even at 25 Gb/s input load, several destinations are fully loaded. With such multiple overloaded destinations, the ports are depleted of buffers, with an ensuing impact on throughput. We run the same experiment without VOQ synchronization, and the results are identical. In this configuration, every source port multiplexes 10 equal-loaded multicast flows, each having a local fanout of 5. Thus, on average, there are 50 VOQs active at every source, which will commonly overflow the sync CAM. Indeed, looking into the simulations, we verified that VOQs were never blocked for notably long periods.

Figure 13(b) presents the average frame delay as a function of the input load. As can be seen, at 5 Gb/s input load the delay is slightly above 4 microseconds, approaching 14 microseconds when the destinations are 82% utilized.

5.3 System-level broadcast

As shown in Fig. 14, a rack consists of two chassis, a chassis consists of four Chassis Interconnect Elements (CIEs), a CIE consists of four edge switches, and each edge switch has 5 user Ethernet ports at 100G. Although, replication trees may be created arbitrarily, we can exploit the topological affinity of ports to tame the configuration complexity. As shown in the figure, a broadcast flow can expand inside a rack using the Rack, Triplet, CIE, and egress-switch surrogates. The latter are not explicitly shown, but one of them is implied in every edge-switch with no outgoing arrows. Optimized configurations can replicate these surrogates in order to increase resiliency and performance.

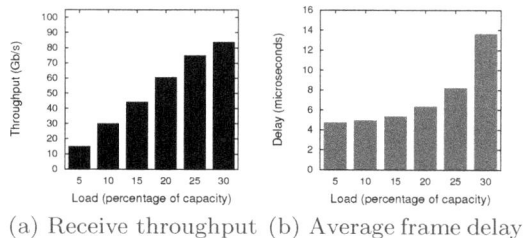

(a) Receive throughput (b) Average frame delay

Figure 13: Performance under uniform multicast traffic. Sources are 6 100G ports. Each source hosts 10 equally-loaded multicast flows targeting 100 destinations in 20 randomly-selected egress switches.

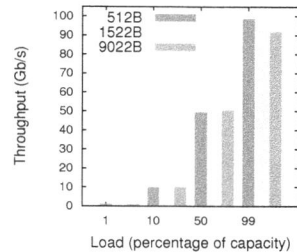

Figure 15: Average receive throughput at the destinations of a (broadcast) flow heading to 640 destinations against its input load.

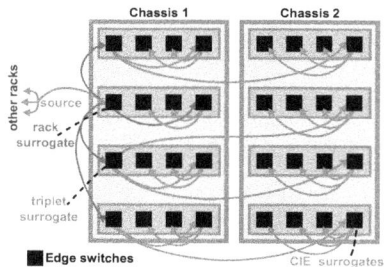

Figure 14: Hierarchical replication inside a rack (two chassis) using the Rack, Triplet, CIE, and egress-switch surrogates.

In our last experiment, we configured a flow broadcasting to all destinations in a full 4-rack system. Figure 15 presents the average receive throughputs at destinations against the input load of the broadcast flow, for 512B, 1522B, and 9022B (Jumbo) frames. As can be seen, in all cases the throughput grows linearly with the input load, with the exception of Jumbo frames that achieve a throughput up to 93 Gb/s.

Figure 16 depicts the average frame delay, measured from source to destination CNA. (Looking at the corresponding zero-load delays of *unicast* frames to remote (local) destinations, we measured 1.88 (0.143), 2.1 (0.35), and 3.6 (1.9) microseconds for 512B, 1522B, and 9022B frames, respectively.) We have separate plots for frames passing through 0, 1, 2, 3, and 4 levels of surrogates. As can be seen, the average delay increases as we move from 1 to 50 Gb/s load, but for 512B and 1522B frames, it stays almost constant when going from 50 to 99 Gb/s. The frame delay also increases with the number of surrogate levels. A significant fraction of these delays is spent scheduling and propagating the frames along the spine-leaf network at each hop of the surrogate tree. While not shown in this paper, our system can lower these delays by avoiding the request-grant admission phase when transmitting frames to non-congested destinations similar to [11, 12].

6. DISCUSSIONS

Implosion of control messages: The multiplication of (unicast) ACK and grant messages is an expected consequence of reliable scheduled multicasting. A similar effect, but which happens in the opposite direction, is due to uni-

cast requests. In our system, we reduce the messages per port and the ensuing bandwidth overhead, through *(a)* hierarchical replication and *(b)* coalescing (combining) of the per-VOQ control messages.

Impact on unicast: One can mitigate the unwanted interferences at the ports by mapping unicast and multicast traffic to separate priority levels, each associated with a configurable service weight used for frame scheduling at fabric egress ports. In our architecture, doing so also segregates the unicast from the multicast VOQs.

Effect on neighbors: The frame replication via the multicast cache harnesses the available crossbar-input bandwidth of the neighboring Ethernet and PCIe ports. To alleviate the burden, we route the local copies, generated at a surrogate or terminal port, through special, one-to-one, crossbar links. This eliminates the impact of these local copies on the neighboring ports. Furthermore, we use (packet-size aware) weighted-round-robin scheduling [13]. One instance of the scheduler is located at every (ingress) crossbar input, and a configurable weight in the range $1 - 99$ defines the proportion of the link bandwidth that multicast copies can appropriate from unicast traffic originating from the corresponding terminal port.

Comparison to other switch architectures: Many Ethernet switch chips available today are based on a shared-memory architecture. These can forward frames copies by "simply" generating the corresponding headers and inserting them in the target output queues [14]. Our design recognizes that hierarchical replication will be indispensable for (reliable or not) hardware multicasting in the emerging high-speed datacenter fabrics. For example, even a moderate switch or fabric with 100 ports at 100G has to generate and process one 512B copy every 0.41 ns.

Variations of the request-grant/credit protocol used here exist in some chassis switch and router products [15, 16]. However, no performance evaluations nor detailed descriptions are available for these systems. In research papers, variations of these protocols have been described and evaluated in [17, 12], showing excellent QoS for unicast traffic. In our system, we use a *request-grant/credit-ACK* protocol to build a reliable server-fabric for performance-optimized datacenter clusters, and consider its multicasting performance. Bianco et. al. have studied multicast support for an asynchronous chassis switch using a request-grant credit protocol [18]. However, that system is remarkably smaller than ours (16 10G ports), and it is built around a single (spine) crossbar. Furthermore, [18] uses FIFO queuing of multicast

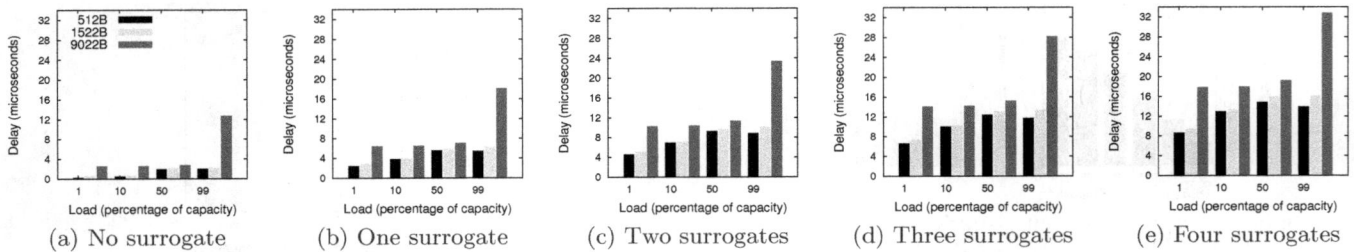

Figure 16: Average frame delay (CNA to CNA) in a broadcast flow heading to 640 destinations. We plot separately the delays for frames passing through 0, 1, 2, 3, and 4 levels of surrogates.

traffic, and cannot replicate delayed copies. Our system applies a favorable VOQ scheme, with accompanying congestion management for lossy and lossless priority levels, and can replicate asynchronously sent copies.

7. CONCLUSIONS

Our work builds upon a massive, performance-optimized server-rack fabric that offers 640, equidistant Ethernet ports at 100G, and provides small buffers and lossless end-to-end scheduled service to avoid backlogs and reduce frame delay. We described the uniform integration of multicast traffic, the obstacles we encountered and the solutions we implemented. We utilize hierarchical replication in hardware, facilitated by specially allocated fabric ports to cope with the enormous processing and forwarding rates. For the efficient replication of the delayed copies, we use a multicast cache together with a VOQ synchronization mechanism. Finally, we developed advantageous flow and congestion control schemes for lossy and lossless multicast traffic classes. Simulations on a detailed computer model evaluated the full 4-rack system, demonstrating the high performance levels that it offers, as well as significant trade-offs.

8. ACKNOWLEDGMENTS

We would like to thank our colleagues in IBM Research–Zurich and in the hardware division of IBM (STG), and Anne-Marie Cromack for proofreading the manuscript. Special thanks to Cyriel Minkenberg, Mitch Gusat, David Shadivy, and Bill Holland, as well as to the anonymous reviewers that helped us improve the manuscript.

9. REFERENCES

[1] P. Radoslavov, C. Papadopoulos, R. Govindan, and D. Estrin, "A Comparison of Application-level and Router-assisted Hierarchical Schemes for Reliable Multicast," *IEEE/ACM Trans. Netw.*, vol. 12, no. 3, pp. 469–482, 2004.

[2] C.-K. Kim and T. T. Lee, "Call Scheduling Algorithms in a Multicast Switch," *IEEE Trans. Commun.*, vol. 40, no. 3, pp. 625–635, 1992.

[3] H. J. Chao, B.-S. Choe, J.-S. Park, and N. Uzun, "Design and Implementation of Abacus Switch: A Scalable Multicast ATM Switch," *IEEE JSAC*, vol. 15, no. 5, pp. 830–843, 1997.

[4] M. A. Marsan, A. Bianco, P. Giaccone, E. Leonardi, and F. Neri, "Multicast Traffic in Input-Queued Switches: Optimal Scheduling and Maximum

Throughput," *IEEE/ACM Trans. Netw.*, vol. 11, no. 3, pp. 465–477, 2003.

[5] F. Neeser, N. Chrysos, R. Clauberg, D. Crisan, M. Gusat, C. Minkenberg, K. Valk, and C. Basso, "Occupancy Sampling for Terabit CEE Switches," in *Proc. IEEE Hot Interconnects*, 2012.

[6] N. Chrysos, F. Neeser, M. Gusat, C. Minkenberg, W. Denzel, and C. Basso, "All Routes to Efficient Datacenter Fabrics," in *Proc. INA-OCMC*, Berlin, Germany, January 2014.

[7] *802.1Qau - Virtual Bridged Local Area Networks - Amendment: Congestion Notification*, IEEE Std., 2010.

[8] B. Prabhakar, N. McKeown, and R. Ahuja, "Multicast Scheduling for Input-Queued Switches," *IEEE JSAC*, vol. 15, no. 5, pp. 855–866, 1997.

[9] D. Pan and Y. Yang, "FIFO-based Multicast Scheduling Algorithm For Virtual Output Queued Packet Switches," *IEEE Trans. Comp.*, vol. 54, no. 10, pp. 1283–1297, 2005.

[10] W. Dally and B. Towles, *Principles and Practices of Interconnection Networks*. San Francisco, CA: Morgan Kaufmann Publishers Inc., 2003.

[11] C. Minkenberg and M. Gusat, "Design and Performance of Speculative Flow Control for High-Radix Datacenter Interconnect Switches," *Elsevier Journal of Parallel and Distributed Computing*, vol. 69, no. 8, pp. 680–695, Aug. 2009.

[12] N. Chrysos, "Congestion Management for Non-Blocking Clos Networks," in *Proc. ACM/IEEE ANCS*, Florida, USA, Dec. 2007.

[13] K. G. Harteros and M. Katevenis, "Fast parallel comparison circuits for scheduling," *Institute of Computer Science, FORTH*, 2002.

[14] F. M. Chiussi, Y. Xia, and V. P. Kumar, "Performance of Shared-Memory Switches under Multicast Bursty Traffic," *IEEE JSAC*, vol. 15, no. 3, pp. 473–487, 1997.

[15] P. Sindhu, P. Lacroute, M. Tucker, J. Weisbloom, and D. Winters, US Patent US 7,102,999 B2, Sep., 2006.

[16] O. Iny, US Patent US 7,619,970 B2, Nov., 2009.

[17] P. Pappu, J. Parwatikar, J. Turner, and K. Wong, "Distributed Queueing in Scalable High Performance Routers," in *Proc. IEEE INFOCOM*, San Francisco, USA, Apr. 2003.

[18] A. Bianco, P. Giaccone, E. M. Giraudo, F. Neri, and E. Schiattarella, "Multicast Support for a Storage Area Network Switch," in *Proc. IEEE GLOBECOM*, 2006.

Marlin: A Memory-Based Rack Area Network

Cheng-Chun Tu
Stony Brook University
1500 Stony Brook Road
New York, U.S.A
u9012063@gmail.com

Chao-tang Lee
Industrial Technology
Research Institute
195 Chung Hsing Road
Hsinchu, Taiwan
marklee@itri.org.tw

Tzi-cker Chiueh
Industrial Technology
Research Institute
195 Chung Hsing Road
Hsinchu, Taiwan
tcc@itri.org.tw

ABSTRACT

Disaggregation of hardware resources that are traditionally embedded within individual servers into separate resource pools is an emerging architectural trend in hyperscale data center design, as exemplified by Facebook's *disaggregated rack* architecture. This paper presents the design, implementation and evaluation of a PCIe-based rack area network system called *Marlin*, which is designed to support the communications and resource sharing needs of disaggregated racks. By virtue of being based on PCIe, *Marlin* presents a memory-based addressing model for both I/O device sharing among multiple hosts and inter-host communications. That is, when a node communicates with other nodes or accesses resources in the same rack, it uses memory read and write operations. In the area of inter-node communications, *Marlin* offers *hardware-based remote direct memory access* (HRDMA) as a first-class communications primitive between servers within a rack. In addition, *Marlin* supports socket-based communications for legacy network applications and cross-machine zero memory copying for applications designed specifically to take full advantage of memory-based communications. Empirical measurements on a fully operational *Marlin* prototype based on 4-lane Gen3 PCIe technology show that the one-way kernel-to-kernel latency is 8.5μsec and the end-to-end sustainable TCP throughput is 19.6 Gbps.

Categories and Subject Descriptors

C.2.1 [**Computer-Communication Networks**]: Network Architecture and Design; B.3.2 [**Memory Structures**]: Shared Memory

Keywords

PCIe Fabric; Rack Disaggregation; Rack-Area Network; RDMA; MR-IOV; SR-IOV; Non Transparent Bridge

1. INTRODUCTION

Hyperscale data centers increasingly use a rack rather than a machine as the basic building block. Recently, Facebook advocated a *disaggregated rack* architecture [8, 9], in which a rack consists not of a set of self-contained hosts, but of a CPU/memory pool, a

disk pool, and a network interface (NIC) pool, which are connected through a high-bandwidth and low-latency rack-area network. A major deployment advantage of the disaggregated rack architecture is that it allows different system components, i.e. CPU, memory, disk and NIC, to be upgraded according to their own technology cycle. From the architectural standpoint, rack disaggregation reduces each "host" to a CPU/memory module, decouples CPU/memory from I/O devices such as disk controllers and network interfaces, and enables more efficient and flexible I/O resource allocation and utilization.

The key enabling technology for the disaggregated rack architecture is the ability for multiple CPU/memory modules to share I/O devices. *Ladon* [46] is a software-only solution that allows multiple servers or multiple virtual machines (VM) running on distinct servers to share PCIe-based I/O devices securely, efficiently and transparently. Specifically, VMs running on distinct servers of a rack are able to use the same PCIe-based NIC to communicate with VMs running on a different rack, without interfering with one another and at native speed. In *Ladon*, servers are connected with the I/O devices they share via a PCIe network.

This paper proposes to take a PCIe-based network that is originally designed for I/O device sharing and extend it into an intra-rack inter-server network system called *Marlin* for the disaggregated rack architecture, and describes two communication mechanisms that are built on top of this architecture: a socket communication mechanism that is meant to support legacy network applications, and a cross-machine memory copying mechanism that is designed to expose *Marlin*'s raw transfer capability to applications that are developed specifically to take advantage of *Marlin*. Logically, *Marlin* offers a *hybrid Ethernet/PCIe switch* to servers in a rack so that they could communicate with one another directly via the PCIe links and with machines outside the rack through Ethernet links. Physically, *Marlin* consists of a management host (MH), a PCIe switch, and a set of Ethernet NICs, and each machine in the rack is connected to a port in the PCIe switch through a PCIe expansion card and a PCIe cable. *Marlin* leverages *Ladon*'s novel multi-root I/O device sharing mechanism [46] to enable servers in a rack to share the Ethernet ports in the hybrid switch.

A distinct feature of the PCIe architecture is its memory-based addressing model. Every interaction with a PCIe device is through a memory read/write operation, including configuring a PCIe device, transferring data to and from a PCIe device via an I/O or memory access instruction, and interrupting a PCIe device. Accordingly, the fundamental communication primitive in *Marlin* is a hardware-based remote direct memory access (HRDMA) mechanism, which allows one machine to initiate a DMA transaction against another machine's memory in the same rack area network *without any software intervention*. To support existing socket-based applications, *Marlin* supports an Ethernet-over-PCIe layer that transfers Ethernet frames using HRDMA. Because of *Marlin*'s memory-based addressing model, this layer features a *sender-based buffer management* scheme [19] that allows a sender machine to manage the receive buffer space that a receiver machine reserves for the sender. To take full advantage of *Marlin*'s underlying HRDMA mechanism, *Marlin* provides a cross-machine memory copying operation (CMMC) that allows an application process running on one machine to copy data from its address space to the address space of another application process running on another machine in the same rack, *without any software in between*. In other words, CMMC is a zero-copy application-level memory copying mechanism, from the sender application's address space to the receiver application's address space.

Marlin is based on the emerging software-defined network (SDN) architecture as exemplified by OpenFlow [35], in that it decouples the network's control plane from data plane, and it centralizes the control plane functionalities into a dedicated controller, specifically, the management host. *Marlin* takes advantage of this central control plane architecture to configure the transparent and non-transparent PCIe switches of a rack's backplane, establish a global address space that is visible to a rack's hosts, and control the accessibility of this address space to specific hosts according to user-specified policies.

2. PCI EXPRESS ARCHITECTURE

2.1 PCIe Architecture

PCIe is a layered protocol consisting of a physical layer, a data link layer and a transaction layer. The transaction layer is responsible for encapsulating high-level PCIe transactions issued by the OS or firmware, i.e., *memory, I/O, configuration* and *message*, into PCIe transaction layer packets (TLP). The data link layer is responsible for sequencing transaction layer packets (TLP) using a sequence numbering mechanism, and ensuring their reliable delivery using CRC and ACK/NACK. In a server, the *root complex* residing in the Northbridge part of the chipset connects CPU and memory with the PCIe network and implements the transaction layer. Each PCIe device in the server is uniquely identified by a bus/device/function ID, and is given a set of *configuration space registers* (CSR) and contains a standardized part (such as device vendor ID, command, *base address register* or BAR, etc.) and a device-specific part. A PCIe card occupying a PCIe slot could function as one or multiple physical functions (PF), each acting like a logical PCIe device with its own device ID and CSR. The PCI-SIG standard on single-root I/O virtualization (SRIOV) [15] virtualizes a PCIe device into multiple virtual PCIe devices, where each of which could be assigned to a distinct VM. SR-IOV separates a physical function (PF) from a virtual function (VF). A PF is a full-function PCI device with its IDs and complete CSR, whereas a VF is a lighter-weight PCIe device with its IDs but without a complete CSR. Instead, each VF only has its own copy of the data plane-related portion of the CSR, but the control plane-related portion is borrowed from its underlying PF's CSR. As a result, SRIOV PCIe devices require special support from BIOS for memory-mapped I/O address range allocation, and from the OS for control plane configuration.

Although PCIe was originally designed to be a system backplane, it is now capable of scaling to a large number of PCIe end points through one or multiple PCIe transparent bridges (TB) or switches. Topologically the end points of a PCIe domain form a tree, whose root is the root complex. To the OS, every operation in a PCIe domain is specified in terms of a memory read or write operation with a target address, which is then translated into a PCIe network packet by the transaction layer and delivered to the target PCIe end point. Routing is based on the address carried in the packet. Unlike Ethernet, PCIe network is lossless at the transport layer; its robust flow-control mechanism prevents packet from being dropped.

2.2 Non-Transparent PCIe Bridging

In the PCIe architecture, at any point in time every PCIe domain has exactly one active root complex. Therefore, in theory, two servers are not allowed to co-exist in the same PCIe domain. Non-transparent bridge (NTB) is a part of the PCI-SIG standard designed to enable two or more PCIe domains to inter-operate together as if they are in the same domain, and thus makes a key building block for the proposed *Marlin* system.

A two-port NTB represents two PCIe end points, each of which belongs to a separate PCIe domain. These two end points each expose a type 0 header type in CSR and thus are discovered and enumerated by their respective PCIe domains in the same way as ordinary PCIe end points. However, an NTB provides additional *memory address translation*, *device ID translation* and *messaging* facilities that allow the two PCIe domains to work together as a whole while keeping them logically isolate from each other. More generally, a PCIe switch with X NTB ports and Y TB ports allows the PCIe domain in which the Y TB ports participates, called the *master* domain, to work with X other PCIe domains, each of which is a *slave* domain and supported by an NTB port. The side of an NTB port that connects to a slave domain is the *virtual* side, whereas the other side is called the *link* side.

The magic of an NTB lies in its ability to deliver a memory read/write operation initiated from one PCIe domain to another PCIe domain, with some translations, and then executed. From the initiating domain's standpoint, the memory read/write operation is logically executed locally within its domain, although physically it is executed in a remote domain. As mentioned earlier, every PCIe end point is equipped with a set of BARs that specify the portions of the physical memory address space of the end point's associated PCIe domain for which it is responsible. That is, all memory read and write operations in a PCIe domain that target at the memory address ranges associated with a PCIe end point's BARs are delivered to that end point. An NTB port associates with every BAR on the link (virtual) side a *memory translation* register, which converts a received memory address at the link (virtual) side into another memory address at the virtual (link) side. The side of an NTB port providing the BAR is the *primary* side whereas the other side is the *secondary* side. For example, an NTB could translate the physical address 0xF8800000 on its link side to the physical address 0xF8A00000 on its virtual side by writing 0xF8800000 to a link-side BAR and 0xF8A00000 to this BAR's memory translation register. In this case, the link side is the primary side and the virtual side is the secondary side.

NTB also contains an ID translation table, which converts the source ID of a PCIe operation as it travels from one domain to another. To allow the two PCIe domains across an NTB port to work more closely, the NTB provides *doorbell* registers for one domain to interrupt the other, and *scratchpad* registers for one domain to pass some information to the other. These two messaging mechanisms provide an out-of-band control path for these two PCIe domains to better communicate with each other.

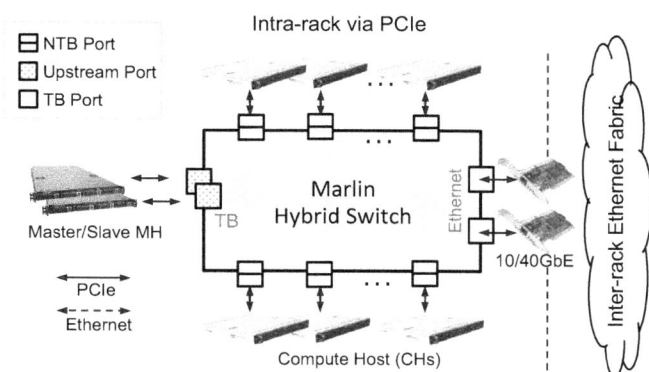

Figure 1: *The key building block of the proposed rack area networking architecture is a hybrid top-of-rack switch that consists of PCIe ports and Ethernet ports.*

3. RACK AREA NETWORKING

3.1 System Architecture

As shown in Figure 1, the key building block of the proposed rack area networking architecture is a hybrid top of rack (TOR) switch consisting of PCIe ports and Ethernet ports. Every machine or compute host in a rack is connected to a port of this *Marlin* switch through a PCIe extender card and a PCIe cable, and communicates with other machines in the rack directly over PCIe and with machines outside the rack through the Ethernet ports. As a rack's server density increases, multiple such TOR switches are needed to connect the machines in a rack. Physically, the *Marlin* switch consists of a management host (MH), a standard PCIe switch with TB and NTB ports, and multiple Ethernet NICs each connected to a TB port of the PCIe switch. The MH is connected to the *Marlin* switch through a TB port, and serves as the root complex of the PCIe domain to which the PCIe switch and Ethernet NICs belong. Other machines or compute hosts in the rack are connected to the *Marlin* switch through the NTB ports.

The MH of the *Marlin* switch maps the main memory of every attached machine to its physical memory address space, and in turn exposes its physical memory address space to every attached machine. For example, assume every machine in the rack including the MH has 32GB worth of local memory. The MH first maps the main memory of the i-th attached machine's local memory to the range from $[32GB + (i - 1) * 32GB, 32GB + i * 32GB)$ of its physical memory address space, as shown in Figure 2(a). Then each attached machine maps the MH's entire physical address space to the range of its physical address space above 32GB. With this set-up, an attached machine could access the i-th attached machine's local memory by reading or writing the $[64GB + (i - 1) * 32GB, 64GB + i * 32GB)$ range of its local physical memory address range, as shown in Figure 2(b). Therefore, an attached machine could access its local memory through either a range below 32GB (directly), or through a range above 64GB (indirectly through the MH's physical address space). Suppose there are 50 machines attached to the *Marlin* switch, including the MH. Then every attached machine could see a 1600GB worth of physical memory, with 32GB local in its own machine (zero hop), 32GB in the MH (one hop) and 1536GB in other attached machines (two hops). Consequently, a *Marlin* switch turns the physical memories of all the machines attached to it into a global memory pool.

Modern BIOS performs physical memory address allocation for PCIe devices at the system boot-up time, but this allocation conflicts with the above design. *Marlin* overcomes this by overriding BIOS's allocation decisions after the kernel takes control. Today's 64-bit servers support at least 48 bits of physical addresses, which are enough to support a 256TB physical address space.

When the *Marlin* switch boots up, its MH enumerates all the devices connected to the PCIe switch, including the Ethernet NICs and NTB ports. Then it sets up the above memory address mappings by programming the BARs, the memory translation registers, and the device ID translation tables on the NTB ports of the PCIe switch. Finally, the MH also exposes the physical memory address range associated with the Ethernet NICs to all attached machines so that they could directly interact with these NICs. To enable attached machines to access these NICs in a way that does not interfere with one another, the MH allocates to each machine one or multiple VFs from the SRIOV-capable Ethernet NICs. This VF allocation mechanism requires a special PCIe driver to be installed in the attached machines [46].

Because every machine connected to a *Marlin* switch could address each physical memory page of every other machine attached to the same switch, data security and safety becomes a critical issue. More specifically, *Marlin* must guarantee that a machine be able to access a remote physical memory page in the global memory pool only when it is explicitly allowed to. *Marlin* leverages IOMMU [16, 27, 48] to provide this security guarantee. When a PCIe device on a machine accesses the machine's physical memory, IOMMU translates the addresses specified in the access operations into the machine's physical memory address space using an IOMMU mapping table. When the target address of a PCIe operation does not match any entry in the IOMMU mapping table, the operation is denied and aborted. IOMMU was originally proposed to prevent one VM in a machine from corrupting another VM in the same machine, but is re-purposed in *Marlin* to prevent one physical machine from accessing the main memory of another physical machine without the latter's permission.

Every machine attached to a *Marlin* switch, including the MH, is assigned a unique PCIe device ID in the MH's PCIe domain, which remains unique after device ID translation across an NTB port. Therefore, the target address of a PCIe operation from Machine A to Machine C is matched against a different IOMMU mapping table in Machine C than that used for a PCIe operation from Machine B to Machine C. To open up a physical memory page P in Machine C only to Machine B, *Marlin* places an entry for P in Machine C's IOMMU mapping table for Machine B, so that memory accesses to P from Machine B could match an entry in this IOMMU mapping table. The above design not only opens up the page P to Machine B, but also restricts P's accessibility to Machine B only, because no other IOMMU mapping tables in Machine C contain an entry for Page P. To close the page P to Machine B, *Marlin* simply removes the entry corresponding to P from Machine C's IOMMU mapping table for Machine B.

3.2 CPU-based Accesses to Remote Memory

Because *Marlin* enables every machine connected to a *Marlin* switch to directly address every other machine's memory, it offers two new ways for machines connected to the same switch to interact with one another. First, a CPU on one machine could use standard remote memory copying API functions such as memcpy to move data between machines. However, because the shared memory abstraction supported by *Marlin* is non-cache-coherent, memory regions that are meant to be accessed by multiple machines must be marked as non-cacheable. Such non-cacheable shared mem-

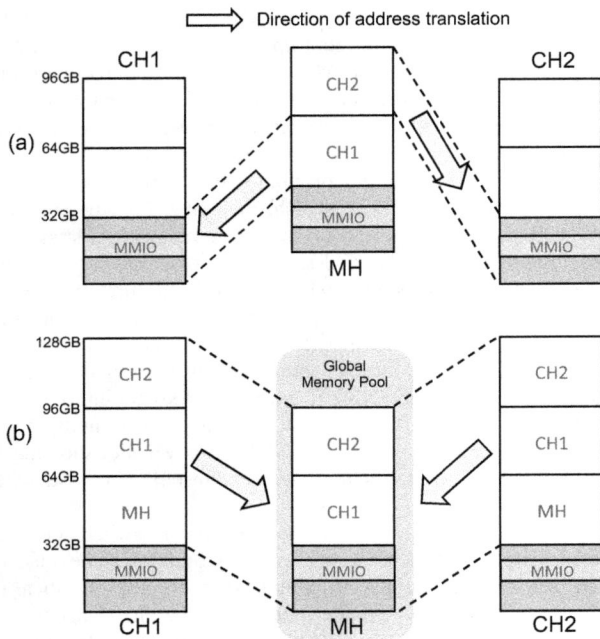

Figure 2: *Construction of* Marlin's *global memory pool requires two address translations; one set up by the MH to map the physical memory of every attached machine, or Compute Host (CH), to the MH's physical memory address space, as shown in (a), and the other done by each CH to map the MH's physical memory address space into its own local physical address space, as shown in (b).*

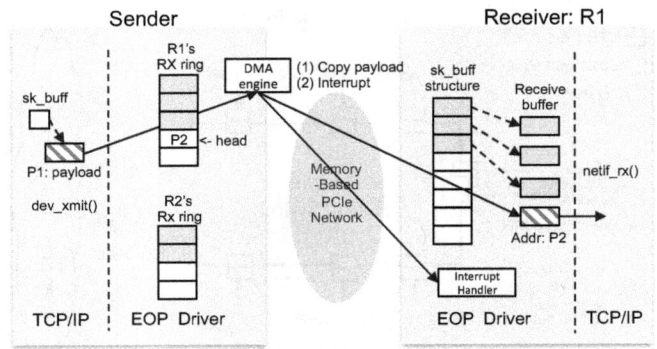

Figure 3: *Transmission and reception of an Ethernet over a PCIe network. The DMA engine copies the payload referenced in an sk_buff structure at the sender side directly to the receiver side, in this case, R1. The sender-side EOP driver on one node keeps track of the head and tail pointer of every receive ring buffer that other nodes allocate for it. Transmitting a packet requires at least two HRDMA operations, one to copy the actual packet and the other to interrupt the receiver to inform it of the transmission completion.*

ory in *Marlin* could be used to implement a memory-based locking mechanism across machines. Second, *Marlin* allows a CPU in one machine to directly send an MSI-X based interrupt to another machine using a single memory write instruction, without relying on any additional I/O device or doorbell mechanism. Once the memory write PCIe packet from the interrupting host gets translated by NTB to the other side, the memory write becomes a legitimate MSI-based write and eventually hits another host's local APIC memory area. For example in Figure 2, CH1 interrupts CH2 by writing to CH2's local APIC memory address space with destination address 96G + 0xFEE00000. The NTB translates ths address from 96G + 0xFEE00000 in CH1 to 0xFEE00000 in CH2, which becomes a legitimate MSI address.

3.3 Hardware-based Remote Direct Memory Access

On each NTB port of the *Marlin* switch is a DMA engine that could initiate a DMA transaction from one local physical address range to another local physical address range. Because the physical memories of the MH and all other attached machines are all mapped to each attached machine's local physical address range, this DMA engine could perform both *local memory copying*, where both the source and target reside in the local machine, and *inter-machine memory copying*, where either the source or target but not both resides in a remote machine. This inter-machine memory copying operation is a form of remote DMA (RDMA) that is completely hardware-based and does not involve any software. It differs significantly from InfiniBand (IB) RDMA, in which the payload at the source is DMAed into an IB interface, fragmented and encapsulated into IB packets, which are sent over IB links, get de-

capsulated and re-assembled, and DMAed to the receive buffers. In contrast, payloads are packaged into PCIe packets which flow from source to destination, and as a result, payloads do not need to experience additional format translation (e.g. between PCIe and Infiniband) and could be moved in a cut-through rather than store-and-forward fashion. This HRDMA mechanism is the fundamental building block of the *Marlin* architecture.

The DMA engine on the PCIe switch supports scatter-and-gather DMA. Therefore, the current HRDMA implementation exploits this capability to aggregate multiple high-level operations issued from the same source node, each destined to a different destination node, into a single DMA transaction. In addition, the DMA engine supports multiple channels, each of which could carry out an independent DMA transaction on its own. The current HRDMA implementation further exploits this fact to issue multiple concurrent DMA transactions at a time. These two aggregation mechanisms significantly improve *Marlin*'s HRDMA throughput.

3.4 Ethernet over PCIe

The Ethernet over PCIe (EOP) interface is positioned as a pseudo device interface similar to an Ethernet NIC. In the IP routing table of every attached machine, all the attached machines that are directly connected to the *Marlin* switch are assumed to be in the same IP subnet and are explicitly routed to the EOP interface, whereas all other machines are routed through the Ethernet interfaces. This way, packets destined to machines attached to the same *Marlin* switch as the home machine are sent out through the EOP interface. In addition, to improve the transport efficiency, the MTU of the EOP interface is set to 64KB, the same as the maximum segment size for IP datagram.

The EOP driver exposes the same interface to the high-level IP protocol stack and uses the same transmission and reception buffer ring as a standard Ethernet driver. A transmission or reception buffer ring is an array of pointers to buffers that is used in a cyclic fashion. In addition to an array of buffer pointers, a receive buffer ring holds two index pointers to the array, *head* and *tail*. Receiver buffer ring entries between *head* and *tail* point to packets that are received and not yet forwarded up to the IP protocol stack. However, there are two key differences between the EOP driver and the standard Ethernet driver. First, each attached machine pre-allocates a receive buffer ring specifically for *every other* attached machine in the rack. Second, the free space in a receive buffer ring reserved on a machine M1 for a remote machine M2 is supplied by M1 but directly consumed by M2.

As shown in Figure 3, when receiving a socket buffer structure, e.g., sk_buff in Linux, that contains a pointer ($P1$) to an Ethernet packet to be transmitted, the sending-side logic of the EOP driver takes control and performs the following steps:

1. Derives from the packet's destination MAC address the corresponding receive buffer ring and then the ring's current *head* pointer ($P2$),

2. Issues an HRDMA transaction using $P1$ as the source address, $P2$ as the target address, and the Ethernet packet's length as the HRDMA transaction size, and

3. Handles the *completion* interrupt when the HRDMA transaction is done by issuing a *packet arrival* interrupt to the destination machine, incrementing (modulo) the *head* pointer of the associated receive buffer ring, and calling on the upper layer to send down the next packet to be transmitted.

In the design above, the sending-side logic of the EOP driver may be blocked at Step 1 because there is no free buffer at the remote receive buffer ring, or at Step 2 because all descriptors in the DMA engine are in use. When the EOP driver on the destination machine receives a packet arrival interrupt, its receiving-side logic comes into play and performs the following:

1. Locates the local receive buffer ring corresponding to the machine issuing the interrupt, then its *tail* pointer and finally the pointer to the buffer actually holding the received packet,

2. Constructs a sk_buff structure that contains the actual receive buffer's pointer among other things, and forwards the sk_buff up to the IP protocol stack, and

3. Allocates a new buffer, puts its pointer into the receive buffer ring entry pointed to by the *tail* pointer, increments (modulo) the *tail* pointer, and informs the associated sender of the new *tail* pointer.

At Step 2, the packet arrival interrupt handler examines the referred buffer to ensure it contains a valid packet before forming a receive sk_buff out of it. When a sender copies an Ethernet packet to a receiver, it encodes the updated *head* pointer, the packet length information and a valid bit flag in the packet's destination MAC address, so that the receiver could determine if a buffer holds a valid packet, derive the size of the transmitted Ethernet packet, and update the *head* pointer of the sender's associated receive buffer ring.

At Step 3, a remote memory access is required to inform the sender of the updated *tail* pointer, which the sender compares with the *head* pointer to detect the situation in which the associated receive buffer ring is filled up. To eliminate this remote memory access in every packet transfer, every machine caches the *tail* pointer of each of its receive buffer rings on remote machines. These cached *tail* pointers may be stale because, to decrease the code path length in the packet arrival interrupt handler, the EOP driver asynchronously allocates new buffers, updates the *tail* pointer and informs the sender of this update in the background. However, the EOP driver ensures that a *tail* pointer and its associated *head* pointer are always sufficiently far apart that such staleness is harmless.

With sender-side caching of the head and tail pointers of receive buffer rings and lazy *tail* pointer updates, every Ethernet packet transmission incurs only two remote memory accesses, one for the packet payload including the embedded EOP header information, and the other for the packet arrival interrupt. In addition, every once in a while, a machine needs to use a remote memory access to update the *tail* pointer cached at every other machine that previously sent packets to it. As a further optimization, when a sender sends a sequence of packets to a receiver, the sender could choose to issue only one packet arrival interrupt for multiple sent packets, essentially implementing *interrupt coalescing*. This requires the packet arrival interrupt handler to process as many received packets as possible when it is invoked.

3.5 Cross-Machine Memory Copying

Application-level cross-machine memory copying (CMMC) allows an application running on one machine to copy data to another application running on another machine connected to the same *Marlin* switch. The design pattern using CMMC works as follows.

1. The sender application first asks the receiver application for an application-level receive buffer of a certain size.

2. The receiver application allocates a page-aligned receive memory area locally, pins it down in memory, derives the physical page numbers of the physical pages backing this receive memory area, and returns to the sender application the pointer to this receive memory area, as well as the physical page number list.

3. When the sender application receives the response returned by the receiver application, it registers the receiver application's IP address, the receiver memory pointer and the physical page number list with its underlying OS.

4. The sender application makes a remote write system call to write to anywhere in this receive memory area in the receive application.

Three new system calls are created to support CMMC. An *address translation* system call is used at Step 2 for a receiver application to derive the physical page number list behind a page-aligned contiguous memory area. A *registration* system call is used at Step 3 for a sender application to register with the underlying OS a remote memory area and its corresponding physical page list, and receive a handle. A *remote write* system call is used at Step 4 for a sender application to write a local buffer to a remote memory area.

The input arguments to a remote write system call are a *handle*, which represents a remote memory area, a *target offset*, which represents the start position in the remote memory area for the write operation, a *source pointer*, which represents the start address of the local source buffer, and *length*. Given a remote write system call, *Marlin*'s CMMC implementation first converts the handle to the corresponding remote memory area, then identifies the sequence of physical page numbers behind the area to be written, and finally sets up a sequence of HRDMA operations using the source pointer and the target physical page numbers. The number of HRDMA operations required to implement a remote write system call depends on the degree of fragmentation, or the number of contiguous physical memory areas behind the source area and the target area. For example, if the source area and the target area of a CMMC operation are backed by 4 and 6 disjoint physical memory regions, respectively, this CMMC operation requires 6 HRDMA operations. Optionally, the remote write system call could include an option that sends a copy completion signal to the receiver application when all of the underlying HRDMA operations are completed.

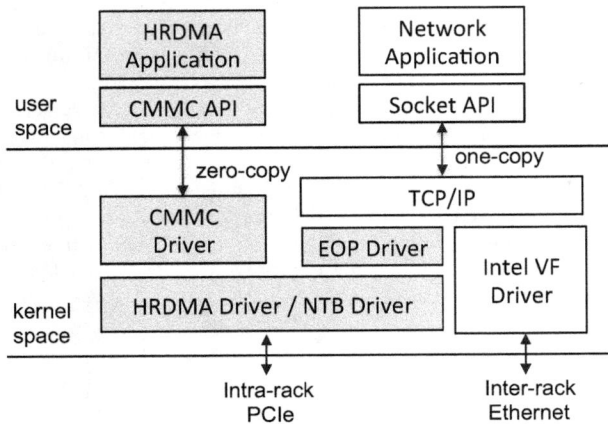

Figure 4: *The software architecture of* Marlin*'s compute host component, where the shaded parts are software introduced by* Marlin

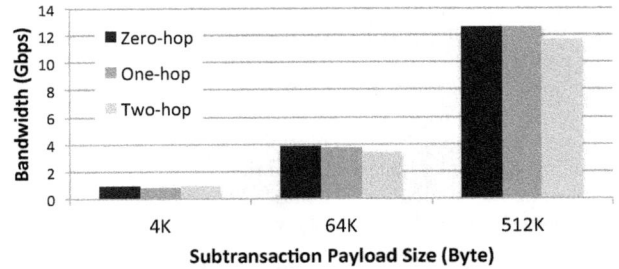

Figure 5: *The throughput comparison among zero-hop, one-hop and two-hop DMA operations with a single source-destination pair when the transfer size is 4KB, 64KB and 512KB*

4. PROTOTYPE IMPLEMENTATION

The hardware test-bed used in the *Marlin* prototype consists of five Intel X86 servers, one 10GE NIC, eight PLX PEX8732, two PLX PEX8717 switches with non-transparent ports, and one PLX PEX8748 PCIe switch. Two servers serve as the master and backup management host, the other two servers serve as compute hosts and the fifth server is a remote server that is not connected to the PCIe switch. All these servers are Supermicro 1U server equipped 8-core Intel Xeon 3.4GHz CPU and 8GB of memory.

Because of signal deterioration concerns [12], each of the two compute hosts is connected to a pair of PEX8732 devices to boost the signals, then a PEX8717 switch, then again connected to a pair of PEX8732 devices, and finally the PEX8748 switch. [1] The PEX8717 device is a 16-lane 10-port switch that supports up to 2 NTB ports and four DMA channels for peer-to-peer data transfers. In addition, an Intel 82599 SRIOV 10GE NIC serves as the out-of-rack Ethernet adapter, is plugged into a downstream TB port of the PCIe switch, and is connected to another Intel 82599 SRIOV 10GE NIC on the fifth server using a duplex fiber optic cable.

The PEX8748 PCIe switch is a 48-lane, 12-port PCIe Gen3 switch, where each lane provides 8Gbits/s raw transfer bandwidth. We assigned 4 lanes of this PCIe switch to the management host, 4 lanes to each of the two compute hosts, and another 4 lanes to the Intel 82599 NIC.

The *Marlin* prototype implementation is based on Fedora 15 with the Linux kernel version 2.6.38, and consists of a management host component and two compute hosts. The management host is responsible for enumerating the PCIe devices, including non-transparent PCIe switches and Ethernet NICs, sets up the BARs and translation registers on NTBs, and allocates and de-allocates virtual PCIe devices to compute hosts for I/O device sharing.

Figure 4 shows the software architecture of *Marlin*'s implementation on compute hosts, which offers two inter-host communications mechanisms: the Ethernet-over-PCIe (EOP) driver supports a socket-based communication mechanism that is meant to support legacy network applications, and the cross-machine memory copying (CMMC) driver is designed to expose *Marlin*'s zero-copy data transfer capability to user applications via a specially designed API.

---

[1]Using additional signal repeaters is a temporary system artifact in *Marlin*'s current test-bed. The production-grade switching such as PLX's Argo series does not require extra switches as signal repeaters.

The NTB driver is invoked at the system start-up time to set up the BARs and translation registers to map the management host's physical address space into a compute host's physical address space. The HRDMA driver sits below the CMMC and EOP driver and exposes a set of remote memory read/write semantics for the CMMC and EOP driver, and performs several optimizations to fully utilize the PCIe link's raw bandwidth.

5. PERFORMANCE EVALUATION

5.1 Hardware-based Remote DMA

The fundamental building block for *Marlin* is a DMA transaction, which could be *local*, where the source and destination memory areas belong to the same compute host, or *remote*, where the source and destination memory areas belong to different machines that are 1 hop (compute host and management host) and 2 hops (compute host to management host to compute host) away. Figure 5 shows the throughput comparison of a single DMA transaction consisting of a *single* source-destination pair of different transfer size when the source and destination memory areas are zero hop, one hop and two hops away. Each reported number is the average of 10 measurements. Except for small transfer size, the throughput of two-hop HRDMA is lower than that of one-hop HRDMA because the former incurs longer latency, and the throughput of one-hop HRDMA is comparable to zero-hop HRDMA because they incur approximately the same latency.

Marlin's HRDMA driver performs the following optimizations to maximize the HRDMA performance: batching, combining and exploitation of multiple DMA channels. Suppose there is a sequence of 10,000 4KB HRDMA requests from one attached compute host to another. In the *baseline* configuration, the HRDMA driver initiates a separate DMA transaction for each of these 10,000 HRDMA requests. In the *multi-channeled* configuration, the HRDMA driver initiates a separate DMA transaction for each of these 10,000 HRDMA requests using multiple DMA channels. In the *batched* configuration, the HRDMA driver exploits the scatter and gather capability of the DMA engine and initiates 40 DMA transactions, each of which consists of 256 subtransactions each with a transfer size of 4KB. The DMA engine pipelines the processing of the subtransactions inside a DMA transaction. In the *combined* configuration, the HRDMA driver combines 32 consecutive memory pages because they are contiguous, and initiates 40 DMA transactions, each of which consists of 8 subtransactions each with a transfer size of 128KB. The measured throughputs of these four configurations are shown in Table 1.

The drastic throughput difference between *baseline* and *batched* shows that batching is very effective because it significantly cuts

Baseline	Multi-Channel	Batched	Combined
1.54 Gbps	2.88 Gbps	20.17Gbps	20.31Gbps

Table 1: *The effectiveness of various optimizations supported by Marlin's HRDMA*

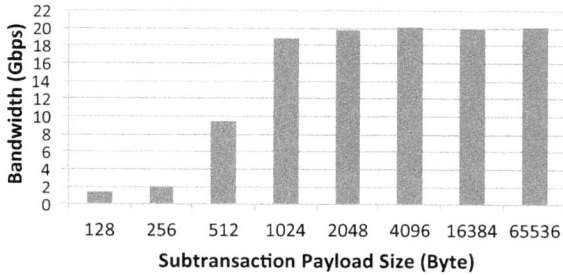

Figure 6: *The throughput comparison among DMA transaction runs that contain the same number of subtransactions but each subtransaction's payload size is varied*

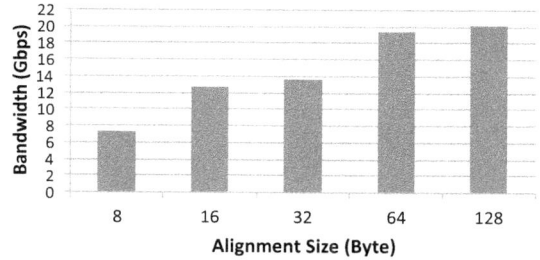

Figure 7: *The throughput comparison among different address alignments.*

down the number of DMA transactions and thus the total per-DMA transaction overhead. The tiny throughput difference between *batched* and *combined* suggests that the number of source-destination pairs in each DMA transaction does not matter much when the total transfer size per DMA transaction is the same. When consecutive DMA payload pages are physically contiguous, the HRDMA driver tries to combine such pages as much as possible. However, combining helps improve the throughput if it reduces the total number of DMA transactions but does not matter much if it just reduces the number of source-destination pairs in a DMA transaction. Finally, the substantial difference between *baseline* and *multi-channel* means that multiple DMA channels does help to mask part of the per-DMA transaction overhead when the DMA transaction size is small.

Considering that data transfer requests from EOP and CMMC may not have large and physically contiguous payloads, we further investigate the impact of memory fragmentation to the HRDMA throughput. We set up a DMA transaction that consists of 2,000 subtransactions, each corresponding to a payload of the same size, varied the per-subtransaction payload size from 128 bytes to 64 Kbytes and measured the total elapsed time of each DMA transaction run. Figure 6 shows the average throughput of 10 runs under different payload size. The HRDMA's throughput saturates at around 20.3 Gbps when the per-subtransaction payload size reaches 4KB. Because the PCIe switch used in our test-bed supports a maximum payload size of 128 bytes and up to 32 outstanding PCIe packets, the maximum amount of data outstanding in each DMA subtransaction is 4KB. Consequently, increasing per-subtransaction payload size beyond 4KB does not lead to any noticeable additional throughput improvement. [2]

5.2 Cross Machine Memory Copying

To measure the latency of CMMC, we created a sender program running on one compute host that writes 4 bytes using CMMC to a pre-defined memory location (say M_r) in a receiver program, which runs on another compute host, polls M_r and writes 4 bytes back using CMMC to a pre-defined memory location (say M_s) in

---

[2]The theoretical bandwidth of a 4-lane Gen3 PCIe link is 32Gbps, whereas *Marlin*'s HRDMA achieves 63.4% link utilization (20.3/32). Generally, closed to full link utilization could be achieved by increasing the maximum payload size [25, 38]. However, our current test-bed machines support up to 128 bytes.

the sender program immediately after detecting a change in M_r. The sender program takes a timestamp before writing the first 4 bytes, polls M_s after writing the first 4 bytes, takes another time stamp after detecting a change in M_s, and finally calculate the difference between these two timestamps. The resulting average round-trip delay for CMMC is 26.9 μsec, among which 11.4 μsec is spent on the two HRDMA operations. The latency penalty of CMMC beyond HRDMA is mainly attributed to virtual-to-physical address translation overhead and system call invocation delay.

To measure the throughput penalty of CMMC when compared with HRDMA, we wrote a sender program running on one compute host that allocates a 4MB contiguous physical memory area, and uses CMMC to copy this memory area to a 4MB contiguous physical memory area allocated by a receiver program, which runs on another compute host. The resulting average throughput for CMMC is 20.11 Gbps, which is 0.98% lower than the throughput of the underlying HRDMA operations (20.31 Gbps). This throughput penalty is again due to address translation and system call overhead.

5.3 Ethernet Over PCIe

To evaluate the performance of EOP, we first measured TCP throughputs using iperf [45]. Initially the measured TCP throughput is below 10 Gbps, which is much less than the underlying HRDMA throughput of 20Gbps. After further investigations, we found that the DMA engine's performance is very sensitive to the alignment of the source and destination addresses used in the DMA transactions. Therefore, we varied the degree of alignment of a DMA transaction's source and destination address but kept the payload size the same, and measured the HRDMA throughput. The results, shown in Figure 7, show that only when source/destination addresses are multiples of at least 64 bytes, the HRDMA performance is able to reach its maximum.

However, assuming the source buffer of an EOP transaction is always 64-byte aligned is impractical. The starting address of the Ethernet packet itself may not be 64-byte aligned because the protocol headers may be of variable length, e.g. both TCP and IP have optional fields. Fortunately, in Linux the gap between an Ethernet packet buffer's starting address and the largest 64-byte multiple that is smaller than the starting address, or *skb headroom*, still belongs to the allocated packet buffer and does not contain any meaningful data. An optimized version of the EOP driver exploits this invariant by using this largest and closest 64-byte multiple associated with a transmitted Ethernet packet as the source address of the corresponding DMA transaction, and embedding the alignment offset information in the headroom, if the transmitted Ethernet packet is not 64-byte aligned. When a user application transmits a sequence of source buffers that are not physically contiguous, modern OS such as Linux explicitly copies them into a contiguous kernel buffer

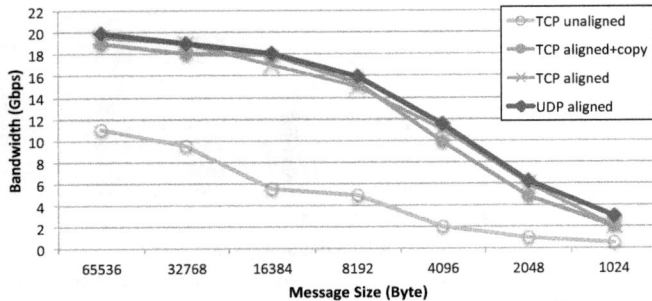

Figure 8: *The TCP/UDP throughput comparison between the vanilla and optimized versions of the EOP driver under MTU sizes.*

	Protocol	Bridges	NTB translation		Total
CPU	0.88 μs	5.2 μs	14.1μs		20.18μs
	Pre-processing	Pre-DMA	DMA	Post-DMA	Total
EOP	2.8 μs	11.4μs	11.5μs	3μs	28.7μs
CMMC	1 μs				26.9μs

Table 2: *The round-trip latency breakdown of sending a 4-byte remote memory read operation using CPU, an 64-byte ping packet using EOP, and a 4-byte remote memory write using CMMC.*

if the underlying NIC does not support scatter/gather DMA, or simply sets up a DMA subtransaction for each source buffer without data copying if the underlying NIC supports scatter/gather DMA. Although the DMA engine in our test-bed supports scatter/gather, the 64-byte alignment requirement suggests that it is more efficient to make a copy of these source buffers than to deal with their alignment issues one by one, especially when the size of these source buffers is small.

Figure 8 shows that when the source and destination address are 64 bytes aligned, the TCP and UDP throughputs of the vanilla EOP driver are effectively the same under different MTU sizes. The TCP and UDP throughputs are measured using iperf and nuttcp [22], respectively. However, when the source address is not aligned, the TCP throughput of the vanilla EOP driver is significantly worse than that when the source address is aligned, sometime by a factor of more than 2. The optimized version of the EOP driver effectively resolves this misalignment-induced performance problem by closing the TCP throughput gap between the aligned source address case and the unaligned source address case to less than 6% when the MTU is 64KB.

When the MTU is 64 KB and the source and destination address are aligned, the TCP and UDP throughputs are 19.6 Gbps and 19.9 Gbps, respectively, which are slightly lower than that of HRDMA (20.3 Gbps). To reach this level of performance, we increased the socket buffer size to 16 Mbytes, turned off SACK and turned on FACK [34]. The performance difference between HRDMA and UDP is due to additional data copying and context switching. The performance difference between UDP and TCP is due to packet losses at the interface between the IP stack and the EOP driver on the sender side. Because such packet losses tend to be bursty, FACK is better at handling such multi-segment losses than SACK.

5.4 Latency Analysis

Using the method in section 5.2, we measured the CPU-based round-trip remote memory write latency. The resulting average of two writes delay reports 17μsec, meaning roughly 8.5μsec one-way remote write latency. To better understand where time is spent, we measured the round-trip delay of a CPU-based memory *read* operation to a configuration register in a local NTB device, and that

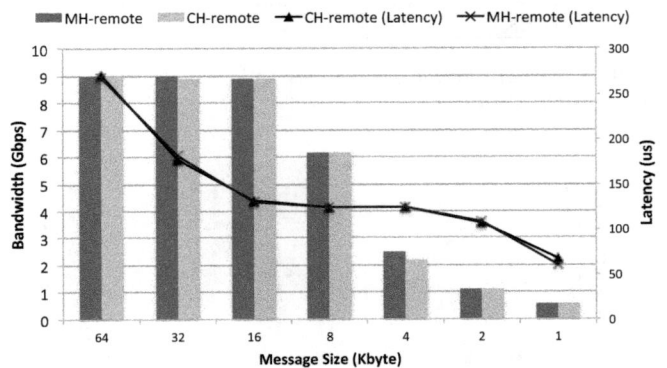

Figure 9: *Throughput and latency of inter-rack communication between a compute host attached to the* Marlin *switch and a remote server in another rack.*

to a remote host's memory location. The first memory read operation takes 2.48μs, which includes the traversal times through 16 PCIe bridges and such PCIe protocol overhead as TLP creation and processing. Because the traversal latency of each PCIe bridge is around 150 ns [11], 0.88μs of this memory read latency is due to PCIe protocol processing. Similar results were reported in [36]. The latency of a CPU-based memory read operation from one attached host to another attached host's memory incurs a round-trip delay of 20.18 μs shown in upper Table 2, which includes the traversal times of 56 PCIe bridges [3] and 4 NTBs, and the PCIe protocol processing overhead. By comparing the latencies of these two memory read operations, we concluded the per-NTB traversal time is 3.52μs, which is spent on PCIe device ID look-up, address translation, and creation of new TLP in the translated domain.

Table 2 shows the latency of sending a 64-byte packet using EOP and performing a 4-byte remote write operation using CMMC, and their break-down. Sending a packet using EOP involves the following steps:

1. *EOP pre-processing*: The EOP driver fetches the packet from the IP layer, and attaches a proper EOP header to it.

2. *Pre-DMA processing*: The HRDMA driver prepares a DMA descriptor for the packet and initiates a DMA transaction based on this descriptor.

3. *DMA transfer*: The DMA engine transfers the packet to the destination according to the DMA descriptor.

4. *Post-DMA processing*: After the DMA transaction is completed, a completion interrupt arrives to notify the sending EOP driver, which in turn triggers a packet arrival interrupt to prompt the receiving EOP driver to pick up the packet.

CMMC follows the same procedure except in the first step the sending CMMC driver performs a virtual-to-physical address translation, and in the last step the receiving CMMC driver delivers a signal to the receiver user application.

5.5 Inter-Rack Socket Communication

The management host of a *Marlin* switch allocates to each attached compute host a *Marlin* switch a VF on an SRIOV-capable

---

[3]Bridges along the path include on-board host bridges, eight PEX8732 switches, two PEX8717 NTBs, and one PEX8748 switch, with each consisting of 4, 16, 4, and 2 P2P bridges, respectively.

	Ethernet[1]	InfiniBand[2]	PCIe[3]
Total Bandwidth (Gbps)	10×24	20×24	32×24
Power per ToR Switch	176	130	90
Power for Adapters	5.5×24	15.5×24	$4.9 \times 24 + 5.5$
Total Power (W)	308	502	213.1
Power/Bandwidth (W)	1.283	1.045	0.277

Table 3: *Power consumption comparison among Ethernet, Infiniband and PCIe as the interconnect for 24 servers.*

[1] 176W: Brocade TurboIron switch, 5.5W: Intel 82599 NIC.
[2] 130W: Mellanox InfiniScale III [6], 15.5W: Mellanox ConnectX MHQH19.
[3] 90W: PLX eFabric switch, 4.9W: PEX8717 NTB adapter [11].

NIC so that the compute host could communicate with a remote host using the standard socket communication interface. We measured the packet latency and throughput of a network connection from a host connected to the *Marlin* switch of one rack to a remote server in another rack, where the source is either a management host or a compute host. The remote server is equipped with another Intel SRIOV NIC, which is connected back-to-back to the SRIOV NIC attached to the PEX8748 switch. To measure the packet latency, we used the NetPIPE benchmarking tool, which employs ping- pong tests and measures the half round-trip time between two servers. To measure the packet throughput, we ran Iperf for 300 seconds and took the average of the highest 90% measurements reported by Iperf. Figure 9 shows the throughput and latency comparison between the following two configurations under various packet sizes: compute host (CH) to remote host and management host (MH) to remote host. The fact that the latency and throughput measurements of these two configurations are almost the same means that sharing an NIC over a PCIe network, as in the case of CH to remote host, does not introduce any noticeable throughput or latency penalty.

5.6 Power Consumption

We compare *Marlin* with existing blade servers in terms of network component expenses and power consumption. Consider a cluster of 24 servers, each of which is equipped with a 10GbE NIC and connected to a top-of-rack 10GbE switch. With server's CPU supporting on-board NTB and DMA channels [43], applying *Marlin*'s architecture immediately saves the cost of 23 NICs by allowing the 24 servers to share one 10GbE NIC via the PCIe switch fabric. The top-of-rack 10GE switch is replaced by the standard PCIe switch, which connects the 24 servers and the built-in layer-2 switch on the shared 10GE NIC, and forwards packets among these 24 servers.

Reducing the number of I/O devices cuts down the hardware, the electricity, and cooling cost, as well as the space requirement. Table 3 lists the power consumption of *Marlin*, compared with Ethernet-based and InfiniBand-based clustering technology. We compare the total power consumption per gigabit bandwidth of a 24-port Ethernet, InfiniBand, and PCIe switch, and their adapters. *Marlin* proves to be a more competitive solution because its I/O sharing and consolidation design affords at least 4 times reduction in power consumption.

6. RELATED WORK

Rack disaggregation, advocated recently by the Virtual I/O group in Open Compute Project [3, 8, 9], proposes open hardware design model to combine and re-combine compute, memory, networking, and storage components as a new path to greater efficiency. By virtue of SAN and technologies such as FCoE, and iSCSI, storage

system is ubiquitously disaggregated from the individual server's hardware. To disaggregate networking components, PCI-SIG defines Multi-Root I/O virtualization (MRIOV) [14], which connects multiple hosts (root complexes) and endpoints with the MRA (Multi-Root Aware) PCIe switch to form a multi-host PCIe fabric. The PCIe-based I/O devices under MRA switch are decoupled from the individual server and shared among multiple hosts by attaching to a virtual PCIe hierarchy. Unfortunately, due to lack of MRA switch in the market, many proprietary attempts have been made to achieve multi-root sharing using SRIOV compliant I/O devices with customized hardware boxes [4, 7, 10, 28, 44] or relying on NTB [32, 40, 41] as an alternative. Besides, PCIe could be an ideal power-efficient interconnect for intra-rack communications [5, 20, 26], by mapping parts of the client host's memory to a global memory address space [23, 24]. As a point of comparison, *Marlin* maps the hosts' *entire* memory address space to avoid extra data copying and guarantees security by leveraging existing hardware components.

SeaMicro [1, 39] proposes a 10U system with disaggregated compute, storage, and network elements. Up to five petabytes of storage and single 10Gbps Ethernet uplink are exposed to each core. EnergyCore system [2, 13] is another I/O disaggregation built on ARM Cortex A9 cores. Its EnergyCoreFabric virtualizes Ethernet interfaces so that the EnergyCards don't need physical network ports. Finally, memory disaggregation allows memory resources to be consolidated in a memory blade. *Marlin*'s memory-based addressing model is native for memory sharing between hosts. However, without installing custom hardware, it's difficult to maintain cache coherence between local memory and remote memory [29–31].

Many studies leverage user-level direct hardware access as a means of achieving high bandwidth transfers and avoid OS's software overheads, such as context switches and data copying [19, 21, 37, 42, 47]. *Marlin*'s CMMC defines the minimum set of interfaces, allowing the user applications to do directly remote memory access. Compared with Intel's PCIe NTB Ethernet driver which uses the sender side CPU to copy payload and requires additional payload copying at the receiver side [33], *Marlin*'s EOP saves the CPU cycles by offloading the operation to the HRDMA and the global memory address allows the sender to directly place the payload into the receiver's buffer, avoiding additional payload copying.

Marlin is capable of mapping the main memory of all the hosts connected to a Marlin switch into a global memory space, and then use a normal DMA engine to copy data within this global memory space efficiently and securely. This approach is architecturally different from InfiniBand (network-oriented) and from SHRIMP (hybrid of network and shared memory) [18]. *Marlin* uses similar ideas in UDMA to reduce the DMA setup overhead [17], but is not as aggressive in pushing these low-level software optimizations. Additionally, the PCIe networking approach of *Marlin* enables not only hardware-based RDMA, but also direct remote I/O device access. That is, one host can directly access another host's disks or SSDs. Most previous works in low-latency networking work did not support such a capability. Finally, as a comparison to Ethernet, *Marlin* enjoys the reliable transmission service over PCIe because PCIe protocol supports end-to-end retransmission and credit-based flow control.

7. CONCLUSION

The emerging *disaggregated rack* architecture requires direct shared accesses from multiple hosts to I/O devices such as SAS controllers or NICs, so as to decouple I/O device upgrades from CPU/memory upgrades. At this point PCIe is the most promising technology to support such I/O device sharing. Moreover, we show in this paper that PCIe could also double as an effective rack area network for both intra-rack and inter-rack communications, without changing the higher-level network software stack. Compared with other system area network technologies, PCIe is more power-efficient because its transceiver is designed for short distance connectivity and thus is simpler and consumes less power. PCIe's memory-based addressing model is especially interesting because it enables one machine to directly address any memory location of another machine. *Marlin* exploits this capability to build a remote DMA mechanism that is truly hardware-based and requires no software involvement in payload transfer. On top of this remote DMA mechanism *Marlin* supports an Ethernet-over-PCIe (EOP) interface for socket-based communications, and a cross-machine memory copying (CMMC) interface for zero-copy application-to-application data transfer. Combining all these technology components leads to a new top-of-rack switch architecture that automatically allows intra-rack communications to go through the PCIe network and inter-rack communications to go through the standard Ethernet. The specific research contributions of this work thus include

- A comprehensive rack area architecture that is built on the same design principles underlying modern software defined networks and effectively combines PCIe network and Ethernet technologies into a coherent whole,

- A hardware-based remote DMA mechanism that allows one application on one machine to copy data to another application on another machine in a secure and efficient way,

- A non-cache-coherent shared memory abstraction that enables a global lock mechanism and a direct inter-CPU interrupt mechanism among nodes connected to a *Marlin* switch, and

- A detailed performance evaluation of the proposed rack disaggregation architecture and the associated intra-rack and inter-rack inter-machine communication method based on a fully operational prototype.

8. REFERENCES

[1] AMD SeaMicro SM15000 Fabric Compute Systems. http://www.seamicro.com/SM15000.

[2] Calxeda ECX1000 Product Brief. http://www.calxeda.com/wp-content/uploads/2012/06/ECX1000-Product-Brief-612.pdf.

[3] Intel shows off Rack Scale Architecture and Rack Disaggregation plans. http://semiaccurate.com/.

[4] I/O Consolidation White Paper, NextIO, Inc. http://www.nextio.com/resources/files/wp-nextio-consolidation.pdf.

[5] kontron VXFabric - PCI Express Switch Fabric for High Performance Embedded Computing. http://www.kontron.com/vxfabric_whitepaper.

[6] Mellanox InfiniScale III. http://www.mellanox.com/related-docs/prod_siliconPB_InfiniScale_III.pdf.

[7] Micron I/O Virtualization White Paper, Micron Technology, Inc. http://www.micron.com/~/media/Documents/Products/White%20Paper/micron_io_virtualization_wp.pdf.

[8] Open Compute Project. http://opencompute.org/.

[9] Open Compute Project Virtual IO Charter. http://www.opencompute.org/wp/wp-content/uploads/2012/10/Open_Compute_Project_Virtual_IO_Charter_2012-09-10.pdf.

[10] PCI Express System Interconnect Software Architecture for x86-based Systems. http://www.idt.com/.

[11] PEX 8717, PCI Express Gen 3 Switch, 16 Lanes, 10 Ports. www.plxtech.com/download/file/2221?

[12] The Case for PCIe 3.0 Repeaters, PCI-SIG Developers Conference, 2011.

[13] The opposite of virtualization: Calxeda's new quad-core ARM part for cloud servers. http://arstechnica.com/.

[14] Multi-Root I/O Virtualization and Sharing 1.0 Specification, PCI-SIG, 2008.

[15] Single-Root I/O Virtualization and Sharing Specification, Revision 1.0, PCI-SIG, 2008.

[16] M. Ben-Yehuda, J. Mason, J. Xenidis, O. Krieger, L. Van Doorn, J. Nakajima, A. Mallick, and E. Wahlig. Utilizing IOMMUs for virtualization in Linux and Xen. In *OLS06*.

[17] M. A. Blumrich, C. Dubnicki, E. W. Felten, and K. Li. Protected, user-level dma for the shrimp network interface. In *High-Performance Computer Architecture, 1996. Proceedings. Second International Symposium on*, pages 154–165. IEEE, 1996.

[18] M. A. Blumrich, K. Li, R. Alpert, C. Dubnicki, E. W. Felten, and J. Sandberg. *Virtual memory mapped network interface for the SHRIMP multicomputer*, volume 22. IEEE Computer Society Press, 1994.

[19] G. Buzzard, D. Jacobson, M. Mackey, S. Marovich, and J. Wilkes. An implementation of the hamlyn sender-managed interface architecture. *ACM SIGOPS Operating Systems Review, 1996*.

[20] J. Byrne, J. Chang, K. T. Lim, L. Ramirez, and P. Ranganathan. Power-efficient networking for balanced system designs: early experiences with pcie. In *Proceedings of the 4th Workshop on Power-Aware Computing and Systems*, page 3. ACM, 2011.

[21] D. Dunning, G. Regnier, G. McAlpine, D. Cameron, B. Shubert, F. Berry, A. M. Merritt, E. Gronke, and C. Dodd. The virtual interface architecture. *Micro, IEEE*, 18(2):66–76, 1998.

[22] B. Fink and R. Scott. nuttcp, v5. 3.1, 2006.

[23] R. Gillett and R. Kaufmann. Using the memory channel network. *Micro, IEEE*, 17(1):19–25, 1997.

[24] R. B. Gillett. Memory channel network for pci. *Micro, IEEE*, 16(1):12–18, 1996.

[25] I. Granovsky. Optimizaing PCIe Port Performance, 2006.

[26] T. Hanawa, T. Boku, S. Miura, M. Sato, and K. Arimoto. Pearl: Power-aware, dependable, and high-performance communication link using pci express. In *Green Computing and Communications (GreenCom), 2010 IEEE/ACM Int'l Conference on & Int'l Conference on Cyber, Physical and Social Computing (CPSCom)*, pages 284–291. IEEE, 2010.

[27] R. Hiremane. Intel Virtualization Technology for Directed I/O (Intel VT-d). *Technology@ Intel Magazine*, 4(10), 2007.

[28] V. Krishnan. Towards an integrated io and clustering solution using pci express. In *Cluster Computing, 2007 IEEE International Conference on*, pages 259–266. IEEE, 2007.

[29] S. Liang, R. Noronha, and D. K. Panda. Swapping to remote memory over infiniband: An approach using a high performance network block device. In *Cluster Computing, 2005. IEEE International*, pages 1–10. IEEE, 2005.

[30] K. Lim, J. Chang, T. Mudge, P. Ranganathan, S. K. Reinhardt, and T. F. Wenisch. Disaggregated memory for expansion and sharing in blade servers. In *ACM SIGARCH Computer Architecture News*, volume 37, pages 267–278. ACM, 2009.

[31] K. Lim, Y. Turner, J. R. Santos, A. AuYoung, J. Chang, P. Ranganathan, and T. F. Wenisch. System-level implications of disaggregated memory. In *High Performance Computer Architecture (HPCA), 2012 IEEE 18th International Symposium on*, pages 1–12. IEEE, 2012.

[32] K. Malwankar, D. Talayco, and A. Ekici. PCI-Express Function Proxy, Oct. 1 2009. WO Patent WO/2009/120,798.

[33] J. Mason. Intel PCIe NTB Driver: ntb_tx_copy_task and ntb_rx_copy_task. `http://lxr.linux.no/linux+v3.9/drivers/ntb/ntb_transport.c`.

[34] M. Mathis and J. Mahdavi. Forward acknowledgement: Refining tcp congestion control. *ACM SIGCOMM Computer Communication Review*, 26(4):281–291, 1996.

[35] N. McKeown, T. Anderson, H. Balakrishnan, G. Parulkar, L. Peterson, J. Rexford, S. Shenker, and J. Turner. Openflow: enabling innovation in campus networks. *ACM SIGCOMM Computer Communication Review*, 38(2):69–74, 2008.

[36] D. J. Miller, P. M. Watts, and A. W. Moore. Motivating future interconnects: a differential measurement analysis of pci latency. In *Proceedings of the 5th ACM/IEEE Symposium on Architectures for Networking and Communications Systems*, pages 94–103. ACM, 2009.

[37] R. OpenFabrics. Protocols through ofed software.

[38] PLX. Draco DMA Performance, 2013.

[39] A. Rao. Seamicro technology overview. Technical report, Technical report, SeaMicro, 2010.

[40] J. Regula. Multi-Root Sharing of Single-Root Input/Output Virtualization, Dec. 28 2010. US Patent App. 12/979,904.

[41] D. Riley. System and Method for Multi-Host Sharing of a Single-Host Device, May 8 2012. US Patent 8,176,204.

[42] L. Rizzo. netmap: a novel framework for fast packet i/o. In *USENIX ATC*, 2012.

[43] M. J. Sullivan. Intel Xeon Processor C5500/C3500 Series Non-Transparent Bridge. *Technology@ Intel Magazine*, 2010.

[44] J. Suzuki, Y. Hidaka, J. Higuchi, T. Baba, N. Kami, and T. Yoshikawa. Multi-Root Share of Single-Root I/O Virtualization (SR-IOV) Compliant PCI Express Device. In *High Performance Interconnects (HOTI), 2010 IEEE 18th Annual Symposium on*, pages 25–31. IEEE, 2010.

[45] A. Tirumala, F. Qin, J. Dugan, J. Ferguson, and K. Gibbs. Iperf: The TCP/UDP Bandwidth Measurement Tool. *http://dast.nlanr.net/Projects*, 2005.

[46] C.-C. Tu, C. tang Lee, and T. cker Chiueh. Secure i/o device sharing among virtual machines on multiple hosts. In *ACM ISCA'13*.

[47] T. Von Eicken, A. Basu, V. Buch, and W. Vogels. U-net: a user-level network interface for parallel and distributed computing (includes url). In *ACM SIGOPS Operating Systems Review*, volume 29, pages 40–53. ACM, 1995.

[48] P. Willmann, S. Rixner, and A. Cox. Protection Strategies for Direct Access to Virtualized I/O Devices. In *USENIX Annual Technical Conference*, pages 15–28, 2008.

Caesar: A Content Router for High-Speed Forwarding on Content Names

Diego Perino, Matteo Varvello
Bell Labs, Alcatel-Lucent
first.last@alcatel-lucent.com

Leonardo Linguaglossa
INRIA
first.last@inria.fr

Rafael Laufer, Roger Boislaigue
Bell Labs, Alcatel-Lucent
first.last@alcatel-lucent.com

ABSTRACT

Internet users are interested in content regardless of its location; however, the current client/server architecture still requires requests to be directed to a specific server. Information-centric networking (ICN) is a recent vein that relaxes this requirement through the use of name-based forwarding, where forwarding decisions are based on content names instead of IP addresses. Despite previous name-based forwarding strategies have been proposed, almost none have actually built a content router. To fill this gap, in this paper we design and prototype a content router called *Caesar* for high-speed forwarding on content names. Caesar introduces several innovative features, including (*i*) a longest-prefix matching algorithm based on a novel data structure called *prefix Bloom filter*; (*ii*) an incremental design which allows for easy integration with existing protocols and network equipment; (*iii*) a forwarding scheme where multiple line cards collaborate in a distributed fashion; and (*iv*) support for offloading packet processing to graphics processing units (GPUs). We build Caesar as an enterprise router, and show that every line card sustains up to 10 Gbps using a forwarding table with more than 10 million content prefixes. Distributed forwarding allows the forwarding table to grow even further, and to scale linearly with the number of line cards at the cost of only a few microseconds in the packet processing latency. GPU offloading, in turn, trades off a few milliseconds of latency for a large speedup in the forwarding rate.

Categories and Subject Descriptors

C.2.1 [**Network Architecture and Designs**]: Network communications, Store and forward networks; C.2.6 [**Internetworking**]: Routers

General Terms

Design; Implementation; Experiments.

Keywords

ICN; forwarding; router; architecture.

1. INTRODUCTION

Internet usage has significantly evolved over the years, and today is mostly centered around location-independent services. However, since the Internet architecture is host-centric, content requests still have to be directed towards an individual server using IP addresses. The translation from content name to IP address is realized through different technologies, e.g., DNS and HTTP redirection, which are implemented by several systems, such as content delivery networks (CDN) [1] and cloud services [2].

Information-centric networking (ICN) offers a radical alternative by advocating name-based forwarding directly at the network layer, *i.e.*, forwarding decisions are based on the content name carried by each packet [3]. Names provide routers with information about the forwarded content, which enables functionalities, such as caching or multicasting, as network-layer primitives. In particular, the use of hierarchical names [4] also allows efficient route aggregation and makes mechanisms to translate content names into IP addresses unnecessary.

At the core of the ICN architecture is a network device called content router, responsible for name-based forwarding. Building a content router is challenging because of two major issues [5, 6]. First, due to the ever-increasing availability of content, the size of the forwarding tables are expected to be from one to two orders of magnitude larger than current tables. Second, content names may be long, having a large number of components as well as many characters per component, which makes several previous hardware optimizations proposed for fixed-length IP prefixes ineffective [7].

In this paper, we address these ICN challenges and introduce *Caesar*, a content router compatible with existing protocols and network equipment. Caesar's forwarding engine features three key optimizations to accelerate name lookups. First, its name-based longest-prefix matching (LPM) algorithm relies on a novel data structure called *prefix Bloom filter* (PBF). The PBF is introduced to achieve high caching efficiency by exploiting the hierarchical nature of content prefixes. Second, a fast hashing scheme is proposed to reduce the PBF processing overhead by a multiplicative factor. Finally, Caesar takes advantage of a cache-aware hash table designed with an efficient collision resolution scheme. The goal is to minimize the number of memory accesses required to find the next-hop information for each packet.

Based on the proposed design, we implement the data plane of Caesar using a μTCA chassis and multiple line cards equipped with a network processor. In its basic design, Caesar maintains a full copy of the forwarding information base (FIB) at each line card. For each received packet, our name-based LPM algorithm runs independently at the input line card, and an Ethernet switch then moves the packet to the output line card following the forwarding decision made. To support large FIBs, we extend Caesar with a distributed forwarding scheme where each line card stores only *part* of the FIB and collaborate with each other to perform LPM. A second extension is also implemented to further increase Caesar's forwarding speed by offloading name-based LPM to a graphics processing unit (GPU), if required.

We evaluate Caesar using our full prototype and a commercial traffic generator that uses synthetic and real traces for the content prefixes and requests. Our main finding is that every line card of Caesar is able to sustain up to 10 Gbps with 188-byte packets and a large FIB with 10 million prefixes. Distributed forwarding over line cards sharing their FIB is shown to allow the the forwarding table to increase linearly with the number of cards at the cost of 15% rate reduction and a few microseconds of additional delay. The GPU extension is also shown to outperform previously proposed designs for the same hardware.

The remainder of this paper is organized as follows. In Section 2, we provide some background and an overview of the work closely related to Caesar. Section 3 presents the design of our name-based LPM algorithm. Section 4 then introduces the implementation of Caesar, while its extensions are presented in Section 5. We evaluate Caesar's performance in Section 6 and, in Section 7, we discuss the design and implementation of additional content router features. Finally, Section 8 concludes the paper.

2. RELATED WORK

This section summarizes the work related to Caesar. Section 2.1 provides a brief background on fundamental NDN concepts, such as name-based longest prefix matching (LPM). Section 2.2 then overviews the state of the art in name-based LPM, and Section 2.3 presents the related work on content router design.

2.1 Background

Caesar uses the hierarchical naming scheme proposed by NDN to address content [4, 8, 9, 10]. In this scheme, each content has a unique identifier composed of a sequence of strings, each separated by a delimiting character (e.g., /ancs2014/papers/paperA). We refer to this identifier as the *content name*, and to each string in the sequence as a *component*. For delivery, content usually has to be split into several different packets, which are identified by appending an extra individual component to the original content name (e.g., /ancs2014/papers/paperA/packet1). For scalability, content routers only maintain forwarding information for *content prefixes* that aggregate several content names into a single entry (e.g., /ancs2014/papers/*).

A content router uses name-based longest prefix matching (LPM) to determine the interface where a packet should be forwarded. Name-based LPM consists in selecting from a local forwarding information base (FIB) the content prefix sharing the longest prefix with a content name. Although the concept is similar to LPM for IP, name-based LPM faces serious scalability challenges [5, 6]. An ICN FIB is expected to be at least one order of magnitude larger than the average FIB of current IP routers. In addition, several hardware optimizations that take advantage of the fixed length of IP addresses are not possible in ICN due to the variable length of content names and prefixes.

2.2 Name-Based LPM

Motivated by these challenges, a few techniques have recently been proposed for name-based LPM. Wang *et al.* [11] propose to use name component encoding (NCE), a scheme that encodes the components of a content name as symbols and organize them as a trie. Due to its goal of compacting the FIB, NCE requires several extra data structures that add significant complexity to the lookup

process, and result in several memory accesses to find the longest prefix match. NameFilter [12] is an alternative name-based LPM algorithm employing one Bloom filter per prefix length, similarly to the solutions proposed in [13, 14] for IP addresses. For lookup, a *d*-component content name then requires *d* lookups in the different Bloom filters. This approach has two intrinsic limitations. First, it cannot handle false positives generated by the Bloom filters, and thus packets can eventually be forwarded to the wrong interface. Second, it cannot support a few important functionalities, such as multipath routing and dynamic forwarding.

In a different approach, So *et al.* [6, 8] implement LPM using successive lookups in a hash table. Instead of using the longest-first strategy (*i.e.*, lookups start from the longest prefix), the search starts from the prefix length where most FIB prefixes are centered, and restarts at a larger or shorter length, if needed. The approach bounds the worst case number of lookups, but cannot guarantee constant performance bounds.

Different from previous work, we reduce the problem of name-based LPM to two stages (cf. Section 3). The first stage finds the *length* of the longest prefix that matches a content name. This stage is accomplished by a Bloom filter variant engineered for content prefixes, which guarantees a constant number of memory accesses. The second stage consists of a hash table lookup to find the output interface where a packet should be forwarded to. This last stage only requires a single lookup with high probability, detects false positives, and supports enhanced forwarding functionalities.

2.3 Content Router Design

To date, the work in [6, 8] is the only previous attempt to build a content router. In this work, the content router is implemented on a Xeon-based Integrated Service Module. Packet I/O is handled by regular line cards, while name-based LPM is performed on a separate service module connected to the line cards via a switch fabric. Real experiments show that the module sustains a maximum forwarding rate of 4.5 Mpps (million packets per second). Simulations without packet I/O show that the the proposed name-based LPM algorithm handles up to 6.3 Mpps.

Different from [6, 8], Caesar supports name-based LPM directly on I/O line cards in order to reduce latency, increase the overall router throughput, and enable ICN functionalities without requiring extra service modules. Real experiments show that, using a single line card based on a cheaper technology than [6, 8], Caesar achieves a comparable throughput (Section 6). Finally, Caesar also allows line cards to share the content of their FIB in order to support the massive FIB expected in ICN, and supports GPU offloading to speed up the forwarding rate (Section 5).

3. NAME-BASED LPM

In this section, we introduce our two-stage name-based longest prefix matching (LPM) algorithm used in the forwarding engine of Caesar. Section 3.1 and 3.2 describe the prefix Bloom filter (PBF) and the concept of block expansion, respectively. Both are used in the first stage to find the length of the longest prefix match. Then, Section 3.3 explains the fast hashing scheme proposed to reduce the hashing overhead of the PBF. Finally, Section 3.4 describes the hash table used in the second stage as well as the optimizations introduced to speed up the lookups.

3.1 Prefix Bloom Filter

For the first stage of our name-based LPM algorithm, we introduce a novel data structure called *prefix Bloom filter* (PBF) and use it as an oracle to identify the length of the longest prefix match. The PBF takes advantage of the semantics in content prefixes to

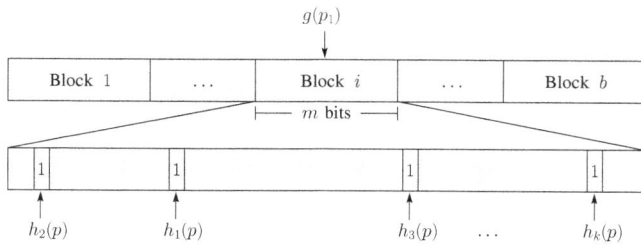

Figure 1: Insertion of a prefix p into a PBF with b blocks, m bits per block, and k hash functions. The function $g(p_1)$ selects a block using the subprefix p_1 with the first component, and bits $h_1(p), h_2(p), \ldots, h_k(p)$ are set to 1.

find the longest prefix match using a single memory access, with high probability.

The PBF is a space-efficient data structure composed of several blocks, where each block is a small Bloom filter with the size of one (or few) cache line(s). Each content prefix in the FIB is inserted into a block chosen from the hash value of its first component. During the lookup of a content name, its first component identifies the unique block, or cache line(s), that must be loaded from memory to cache before conducting the membership query.

Figure 1 shows the insertion of a content prefix p into a PBF composed of b blocks, m bits per block, and k hash functions. Let $p = /c_1/c_2/ \ldots /c_u$ be the u-component prefix to be inserted into the PBF, and let $p_i = /c_1/c_2/ \ldots /c_i$ be the subprefix with the first i components of p, such that $p_1 = /c_1$, $p_2 = /c_1/c_2$, and so on. A uniform hash function $g(\cdot)$ with output in the range $\{0, 1, \ldots, b - 1\}$ is used to determine the block where p should be inserted. The hash value $g(p_1)$ is computed from the subprefix p_1 defined by the first component. This guarantees that all prefixes starting with the same component are stored in the same block, which enables fast lookups. Once the block is selected, the hash values $h_1(p), h_2(p), \ldots, h_k(p)$ are computed using the complete prefix p, resulting in k indexes within the range $\{0, 1, \ldots, m-1\}$. Finally, the bits at the positions $h_1(p), h_2(p), \ldots, h_k(p)$ in the selected block are set to 1.

To find the length of the longest prefix in the PBF that matches a content name $x = /c_1/c_2/ \ldots /c_d$, the first step is to identify the index of the block where x or its subprefixes may be stored. Such block is selected using the hash of the first component of the content name, $g(x_1)$. Once this block is loaded, a match is first tried using the full name x, *i.e.,* maximum length. The bits of the positions $h_1(x), h_2(x), \ldots, h_k(x)$ are then checked and, if all bits are set to 1, a match is found. Otherwise, or if a false positive is detected (cf. Section 3.4), the prefix x_{d-1} is checked using the same procedure and, if there is no match, x_{d-2} is then checked, and so on until a match is found or until all subprefixes of x have been tested. At each membership query, the bits of the positions $h_1(x_i), h_2(x_i), \ldots, h_k(x_i)$ are checked, for $1 \leq i \leq d$, accounting for a maximum of $k \times d$ bit checks per name lookup in the worst case. Bits checks require only a single memory access as the bits to be checked reside in the same block.

The false positive rate of the PBF is computed as follows. If n_i is the number of prefixes inserted into the i-th block, then the false positive rate of this block is $f_i = (1 - e^{-kn_i/m})^k$. We consider two possible cases of false positives. First, assume the worst-case scenario where the name to be looked up and all of its subprefixes are *not* in the FIB. In this case, assuming a content name with d components, the number F_i of false positives in the i-th block fol-

lows the binomial distribution $F_i \sim B(d, f_i)$. The average number of false positives in this block is then $d \times f_i$. Since the function $g(\cdot)$ is uniform, each block is chosen with probability $1/b$, where b is the number of blocks, and thus the average number of false positives in the PBF for a content name with d components and no matches is $d \times f$, where $f = (1/b) \sum_{i=1}^{b} f_i$ is the average false positive rate.

Consider now the case where either the content name or at least one of its subprefixes *are* in the table, and let l be the lenght of its longest prefix match. In this case, a false positive can only occur for a subprefix whose length is larger than l, i.e., the l-component subprefix is a real positive and the search stops. The number F_i of false positives in the i-th block then follows the binomial distribution $F_i \sim B(d - l, f_i)$, and the average number of false positives in this block is $(d - l) \times f_i$. In general, for a d-component name whose longest prefix match has length l, the average number of false positives in the PBF is $(d - l) \times f$.

3.2 Block Expansion

For fast lookups, the PBF is designed such that prefixes sharing their first component are stored in the same block. It follows that if many prefixes in the FIB share the same first component, then the corresponding block may yield a high false positive rate. To address this, we propose a technique called *block expansion* that redirects some content prefixes to other blocks, allowing the false positive rate to be reduced in exchange for loading a few additional blocks from memory.

Block expansion is used when the number n_i of prefixes in the i-th block exceeds the threshold $t_i = -(m/k)\log(1 - \sqrt[k]{f_i})$ selected to guarantee a maximum false positive rate f_i. For now, assume that prefixes are inserted in order from shorter to longer lengths[1]. Let n_{ij} be the number of j-component prefixes stored in the i-th block. If at a given length l the number $\sum_{j \leq l} n_{ij}$ exceeds the threshold t_i, then a block expansion occurs. In this case, each prefix p with length l or higher is redirected to another block chosen from the hash value $g(p_l)$ of its first l components. To keep track of the expansions, each block keeps a bitmap with w bits. The l-th bit of the bitmap is set to 1 to notify that an expansion at length l occurred in the block. If the new block indicated by $g(p_l)$ already has an expansion at a length e, with $e > l$, then any prefix p with length e or higher is redirected again to another block indicated by $g(p_e)$, and so on.

Figure 2 shows the insertion of a prefix $p = /c_1/c_2/ \ldots /c_u$ in a PBF using block expansion. First, block $i = g(p_1)$ is identified as the target for p. Assuming that the threshold t_i is reached at prefix length l, block i is expanded and the l-th bit of its bitmap is set. Since $l \leq u$, a second block $j = g(p_l)$ is then be computed from the first l components of p and, assuming block j is not expanded, positions $h_1(p), h_2(p), \ldots, h_k(p)$ of this block are set to 1.

The lookup process works as follows. Let x be the prefix to be looked up, and $i = g(x_1)$ be the block where x or its LPM should be. First, the expansion bitmap of block i is checked. If the first bit set in the bitmap is at position l and x has l or more components, then block $j = g(x_l)$ is also loaded from memory. Assuming that no bits are set in the bitmap of j, prefixes x_l and higher are checked in block j. In case there are no matches, then prefixes x_{l-1} and lower are checked in block i.

The false positive rate of the PBF with block expansion is similar to the case without expansion, except for two key differences. First, the filter size is now $m - w$ bits, since the first w bits of the block are used for the expansion bitmap. The range of the hash

---

[1]The dynamic case, where the prefixes in the FIB change over time, is addressed by the control plane, and explained in Section 4.3.

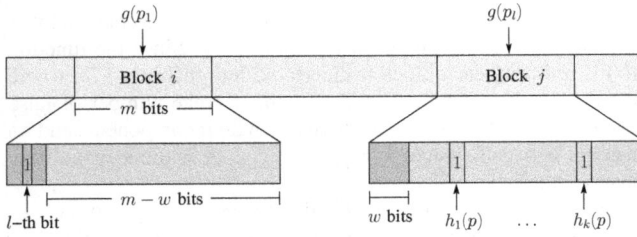

Figure 2: Insertion of a prefix $p = /p_1/p_2/\ldots/p_d$ into a PBF using block expansion. If block $i = g(p_1)$ reached its insertion threshold or if the l-th bit is set in its bitmap and $l \leq d$, then p is inserted into block $j = g(p_l)$.

functions h_i is thus $\{0, 1, \ldots, m - w - 1\}$. Second, the number n_i of prefixes inserted in each block i is now computed from the original insertions, minus the prefixes redirected to other blocks, plus the prefixes coming from the expansion of other blocks.

3.3 Hashing

Hashing is a fundamental operation in our name-based LPM algorithm. For the lookup of a content name $p = /c_1/c_2/\ldots/c_d$ with d components and k hash functions in the PBF, a total of $k \times d$ hash values must be generated for LPM in the worst case, *i.e.*, the running time is $O(k \times d)$. Longer content names thus have a higher overall impact on the system throughput than shorter names. To reduce this overhead, we propose a linear $O(k + d)$ run-time hashing scheme that only generates $k + d - 1$ seed hash values, while the other $(k - 1)(d - 1)$ values are computed from XOR operations.

The hash values are computed as follows. Let H_{ij} be the i-th hash value computed for the prefix $p_j = /c_1/c_2/\ldots/c_j$ containing the first j components of p. Then, the $k \times d$ values are computed on demand as

$$H_{ij} = \begin{cases} h_i(p_j) & \text{if } i = 1 \text{ or } j = 1 \\ H_{i1} \oplus H_{1j} & \text{otherwise} \end{cases}$$

where $h_i(p_j)$ is the value computed from the i-th hash function over the j-component prefix p_j, and $\oplus$ is the XOR operator. The use of XOR operations significantly speeds up the computation time without impacting hashing properties [14].

3.4 Hash Table Design

After the PBF identifies the longest prefix length, the second stage of our name-based LPM algorithm consists of a hash table lookup to either fetch the next hop information or to rule out false positives.

Figure 3 shows the structure of the hash table used in our system, which consists of several buckets where the prefixes in the FIB are hashed to. Our first design goal is to minimize memory access latency. For this purpose, each bucket is restricted to the fixed size of one cache line such that, for well-dimensioned tables, only a single memory access is required to find an entry. In case of collisions, entries are stored next to each other in a contiguous fashion up to the limit imposed by the cache line size. Bucket overflow is managed by chaining with linked lists, but this is expected to be rare if the number of buckets is large enough.

Our second design goal is to reduce the string matching overhead required to find an entry. As a result, each entry stores the hash value h of its content prefix in order to speed up the matching process. String matching on the content prefix only occurs if there is a match first on this 32-bit hash value. Due to large output

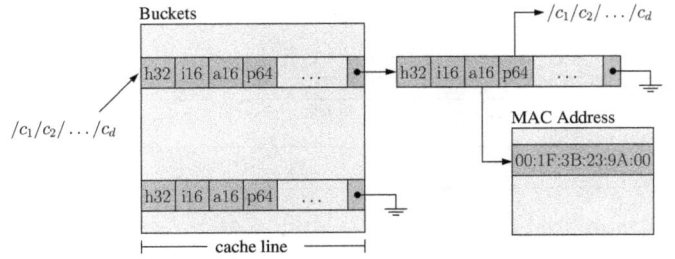

Figure 3: The structure of the hash table used to store the FIB. Each bucket has a fixed size of one cache line, with overflows managed by chaining. Each entry consists of a tuple $\langle h, i, a, p \rangle$ that stores the next hop information.

range of the hash function, an error is expected only with a small probability of 2^{-32}, assuming uniformity.

Finally, our last goal is to maximize the capacity of each bucket. For this purpose, the content prefix is not stored at each entry due to its large and variable size. Instead, only a 64-bit pointer p to the prefix is stored. To save space, next-hop MAC addresses are also kept in a separate table and a 16-bit index a is stored in each entry. A 16-bit index i is also required per entry to specify the output line card of a given content prefix. Each entry in the hash table then consists of a 16-byte tuple $\langle h, i, a, p \rangle$, where h is the hash of the content prefix, i is the output line card index, a is index of the next-hop MAC address, and p is the pointer to the content prefix.

4. CAESAR

This section explains the design and implementation of Caesar, our high-speed content router prototype. Section 4.1 overviews the hardware setup of Caesar, while Section 4.2 and 4.3 present its data and control plane, respectively.

4.1 Hardware

Caesar's hardware is chosen with three key goals in mind:

Enterprise router: Caesar is a router for an enterprise network, *i.e.*, few 10 Gbps ports. This impacts the choice of router chassis as well as the selection of the type and number of line cards used.

Easy deployment: Caesar is easily deployable in current networks, e.g., via a simple firmware upgrade of existing networking devices. This constraints the hardware choice to programmable components already widely adopted by commercial network equipment. We thus resort to network processors optimized for packet processing.

Backward compatibility: Caesar is designed to be backward compatible with existing networking protocols. In particular, its switch fabric is based on regular Ethernet switching, and thus name-based forwarding is implemented on top of existing networking protocols (e.g., Ethernet and IP) in a transparent fashion, without requiring a clean slate approach.

Figure 4 shows the hardware architecture of Caesar. It consists of a micro telecommunications computing architecture (μTCA) chassis with slots for advanced mezzanine cards (AMCs). Four slots of the chassis are occupied by line cards, each equipped with a network processor unit (NPU), a 4-GB off-chip DRAM, a SFP+ 10GbE interface, and a 10 Gbps interface to the backplane. Each NPU has a 10-core 1.1 GHz 64-bits MIPS processor with 32-KB L1 cache per core, and 2-MB L2 shared cache. Some of the remaining slots of the chassis are occupied by an Ethernet switch with 10GbE ports, one connected to each slot via the backplane, and the route

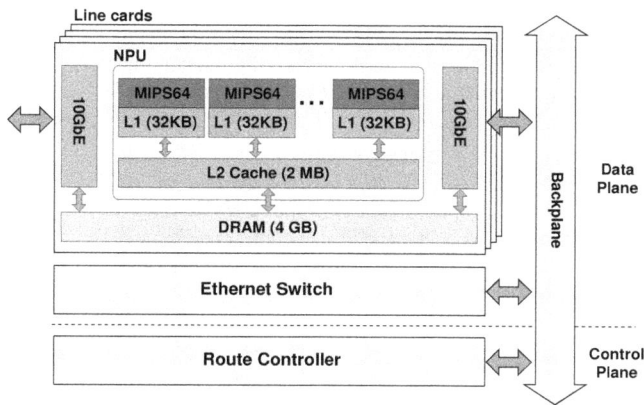

Figure 4: The hardware architecture of Caesar.

controller, composed of an Intel Core Duo 1.5 Ghz processor, 4-GB off-chip DRAM, and a 300-GB hard disk.

4.2 Data Plane

Caesar's data plane is responsible for forwarding packets received by the line cards. Next, we describe the path of packet within Caesar, from the moment it is received until it leaves the system.

Packet input: As a packet is received from the SFP+ 10GbE external interface, it is stored in the off-chip DRAM of the line card. A hardware load balancer then assigns the packet to one of the available cores for processing.

Header parsing: A standard header format for ICN is currently under debate in the ICN research group at the IRTF [15]. In absence of such standard, we use our own header which consists of four fields. First, the 16-bit *length* field specifies the size of the following *content name* field. To expedite parsing, we also include an 8-bit *components* field, which specifies the number of components in the content name, and several *offset* fields, each containing an 8-bit offset for each component in the content name. For backward compatibility, the name-based header is placed after the IP header, which allows network devices to operate with their standard forwarding policy, e.g., L2 or L3 forwarding.

Once dispatched to a core, each packet is checked for the presence of a name-based header by inspecting the protocol field of the IP header. If a name-based header is present, pointers to each field are extracted and stored in the L1 cache. Otherwise, regular packet processing is performed, *i.e.,* LPM on the destination IP address.

Name-based LPM: If such a header is found, our name-based LPM algorithm is used (cf. Section 3). The size of each PBF block is set to one cache line, which is 128 bytes in our architecture (cf. Section 6). To ensure fast hashing calculations, Caesar takes advantage of the optimized instruction sets of the NPU; the $k + d - 1$ seed hash values are computed using the CRC32 optimized instructions, whereas the remaining $(k - 1)(d - 1)$ hash values are computed from XOR operations. In case of a match in the PBF, the content prefix is looked up in the hash table stored in the off-chip DRAM to determine its next hop information, or to rule out false positives. Each table entry has a fixed size of 16 bytes, which, for a bucket of 128 bytes, results in a maximum of 7 entries per bucket in addition to the 64-bit pointer required by the linked list (cf. Section 3.4). We dimension the hash table to contain 10 million buckets, requiring a total of 1.28 GB to store the buckets. An additional 640 MB are required to store the content prefixes, for a total of 1.92 GB of storage.

Switching: The LPM algorithm returns the index of the output line card and the MAC address of the next hop for a packet. The source MAC address of the packet is then set to the address of the backplane interface, and its destination MAC address is set to the address of next hop. Finally, the packet is placed into a per-core output queue in the backplane interface and waits for transmission. Each NPU core has its own queue in the backplane interface to enable lockless queue insertions and avoid contention bottlenecks. Once transmitted over the backplane, the packet is received by the Ethernet switch, and regular L2 switching is performed. The packet is then sent to the output line card over the backplane once again.

Packet output: Once received by the backplane interface of the output line card, the packet is assigned to a NPU core and the source MAC address is overwritten with the address of the SPF+ 10GbE interface. The packet is then sent to the interface for transmission.

4.3 Control Plane

Caesar's control plane is responsible for periodically computing and distributing the FIB to line cards. These operations are performed by the route controller, a central authority that is assumed to participate in a name-based routing protocol [16] to construct its routing information base (RIB). The RIB is structured as a hash table that contains the next hop information for each reachable content prefix.

The FIB is derived from the RIB and is composed of the PBF and the prefix hash table (cf. Section 3). To allow prefix insertion and removal, the route controller maintains a mirror counting PBF (C-PBF). For each bit in the PBF, the C-PBF keeps a counter that is incremented at insertions and decremented at removals. Only when a counter reaches zero the corresponding bit in the PBF is set to 0. The C-PBF enables prefix removal while avoiding to keep counters in the original PBF, which saves precious L2 cache space.

The C-PBF is updated on two different timescales. On a long timescale (*i.e.,* minutes), the C-PBF is recomputed from the RIB with the goal to improve prefix distribution across blocks. On a short timescale (*i.e.,* every insertion/removal) the C-PBF is greedily updated. When inserting a new prefix, additional expansions are performed on blocks that exceed the false-positive threshold. When removing a prefix, block merges are postponed until the next long-timescale update.

The content prefixes stored in the i-th block of the PBF are hierarchically organized into a prefix tree to (1) easily identify the length at which the threshold t_i is exceeded, and (2) efficiently move prefixes during block expansions with a single pointer update operation. The prefix tree of each block is implemented as a left-child right-sibling binary tree for space efficiency.

5. CAESAR EXTENSIONS

In this section, we introduce two Caesar extensions in order to support (1) large FIBs (*i.e.,* tens of gigabytes), and (2) high-speed forwarding (*i.e.,* tens of Mpps). Large FIBs are supported by having each line card store only part of the entire FIB and collaborate with each other in a distributed fashion. High-speed forwarding is supported by offloading large packet batches to a graphics processing unit (GPU). Although efficient, these solutions may introduce additional latency during packet processing and thus are presented here as extensions that can be activated at the operator's discretion.

Large FIBs: In its original design, Caesar stores a full copy of the FIB at each line card, as commonly done by commercial routers. Although this allows each line card to independently process packets at the nominal rate, it also results in FIB replication and waste of storage resources. For IP prefixes, this is usually not a concern, as a typical FIB contains less than one million entries. In ICN, however, the FIB can easily grow past hundreds of millions of content prefixes [5, 6] and memory space becomes a real concern.

To address this issue, we propose a Caesar extension in Section 5.1 that allows line cards to share their FIB entries. FIBs at different line cards are populated with a unique set of prefixes such that, overall, Caesar is able to store N times more content prefixes, where N is the number of line cards. Since the individual FIB size at each card does not change, line cards are still able to operate at their nominal rate. The key challenge is then how to use a shared FIB to perform LPM on each received packet.

High-speed forwarding: The classic strategy to increase forwarding speeds in routers is a hardware update. However, there is an intrinsic scalability limitation to this approach, in addition to high costs of both hardware and reconfiguration. For instance, upgrading Caesar's line cards from 10 to 40 Gbps requires changing the hardware architecture, with a 10x impact on cost. While this is an option for the deployment of edge/core routers with a large set of networking features, such cost is prohibitive for an enterprise router.

In Section 5.2, we propose an alternative strategy that does not incur such a high cost. Wang *et al.* [9] have recently shown that high-speed LPM on content names is possible by exploiting the parallelism of popular off-the-shelf GPUs. As a second Caesar extension, we propose to use GPUs to accelerate packet processing. Currently, each GPU has an average cost of 10% of the aforementioned architecture upgrade. The challenge is then how to efficiently leverage a GPU to guarantee fast name-based LPM.

For this extension, we assume that a GPU is associated to each line card and that it stores the same FIB entries as the line card. In our platform, a GPU is installed in an external device and connected to a line-card via the switch for power budget reasons. In other platforms (e.g., Advanced Telecommunications Computing Architecture ATCA with enhanced NPU), a GPU can be directly connected to a line card using a regular PCIe bus .

5.1 Distributed Forwarding

To share a large FIB among line cards, we implement a forwarding scheme where LPM is performed in a distributed fashion. The idea is for each packet to be processed at the line card where its longest prefix match resides, *i.e.,* not necessarily the line card that received the packet. A fast mechanism must then be in place for each received packet to be directed to the correct line card for LPM. For this extension, the following modifications to Caesar's control and data planes are required.

Control plane: The route controller now has to compute a different FIB per line card. Each content prefix p in the RIB is assigned to a line card L_i, such that $i = g(p_1) \bmod N$, where $g(p_1)$ is the hash of the subprefix p_1 defined by the first component of p. The rationale here is the same used in the PBF for block selection (cf. Section 3.1); by distributing prefixes to line cards based on their first component, it is possible for an incoming packet to be quickly forwarded to the line card where its longest prefix match resides.

In addition to distributing the FIB, the route controller also maintains a *Line card Table* (LT) containing the MAC address of the backplane interface of each line card. The LT is distributed to each line card along with their FIB, and serves two key purposes.

First, the LT is used by each line card to delegate LPM to another card (see data plane). Second, the LT allows the router controller to quickly recover from failures. With distributed forwarding, the failure of a line card may jeopardize the reachability to the prefixes it manages. We solve this issue by allowing redirection of traffic

---

Algorithm 1: Kernel description

Input: Bloom filters B, hash tables H, content names C
Output: Lengths L of the LPM for each name $c \in C$

1   *prefixLength* ← blockIdx div *blocksPerLength*
2   *blockIdxLength* ← blockIdx mod *blocksPerLength*
3   *namesPerBlock* ← $\lceil |C|/blocksPerLength \rceil$
4   *namesOffset* ← *blockIdxLength* × *namesPerBlock*
5   *namesLast* ← MIN(*namesOffset*+*namesPerBlock*, $|C|$)
6   *tid* ← namesOffset+*threadIdx*
7   **while** *tid* < *namesLast* **do**
8 | c ←READNAME(C, *tid*)
9 | p ←MAKEPREFIX(c, *prefixLength*)
10 | m ← BFLOOKUP(B[*prefixLength*], p)
11 | **if** m = TRUE **then**
12 | | *interface* ← HTLOOKUP(H[*prefixLength*], p)
13 | | **if** *interface* ≠ NIL **then**
14 | | ⌊ ATOMICMAX(L[*tid*], *PrefixLength*)
15 | *tid* ← *tid*+ threads

---

from a failing line card to a backup line card. Once Caesar detects a failure at a line card L_i, the route controller sends the FIB of L_i to one of the additional pre-installed line cards and updates the LT to reflect the change. The updated table is then distributed to all line cards to complete the failure recovery.

Data plane: Upon receiving a packet with content name x, an available NPU core computes the target line card L_i to process the packet, with $i = g(x_1) \bmod N$. If L_i corresponds to the local line card, then the regular flow of operations occurs, *i.e.,* header extraction, name-based LPM, switching, and forwarding (cf. Section 4). Otherwise, the destination MAC address of the packet is overwritten with the address of the backplane interface of L_i fetched from the LT, and the packet is transmitted over the backplane. LPM then occurs at L_i and the packet is sent once again over the backplane to the output line card (if different than L_i) for external transmission.

Distributed forwarding imposes two constraints as tradeoffs for supporting a larger FIB. First, it introduces a short delay caused by packets crossing the backplane twice. Second, extra switching capacity is required. In the worst case, *i.e.,* when a packet is never processed by the receiving line card, the switch must operate twice as fast at a rate $2NR$, where R is the rate of a line card, instead of NR. Nonetheless, as showed in [17], it is possible to combine multiple low-capacity switch fabrics to provide a high-capacity fabric with no performance loss at the cost of small coordination buffers. This is a common approach in commercial routers, e.g., the Alcatel 7950 XRS leverages 16 switching elements to sustain an overall throughput of 32 Tbps [18].

5.2 GPU Offloading

We also propose a Caesar extension to accelerate packet forwarding using a GPU. First, a brief background on the architecture and operation of the NVIDIA GTX 580 [19] used in our implementation is provided. Then, a discussion on our name-based LPM solution using this GPU is presented.

GPU background: The NVIDIA GTX 580 GPU is composed of 16 streaming multiprocessors (SMs), each with 32 stream processors (SPs) running at 1,544 MHz. This GPU has two memory types: a large, but slow, *device memory* and a small, but fast, *shared memory*. The device memory is an off-chip 1.5 GB GDDR5

DRAM, which is accelerated by a L2 cache used by all SMs. The shared memory is an individual on-chip 48 KB SRAM per SM. Each SM also has several registers and a L1 cache to accelerate device memory accesses.

All threads in the GPU execute the same function, called *kernel*. The level of parallelism of a kernel is specified by two parameters, namely, the number of *blocks* and the number of *threads per block*. A block is a set of concurrently executing threads that collaborate using shared memory and barrier synchronization primitives. At run-time, each block is assigned to a SM and divided into *warps*, or sets of 32 threads, that are independently scheduled for execution. Each thread in a warp executes the same instruction in lockstep.

Name-based LPM: We introduce few modifications made to the LPM algorithm to achieve efficient GPU implementation. Due to the serial nature of the NPU, the original algorithm uses a PBF to test for several prefix lengths in the same filter (Section 3). However, to take advantage of the high level of parallelism in GPUs, a LPM approach that uses a Bloom filter and hash table per prefix length is more efficient. Since large FIBs are expected, both the Bloom filters and hash tables are stored in device memory.

For high GPU utilization, multiple warps must be assigned to each SM such that, when a warp stalls on a memory read, other warps are available waiting to be scheduled. The GTX 580 can have up to 8 blocks concurrently allocated and executing per SM, for a total of 128 blocks. Content prefixes are assumed to have 128 components or less, and thus we have one block per prefix length in the worst case. Since such a large number of components is rare, we allow a higher degree of parallelism with multiple blocks working on the same prefix length. In this case, each block operates on a different subset of content names received from a line card.

Algorithm 1 shows our GPU kernel. As input, it receives arrays B, H, and C that contain the Bloom filters, hash tables, and content names to be looked up, respectively. The kernel identifies the length of the longest prefix in the FIB that match each content name $c \in C$ and stores it in the array L, which is then returned to the line card. All these arrays are located in the device memory. We take advantage in the algorithm of a few CUDA variables available to each thread at run-time: blockIdx and threadIdx, which are the block and thread indexes, and blocks and threads, which are the number of blocks and the number of threads per block, respectively.

At line 1, each block uses its blockIdx index to compute the prefix length that it is responsible for. The parameter *BlocksPerLength* is passed to the kernel in order to control how many blocks are used per prefix length. Line 2 computes the relative index (*i.e.*, from 0 to *BlocksPerLength*−1) among the blocks responsible for this prefix length. Line 3–5 show the partitioning of the content names among these blocks. Line 3 uses the batch size $|C|$ to compute the number of content names that each block must look up. Line 4 computes the offset of the current block in C, and line 5 computes the index of the first name outside the block range. The index of the first content name to be read by the thread is computed in line 6.

Lines 7–15 are the core of the LPM. In each iteration, a thread loads a different content name c (line 8), transforms it into a prefix p (line 9), and performs a Bloom filter lookup (line 10). If a match is found, a hash table lookup is performed (line 12), and line 13 makes sure that the match is not a false positive. Finally, if an entry was found, the prefix length is written to $L[tid]$ using the ATOMICMAX call (line 14). The ATOMICMAX(a, v) call is provided by the GPU to write a value v to a given address a only if v is higher than the contents of a. The operation is atomic across all SMs, and thus line 14 ensures LPM is realized. The thread index is then increased in line 15 and matching is initiated on the next content name.

6. EVALUATION

This section experimentally evaluates Caesar along with its extensions and the name-based LPM algorithm. First, Section 6.1 presents the experimental setting and methodology. Section 6.2 then presents results from a series of microbenchmarks to properly dimension the PBF, key data structure in our name-based LPM algorithm. Finally, Section 6.3 and 6.4 evaluate both Caesar and its extensions, namely distributed forwarding and GPU offloading.

6.1 Experimental Setting

Using optical fibers, we connect Caesar to a commercial traffic generator equipped with 10 Gbps optical interfaces. For easy of presentation, we assume that the four line cards in Caesar work in half-duplex mode, two for input traffic and two for output traffic. Nevertheless, results can be extended to full-duplex configurations, as well as to a larger number of line cards. To support content names, the traffic generator produces regular IP packets with our name-based header as payload (cf. Section 4). Each experiment then consists of three parts: (1) traffic with desired characteristics is originated at the traffic generator and transmitted to Caesar; (2) packets are received by Caesar's line cards and content names are extracted; and (3) forwarding decisions are made and packets are sent back to the generator. For each experiment, we mainly measure the *forwarding rate* and *packet latency*. The forwarding rate is measured as the highest input rate that Caesar can handle, during 60 seconds with no losses. Packet latency is described by the minimum, maximum, and average latency of the packets forwarded within the selected 60 seconds time-frame.

We call *workload* the combination of a set of content prefixes stored in Caesar's FIB, and content names requested via the traffic generator. We derive a *reference* workload from the trace described in [9]; this trace contains 10 million URLs collected by crawling the Web. The assumption here is that the hostname extracted from an URL is representative of a content prefix in ICN. Content names are then generated by adding random suffixes to content prefixes randomly selected from the trace; this is the same procedure used in [9], and produces content names that are 42-Bytes long. Overall, most content prefixes in the reference workload are short, with only 2 components on average, whereas content names have between 3 and 12 components, with 4 components on average. The *average distance* Δ between content names and their matching prefixes is only equal to 2 components. To avoid the effect of congestion and traffic management, we assume next hops associated with content prefixes are uniformly distributed over the two output line cards.

Throughout the evaluation, we also use *synthetic* workloads to assess the impact of system parameters and traffic characteristics on Caesar's performance. Synthetic workloads are generated from the reference workload by varying the following parameters: (1) the average distance Δ, which affects the number of potential PBF/hash table lookups, as well as the complexity of the hashing operation; (2) the number of content prefixes in the FIB, which affects the FIB size and access speed; and (3) the number of content prefixes sharing the first component, which affects the distribution of prefixes among PBF blocks, and thus the false positive rate.

6.2 PBF Dimensioning

We start by motivating the choice of the number of hash functions k used in the PBF. The goal is to minimize the cost of computing seed hash values, as this operation has a high computation time (cf. Table 2). After extensive investigation, we set $k = 2$ since the generation of additional seed hash values significantly hurts Caesar's forwarding rate, with only a marginal false positive reduction.

(a) Single input line card.

(b) Single input line card.

(c) Two input line cards.

(d) Two input line cards.

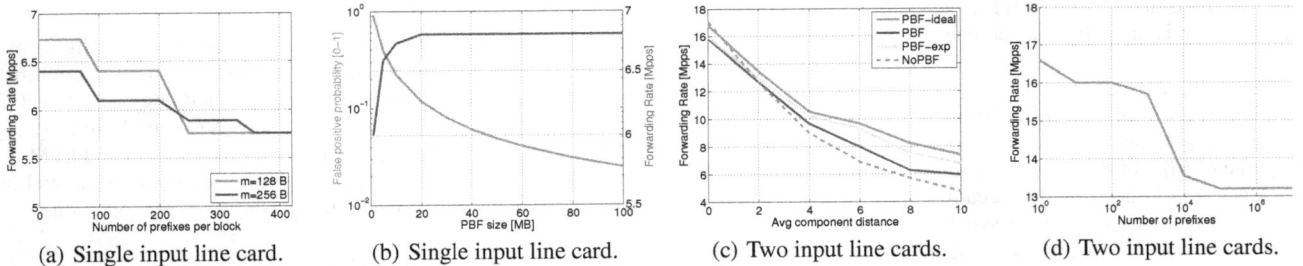

Figure 5: PBF dimensioning and Caesar's evaluation. (a) Forwarding rate as a function of the number of prefixes per block. (b) False positive and forwarding rate as a function of the total PBF size. (c) Forwarding rate as a function of average component distance Δ. (d) Forwarding rate as a function of the number of prefixes.

We now focus on PBF dimensioning. Figure 5(a) shows Caesar's forwarding rate in millions of packets per second (Mpps) as a function of the number of content prefixes per PBF block. The block size is set to one and two cache lines, corresponding to 128 and 256 bytes, respectively, For simplicity, we assume a single line card is active, and use synthetic workloads. The figure shows a key result: *the fastest forwarding rate is measured when a block fits in a single cache line and there are less than 100 content prefixes per block.* Therefore, for the rest of the evaluation we set the block size m equal to 128 bytes and the expansion threshold t_i for a block i to 75 prefixes, *i.e.,* the largest value which does not reduce the forwarding rate, cf. Figure 5(a).

Figure 5(a) shows another interesting result. When a block contains less than 200 prefixes, increasing the block size slightly reduces Caesar's forwarding rate. A larger block size is instead beneficial to the forwarding rate when the block contains more than 200 prefixes. It comes with no surprise that, overall, a larger block size provides a lower false positive rate for the same amount of content prefixes per block. Accordingly, 200 prefixes per block is the threshold for which the additional memory accesses required to load a larger block are amortized by the lower false positive rate.

Figure 5(b) shows Caesar's forwarding rate as a function of the total PBF size $s = m \times b$, where b is the number of PBF blocks, for the reference workload, *i.e.,* 10 million content prefixes. As above, just one line card is active. When $s < 20$ MB, the forwarding rate quickly grows from 6 to 6.7 Mpps. For $s > 20$ MB, the forwarding rate is constant at 6.7 Mpps. As above, this effect is due to the fact that the false positive rate quickly flattens out as s increases. Accordingly, we set the PBF size s to 30 MB, which is the minimum PBF size that maximizes the forwarding rate.

Based on these parameters ($k = 2$, $m = 128$ bytes, $t_i = 75$), we compute the number of expansions required per prefix in the reference workload. We find that a single expansion is enough to handle 95% of the content prefixes; however, 1% of the prefixes incur four expansions, which is the maximum number of expansions required to handle content prefixes from the reference workload.

6.3 Caesar

This section evaluates Caesar. For completeness, we consider several variants of the first stage of our name-based LPM algorithm (cf. Section 3): (1) *PBF*, where the PBF is used without expansion, (2) *PBF-exp*, where PBF expansion is enabled, (3) *NoPBF*, where no PBF is used. In the *NoPBF* case, all possible content prefixes originated from a requested content name are looked up directly in the hash table, from the longest to the shortest prefix. As an upper bound for performance, we introduce the *PBF-ideal*. This consists of using a PBF with expansion while assuming an ideal synthetic

workload where all content prefixes differ in their first component. In this case, content prefixes are uniformly distributed among PBF blocks.

In the remainder of this section, we first evaluate Caesar's performance assuming the reference workload. Then, we present a sensitivity analysis that leverages several synthetic workloads to quantify the impact of workload characteristics on Caesar.

Reference workload: We start by measuring Caesar's forwarding rate under each of the four variants: *PBF*, *PBF-exp*, *NoPBF*, and *PBF-ideal*. The reference workload is used for all variants, with the exception of *PBF-ideal*, that uses the ideal workload. Table 1 summarizes the results from these experiments, differentiating between the cases of one and two active line cards for the forwarding rate. We first focus on the forwarding rate achieved under the *PBF-exp* variant. Assuming a single line card, the table shows that Caesar supports a maximum of 6.6 Mpps when a matching content prefix is found in the FIB (*Match*), and up to 7.5 Mpps when no matches are found (*No Match*), *i.e.,* the corresponding packet is forwarded to a default route. At 10 Gbps, 6.6 Mpps translates to a minimum packet size of 188 Bytes. The table also shows that doubling the active line cards doubles the overall forwarding rate. Accordingly, *Caesar sustains up to 10 Gbps input traffic per line card assuming a minimum packet size of 188 Bytes, and a FIB with 10 million content prefixes.* In the remainder of this paper, we focus on results and experiments where two line cards are active.

Table 1 also shows that *PBF-exp* pays only a 2% reduction of the forwarding rate compared to the ideal case (*PBF-ideal*). This reduction of the forwarding rate is due to the additional memory accesses and complexity required by *PBF-exp* to deal with the non-uniform distribution of content prefixes among blocks. Compared to the *PBF-exp* variant, the absence of the expansion mechanism (*PBF*) costs an additional 2% reduction of the forwarding rate; this is due to the high false positive rate in overloaded PBF blocks. Surprisingly, Table 1 shows that *PBF-exp* only gains about 5% on a solution without a PBF (*NoPBF*), *i.e.,* a forwarding rate of 13.1 Mpps

	PBF-ideal	PBF-exp	PBF	NoPBF
Fwd Rate *Match* (Mpps)	6.7/13.3	6.6/13.1	6.3/12.5	6.3/12.5
Fwd Rate *No Match* (Mpps)	7.5/14.9	7.5/14.9	6.3/12.5	5.2/10.2
Min. latency (μs)	5.4	5.6	5.8	5.8
Avg. latency (μs)	6.4	6.5	6.9	7.0
Max. latency (μs)	8.1	8.1	9.4	9.9

Table 1: Caesar's forwarding rate (Mpps) and latency (μs) with the reference workload. For the forwarding rate, we differentiate between experiments with one and two line cards.

	Total	I/O processing	Hashing	HT lookup	*PBF* lookup
PBF-ideal	1412	371	363	384	294
PBF-exp	1553	371	440	385	357
PBF	1763	371	440	656	294
NoPBF	1781	371	462	948	-
Atomic	-	371	107	251	129

Table 2: CPU cycles per operation.

versus 12.5 Mpps. Such small gain is due to the simplicity of the reference workload where Δ, the average distance between a name and its matching prefix, is low (*i.e.,* 2 components on average). In this case, the *NoPBF* variant requires, on average, only two extra hash table lookups to perform LPM compared to both *PBF* and *PBF-exp*. Larger gains from the *PBF* data structure are showed later under the presence of adversarial workloads. Nevertheless, Table 1 shows that *PBF-exp* gains about 30% over *NoPBF* when none of the incoming content names matches a FIB entry. This result suggests that *the PBF-exp is robust to DoS attacks, where an attacker generates non-existing content names to slow down a content router.*

We now focus on packet latency. Table 1 indicates that *PBF-exp* provides a slightly lower latency than both *PBF* and *NoPBF*, on average. In fact due to the simplicity of the reference workload, the switch is responsible for most of the packet latency, and the impact of the name-based LPM variant on the average latency is minimal. The maximum latency, however, shows significant difference. *PBF-exp* reduces the maximum latency by more than 15% compared to both *PBF* and *NoPBF*. The maximum latency is due to packets whose content names have many components (e.g., 12), and a high average distance Δ from prefixes in the FIB. In this case, the algorithmic benefit of *PBF-exp* plays a role as LPM starts contributing to the overall latency. The table also shows that the expansion mechanism only causes a 2-4% latency increase with respect to the ideal case.

We dissect Caesar's performance bottlenecks by tracking the total number of CPU cycles per major operation, assuming the reference workload. Table 2 reports the number of CPU cycles spent, on average, in the execution of the following operations: I/O processing[2], hashing, hash table lookup, and *PBF* lookup. We differentiate between *PBF*, *PBF-exp*, *NoPBF*, and *PBF-ideal*; we also investigate the cost of each operation in isolation (*Atomic* in the table), *i.e.,* the CPU cycles for a single execution of an operation.

Overall, the results for the total CPU cycles in Table 2 confirm the trend showed in Table 1, with *PBF-ideal* being the least and *NoPBF* being the most CPU hungry. In isolation (the *Atomic* row), I/O processing and hash table lookup require the most CPU cycles. However, while I/O processing is performed once per packet, hash table lookup might be performed multiple times according to the LPM variant adopted. Accordingly, the hash table lookup operation accounts for a minimum of 25% (*PBF-exp*) and a maximum of 50% of the CPU cycles (*NoPBF*). This result showcases the algorithmic advantage of the *PBF-exp* in reducing the number of hash table lookups. Conversely, *PBF-exp* requires some additional CPU cycles for the PBF lookup, since occasionally more than one block might be loaded, e.g., *PBF-exp* requires on average 357 CPU cycles whereas both *PBF* and *PBF-ideal* require only 294 cycles. Finally despite hashing per se is not CPU-intensive, on average, it accounts for 25% of the total number of cycles since several seed hash values are computed (cf. Section 3.3).

---

[2]I/O processing consists of header parsing, MAC address lookup, and header rewriting for packet switching.

Sensitivity analysis: We now analyze the impact of different workload characteristics on Caesar's performance. We start by varying the average distance Δ between the content prefixes in the FIB and the requested content names. The parameter Δ is key to properly characterize a given workload, since it defines the complexity of the LPM operation.

Figure 5(c) shows Caesar's forwarding rate as Δ grows from 0 (equivalent to exact matching) to 10 (highly adversarial workload); as usual, we distinguish between *PBF-ideal*, *PBF*, *PBF-exp* and *NoPBF*. Overall, the rate decreases as Δ increases, which is expected since the number of seed hash values increases linearly with Δ. As Δ increases, the performance gap between *PBF-exp* and *NoPBF* increases too, *i.e.,* when $\Delta = 10$, *PBF-exp* guarantees a forwarding rate twice as fast as the *NoPBF* variant. Compared to *PBF*, *PBF-exp* adds a penalty when Δ is small, which is absorbed as Δ increases. This set of results suggests that *the PBF-exp is robust to adversarial workloads and variable traffic patterns.*

We now investigate the impact of the number of content prefixes n in the FIB. Figure 5(d) plots the evolution of the forwarding rate as n grows from 1 content prefix up to 10 million, as in the reference workload. Overall, the forwarding rate follows a step function, with a large drop in the forwarding rate for $n > 1000$, *i.e.,* from 8.3 to 6.6 Mpps. This phenomenon depends on the hierarchical memory organization of the NPU. When $n = 1$, the only content prefix quickly propagates from DRAM to the L1 cache of every core. As the number of prefix grows, the network processor efficiently stores the prefixes in the L2 cache; after 1,000 prefixes, the L2 caches is exhausted and most prefixes are fetched from the off-chip DRAM, which causes the rate drop. After the 1,000 prefixes threshold, the forwarding rate is almost constant: this indicates that *the amount of prefixes that Caesar support is limited by the amount of off-chip DRAM.* Therefore, with additional DRAM, Caesar could support more content prefixes with little impact on the forwarding rate. Such additional memory is largely available in both edge and core routers. Implementing Caesar on such platforms would allow storing one to two orders of magnitude more prefixes, while still guaranteeing name-based forwarding at wire speed. This is part of our future work.

6.4 Distributed Forwarding

This section evaluates the distributed forwarding extension used by Caesar to allow very large FIBs without requiring additional DRAM (cf. Section 5.1). We populate each input line card with a disjoint set of 10 million content prefixes, 20 millions in total, originated by modifying few characters from the 10 million prefixes in the reference workload. Since Caesar has a switch with a capacity of 10 Gbps per line card, and distributed forwarding requires twice the overall switching speed in the worst case (cf. Section 5.1), we limit the traffic at 5 Gbps per line card and halve the minimum packet size from 188 to 94 bytes.

Figure 6(a) shows Caesar's forwarding rate as a function of ρ, the fraction of packets that require going to another line card for name-based LPM. Overall, the forwarding rate slowly decreases as ρ increases. In the worst-case scenario, $\rho = 100\%$ and these operations account for a drop of only 15% in the rate *i.e.,* from 13.2 to 11.5 Mpps for *PBF-exp*. This reduction of the forwarding rate is due to additional operations required by distributed forwarding, namely packet dispatching, and MAC address rewriting.

We also estimate the impact of distributed forwarding on packet latency in the worst case, *i.e.,* $\rho = 100\%$. We find that distributed forwarding causes an increase of the average and minimum latency in Caesar by 50%. As previously discussed, minimum and average latency mostly derives from the switching latency which doubles

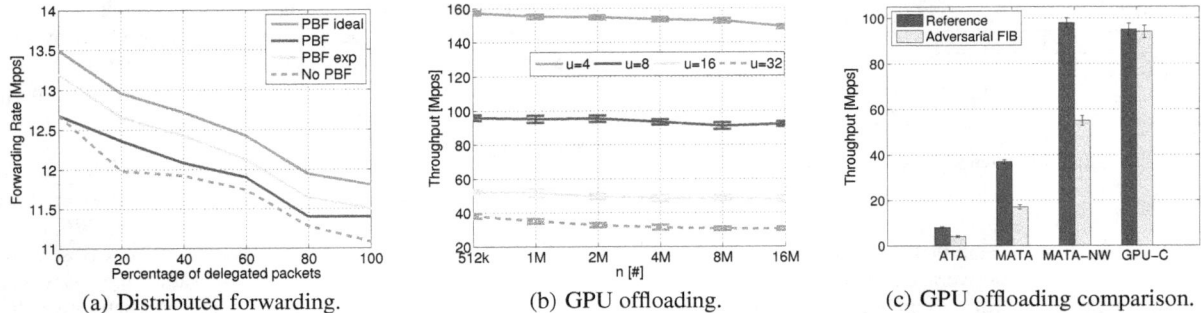

(a) Distributed forwarding.

(b) GPU offloading.

(c) GPU offloading comparison.

Figure 6: Evaluation of Caesar's extensions. (a) Forwarding rate as a function of ρ in distributed forwarding. (b) Throughput as a function of FIB size n and maximum prefix length u in GPU offloading. (c) GPU offloading comparison with [9].

with distributed forwarding. The maximum latency grows instead by about 30%, and this happens when LPM latency overcomes the switching latency, *i.e.*, in presence of large values of Δ. In any case, the additional latency remains in the order of microseconds and it is thus tolerable even for delay-sensitive applications.

To summarize, *distributed forwarding extends Caesar to support twice as many content prefixes with a reduction of only 15% in the forwarding rate and an additional delay of a few microseconds.*

6.5 GPU Offloading

This section quantifies the speedup that GPU offloading provides to Caesar's forwarding rate. We assume a line card offloads a batch of 8K content names to a GTX 580 GPU [19]. Such batch ensures high GPU occupancy, and a maximum buffering delay of about 1 ms, assuming 188-byte packets and 10 Gbps. Larger packet sizes or slower speeds, which both cause higher delay in forming a batch, can be easily handled by Caesar without the GPU (Section 6.3).

We first measure how many packets per second the GPU can match as a function of the number of content prefixes n in the FIB. Figure 6(b) reports the *throughput* only from the kernel execution time, *i.e.*, we omit the transferring time between line card and GPU, and vice-versa, to be comparable with [9] and not limited by the PCIe bandwidth problem discussed therein. We generate several synthetic FIBs where the number of content prefixes grow exponentially from 0.5 to 16 million, the maximum number of prefixes that fits in the GPU device memory. We also vary the maximum length u of the prefixes in the FIB between 4 and 32 components. For each value of u, content prefixes in the FIB are equally distributed among the possible lengths, e.g., when $u = 4$, a quarter of the prefixes have a single component. Finally, we assume that all content names have 32 components, *i.e.*, $d = 32$.

Figure 6(b) shows two main results. First, the throughput is mostly independent from the number of prefixes n; overall, growing the FIB size from 0.5 to 10 million prefixes causes less than a 10% throughput decrease. Second, the throughput largely depends on u. For example, when $n = 16$ M, increasing u from 4 to 32 components reduces the throughput by 5x, from 150 to 30 Mpps.

We now compare our implementation with the work in [9], which also explores the usage of GPU for name-based forwarding. Their GPU code is open-sourced, which allows us to perform a fair comparison with our implementation. The key idea of the work in [9] is to organize the FIB as a trie as done today for IP. They thus introduce a character trie which allows name-based LPM. Then, they introduce three optimizations, namely the aligned transition array (ATA), the multi-ATA (MATA) and MATA with interweaved name storage (MATA-NW), which leverage a combination of hash-

ing and the hierarchical nature of the content names to realize efficient compression and lookup.

Figure 6(c) compares the performance of our kernel (GPU-C) with the kernels proposed in [9], namely ATA, MATA and MATA-NW by running their code on our GPU. For such comparison we use the reference workload, where $u \sim 3$, as well as a more adversarial workload where $u = 8$. We refer to this adversarial workload as "adversarial FIB."

Compared to the results presented in [9], we measure less than half the throughput for ATA, MATA and MATA-NW. This is expected, since our GPU has half the cores than the GTX 590 GPU used in [9]. The figure also shows that the throughput measured for Caesar, about 95 Mpps, matches the results from the synthetic traces when $u = 8$ and $n = 10$ M, cf. Figure 6(b). MATA-NW is slightly faster than Caesar, 100 versus 95 Mpps, assuming the reference workload. This happens because MATA-NW exploits the fact that most of the content prefixes in the FIB are very short, e.g., 2 or 3 components, to reduce LPM to (mostly) an exact matching operation. Instead, our algorithm does not rely on such assumption; this design choice makes it resilient to more diverse FIBs at the expense of a performance loss with a simplistic FIB. Such feature is visible in the presence of the adversarial FIB, where Caesar is twice as fast as MATA-NW.

To summarize, *GPU offload augments Caesar's forwarding rate by an order of magnitude, with a small penalty in packet latency, and our GPU-based LPM algorithm is resilient to adversarial traffic workloads.*

7. ADDITIONAL FEATURES

Name-based forwarding is the key task of a content router. Additional features are caching, multicasting, and dynamic multipath forwarding. To support these features, a Pending Interest Table (PIT) and a Content Store (CS) are required. The PIT keeps track of pending content requests, or "Interest" in the NDN terminology, already forwarded by the content router. The CS stores a copy of forwarded data packets to satisfy eventual future requests.

The design, implementation, and evaluation of PIT and CS is out of the scope of this paper, and left as future work. However, we have recently started extending Caesar with both PIT and CS based on a set of design guidelines derived in our previous work [20, 5]. In the following, we briefly summarize such integration.

In [20], we identify two challenges in PIT design: *placement* and *data structure*. Placement refers to where in the content router the PIT should reside. Data structure refers to how the PIT entries should be stored and organized to enable efficient operations. The paper concludes that the best approach is a third-party placement leveraging the semantic of content names to select a line card where PIT matching is performed. This idea fits well the distributed forwarding scheme used by Caesar, which we plan to piggyback for the PIT implementation. As data structure, we use an open-addressed hash table (cf. Section 3.4).

The CS consists of a packet store, where data packets are physically stored, and an index table, that keeps track of data packet memory locations in the packet store. Similar to the PIT, the index table is implemented as an open-addressed hash table. In addition to pointers to data packets, the index table stores data statistics, e.g., access frequency and timestamps, to enable replacement policies like FIFO or LRU. We implement the packet store by an extension to Caesar's packet buffer in order to allow Caesar to store data packets after forwarding as well as serve them when needed. An evinction mechanism was also added to support the removal of data packets according to the replacement policy. The CS is physically allocated on the off-chip DRAM memory. Additional levels of storage on lower throughput/higher capacity technologies (e.g., SSD) can complement the packet store design; however, this optimization is not supported by our current hardware setup.

8. CONCLUSION

The Internet usage is currently centered around content distribution, instead of the original host-to-host communication. Future Internet architectures are thus expected to depart from a host-centric design to a content-centric one. Such evolution requires routers to operate on content names instead of IP addresses. A high burden is expected on the routers due to the explosion of the address space, both in number of content prefixes, which are hard to aggregate compared to IP, and their length, expected to be on the order of tens of bytes as opposed to 32 or 128 bits for IPv4 and IPv6, respectively. Our paper investigates the design and implementation of Caesar, a content router capable of forwarding packets based on names at wire speed. Caesar advances the state of the art in many ways. First, it introduces the novel prefix Bloom filter (PBF) data structure to allow efficient longest prefix matching operation on content names. Second, it is fully compatible with current protocols and network equipment. Third, it supports packet processing offload to external units, such as graphics processing units (GPUs), and distributed forwarding, a mechanism which allows line cards to share their FIBs with each other. Our experiments show that Caesar sustains up to 10 Gbps input traffic per line card assuming a minimum packet size of 188 bytes, and a FIB with 10 million content prefixes. We also show that the two proposed extensions allow Caesar to support both a larger FIB and higher forwarding speed, with a small penalty in packet latency.

ACKNOWLEDGMENTS

This work has been partially carried out at the Laboratory of Information, Networking, and Computer Science (LINCS), and results have been partially produced in the framework of the common research laboratory between INRIA and Bell Labs, Alcatel-Lucent.

9. REFERENCES

[1] "Akamai," http://www.akamai.com/.

[2] "Amazon elastic compute cloud (amazon ec2)," http://aws.amazon.com/ec2/.

[3] G. Carofiglio, G. Morabito, L. Muscariello, I. Solis, and M. Varvello, "From Content Delivery Today to Information Centric Networking," *Computer Networks*, 2013.

[4] V. Jacobson, D. K. Smetters, J. D. Thronton, M. F. Plass, N. H. Briggs, and R. L. Braynard, "Network Named Content," in *Proc. ACM CoNEXT*, Rome, Italy, Dec. 2009.

[5] D. Perino and M. Varvello, "A Reality Check for Content Centric Networking," in *Proc. ACM ICN*, Toronto, Canada, Aug. 2011.

[6] W. So, A. Narayanan, and D. Oran, "Named Data Networking on a Router: Fast and DoS-Resistant Forwarding with Hash Tables," in *Proc. IEEE/ACM ANCS*, San Jose, California, USA, Oct. 2013.

[7] G. Pankaj, L. Steven, and M. Nick, "Routing Lookups in Hardware at Memory Access Speeds," in *Proc. IEEE INFOCOM*, San Francisco, CA, Mar. 1998.

[8] W. So, A. Narayanan, D. Oran, and M. Stapp, "Named Data Networking on a Router: Forwarding at 20Gbps and Beyond," in *Proc. ACM SIGCOMM (demo)*, Honk Kong, China, Aug. 2013.

[9] Y. Wang, Y. Zu, T. Zhang, K. Peng, Q. Dong, B. Liu, W. Meng, H. Dai, X. Tian, Z. Xu, H. Wu, and D. Yang, "Wire Speed Name Lookup: a GPU-Based Approach," in *Proc. NSDI*, Lombard, IL, Apr. 2013.

[10] H. Yuan, T. Song, and P. Crowley, "Scalable NDN forwarding: Concepts, Issues and Principles," in *Proc. ICCCN*, Bundeswehr Munchen, Jul. 2012.

[11] Y. Wang, K. He, H. Dai, W. Meng, J. Jiang, B. Liu, and Y. Chen, "Scalable Name Lookup in NDN Using Effective Name Component Encoding," in *Proc. ICDCS*, Macau, China, Jun. 2012.

[12] Y. Wang, T. Pan, Z. Mi, H. Dai, X. Guo, T. Zhang, B. Liu, and Q. Dong, "NameFilter: Achieving Fast Name Lookup with Low Memory Cost via Applying Two-Stage Bloom Filters," in *Proc. IEEE INFOCOM*, Turin, Italy, Aug. 2013.

[13] S. Dharmapurikar, P. Krishnamurthy, and D. E. Taylor, "Longest Prefix Matching Using Bloom Filters," in *Proc. ACM SIGCOMM*, Karlsruhe, Germany, Aug. 2003.

[14] H. Song, F. Hao, M. S. Kodialam, and T. V. Lakshman, "IPv6 Lookups using Distributed and Load Balanced Bloom Filters for 100Gbps Core Router Line Cards," in *Proc. IEEE INFOCOM*, Rio de Janeiro, Brazil, Jul. 2009.

[15] "Information centric networking research group (icnrg)," http://irtf.org/icnrg.

[16] A. K. M. M. Hoque, S. O. Amin, A. Alyyan, B. Zhang, L. Zhang, and L. Wang, "NLSR: Named-data Link State Routing Protocol," in *Proc. ACM ICN*, Hong Kong, China, Aug. 2013.

[17] S. Iyer and N. W. McKeown, "Analysis of the Parallel Packet Switch Architecture," *IEEE/ACM Transactions on Networking*, vol. 11, no. 2, pp. 314–324, Apr. 2003.

[18] "Alcatel 7950," http://www.alcatel-lucent.com/products/7950-extensible-routing-system.

[19] "nvidia. gtx 580," http://geforce.com/hardware/desktop-gpus/geforce-gtx-580/.

[20] M. Varvello, D. Perino, and L. Linguaglossa, "On the Design and Implementation of a Wire-Speed Pending Interest Table," in *Proc. IEEE NOMEN*, Turin, Italy, Aug. 2013.

Design Patterns for Tunable and Efficient SSD-based Indexes

Ashok Anand[†], Aaron Gember-Jacobson*, Collin Engstrom*, Aditya Akella*
[†]Instart Logic   *University of Wisconsin-Madison
[†]ashok.anand@gmail.com   *{agember,engstrom,akella}@cs.wisc.edu

ABSTRACT

A number of data-intensive systems require using random hash-based indexes of various forms, e.g., hash tables, Bloom filters, and locality sensitive hash tables. In this paper, we present general SSD optimization techniques that can be used to design a variety of such indexes while ensuring higher performance and easier tunability than specialized state-of-the-art approaches. We leverage two key SSD innovations: a) rearranging the data layout on the SSD to combine multiple read requests into one page read, and b) intelligently reordering requests to exploit inherent parallelism in the architecture of SSDs. We build three different indexes using these techniques, and we conduct extensive studies showing their superior performance, lower CPU/memory footprint, and tunability compared to state-of-the-art systems.

Categories and Subject Descriptors

C.2.m [**Computer Communication Networks**]: Miscellaneous; D.4.2 [**Operating Systems**]: Storage Management; E.2 [**Data**]: Data Storage Representations

Keywords

Solid state drives (SSDs), hashtables, bloom filters, memory efficiency, CPU efficiency, parallelism

1. INTRODUCTION

Data-intensive systems are being employed in a wide variety of application scenarios today. For example, key-value systems are employed in cloud-based applications as diverse as e-commerce and business analytics systems, and picture stores; and large object stores are used in a variety of content-based systems such as network deduplication, storage deduplication, logging systems, and content similarity detection engines. To ensure high application performance these systems often rely on random hash-based indexes whose specific design may depend on the system in question. For instance, WAN optimizers [5, 6], Web caches [4, 7], and video caches [2] employ large streaming hash tables. De-duplication systems [28, 30] employ Bloom filters. Content similarity engines and

some video proxies [2, 11] employ locality sensitive hash (LSH) tables [24]. Given the volume of the underlying data, the indexes often span several 10s to 100s of GB, and they continue to grow in size.

Across these systems, the index is the most intricate in design. Heavy engineering is often devoted to ensure high index performance at low cost and low energy footprint. Most state-of-the-art systems [14, 15, 21, 25] advocate using SSDs to store the indexes, given flash-based media's superior density, 8X lower cost (vs. DRAM), 25X better energy efficiency (vs. DRAM or disk), and high random read performance (vs. disk) [25]. However, the commonality ends here. The conventional wisdom, which universally dictates index design, is that domain- and operations-specific SSD optimizations are necessary to meet appropriate cost-performance trade-offs. This poses two problems: (1) *Poor flexibility:* Index designs often target a specific point in the cost-performance spectrum, severely limiting the range of applications that can use them. It also makes indexes difficult to tune, e.g., use extra memory for improved performance. Finally, the indexes are designed to work best under specific workloads; minor deviations can make performance quite variable. (2) *Poor generality:* The design patterns employed apply only to the specific data structure on hand. In particular, it is difficult to employ different indexes in tandem (e.g., hash tables for cache lookup alongside LSH tables for content similarity detection over the same underlying content) as they may employ conflicting techniques that result in poor SSD I/O performance.

Our paper questions the conventional wisdom. We present different indexes that all leverage a common set of novel SSD optimizations, are easy to tune to achieve optimal performance under a given cost constraint, and support widely-varying workload patterns and applications with differing resource requirements; yet, they offer better IOPS, cost less, and consume lower energy than their counterparts with specialized designs.

We rely on two key innovations. (1) We leverage a unique feature of SSDs that has been overlooked by earlier proposals, namely, that the internal architecture of SSDs offers parallelism at multiple levels, e.g., channel-, package-, die-, and plane-level. Critically, the parallelism benefits are significant only under certain I/O workloads. Our key contribution lies in identifying these parallelism-friendly workloads and developing a set of design patterns for encapsulating the input workload for an index into SSD parallelism-friendly forms. (2) Based on the design patterns, we develop a new primitive called *slicing* which helps organize data on the SSD such that related entries are co-located. This allows us to combine multiple reads into a single "slice read" of related items, offering high read performance. We show how our design patterns inform slice size, the number of slices to co-locate at a particular SSD block, and the techniques to use for reading from and writing to slices. A key feature of slicing is that slice size/composition (i.e., how many elements constitute a slice) offers simple knobs to trade off I/O performance for the memory overhead of any index data structure.

In §4, we conduct several experiments to profile the internal parallelism behavior on a desktop-grade SSD to identify parallelism-friendly I/O patterns, and derive the appropriate design patterns that guide the composition, configuration and use of slices. Then, we present the design of three random-hash based indexes that leverage our design patterns and slicing: a streaming hash table called SliceHash (§5), large Bloom filters called SliceBloom, and locality-sensitive hash tables called SliceLSH (§6).

Our index designs can be sketched as follows: We use small in-memory data structures (hash tables, Bloom filters, or LSH tables, as the case may be) as *buffers* for insert operations to deal with the well-known problem of slow random writes on SSDs. When full, these are flushed to the SSD; each of these flushed data structures is called an "incarnation". A similar approach has also been used in state-of-the-art techniques, e.g., [14, 25], to deal with slow random writes. However, they need to maintain complex metadata for lookups, which imposes high memory overhead or CPU cost. In contrast, we use a simple reorganization of data on the SSD such that all related entries of different incarnations are located together in a slice, thereby optimizing lookup and eliminating the need for maintaining complex metadata. We show that this frees memory and compute resources for use by higher layer applications. Further, based on an understanding of the SSD's writing policy, we appropriately reorder lookups, without violating application semantics, to distribute them uniformly across different channels and extract maximal parallelism benefits.

Our parallelism-centered design patterns and the slicing primitive together offer good performance at relatively low CPU or memory overhead in comparison to state-of-the art techniques. We show that our design techniques facilitate extending the indexes to use multiple SSDs on the same machine, offering linear scaling in performance while also *lowering* per-key memory overhead. State-of-the-art techniques cannot be scaled out in a similar fashion.

We build prototype indexes using a 128GB Crucial SSD and at most 4GB of DRAM. We conduct extensive experiments under a range of realistic workloads to show that our design patterns offer high performance, flexibility, and generality. Key findings from our evaluation are as follows: On a single SSD, SliceHash can provide 69K lookups/sec by intelligently exploiting parallelism which is 1.5X better than naively running multiple lookups in parallel. Lookup performance is preserved even with arbitrarily interleaved inserts, whereas state-of-the-art systems take up to a 30% performance hit. SliceHash has low memory footprint and low CPU overhead, yet it provides high lookup performance. Furthermore, SliceHash can be tuned to use progressively more memory (from 0.27B/entry to 1.1B/entry) to scale performance (from 70K to 110K ops/s) for mixed (50% lookup, 50% insert) workloads. When leveraging 3 SSDs in parallel, SliceHash's throughput improves to between 207K (lookup-only) and 279K (lookup/insert) ops/sec. Slice-Bloom performs 15K ops/sec with a mixed lookup/insert workload, whereas the state-of-the-art [22] achieves similar performance on a high-end SSD that costs 30X. SliceLSH performs 6.9K lookups/s.

2. DESIGN REQUIREMENTS AND EXISTING SYSTEMS

Our goal is to develop *generic* SSD design optimizations that can be applied *nearly universally* to a variety of random hash-based indexes that each have the following requirements:

Large scale: A number of data-intensive systems require large indexes. For example, WAN optimizer [5, 6] indexes are ≥32GB; data de-duplication indexes are ≥40 GB [3]. In keeping with the trend of growing data volumes, we target indexes that are an order-of-magnitude larger, i.e., a few hundred GB.

High performance and low cost: The index should provide high throughput, low per-operation latency, and low overall cost, memory, and energy footprint. To apply to a wide-variety of content-based systems, the index should provide good performance under both inserts/updates and reads. State-of-the art techniques for hash tables offer 46K IOPS [14, 25]; those for bloom filters offer 12-15K IOPS [22]. Our indexes should match or exceed this performance.

Flexibility: This covers various aspects of how easy the index is to use, as we discuss below.

Applications leveraging a given index may require significant CPU and memory resources for their internal operations. For example, data de-duplication applications require CPU resources for computing SHA-1 hashes of fingerprints [12]. Various image and video search applications require CPU resources for computing similarity metrics after they find potential matches. Caching applications may want to use memory for caching frequently accessed content. To ensure that the applications can flexibly use CPU and memory and that their performance does not suffer, the index should impose low CPU and memory overhead. Unfortunately, many prior index designs ignore the high CPU overhead they impose in their singular quest for, e.g., low memory footprint, and high read performance (e.g., SILT [25]), which makes application design tricky. Equally importantly, application designers should be able to easily extend the index with evolving application requirements, e.g., add memory or CPU cores at a modest additional cost to obtain commensurately better performance. Finally, the index should work well under a variety of workload patterns.

In the rest of this section, we survey other related hash-based systems that employ flash storage. As stated earlier, none of these studies use techniques that are all generally applicable across different random hash-based indexes. Even ignoring this issue, all prior designs fall short on one or more of the above requirements.

2.1 SSD-Based Hash Tables

We start by reviewing a specific class of indexes, namely those based on hash tables. We review several prior systems each designed for a specific application domain. We highlight the design choices made in each case and the restrictions they impose.

Many recent works [14, 15, 20, 21, 25] have proposed SSD-based indexes for large key-value stores. As Table 1 shows, each design optimizes for a subset of metrics that matter in practice (i.e., high throughput, low latency, low memory footprint or low computation overhead). Unfortunately, these optimizations come at the expense of significantly impacting other metrics and they may impact the applications that use the indexes, as we argue below.

FlashStore[20] stores key-value pairs in a log-structured fashion on SSD storage, and uses an in-memory hash table to index them. It optimizes for lookup (on average, one SSD read per lookup), but imposes high memory overhead (~6 bytes/key). *SkimpyStash* [21] uses a low amount of memory—1 byte/key—to maintain a hash table with linear chaining on the SSD. However, it requires 5 page reads/lookup on average.

BufferHash [14] buffers all insertions in memory, and writes them in a batch to the SSD. It maintains in-memory Bloom filters [8] to avoid spurious lookups to any batch on the SSD. BufferHash requires ~1 page read per lookup on average and works well across a range of workloads. However, it may need to read multiple pages in the worst case due to false positives of the Bloom filters. Buffer-

	FlashStore	SkimpyStash	BufferHash	SILT
Avg Lookup (#page read)	~1	~5	~1	~1
Worst Lookup (#page read)	1	10	16	33
Memory (# bytes/entry)	~6	~1	~4	~0.7
CPU overhead	Low	Low	Low	High

Table 1: Comparison of different SSD-based Hash tables under different metrics. The worst-case lookups are based on default prototype configurations of these systems. Existing SSD-based Hash tables are optimized for one set of metrics, but incur additional overhead or perform poor under other metrics (shown in bold red).

Hash also has a high memory overhead (~4 bytes/key) due to in-memory Bloom filters. Finally, BufferHash is difficult to tune: it requires a predetermined amount of memory (a function of SSD size) to ensure that the false positive rate is low and worst-case lookup cost is small.

SILT [25] offers a better balance across the different metrics than any of the above systems. SILT achieves a low memory footprint (0.7 bytes/entry) and requires a single page lookup on average. However, SILT uses a much more complex design than the systems discussed above. It employs three data structures: one of them is highly optimized for a low memory footprint, and the others are more write-optimized but require more memory. SILT continuously moves data from the write-optimized data structures to the memory-efficient one. In doing so, SILT has to continuously sort newly written data and merge it with old data. This increases the computation overhead, which may impact the applications that use SILT. Furthermore, these background operations affect the performance of SILT under a workload of continuous inserts and lookups as is common with, e.g., WAN optimizers. For example, the lookup performance drops by 21% for a 50% lookup-50% insert workload on 64B key-value pairs. While SILT is somewhat tunable—e.g., it is possible to tune the memory overhead between 0.7 and 2B per entry [25]—it doesn't permit configurations with arbitrarily low memory footprint contrary to our index designs.

Also, none of the above systems are designed for exploiting the intrinsic parallelism of SSDs. As we show in §4, lookup performance can improve by 5.2X if the underlying parallelism is optimally exploited.

2.2 Other Indexes

Other hashing-based data structures have received less attention than hash tables. But there has been growing interest in using SSDs to support them when the scale is large, especially for Bloom filters.

Buffered Bloom Filter [17] is an approach for SSD-resident Bloom filters that targets initial construction of Bloom filters to ensure a low memory footprint. However, this data structure cannot handle updates over time. BloomFlash [22] is an approach for SSD-resident Bloom filters that optimizes for writes. BloomFlash buffers bit updates in DRAM to avoid random writes to the SSD. It also uses a hierarchical organization to manage writes. Neither approach leverages parallelism intrinsic to SSDs. In particular, our experiments show that by adapting BloomFlash's design using our parallelism-centered patterns and techniques, we can achieve the same I/O performance using a commodity SSD that their design achieves with a high-end SSD costing 30X more.

The critical takeaways from the above discussion are that the individual designs are targeted to specific scenarios and workloads; they are often not easy to tune, e.g., to trade-off performance for

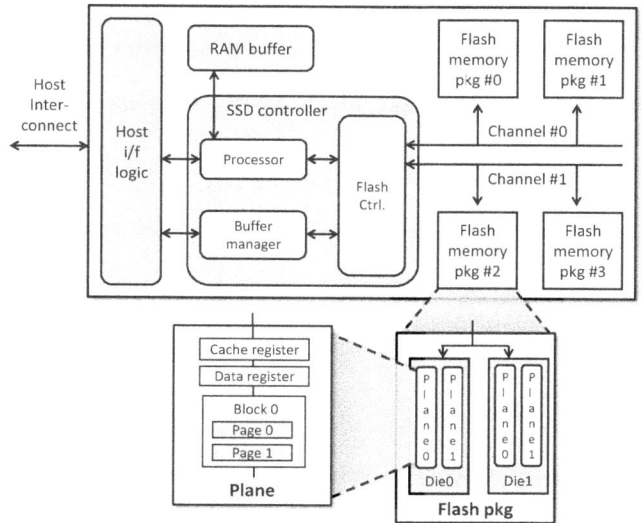

Figure 1: SSD internal architecture

memory; they are CPU intensive; and techniques used in one often don't extend to another.

Our goal is to develop guidelines to design indexes that offer high I/O performance and low memory overhead, are easy to tune, work well under a variety of workloads, and apply to a variety of indexes based on random hashing, including hash tables, locality-sensitive hash tables, and Bloom filters.

3. PARALLELISM IN SSD ARCHITECTURE

To meet our goal, we must first understand key properties of SSDs that influence the design and performance of random hash-based indexes. To this end, we describe the internal architecture of SSDs. We then describe the different forms of parallelism available within SSD architectures.

Figure 1 shows an illustration of a SATA-based SSD architecture. SSDs provide logical block addresses (LBAs) as an interface to the host. All I/O requests for LBAs are processed by an SSD controller. The controller receives I/O requests from the host via an interface connection (i.e., the SATA interface). The controller uses the flash translation layer (FTL) to translate logical pages of incoming requests to physical pages. It issues commands to *flash packages* via flash memory controllers. The flash memory controller connects to flash packages via *multiple channels* (generally 2-10).

Each package has two or more *dies* or chips. Each die is composed of two or more *planes*. On each plane, memory is organized into *blocks*; each block consists of many *pages*. Each plane has a data register to temporarily store the data page during reads or writes. For a write command, the controller first transfers data to a data register on a channel, and then the data is written from the data register to the corresponding physical page. For a read command, the data is first read from the physical page to the data register, and then transferred to the controller on a channel.

Different Forms of Parallelism. The internal architecture of SSDs incorporates varying degrees and levels of parallelism. Each of an SSD's channels can operate in parallel and independently of each other. Thus, SSDs inherently have *channel-level parallelism*. Typically, the data transfers from/to the multiple packages on the same channel get serialized. However, data transfers can be interleaved with other operations (e.g., reading data from a page to the data register) on other packages sharing the same channel [10, 29]. This interleaving provides *package-level parallelism*. The FTL stripes consecutive logical pages across a gang of different packages on the same channel [10] to exploit package-level parallelism. Furthermore, the command issued to a die can be executed independently of the others on the same package. This provides *die-level parallelism*.

Multiple operations of the same type (read/write/erase) can happen simultaneously on different planes in the same die. Currently, a *two plane command* is widely used for executing two operations of the same type on two different planes simultaneously. This provides *plane-level parallelism*. Furthermore, the data transfers to/from the physical page can be *pipelined* for consecutive commands of the same type.

4. PARALLELISM-FRIENDLY DESIGN PATTERNS

At the heart of our work lies a generic set of techniques for carefully extracting the above intrinsic parallelism of SSDs to ensure high performance without sacrificing generality and tunability. In what follows, we first outline known properties of SSD I/O, and techniques for accommodating them (§4.1). We then describe design patterns that help account for both the known properties as well as the available forms of parallelism (§4.2).

4.1 Reads and Writes

The read/write properties of SSDs are well known. In particular, a page is the smallest unit of read or write operations, meaning that reading a 16B entry (such as a key-value pair in a hash table) is as costly as reading an entire page. Also, the performance of random page reads is comparable to that of sequential page reads. Thus, we arrive at design pattern **DP1**: *Organize data on the SSD in such a way that multiple entries to be read reside on the same page.*

SSDs show poor performance under a heavy random write workload [27]. Even the random read performance is affected in a mixed workload of continuous reads and writes [14]. A common design pattern, which we call **DP2**, used to accommodate this property is: *Leverage a small amount of memory to buffer writes and flush data out to the SSD at a granularity lower bounded by the size of a block (typically 128K)*; we adopt this in our design.

We now describe the benefits of, and techniques for, applying these insights along with leveraging SSD parallelism.

4.2 Extracting Parallelism

Channel-level Parallelism. The throughput of page reads can be significantly improved by leveraging channel-level parallelism. However, a simple way of using multiple threads to issue requests in parallel does not work in the general case: when a sudden skew in input keys forces all requests to go to the same channel, naive parallel lookups will obviously not provide any benefits. To extract the benefits of parallelism under a wide-range of workloads and workload variations, we need to ensure that the requests issued to the SSD are spread uniformly across the channels. This becomes possible if we know the mapping between pages and channels. Armed with this knowledge, we can then reorder lookup requests to ensure that those issued concurrently to the SSD are uniformly spread across channels.

However, the mapping is often internal to SSDs and not exposed by vendors. Recent work [18] has shown that this mapping can be reverse engineered. As mentioned earlier, the FTL stripes a group of consecutive logical pages across different packages on the same channel. The authors in [18] discuss a technique to determine the size of the group that gets contiguously allocated within a channel; they call this logical unit of data a *chunk*. They show how to determine the chunk size and the number of channels. Using this, they also show how to derive the two common mapping policies: (1) *write-order mapping*, where the ith chunk write is assigned the channel $i \% N$, assuming N is the number of channels, and (2) *LBA-based mapping*, where the logical block address (LBA) is mapped to channel number $LBA \% N$.

As an example, we employed the technique in [18] with a Crucial SSD. We estimated the chunk size and number of channels to be 8KB and 32, respectively. We further found that the Crucial SSD follows write-order mapping. Figure 2a shows the lookup performance of the our channel-aware technique that uses the above estimates of the SSD channel count and mapping policies, for different numbers of threads (labeled "Best"). We also show the worst case (labeled "Worst"), where we force requests to go to the same channel. We find that the gap between the two is quite substantial—nearly 5.2X. As a point of comparison, we also show the performance of simply issuing multiple requests using multiple threads without paying attention to channel-awareness (labeled "Rand"): we see that this is up to 1.5X worse for this workload.

Thus, we arrive at the following design pattern **DP3**: *when performing lookups, rearrange them such that the requests are evenly spread across channels.*

We further investigate if issuing concurrent writes leads to similar benefits as concurrent reads; as stated above, each write should be at least the block size (DP2). Figure 2b shows results for the Crucial SSD. We see that parallelism offers marginal improvement at best. The reason is that the Crucial SSD's write-order-based mapping assigns consecutive chunks (8KB) to different channels, and so, by default, any write larger than the chunk size is distributed over multiple channels. Thus, we arrive at **DP4**: *simply issuing large bulk writes suffices - issuing writes concurrently is not essential to improving write throughput.*

Package-level parallelism: Figure 2c shows the random read performance for different read sizes. We observe high read bandwidth when large reads are issued. This is because reads up to the chunk size (8KB) can exploit package-level parallelism. Reads larger than the chunk size can exploit both channel-level and package-level parallelism. Thus, we have **DP5**: *when possible, it helps to issue large reads.*

Note that this design pattern cannot be used for regular lookups into an index data structure, as issuing large reads may retrieve useless data resulting in low system goodput. However, as we will show later, this design pattern aids in instrumenting patterns 1–4.

Plane-level parallelism: Earlier works [18, 29] have shown that intermingling small reads and small writes affects plane-level parallelism, leading to a performance drop of up to $1.3X$ in throughput compared to issuing consecutive small reads followed by consecutive small writes. However, the above design patterns already dictate that we issue large writes (DP2) and small reads (small page reads for lookup requests; DP1), which already ensure that small reads and small writes are not intermingled by default. Thus, there are no further undesirable interactions with plane-level parallelism.

5. STREAMING HASH TABLES: SLICEHASH

In this section, we discuss how, using the design patterns (DP1–5), we can develop techniques for building high-performance large streaming hash tables where <key, value> pairs can be looked up, inserted, updated and evicted over time. We call our index Slice-Hash. We will describe how to build other index data structures in §6.

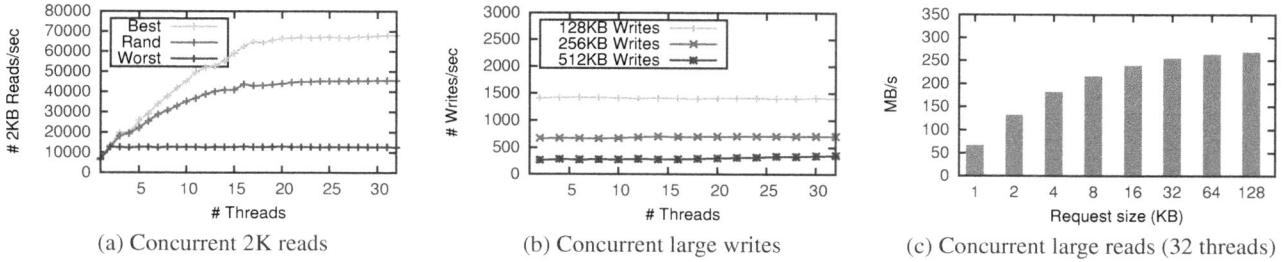

(a) Concurrent 2K reads

(b) Concurrent large writes

(c) Concurrent large reads (32 threads)

Figure 2: Concurrent I/O performance

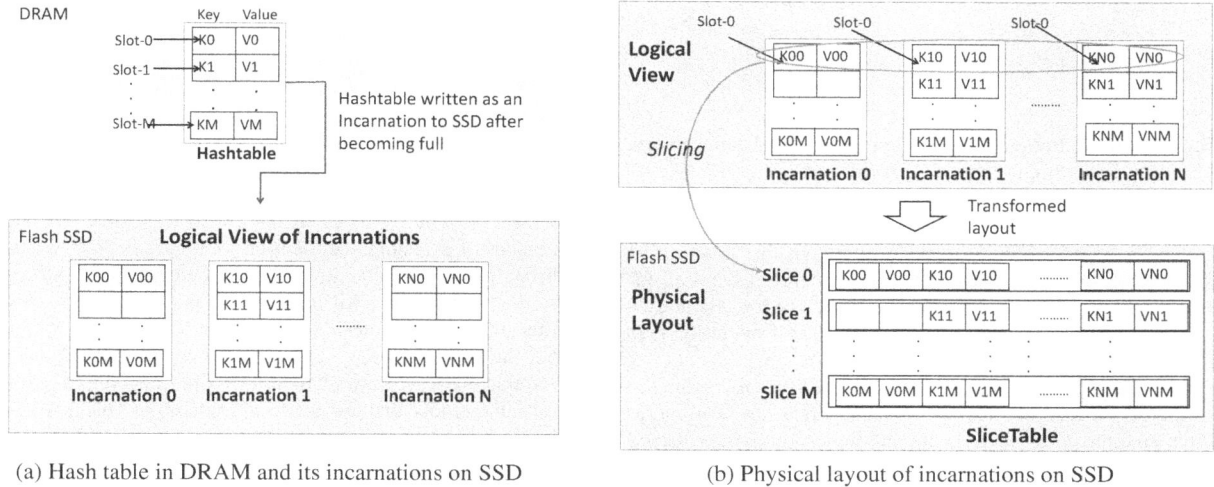

(a) Hash table in DRAM and its incarnations on SSD

(b) Physical layout of incarnations on SSD

Figure 3: Basic SliceHash structure

Our key innovation, which applies across all the data structures, is the use of a *slicing* primitive for storing multiple related entries on the same page (DP1) thereby helping combine multiple index lookups into one page read. We use known techniques for dealing with random writes (DP2) but adapt them to work with slicing (based on DP4 and DP5). Finally, we discuss how we implement support for concurrent I/O in SliceHash (based on DP3). We show how the design patterns influence key aspects of the configuration of the data structure as well as the techniques we use to read from and write to the SSD.

5.1 Basic SliceHash

Figure 3 shows the basic overview of SliceHash. SliceHash hierarchically organizes the hash table across DRAM and SSD. We maintain an in-memory hashtable, and inserts *only* happen in this in-memory table. After the in-memory table is full, it is written as an *incarnation* to the SSD in a batch. Over time, multiple incarnations are written to the SSD. This aspect of the design is motivated by DP2 for avoiding slow writes/updates to random SSD locations during insertion of keys. BufferHash [14] also uses a similar design principle, but SliceHash differs in how the data in the incarnations is laid out on the SSD.

SliceHash uses the idea of slicing to lay out the data. Figure 3b shows the physical layout of the data in incarnations in the form of a slicetable. Before describing construction of the slicetable, we define a few key terms:

- A *slot* is an index into the in-memory hash table or an on-SSD incarnation, where an entry (i.e., a key-value pair) is or can be stored.
- For a given slot, a *slice* is a list of all entries located at the slot within all on-SSD incarnations. In Figure 3b, the slice for slot-0, i.e., *slice-0*, contains entries from slot-0 from each incarnation, e.g., <K00,V00> from incarnation-0, <K10,V10> from incarnation-1, and <KN0 ,VN0> from incarnation-N.
- A *slicetable* then refers to a sequential arrangement of slices on the SSD, each slice corresponding to a given slot. A slicetable can span multiple SSD blocks. In Figure 3b, the slicetable contains slice-0, slice-1, ..., slice-M.
- A *SliceHash* is comprised of both the in-memory hash table and the on-SSD slicetable.

Slicing improves lookups. The main advantage of using slicing is that lookup is vastly simplified and more efficient compared to storing incarnations directly on the SSD.

When incarnations are stored directly on the SSD, we may have to examine all incarnations since the key may be present in any of them. Since each incarnation occupies a different set of SSD pages, a key lookup may incur multiple SSD page reads.

In contrast, using slicing simplifies lookups: we hash a key to obtain the slot, and simply read the corresponding slice. We then compare the input key against the entries in the slice to obtain the relevant value. For example, in Figure 3b, look ups for keys in the slot-0 of all incarnations only require reading the corresponding

153

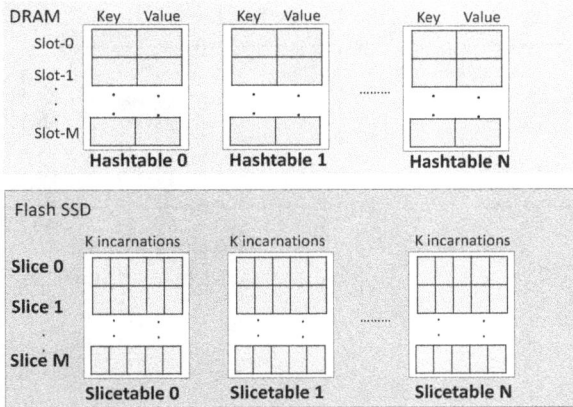

Figure 4: Partitioned SliceHash

slice-0. By limiting the size of a slice to be one or a few pages (DP1), we correspondingly limit the cost of lookup.

Impact on inserts. While slicing positively impacts lookups, it makes inserts complex. In particular, when flushing a full in memory hash table to the SSD, we need to maintain the structure of the slicetable on the SSD. Because a slice has entries from all incarnations, we would need to modify each slice to include entries from the new incarnation. However, the cost of this operation gets amortized over multiple inserts.

We first read as many blocks of a slicetable as possible from the SSD to memory (since, the entire slicetable might not fit in memory). This amounts to a "large" read and hence can be performed at high throughput (DP5). We then modify these blocks at the appropriate positions for each slice, and write back to the SSD; as DP4 indicates, such large writes help leverage channel-level parallelism. We continue reading, modifying and writing back the subsequent remaining blocks of the slicetable, till the whole slicetable is modified on SSD.

While this imposes a high overhead, it is only incurred when the in-memory hash table is full. Since the vast majority of insert operations still happen in memory, the impact of this flush operation on an average insert is small. We further discuss in §5.1.1 how we reduce these overheads.

To summarize, the basic operations in SliceHash are as follows:

Inserts and updates: Keys are inserted only into the in-memory hash table. When this becomes full, we flush it to the SSD while maintaining the slicetable structure. When the on-SSD slicetable becomes full, we employ the simple "eviction policy" of overwriting the oldest incarnation. For updates, we simply insert the new key-value pair in the in-memory hash table.

Lookups: We first look up the key within the in-memory hash table. If the key is not found, we read the corresponding slice from the SSD, scan the entries for all incarnations *from the latest to the oldest*. This ensures that the lookup does not return stale values in the face of updates.

5.1.1 Partitioning SliceHash

Maintaining a single large slicetable spanning the entire SSD is not scalable: in particular, this can cause the flush of the in-memory hash table to take an undue amount of time during which lookup operations can also be blocked (note that SSD I/Os are blocking). Further, it requires multiple SSD I/Os for reading, modifying and writing back the single large slicetable to SSD. To mitigate this and control the worst case insertion cost, we adopt a strategy similar

to BufferHash: We partition the in-memory hash table to multiple small in-memory hash tables based on the first few bits of the keys' address space. We then maintain a separate slicetable for each in-memory hash table (shown in Figure 4). If an in-memory partition becomes full, we only need to update the corresponding (smaller) slicetable on the SSD. Thus, we can read the smaller slicetable entirely in memory, modify it at appropriate positions, and write it back to SSD.

Henceforth, we assume a partitioned SliceHash is in use. Furthermore, we use the term "in-memory hash table" to refer to one of the partitions in memory (Figure 4).

5.1.2 Some Optimizations

Note that, for ease of explanation, we present the case of a simple hash table with a single entry per slot. However, we can trivially support hash tables with a fixed-size bucket of entries for every slot; in this case, each slice will have buckets of entries from all incarnations for a given slot. We can also support an N-function Cuckoo hash table [23]; in this case, a key lookup may need to read up to N slots in the worst case (when the key is not found in the first $N-1$ slots). Lookup cost is bounded by N page reads.

SliceHash may require an SSD page read for a key lookup even if the key is not present in the entire data structure. Additional memory, if available, can be used to reduce such spurious lookups through the use of a summary data structure, such as a Bloom filter, for every slicetable. All lookups are first checked against Bloom filters. SSD operations are issued only if the Bloom filters indicate that the key is present. Crucially, our design can use memory opportunistically: e.g., we maintain Bloom filters only for some partitions, e.g., those that are accessed frequently. This gives SliceHash the ability to adapt to memory needs, while ensuring that in the absence of such additional memory, application performance targets are still met.

5.2 Adding concurrency to SliceHash

In order to leverage the parallelism inherent to SSDs, I/O requests should be issued in such a manner that they are spread uniformly across channels (DP3). We use two components to achieve this: (1) a *scheduler* for request selection, and (2) a *worker* for SSD reads/writes.

The scheduler processes requests in batches. It first process all requests that can be instantly served in memory. Then, it processes lookup requests which require reading from the SSD. We have developed a channel-estimator (described later) to estimate the mapping between read requests and channels. Using these estimates, the scheduler finds a set of K requests (we choose K as the size of the SSD's NCQ (native command queue)).

The request selection algorithm works as follows. The goal here is to ensure that requests get uniformly distributed across channels to optimally exploit channel parallelism offered by NCQ. To meet this objective, we maintain a "depth" for each channel, which estimates the number of selected requests for a channel. We take multiple passes over the request queue until we have selected K requests (size of SSD's NCQ). In each pass, we select requests that would increase the depth of any channel by at most 1. In this manner, we first find the set of read requests to be issued.

The scheduler then instructs the worker to process the chosen read requests in parallel. The worker simply employs multiple threads to issue requests to the SSD. Each thread is "associated" with a channel and is assigned requests that correspond to this channel. When a thread completes a request, it accepts new requests for the channel. As the SSD page reads complete, the worker searches the entries of all incarnations on the pages for the input key. After pro-

154

Symbol	Meaning	Symbol	Meaning	Symbol	Meaning
n	Number of partitions	F	Total SSD size	r_p	Page read latency
s	Size taken by a hash entry	M	Total memory size	r_b	Block read latency
u	Utilization of the hash table	N	Number of SSDs	w_b	Block write latency
s_{eff}	Effective size of the hash entry ($= s/u$)	P	Size of an SSD page/sector		
k	Number of incarnations ($= F/M$)	B	Size of an SSD block		
r_{write}	Ratio of insertions to block writes	H	Size of a single hash table ($= M/n$)		
R	Insert rate	S	Size of slicetable ($= H \times k$)		

Table 2: Notations used in cost analysis

cessing lookups, the scheduler assigns SSD insert requests to the worker soon after an in-memory hash table fills up and needs to be flushed to the SSD. The worker accordingly reads/writes slicetables from/to the SSD.

Channel Estimation. We now describe a simple technique to estimate the channels corresponding to the read requests issued to the SSD, which is a crucial component in performing concurrent I/O on the SSD (DP3). We focus on SSDs that use write-order mapping (the mapping strategy can be inferred using the techniques in [18] as mentioned in §4). Similar approaches can be employed for SSDs that use other write policies.

As discussed in §4, chunk writes in write-order mapping are striped across channels, i.e., the first write goes to the first channel, the second write goes to the second channel, and so on. We leverage this property and restrict the size of a slicetable to be a multiple of $N \times ChunkSize$, where N is the number of channels. Thus, whenever a slicetable is written to the SSD, there will be N chunk writes, with the ith chunk write going to the ith channel. In other words, once we determine the relative chunk identifier (first, or second, or N^{th}) for an offset in the slicetable, we can determine the channel. The relative chunk identifier can be determined as the offset modulo chunk size. Although this is a heuristic, experiments show that it is remarkably effective at helping the scheduler schedule requests across channels (§7).

5.3 Leveraging multiple SSDs

Due to its simple design and low resource footprint, SliceHash can be easily extended to run across multiple SSDs attached to a single machine. We elaborate below on two possibilities: one that offers high throughput and the other that offers low memory footprint.

Throughput-oriented design. We can exploit multiple SSDs to increase parallelism and obtain high throughput. To do this, we partition the key-space across multiple SSDs so that incoming requests are distributed across SSDs and can be processed by SSDs in parallel.

Memory-oriented design. We can also exploit multiple SSDs to lower the memory footprint of SliceHash. In this design, a slicetable for an in-memory hash table expands across multiple SSDs, i.e., each slice has its entries stored across multiple SSDs. So the slicetable can contain a larger number of incarnations compared to the number of incarnations when using a single SSD. As the number of incarnations increases, the memory footprint is reduced (§7.4). Although more incarnations must be read when reading a slice, lookups can be issued to multiple SSDs in parallel, avoiding any loss in performance.

5.4 Analysis

In this section, we analyze the I/O latency and the memory overhead of SliceHash. We also estimate the number of writes to the SSD per unit time, and its impact on SSD lifetime. Alongside, we illustrate the knobs SliceHash offers to easily control cost-perform-ance trade-offs; such tunability is missing from almost all prior designs. Table 2 summarizes the notation used.

Memory overhead per entry. We estimate the memory overhead per entry. The total number of entries in an in-memory hash table is H/s_{eff}, where H is the size of a single hash table and s_{eff} is the effective average space taken by a hash entry (actual size (s)/utilization (u)). The total number of entries overall in SliceHash for a given size F of the SSD is: $(\frac{F+M}{H}) \times \frac{H}{s_{eff}} = \frac{F+M}{s_{eff}}$.

Here, M is the total memory size. Hence, the memory overhead per entry is, $\frac{M}{\#entries}$, i.e., $\frac{M}{F+M} \times s_{eff}$, or $\frac{1}{k+1} \times s_{eff}$, where k is the number of incarnations.

For $s = 16B$ (key 8 bytes, value 8 bytes), $u = 80\%$, $M = 1GB$, and $F = 32GB$, the memory overhead per entry is *0.6 bytes/entry*.

In contrast, state-of-the-art approaches for SSD-based hash tables, e.g., SILT [25] and BufferHash [14] have memory overheads of *0.7 bytes/entry* and *4 bytes/entry*, respectively. The use of Bloom filters (used to prevent lookups from incurring multiple SSD reads across incarnations) in BufferHash imposes high memory overhead.

Insertion cost. We estimate the average time taken for insert operations. We first calculate the time taken to read a slicetable and then write it back. This is given by: $(\frac{S}{B} \times r_b + \frac{S}{B} \times w_b)$, where S is the size of the slicetable, B is the size of an SSD block, and r_b and w_b are the read and write latencies per block, respectively. This flushing happens after H/s_{eff} entries are inserted to the hash table; all insertions up to this point are made in memory. Hence, the average insertion cost is $(\frac{S}{B} \times r_b + \frac{S}{B} \times w_b) \times \frac{s_{eff}}{H}$

Replacing S by $H*k$, we get $\frac{(r_b+w_b) \times s_{eff} \times k}{B}$, which is independent of the size of the hash table.

For a typical block read latency of 0.31ms [13], a block write latency of 0.83ms [13], $s = 16B$, $M = 1GB$, $F = 32GB$, and $u = 80\%$, the average insertion cost is $\sim 5.7\mu s$. Similarly, the worst case insertion cost of SliceHash is $(0.31+0.83) \times \frac{S}{B}$ms. By configuring S to be same size as B, we can control the worse case insertion cost to $(0.31+0.83) = 1.14ms$.

In contrast, BufferHash has average and worst case insertion latencies of $\sim 0.2\mu s$ and $0.83ms$, both of which are better than Slice-Hash. We believe that the somewhat higher I/O costs are an acceptable trade-off for the much lower memory footprint in SliceHash.

Lookup cost. We consider a Cuckoo hashing based hash table implementation with 2 hash functions. Suppose that the probability of success for the first lookup is p. For each lookup, a corresponding slice is read. Configuring H, the size of an in-memory hash table, to match that of a page, the average lookup cost becomes $r_p + (1-p) \times r_p$ or $(2-p) \times r_p$, assuming that all of the lookups go to the SSD. For $p = 0.9, r_p = 0.15$ ms, the average lookup cost is 0.16 ms. SILT and BufferHash have a similar average lookup cost.

The worst case happens when we have to read both pages corresponding to the two hash functions. Thus, the worst case lookup latency is $2 \times r_p$. For $r_p = 0.15$ ms, this cost is 0.3 ms. In contrast,

BufferHash may have very high worst case lookup latency because it may have to scan all incarnations due to the false positives of Bloom filters. For $k = 32$, this cost would be as high as 4.8 ms.

Frequency of SSD writes, and knobs for tunability. We estimate the ratio of the number of insertions to the number of block writes to the SSD; we denote this as r_{write}. A hash table becomes full after every H/s_{eff} inserts, after which the corresponding slicetable on the SSD is modified. The number of blocks occupied by a slicetable is S/B or $k \times H/B$. Thus, $r_{write} = \frac{H}{s_{eff}} \times \frac{B}{k \times H} = \frac{B}{k \times s_{eff}}$

Thus, by increasing the number of incarnations k, the frequency of writes to the SSD (which is inversely proportional to r_{write}) also increases. This in turn affects the overall performance.

Note, however, that increasing the number of incarnations also decreases the memory overhead as shown earlier. We investigate this dependency in more detail in §7.4 and find that our design provides a smooth trade-off between memory overhead and performance, allowing designers the flexibility to pick a point in the design space that best fits their specific cost-performance profile.

Effect on SSD lifetime. SliceHash increases the number of writes to the SSD which may impact its overall lifetime. We now estimate the lifetime of an SSD as follows. For a given insert rate of R, the number of block writes to the SSD per second is $\frac{R}{r_{writes}}$ or the average time interval between block writes is $\frac{r_{writes}}{R}$. Say the SSD supports E erase cycles. Also, assume that the wear leveling scheme for the SSD is perfect. Then, the lifetime (T) of the SSD could be approximately estimated as number of blocks, $\frac{F}{B}$, times erase cycles, E, times the average time interval between block writes, $\frac{r_{writes}}{R}$, i.e., $T = \frac{F \times E \times r_{writes}}{R \times B}$

Consider a 256GB MLC SSD drive that supports 10000 erase cycles [16]. We use SliceHash on this SSD with $M = 4$GB of DRAM, i.e., $k = 64$. With a 16B entry size and utilization of 80%, the ratio r_{write} would be 102.4. Even with $R = 10K$ inserts/sec (required, e.g., for a WAN optimizer connected to 500 Mbps link), the SSD would last 6.8 years. Thus, despite an increase in the writes to SSD, its lifetime would still be reasonably long.

In sum, our analysis shows that our design patterns help SliceHash to reduce the memory overhead to 0.6 bytes/entry and limit the lookup cost to 1 page read on average, without significantly affecting the average insert performance or SSD lifetime. A simple knob—the number of incarnations—helps control the performance-cost trade-off in a fine-grained fashion. We empirically study the performance and flexibility benefits of SliceHash in §7.

Next, we discuss how our key techniques can also be applied to other (hashing-based) data structures.

6. GENERALITY

In this section, we discuss how the five design patterns discussed in §3 and the slicing primitive discussed in §5, can be used to design other hashing-based data structures, particularly, Bloom filters and locality sensitive hashing (LSH)-based indexes. Many of the supporting design techniques we used in SliceHash—the use of incarnations, slices, slicetables, and optimizations for multiple SSDs—are derived directly from the design patterns and hence, as argued below, they also apply directly to other data structures.

Bloom Filters. Bloom filters have traditionally been used as in-memory data structures [8]. As some recent studies have observed [17, 22], with storage costs falling and data volumes growing into the peta- and exa-bytes, space requirements for Bloom filters constructed over such datasets are also growing commensurately. In limited memory environments, there is a need to maintain large

Bloom filters on secondary storage. We show how we can apply our techniques for supporting Bloom filters on SSD storage effectively.

Similar to SliceHash, we maintain several in-memory Bloom filters and corresponding slicefilters on the SSD; the in-memory Bloom filters are written to the SSD as incarnations. Each slice in a slicefilter contains the bits from all incarnations taken together for a given slot.

In traditional Bloom filters, a key lookup requires computing multiple hash functions and reading entries corresponding to the bit positions computed by the hash functions. In our case, for each hash function we first look up the corresponding in-memory Bloom filter and then the corresponding slicefilter on the SSD.

The number of hash functions would determine the number of page lookups, which could limit the throughput. We now argue how this cost can be controlled.

Since SSD storage is much cheaper than DRAM, we can use more space per entry on the SSD – i.e., use a large m/n where m and n are the Bloom filter size and the number of unique elements, respectively; this allows us to use fewer hash functions (smaller h) while maintaining similar overall false positive rate [1]. For example, for a target false positive rate of 0.0008, instead of using $m/n = 15$ and $h = 8$, we can use $m/n = 32$ and $h = 3$. By reducing h, we can reduce the number of page lookups and improve performance.

Our design patterns and the techniques we derive from them enable us to reduce the effective memory footprint per key (where a "key" refers to a unique element inserted into the Bloom filter) while achieving high performance, similar to the trade-offs we were able to achieve with SliceHash. For example, choosing $m/n = 32$, we can use a combination of a 256MB DRAM and a 64GB SSD (leading to 256 incarnations per Bloom filter) to store Bloom filters. This results in an effective memory overhead of 0.125 bits per entry and causes block writes to the SSD every 128 key insertions. Our evaluation in §7.5 shows that we achieve good throughput with this configuration.

LSH-based index. Locality sensitive hashing [24] is a technique used in the multimedia community [26, 9] for finding duplicate videos and images at large scale. LSH systems use multiple hash tables. For each key, the corresponding bucket in each hash table is looked up. Then, all entries in the buckets are compared with the key to find the nearest neighbor based on a certain distance metric.

In SliceLSH, each LSH hash table is designed using SliceHash. When a query arrives, it is distributed to all SliceHash instances. Leveraging the design patterns, we can subtly tweak the data structure to more closely align with how LSH works and ensure improved I/O performance. Specifically, when we write in-memory LSH hash tables to the SSD, we arrange them such that: (1) all chunks (group of consecutive logical pages assigned to same channel, as defined in §4.2) of each slicetable get mapped to the same channel (this is in contrast with SliceHash where each chunk in a slicetable may go to a different channel), and (2) the chunks corresponding to different LSH hash tables map to different channels. We write in-memory LSH hashtables to the SSD together; while writing to the SSD, we rearrange the chunks of LSH slicetables to satisfy the above properties. The benefit of this approach is that multiple LSH hash table lookups for a given key will be uniformly distributed over multiple channels. This helps us maximally leverage the intrinsic parallelism of SSDs resulting in high lookup throughput (§7).

7. EVALUATION

In this section, we measure the effectiveness of our design patterns as applied to the three different indexes described above, and we show the flexibility offered and the generality of our design choices. For simplicity, a majority of our evaluation focuses on SliceHash.

7.1 Implementation and Configuration

We have implemented SliceHash in C++ using ~3K lines of code. I/O concurrency is implemented using the pthread library. We use direct I/O for access to the SSD. We use the simple "noop" scheduler in the Linux kernel (which implements basic FIFO scheduling of I/O requests) for leveraging the intrinsic parallelism of SSDs.

Each hash table is implemented using Cuckoo hashing [23] with 2 hash functions and 3 entries per bucket, which corresponds to 86% space utilization. As mentioned in §5, we have multiple in-memory hash tables. The size of each of these is 128KB, so each can hold ~7K key-value entries of size 16B each. Slicetables corresponding to different in-memory hash tables are arranged across continuous logical block addresses on the SSD.

We evaluate SliceHash on a 128GB Crucial M4 SSD attached to a desktop with dual 2.26 GHz quad-core Intel Xeon processor. We use 32 threads for issuing concurrent I/O requests, corresponding to the number of channels in the Crucial SSD. The size of the NCQ is also 32.

Unless otherwise specified, the size of each slicetable is 4096 KB and the slicetable contains 32 incarnations of an in-memory hash table. This amounts to using 4GB DRAM in total toward the SliceHash data structure.

7.2 SliceHash Performance

We evaluate the lookup and insert performance of SliceHash, examining its throughput, memory footprint, and CPU overhead under different mixes of read and write workloads. We compare SliceHash with BufferHash and SILT.

Methodology. BufferHash [14] does not consider concurrent I/O access. For a fair comparison against SliceHash, we added concurrency to BufferHash using the pthread library. We also added locking mechanisms to ensure that no two threads access the same in-memory hash table of BufferHash at the same time. We use a similar configuration as in [14], i.e., 16 incarnations and 128 KB in-memory hashtable partition with maximum of 4096 entries. We use 8GB DRAM for in-memory hashtables, 8GB DRAM for Bloom filters and 128 GB for flash SSD. The memory footprint of this configuration is ~ 4 byte/entry.

SILT [25] considers concurrent access by default. We use 4 SILT instances with 16 client threads concurrently issuing requests. A merge operation is triggered when a partition has one or more Hash-Stores; we do not limit the convert or merge rates. At the beginning of each experiment, we insert 1 billion random key-value pairs to "warm-up" SILT's stores.

We use YCSB [19] to generate uniformly random key-value workloads with varying lookup and insert ratios.[1] Each workload consists of 1 billion operations, unless otherwise noted.

Lookup performance. Figure 5a shows the performance of the three systems—SliceHash (*SH*), multi-threaded BufferHash (*BH+MT*), and SILT (*SILT*)—for a lookup-only workload. We observe that SliceHash achieves 69K lookups/sec while SILT and BH+MT achieve only 62K lookups/sec (10% lower) and 57K look-

Percentage Inserts	Memory Footprint (bytes/entry)		
	SliceHash	BH+MT	SILT
0%	0.6	4	0.21
50%	0.6	4	0.21–0.57
100%	0.6	4	0.21–1.46

Table 3: Memory footprint under various workloads

Percentage Inserts	CPU Utilization (%)		
	SliceHash	BH+MT	SILT
0%	16	18	27
50%	12	24	67
100%	8	92	72

Table 4: CPU utilization under various workloads

ups/sec (12% lower), respectively. *SliceHash achieves higher lookup performance because it exploits channel-level parallelism by running multiple threads accessing different channels in parallel.* In contrast, neither SILT nor BH+MT are designed to exploit such channel-level parallelism.

Insert performance: We now study the insert throughput of Slice-Hash. Figure 5b shows the performance of the three systems for a continuous insert-only workload. We observe that SliceHash can achieve 125K inserts/sec. In contrast, BufferHash can achieve almost 1100K inserts/sec for the same configuration (i.e., 128 KB in-memory hash table), and SILT can achieve 254K inserts/sec.

BufferHash achieves much better insert performance, since it is write-optimized structure. However, BufferHash imposes very high memory footprint (~4 bytes/entry). SILT achieves better insert performance but at the expense of an /increase in memory footprint (0.21 - 1.46 bytes/entry) due to a backlog of HashStores, as shown in Table 3. In contrast, SliceHash keeps the memory footprint small (0.6 bytes/entry) while achieving reasonably good insert performance. In fact, by bounding SILT's memory footprint to 0.6 bytes/entry, the insert rate of SILT is significantly impacted and reduced to only 46K inserts/s (as shown by "SILT-cap" in Figure 5b). Thus, *under same memory footprint, SliceHash is ~3X better than SILT.*

We believe that the reduced insert performance of SliceHash is an acceptable trade-off for the significantly low memory overhead (Table 3) and better/more consistent lookup performance offered by SliceHash.

Moreover, SliceHash can be augmented with a small write-optimized table (using a BufferHash-like data structure) for handling bursts of writes; this table can be written back to SliceHash during a low I/O activity period. SILT uses a similar idea; it uses a write-optimized data structure for handling writes, which is later merged into SILT's read-optimized data structures. However, merging in SILT is far more compute-intensive (needs sorting) than writing a hash table back to a slicetable with SliceHash, which just requires copying entries to appropriate positions. As shown in Table 4, the average CPU utilization[2] during an insert-only workload is 72% when running SILT and 8% when running SliceHash.

Mixed workload. Finally, we investigate how SliceHash performs under a continuous workload of 50% lookups and 50% inserts. Figure 5c shows the performance of the three systems in this mixed workload setting. We observe that SliceHash provides 105K ops/sec, versus 121K ops/sec for BH+MT and 92K ops/sec for SILT.

BH+MT only has to write the buffer to the SSD when the buffer becomes full, while SILT and SliceHash have to perform extra operations, which affect their performance. SliceHash performs 14%

---

[1]We use the upper 8 bytes of the SHA1 hash of each YCSB-generated key as our 8 byte key.

[2]Utilization is the sum of %user, %nice, and %system as reported by iostat at 1 second intervals.

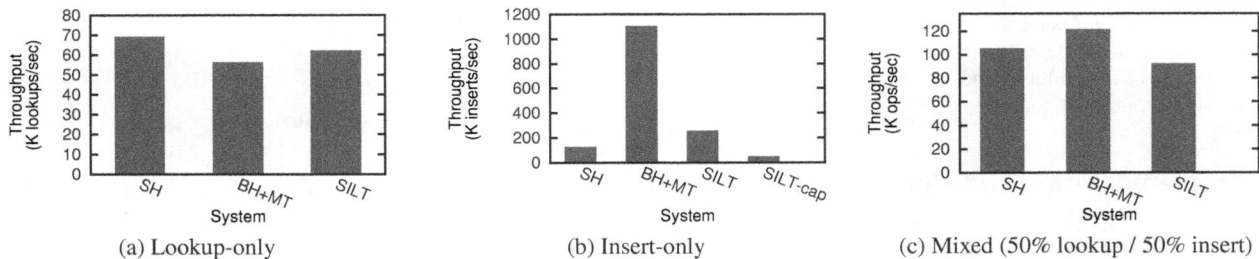

Figure 5: Performance under varying workloads and systems

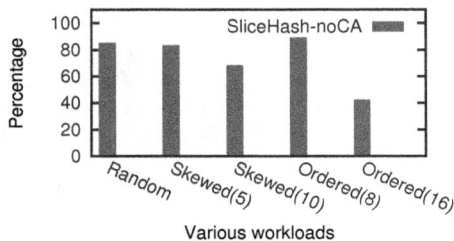

(a) Lookup-only

(b) Insert-only

(c) Mixed (50% lookup / 50% insert)

Figure 6: SliceHash-noCA relative to SliceHash

# Incarnations	Insert-only (ops/sec)	Mixed (ops/sec)	Memory footprint (B/entry)
16	207K	110K	1.1
32	139K	93K	0.6
48	85K	79K	0.38
64	66K	70K	0.27

Table 5: Memory vs. performance trade-off

better than SILT, and imposes very little CPU overhead (12%). In contrast, SILT imposes high CPU overhead (67%) due to its background converting and merging operations (Table 4).

7.3 Contribution of Optimizations

We now study how the two main parallelism-centered optimizations—request-reordering and slice-based data layout—contribute to SliceHash's performance.

Request-reordering. We study the extent to which reordering can be beneficial compared to a naive scheme of issuing requests in FIFO order. SliceHash-noCA (i.e., SliceHash with no channel-awareness) does not consider the request-to-channel mapping when assigning requests to a thread; requests are simply assigned to threads in the order the requests are made.

We consider three types of workloads to study the impact: (1) *Random:* the keys are generated randomly, so the distribution of requests among channels is also random; (2) *Skewed:* the channel distribution is skewed, i.e., a certain number of requests (configured by the skew parameter S) go to the same channel, while the remaining requests are evenly distributed across channels; and (3) *Ordered:* the requests are uniformly distributed across channels, however their ordering is such that the first K requests go to first channel, the second K requests go to second channel and the ith set of K requests go to channel $i \bmod N$ (where N is the number of channels; $N = 32$ for Crucial SSD). Essentially, if $K = 1$, even a FIFO scheme would have all 32 requests going to different channels (the best case), while if $K = 32$, it would result in all flash page read requests going to the same channel (the worst case).

Figure 6 shows the performance of SliceHash-noCA relative to the performance of SliceHash. In the worst case (Ordered (K=16)), SliceHash-noCA can only achieve 42% of SliceHash performance. Under a small skew of 5 requests (S=5), the performance drops by 17%; larger skew (S=10) deteriorates performance by almost 30%. Even with a random workload, where keys are likely to be evenly distributed across channels, we see a performance drop of 15%. These results indicate that channel-awareness is crucial to high performance in SliceHash.

Slicing. Slicing helps in reducing SliceHash's memory footprint compared to BufferHash's use of Bloom filters. In principle, BufferHash could avoid using Bloom filters and maintain the same memory footprint as SliceHash while leveraging concurrency to obtain good performance. However, we show that doing so has a severe performance impact.

We use the lookup-only workload from §7.2 to measure the throughput. We observe that BufferHash without Bloom filters achieves very low performance, only 8K lookups/sec. In contrast, SliceHash-noCA achieved 57K lookups/sec. Since the central difference between SliceHash-noCA and Bufferhash without Bloom filters is the use of slicing, this result shows that slicing is crucial for collectively achieving high performance and a low memory footprint.

7.4 Tuneability in SliceHash

SliceHash is highly flexible and can be tuned to match application requirements. SliceHash has a very small memory footprint (~0.6 bytes/entry), and it can leverage additional memory to improve lookup performance, e.g., by using Bloom filters (§5.1.2). It also has a small CPU footprint, so it can easily be used with other applications requiring compute-intensive tasks. In contrast, BufferHash has a high memory footprint (Table 3), and SILT imposes high CPU overhead due to continuous sorting (Table 4); these aspects limit their suitability to a range of important applications.

In addition, SliceHash provides the flexibility to tune the memory footprint at the cost of performance, and it can scale to multiple SSDs without usurping memory/CPU, as we show below.

Memory footprint vs. Performance. By increasing the number of incarnations for a given SSD size and hence, using larger slicetable, we can reduce the memory footprint of SliceHash (memory footprint depends on the ratio of size of the in-memory hashtable and size of the slicetable). The side effect is that the number of block writes to flash SSDs is higher (since larger slicetable gets written to SSD when hashtable becomes full), which can affect the performance. Table 5 shows this trade-off for mixed (50% lookup/50% insert) and insert-only workloads. SliceHash provides a throughput between 110K-70K operations/sec for a mixed workload and 207K-66K operations/sec for an insert-only workload; SliceHash's memory footprint ranges from 1.1 bytes/entry to 0.27 bytes/entry. The lookup-only workload is not shown here, as performance re-

# SSDs	Lookup-only (ops/sec)	Mixed (ops/sec)	Memory footprint (B/entry)
1	69K	93K	0.6
2	138K	186K	0.3
3	207K	279K	0.2

Table 6: Leveraging multiple SSDs

mains close to 69K lookups/sec regardless of the number of incarnations.

Scaling using multiple SSDs. We evaluate SliceHash on our Intel Xeon machine using up to 3 SSDs for both the high-throughput and low memory footprint configurations outlined in §5.3.

We find that SliceHash can provide linear scaling in performance with the throughput-oriented configuration (Table 6). With 3 SSDs, SliceHash offers 207K ops/sec for a lookup-only workload, and 279K ops/sec for a mixed workload. Because of its low CPU and memory footprint, SliceHash can easily leverage multiple SSDs on a single physical machine to match higher data volumes and provide higher overall throughput without usurping the machine's resources. Neither SILT nor BufferHash can scale in this fashion: the former due to high CPU overhead (67% CPU utilization when one SSD is used; 3 SSDs exceed the CPU budget for a single machine) and the latter due to high memory overhead (48 GB for 3 SSDs).

In the memory-oriented configuration, SliceHash's memory overhead falls as the number of SSDs is increased, to 0.2 B/entry when 3 SSDs are used. But the throughput stays the same as using a single SSD. Neither SILT or BufferHash can offer similar scale down of memory.

7.5 Generality: SliceBloom and SliceLSH

We now show how our general design patterns improve the performance of other indexes.

We evaluate SliceBloom on the 128GB Crucial SSD using 512 MB DRAM. We use $m/n = 32$ and $k = 3$ hash functions with a memory overhead of 0.1 bits/entry. Under a continuous mixed workload, our system can perform 15K ops/sec. With naive parallelism, the system performance can drop to 5K ops/sec, especially when all requests go to the same channel. In contrast, Bloom-Flash [22] achieves similar performance for a mixed workload, but on a high-end Fusion-io SSD (100,000 4KB I/Os per sec) that costs 30X more ($6K vs. $200). Furthermore, on a low-end Samsung drive, BloomFlash only provides 4-5K lookups/sec.

We also evaluate SliceLSH on the Crucial SSD. We use 10 hash tables, where each hash table uses 256MB in memory, and the corresponding slicetable occupies 8GB on flash. SliceLSH can perform 6.9K lookups/sec, as it has to look up each hash table. By design, SliceLSH can intrinsically exploit channel parallelism. Hence, our system consistently offers similar performance under various workload patterns (results omitted for brevity).

7.6 Summary of key results

Our evaluation results show that our general design patterns improve the performance as well as tunability and flexibility of various indexes. Specifically,

- On a single SSD, SliceHash can achieve 69K lookups/sec, 10-12% higher than SILT and BufferHash. SliceHash can retain high lookup performance under different workloads by exploiting the internal parallelism of an SSD, while SILT's and BufferHash's performance can drop by 30%.
- SliceHash has much lower memory overhead (0.6 bytes/entry) compared to BufferHash (4 bytes/entry) and SILT (0.7 bytes/entry). Further, it has much lower CPU utilization (12%)

in comparison to SILT (67%) and BufferHash (24%) under mixed lookups and inserts.

- SliceHash is highly flexible and tunable. SliceHash can be easily tuned to vary the memory footprint from 0.6 bytes to 0.27 bytes/entry, with slight degradation in performance from 93K to 70K operations/sec under mixed lookups and inserts. In addition, due to its low memory footprint and CPU overhead, SliceHash can be easily scaled using multiple SSDs, unlike other index designs.
- We also show that our design patterns are applicable to other indexes (SliceBloom and SliceLSH), and can improve their effectiveness.

8. DISCUSSION

Generality of SSD mapping policy. Using knowledge of the mapping policy for a Crucial SSD, we have shown how we can exploit its internal parallelism to get high performance for our index designs. Other SSDs may have different mapping policies, and similar techniques can be used to exploit their intrinsic parallelism. Even if the mapping policies are not completely known, certain patterns can be learned to understand how to exploit intrinsic parallelism. In addition, we can also consider designing new interfaces for SSDs, which could help applications leverage the underlying parallelism without revealing its internal mapping policies. We keep these problems open for future research.

Tolerating failures. Our designs maintain in-memory data structures which are vulnerable to system failures or crashes. This can be addressed using standard techniques, such as, appending in-memory inserts to a log file on an additional small SSD (similar to SILT [25]). In the event of crashes, this log file can be used to reconstruct the in-memory hash tables.

Large key-value pairs. Our designs are suited for small key-value pairs so that the size of a slice is limited to one or a few pages for a given number of incarnations. To accommodate large key-value pairs (e.g., few KBs or more), our designs can be extended by having additional indirection. Instead of storing the large value in the slice, we can only store the location information of the large value stored elsewhere on the SSD. This requires additional lookup, however, it keeps the insertion cost small.

9. CONCLUSION

A key impediment in the design of emerging high-performance data-intensive systems is the design of large hash-based indexes that offer good throughput and latency under specific workloads and at specific cost points. Prior works have explored point solutions using SSDs that are each suited to a narrow setting and crucially lack flexibility and generalizability.

In this paper, we develop a set of general techniques for building large, efficient and flexible hash-based systems by carefully leveraging unique properties of SSDs. Using these techniques, we first build a large streaming hash table, called SliceHash, that provides higher performance, while imposing low computation overhead and low memory overhead, compared to the state-of-the-art. Developers can easily tune SliceHash to meet performance goals under tight memory constraints and satisfy the diverse requirements of various data-intensive applications. The indexes also perform well under a range of workloads. We illustrate the generality of our ideas by showing that they can be applied to building other efficient and flexible hash-based indexes.

Additionally, our work shows the promise of adopting the design patterns and primitives we advocate to develop other general SSD-based indexes.

10. ACKNOWLEDGEMENTS

We would like to thank the anonymous reviewers for their insightful feedback. This work is supported in part by National Science Foundation grants CNS-1302041, CNS-1314363, CNS-1330308, CNS-1040757, and CNS-1065134. Aaron Gember-Jacobson is supported by an IBM PhD Fellowship.

11. REFERENCES

[1] Bloom filters – the math.
http://cs.wisc.edu/~cao/papers/summary-cache/node8.html.

[2] BlueCoat video caching appliance.
http://www.bluecoat.com/company/press-releases/blue-coat-introduces-carrier-caching-appliance-large-scale-bandwidth-savings.

[3] Disk backup and deduplication with DataDomain.
http://datadomain.com.

[4] Memcached: A distributed memory object caching system.
http://memchached.org.

[5] Peribit Networks (acquired by Juniper in 2005): WAN optimization solution. http://www.juniper.net.

[6] Riverbed: WAN optimization. http://riverbed.com/solutions/wan_optimization.

[7] A. Badam, K. Park, V. S. Pai and L. Peterson. HashCache: Cache storage for the next billion. In *NSDI*, 2009.

[8] A. Broder and M. Mitzenmacher. Network applications of bloom filters: A survey. *Internet Mathematics, 2005*, 1(4):485–509.

[9] A. Torralba, R. Fergus, and Y. Weiss. Small code and large image databases for recognition. In *CVPR*, 2008.

[10] N. Agrawal, V. Prabhakaran, T. Wobber, J. D. Davis, M. S. Manasse, and R. Panigrahy. Design tradeoffs for SSD performance. In *USENIX ATC*, 2008.

[11] A. Anand, A. Akella, V. Sekar, and S. Seshan. A case for information-bound referencing. In *HotNets*, 2010.

[12] A. Anand, A. Gupta, A. Akella, S. Seshan, and S. Shenker. Packet caches on routers: The implications of universal redundant traffic elimination. In *SIGCOMM 2008*.

[13] A. Anand, S. Kappes, A. Akella, and S. Nath. Building cheap and large CAMs using BufferHash. Technical Report 1651, University of Wisconsin, 2009.

[14] A. Anand, C. Muthukrishnan, S. Kappes, A. Akella, and S. Nath. Cheap and large CAMs for high performance data-intensive networked systems. In *NSDI*, 2010.

[15] D. Andersen, J. Franklin, M. Kaminsky, A. Phanishayee, L. Tan, and V. Vasudevan. FAWN: A fast array of wimpy nodes. In *SOSP*, 2009.

[16] M. Balakrishnan, A. Kadav, V. Prabhakaran, and D. Malkhi. Differential RAID: rethinking RAID for SSD reliability. In *EuroSys*, 2010.

[17] M. Canim, G. A. Mihaila, B. Bhattacharjee, C. A. Lang, and K. A. Ross. Buffered bloom filters on solid state storage. In *ADMS*, 2010.

[18] F. Chen, R. Lee, and X. Zhang. Essential roles of exploiting internal parallelism of flash memory based solid state drives in high-speed data processing. In *HPCA*, 2011.

[19] B. F. Cooper, A. Silberstein, E. Tam, R. Ramakrishnan, and R. Sears. Benchmarking cloud serving systems with YCSB. In *SoCC*, 2010.

[20] B. K. Debnath, S. Sengupta, and J. Li. FlashStore: High throughput persistent key-value store. *PVLDB*, 3(2):1414–1425, 2010.

[21] B. K. Debnath, S. Sengupta, and J. Li. SkimpyStash: RAM space skimpy key-value store on flash-based storage. In *SIGMOD*, 2011.

[22] B. K. Debnath, S. Sengupta, J. Li, D. J. Lilja, and D. H.-C. Du. BloomFlash: Bloom filter on flash-based storage. In *ICDCS*, 2011.

[23] U. Erlingsson, M. Manasse, and F. McSherry. A cool and practical alternative to traditional hash tables. In *Workshop on Distributed Data and Structures (WDAS)*, 2006.

[24] A. Gionis, P. Indyk, and R. Motwani. Similarity search in high dimensions via hashing. In *VLDB*, 1999.

[25] H. Lim, B. Fan, D. G. Andersen, and M. Kaminsky. SILT: a memory-efficient, high-performance key-value store. In *SOSP*, 2011.

[26] Q. Lv, M. Charikar, and K. Li. Image similarity search with compact data structures. In *CIKM*, 2004.

[27] S. Nath and P. B. Gibbons. Online maintenance of very large random samples on flash storage. In *VLDB*, 2008.

[28] S. Quinlan and S. Dorward. Venti: A new approach to archival storage. In *FAST*, 2002.

[29] H. Roh, S. Park, S. Kim, M. Shin, and S.-W. Lee. B+-tree index optimization by exploiting internal parallelism of flash-based solid state drives. *PVLDB*, 5(4):286–297, 2011.

[30] B. Zhu, K. Li, and H. Patterson. Avoiding the disk bottleneck in the data domain deduplication file system. In *FAST*, 2008.

CoRC: Coordinated Routing and Caching for Named Data Networking

Hoon-gyu Choi
School of Computer Science
and Engineering
Seoul National University
Seoul, Korea
hgchoi@mmlab.snu.ac.kr

Jungmin Yoo
School of Computer Science
and Engineering
Seoul National University
Seoul, Korea
jmyoo@mmlab.snu.ac.kr

Taejoong Chung
School of Computer Science
and Engineering
Seoul National University
Seoul, Korea
tjchung@mmlab.snu.ac.kr

Nakjung Choi
Bell Labs
Alcatel-Lucent
Seoul, Korea
nakjung.choi@alcatel-
lucent.com

Ted "Taekyoung" Kwon
School of Computer Science
and Engineering
Seoul National University
Seoul, Korea
tkkwon@snu.ac.kr

Yanghee Choi
School of Computer Science
and Engineering
Seoul National University
Seoul, Korea
yhchoi@snu.ac.kr

ABSTRACT

Named Data Networking (NDN) uses content names as routing entries, and thus the scalability of NDN routing is of primary concern. NDN allows in-network caching as a built-in functionality; however, if network nodes make caching decisions individually, duplicate copies of the same content may exist among nearby nodes. To address these problems, we propose Coordinated Routing and Caching (CoRC) that mitigates routing scalability and enhances the efficiency of the in-network storage. CoRC aligns the routing and caching mechanisms to manage the same content namespace for better performance. We evaluate CoRC (and its variants) with Vanilla NDN in terms of the cache hit ratio, hop count, and traffic load by running software routers on Amazon EC2. To demonstrate the feasibility of CoRC, we also implement and test the processing time of CoRC forwarding in Linux machines.

Categories and Subject Descriptors

C.2.1 [**Computer-Communication Networks**]: Network Architecture and Design

Keywords

Named Data Networking; Content Oriented Networking; Routing; Caching

1. INTRODUCTION

Due to the flexible design of the TCP/IP protocols, a wide range of new applications and services has been proliferated

on the Internet over the decades. According to the Cisco report [1], the recent surge of Internet traffic is mainly attributed to applications such as web, P2P file sharing, and video streaming. In such applications, an end user is mostly interested in content itself, not in a particular host or its location.

The gap between the original host-to-host Internet design and the current content-oriented usage patterns causes many problems such as inefficient content delivery and flash crowds. For example, when thousands of people request the same content, it might be forwarded over the same link thousands of times. This is because ordinary network nodes are not aware of the content due to the host-based IP routing. Content Delivery Networks (CDNs) [2] mitigate this inefficiency by locating popular contents to nearby storages. However, relying on CDN providers is not considered a fundamental and general solution, as (i) it requires substantial monetary cost to content providers of various sizes, (ii) it may burden Internet service providers (ISPs) depending on the locations of CDN storages, and (iii) it may not adapt to the time-varying content popularity (e.g., flash crowds). Also, the host-based TCP/IP protocol suite cannot handle mobility and security properly.

Over the past few years, there have been many efforts to address the above issues from a content centric perspective. Those proposals are collectively called Information Centric Networking (ICN), which is largely deemed as a clean-slate approach. Most of the ICN studies think of content as a key element and hence assume a new paradigm by shifting from host-oriented communications to content-oriented communications [3–7]. One of the key advantages in ICN comes from in-network caching; when a request encounters a network node that caches the content of interest, the node sends back the content immediately without contacting the original server. The more frequently an item is requested, the more likely the item is to be retrieved from a close in-network cache, not from the original publisher. By decoupling content production and consumption in the time and space domains, ICN enhances content availability and naming persistency, and naturally supports mobility, security and multicast.

While there are subtle differences among those ICN proposals, we focus on Named Data Networking (NDN) [4, 8] as a basic architecture because it is the most recent and well-known proposal that specifies technical details under the ICN philosophy. Despite its clear advantage and wide acceptance in the research community, there are still many hurdles to deploy in the current Internet. In this paper, we propose a framework of Coordinated Routing and Caching (CoRC) to address the following challenges in NDN. (i) How to maintain Forwarding Information Bases (FIBs) scalable?, (ii) Which content will be cached by which node in order to efficiently utilize the network-wide storage?, and (iii) How to reach a nearby cached item without additional signaling overhead? By partitioning the whole content namespace and assigning each partition to a dedicated node, CoRC mitigates routing scalability and enhances caching efficiency with no control message exchanges. We combine routing and caching into a unified framework, while many prior proposals deal with routing and caching separately.

The rest of this paper is organized as follows. In Section 2, we describe design principles behind CoRC. The routing and caching mechanisms in the CoRC framework are detailed in Section 3. Optimization methods are discussed to reduce the route stretch of CoRC in Section 4. The FIB size of a router in CoRC is analyzed in Section 5, and the network performance of the CoRC framework is evaluated in Section 6. Packet processing time of CoRC forwarding in Linux machines is shown in Section 7. Related studies that seek to solve the NDN routing and caching issues are reviewed in Section 8, and additional design issues to accommodate realistic conditions are discussed in Section 9. The concluding remarks are given in Section 10.

2. CHALLENGES AND PRINCIPLES

The NDN project [8] was launched to develop a full-fledged architectural framework based on Van Jacobson's architecture – Content-Centric Networking (CCN) [4]. NDN defines two kinds of packets: interest and data packets. A consumer sends out an interest packet, which specifies the content name of her interest. On receiving the interest packet, an NDN router records the interface from which the interest comes into its Pending Interest Table (PIT), and then forwards the interest by looking up the content name in its Forwarding Information Base (FIB). When the interest reaches the original server (that has published the content) or an NDN router (that caches the content, or its segment), the data packet is sent back. The data packet includes both the content name and the requested content[1]. When a data packet is relayed back to the consumer, each NDN router along the path finds the matching PIT entry and forwards the data to the interface in the PIT entry. The router then removes the corresponding PIT entry, and may cache the data in the Content Store (CS) depending on its caching policy.

The following challenges are considered to design our CoRC framework.

2.1 How to Make FIBs Scalable?

Each router in NDN should be able to interpret a content name (instead of an IP address) in its FIB. Though

NDN takes a hierarchical name structure that can be aggregatable for routing scalability, making FIBs scalable is still a problem. For example, two routing entries in an FIB for content items whose names are *cnn.com/us/news* and *cnn.com/eu/news* can be aggregated to *cnn.com*. Assuming that content names are aggregated to their publisher names (e.g., *cnn.com*), a FIB needs to contain as many entries as the number of domain names. According to [9], the number of domain names currently registered with the Domain Name System (DNS) is approximately 10^9, which means a router should have 10^9 entries in its FIB. Thus, even if we assume only publisher names in a FIB, its size is order of magnitude higher than that of a current IP router in the default-free zone. Unfortunately, the current hardware capability of network nodes can hardly meet this requirement [10]. To reduce the FIB size of an NDN router to the level of that of an IP router, CoRC is designed based on the following two principles: (i) exploiting the hierarchy of current Internet and (ii) partitioning the FIB space (e.g., the whole content namespace) among NDN routers.

2.2 Where to Place the Cached Item?

Cache storage in a router is a limited resource, hence it is desirable to avoid caching duplicate copies of the same content across NDN routers for cache utilization. When data is sent back in NDN, each router on the path may cache the item in its local storage. If routers (with in-network storage modules) make caching decisions individually, caching redundant copies of the same content will happen frequently. In this case, the cache hit ratio for popular items will be high, and a small number of selected items can be fetched from a close router. However, a large number of non-cached items (which correspond to the tail part of the Zipf distribution) may have to be downloaded from a distant place, and its delivery cost is not marginal. Moreover, most of the cache hits occur at the network edge (the so-called filter effect) [11], thus the storage modules in upstream routers may not be efficiently utilized. CoRC seeks to make routers cache as diverse content items as possible, so that the network-wide in-network storages are efficiently utilized.

2.3 How to Coordinate between Routing and Caching?

The so-called on-path caching mechanism (which is adopted in most NDN studies) causes inefficient cache utilization because only the cache space in the nodes en route to the publisher of the requested item is checked for cache hits. If a router caches an item and wishes to allow other routers (i.e., off-path routers) to access the cached item, the off-path routers should populate a routing entry for the cached item, which worsens the above FIB scalability issue. What is worse, whenever items are cached and replaced, the change in the cache repository of a router should be advertised to other routers, which may result in substantial signaling traffic, not to mention the update overhead of FIBs. To minimize such overhead to utilize cached items by off-path routers, CoRC makes each and every router know which router is to cache the item of interest.

2.4 How to Reflect the Current Internet Infrastructure and Business?

The current Internet consists of a number of independent networks, which are called Autonomous Systems (ASes).

---
[1]Each interest is assumed to specify a single segment (of the whole content) that can be contained in a data packet.

The current routing infrastructure and AS relations should be considered for practical deployment of CoRC. Also, the relations and businesses among Internet stakeholders like ISPs, CPs, and users should be taken into account. We design CoRC based on the following principles. First, we reflect the separation of inter-domain routing and intra-domain routing in the current IP routing. Second, we should design CoRC in such a way that the business models like CDNs can be easily accommodated. Because, ISPs now try to offer CDN-like services. We will discuss how ISPs can leverage the CoRC framework to offer such content business later. Without such economic incentives, the deployment of NDN technologies may not be realized in the foreseeable future. Also, it should be considered to minimize the inter-AS traffic because the transit cost across ASes is typically charged based on the traffic volume [12].

3. CORC FRAMEWORK

Based on the principles in the previous section, we detail the CoRC framework.

3.1 Name Resolution

In addition to hierarchical naming in NDN, we make the following assumptions: (i) a content name always contains a publisher part, (e.g., the domain name in the URL), (ii) every AS has its own unique name, (iii) each publisher is a customer of a single AS. (Later, we will discuss site multi-homing cases.) Figure 1 illustrates the case in which two publishers (*abc.com* and *cnn.com*) are connected to two ASes (sprint and att), respectively. For the sake of simplicity, an ISP is assumed to be an AS throughout this paper.

The name of the AS (e.g. *att*) that provides the Internet connectivity to a given publisher (e.g. *cnn.com*) can be retrieved by looking up a name resolution system. The DNS is a good candidate to provide this functionality due to its flexibility, which is adopted in the CoRC framework. To obtain the AS name of a publisher (of a content item to be requested), a host sends an interest packet (i.e., a query) to its local resolution server (i.e., the local DNS server). The local DNS server will obtain the AS name of the publisher iteratively by exchanging interest and data packets with the corresponding mapping servers along the DNS hierarchy. After obtaining the AS name for the item, the host issues an interest for the item; the AS name is also included in the interest packet for inter-domain routing (to be detailed below).

3.2 Routing

CoRC routing has two parts: intra-domain routing and inter-domain routing. For a given interest, intra-domain routing is performed to find the requested item if the publisher is within the local AS. The item can then be retrieved from the publisher (i.e., its server) located in the AS. Otherwise, the interest will be forwarded to the AS of the publisher by inter-domain routing.

3.2.1 Intra-domain Routing

For (the items of) a given publisher in an AS, all the routers in the AS should know how to forward interests to the publisher for intra-domain routing. One naive option is to populate as many entries in the FIB of every router as the number of local publishers. According to our estimation (to be detailed later), a few hundreds of millions of publishers

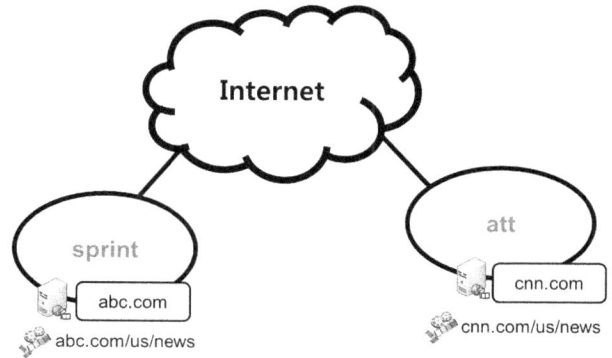

Figure 1: Each publisher is connected to its AS. For a given publisher name, its AS name can be retrieved by extending DNS.

are expected to be connected to the largest AS in year 2030, which is not scalable. To make FIBs scalable, we adopt the ViAggre approach [13], where the entire namespace is split into partitions, and each router contains only its partition in its FIB.

A publisher name in an interest is hashed to a fixed-length value (say, 128 bits), which is called a publisher identifier (PID). Then the PID space becomes the namespace to be covered by FIBs of routers. Let a partition of the PID space be represented by a PID prefix (like an IP prefix in BGP routing). A set of routers in an AS is selected as responsible routers (RRs), each of which is to maintain its own PID prefix. Each RR advertises its PID prefix throughout its AS, so that other routers populate the corresponding FIB entry (in PAR-FIB) for intra-domain routing. A PAR-FIB entry contains <PID prefix, next hop interface>. Each publisher calculates its PID and registers the PID prefix of its access router with the RR whose partition includes the PID. Each RR also maintains a Publisher Information Base (PIB), which is a mapping table whose entry contains <PID of a publisher, PID prefix of its access router>.

In Figure 2, let us illustrate how CoRC intra-domain routing operates. Suppose that four routers are RRs whose PID prefixes are 0b00, 0b01, 0b10, and 0b11, respectively. R01 is responsible for all the PIDs starting with prefix 0b01; that is, R01 should know the locations of all the publishers whose PIDs start with 0b01. Here, the location of a publisher means the PID prefix of the access router of the publisher. Likewise, R00 knows the locations of publishers whose PIDs start with 0b00, and so on.

The interest to retrieve *cnn.com/us/news* will be first forwarded to R01 because the PID of cnn.com starts with 0b01 in this example. On the path from access router to R01, there can be multiple non-RRs which use PAR-FIB to forward the interest to R01.[2] By looking up the PIB, R01 tunnels the interest to the access router (R11) of the publisher *cnn.com*. In Figure 2, the PID prefix of the access router of *cnn.com* is 0b11. It is not straightforward to perform tunneling as there is no locator in NDN. We slightly abuse the PID prefix of a router as the router's identifier for this purpose. That is, the RR will tunnel an interest toward the access router of the corresponding publisher by adding

---

[2] Non-RRs are not visible in Figure 2 for the sake of simplicity.

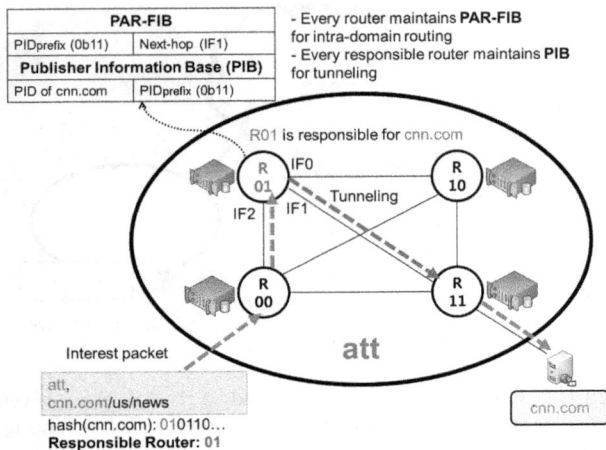

PAR-FIB	
PIDprefix (0b11)	Next-hop (IF1)
Publisher Information Base (PIB)	
PID of cnn.com	PIDprefix (0b11)

- Every router maintains **PAR-FIB** for intra-domain routing
- Every responsible router maintains **PIB** for tunneling

R01 is responsible for cnn.com

Interest packet

att,
cnn.com/us/news
hash(cnn.com): 010110...
Responsible Router: 01

att

cnn.com

Figure 2: Intra-domain routing of CoRC is illustrated.

the PID prefix of the access router into the interest. The routers forward the interest by looking up their PAR-FIBs with the PID prefix (added for tunneling).

3.2.2 Inter-domain Routing

When the interest packet arrives at the RR, the router knows whether the publisher (of the requested item) belongs to its local AS or not. If the router finds that the item is not in its cache and the publisher belongs to another AS, it will forward the interest to the neighbor AS toward the AS of the publisher. Every router also maintains an AS-FIB whose entry contains <AS name, next-hop interface> for inter-domain routing. Each entry in the AS-FIB is assumed to be populated by receiving an advertisement message from each AS by an inter-domain routing protocol such as BGP. Thus, the number of AS-FIB entries is the same as the number of ASes in the Internet. Note that the number of ASes currently is around a few tens of thousands and increases relatively slowly. Thus, the scalability of the AS-FIB is sustainable in the foreseeable future. In Section 5, we will estimate the number of AS-FIB entries until the year 2030.

3.3 Caching

In the process of routing, an interest packet will visit the corresponding RR first. That is, requests with different PID prefixes are forwarded to the corresponding (and hence different) RRs whose PID partitions are non-overlapping. In CoRC, each RR caches only items whose PID belongs to its PID partition. We align the caching and routing functionalities into the same router, so that interests for the items and their corresponding data packets (which may be cached) are all handled by the same router. As shown in Figure 2, an item whose content name starts with *cnn.com* is cached only at router R01 as R01 is in charge of routing all the interests whose PIDs start with 0b01.

4. CORC OPTIMIZATION

CoRC coordinates each RR to perform routing and caching together for the same partition of the PID namespace. The advantages of this alignment are two-fold: (i) there is no advertisement signaling overhead to announce cached items in in-network storages, and (ii) there is no duplicate copy

of the same item among RRs from a network-wide perspective. However, this kind of indirect routing (i.e., stopping by RRs) causes a longer delivery path. Hence, in this section, we propose two optimization methods which mitigate this stretch issue.

4.1 Assigning PID prefix to RR

The route stretch strongly depends on the location of the RR in charge of each request. Therefore, we need to carefully assign PID prefixes to RRs. We propose a simple but powerful prefix assignment algorithm with the following assumptions. First, the popularity distribution of prefixes is given. Second, requests are uniformly distributed among all edge routers. Last, RRs cache popular items depending on the content popularity. Unpopular items not cached in RRs represent the long-tailed part of the Zipf distribution, which can be assumed to be uniformly distributed to all edge routers of publishers.

Let $R = \{r_1, r_2, ..., r_k\}$ and $P = \{p_1, p_2, ..., p_k\}$[3] be the sets of RRs and PID prefixes, respectively. The function $f(k)$ represents the request frequency of each PID prefix, which satisfies $f(p_1) \geq f(p_2) \geq ... \geq f(p_k)$. In addition, if hop_n is defined as the number of hops traversed by the nth request, the optimal prefix assignment problem is to map P to R such that $\sum_{x=1}^{n} hop_x$ is minimized for n requests. Algorithm 1 first sorts R by the sum of distances to all edge routers in non-decreasing order and then iteratively assigns the most to least popular PID prefixes to the sorted R.

Algorithm 1 Prefix assignment algorithm

Require: Set of edge routers $E = \{e_1, e_2, ..., e_m\}$; Set of responsible routers $R = \{r_1, r_2, ...r_k\}$;
1: **for all** $r_k \in R$ **do**
2:     $sum = \sum_{i=1}^{m} distance(e_i, r_k)$
3:     $Array[k].r \leftarrow r_k$
4:     $Array[k].s \leftarrow sum$
5: **end for**
6: Sort $Array[k]$ by s in a non-decreasing order
7: **for all** $p_k \in P$ **do**
8:     Assign p_k to $Array[k].r$
9: **end for**

Proof of optimality: each of n requests is hashed into each of k PID prefixes. By the assumption, $n = n_{p_1} + n_{p_2} + ... + n_{p_k}$ where $n_{p_1} \geq n_{p_2} \geq ... \geq n_{p_k}$. If c_k items are cached at r_k and n_{c_k} is the number of requests to c_k among n_{p_k} requests, n_{c_k} requests are satisfied by r_k while $n_{p_k} - n_{c_k}$ requests are forwarded to the original publisher. Therefore, the expected number of hops for a request whose PID prefix is p_k is defined as follows.

$$AvgHop_{p_k} = \frac{\sum_{i=1}^{n_{c_k}} d(e_r(i), r_k) + \sum_{j=1}^{n_{p_k}-n_{c_k}} d(e_r(j), r_k, e_o(j))}{n_{p_k}}$$

$$(d(u, v, w) = d(u, v) + d(v, w))$$

$$(1)$$

---

[3] P is sorted in a popularity order of PID prefixes.

Here, $e_r(i)$ and $e_o(i)$ represent edge routers attached to the requester and the original publisher for the ith request, respectively. The function $d(u, v)$ is defined as the shortest distance between u and v. Accordingly, the total number of hops for n requests is defined as follows.

$$\sum_{x=1}^{n} hop_x = \sum_{y=1}^{k} n_{p_y} \cdot AvgHop_{p_y} \qquad (2)$$

By the inequality of rearrangement, $\sum_{x=1}^{n} hop_x$ is minimal. ($\because n_{p_1} \geq ... \geq n_{p_k}$ and $AvgHop_{p_1} \leq ... \leq AvgHop_{p_k}$.)

4.2 Hybrid Approach

Although CoRC improves the total cache hit ratio due to the network-wide aggregated cache utilization, independent caching may be more beneficial for popular items. In practice, it is reported that the popularity of items follows the Zipf distribution [14]. With independent caching, the popular items can be retrieved from any intermediate routers that their interests encounter. To leverage both independent and coordinated caching, we propose a hybrid approach, dubbed CoRC-HBD.

In CoRC-HBD, edge routers (access routers attached to requesters) perform individual and independent caching and only non-edge routers collaborate for coordinated caching. Edge routers cache every item being forwarded based on their own replace strategies, e.g. Least Recently Used (LRU). As most of the popular items accouting for the majority of traffic are likely to be retrieved from edge routers, the route stretch problem can be alleviated. Non-edge routers cache only items whose PIDs belong to individual partitions, and thus the network-wide cache diversity is somewhat retained. Note that a unique tag like the RR's PID prefix should also be assigned to each edge router and populated in a PAR-FIB (of every RR) in order to tunnel interests to non-RRs (i.e., edge routers).

5. ROUTING SCALABILITY

A router in the CoRC framework has three tables for request routing: (i) AS-FIB, (ii) PAR-FIB, and (iii) PIB. In this section, we estimate the number of ASes and domain names expected in year 2030 and then analyze how large each table will be in year 2030 to investigate a routing scalability.

5.1 AS-FIB

A router maintains AS-FIB to forward interests toward any ASes, so its size depends on the number of ASes. According to [15], there are currently more than 45,000 active ASes advertised in the Internet as of July 2013. Figure 3 shows that the number of ASes will be expected to reach around 120,000 by the year 2030, which is projected based on the recent history of AS numbers. Accordingly, we claim that AS-FIB will contain around 120K routing entries by the year 2030.

5.2 PAR-FIB and PIB

To estimate the size of a PAR-FIB, the total number of domain names should be analyzed at first. As of July 2012, around 0.9 billion domain names are registered according to Internet systems consortium [9]. Figure 4 shows that the

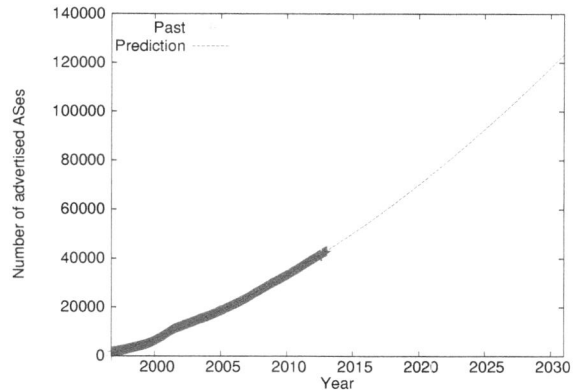

Figure 3: The number of ISPs is predicted to reach around 120,000 by the year 2030.

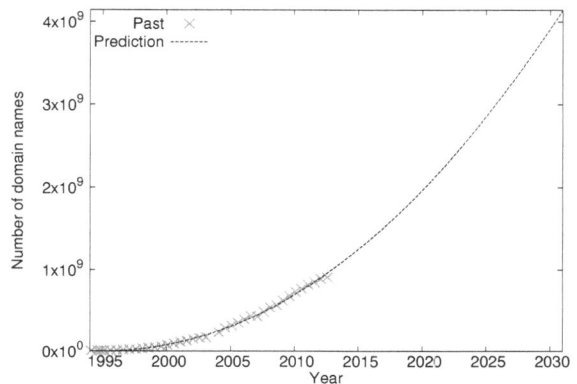

Figure 4: The number of domain names is predicted to reach around 4 billion by the year 2030.

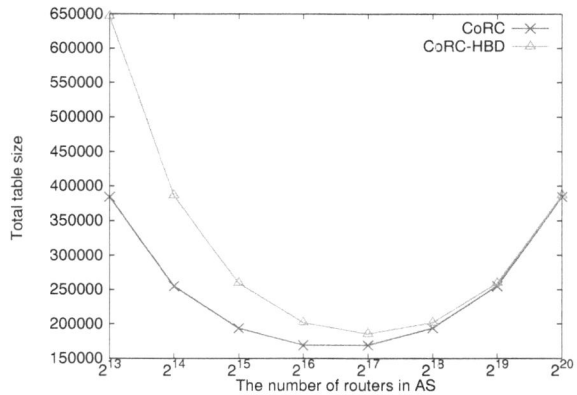

Figure 5: The total number of entries in each of CoRC and CoRC-HBD routers is estimated.

total number of domain names is expected to reach almost 4B (or 2^{32}) by the year 2030. Note that we have to consider the total numbers of both domain names and ASes to calculate the number of domain names per AS. Definitely, larger ASes would have more domain names than smaller ASes.

It is reported that the number of connections among ASes (or AS degree) follows a Zipf distribution [14, 16]. In addition, according to [17], the number of routers per AS is positively correlated to the AS degree. If we make a similar conjecture with respect to the distribution of the numbers of domain names among ASes, we can assume that the number of domain names per AS also follows a Zipf distribution. We apply a Zipf distribution (its exponent is 1.0) to 4 billion domain names among 120K ASes. The maximum number of domain names per AS is estimated to be around 330M domain names in year 2030. Thus, we expect that the maximum number of domain names per AS will be less than 2^{29} until 2030.

The sizes of a PAR-FIB and a PIB also depend on the number of routers (of an AS) that can serve as RRs. According to [18], some large ASes currently contain around 2^{20} routers. Let us make the following assumptions to estimate the sizes of a PAR-FIB and a PIB in year 2030: (i) the largest AS (in terms of number of domain names) has up to 2^{20} routers, (ii) a quarter of all routers in the AS serve as RRs in CoRC, and (iii) one eighth of all routers serve as RRs and another eighth as edge routers in CoRC-HBD. Also, 2^{29} domain names (actually PIDs) are estimated to be evenly distributed among RRs, which determines the size of a PIB.

5.3 Numbers of Entries of Three Tables

Figure 5 shows the total number of entries of AS-FIB, PAR-FIB, and PIB depending on n routers in a extremely large AS with 2^{29} domain names, varying n from 2^{13} to 2^{20}. The total number of routing table entries of a CoRC router in year 2030 is bounded to the same level of the current number of IP prefixes (i.e., the FIB size of a DFZ router). However, a single PID requires at least a 128-bit hash value to guarantee the probability of hash collision negligible. Thus, the overall memory space for a CoRC router may be greater than that of the current IP router. There should be a trade-off between the size of PAR-FIB and that of PIB. If more routers participate in CoRC as RRs, each router has the larger PAR-FIB and the smaller PIB. Each AS can adjust the number of RRs in accordance with the network size.

6. NETWORK PERFORMANCE

Splitting the whole namespace into the FIBs (of RRs) achieves the scalable FIB size at the cost of route stretch as explained earlier. In addition, it can efficiently exploit in-network storages across the given network by dividing the PID namespace among caches. To fully understand CoRC, we first conduct comprehensive emulations with 4 stub topologies. Then, we investigate the route stretch within a single AS.

6.1 Performance Metrics

Cache hit ratio: Assigning partitions of the whole caching space to individual RRs enables more items to be cached at in-network storages (in RRs).

Content delivery latency: Two specific metrics are considered: (i) the average delivery hop and (ii) the average content retrieval time, which are directly impacted by route stretch.

Traffic load: We focus on inter-AS traffic because stub ASes should generally pay transit fees which is normally proportional to the cross-AS traffic volume. We also investigate total traffic to study how much traffic is stretched.

6.2 Performance on Transit-stub Topology

6.2.1 Compared Schemes

We consider five different schemes based on routing and caching strategies, which are to be compared in terms of above metrics.

Vanilla NDN: In Vanilla NDN, routers forward interest packets to the publisher of the content along the shortest path by looking up flat FIB entries. We assume that each router makes independent caching decisions with LRU replace strategy. Vanilla NDN has the routing scalability problem as every router maintains the entire FIB, and is deemed as a baseline.

Coordinated Routing/Individual Caching (CRIC): CRIC is a modified Vanilla NDN scheme where splitting FIB is used to address the routing scalability issue. In CRIC, interest packets are first sent to RRs, and then delivered to publishers via tunneling. When data packets are relayed back to the requesters, the routers on the path cache content individually. CRIC is meaningful in examining the impact of the lengthened path and the limited cache diversity.

CoRC and CoRC-HBD: CoRC achieves the cache diversity by performing coordinated caching at the cost of longer route stretch. CoRC-HBD mitigates the route stretch issue while the network-wide cache diversity is somewhat degraded by combining both individual and coordinated caching strategies.

Oracle: As another reference, the oracle version of caching is also evaluated. A border router in each AS has its own storage whose size is the sum of all the cache sizes within the AS in other schemes. The gateway router's storage is filled with the most popular items based on the knowledge of the popularity distribution. Oracle is deemed to achieve the best performance since flat routing (i.e., the shortest path routing) is used, and the cache utilization is the best.

Note that we do not directly compare our CoRC with previous proposals. We highlight that CoRC outperforms the reference schemes in terms of above metrics, even though CoRC uses indirection to address the routing scalability.

6.2.2 Experimental Setting

We implemented software routers running on Amazon Elastic Compute Cloud (EC2) [19] to emulate CoRC and the other schemes. In our experiments, 60 routers are installed as 60 virtual machines in Amazon data centers in five different regions: Oregon, North California, North Virginia, Sao Paulo, and Ireland. We assume that each of four regions represents a stub AS and the other region (North Virginia) represents a transit AS that interconnects the four stub ASes. We constructed a tree topology whose mean degree is 2.42 at the router level in each stub AS by referring to [20]. Every stub AS consists of 14 routers: 8 edge, 4 backbone, and 2 border routers. The transit AS has 4 routers.

Content items are uniformly distributed over four ASes, each of which is configured with a total cache space equal to 0.5%, 1.0% and 1.5% of the total content volume[4]. In Oracle, the whole cache space is allocated to a border router. In the other schemes, by taking into account the difference of

---

[4]We omit the cases of 0.5% and 1.5% due to the marginal difference.

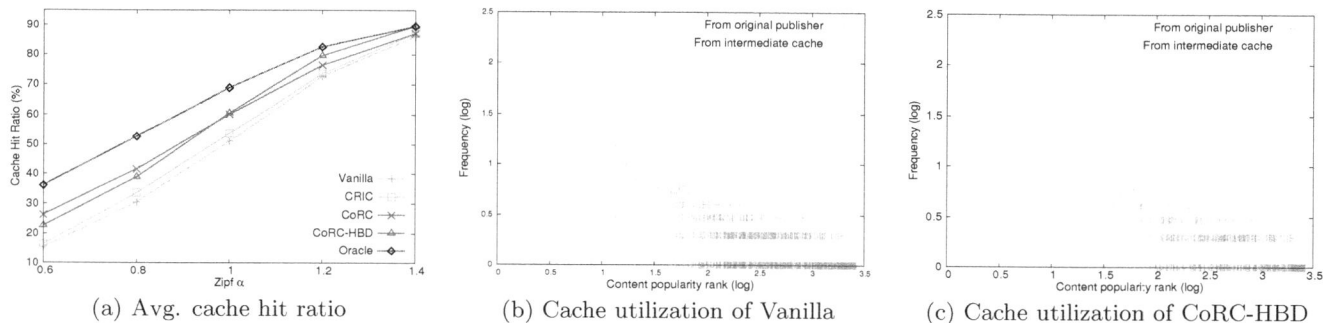

(a) Avg. cache hit ratio   (b) Cache utilization of Vanilla   (c) Cache utilization of CoRC-HBD

Figure 6: (a) The comparison of cache hit ratio of CoRC and other schemes is shown. (b) and (c) CoRC can serve more diverse items than Vanilla, which results in higher cache hit ratio.

router capability, each of backbone, border, and edge routers has one eighth, one eighth, and one thirty-second of a total cache space, respectively. Note that the FIB is also split with the same ratio. PID prefixes are generated by modular hashing and assigned to the corresponding RRs by the Algorithm 1. A request for 10 MB data is generated at each edge router with a poisson arrival rate 0.1 (per second), which means 32 data items are requested per every ten seconds on average. Users (generating interests) belonging to an edge router are running in the same virtual machine as their edge router. The skewness of the popularity distribution is determined by the Zipf exponent α: 0.6, 0.8, 1.0, 1.2, and 1.4.

6.2.3 Average Cache Hit Ratio

Figure 6a shows the average cache hit ratio with a cache space ratio of 1.0%, varying α. Obviously, splitting the whole cache space into non-overlapping partitions in CoRC allows more items to be stored in the caches, resulting in a higher cache hit ratio. There are two interesting observations. First, CoRC-HBD achieves almost similar performance to Oracle as α increases from 1.2 to 1.4. Note that the cache hit ratio of CoRC is higher than that of CoRC-HBD when α is 0.8 but the performance gain is reversed as α increases to 1.2. It is because with highly skewed requests (e.g., α is 1.2 or 1.4), popular items have more requests while non-popular items have less requests. Accordingly, the effect of partitioning a cache space is mitigated. Second, CRIC exhibits the higher hit ratio than Vanilla because CRIC routes interests via RRs, which gives a higher cache hit chances at RRs.

To better understand the splitting effect, we investigated the frequency of content requests which arrive at each router, which is plotted according to their popularity in a log-log scale. We distinguished items which are retrieved from intermediate caches and original publishers by color. Figures 6b and 6c reveal that only popular items are mostly cached in Vanilla while CoRC can cache much more items than Vanilla.

6.2.4 Content Delivery Latency

Figure 7 shows the ratio of the average hop count of each scheme to that of Vanilla, and Figure 8 is the average route stretch which is the (hop count) ratio of a path taken by each scheme to retrieve an item to the shortest path to its publisher, as α varies. Vanilla has a fairly low hop count throughout α since it takes the shortest path to the original

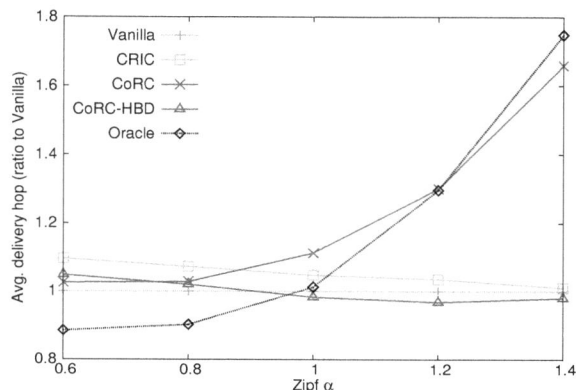

Figure 7: The average hop count of each scheme is plotted. CoRC-HBD achieves the near-optimal performance.

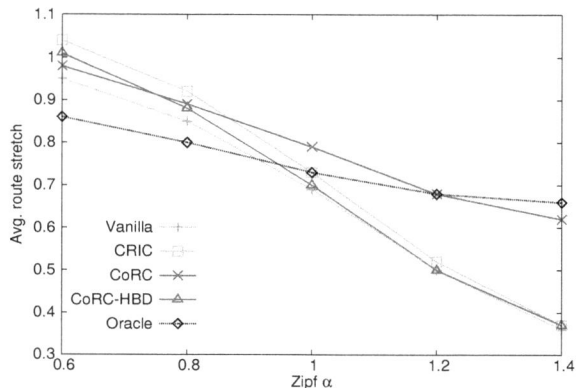

Figure 8: The relative path length of each scheme is plotted. CoRC-HBD achieves the near-optimal performance.

servers (in cases of cache misses). With not-so-skewed popularity distributions (e.g., α is 0.6 or 0.8), Oracle achieves the lowest hop count since it caches most popular items while the other schemes may suffer from cache misses due to relatively small popularity differences among items. CoRC and CoRC-HBD show a slightly longer hop count than Vanilla due to route stretch. As α increases, however, CoRC-HBD outperforms the other schemes since (i) popular items get

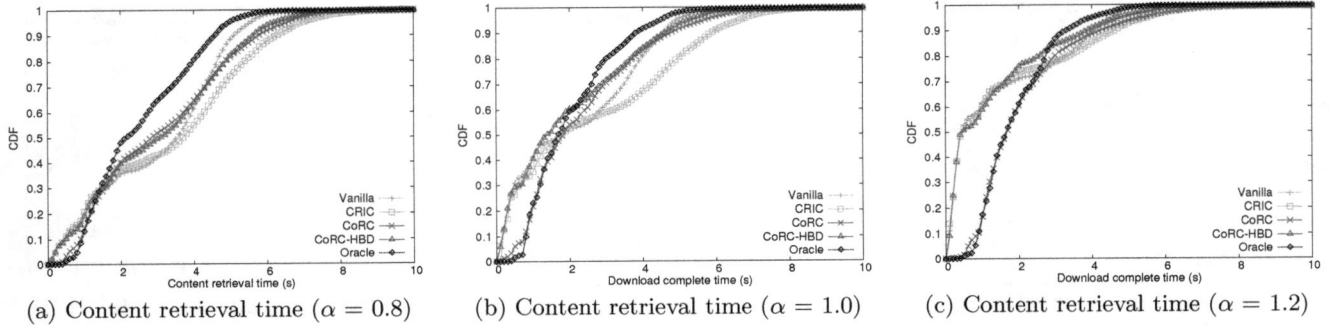

(a) Content retrieval time ($\alpha = 0.8$) (b) Content retrieval time ($\alpha = 1.0$) (c) Content retrieval time ($\alpha = 1.2$)

Figure 9: The content retrieval time of each scheme is illustrated. CoRC-HBD achieves the near-optimal performance.

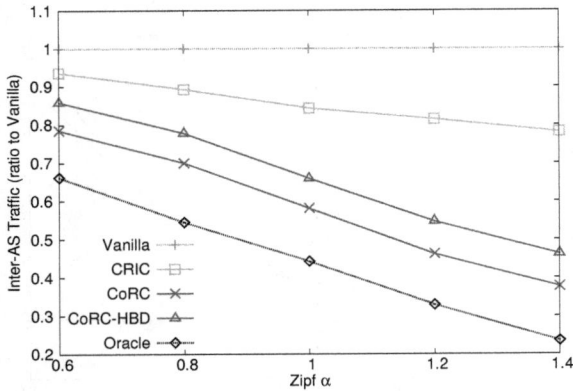

Figure 10: Inter-AS traffic is plotted for each scheme. Traffic reduction comes from caching diversity.

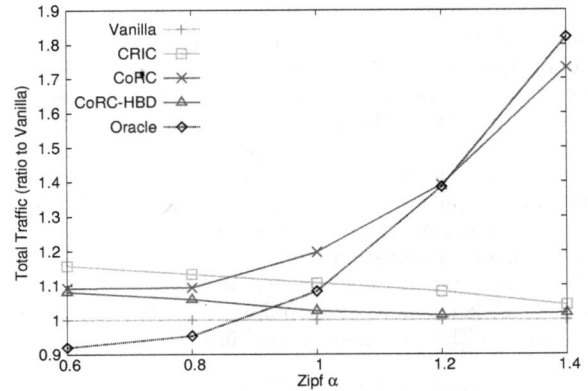

Figure 11: Total traffic is plotted for each scheme. CoRC-HBD achieves the near-optimal performance.

more requests and are cached at edge routers, and (ii) cache diversity is somewhat retained. Note that Oracle performs poorly with the highly skewed popularity distribution (e.g., α is 1.2 and 1.4), since a single cache is located at the border router; popular items in the other schemes are likely to be cached at edge and backbone routers.

Figure 9 show the CDF of the content retrieval times of each scheme when α is 0.8, 1.0, and 1.2, respectively. Regardless of the skewness of the popularity distribution, CoRC-HBD achieves mostly shorter retrieval time by taking advantage of both independent and coordinated caching. When α is 1.0, for example, about half of all requested items (that are more popular) are retrieved from (closer) edge routers in Vanilla, CRIC, and CoRC-HBD due to the independent caching, which shows shorter retrieval time. For the other half (i.e., items less popular), they are retrieved from caches in RRs in CoRC and CoRC-HBD due to the cooperative caching, compared to Vanilla and CRIC. While Oracle shows the shortest retrieval time for the less popular items (but located in the cache storage), it performs poor for the popular items. To summarize, CoRC-HBD achieves the low route stretch, and hence the low delivery latency while mitigating the routing scalability issue.

6.2.5 Traffic Load

Figures 10 shows the traffic load over inter-AS links, which is normalized to the Vanilla case. As expected, Oracle achieves

the smallest inter-AS traffic due to the omniscient knowledge of content popularity, while Vanilla shows the highest inter-AS traffic due to poor cache diversity and cache hit ratio. We have two observations: (i) CoRC performs better than CoRC-HBD, which is in turn better than CRIC, and (ii) as α increases, the reduction of inter-AS traffic also increases. It can be explained by the degree of cache diversity in these schemes.

Figure 11 shows the total amount of traffic, which is normalized to the Vanilla case. The total traffic is the sum of transferred traffic for all the links. Notice that Oracle and Vanilla NDN reveal interesting patterns. With not-so-skewed popularity distributions (e.g., α is 0.6 or 0.8), Oracle is better than Vanilla since the cache utilization is more important when content items exhibit relatively small popularity differences. However, with the highly skewed popularity distribution (e.g., α is 1.2 or 1.4), Vanilla NDN is better than Oracle since popular items have more requests, and hence interests for popular items are more likely to be hit on cache. The similar pattern is observed between CoRC and CRIC. When α is 0.8, CoRC is better than CRIC since the cache diversity is more effective to reduce traffic. Meanwhile, when α is larger than 1.2, CoRC is worse than CRIC since every interest should visit its RR first. Overall, CoRC-HBD reduces the effect of route stretch caused by RRs.

Figure 12 shows traffic load of each link when α is 1.0. Splitting the whole cache space to routers helps spread traf-

168

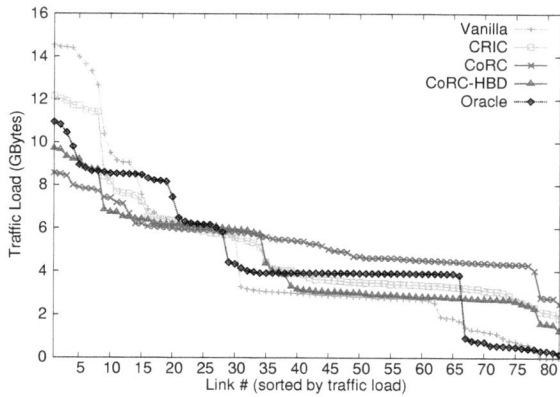

Figure 12: Traffic load of each link is plotted for each scheme. Traffic load is balanced in CoRC and CoRC-HBD.

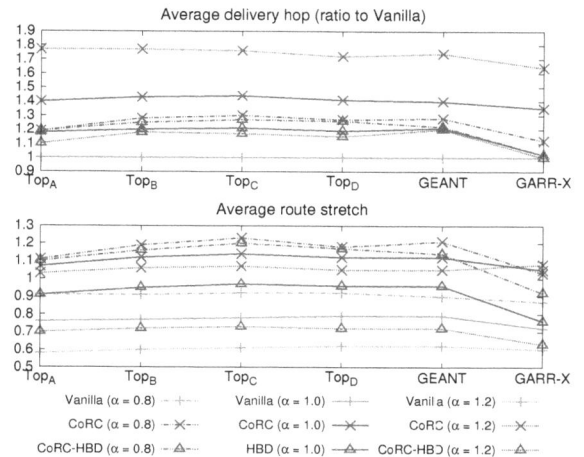

Figure 13: Route stretch is almost irrespective of a topology.

fic over all links. It is another advantage for network management.

6.3 Route Stretch vs. Topology

According to the CAIDA's analysis [21], the number of routers and their degree distribution in each AS are different. To study how route stretch is affected by a topology in a single AS, we evaluate the above schemes with six different topologies (see Table 1). Four router-level topologies are generated by IGen [22] with 64 nodes. We vary the node degree distribution of each topology by changing the number of links between access and backbone routers and between clusters. In addition, two real topologies are considered: GEANT (pan-European research and education network) and GARR-X (Italian research and education network).

In this experiment, an interest packet is generated by a randomly selected node with a poisson arrival rate 0.1 (per second). In CoRC, all nodes in each topology are in charge of non-overlapping parts of the whole cache space while a half of them are selected as RRs in CoRC-HBD. Figure 13 shows the relative path length of CORC and CoRC-HBD with the cache space ratio of 1.0%. We made two observations. First, regardless of a topology, route stretch does not exceed a certain level, which gives an incentive to the AS that adopts CoRC. Second, route stretch affected by the skewness of content popularity can be alleviated by CoRC-HBD.

Table 1: Topology properties

Name	Top_A	Top_B	Top_C	Top_D	GEANT	GARR-X
Nodes	64	64	64	64	40	34
Mean Degree	2.84	4.34	5.87	7.41	2.98	2.70
Std.dev	3.57	4.51	5.45	6.58	2.01	1.53
Min	1	2	3	4	1	1
Max	12	18	22	27	10	6

7. PACKET PROCESSING TIME

In Vanilla NDN routing, an incoming interest packet can be forwarded by looking up the FIB once. Forwarding an interest packet in the CoRC framework may take longer time since there are more actions. In this section, we evaluate the interest packet processing time in a router with the CoRC framework.

7.1 Methodology

We implement Vanilla routing and CoRC in two different settings: (i) the CCNx framework over UDP/IP/Ethernet [23], and (ii) the Linux kernel over the Ethernet link layer. In both settings, we increase the number of incoming interest packets per time and measure the packet drop rate, which is the percentage of dropped interest packets among all the incoming interest packets.

Also, we use another PC to generate interest packets. Thus, depending on the settings, the interest packet generator is implemented in user space (i.e., in the CCNx framework), or in kernel space. The number of generated interest packets per time is varied to see the relation between the traffic rate (incoming interest packets per second) and the drop rate. As a data packet is forwarded by the same PIT mechanism in CoRC and Vanilla NDN routing, the forwarding mechanism of data packets is not implemented, and data packets are not generated. Each PC has an Intel Core i3-2100 CPU running at 3.10 GHz with 3 MB L2 cache and 3 GB memory.

7.2 Drop Rate vs. Interest Packet Rate

The drop rate of interest packets in the CCNx framework (in user space) is shown in Figure 14. Interest packets start being dropped at 6000 packets per sec (pps) with Vanilla routing, while CoRC shows packet drops at 4000 pps. This result reveals that there is additional forwarding delay in CoRC with the first setting due to two actions: (i) checking the AS name, and (ii) looking up the PIB and performing tunneling.

In the second setting, both CoRC and Vanilla NDN routing schemes are implemented in Linux kernel space. The drop rates of both schemes start at significantly higher interest packet rate (40K pps), and there are marginal differences as shown in Figure 15. This result indicates two observations. First, by implementing routing schemes in kernel space, the processing overhead (e.g., context switching) for the additional actions in forwarding interest packets becomes marginal. While CoRC requires more actions in forwarding interests, the additional processing delay is not significant even with software implementation (in kernel). We believe that forwarding speed of interest packets on the

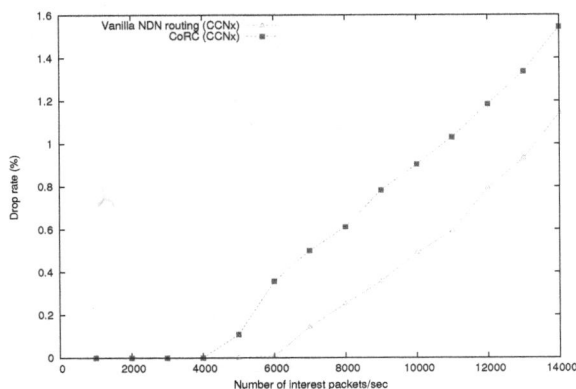

Figure 14: Drop rate versus interest packet rate in CCNx is plotted.

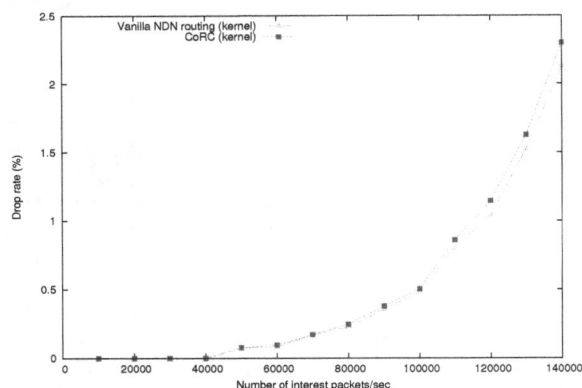

Figure 15: Drop rate versus interest packet rate in kernel is plotted.

hardware implementation of CoRC would be comparable to that of Vanilla routing on the hardware implementation.

8. RELATED WORKS

Routing scalability: Various solutions are proposed to reduce the FIB size in the ICN environment. Greedy routing [24] and an ISP-based name aggregation are suggested in the NDN project [8] but they did not detail how actually to be adapted in NDN. A local FIB aggregation technique is proposed to scale IP forwarding tables [25] by aggregating entries with the same next-hop. However, this reduction is not enough for larger-scale NDN FIBs. In [26], the Lookup-and-Cache solution is proposed, where routers cache the fixed number of router records as the FIB. When a router has no FIB record for the given request, it sends a query to a centralized Routing Information Base (RIB), whose response is then cached in its FIB. However, there is no consideration how to disseminate such huge RIBs among ISPs. DHT-based routing [27, 28] constructs a virtual DHT to fully exploit the underlying hierarchical structure of the Internet. However, [27] requires multiple resolution stages to retrieve an item and αRoute [28] did not consider routing scalability within an AS.

Caching efficiency: In-network caching approaches are classified into two categories: explicit and implicit. Gen-

erally, explicit solutions advertise or explore cached items over the network within a limited range by exploiting the knowledge of a network topology, a storage capacity, and even a content popularity. They make it easy for requesters retrieve interesting items from nearby nodes. However, they may incur (i) considerable advertisement traffic to share the information of the cache repositories [29, 30], or (ii) probing delay/traffic whenever a content request arrives [31]. Meanwhile, implicit solutions aim to realize efficient content placement without any additional signaling overhead. However, they typically have difficulties in locating items because each of items is cached in an independent and distributed manner [32, 33]. Similar cooperative caching techniques have been proposed in the web cache area whose characteristics are significantly different because they are based on an overlay environment [34].

Closer to our work, there exist two recent proposals to map the dedicated node to a non-overlapping cache space [35, 36] using hash function to maximize the aggregated cache capacity. However, they did not consider routing scalability in both intra- and inter-domain routing, and restrictively investigated the impact of route stretch. CoRC is designed to perform routing and caching in an aligned fashion, which improves routing scalability and cache efficiency at the same time.

9. DISCUSSIONS

9.1 Hashing by Publisher Name

CoRC generates a PID by hashing a publisher name, which has the following two advantages. First, routing scalability is enhanced by aggregation. Second, a particular node is in charge of all contents with the same publisher, which is advantageous in terms of network management and business with content providers. However, hashing can cause collisions, which may have a marginal effect on the routing and caching performance in CoRC. First of all, the PID collision probability is extremely low with long hash length (say, 128 bits). Suppose two different publisher names are hashed into the same PID. An interest packet for either of the two publishers is delivered to the same RR by intra-domain routing in CoRC. The RR will look up its PIB to find out the access router of the correct publisher. When the corresponding PIB entry were populated, the RR already knows there is a hash collision for the entry. To differentiate the two publisher names mapped to the same PID, we need another field (say, the string of the publisher name) in the PIB only for the collided entries.

9.2 Dealing with Router Failure

Like ViAggre [13], multiple replicas with the same PID prefix can be allocated for availability. When any RR is down, its backup can come to the front by advertising the PID prefix over the network. In this case, the caching procedure should be restarted. Note that caching is less crucial than routing in case of node failures, and eventually most of popular items will be cached in a relatively short time.

9.3 Resolution System

Most of organizations are connected to multiple ASes for availability and traffic engineering purposes. Suppose *cnn.com* is connected to AS1 and AS2. The publisher may want to receive interests for *cnn.com/video* via AS1, and other interests for *cnn.com* via AS2. To support, the DNS should be able to map AS names not just at the level of publisher names but also at a finer granularity, e.g., directory under the same publisher. Hence, we can keep maintaining two mapping entries for *cnn.com* and *cnn.com/video* in the DNS. Moreover, multiple AS names may have to be dynamically selected, depending on the purposes such as load balancing and failover. For this purpose, a possible option for reliable communications is to send multiple AS names to a requester at once, and then the requester can control how to use multiple ASes to access the particular publisher, which requires a further study.

10. CONCLUSION

We proposed the CoRC framework in Named Data Networking (NDN) for: (i) routing scalability, (ii) caching efficiency, and (iii) coordination between routing and caching. With the AS name-based inter-domain routing, a router in an AS needs to handle routing packets only for the publishers belonging to the local AS. For the purpose of scalable intra-domain routing, CoRC partitions a forward information base (FIB) among routers so that every router maintains only a partition of the entire FIB. To maximize cache diversity, CoRC makes each router cache content items whose names belong to its own partition of the content namespace. We implemented an overlay testbed of 60 routers, which runs on Amazon EC2 in five regions. Our results revealed that the proposed CoRC achieves the higher cache hit ratio, and hence reduce the inter-AS traffic, compared to Vanilla NDN. The route stretch caused by CoRC can be alleviated by applying optimizations. Considering that the routing table size in CoRC is significantly reduced compared with Vanilla NDN, it is worthwhile to deploy CoRC and its variants.

11. ACKNOWLEDGMENTS

This work was supported by the ICT R&D program of MSIP/IITP, Republic of Korea. (2014-044-011-003, Open control based on distributed mobile core network) This research was funded by the MSIP (Ministry of Science, ICT & Future Planning), Korea in the ICT R&D Program 2014.

12. REFERENCES

[1] Cisco Visual Networking Index: Forecast and Methodology, 2012-2017, May 2013.

[2] Andrea Passarella. Review: A Survey on Content-centric Technologies for the Current Internet: CDN and P2P Solutions. *Computer Communications*, 2012.

[3] Teemu Koponen *et al.* A Data-oriented (and Beyond) Network Architecture. In *Proceedings of ACM SIGCOMM*, 2007.

[4] Van Jacobson *et.al.* Networking Named Content. In *Proceedings of ACM CoNEXT*, 2009.

[5] PURSUIT. http://www.fp7-pursuit.eu/.

[6] SAIL. http://www.sail-project.eu/.

[7] 4WARD. http://www.4ward-project.eu/.

[8] Named Data Networking. http://www.named-data.net/.

[9] The ISC domain survey. http://www.isc.org/solutions/survey.

[10] Diego Perino *et al.* A Reality Check for Content Centric Networking. In *Proceedings of the ACM SIGCOMM Workshop on Information-Centric Networking*, ICN, 2011.

[11] Carey Williamson *et al.* On Filter Effects in Web Caching Hierarchies. *ACM Transactions on Internet Technology*, 2002.

[12] Steven DiBenedetto *et al.* Routing Policies in Named Data Networking. In *Proceedings of the ACM SIGCOMM Workshop on Information-Centric Networking*, ICN, 2011.

[13] Hitesh Ballani *et al.* Making routers last longer with ViAggre. In *Proceedings of USENIX NSDI*, Boston, Massachusetts, 2009.

[14] Lada A. Adamic *et al.* Zipf's Law and the Internet. *Glottometrics*, 2002.

[15] AS Number Analysis Reports. http://bgp.potaroo.net/.

[16] Michalis Faloutsos *et al.* On power-law relationships of the Internet topology. *SIGCOMM Computer Communications Review*, 1999.

[17] Hongsuda Tangmunarunkit *et al.* Does AS size determine degree in as topology? *ACM SIGCOMM Computer Communications Review*, 2001.

[18] Bradley Huffaker *et al.* Toward Topology Dualism: Improving the Accuracy of AS Annotations for Routers. In *Proceedings of PAM*, 2010.

[19] Amazon Elastic Compute Cloud (Amazon EC2). http://aws.amazon.com/ec2/.

[20] Ingo Scholtes *et al.* TopGen - Internet Router-Level Topology Generation Based on Technology Constraints. In *Proceedings of SIMULTOOLS*, 2008.

[21] Internet topology at router- and AS-levels, and the dual router+AS Internet topology generator. http://www.caida.org/research/topology/generator/.

[22] Bruno Quoitin *et al.* IGen: Generation of Router-level Internet Topologies through Network Design Heuristics. In *Proceedings of ITC*, 2009.

[23] CCNx. http://www.ccnx.org/.

[24] Fragkiskos Papadopoulos *et al.* Greedy Forwarding in Dynamic Scale-Free Networks Embedded in Hyperbolic Metric Spaces. In *Proceedings of IEEE INFOCOM*, 2010.

[25] Xin Zhao *et al.* On the Aggregatability of Router Torwarding Tables. In *Proceedings of IEEE INFOCOM*, 2010.

[26] Andrea Detti *et al.* Supporting the Web with an Information Centric Network that Routes by Name. *Computer Networks*, 2012.

[27] Hang Liu *et al.* A Multi-Level DHT Routing Framework with Aggregation. In *Proceedings of the ACM SIGCOMM Workshop on Information-Centric Networking*, ICN, 2012.

[28] Reaz Ahmed *et al.* αRoute: A Name Based Routing Scheme for Information Centric Networks. In *Proceedings of IEEE INFOCOM*, 2013.

[29] Yaogong Wang *et al.* Advertising Cached Contents in the Control Plane: Necessity and feasibility. In *Proceedings of INFOCOM NOMEN Workshop*, 2012.

[30] Suyong Eum *et al.* CATT: potential based routing with content caching for ICN. In *Proceedings of the ACM SIGCOMM Workshop on Information-Centric Networking*, ICN, 2012.

[31] Munyoung Lee *et al.* SCAN: Scalable Content Routing for Content-Aware Networking. In *Proceedings of IEEE ICC*, 2011.

[32] Zhongxing Ming *et al.* Age-based cooperative caching in Information-Centric Networks. In *Proceedings of INFOCOM NOMEN Workshop*, 2012.

[33] Ioannis Psaras *et al.* Probabilistic In-Network Caching for Information-Centric Networks. In *Proceedings of the ACM SIGCOMM Workshop on Information-Centric Networking*, ICN, 2012.

[34] Jia Wang. A Survey of Web Caching Schemes for the Internet. *ACM Computer Communication Review*, 1999.

[35] Lorenzo Saino *et al.* Hash-routing Schemes for Information Centric Networking. In *Proceedings of the ACM SIGCOMM Workshop on Information-Centric Networking*, ICN, 2013.

[36] Sumanta Saha *et al.* Cooperative Caching through Routing Control in Information-Centric Networks. In *Proceedings of IEEE INFOCOM*, 2013.

Secure Remote Sensing and Communication using Digital PUFs

Teng Xu, James B. Wendt, and Miodrag Potkonjak
Computer Science Department
University of California, Los Angeles
{xuteng, jwendt, miodrag}@cs.ucla.edu

ABSTRACT

Small form, mobile, and remote sensor network systems require secure and ultralow power data collection and communication solutions due to their energy constraints. The physical unclonable function (PUF) has emerged as a popular modern low power security primitive. However, current designs are analog in nature and susceptible to instability and difficult to integrate into existing circuitry. In this paper, we present the digital PUF which is stable in the same sense that digital logic is stable, has a very small footprint and very small timing overhead, and can be easily integrated into existing designs. We demonstrate the use of the digital PUF on two applications that are crucial for sensor networks: trusted remote sensing and logic obfuscation. We present our security analysis using standard randomness tests and confusion and diffusion analysis, and apply our new obfuscation approach on a set of standard design benchmarks.

Categories and Subject Descriptors

B.7 [**Hardware**]: Integrated Circuits; C.2.0 [**Computer-Communication Networks**]: General—*Security and Protection*

General Terms

Security.

Keywords

Sensor networks, digital PUFs, trusted sensing, hardware logic obfuscation.

1. INTRODUCTION

Sensor networks have been widely researched over the last decade but have received new interest and a fresh perspective with emerging trends and developments in the Internet of Things (IoT). Sensor networks are comprised of small

form, mobile, and remote devices. They are also often placed in unattended locations, and sometimes even in hostile environments. Due to their remote and unattended nature, they are susceptible to physical and side-channel attacks. Thus, it is crucial that these devices be developed with security in mind. Specifically, both the device itself as well as the data it collects must be secured.

The physical unclonable function (PUF) is a cryptographic primitive that has been suggested for sensor network security due to its low power requirements. PUFs are physical devices that have a random but deterministic mapping of inputs to outputs. Their unclonability—and functionality—are often inextricably tied to the physical characteristics of the device components (e.g. gate delay, leakage energy). While PUFs receive and generate digital inputs and outputs, they are analog in nature due to their reliance and design based on their inherent physical characteristics. Thus, current PUFs have many limitations. The most limiting of which includes stability and susceptibility to environmental and operational conditions. Many PUFs, including the standard delay-based PUF require arbiters to operate. These memory components limits the PUF in terms of placement and coordination in circuitry since their outputs cannot be used directly in the current cycle like a combinational module, but require an additional clock cycle to be used.

These main limitations can be removed by creating a purely digital PUF. The digital PUF must be stable in the same sense that digital logic is stable against environmental and operational conditions and must produce deterministic outputs for all input vectors. The digital PUF must integrate with existing combinational logic without requiring additional clock cycles to use its outputs. And lastly, the digital PUF must be flexible in the sense that its structure can be altered for different tradeoffs between security, energy, and delay as required by the pertinent task.

In this paper, we present a digital PUF design with such characteristics. Its underlying architecture consists of a series of lookup tables (LUTs) which are initialized using standard delay-based PUFs. The standard PUFs enable both unclonability and configurability in our design. Despite the inherent instabilities known to exist in them, we ensure stability through two means: (a) through a slight modification in the standard delay-based PUF design that enables stable output validation and input selection, and (b) through a reduction in use to only circuit initialization, thus tremendously reducing the impact of device aging on its gate delays.

We analyze the security of the digital PUF as it stands alone by applying the NIST randomness benchmark test suite [1] and demonstrating that it passes all tests. We also analyze the outputs of our digital PUF using the security principles of confusion and diffusion, as presented by Shannon [2], through demonstration of the avalanche criterion.

However, despite the theoretically sound and mathematically proven security properties of many digital cryptographic systems, there exist many potential side-channels which can effectively bypass these mathematical constructs altogether by reading internal memory or inferring internal procedures through power analysis and memory attacks. Since our digital PUF utilizes memory cells, such as arbiters, SRAM, and flip-flops in its LUTS, it is potentially susceptible to side-channel attacks [3]. We demonstrate that these attacks can be prevented through analysis of modern feature sizes, the use of 3D integrated circuitry, and the use of inspection resistent memory [4].

Finally, we explore two important applications of the digital PUF. Due to the unattended nature of a sensing node, it is possible that an attacker tamper with it in such a way so as to alter the data it is sensing. Thus, our first application is secure data collection, or trusted sensing.

The second application we present is secure information flow through hardware logic obfuscation. Hardware obfuscation is an essential task for the protection of hardware intellectual property (IP). An unattended sensing node can easily be stolen by an attacker with the hopes of learning secure or private information. Through logic obfuscation we prevent the attacker from knowing what the actual functionality of the node is, thus preventing an attacker from being able to learn anything.

The digital PUF enables actual integration with digital circuitry, and most importantly, the actual implementation of logic. The essential idea behind our hardware obfuscation approach is to replace an arbitrary piece of logic with a digital PUF and programmable fabric. The digital PUF serves to obfuscate the inputs in an unpredictable way, while the programmable fabric produces the correct outputs as defined by the original replaced logic. Our PUF is particularly favorable for this application because its digital and combinational nature allow us to obfuscate any arbitrary piece of logic anywhere in a circuit without inducing additional cycles. To analyze our techniques we introduce new metrics for measuring the difficulty in reverse engineering the obfuscated logic.

2. RELATED WORK

Pappu et al. introduced the concept of the first PUF and demonstrated it using mesoscopic optical systems [5]. Devadas' research group at MIT developed the first family of silicon PUFs through the use of intrinsic process variation in deep submicron integrated circuits [6]. Guarardo and his coworkers at Philips Research in Eindhoven demonstrated how PUFs can create unique startup values in SRAM cells [7]. Consequently a great variety of technologies were used for PUF creation including IC interconnect networks, thyristors, memristors, and several nanotechnologies. Although a variety of PUF structures have been proposed, arbiter-based (APUF) [6], ring oscillator-based (RO-PUF) [8], and SRAM PUFs [7] are by far most popular.

PUFs were immediately applied to a number of applications including authentication, cryptographic key generation and secure storage [9], anti-counterfeiting [10], FPGA intellectual property (IP) protection [11], remote enabling and disabling of integrated circuits [12], and remote trusted sensing [13] [14]. PUFs are also used in conjunction with traditional creation and operation of remote secure processors [15]. The security role of the PUF has been greatly enhanced with several proposals for employing PUFs in public key security protocols in systems such as the public PUF (PPUF), SIMPL, and one time pads [16] [17].

There have been two efforts that aim to remove the limitations of analog PUFs. The first is the digital bimodal function (DBF) [18]. The DBF easily passes several security and randomness tests, but is not unclonable and cannot be integrated with regular digital logic without significant time overhead. In the second effort, Fyrbiak et al. proposed the creation of software security primitives using hardware random generators [19]. Hardware-software security primitives require relatively long execution times and depend on unspecified reproducible random generators.

A large number of security attacks on essentially all types of PUFs have been explored. They can be classified into two groups: reverse engineering (also called characterization) and manufacturing or emulation attacks. Non-invasive characterization attacks mainly target the delay-based PUFs (e.g. APUF and RO-PUF). These attacks mainly use numerical algebra and machine learning techniques. For example, Majzoobi et al. demonstrated how linear programming can be used to characterize delay PUFs [20]. By far the most popular statistical attack was reported by Rührmair at al. in which a relatively small number of challenge-response pairs yielded highly accurate prediction models [21]. Most recently, Xu and Burleson proposed coordinated side-channel and machine learning attacks [22].

There are a number of well studied side-channel attacks either on cryptographical protocols and devices or directly on PUFs including timing, power, electromagnetic emanation, optical, and variety of memory reading attacks including the use of focused ion beams [23] [24]. Note that attacks such as cache behavior attacks are not applicable to PUFs. For instance, it has been practically demonstrated that several side-channel attacks can read data stored in DRAM and SRAM cells [25]. For example, the security research group at Technische Universität Berlin reported successful physical cloning of SRAM PUFs [3].

Side-channel attacks use a variety of physical phenomena and sophisticated engineering approaches, often with high effectiveness. Still, there is a strong belief that APUFs and other delay-based PUFs are either safe or at least much more resilient against side-channel attacks due to their small difference in physical signals and dependency on difficult-to-measure threshold voltages that depend on the number of dopants and their distribution in transistor channels along with other physical characteristics of the device.

A multitude of techniques for layout reconstruction and reverse engineering of integrated circuit functionality have been proposed and demonstrated over the last couple decades [26]. The goal of hardware obfuscation is to prevent reverse engineering. One popular approach is to append unique structures to the design in such a way that only the designer of the circuit can enable the correct functional execution [12]. Another approach harnesses the physical structure of gates, specifically differences in small implementation details that cannot be easily deduces using existing reverse engineering techniques [27]. We demonstrate that it is possible with very low overhead to make each integrated circuit of a particular

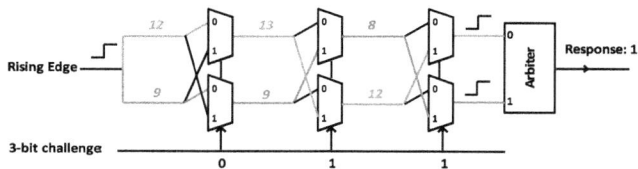

Figure 1: Applying a 3-bit input challenge to a delay-based PUF. The challenge is intentionally chosen in this example in such a way that the delay difference between the two paths (red and blue) are maximized.

Challenge	Delay Difference
000	3
001	-3
010	-11
011	11
100	-3
101	3
110	-5
111	5

Table 1: Delay differences between all possible paths in the example delay-based PUF in Figure 1.

design unique and therefore greatly increase the difficulty of reverse engineering because reverse engineering one IC does not help in reverse engineering a second. Another beneficial side effect is that now energy consumption of each circuit becomes unique.

In this paper we present three primary contributions that differentiate our work from prior art: (i) the digital PUF, (ii) logic obfuscation, and (iii) remote sensing and communication. The current state-of-the-art PUF, in particular, the SRAM PUF, has two problems, the first is that it is susceptible to side-channel attacks, and the second is that it is unstable. Our digital PUF outperforms the SRAM PUF because no one can reverse engineer the digital PUF due to storing its secret key in a stable analog delay-based PUF. In terms of state-of-the-art ring oscillator based and delay based PUFs, we demonstrate that the digital PUF is not only stable, but also digital, which means that we can easily integrate the system into existing logic.

Recently, Zheng et al. has proposed a reconfigurable digital PUF [28]. Our design differs in three regards. The first is that Zheng's digital PUF requires significantly more resources and real-time configuration mechanisms which limits its implementation to only FPGA systems, while our digital PUF can be implemented on any platform, including ASIC and programmable processors, and is much smaller and faster. The second difference is that Zheng focuses on code obfuscation and protection of software which cannot be done using our system because we assume that one will change the primary inputs to the system. However, our digital PUF design can be operated externally as any other system, the only difference is that internally it is very different. The final difference is that we enable two distinctly different applications that the reconfigurable PUF cannot implement without very large overhead.

Regarding our second main contribution, logic obfuscation, existing solutions utilize special implementations, and often obfuscate using techniques external to the actual logic mechanisms. Our system allows for obfuscation of any sys-

tem regardless of what kinds of gates it uses and does so by putting the mechanism inside of the logic.

As for our third contribution, no one else has implemented remote secure trusted communication using PUFs that enables that the source of the transmissions can be trusted. For example, this could be essential for secure remote access of files on the web through FTP. Furthermore, the use of the digital PUF enables for low overhead and, more importantly, resiliency with respect to operational and environmental conditions and aging.

3. PRELIMINARIES

3.1 Delay-based PUF Stability

Figure 1 depicts an example of a 3-bit delay-based PUF. Each challenge bit controls the inputs of two multiplexers. An output bit is generated by assigning a challenge vector and sending a rising edge through the PUF. The two paths traverse the three delay segments, swapping positions (top and bottom) depending on the input bit at each segment, before arriving at the arbiter which determines the final output. For example, an input challenge of 011 generates the blue and red paths depicted. An arbiter will set its value to 0 or 1 depending on which path (top or bottom) arrives first, effectively selecting the path that has the smaller delay. Table 1 consists of the delay differences between the top and bottom paths for all possible paths in the example PUF in Figure 1.

A key observation is that for each unique delay-based PUF there exists a set of challenges that produce stable outputs. Consider the situation in which environmental conditions affect the physical characteristics of the circuit. For example, variations in temperature cause variations in individual gate delays, thereby affecting the overall path delays in the analog PUF. Since challenges 011 and 010 result in a large difference in delay between the two racing paths, it is still with high possibility that the red path will have a larger delay compared to the blue path despite the effects temperature may have on the individual gate delays. We label this challenge, and any other challenges that are resilient to such environmental changes, as stable inputs.

For path delay analysis we introduce a *delay ratio* metric, which is defined as the delay differences of two paths divided by the delay of the shorter path. For the purposes of testing, we assume that gate delays follow a normal distribution due to the effects of process variation.

For different original delay ratios and varying temperatures we use the Hotspot tool [29] to simulate the standard delay-based PUF and measure the probability that its output is stable. Table 2 shows the results of a 32-bit delay-based PUF. As expected, a higher original delay ratio yields higher probabilities for stable outputs. For example, for an original delay ratio of 0.1, the probability that the PUF output remains stable across temperatures ranging from 250K to 400K remains 1.

The results of our 64-bit PUF tests are shown in Table 3. Compared to the 32-bit test case, the 64-bit test case demonstrates a similar trend and exhibits even better stability under the same conditions. As long as the original delay ratio reaches a particular threshold (e.g. 0.1 in this experiment), the outputs remain stable for a wide range of temperatures. Hence, we select those challenges that satisfy this delay ratio threshold as the stable challenges.

Temperature	Delay Ratio (T=300K)						
	0.04	0.05	0.06	0.07	0.08	0.09	0.1
250K	0.979	0.987	0.994	0.997	1	1	1
350K	0.969	0.975	0.989	0.994	0.997	1	1
400K	0.937	0.951	0.959	0.977	0.988	0.996	1

Table 2: Probability that outputs of the 32-bit PUF are stable over varying temperatures for different delay ratios.

Temperature	Delay Ratio (T=300K)						
	0.04	0.05	0.06	0.07	0.08	0.09	0.1
250K	0.984	0.986	0.996	0.998	1	1	1
350K	0.982	0.986	0.993	0.998	1	1	1
400K	0.954	0.974	0.986	0.991	0.997	1	1

Table 3: Probability that outputs of the 64-bit PUF are stable over varying temperatures for different delay ratios.

	$P(R \geq 0.04)$	$P(R \geq 0.06)$	$P(R \geq 0.08)$	$P(R \geq 0.1)$
32-bit PUF	12.51%	4.27%	1.07%	0.21%
64-bit PUF	9.34%	2.44%	0.43%	0.05%

Table 4: Probability that the delay ratio (R) is larger than the labelled threshold value for a 32-bit and 64-bit PUF.

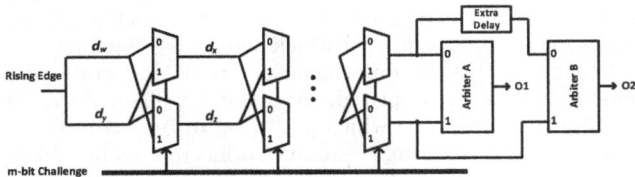

Figure 2: Architecture for stable challenge-response testing.

An important issue to address is how to obtain these stable challenges. Gate level characterization is possible but may require expensive efforts and costs. We have proposed an easy but feasible alternative. As shown in Figure 2, before the two paths reach the arbiter, we intentionally place extra delays within one of the paths. Assuming we are measuring an m-bit PUF, and assuming the expected delay of each stage is D (since delays are distributed normally in the presence of process variation), the expectation of the total delay for each path is $m \times D$. Therefore, we intentionally add $0.1 \times m \times D$ delay to one of the paths using our additional architecture. When applying a challenge, if the path with extra delay still reaches Arbiter B earlier than the other path reaches both Arbiter A and B (i.e. both O_1 and O_2 are 0), then we can claim with certainty that the challenge coupled with this particular PUF produces a path difference of 0.1 or greater and can thus be regarded as a stable input.

We search for stable inputs in this manner by applying many random challenges to the delay-based PUF. Table 4 shows the probability that for a random input challenge the corresponding *Delay Ratio* is larger than a particular threshold value. Although the portion of stable challenges is small, the time required to build a reasonable amount of stable challenges is negligible due to the fact that each test only requires a single clock cycle.

3.2 Digital Bimodal Function

The concept of the digital bimodal function (DBF) was first proposed by Xu et al. [18]. The essential idea behind the DBF is to represent a set of binary functions in two forms, one which is fast and compact ($f_{compact}$) and the other which is slow and complex ($f_{complex}$). Both forms have exactly the same functionality, in other words, given the same inputs, both forms produce the same outputs.

Equation 1, 2, and 3 illustrate an example of a DBF. As a prerequisite, a_i, b_i, and c_i are binary values, and the function sets f and g are Boolean functions in the form of sums of products (SOP) and/or products of sums (POS) representing $f_{compact}$ and $f_{complex}$, respectively. Equation 1 represents the relationship between a_i and b_i and Equation 2 represents the relationship between b_i and c_i. Note that each function f has 4 binary inputs assigned in a random and permanent order.

Equation 3 is generated by substituting 1 into 2, yielding a direct relationship between a_i and c_i. Note that substitutions are expanded and simplified so that each sub function in g is in the form of a SOP or a POS. The key observation here is that while both f and g implement the same functionality, f can be computed much more rapidly than g since it is in a compact format in which each subfunction requires only four inputs, while g is in an expanded format in which each subfunction requires up to n variables. It has been shown that the size difference between $f_{compact}$ and $f_{complex}$ increases exponentially with an increase in input variables and additional levels of substitution [18].

Figure 3 depicts the FPGA-based implementation of the DBF example defined in Equations 1, 2, and 3. The architecture is composed of two levels of 4-input LUTs. Note that each 4-input LUT implements a 4-input Boolean function from f. A hierarchy structure is constructed by feeding the outputs of the previous level of LUTs to the inputs of the next level of LUTs which is equivalent to the function substitution. Therefore, the LUT network directly implements $f_{compact}$ in the DBF. As the number of inputs and number of levels in the LUT network grows, the expanded form of $f_{complex}$ becomes very difficult to implement in hardware (grows exponentially) while $f_{compact}$ remains in a relatively compact form (grows linearly).

Unfortunately, one significant drawback of the DBF is that it can easily be reverse engineered once an attacker gains access to the configuration of the LUT network. Our digital PUF solves this problem by integrating the delay-based PUF into the design and using only stable challenge-response pairs to initialize a random subset of LUTs comprising the DBF.

Inputs: $a_i \in \{0,1\}, i \in \{0,1,2...n-1\}$
Outputs: $c_i \in \{0,1\}, i \in \{0,1,2...n-1\}$
Variables: $b_i \in \{0,1\}, i \in \{0,1,2...n-1\}$
$r_j \in \{0,1,2...n-1\}, j \in \{0,1,2...8n-1\}$

$$
\begin{cases}
b_0 = f_0(a_{r_0}, a_{r_1}, a_{r_2}, a_{r_3}) \\
b_1 = f_1(a_{r_4}, a_{r_5}, a_{r_6}, a_{r_7}) \\
b_2 = f_2(a_{r_8}, a_{r_9}, a_{r_{10}}, a_{r_{11}}) \\
\dots \\
b_{n-1} = f_{n-1}(a_{r_{4n-4}}, a_{r_{4n-3}}, a_{r_{4n-2}}, a_{r_{4n-1}})
\end{cases} \quad (1)
$$

$$
\begin{cases}
c_0 = f_n(b_{r_{4n}}, b_{r_{4n+1}}, b_{r_{4n+2}}, b_{r_{4n+3}}) \\
c_1 = f_{n+1}(b_{r_{4n+4}}, b_{r_{4n+5}}, b_{r_{4n+6}}, b_{r_{4n+7}}) \\
c_2 = f_{n+2}(b_{r_{4n+8}}, b_{r_{4n+9}}, b_{r_{4n+10}}, b_{r_{4n+11}}) \\
\dots \\
c_{n-1} = f_{2n-1}(a_{r_{8n-4}}, a_{r_{8n-3}}, a_{r_{8n-2}}, a_{r_{8n-1}})
\end{cases} \quad (2)
$$

$$
\begin{cases}
c_0 = g_0(a_0, a_1, a_3, \dots, a_{n-1}) \\
c_1 = g_1(a_0, a_1, a_3, \dots, a_{n-1}) \\
c_2 = g_2(a_0, a_1, a_3, \dots, a_{n-1}) \\
\dots \\
c_{n-1} = g_{n-1}(a_0, a_1, a_3, \dots, a_{n-1})
\end{cases} \quad (3)
$$

4. DIGITAL PUF

4.1 Architecture

Figure 4 depicts the architecture of the digital PUF. At startup, the user selects and applies stable challenge vectors, supplied by the digital PUF manufacturer, to an array of delay-based PUFs. The resultant stable outputs are then used to initialize and configure individual LUT cells in the DBF. This procedure is applied to a random subset of LUT cells, while the remaining cells are initialized by the user. This bifurcation in initialization enables self trust by preventing malicious manufacturers from completely controlling the DBF configuration process.

After PUF initialization, the user generates an input-output mapping for the DBF which serves as a specification of $f_{complex}$. This is easily done by traversing all the possible inputs and generating the corresponding output. The mapping is stored as Boolean functions in both SOP and POS forms.

By applying only stable challenges to the delay-based PUF at initialization we ensure that the entire digital PUF system is completely stable. Furthermore, the intrinsic unclonability of the delay-based PUF along with its integration with the DBF guarantees that the overall architecture is unclonable. Since the delay-based PUF is used only at initialization and is subsequently disregarded and the rest of the digital PUF operation is delegated to the DBF, we inherit the small power, area, and low delay properties of the DBF as discussed by Xu et al. [18].

4.2 Side-channel Attacks

In this section we discuss solutions for protecting the digital PUF against side-channel attacks on the LUT memory cells.

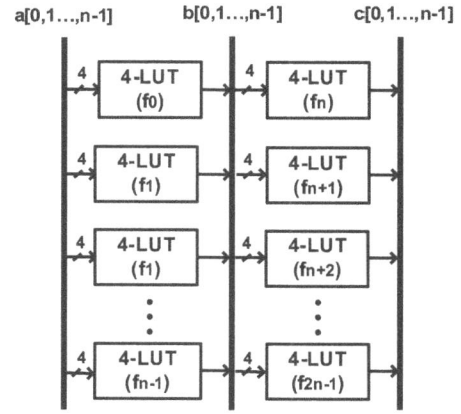

Figure 3: An example of the FPGA-based DBF LUT network.

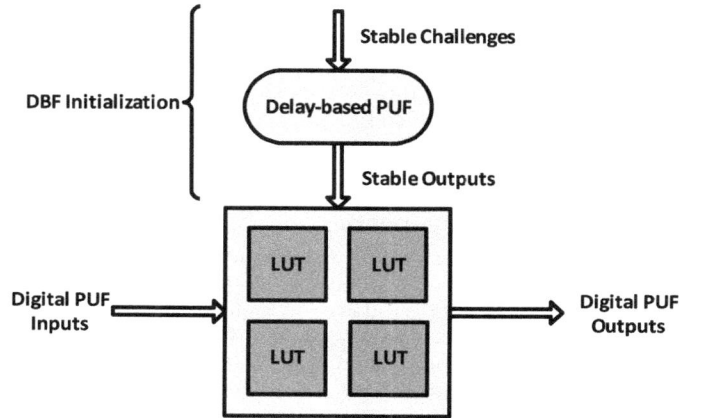

Figure 4: Architecture of the digital PUF. Note that the stable outputs from the analog PUF are used only once at startup to initialize and configure the LUTs in the DBF.

MicroSemi/Actel's antifuse-based FPGA employs one-time programmable connections that are non-volatile [30]. After each fuse is programmed, its probe and programming interface is automatically disabled. Actel fuses are smaller than the regular feature size of the FPGA and therefore are much less susceptible to destructive reverse engineering techniques. They have a very small power footprint (below 40 µJ) that is significantly smaller than the footprint of a transistor. There are many millions or fuses and recovering their values is at best a very time consuming task. Note that in our approach, the fuses would be programmed in a unique way for each circuit. While dynamic reprogramming of fuses is not feasible, one can easily organize several combinations of fuses in such a way that their software activated combination produces a unique digital PUF.

The second potential approach to side-channel prevention is the use of inspection resistant memory proposed by Valamehr et al. [4]. They employ a combination of secret sharing and secure hashing to reduce the probability of correct key or device recovery to 10^{-12} even if the probability of incorrectly recovering a value from a particular location is only 5%. The overall hardware overhead is equal to slightly more than 7 SRAM cells. Note that as observed by Valamehr et al. their techniques can be combined with antifuse mechanisms.

Our most preferable solution against side-channel attacks is the use of 3D integrated circuit technology [31]. Recently, 3D integrated circuits have emerged as a practical industrial option that reduces some design constraints, such as long interconnect, yield, and levels of integration. 3D has been proposed several times for security application [32] [33], but only very recently has it been advocated as a platform for the detection of intrusive side-channel attacks [34]. Also, the use of configurable shields against side-channel attacks has been explored [35].

We propose the use of 3D implementation in which the security device, in our case, the digital PUF, is placed in the middle-most layers. Devices with the same architecture but with randomly selected parameters are placed both above and below the actual device. Another alternative is that all these devices are used in a standard secret sharing mode. Therefore, no backside access is possible, and the performance of electromagnetic attacks are drastically reduced or even eliminated. Finally, to prevent attacks through the same layers we can employ an active shield [35]. Our final observation is that all three discussed techniques are orthogonal and can be combined. Each technique does introduce some overhead but is relatively small. 3D techniques are applicable only if 3D technology is used.

4.3 Security Properties

In this section, we adopt a set of standard statistical tests to analyze the security properties of the digital PUF. We describe possible statistical attacks and test the resilience of our digital PUF against such attacks. We use the standard digital PUF structure with 64-bit inputs and outputs and 32 levels of substitution. We assume that the digital PUF is initialized randomly.

4.3.1 Output Randomness

We quantify the output randomness of the digital PUF by applying the industry standard statistical test suite provided by the National Institute of Standards and Technology (NIST). We generate a stream of outputs in the following way: a random seed is used as the primary inputs to the digital PUF after random configuration and the corresponding outputs are generated. In each subsequent clock cycle, the outputs are XORed with the previous inputs to generate the inputs for the next clock cycle. We repeat the process until we collect enough outputs required by the benchmark suite. The results in Table 5 indicate that the output stream of the digital PUF passes the NIST randomness tests.

4.3.2 Avalanche Effect

In this attack, an adversary attempts to predict the outputs of the digital PUF using the knowledge of outputs for similar inputs. This attack is only dangerous for systems in which output vectors of similar inputs are highly correlated with one another. In cryptography, cipher diffusion is achieved if a change in the input by one bit results in a dramatic change in the outputs in an unpredictable manner. This is otherwise known as the avalanche effect. To test this, we measure the hamming distance between two output vectors whose input vector differ by one bit. Ideally, the distribution should be in the form of a binomial distribution with the peak at half of the number of output bits. The

Statistical Test	Avg. Success Ratio
Frequency	100%
Block Frequency (m=128)	98.7%
Cusum-Forward	97.8%
Cusum-Reverse	97.9%
Runs	98.4%
Longest Runs of Ones	97.9%
Rank	99.3%
Spectral DFT	97.5%
Non-overlapping Templates ($m = 9$)	97.5%
Overlapping Templates ($m = 9$)	97.5%
Universal	100%
Approximate Entropy ($m = 8$)	98.1%
Rand. Excursions ($x = 1$)	98.8%
Rand. Excursions Variant ($x = -1$)	97.6%
Serial ($m = 16$)	99.3%
Linear Complexity ($M = 500$)	98.0%

Table 5: NIST randomness test results on the digital PUF. 1,000 bitstreams of 10,000 bits are provided to each test. Each test passes for p-value$\geq \sigma$, where $\sigma = 0.01$.

result in Figure 5a shows an almost perfect binomial distribution which indicates our matched device satisfies the avalanche criterion and is highly resilient against this type of attack.

4.3.3 Input-based Correlation

Another type of attack utilizes correlations between individual output bits, O_i, and input bits, I_j, for prediction. The goal in this attack is to predict the conditional probability, $P(O_i = c_1 | I_j = c_2)$, where c_1 and c_2 are either 1 or 0. For example, if the attacker observes that output O_i is equal to 1 when the input I_j is 1 a large majority of the time, then he can guess with a high probability that output O_i is 1 when I_j is 1. The ideal situation is when all conditional probabilities are 0.5. Figure 5b depicts the distribution of conditional probabilities, $P(O_i = 1 | I_j = 1)$, for the digital PUF. The majority of probabilities cluster around 0.5, thus indicating low potential for prediction.

4.3.4 Output-based Correlation

Similar to the previously described attack, this attack attempts to predict an output bit O_i according to the value of a corresponding output bit O_j. In this case, if two output bits have a strong correlation, then the attacker can deduce the output vector through knowledge of a subset of output bits. We present the distribution of conditional probabilities, $P(O_i = 1 | O_j = 1)$, in Figure 5c which depicts low potential for prediction based on output to output correlation.

4.4 Structure Exploration

The core architecture of the digital PUF is the randomly connected LUT network. In this section we address how to connect the LUTs to achieve optimal security, while ensuring that the the structure has a small area and delay overhead. The following factors can directly influence the LUT structure:

- **Number of Inputs.** The size and the complexity of $f_{complex}$ is directly dependent on the number of inputs to $f_{compact}$. Thus, the number of inputs should be

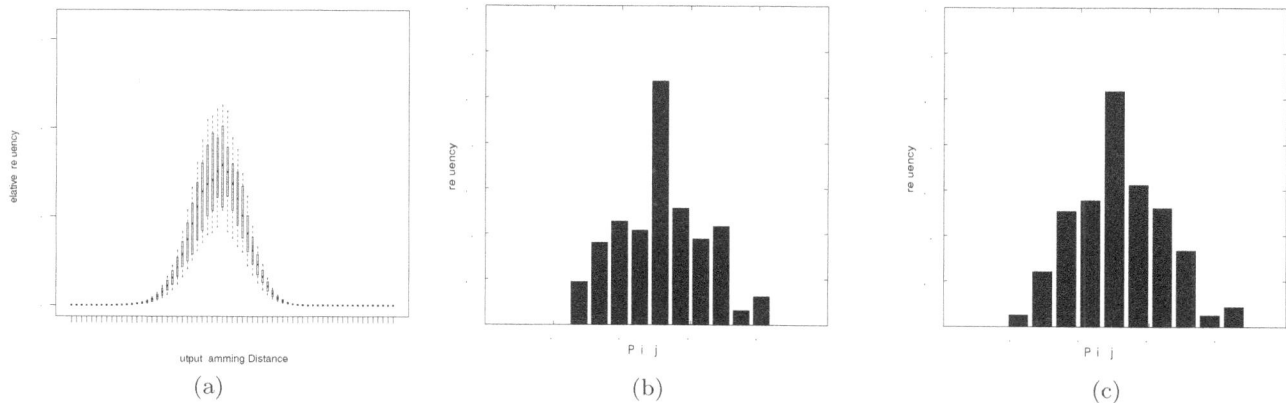

Figure 5: (a) Distribution of output hamming distances testing the avalanche effect. The error bars depict the max, 0.75 quantile, mean, 0.25 quantile, and min frequencies. (b) Probability distribution of conditional probabilities between output bits O_i and input bits I_j. (c) Probability distribution of conditional probabilities between output bits O_i and output bits O_j.

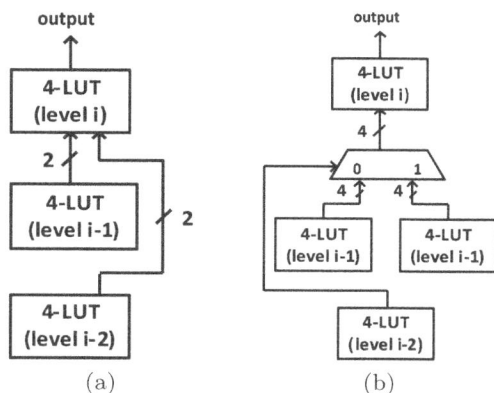

Figure 6: Examples of feed forward structures applied to the digital PUF. (a) Inputs arrive from all previous levels. (b) Inputs arrive from and are controlled by previous levels.

selected in such a way so as to satisfy the application requirements for security, delay, and area.

- **Number of Levels.** Adding more LUT levels to the digital PUF causes more diffusion, however, also increases the delay and area costs.

- **LUT Connections.** In Figure 4, LUTs are connected in such a way that all the outputs feed into the inputs of the next level. However, this is not a mandatory requirement for the digital PUF. For example, feed forward structures can be used. Specifically, the inputs to a specific level of LUTs can come from or be controlled by the outputs from any previous level up to and including the primary inputs. Figure 6 illustrates two examples of feed forward structures for the digital PUF.

We explore the impact of input size on the digital PUF by measuring the success of the NIST tests for varying input sizes. Only when the digital PUF's output stream can pass all NIST tests do we claim that the configuration is acceptable. We begin with a digital PUF with 8 bit inputs and

increment its input size by 8 after each test. We find that once the digital PUF reaches an input size of 32 bits it can consistently pass all NIST randomness tests.

We compare the different structures depicted in Figure 6 against the original digital PUF with varying levels of LUTs. We use the output hamming distance test from the avalanche criterion to compare the structures. Since the input size of each structures is 32 bits, the best structure will yield an average output hamming distance of close to 16.

Table 6 shows the results across the three types of structures. Two observations can be drawn from this table. The first is that the average hamming distance increases with more LUT levels for smaller sized digital PUFs but eventually stabilizes as the digital PUF grows. It can be concluded that after some growth, more levels would not significantly increase overall input diffusion. The second observation is that the feed forward structure in Figure 6b is the most secure of the three structures (in terms of satisfying the avalanche criterion) since its average output hamming distance reaches closest to 16.

5. APPLICATIONS

In this section we present two applications of the digital PUF. The first application is logic obfuscation. In this application we replace a portion of logic within a circuit with a digital PUF and a supporting programmable fabric in order to hide the functionality of the circuit and thus eliminate the possibility of reverse engineering attacks. The second application is trusted remote sensing which enables that the base station of a sensor network can fully trust that the data collected and transmitted from each node is valid and not tampered with, and furthermore, that the node itself has not been tampered with.

5.1 Hardware Logic Obfuscation

Reverse engineering attacks are so advanced nowadays that even integrated circuits containing on the order of 10^9 transistors can be reverse engineered in a matter of weeks. Techniques for hardware obfuscation attempt to prevent reverse engineering attacks by obscuring the functionality of

Levels	4	8	12	16	20	24
Original Structure	8.8 ± 0.6	12.7 ± 0.2	12.8 ± 0.5	13.1 ± 0.4	13.3 ± 0.5	12.9 ± 0.7
Feed Forward in Figure 6a	6.7 ± 0.4	10.9 ± 0.7	12.6 ± 0.6	13.3 ± 0.4	12.9 ± 0.5	13.1 ± 0.9
Feed Forward in Figure 6b	9.9 ± 0.9	13.9 ± 0.8	14.8 ± 0.8	15.1 ± 0.5	15.1 ± 0.5	14.8 ± 0.7

Table 6: Output hamming distance averages and standard deviations across 20 random instances of each digital PUF structure. The input size is 32 bits. Each column corresponds to a given number of LUT levels in the PUF structure.

a portion of logic within the circuit from an attacker while maintaining that the circuit performs its intended function.

Through the use of the digital PUF we demonstrate that we can obfuscate the functionality of a circuit by obscuring a portion of circuitry in such a way that the original circuit functionality is maximally difficult to reverse engineer. Specifically, we combine the digital PUF with a programmable fabric that, together, implement the originally intended functionality of the original circuitry while its function remains unknown. What is most unique about our approach in comparison to previous obfuscation techniques is that our digital PUF is able to integrate directly into the circuit and actually directly obfuscate logic.

5.1.1 Architecture

We obfuscate a piece of arbitrary logic by completely replacing it with a digital PUF and a supporting programmable fabric using the architectures shown in Figure 7. Obfuscation is accomplished by connecting the original logic inputs as the challenge to the digital PUF. The configurable fabric is necessary since the actual function of the digital PUF is configured post-fabrication. This is done by first characterizing the supporting delay-based PUFs that determine the digital PUF's LUTs. Characterization of these initialization PUFs is carried out as described previously in Section 3.1. Then, the digital PUF is configured following the procedure outlined in Section 4.1.

It is important to note that it is feasible to use only the standard delay-based PUF for logic obfuscation. However, given its limitations, it can only be applied using the architecture depicted in Figure 7a. This is due to two reasons. The first is because the standard delay-based PUF is unstable for some set of inputs. If the post-logic architecture from Figure 7b is used, it is possible that an input vector for which the analog PUF has an unstable output could arrive at the PUF in which case the obfuscated block would fail to produce the correct circuit functionality due to the PUF's instability. The second reason the analog PUF must be placed after the programmable fabric is because of its required arbiter which effectively acts as a flip-flop, thus ending the flow of logic for the given clock cycle. Assuming that an attacker can read this flip-flop and an attacker knows the structure of the configurable fabric, then his task is simplified to recording input-output pairs to build a representation of the PUF's functionality.

Since the digital PUF can be employed just like any other combinational component, it can be applied to the post-logic architecture depicted in Figure 7b. The biggest benefit of this architecture is that the PUF outputs cannot be measured directly as they can be in the pre-logic case. In the post-logic design, we can select the output wires of the obfuscated circuit in such a way that the remaining circuitry that the signals propagate through are difficult for an attacker to reverse engineer.

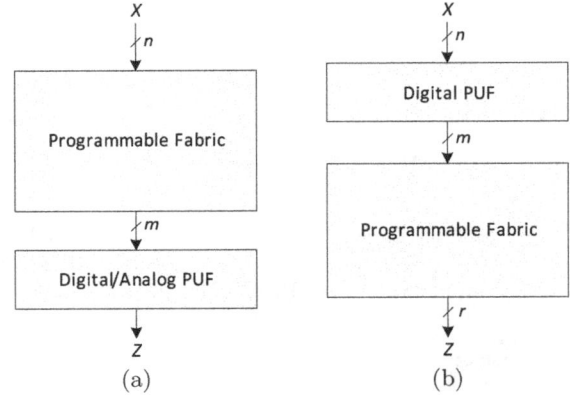

Figure 7: Hardware logic obfuscation architecture. (b) Pre-logic is required for the analog PUF to ensure input-output stability. (c) Post-logic is enabled through the use of the digital PUF since it is stable for all inputs.

Note that utilizing the digital PUF enables us to place the PUF anywhere in the circuit without the need of flip-flops or arbiters. Also note that flip-flops in this case are not primary inputs or outputs and cannot be directly controlled. Hence, we can obfuscate any connected subset of combinational circuitry anywhere in the design. In order to make the reverse engineering task difficult for an attacker, we select for replacement a portion of circuitry whose inputs that are difficult for the attacker to control as well as whose outputs are are difficult for the attacker to reverse engineer. We discuss the specifics of our heuristics in Section 5.1.3

In Figure 8 we present a motivational example using the s27 circuit from the ISCAS'89 benchmark suite [36]. In this example we obfuscate the circuitry consisting of the G9 and G11 gates. Note that by selecting this portion of circuitry for obfuscation we affect a portion of flip-flops which cannot be directly controlled, G5 and G6. In this case G6 is simply a direct output of the obfuscated block.

This is a small circuit with as many primary inputs as their are flip-flops (specifically, flip-flops that cannot be directly controlled). In larger circuits we find it is much easier to find portions of circuitry that are influenced by a larger majority of flip-flops than primary inputs and also affect a larger number of flip-flops than primary outputs.

Once the digital PUF is configured in Figure 8b we synthesize the configurable fabric to map the PUF outputs to the original replaced circuitry outputs using traditional FPGA design tools.

5.1.2 Attack

We assume that an adversary has complete knowledge of the design of the circuit even including knowledge of the design of the supporting configurable fabric. We assume

(a)

(b)

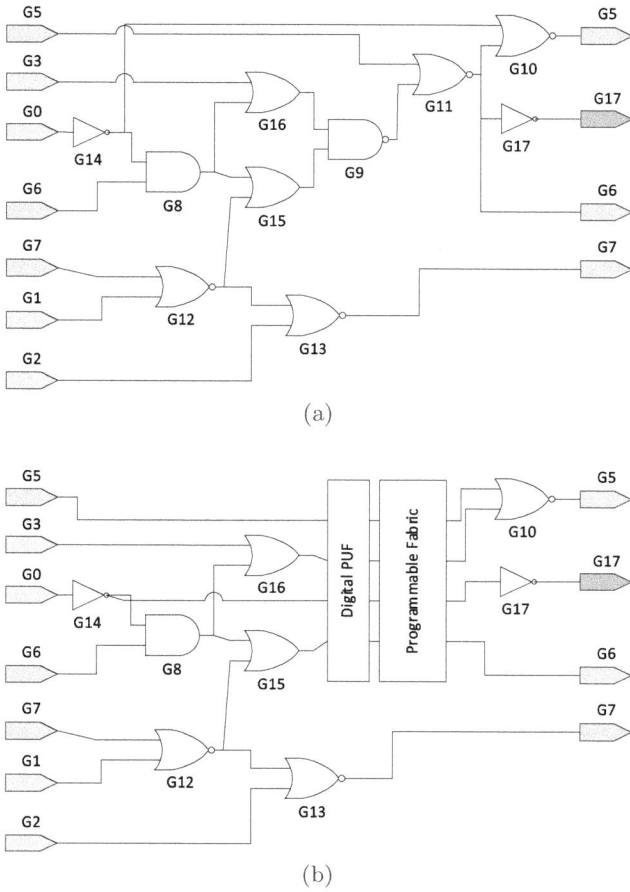

Figure 8: Motivational example using the (a) s27 circuit from the ISCAS'89 benchmark suite [36]. (b) Obfuscated form using the post-logic architecture from Figure 7b. The blue pins denote primary inputs. The red pin denotes a primary output. The green pins represent flip-flops.

that he has read access to all flip-flops in the circuit, but only write access to those flip-flops which are primary inputs to the system.

The job of the attacker is to reverse engineer the functionality of the entire circuit. Specifically, he will focus on the part that is obfuscated. Since we allow him to know the design of the configurable fabric, this leaves him with the task of fully characterizing the digital PUF.

This task is made more difficult by strategically selecting logic for obfuscation in such a way to reduce the attacker's ability to control the inputs to the obfuscating PUF as well to diffuse the outputs of the PUF before they arrive at a readable flip-flop.

5.1.3 Logic Selection

The digital nature of our PUF enables us to treat it as a combinational component. This gives us almost complete freedom to select any piece of arbitrary combinational logic for obfuscation. In assigning placement of obfuscated circuitry we consider the attack outlined above. Ultimately, the obfuscated logic is a black box in which the attacker can

measure the inputs and outputs but is unaware of the internal functionality (e.g. digital PUF configuration). Thus, in logic selection for obfuscation we purposefully select a portion of logic for obfuscation whose inputs are difficult to control and whose outputs are as difficult as possible to measure. In this way we prevent an attacker from reconstructing a complete input-output switching expression of the obfuscated block.

Choosing inputs is accomplished by selecting wires that are dependent upon many flip-flops. By selecting the inputs to the obfuscated block in this manner we ensure that an attacker cannot directly control its input vectors. For example, in the obfuscated circuit example in Figure 8b, the obfuscated block is dependent upon six flip-flops, three of which cannot be directly controlled (G5, G6, G7) and two of which are also obfuscated (G5, G6). In order to reduce delay overhead we select sets of input wires which contain positive slack and whose ASAP and ALAP delays overlap.

The outputs of the obfuscated block are selected in such a way so as to maximize the reverse engineering task of the attacker. We assume that an attacker has full knowledge of the netlist of the circuit as well as read access to all flip-flops. In order to hide the outputs of the obfuscated block from the attacker we select output wires that combine together through regular circuitry into one flip-flop. This forces the attacker to reverse engineer the original output through the circuitry from a minimal amount of information

Note that the reverse engineering task is equivalent to the satisfiability (SAT) problem and is thus NP-complete. Hence, we increase the level of difficulty by selecting n obfuscated logic block outputs that combine maximally to k flip-flops, thus increasing the total number of clauses and variables comprising the SAT instance that must be solved by the attacker.

5.1.4 Obfuscation and Overhead

In this section we analyze and measure the overhead requirements and feasibility of attacking obfuscated circuits from the ICSACS'89 benchmark suite [36].

Figure 9 depicts the number of clock cycles required to fully characterize a fraction of input-output mappings of the pertinent obfuscated logic for three example benchmarks. In each case we analyze 100 different obfuscation configurations with the corresponding input bit size and plot the average number of characterized input-output mappings over time.

In these examples we assume an even more powerful attack than described above in which the attacker knows the output of the obfuscated block without the need to reverse engineer it. Note that even with this knowledge the number of characterized input-output mappings increases only linearly with an order of magnitude increase in cycles observed. Furthermore, by increasing the input size of the obfuscated logic block we reduce the absolute fractional number of input-output mapping characterizations by the same order of magnitude increase in input size, rendering complete specification of the obfuscated logic block infeasible.

We measure the area overhead required by the varying input sizes on different gates and depict the results in Figure 10 and Table 7. Our technique ensures that area overhead remains approximately the same order of magnitude for a given input set size in absolute terms, and thus, decreases tremendously with the size of the obfuscated circuit.

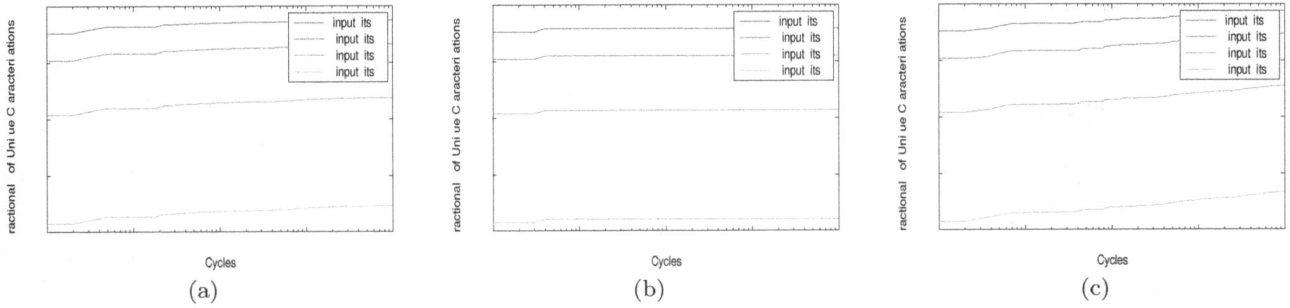

Figure 9: Fraction of correctly characterized PUF obfucated logic input-output mappings for the (a) s5378, (b) s9234, and (c) s38417 circuits from the ISCAS'89 benchmark suite [36].

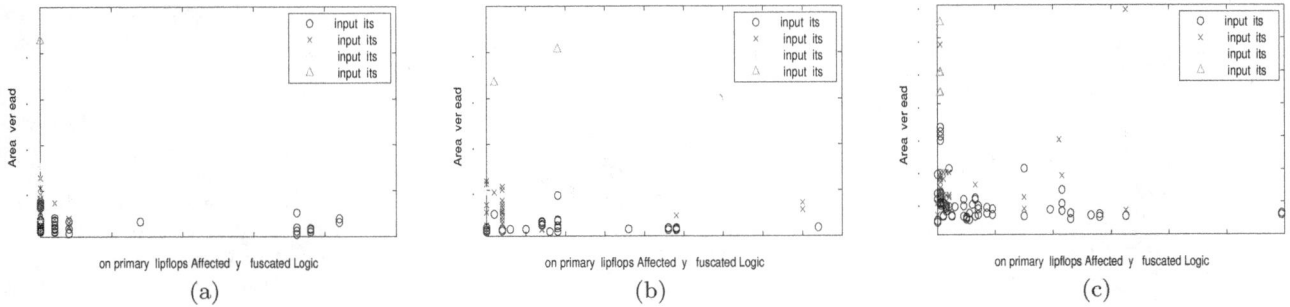

Figure 10: Area overhead of circuit obfuscation as a fraction of the original size of a 90nm circuit for the (a) s5378, (b) s9234, and (c) s38417 circuits from the ISCAS'89 benchmark suite [36].

Circuit	Gates	Average Area Overhead			
		8	16	32	64
s1488	653	13.55 %	58.96 %	-	-
s5378	2,779	5.48 %	11.25 %	16.09 %	85.46 %
s9234	5,597	4.14 %	11.42 %	18.87 %	74.15 %
s35932	16,065	2.27 %	2.68 %	-	-
s38417	22,179	0.82 %	2.34 %	2.69 %	4.85 %

Table 7: Average area overhead for obfuscated logic with input sizes of 8, 16, 32, and 64 for the pertinent benchmark circuits. The dashed placeholders represent input set sizes that could not be found for the corresponding circuit.

5.2 Remote Trust

Trust is an essential component for many remote systems. It is even more essential for sensor networks which are often left unattended and installed in potentially hostile environments. The notion of trust in such systems enables that a communicating party know with certainty that a sensor node's data being transmitted has indeed been collected by that sensor which has not been tampered or compromised in any way. While public key cryptography ensures that no information is snooped over an insecure line, it does not protect against physical attacks to the sensing node. For example, if an attacker were to move a sensing node from its intended location, the node will continue to record and send its data over a secure channel to the base station, while the base station is unaware of the attack.

The key to enabling remote trust is through the integration of the system's core functionality along with pertinent parts of trustworthy circuitry with a PUF. The idea is that by combining the PUF with these data collecting elements (i.e. sensors, GPS, clock), any tampering of the PUF and/or data elements will affect the PUF outputs, effectively changing its functionality.

Previous approaches to trusted remote sensing utilize analog PUFs as the trust mechanism [13]. In addition to a susceptibility to environmental and operational variations, these devices are also susceptible to glitching. Since these devices are analog in nature, they rely on signal path propagation races throughout the PUF network. Between clock cycles and applications, some signals remain inside the PUF, ultimately affecting the next clock cycle. A zeroing procedure has yet to be presented for these architectures that is low in latency and effective at removing glitching between uses, however it is assumed that at least half of the throughput of the device is lost in practical operation since in at least every other clock cycle it is necessary that the PUF be zeroed, possibly more.

The digital PUF requires only a single cycle to initialize at power-up and only a single cycle to function and requires no additional clock cycles for resetting. Not only is it a low latency, high throughput, and low energy primitive, but it is also completely integrable with digital logic. Similar to our

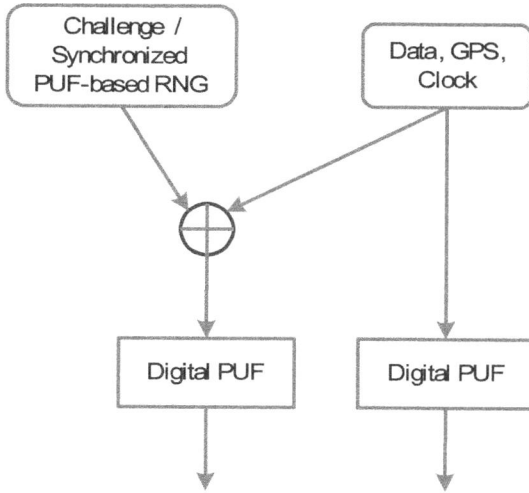

Figure 11: Trusted remote sensing computation flow at the sensor node. The base station provides the challenge.

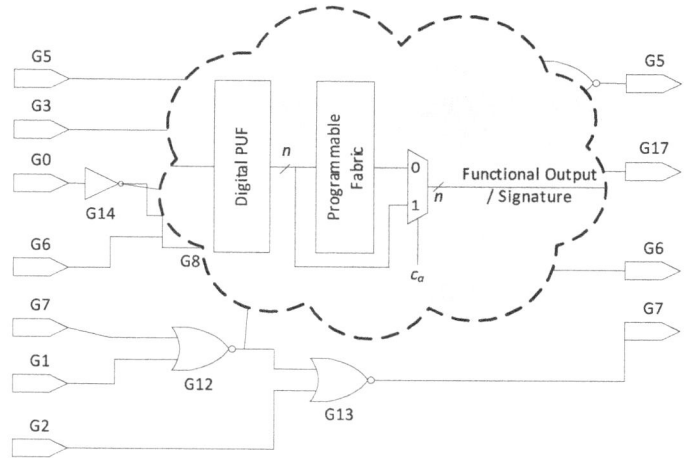

Figure 12: Variant of the hardware obfuscation architecture applied to the s27 benchmark suite enabling hardware attestation. The control signal c_a determine whether the circuit operates in normal functional mode or in attestation mode.

logic obfuscation application, we can place digital PUFs in the middle of digital logic, completely integrating with data collection elements such as sensory circuitry.

Figure 11 depicts the trusted remote sensing computation flow performed by each sensor node. The challenge provided to the sensor node can either be sent directly by the base station or—since the digital PUF passes all NIST tests—can be supplied using a digital PUF as a synchronized random number generator (RNG). At installation, the digital PUF-based RNG is synchronized with the digital PUF-based RNG at the base station. Since the system operator is the only entity that knows the functionality of both PUFs, only he can select seeds for each PUF that synchronizes their functionality. Note that the seeds are in fact challenge vectors to the analog parts of the digital PUF for initialization and hence, are unique. Thus, the seeds can even be made public since their use in initializing any other digital PUF would produce a completely different random number generator.

The remaining digital PUFs are also configured at installation and their functionality is recorded at the base station. At transmission time, the sensor node sends its data, timestamp, GPS coordinates, and two digital PUF outputs as illustrated in Figure 11. Since the base station knows the configuration of the sensor, it validates the data in a single cycle. A man-in-the-middle attack is easily caught since any alterations to any of the transmitted data will cause a vastly different PUF output which cannot be computed by an attacker without having reverse engineered the pertinent digital PUF.

5.2.1 Hardware Attestation

A requirement of the trusted remote sensing computation flow depicted in Figure 11 is that the digital PUF and circuitry (e.g. sensing, GPS, clock) must be physically coupled together to prevent physical attacks. Specifically, the boundaries between these two components should not be easily read or, more importantly, written to by an attacker.

We enable physical coupling by incorporating a variant of our hardware obfuscation architecture into the pertinent circuit as depicted in Figure 12. The control signal c_a selects whether the circuit operates in functional mode, in which the circuit operates as normal, or attestation mode, in which the circuit outputs a unique signature for verification.

The most important property of the generated signature is that it simultaneously and uniquely entangles the input data, logic, and digital PUF into one signal, and does so in a single clock cycle. Since the digital PUF functionality is known only by the remote operator, only he can verify the output signature given the inputs. By integrating this architecture into pertinent components of the device (e.g. sensing circuitry, GPS, clock), we enable that these components and their outputs can be remotely trusted.

6. CONCLUSION

We have presented a digital PUF which leverages a stable delay-based PUF for initializing its connected network of LUTs. Stability in the delay-based PUF is ensured by selecting challenges that have a delay ratio of 10% which ensures that the output is always stable for temperatures ranging from 250K to 400K. We demonstrated the security properties of the digital PUF by passing all benchmark tests from the NIST randomness suite, passing the avalanche criterion, and subjecting the digital PUF to a host of statistical attacks. Finally, we have demonstrated the application of the digital PUF in a remote secret key exchange protocol in which both communicating parties experience very low overhead in terms of both time and energy. Furthermore, while previous PUFs have been designed for remote enabling and communication tasks, the digital PUF enables the actual implementation of logic. We use this capability in a novel logic obfuscation technique and demonstrate that for large circuits we can successfully obfuscate circuit functionality while imposing less than 5% overhead in terms of area.

7. ACKNOWLEDGEMENTS

This work was supported in part by the NSF under award CNS-0958369, award CNS-1059435, and award CCF-0926127, and by Samsung under award GRO-20130123.

8. REFERENCES

[1] A. Rukhin, J. Soto, J. Nechvatal, M. Smid, and E. Barker, "A statistical test suite for random and pseudorandom number generators for cryptographic applications," tech. rep., DTIC Document, 2001.

[2] C. E. Shannon, "Communication theory of secrecy systems," *Bell System Technical Journal*, vol. 28, no. 4, pp. 656–715, 1949.

[3] C. Helfmeier, C. Boit, D. Nedospasov, and J.-P. Seifert, "Cloning physically unclonable functions," in *HOST*, pp. 1–6, 2013.

[4] J. Valamehr *et al.*, "Inspection resistant memory: architectural support for security from physical examination," in *ACM SIGARCH Computer Architecture News*, vol. 40, pp. 130–141, 2012.

[5] R. Pappu, B. Recht, J. Taylor, and N. Gershenfeld, "Physical one-way functions," *Science*, vol. 297, no. 5589, pp. 2026–2030, 2002.

[6] B. Gassend *et al.*, "Silicon physical random functions," in *Computer and Communications Security*, pp. 148–160, 2002.

[7] J. Guajardo, S. S. Kumar, G.-J. Schrijen, and P. Tuyls, "FPGA intrinsic PUFs and their use for IP protection," in *CHES*, pp. 63–80, 2007.

[8] G. E. Suh and S. Devadas, "Physical unclonable functions for device authentication and secret key generation," in *DAC*, pp. 9–14, 2007.

[9] J. W. Lee *et al.*, "A technique to build a secret key in integrated circuits for identification and authentication applications," in *Symposium on VLSI Circuits*, pp. 176–179, 2004.

[10] S. Devadas *et al.*, "Design and implementation of PUF-based 'unclonable' RFID ICs for anti-counterfeiting and security applications," in *IEEE International Conference on RFID*, pp. 58–64, 2008.

[11] E. Simpson and P. Schaumont, "Offline hardware/software authentication for reconfigurable platforms," in *CHES*, pp. 311–323, 2006.

[12] Y. Alkabani and F. Koushanfar, "Active hardware metering for intellectual property protection and security," in *USENIX Security Symposium*, pp. 291–306, 2007.

[13] M. Potkonjak, S. Meguerdichian, and J. L. Wong, "Trusted sensors and remote sensing," in *IEEE Sensors*, pp. 1104–1107, 2010.

[14] J. B. Wendt and M. Potkonjak, "Nanotechnology-based trusted remote sensing," in *IEEE Sensors*, pp. 1213–1216, 2011.

[15] G. E. Suh *et al.*, "Design and implementation of the AEGIS single-chip secure processor using physical random functions," in *ACM SIGARCH Computer Architecture News*, vol. 33, pp. 25–36, 2005.

[16] N. Beckmann and M. Potkonjak, "Hardware-based public-key cryptography with public physically unclonable functions," in *Information Hiding*, pp. 206–220, 2009.

[17] U. Rührmair, "SIMPL systems, or: can we design cryptographic hardware without secret key information?," in *SOFSEM*, pp. 26–45, 2011.

[18] T. Xu, J. B. Wendt, and M. Potkonjak, "Digital bimodal function: an ultra-low energy security primitive," in *ISLPED*, pp. 292–296, 2013.

[19] M. Fyrbiak, C. Kison, and W. Adi, "Construction of software-based digital physical clone resistant functions," in *International Conference on Emerging Security Technologies*, pp. 109–112, 2013.

[20] M. Majzoobi, F. Koushanfar, and M. Potkonjak, "Techniques for design and implementation of secure reconfigurable PUFs," *ACM Transactions on Reconfigurable Technology and Systems*, vol. 2, no. 1, p. 5, 2009.

[21] U. Rührmair *et al.*, "Modeling attacks on physical unclonable functions," in *Computer and Communications Security*, pp. 237–249, 2010.

[22] X. Xu and W. Burleson, "Hybrid side-channel/machine-learning attacks on PUFs: a new threat?," in *DATE*, p. 349, 2014.

[23] D. Agrawal, B. Archambeault, J. R. Rao, and P. Rohatgi, "The EM side-channel(s)," in *CHES*, pp. 29–45, 2003.

[24] S. P. Skorobogatov and R. J. Anderson, "Optical fault induction attacks," in *CHES*, pp. 2–12, 2003.

[25] J. A. Halderman *et al.*, "Lest we remember: cold-boot attacks on encryption keys," *Communications of the ACM*, vol. 52, no. 5, pp. 91–98, 2009.

[26] Y. Ren, Y. Shi, and B.-H. Gwee, "A novel gate-level to behavior-level conversion algorithm with high microcell identification rate," in *IASTED International Conference*, vol. 712, p. 138, 2010.

[27] J. Rajendran, Y. Pino, O. Sinanoglu, and R. Karri, "Security analysis of logic obfuscation," in *DAC*, pp. 83–89, 2012.

[28] J. Zheng and M. Potkonjak, "DPUF: A reconfigurable IP protection architecture for embedded systems," in *ANCS*, pp. 1–2, 2014.

[29] W. Huang *et al.*, "Hotspot: A compact thermal modeling methodology for early-stage VLSI design," *IEEE Transactions on Very Large Scale Integration Systems*, vol. 14, no. 5, pp. 501–513, 2006.

[30] "Implementation of security in Actel's ProASIC and ProASICPLUS flash-based FPGAs." http://www.actel.com/documents/Flash_Security_AN.pdf, 2003.

[31] D. H. Kim, K. Athikulwongse, and S. K. Lim, "A study of through-silicon-via impact on the 3D stacked IC layout," in *ICCAD*, pp. 674–680, 2009.

[32] T. Huffmire *et al.*, "Hardware trust implications of 3-D integration," in *Proceedings of the 5th Workshop on Embedded Systems Security*, p. 1, 2010.

[33] J. Valamehr *et al.*, "A qualitative security analysis of a new class of 3-D integrated crypto co-processors," in *Cryptography and Security: From Theory to Applications*, pp. 364–382, 2012.

[34] S. Briais *et al.*, "3D hardware canaries," in *CHES*, pp. 1–22, 2012.

[35] U. Guvenc, "Active shield with electrically configurable interconnections," in *SECUREWARE*, pp. 43–45, 2013.

[36] F. Brglez, D. Bryan, and K. Kozminski, "Combinational profiles of sequential benchmark circuits," in *ISCAS*, pp. 1929–1934, 1989.

Thermal-Aware Vacation and Rate Adaptation for Network Packet Processing*

Chih-Hsun Chou
Department of Computer
Science and Engineering
University of California, Riverside
cchou011@cs.ucr.edu

Laxmi N. Bhuyan
Department of Computer
Science and Engineering
University of California, Riverside
bhuyan@cs.ucr.edu

ABSTRACT

As processor power density increases, thermal and power control becomes critical for packet processing on a processor. In "run-to-finish" applications, power consumption is stable and temperature simply rises to saturation point and then stabilizes. But, network applications feature ON/OFF execution pattern, which causes frequent temperature and power consumption changes in the processor. We propose a thermal aware scheduler, *TrafficLight*, which achieves power saving by employing vacation and rate adaptation techniques. We implement these through the idle states (C-state) provided by the OS in a CPU and show their effectiveness through experimental data. Then we build power, thermal and latency models based on the vacation queuing theory, which estimates the performance of our proposed techniques. Finally, we design, implement and evaluate an on-line algorithm to dynamically choose the proper power/thermal management technique based on the traffic variation. The technique maintains the processor temperature below the temperature constraint and achieves power saving. To the best of our knowledge, this is the first work to provide the theoretical analysis as well as the experimental results for the vacation and rate adaptation schemes considering power, temperature and latency in the packet processing on a general purpose processor.

Categories and Subject Descriptors

C.4 [PERFORMANCE OF SYSTEMS]: *Modeling techniques*.

General Terms

Design, Reliability, Experimentation, Performance.

Keywords

Network application; Packet processing, Power saving; Thermal aware technique, vacation and Rate adaptation.

1. INTRODUCTION

The explosive growth of network bandwidth requires orders-of-magnitude increase in packet processing throughput. In addition, many applications (e.g., fast IP-lookup, real-time video streaming, packet classification and deep packet inspection) demand not only high throughput but also low latency. The network industry is aggressively scaling the capability of network processing by employing high-performance off-the-shelf computers to meet this challenge. However, high power consumption in these computers while processing network applications poses a significant challenge to scalable network system design.

Several research prototypes have demonstrated that chip multiprocessor (CMP) is capable of high-performance packet processing (line rates of 10 Gbps or more) for IP forwarding [1], packet classification [2], and cryptographic operations [3]. These systems not only provide the flexibility to deploy new packet processing algorithms; they also incorporate parallel scheduling to exploit packet-level parallelism on multiple cores for higher throughput and lower latency. Along with increased throughput, however, comes significantly increased power consumption [4]. Collectively, millions of servers in the global network consume a great deal of power [5].

Some studies proposed power saving for the network devices, such as network interface card, routers and mobile platform through sleep and rate adaptation. Some of the early work was done for mobile devices. In [6, 7], the authors proposed to put the network devices into power saving mode during the OFF period, and wake up the processor when a packet arrives. However, this approach highly depends on the incoming traffic pattern and the transition overhead of entering/exiting the power saving mode. It achieves good energy efficiency only when the OFF period is larger than transition overhead. Yuan et al. [8] proposed to decrease the operating voltage in the mobile multimedia system to achieve power saving. Since the active power consumption is proportional to the square of operating voltage, they can achieve power saving by reducing the voltage. In [9, 10], the authors show the experimental results for the latency, power consumption and temperature under the effect of deferred execution. However, how to balance the

*The research was supported by NSF grants CSR 0912850 and 1216014.

trade-off between these three major performance metrics in remains unclear. This further motivates our work to develop a thermal and power aware scheduling algorithm to achieve power saving under certain latency requirement, while maintaining temperature below the thermal constraint.

In [10], Nedevschi et al. give the comparison between two power saving techniques on network interface card — "buffer and burst" and "rate adaptation". "Buffer and Burst" refers to letting the devices go into power saving mode, buffer the incoming packets, and transmit the buffered packets as a burst after a period of time. "Rate adaptation" achieves power saving by lowering the linecard operating voltage. Their result shows that "Buffer and Burst" can achieve better power saving than "Rate adaptation". However, power savings never come for free. These techniques will introduce some additional packet latency and poorer application quality, thus it is important to understand the trade-off between power saving and performance degradation.

In addition, while power consumption remains the major challenge, another factor that must be considered is operating temperature. It is known that high operating temperature adversely affects not only the system performance and leakage power, but also the throughput [11], circuit reliability and chip lifetime [12]. In addition, the cooling and packaging cost for heat dissipation increases exponentially with the power and peak temperature [13]. However, no work has been done on addressing the problem of high operating temperature, as well as the trade-off between thermal constraint, power reduction and packet latency on a processor.

We focus our attention only to packet processing in a general-purpose CPU with single core and reveal many interesting relationship between power saving and sleep states (C-states) in the OS. We also derive approximate analytical models based on M/G/1 queuing theory with vacation to be used later in the paper for developing a runtime scheduling algorithm.

Finally, we propose *TrafficLight*, a thermal and power aware runtime, which measures the packet intensity and predicts the power consumption, latency and temperature using our analytical techniques. Then it chooses one among the vacation and rate adaptation techniques to achieve power saving through existing sleep states (C-states) on a processor without violating a predefined thermal constraint. Besides, the scheme provides maximum power saving under different latency requirements. To the best of our knowledge, *TrafficLight* is the first to explore the trade-off between power, temperature and latency in the network packet processing on a general purpose processor in the context of vacation and rate adaptation schemes.

This paper considers packet processing at the application layer only. In order to avoid the effect of power consumption and temperature rise due to packet interrupts and TCP/IP processing, we use an idle core inside the CPU to generate these packets. Our measurements are carried out only for the core processing those packets.

This paper makes the following contributions. (1) We implement sleep and rate adaptation through the idle states (C-states) and dynamic frequency scaling, provided by the OS and observe the packet processing characteristics under different traffic load. (2) We derive analytical models for power, thermal and latency characteristics for the vacation and rate adaptation based on the vacation queuing theory.(3) We design, implement and evaluate an on-line algorithm to dynamically choose the proper power/thermal management technique based on the traffic variation to achieve power saving under a temperature constraint. (4) We verify the operation by implementing various applications from NetBench [14] on an Intel Ivybridge processor.

2. PACKET PROCESSING ON A SERVER
This section describes the high-level network application characteristic and relate it to the power and thermal behavior while packet processing on a processor. Also, we study the default operations to the C states in OS.

2.1 Packet Processing Characteristics

The "run-to-finish" applications always consume active power while running, and the temperature simply rises to saturation point until it stabilizes. But network packet processing exhibit an ON/OFF pattern [15,16], where the CPU core temperature rises and consumes active power during the ON period, (also known as *busy period)* when the packet is being processed. During the OFF period when no packet arrives, the CPU still runs and consumes idle power which is less than the active power. It allows the CPU to cool down. The OFF period in-between packet processing provides the opportunities to do power and thermal management. The length of ON/OFF period is not deterministic, and depends on the packet arrival and service rates. Also, latency is an important performance metric of the network application. Thus, the main objective of the thermal management of network applications is to achieve an optimal tradeoff between latency, and power consumption, while ensuring safe working temperature at the same time.

To create long enough time window for the power saving mode, the authors proposed "buffer and burst" [10], a technique that buffers the incoming packets for a period of time, during which the network devices will stay idle. With this approach, the incoming traffic is reshaped into small bursts of arrival; devices wake up to transmit a burst of packets, and then sleep until the next burst arrives. The intent is to provide sufficient time for devices to enter the deeper sleep state with lower power consumption, and for the processors to cool down. We follow similar techniques, but introduce variations by limiting our study to packet processing only. In addition, we consider the thermal behavior, which is very important in network system design [15].

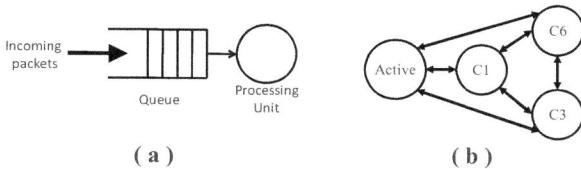

Figure 1. (a) Classical single server queue. (b) State diagram for the CPU active and C states.

Table 1. CPU C-states.

State	Description	Overhead	Residency	Power
P	Active state.	N/A	N/A	10.1W
C1	core clocks stop.	1μs	1 μs	5.1W
C3	core clocks stop and flush core cache.	59 μs	156 μs	1.8W
C6	Turn off the core power and save the core state in main memory.	80 μs	300 μs	0W

2.2 Power Consumption and Thermal Behavior

We start by considering how packets arrive and are served. Fig. 1a shows the general packet processing system. It consists of a queue and a processing unit (PU), which is the CPU core in our case. Incoming packets are stored in the queue, and the PU constantly checks whether the queue is empty or not. If the queue is not empty, PU will fetch and process a packet in the queue in an FIFO fashion driving the CPU to the active state. On the other hand, while PU finds no packet in the queue, it will become idle until the next packet arrives and stored in the queue.

In the idle state, CPU still consumes power but doesn't do meaningful work. Modern CPUs provide succession of idle states (called sleep states or C-states) to save power. As shown in Fig. 1b, there are three CPU idle power states, C1, C3 and C6, which are achieved by disabling different CPU components. The higher the C state is numbered, the deeper the CPU will sleep and lower is the power consumption. For instance, in the state C1 only the CPU clocks are disabled, in C3 the CPU caches are also flushed and disabled, and in C6 the CPU core is turned off. Every state can enter/exit to all other states as long as it satisfies the target residency. By enabling each of the idle states separately, we have measured the CPU idle state power on Intel Ivybridge i7-3770. As a comparison, we also measured the case when the CPU is in the active state. Table 1 shows that the C-states consume much lower power than the active state and the power consumption of different idle states are also very different.

We can also see that as the number of disabled components increases, the transition overhead of entering that C state increases, from 1 to 80μs. Furthermore, to avoid inefficient usage of deeper C-state, the time that the CPU needs to stay in the C-state, defined as residency, will also increase. The Intel auto-demotion [17] will prevent CPU from entering deep C-state if it predicts that the idle time is shorter than the target residency. For example, upon each core C3 request, the core C-state is demoted to C1 until a sufficient amount of residency has been established.

Let us now discuss how the power consumption and temperature will behave in a CPU-based packet processing system. Fig. 2a depicts the amount of work presented in the queue while time is advanced. The up arrows under the x-axis represent the packet arrivals, which cause the step increase of the work in the queue. The slant line represents the packet being processed by the processor with the slope representing the service rate. We can clearly see the busy and idle (vacation) periods during packet processing. Although the lengths of these periods are random variables, the average length can be easily found as $\frac{1}{\mu-\lambda}$ and $\frac{1}{\lambda}$ corresponding to an arrival rate of λ and service rate of μ. Fig. 2b shows the power and thermal behavior of the CPU for the same packet arrival pattern. We can see that the longer the busy period, the higher the temperature will rise until a steady state. On the contrary, the longer the idle period, the lower the temperature will fall. Because of the randomness of both periods, the temperature will also behave randomly, and become a major challenge for the temperature management. For the power consumption, the probability that the processor is idle is $1 - \frac{\lambda}{\mu}$, and is too short and frequent, so the CPU can only go into C1 state, which is idle state with least power saving. It rarely achieves long enough idle time for the target residency and prevents the CPU from taking power savings of deeper C-states (C3 and C6). Our experimental result, given in Section 4, shows that CPU spends at least 90% of idle time in C1 state, which is the least power saving mode. Using the deeper C-states to achieve better power saving becomes a significant challenge in power management.

3. THERMAL AWARE POWER MANAGEMENT

In this section we first propose a vacation scheme, where the CPU goes serving the packets in the queue for a fixed time period and then goes on a vacation (idle state) also for a fixed period. We then modify the scheme where the CPU goes on vacation as soon as the queue becomes empty. Finally, we propose a rate adaptation scheme through frequency scaling

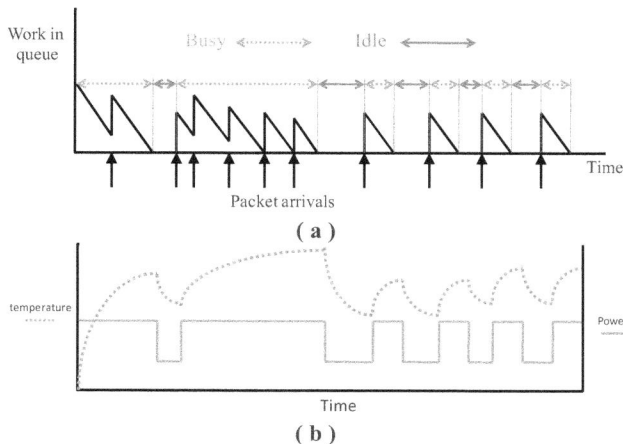

Figure 2. (a) Packets processing pattern. (b) Temperature and power consumption of packet processing.

3.1 Power Saving though Vacation

Fixed Service and Vacation Scheme:

In the original system, servers are busy processing packets as long as there are packets in the queue, and become idle when the queue is empty. Although servers spend most of their time idle, conventional energy-conservation techniques are unable to exploit these brief idle periods. We propose an approach to reshape the packet processing pattern that creates longer idle period and allows the processors to enter low-power state which consumes less power. We call this approach *vacation*. We also use the terms sleep or idle state alternatively.

Fig. 3a shows the flow chart of the vacation approach. In working state, the processor works as in the original case for a time period t_{work}, which prevent the processor from exceeding the given temperature threshold. In the sleep state, the server takes a vacation for time t_{vac}, during when the server will buffer all the incoming packets in the queue. After t_{vac} expired, the server wakes up and goes back to the working state, and continues serving packets in the queue. The approach is similar to the "buffer and burst approach", described in [10] except that the details of the sleep approach here are different. In buffer and burst approach, the incoming packets are buffered during the buffer period, and these buffered packets are transmitted only in the burst period. We process those packets if they arrive during the working period subject to t_{work}. Also, their approach did not include the thermal consideration like temperature threshold.

In the original system, the idle period is too short to allow the processor enter deep sleep state. In our vacation approach, the incoming traffic, form processor's perspective, is reshaped into short bursts of arrival. Processors wake up to process bursts of packets, and then sleep for a long time. The intent is to provide sufficient time for processors to enter the deeper sleep state with lower power consumption, and temperature cool down. Fig. 3b shows the amount of work presented in the queue while time advances. Compared with Fig. 2a, we can see that the amount of work increases due to the buffering during the vacation. In the working state, instead of many short packet processing time periods, it's now a long busy period.

Several competing factors influence the efficiency of this approach. The idle periods between packet processing provides natural thermal modulation and Vacation alters the distribution of these idle periods. The power and thermal behaviors are shown in Fig. 3c; where the deeper idle states during vacation decrease the power consumption, and cause the temperature to cool down faster. However, since the incoming packets are "pushed" into vacation state, there may be higher load on the system during the working period. This leads to increased average power consumption and heat generation during the period. Longer busy period means that the temperature could rise to a higher level, but longer sleep (vacation) state helps lower temperature.

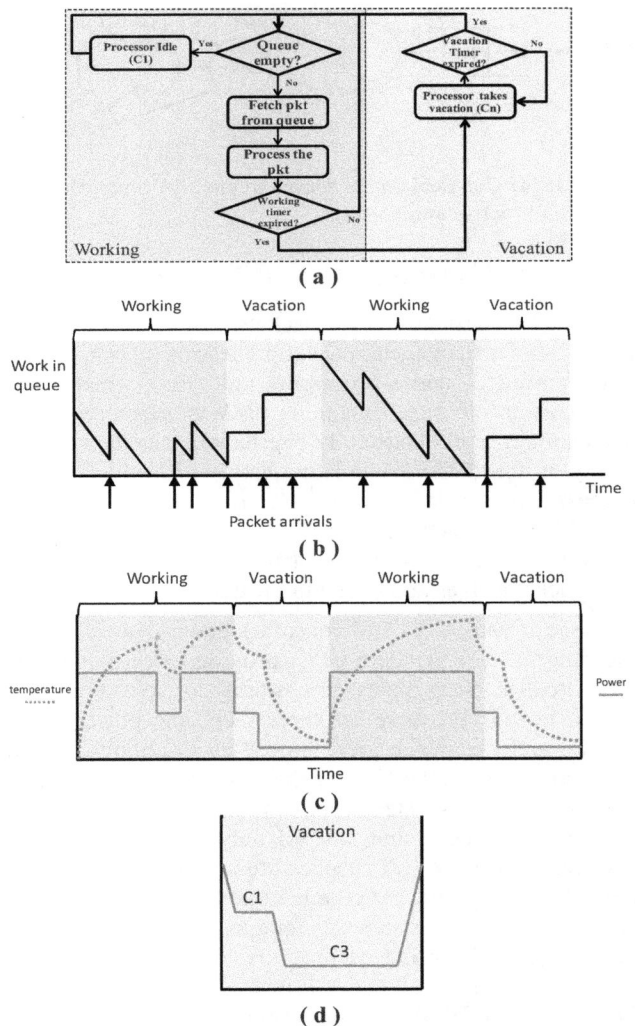

(a)

(b)

(c)

(d)

Figure 3. (a) Vacation approach flows. (b) Packets processing pattern with vacation approach. (c) Temperature and power consumption. (d) C-state transition during vacation period.

Therefore, the efficiency depends on balancing the working and vacation states.

Fig. 3d shows the magnified vacation period, where we can see that the CPU first enters to C1 state when the vacation begins. When the residency is satisfied, it enters to C3 state for more power saving. When the vacation is close to the end, it transits back to the active state. By doing so, we can hide the transition overhead between C states within vacation period without increasing the execution time.

Modified Vacation Approach:

In vacation scheme, there will be cases that the processor will experience short idle time during the working period, as shown in Fig. 3b. To further achieve power saving, we propose a modified vacation scheme with the flowchart shown in Fig. 4a. The processor now will switch into vacation state not only when the timer expired, also when the processor finds out that the queue is empty during the working period. In Fig. 4b, we can see that once the work

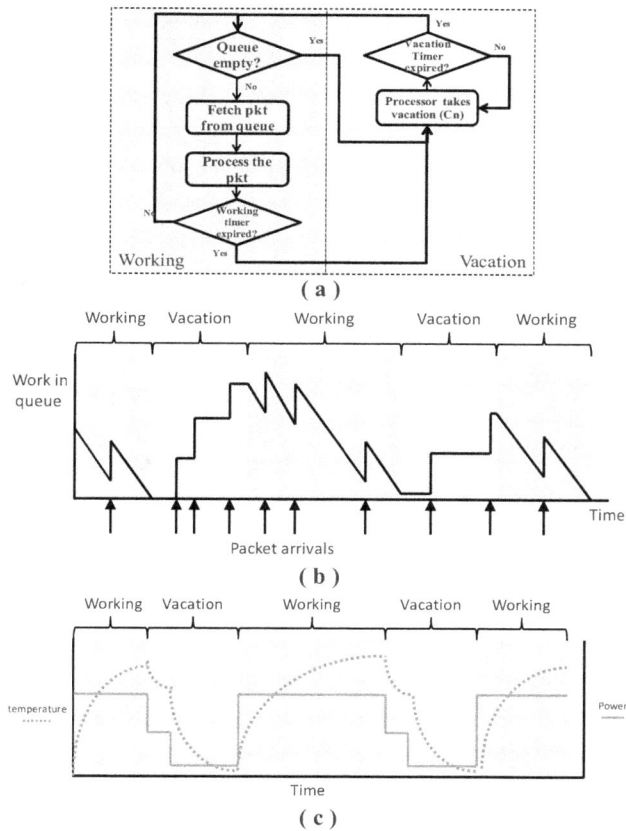

Figure 4. (a) Modified Vacation approach flows. (b) Packets processing pattern with modified vacation approach. (c) Temperature and power consumption.

in queue becomes zero, the processor immediately takes a vacation, and packets accumulate in the queue until the vacation time expires. Also, since the working period ends when queue is empty, the length of working period becomes non-deterministic and is dependent on the incoming traffic and the length of vacation. However, the working period is always less than or equal to the previously fixed time period, t_{work}.

Fig. 4c depicts the power and temperature behavior under modified vacation; we can see that there is no short idle period during the working period, and the power consumption is purely active state power. The thermal behavior is now simpler, without any short cool-down period, the temperature rise until the end of working period, and cool-down during the vacation period.

In modified vacation approach, the length of vacation period becomes more critical to the performance than the original approach. Longer vacation time will reduce the temperature and power consumption. On the other hand, long vacation period will introduce higher packets latency. Thus experimental data and analysis in the next section show the effectiveness of this approach.

3.2 Rate adaptation Approach

In this section, we propose a rate adaptation approach which achieves power saving by decreasing the packet processing rate, and thus reduce the active power consumption

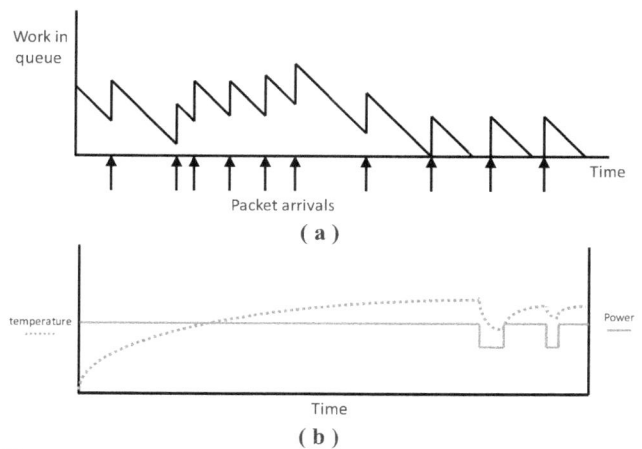

Figure 5. (a) Packets processing pattern with rate adaptation approach. (b) Temperature and power consumption.

in a processor. Rate adaptation is achieved through dynamic voltage and frequency scaling (DVFS) provided in all modern CPUs. Usually, it is just called as frequency scaling, although the voltage is correspondingly reduced. Then, active power being proportional to the cube of frequency reduces significantly when frequency is reduced. Fig. 5a shows packet processing pattern under the DVFS approach. We can see that the slope of the slash line is decreased, which represents decrease in the packet processing rate. In this case, the busy period is prolonged. Still there will be some idle time when all the packets in the queue are finished, but the length of such idle state is decreased compared to the default (no rate adaptation) case. Fig. 5b gives the power and temperature variation under rate adaptation approach. It is obvious that there exist some competing factors that influence the efficiency of this approach. Since the active power consumption is reduced, the heat generated by the power consumption is also reduced. However, the decreasing processing rate causes prolonged busy period, and leads to longer heat up time duration, and less idle period for the temperature to cool down. In addition, the longer packet processing time will cause more packets to be buffered in the queue, and increase the packet latency.

4. PERFORMANCE EVALUATION

In the previous sections, we proposed two different approaches to achieve power saving, and both of them have some trade-off between power, temperature and latency. In this section, we present the experimental results of these approaches and provide some insight on how to effectively use them in practice. We conduct the experiments on Intel i7-3770 quad-core processor with three cores power gated. Power gating is achieved by removing cores from active working set based on kernel's built-in CPU "hotplug" support. Power consumption and temperature readings are collected from the machine specific register (MSR). Also, in vacation and modified vacation approach, the CPU frequency is set as 3.4 GHz. For machine measurement, we use one core of the Intel Ivybridge to run benchmark applications, and another core to generate packets based on the load. Our experiments are based on six benchmarks from

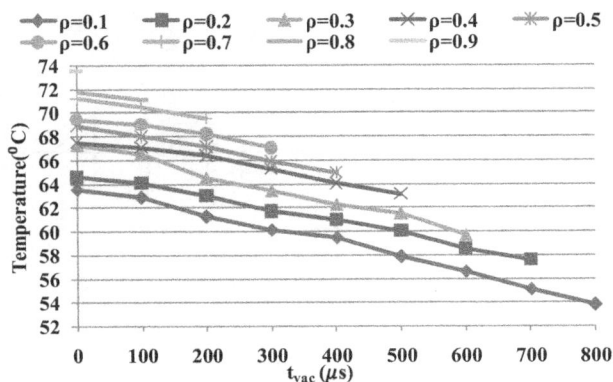

Figure 6. Temperature reduction under vacation approach for CRC.

the NetBench suite [14] that represent various real-life network applications. In this section, we examine how the temperature, power consumption and latency are affected when the vacation period is varied. Since we also measure the impact of arrival rate of the packets, we take only one application, CRC, as an example from the NetBench. Later, we compare the results across all applications for a fixed arrival rate.

4.1 The Vacation Approach

In the vacation approach, design parameters which will affect the packet processing performance are the length of working period (t_{work}) and vacation period (t_{vac}). Let t_{cycle} be the cycle time period, defined as $t_{cycle} = t_{work} + t_{vac}$. For stability of the system, we need to satisfy the condition that $\frac{t_{vac}}{t_{cycle}} < 1 - \rho$, where ρ is the incoming traffic load, defined as $\frac{\lambda}{\mu}$.

Fig. 6-8 shows the experimental results of CRC from Net-Bench with the vacation approach. In these experiments, we fix the cycle time to 1ms (t_{cycle} = 1ms), and vary t_{vac} from 0 to 800 μs, where t_{vac} = 0 represents the default scenario without applying our approach.

In Fig. 6, we can see that the temperature decreases as t_{vac} increases. Although the busy period is prolonged due to forced vacation, which causes the longer heat up, the temperature cool-down brought from continuous idle period

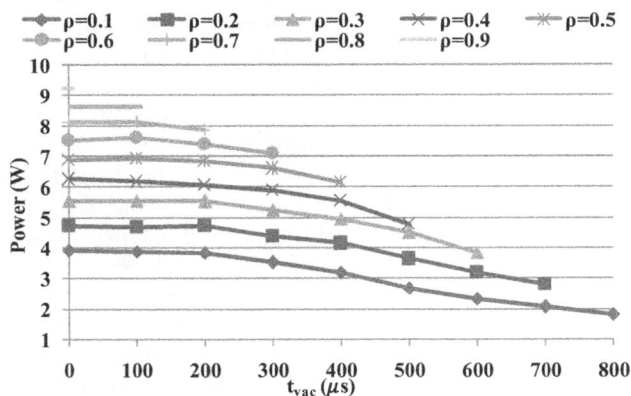

Figure 7. Power consumption under vacation approach for CRC.

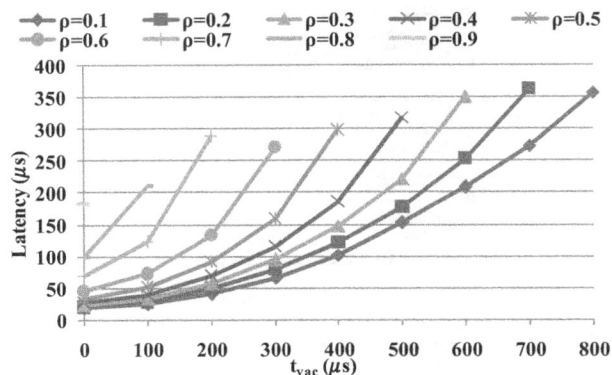

Figure 8. Packet latency under vacation approach for CRC.

and deeper idle state is more significant. Also, when ρ increases, load during the working period increases, which causes the temperature to increase.

The power consumption results are given in Fig. 7. We can see that it achieves more than 20% of power saving under low traffic load ($\rho<0.4$), and 50% when $\rho=0.1$. However, the effect of power saving is diminished when traffic load is high. The reason is that under low traffic load, there exists a large amount of short idle period. These short idle periods are packed into a long idle period in the vacation state, and allow the processer to have enough time to enter deeper C-state. On the other hand, under high traffic load, the idle period is still not long enough because working period increases. We can also observe this through t_{vac}. When t_{vac} is smaller than 200 μs, we can see that the power saving is insignificant, because the short t_{vac} will stop the processer from entering deep C-states (C3 and C6).

The down side of the vacation approach is that it will increase the overall packet latency. Fig. 8 shows that the latency increases quickly as t_{vac} decreases. There are two factors that will cause this latency to increase. First, when t_{vac} is larger, which means longer vacation period, the packets arriving during vacation will have to wait for longer time for processing. Second, since all packets arriving during the vacation period are queued, the packets arriving during working period will have to wait for the packets already in the queue to be processed. The longer the vacation period, the more packets are in the queue, thus longer is the waiting period.

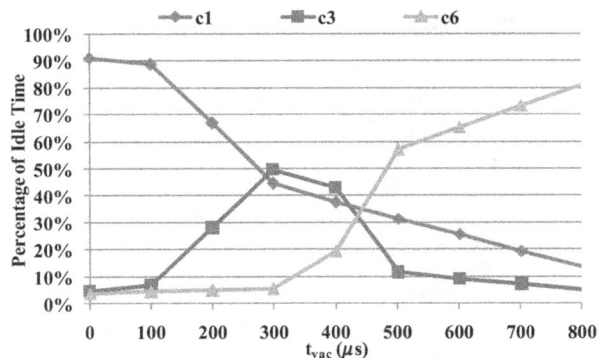

Figure 9. Percentage of idle period that the processor resides in the C-states under vacation for CRC. ($\rho=0.1$)

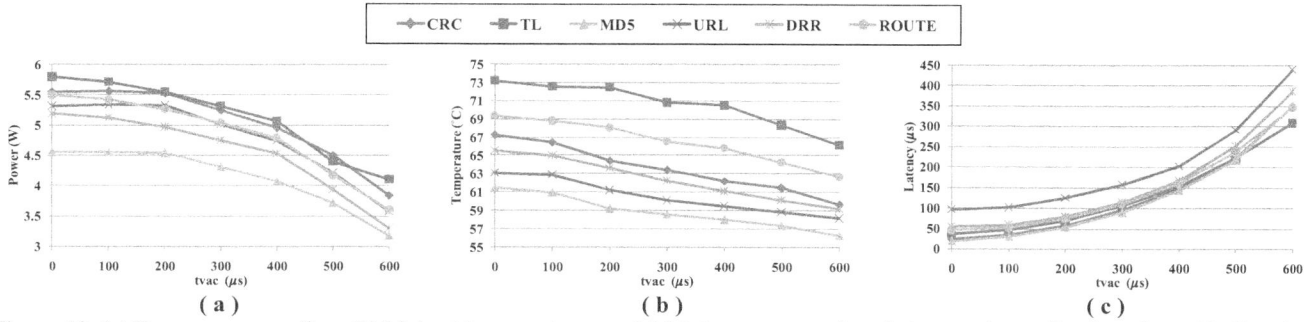

Figure 10. (a) Power consumption, (b) highest temperature, and (c) latency comparison between six applications from NetBench (ρ=0.3).

To further show that vacation approach achieves power saving through the use of processer C-states, we record the percentage of the idle time that the processer resides in different C-states under low traffic load. In Fig. 9, we can see that when $t_{vac} = 0$ and $\rho = 0.1$, processor spends more than 90% of the idle time in C1 state, the least power saving mode. When t_{vac} increases to 200μs, the processor starts to enter C3 state. When t_{vac} further increases beyond 500, processor enters C6 state and achieves higher power saving because there is long enough idle time. The slope of the power consumption in Fig. 7 increases between $t_{vac} = 400$ and 500μs, the processor spends majority of idle time in C6 states. As a result, the processor can't enter deeper C-state during these idle periods.

Fig. 10 shows the power consumption, temperature and latency for all six applications from NetBench. These applications are: *Cyclic Redundancy Check (CRC), Table lookup (TL), IPv4 Routing (Route), Deficit-Round Robin (DRR) scheduling, URL-based switching (URL), and Message Digest algorithm (MD5)*. We can see that except for the quantity, the performance curves are very similar for all applications. It's because the results are the average performance over a long run (processing over 10 million packets), and are dependent on the expected value of service time and active power consumption. The larger the active power of the application is, the higher the power saving and temperature reduction are after applying vacation. Also, the longer the packet processing time, the larger the latency will be.

4.2 Modified Vacation Approach

We modified the vacation scheme so that the processor will start vacation as soon as the queue becomes empty. Since there is no more packet to be processed we forcibly end the working period, so we should be able to observe more power saving. The comparison between vacation (VAC) and modified vacation (mVAC) scheme are shown in Fig. 11. Fig. 11a shows the experimental result of power consumption with different vacation time for modified vacation. We can see that the power consumption drops when t_{vac} reaches 200μs corresponding to the processor entering C3 state in the vacation period. The power consumption further drops when t_{vac} reaches 400μs, when the processor starts to enter C6 state. Also, modified vacation approach can achieve higher power saving because there is no short idle time, which prevents the processor from entering deep C states during the working period. To confirm the power consumption is actually coming from the use of deeper C-state, the percentage of idle time that the processor spent in each C-state is shown in Fig. 12. We can see that the C3 and C6 residencies increase at t_{vac}= 200 and 400μs, which confirms our statement for the power consumption. Also, compared with Fig. 9, we can see that the C1 residency is less than 5% when t_{vac} is greater than 300μs, which suggests that the modified vacation approach indeed packed all the idle periods into vacation period, and effectively uses the deep C state for power saving.

The temperature reduction results are shown in Fig. 11b. We can see that the modified vacation approach achieves better temperature reduction than the original one, especially when t_{vac} is large (2°C more temperature reduction when $t_{vac} = 800\mu$s). It's because at high t_{vac}, the heat up duration is significantly shorter, 200μs in original and 90μs in modified vacation, but with less than 25% power consumption increasing, which is the source of heat generation. When t_{vac} is smaller, the benefit of shorter heat up duration and

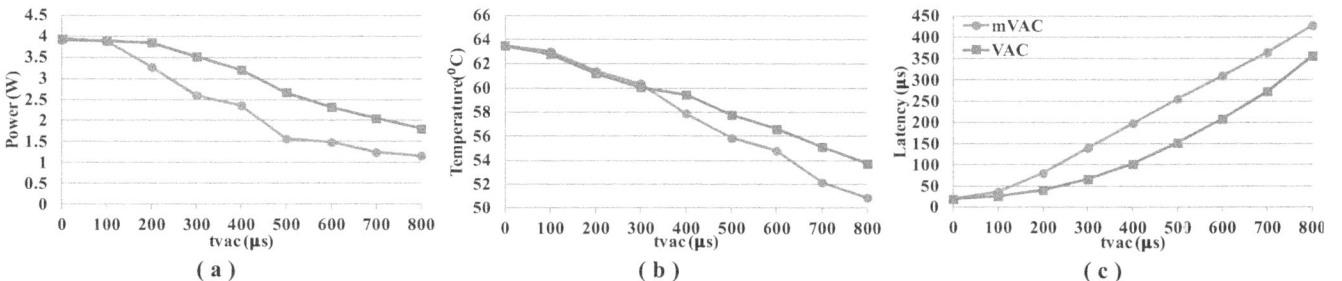

Figure 11. (a) Power consumption, (b)highest temperature, and (c) latency comparison between modified vacation (blue line) and original vacation approach (red line) with CRC form NetBench ($\rho = 0.1$).

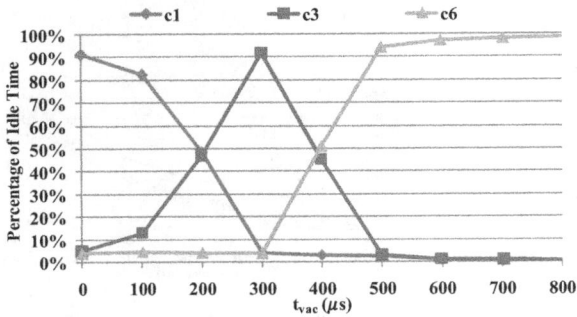

Figure 12. Percentage of idle period that the processor resides in the C-states under modified vacation for CRC. (ρ=0.1)

the harm of higher heat generation are close to each other, so the temperature reduction of modified vacation is similar to the original vacation.

Although modified vacation outperforms the original vacation in both power saving and temperature reduction, it suffers from higher latency. Fig. 11c shows the latency comparison between two approaches. When ρ is low, the working period is shortened, the possibility that the packet arrives during vacation period is increased, and those packets will have to wait for the vacation to end, which causes higher latency.

4.3 Rate adaptation Approach

In rate adaptation approach, the performance is dependent on the operating frequency of the processor, and the incoming traffic rate. In our experimental platform, we have 15 different frequency settings from 1.6 to 3.4GHz.

Fig. 13a shows the power consumption with different frequency and traffic load. We can see that the power consumption does not decrease significantly compared with the previous two approaches. It is because the idle time decreases and reduces the chance for processor to enter C state to save power. On the other hand, this approach can achieve power saving while the traffic load is high. In the previous approaches, for the system stability, the length of vacation period is limited while the traffic load is high. The period is not long enough to utilize deeper C state. However, rate adaptation can achieve power saving through reducing active power consumption.

The temperature result and the comparison are shown in Fig. 13b; the temperature reduction is less compared with the previous two approaches because of the active power consumption. Due to the nature of the processor thermal behavior [13], the temperature will vary around the steady state temperature depending on the average power consumption. Since the idle time is short, there is almost no cooling, and the temperature can be approximated as the steady state temperature. In rate adaptation approach, less power consumption decreasing results in smaller temperature reduction compared with vacation approach.

Although the power saving and temperature reduction are not as good as previous two approaches, the advantage of rate adaptation is that it has less packet latency. Fig. 13c gives the packets latency with different frequency and traffic load. We can see that the latency is considerably less than those in the vacation approaches. It's because the packet doesn't have to wait for the vacation, it can be processed as long as there is no packet in front of it in the queue.

Fig. 14 shows the power consumption, temperature and latency for all six applications we choose from NetBench. The result shows that the power saving and temperature reduction of TL, DRR and Route are worse than the other three applications. It's because that these three applications exhibit large amount of memory access. Since the power consumed by the memory access will not benefit from decreasing the operating frequency, power saving and temperature reduction are decreased. For the latency, all six applications behave similarly except for the quantity, which is determined by the expected value of the packet processing time.

5. PERFORMANCE ESTIMATION

5.1 Queuing Analysis

In Section 4.1-4.3, we show that the performances of our proposed approaches are highly dependent on the traffic load and the design parameters. To predict performance without conducting experiments, we propose the performance estimation model by applying queuing theory. The model will be used to develop a runtime scheduler in the next section.

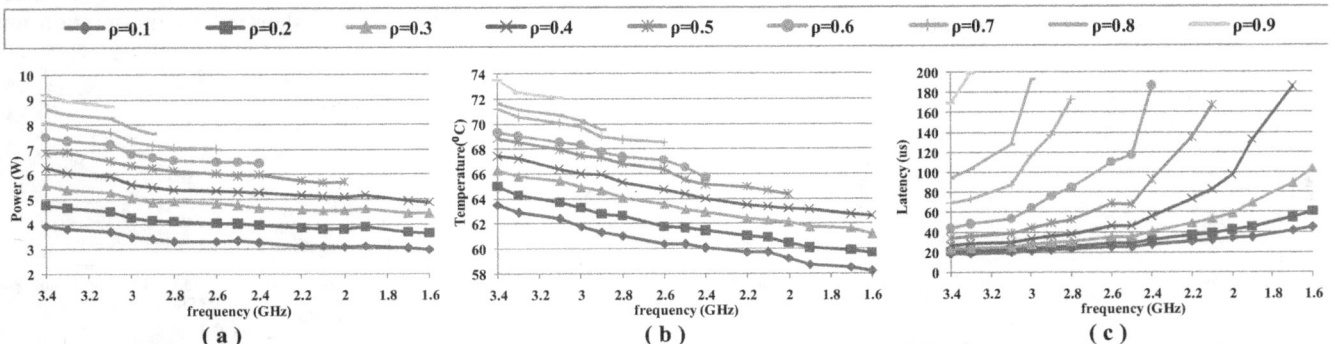

Figure 13. (a) Power consumption, (b) highest temperature, and (c) latency under rate adaptation approach with CRC form Net-Bench.

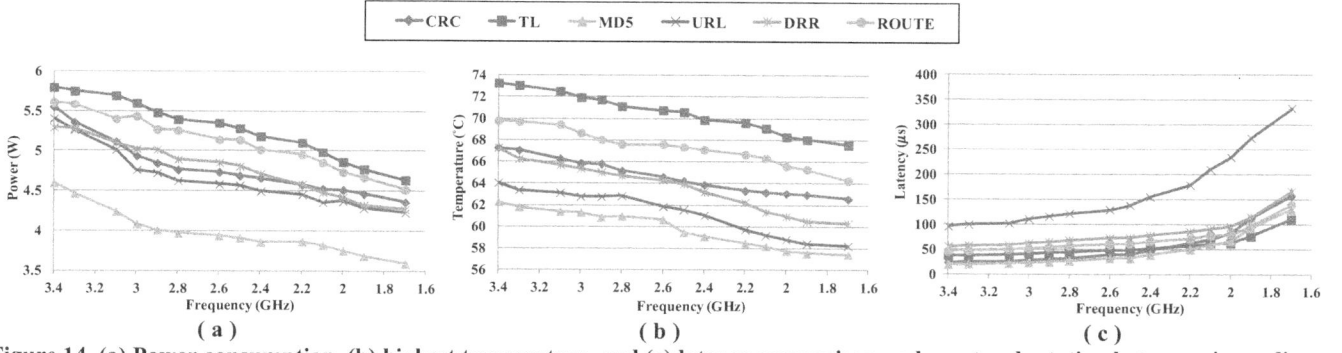

Figure 14. (a) Power consumption, (b) highest temperature, and (c) latency comparison under rate adaptation between six applications from NetBench ($\rho=0.4$).

5.1.1 Vacation approach

As mentioned previously, there are two states in vacation approach, working and vacation. In vacation state, the processor stays in the idle state (C1, C3 or C6), with power consumption P_s, for t_{vac}. On the other hand, in the working period, the processor is either active when processing packet, or idle when the queue is empty. Thus, we compute the power model as

$$
\begin{aligned}
P_{avg} &= \frac{P_{work} \times t_{work} + P_s \times t_{vac}}{t_{cycle}} \\
&= \frac{\left(P_a \times \frac{\rho}{\alpha} + P_i \times \left(1 - \frac{\rho}{\alpha}\right)\right) \times t_{work} + P_s \times t_{vac}}{t_{cycle}} \\
&= P_a \times \rho + P_i \times (\alpha - \rho) + P_s \times (1 - \alpha)
\end{aligned}
\tag{1}
$$

, where $t_{cycle} = t_{work} + t_{vac}$, $\alpha = \frac{t_{work}}{t_{cycle}}$ and $\frac{\rho}{\alpha}$ is the effective load in the working state. Thus, for the system to be stable, the condition $\rho < \alpha$ needs to be satisfied.

To derive the general temperature behavior model, we use the thermal equivalent lumped RC model [13] and simplified to the core level. Due to the two states, the temperature will rise and fall constantly and can be formulated as

$$
\begin{aligned}
T_{vac}(t) &= T_{vac}(0) e^{-\frac{t}{RC}} + P_s R \left(1 - e^{-\frac{t}{RC}}\right) && ,0 \le t \le t_{vac} \\
T_{work}(t) &= T_{work}(0) e^{-\frac{t}{RC}} + P_{work} R \left(1 - e^{-\frac{t}{RC}}\right) && ,0 \le t \le t_{work}
\end{aligned}
\tag{2}
$$

, where R and C are thermal resistance and capacitance, respectively.

Although the temperature will not converge to steady state, we could derive the thermal behavior in the equilibrium state. By letting $T_{vac}(t_{vac})=T_{work}(0)$, and $T_{vac}(0)=T_{work}(t_{work})$, we can have the maximum temperature, T_h, as

$$
T_h = \left(P_s(1-\alpha)\left(1 - \frac{\alpha t_{cycle}}{RC}\right) + P_a \times \rho + P_i \times (\alpha - \rho) \right) R
\tag{3}
$$

, where we took the first two term of Taylor expansion of exponential function.

The vacation approach achieves power saving by altering the distribution of the idle periods between packet pro-

cessing. However, it also introduces additional latency. When a packet arrives during the vacation state, it's processing is delayed until the next working state. For a packet arriving during the working state, it needs to wait until the previously buffered packets are all processed. We follow a walking (vacation) server queuing model to model the behavior [5]. Basically, the service rate of the server is modified to account for the fixed sleep or vacation time. The behavior is similar to the single token ring network, which is widely used in telecommunication system. In ring network, each station can transmit packets only when it has the token, and token will be passed to the next station after a period of time. The station will acquire the token after the token have rotated through all other stations. The vacation approach is equivalent to the station in single token ring network with fix token held time and rotation time, thus we can use the technique proposed in [18,19] to analyze the latency. The latency model is given as

$$
E(W) = \frac{E(S_r)}{\rho(\alpha - \rho)} + (2 - \alpha)\left(E(S) - E(S_r)\right)
\tag{4}
$$

, where S_r is the mean residual service time.

5.1.2 Modified Vacation approach

In modified vacation scheme, the processor is always busy during working period, so the problem becomes how to estimate the length of working period. We choose to use mean value analysis to get the average working period time, and derive the average power consumption as:

$$
\begin{aligned}
t_{work} &= \frac{\rho}{1-\rho} t_{vac} \\
P_{avg} &= \frac{P_a \times \frac{\rho}{1-\rho} t_{vac} + P_s \times t_{vac}}{\frac{\rho}{1-\rho} t_{vac} + t_{vac}} \\
&= P_a \times \rho + P_s \times (1-\rho)
\end{aligned}
\tag{5}
$$

For the temperature, we use the same analysis as in equation 6-7, and have the maximum temperature, T_h, as

$$
T_h = \left(P_s\left(1 - \frac{\rho t_{vac}}{RC}\right) + P_a \times \rho \right) R
\tag{6}
$$

In order to estimate the latency of packets, we find out that since the working period will end when the queue becomes empty or timer expired, the system is equivalent to a single-server queue with vacation and non-gated time-limited service. Since there is no close form solution of the latency, the authors in [4] proposed an approximate solution to it. However, this solution requires solving a large amount of linear equations, which make it time consuming and not suitable in our case.

We propose to use mean value analysis to analyze the packet latency in modified vacation approach. We assume that the working period time limit is large enough to avoid packet being deferred to the next working period. Under this assumption, we can have latency as

$$E(W) = \frac{E(S_r)}{(1-\rho)} + \frac{t_{vac}}{2} \tag{7}$$

In section 4, we will show that this assumption is valid in most of cases, which makes our analysis useful.

5.1.3 Rate adaptation approach

Since we change the operating frequency in rate adaptation approach, the packet processing time will be affected and the relation is given as

$$E(S_f) = \left(\frac{1}{\beta} + \left(1 - \frac{1}{\beta}\right)\gamma\right)E(S) \tag{8}$$

, where β is the ratio of the chosen operating frequency to the maximum frequency, and γ is the portion of the packet processing time that does not scale with frequency change.

The difference between rate adaptation and base line case is that the packet processing time is now longer. In addition, the active power P_a is proportional to the frequency, thus we can have the power consumption estimation:

$$P_{avg} = \beta P_a^{max} \times \rho_f + P_i \times (1 - \rho_f)$$
$$\rho_f = \lambda E(S_f) \tag{9}$$

, where P_a^{max} is the power consumption under maximum operating frequency.

For the temperature and latency, they follow the same principle of base line case:

$$\max(T_f(t)) = P_{avg}R \tag{10}$$
and

$$E(W) = \frac{\rho_f E(S_f^2)}{2(1-\rho_f)E(S_f)} + E(S_f) \tag{11}$$

5.2 Model Verification

In this subsection, we compare the results of our analytical model with the experimental results to show the accuracy of our models.

Since our proposed approaches are based on the mean value analysis of the non-deterministic queuing system, the accuracy is dependent on the amount of randomness. Fig. 15 shows the average estimation error of our three proposed approaches for different NetBench applications. The bar gives the average error of all the configurations (incom-

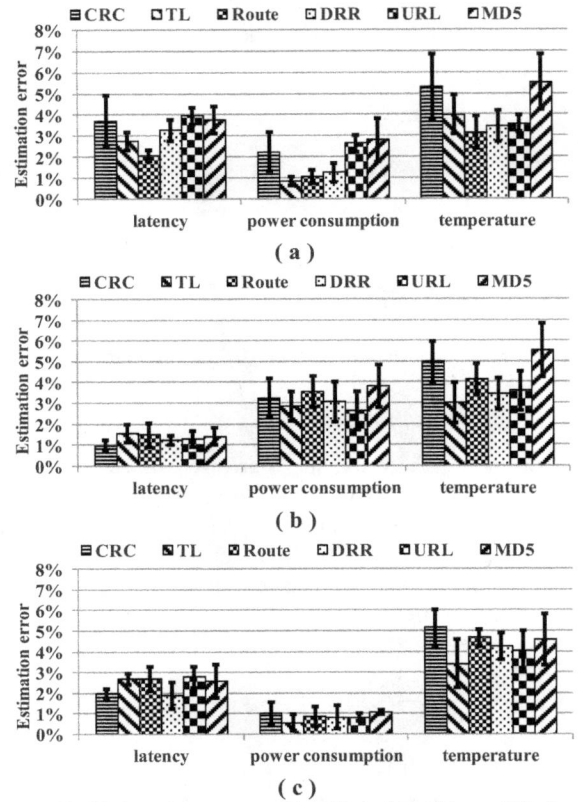

Figure 15. Estimation error of (a) Vacation, (b) modified vacation, and (c) rate adaptation approach.

ing traffic, t_{vac}, and frequency), and the dark line at the top gives the standard deviation. First, our models have high accuracy, with less than 6% of estimation error for all the six applications with three approaches (Fig. 15 a, b, and c).

In modified vacation, the model gives the lowest error of latency among all three approaches. It's because the latency is mainly caused by the waiting time during the vacation period, which can be modeled accurately. The rate adaptation model has the lowest power consumption estimation error, it's because the prolonged packet processing time reduces the amount of processor idle period.

The temperature error is the highest among all three performance matrices in all three models. It's because we simplified the temperature behavior by taking the first two terms of Taylor expansion of exponential function, which work as a linearization of a non-linear function. Also, temperature is more sensitive to the unpredictable system event, such as OS interrupt, which will affect the accuracy of the temperature models.

6. RUNTIME DEVELOPMENT

In section 4, we showed the effectiveness of our proposed three approaches, and in section 5, we developed an estimation model for performances under different incoming traffic. In this section, we propose *Trafficlight*, a thermal and power aware scheduler for packet processing, which moni-

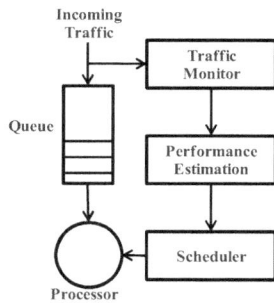

Figure 16. Overview of *trafficLight*.

tors the incoming traffic, estimates the working and vacation periods, and compares with DVFS using the analytical models. Then it dynamically chooses the one of the three approaches to achieve either highest power saving or lowest latency while satisfying the latency requirement and power budget, respectively, without violating the temperature constraint.

6.1 Trafficlight overview

Fig. 16 shows the overview of the proposed runtime *trafficlight* consisting of three major components: *traffic monitor, performance estimator and scheduler*. The traffic monitor will continuously record the arrival packet count and a timer. By dividing the number of the arrival packets and the time, it can have the traffic load within the monitoring period. Also, it will compare the traffic load with the previous monitoring period; if the difference is larger than a threshold σ, it will pass the new traffic load to the performance estimator.

Based on the incoming traffic load, the performance estimator will calculate the design parameter (t_{vac} in vacation and frequency in rate adaptation) by using the performance model proposed in section 5. We implement two different performance requirement scenarios: (1) achieve maximum power saving under latency constraint, and (2) achieve lowest latency under power budget. Also, the temperature constraint cannot be violated under both scenarios. In the first scenario, the estimator will calculate the boundary values of the design parameters, lower bounds for vacation or upper bound for rate adaptation, which satisfy the temperature constraint. Then it calculates the upper bound for vacation or lower bound for rate adaptation to meet the latency constraint. At last, it finds the configuration with the highest power saving within the boundary, and passes it to the scheduler. In the second scenario, after calculating the boundary to satisfy the temperature constraint, the estimator will find the boundary to satisfy the power budget, and then find the lowest latency within the range of the intersection of those two boundaries. At the final step, the scheduler will choose the highest power saving or lowest latency among all three approaches, and apply the approach with the design parameters to the processor.

Table 2. Characteristics of six network applications from NetBench.

Name	Power (watt)	Time E_i (μs)	T_{ss}(°C)
CRC	10.3	0.004×pkt size+0.34	83
TL	11.6	24.13	84
Route	9.8	18.66	82
DRR	10.1	15.320	83
URL	9	0.003×pkt size+13.54	82
MD5	7.2	0.0049×pkt size+3.64	81

6.2 Trafficlight Performance Evaluation

For performance evaluation, we implement the *trafficlight* on an Intel Ivybridge processor, and the experiments are conducted with six network application benchmarks from the NetBench suite [14] on a real Linux operating system. The six benchmarks we choose are listed in Table 2. The packet size ranges from 40 bytes to 1500 bytes with an average of 743 bytes. For the incoming traffic load, we run our benchmark applications with the 24-hour traffic trace from Equinix [20]. The traffic variation is drawn in Fig. 17. Also, the arrival pattern is Poisson arrivals, which means that the packets inter-arrival time is exponential distribution. For machine measurement, we use one core of the Intel Ivybridge to run benchmark applications, and one core to generate packets based on the traffic traces. Power consumption and temperature readings are collected from the machine specific register (MSR).

In this section, we first show the effectiveness of *trafficlight* for the scenario that achieves the highest power saving while satisfying latency and temperature constraints. The thermal constraint is set to be 10°C below the T_{ss}, which is the steady state temperature of the continuous packet processing, and the latency constraint is set to be 150μs. Fig. 17 shows the power saving of taking three approaches individually and the *trafficlight* as time proceeds and traffic load changes. The figure shows the average values of all the applications, presented in Table 2. We can see that the rate adaptation outperforms the other two approaches during hours 1-6 and 13-15, when the traffic load is high ($\rho > 0.6$). The original vacation and modified vacation can

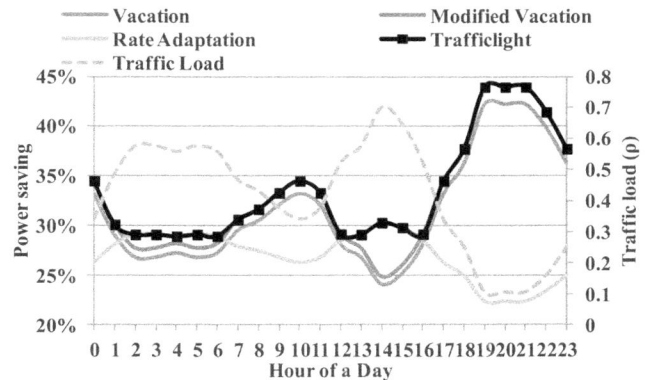

Figure 17. Trafficlight power saving under temperature and latency constraint.

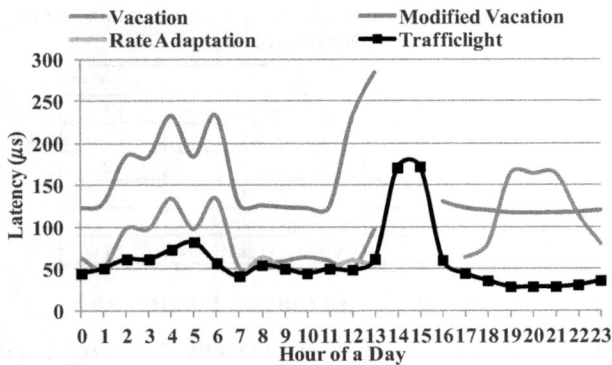

Figure 18. Trafficlight latency under temperature constraint and power budget.

achieve significant power saving when traffic is low, during hours 19-21, by effectively using processor C-states.

In Fig. 18, we show the *trafficlight* performance, average over all applications, under the scenario to achieve the lowest latency while satisfying power budget and temperature constraint. The thermal constraint is set to be 10°C below the T_{ss}, and the power budget is set to be 70% of the active power consumption of the application. We can see that *trafficlight* will select rate adaptation most of the time, because at high traffic load ($\rho > 0.5$), the vacation and modified vacation can only satisfy power budget by using large t_{vac}, which leads to high latency. Also, these two approaches failed to meet power budget when $\rho > 0.6$.

7. CONCLUSION

In this paper, we propose a thermal aware scheduler, *TrafficLight*, which achieves power saving by employing vacation and rate adaptation techniques. We implement these through the idle states (C-state) provided by the OS in a CPU and show their effectiveness through experimental data. Then we build power, thermal and latency models based on the vacation queuing theory, which estimates the performance of our proposed techniques. Finally, we design, implement and evaluate an on-line algorithm to dynamically choose the proper power/thermal management technique based on the traffic variation. To verify the model and evaluate the scheduler, we use a real Linux server to run six applications chosen from NetBench benchmark suite. Extensive results showed that our scheduler is capable of maximizing power saving while satisfying latency requirements and minimizing latency under power budget without violating thermal constraint. Future work includes evaluating the proposed method in a CMP with three or more cores, investigating the effectiveness of the method with packet transmitting over real network, and the impact of TCP/IP protocol.

REFERENCES

[1] M. Dobrescu, N. Egi, K. Argyraki, B.-G. Chun, K. Fall, G.Iannaccone, A. Knies, M. Manesh, and S. Ratnasamy. RouteBricks:Exploiting Parallelism to Scale Software Routers. SOSP,2009.

[2] Y. Ma, S. Banerjee, S. Lu, and C. Estan. Leveraging Parallelismfor Multi-dimensional Packet Classification on Software Routers. SIGMETRICS, 2010.

[3] K. Jang, S. Han, S. Han, S. Moon, and K. Park. SSLShader:Cheap SSL Acceleration with Commodity Processors. NSDI, 2011.

[4] M. Eisenberg and K.K. Leung, A single-server queue with vacations and non-gated time-limited service, Performance Evaluation, 1991.

[5] N. Tian, andZ.G. Zhang, Vacation queueing models: theory and applications . Springer,2006.

[6] R. Kravetsa, and P. Krishnanb. Application-driven power management for mobile communication. Wireless Networks, 2000.

[7] D. Meisner, B. Gold, and T. Wenisch. PowerNap: Eliminating Server Idle Power. ASPLOS, 2009.

[8] W. Yuan and K. Nahrstedt. Energy-efficient Soft Real- time CPU Scheduling for Mobile Multimedia Systems. SOSP. 2003.

[9] Y. Luo, J. Yu, J. Yang, and L. Bhuyan. Conserving network processor power consumption by exploiting traffic variability. TACO, 2007.

[10] S. Nedevschi, L. Popa, G. Iannaccone, S. Ratnasamy, and D. Wetherall. Reducing Network Energy Consumption via Sleeping and Rate-Adaptation. NSDI, 2008.

[11] N. El-Sayed, I. A. Stefanovici, G. Amvrosiadis, A. A. Hwang, and B. Schroeder, "Temperature Management in Data Centers: Why Some (Might) Like It Hot," SIGMETRICS, 2012.

[12] J. Srinivasan, S. V. Adve, P. Bose, and J. A. Rivers, "The Case for Lifetime Reliability-Aware Microprocessors," in ISCA, 2004.

[13] K. Skadron, T. Abdelzaher, M.R. Stan, Control-theoretic techniques and thermal- RC modeling for accurate and localized dynamic thermal management, HPCA, 2002.

[14] G. Memik, W. H. Mangione-Smith, and W. Hu, "Netbench:A benchmarking suite for network processors," ICCAD, 2001.

[15] J. Kuang, L. Bhuyan "Thermal-aware Scheduling of Network Applications on Multicore Architecture," ANCS, 2009.

[16] T. Benson, A. Akella, and D. Maltz. Network traffic characteristics of data centers in the wild. IMC, 2010.

[17] Desktop 3rd Gen Intel® Core™ Processor Family: Datasheet.http://www.intel.com/content/www/us/en/processors/core/3rd-gen-core-desktop-vol-1-datasheet.html

[18] L. N. Bhuyan , D. Ghosal and Q. Yang "Approximate analysis of single and multiple ring networks", *IEEE Trans. Comput.*, vol. 38, no. 7, pp.1027 -1040 1989

[19] J. Xie, M. J. Fischer, and C. M. Harris. "Workload and waiting time in a fixed-time loop system." Computers & operations research, 1997.

[20] "Equinix", http://www.caida.org/

Fine-Grained Power Scaling Algorithms for Energy Efficient Routers

Tian Song
School of Computer Science
Beijing Institute of Technology
Beijing, P.R.China 100081
songtian@bit.edu.cn

Xiangjun Shi
School of Computer Science
Beijing Institute of Technology
Beijing, P.R.China 100081
shixiangjun@bit.edu.cn

Xiaowei Ma
School of Computer Science
Beijing Institute of Technology
Beijing, P.R.China 100081
xwma@bit.edu.cn

ABSTRACT

Energy efficient router is one of the most important and promising devices in the roadmap towards green communication and networking. In recent years, automatic power scaling adapting with real-time network traffic in a router has been proved to be practical on real hardware, which is an implementation under the traffic aware philosophy. In this paper, we further explore this direction, and present four real-time power scaling algorithms for the fine-grained energy management within a router. These algorithms are all based on the traffic aware philosophy. We first classify the traffic characteristics into three categories of the core router, access router and home router and analyze the differences among them. Then, we propose two design methodologies, periodical scaling and threshold scaling, and address four algorithms in details. Finally, we use real network traffic to evaluate these algorithms and draw the conclusions. The experiments on real traffic show that more than 40% of the energy in a router can be saved by using proposed system-level power scaling methods. Based on those evaluations, we also find that three status modes with two working frequencies and a sleep in a router are enough to achieve near-optimal energy efficiency by using our algorithms, which indicates an easy and practical hardware modification.

Categories and Subject Descriptors

C.2.6 [**Computer-Communication Networks**]: Internetworking; C.2.1 [**Computer-Communication Networks**]: Network Architecture and Design; C.2.0 [**Computer-Communication Networks**]: General

General Terms

Algorithms; Measurement; Performance

Keywords

green network; traffic analysis; energy efficient router; frequency scaling

1. INTRODUCTION

As the growth of Internet traffic is taking shape, the concern of energy consumption in network infrastructure, especially wired networks, is becoming increasingly important for network operators. Economizing the energy consumption not only can help to reduce CO_2 emissions but also can significantly reduce the ISP's cost. The energy consumption accounts for approximate 1% of the total energy demand in one country, and it costs about 70% of the ISP's operating cost [1], which indicates a direction of green networking.

The establishment of a standard for Energy Efficient Ethernet (EEE), IEEE 802.3az, was a great step in this area [2] in 2010. Two years later, Ethernet NICs with EEE were available in real life in 2012. EEE exploits an automatical sleep-wake mechanism to switch between an active awake and a low power sleep mode in a network device in order to gain energy efficiency in the link layer. Experiments show that EEE is efficient in most of cases.

Our work takes a step further in the network layer. The router, as one of the basic elements in the network infrastructure, is one of the promising devices towards green networking and is worth re-thinking to design as being energy efficient [3]. To achieve system-level energy efficiency, rather than port-level saving in EEE, *energy efficient router*(EER) is suggested to be designed as self-control devices based on the traffic aware philosophy, in which they can automatically adapt their performance, further energy, according to the actual load of the network traffic.

Fig.1 summarizes a general architecture of contemporary high-speed routers, where line cards or ports are abstracted as parallel pipelines. When an incoming traffic arrives, the router buffers packets to the FIFOs, processes them one by one, performs the lookup by forwarding engines, and forwards them appropriately.

According to the definition, an energy efficient router should be aware of the actual load of network traffic. Thus, a traffic aware power scaling module is added to the general architecture of routers to bridge the gap between the processing capacity and the actual traffic load, as shown in Fig.1. This module monitors the input packet FIFOs and dynamically adapts the processing capacity of the internal components (in the scaling zone) to achieve lower energy consumption. Besides, some modules in the fixed zone should keep unchange in order to communicate with outside devices.

Two important questions should be answered in practice for Fig.1-like architecture design: how to engineer the internal components to output different capacities? and how to

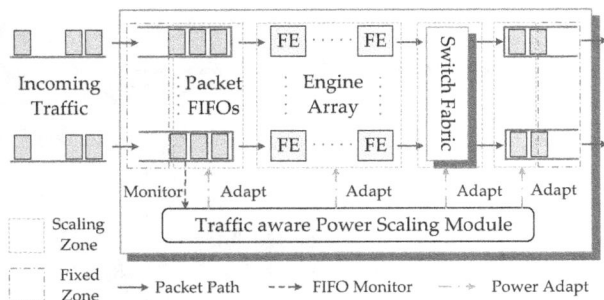

Figure 1: The architecture of power-scaling energy efficient routers.

dynamically adapt the processing capacity to achieve maximum energy efficiency according to the traffic?

For the first question, inspired by the DVFS (dynamic voltage and frequency scaling) techniques in Intel CPU, our vision is to engineer the internal components to work on multiple frequencies for energy efficient routers, so that the internal capacity, therefore the energy consumption, could be scaled according to the load of the network traffic. Our previous work [4] [5] [6] implemented a proof-of-concept prototype, an energy efficient reference router with frequency scaling, on NetFPGA platform [7], showing the feasibility and stability of the design. This prototype can adapt its frequency dynamically on five stages, from 125MHz to 42MHz.

This paper mainly focuses on the solution to the second question, i.e., to find easy and elegant traffic aware approaches to dynamically adapt the processing capacity to achieve maximum energy efficiency for the router.

Based on the implementation of our prototype, we found an important fact that further directs our work. The fact is that every switch of frequencies can be achieved within 160 ns (20 clock cycles in the 125MHz frequency). During the switch, the hardware data path is stopped and no packets can be processed. This incapable time is the cost for every frequency switch.

Given the incapable time of data path, the switch cost is small enough for the system to perform *fine-grained switching* on the scale of microsecond, compared to the millisecond scaling in Intel CPU. Fine-grained switching can harvest tiny spare time in an energy efficient router and save energy by scaling down the capacity. However, more switches also introduce more overhead. Our work is to design and evaluate power-scaling algorithms to balance the gains and costs to achieve maximum energy efficiency. Although our methods are proposed towards the frequency scaling, they can also be applied to other power-scaling scenarios, such as voltage scaling. Our work is carried out step by step as follows.

Firstly, we collected and analyzed three types of network traffic from the core routers (10Gbps), access/metro routers (2.5Gbps) and home routers (100Mbps). Statistics show that the average bandwidth is less than 30% of the maximum capacity for each type. Together with the calculation of ON/OFF periods, our observations on real traffic form the design space for scaling based energy efficiency.

Then, we proposed two design methodologies, periodical scaling and threshold scaling, on behalf of time and space design ideas separately. Periodical scaling triggers the frequency switching in a regular period of time. While, threshold scaling triggers the switching by setting multiple thresholds in the packet FIFOs. They are feasible and reachable approaches in practice.

We also introduced two modes, active and passive, to the algorithms. In active mode, routers tend to process arrived packets at the earliest time and adapt the capacities more frequently. While in passive mode, routers tend to accumulate packets and process them in shorter time with high capacity and keep more time in the sleep mode. Two modes were foreseen in [1], but it is still an open question till now, i.e., which one is better in the energy consumption for real traffic? In details, we presented and formulated four power-scaling algorithms, and tried to answer this question by using real traces.

The main contributions of this paper are as followings:

- We analyzed three types of real traffic from the core routers, access routers and home routers, and showed the design opportunities for the energy efficient routers with scaling in the view of network loads.

- We studied the principles to implement frequency scaling for routers in practice, and proposed four algorithms in detail based on two design methodologies, periodical scaling and threshold scaling.

- We simulated the four algorithms using real network traffic in two cases, three frequencies and six frequencies, and drew the conclusion that our methods can generally save 40% power consumption. We also addressed the algorithm choices for different situations.

- We compared and evaluated the active and passive modes in power scaling. Results show that active methods have shorter packet latency and buffer length. Both active and passive modes are useful to achieve energy efficiency. In the case of six frequencies, all algorithms perform well enough in power consumption.

The remainder of the paper is organized as follows. In Section 2, we review some works related to this paper. Section 3 analyzes three different network traffic and shows the power scaling design space from coarse-grained power scaling to fine-grained scaling methods. In Section 4, we study the principles to adapt the performance according to the network traffic, and propose four practical algorithms. Section 5 presents some numerical results that illustrate our finding and evaluate our algorithms. Section 6 concludes our work.

2. RELATED WORKS

Green network devices have attracted a lot of research attentions in recent years [1] [8] [9]. The first step is the energy efficient ethernet, which has been solved by establishing an IEEE standard [2]. The second step is the energy efficient devices, including system-level methods [10] and optical devices [11]. The proposed methods can be classified into two categories: *smart standby* and *dynamic power scaling*.

2.1 Smart Standby

Smart standby approaches allow devices or part of them fall asleep and enter low energy state to conserve energy. In 2003, M.Gupta *et al.* first explored a method to determine whether the interfaces should sleep by predicting packets interval [12] [13]. This method relies on the distribution of the interval of packets arrival. The method is improved by storing packets in the buffer temporarily. The interfaces will stay in a low-power state until the queue of buffer exceeds a set threshold. G.Ananthanarayanan *et al.* proposed a novel architecture for buffering ingress packets using shadow ports which can receive packets when conventional ports are in low-power state [14].

A.Vishwanath *et al.* [15] introduced an algorithm that activates buffers incrementally as needed and puts them to sleep when not in use. Thresholds are set to trigger on-chip buffers, SRAM and DRAM dynamically. The experiments prove that 10% of the total line-card energy can be saved.

2.2 Dynamic Power Scaling

Dynamic power scaling approaches, also known as dynamic adaptation, allow the software or devices to dynamically modulate capacities according to the actual (or predicted) traffic load and service requirements.

M.Mandviwalla *et al.* studied the linecards of backbone routers and scaled the voltage dynamically by using prediction methods. Because the consumption of multiprocessor-based linecards accounts for the most in power consumption of routers, their results showed that the power consumption can be saved up to 60% by scaling the voltage [16]. However, the results are specific to some platforms.

S.Nedevschi *et al.* considered both sleeping scheme and rate-adaptation for different modules to reduce network energy consumption [17]. Besides, they showed the potential of energy saving with a small and bounded impact on performance by dynamic power scaling in specific hardware.

W.Fu *et al.*, our group, implemented a dynamic frequency scaling reference router on NetFPGA platform, which proved the feasibility of the concept [4] [5].

Previous works provided insight visions but lacked the practical level considerations. For example, traffic prediction based scaling methods introduce complicated calculation and unnecessary metempirical feedback, although they have good theoretical results. Our work tries to present feasible algorithms that can be used in the real systems.

3. POWER SCALING DESIGN SPACE

In this section, we analyze the real traffic from different types of routers and show the power scaling design space.

3.1 Understanding the Traffic on Routers

3.1.1 Data Collection

We collected traffic data for three sources. One is a seven-day traffic from a 100 Mbps router in our laboratory, which can be regarded as the trace of *home router*. The other two data, 2.5 Gbps [18] and 10 Gbps [19], are one-day traffic obtained from CAIDA, and they represent data from *access router* and *core router* respectively.

3.1.2 Traffic Overview

Fig.2 gives a one-hour overview from the three network traffic in the scale of second. Statistical results show that the average bandwidth utilization (flow rate) of three types of real traffic, from the core router, access router and home router, are 3.71 Gbps (37.1%), 612 Mbps (24.5%) and 4.4 Mbps (4.4%), as shown in Table 1. The actual bandwidth utilization are all far less than the maximum bandwidth of

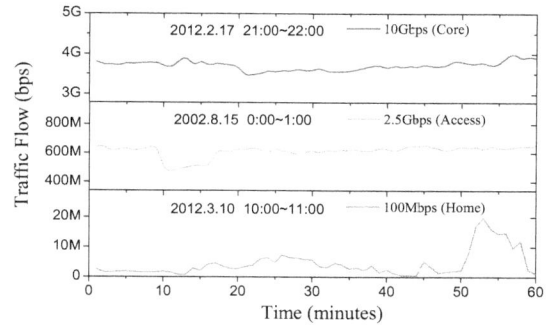

Figure 2: The overview of three types of network traffic in the scale of second.

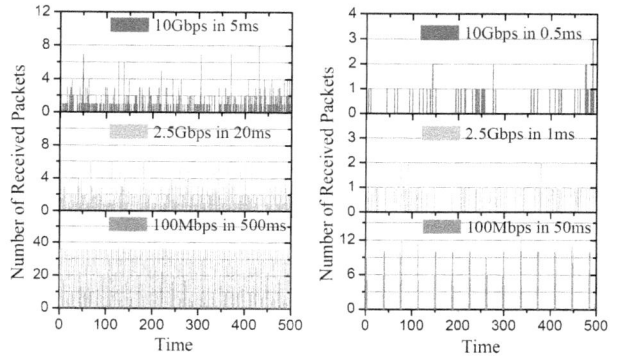

Figure 3: (a) Staging and (b) ON/OFF features in the scale of microsecond.

devices, which gives the opportunities to gain energy efficiency for routers.

We also found that the small packets (less than 100 bytes) and large packets (more than 1450 bytes) account for a great part of packets in all traces. In the seven-day trace from home router, the average length of all packets is 929 bytes. Similarly, the average length of the one-day 2.5 Gbps and 10 Gbps traffic are 656 bytes and 872 bytes respectively.

3.1.3 ON/OFF Period

The traffic on routers can be regarded as the superposition of multi-source ON/OFF traffic [20]. This model helps to understand and measure traffic theoretically. Here we only observe the traffic in time scale instead of discussing the model. During the ON periods, packets arrive at the router, while there is no packet during the OFF periods.

Fig.3 shows the staging and ON/OFF features of traffic in the time scale of microsecond, even for 10 Gbps traffic. Taking one ON and the next OFF as a period, Table 1 shows the average period and proportion for the three traces.

For the 10 Gbps trace, the average ON/OFF period is 4.1 μs, and the proportion of ON against OFF is 1:1.2, i.e., there is about 50% idle time every 4 μs. For 2.5 Gbps, the average ON/OFF period is 10.2 μs, and the proportion of ON against OFF is 1:8. More idle time can be found. For 100 Mbps traces, the potential is much more than that.

To achieve energy efficiency, we should find and harvest any possible idle time or lower load of traffic with scaling if the scaling cost is economic. The above observations intro-

Table 1: Characteristics of three types of network traffic.

Traffic type	Sources	Max. Bandwith	Avg. bandwidth util.	ON/OFF period	ON/OFF proportion	Avg. packet length
Core router	one-day, CAIDA [19]	10 Gbps	37.1%	4.1 μs	1:1.2	872 B
Metro/access router	one-day, CAIDA [18]	2.5 Gbps	24.5%	10.2 μs	1:8	656 B
Home router	seven-day, author's lab	100 Mbps	4.4%	1.7 ms	1:1650	929 B

duce us to use capacity scaling (in the grain of staging) and smart standby (in the grain of ON/OFF) for energy efficient routers. In the rest of the paper, we describe our methods by using frequency scaling, instead of power scaling.

3.2 Design Space for Energy Efficient Routers

There are several opportunities to design energy efficient routers. As Fig.2 shows, the average traffic loads are around 30% for 10 Gbps and 2.5 Gbps networks, 5% for 100 Mbps network. That is, the maximum frequency has no need on average. We can save the energy reduced from the maximum frequency to the frequency with average workload.

Switching the maximum frequency to the average frequency according to the workload is a coarse-grained scaling opportunity. Furthermore, the staging feature in Fig.3 introduces a fine-grained frequency scaling opportunity that can save energy from the frequency with average workload to multiple frequencies working with different levels of workloads. ON/OFF feature gives the finest opportunity to switch frequency to sleep fragmentarily, saving more energy in the level of microsecond.

The application of the coarse- and fine-grained frequency scaling depends on several factors, such as the time and energy cost of frequency switching, the energy consumptions related to different frequencies, the implementation cost in the architecture of routers, and frequency scaling algorithms. Intuitively, fine-grained frequency scaling can save more energy since it digs into the microsecond level time interval and finds more opportunities than coarse-grained scaling. However fine-grained scaling has more switchings that can neutralize the (partial) benefits.

In the real system, referring to our prototype implementation [4] [5], the frequency switching needs only 160 ns. For 10 Gbps real traffic, there are only one to three packets arrived within 1 μs on average. Thus 160 ns is an acceptable switching cost that may introduce fine-grained frequency scaling to core, access and home routers.

4. FINE-GRAINED POWER SCALING ALGORITHMS

Power scaling can be achieved by many ways, such as smart standby by Ethernet when there is no traffic on the link, or scaling the CPU frequency depending on the number of issued instructions. Most of those methods will perform scaling after staying still for at least tens of milliseconds or even seconds because of the considerable switching time and cost. We named these scaling with the period of milliseconds and above as coarse-grained methods. While in fine-grained methods, the possible interval between every two scalings should be less than one millisecond, tens of microsecond in our work. Fine-grained scaling also means that we can use near real-time conditions to trigger the switching.

As Fig.1 shows, actual FIFOs (buffers) occupancy is considered as an indicator to measure the link speed in the

Table 2: Parameters

Notation	Meaning
Δt	the sampling interval
$\alpha \Delta t$	the maximum tolerant delay of packets
δ	the incapable time during frequency scaling
l_{max}	the maximum length of buffer
f_i	the ith frequency, defined as processing ability (packets) per unit of time. f_0 presents the sleep state ($f_0=0$) and f_m is the maximum frequency ($0 \leq i \leq m$)
$p(f_i)$	the power consumption at frequency f_i
$p(\delta)$	the additional energy consumption of each frequency scaling. The total cost also includes sleep mode energy during the switching time, as $p(f_0)\delta + p(\delta)$
th_i	the ith threshold in threshold scaling polies
$n(t)$	the number of packets arrived at time t
$l(t)$	the length of FIFO at t, defined as the number of packets
$f(t)$	the working frequency at time t

architecture of energy efficient routers. Then, the power scaling methods could be aware of the real traffic. All our power scaling methods in the following are based on this model. It is a posteriori way without any traffic predicting.

Based on the actual buffer indication, two design methodologies are used as trigger methods: periodical scaling and threshold scaling. In periodical scaling methods, a fixed period of time, Δt, is used as an interval between every two scaling judgements. At the end of Δt, the buffer occupancy is measured and frequency scaling is possibly triggered. While in threshold scaling methods, the buffer is partitioned by several thresholds, and scaling occurs when the actual buffer occupancy crosses those thresholds. The two trigger methodologies represent time and space partition separately.

We also introduce two working modes, active (diligent) and passive (lazy), to the algorithms. In active modes, algorithms tend to process the arrived packets as much as possible to make the buffer empty before the next trigger event. In passive modes, algorithms tend to get more time at the sleep state, so they accumulate packets and wait till some future trigger event to scale to the maximum capacity in which packets can be processed in shorter time.

The above design methods can be used in many power-scaling scenarios. To simplify our description, we take frequency scaling as an example to propose, formulate and evaluate detailed algorithms.

4.1 The Problem Definition

Our question towards frequency scaling can be described as the energy calculation of routers based on some traffic. The energy consumption is formulated as the following by using the parameters shown in Table 2.

$$minimum\{\sum_{t=0} p(f_i) + p(\delta) * W\} \qquad (1)$$

Here, W is the number of switchings from time 0 to t.

The question is to find the minimum energy consumption by using multiple frequencies. The energy consumption from 0 to time t consists of two parts in Eq.1: energy consumption contributed by multiple frequencies including sleep mode and the additional energy cost for frequency scaling. Here, we take three assumptions: 1) every frequency scaling, from f_i to f_j ($i \neq j$), has the same time and energy cost, where the energy cost includes a sleep mode energy consumption and additional energy cost, as $p(f_0)\delta + p(\delta)$; 2) the energy consumption of FIFOs are not related to the actual occupancy of packets, i.e., we do not consider dynamic buffer in [21]; 3) every calculation of power-scaling algorithms consumes no energy and time.

Energy efficient scheduling is generally a NP-hard problem [22]. All the proposed algorithms in our work are oriented to easy implementation based on Markov process. Essentially, they all belong to greedy type heuristic optimization.

4.2 Periodical Scaling

Periodical scaling takes a fixed time working period, Δt, as the scale of power scaling. Given the frequency of time t is f_i. If no scaling occurs, there is no additional time and energy cost, so the router can process packets in the next Δt time with f_i. If scaling occurs from f_i to f_j, there is δ incapable time, so the router can only handle packets in the next $(\Delta t - \delta)$ time with f_j. Therefore, algorithms have to balance this tradeoff.

Considering the active and passive mode, periodical scaling includes two algorithms, MinLP (Minimum Latency Periodical) and MaxLP (Maximum Latency Periodical).

MinLP takes the idea to make the packet delay as short as possible and minimize the frequency used as low as possible. It adapts frequency to an appropriate capacity level which can deal with all the existing packets of the current buffer in the next Δt. Suppose MinLP is invoked at time t, with $l(t)$ buffer length and $f_i(= f(t))$ working frequency, to resolve the frequency of next Δt interval, $f(t + \Delta t)$, MinLP has two steps as follows, and the detailed algorithm is shown in Alg.1.

Step 1: Assuming that the router has to adapt frequency, find a minimum (also energy efficient) frequency, f_k, that can process $l(t)$ packets in the next $\Delta t - \delta$ period.

Step 2: Adapt the frequency as the following. If the queue is empty, adapt frequency to f_0 (sleep mode). Although $f_k > f_i$, meaning a higher frequency is needed, we can still maintain current frequency, f_i, if it can process all $l(t)$ packets in Δt time. If no frequency can process all packets in the next $\Delta t - \delta$ period, adapt to the highest frequency, f_m. Otherwise, the frequency in the next period should be scaled to f_k.

MaxLP is designed on the work-hard and sleep-deep policy. It favors buffering the packets as long as possible and invokes the higher frequency to process the packets in stock to gain more sleep time. It works with the requirement of maximum tolerant latency, $\alpha\Delta t$, of the system. Here, we define the *timestamp* of the buffer $l(t)$ as the timestamp of the first packet in it. MaxLP has two steps as follows based on MinLP, and the detailed algorithm is shown in Alg.2.

Algorithm 1 *MinLP* (Minimum Latency Periodical)

1: **Given** $f(t){=}f_i$, $l(t)$; **Output** $f(t + \Delta t)$;
2: **Solve** f_k, if $(\Delta t\text{-}\delta)^* f_{k-1} < l(t) \leq (\Delta t\text{-}\delta)^* f_k$ ($0 < k \leq m$);
3: **if** $l(t) == 0$ **then**
4:     $f(t + \Delta t) = f_0$;
5: **else if** $l(t) \leq \Delta t * f_i$ and $k > i$ **then**
6:     $f(t + \Delta t) = f_i$;
7: **else if** $l(t) > (\Delta t - \delta) * f_m$ **then**
8:     $f(t + \Delta t) = f_m$;
9: **else**
10:     $f(t + \Delta t) = f_k$;
11: **end if**

Step 1: Check the timestamp of the buffer every Δt interval. Wait and accumulate packets till the timestamp equals or exceeds the maximum latency at the check time.

Step 2: Adapt the frequency as the following. If the maximum latency is achieved, solve and adapt to a frequency by using MinLP algorithm (Alg. 1). Process the packets till the buffer is empty. Then adapt to sleep mode. Otherwise, keep the current status.

Algorithm 2 *MaxLP* (Maximum Latency Periodical)

1: **Given** $\alpha\Delta t$, $l(t)$; **Output** $f(t + \Delta t)$;
2: **if** $|timestamp(l(t)) - t| \geq \alpha\Delta t$ **then**
3:     **Solve** $f(t + \Delta t)$ by using MinLP (Alg.1);
4: **else if** $l(t){==}0$ **then**
5:     $f(t + \Delta t) = f_0$;
6: **else**
7:     **Remain** the current status
8: **end if**

Suppose we evaluate time from 0 to $\alpha\Delta t + s$, and s is the time for MaxLP to process all existing packets using maximum frequency and switch back to sleep mode. MinLP and MaxLP perform the scaling as the following separately.

$$\sum_{t=0}^{\alpha\Delta t + s} n(t) \leq \sum_{t=0}^{\alpha\Delta t + s} f(t); \quad \sum_{t=0}^{\alpha\Delta t + s} n(t) \leq s * f((\alpha + 1)\Delta t) \quad (2)$$

Based on Eq.2, the energy consumption for a given number of packets by using MinLP and MaxLP are shown in Eq.3 and Eq.4 separately.

$$\sum_{t=0}^{\alpha\Delta t + s} p(f(t)) + p(\delta) * W \qquad (3)$$

Here, $0 \leq W \leq \alpha + \frac{s}{\Delta t}$

$$\alpha\Delta t * p(f_0) + s * p(f((\alpha + 1)\Delta t)) + p(\delta) * 2 \qquad (4)$$

The above equations can be used to estimate energy consumptions for real traffic in the two algorithms of MinLP and MaxLP .

Obviously, as its definition, MinLP produces a shorter packet latency than MaxLP to process packets, while MaxLP may have better energy efficiency since the maximum tolerant latency, $\alpha\Delta t$, may help the router to gain more time in sleep mode. Section 5 will give further comparison based on results from real data set.

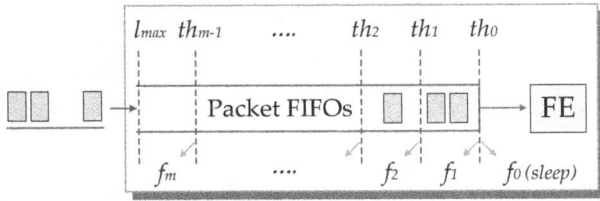

Figure 4: The description of threshold scaling.

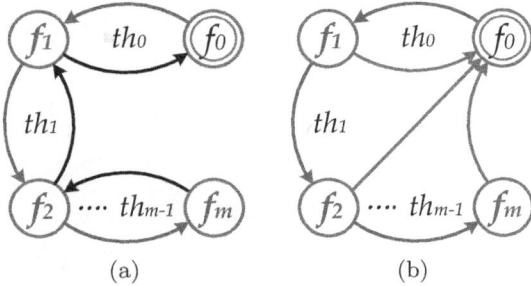

(a)   (b)

Figure 5: The state diagram of (a) SFT algorithm (b) MCT algorithm.

4.3 Threshold Scaling

In threshold based methods, there is no sampling period and the queue is monitored by using multiple thresholds. A threshold is set in the FIFO queue (buffer), defined as a percentage of the maximum length. It monitors the actual occupancy of the buffer. The different frequencies are set between thresholds as their working zones. When the actual length falls into a certain working zone, the frequency will be adapted to the corresponding level. The scaling algorithms can be triggered when the actual occupancy passes the threshold, as shown in Fig.4.

Threshold scaling includes two algorithms: Step-Followed Threshold (SFT) and Max-Cascade Threshold (MCT), representing active and passive modes.

SFT, as its name implies, adapts the frequency step by step to the actual occupancy of queue. Its policy to the length of queue demonstrates the faster processing for a longer buffer and the slower processing for a shorter one, showing energy efficiency in a heuristic way. Suppose there are m working frequencies, f_1, f_2, ..., f_m, and one sleep mode, f_0. m thresholds are required to distinguish them. The frequency is stepwise increased or decreased. The state diagram of SFT is shown in Fig.5(a), and the detailed algorithm is in Alg.3.

Algorithm 3 *SFT*, Step-Followed Threshold

1: **Given** $f(t)=f_i$, $l(t)$; **Output** $f(t+1)$;
2: **if** $l(t) < th_0$ **then**
3:     $f(t+1) = f_0$;
4: **else if** $th_0 \leq l(t) < th_1$ **then**
5:     $f(t+1) = f_1$;
6:     $\vdots$
7: **else if** $l(t) \geq th_{m-1}$ **then**
8:     $f(t+1) = f_m$;
9: **end if**

MCT separates the frequency increasing and decreasing apart. It allows the frequency to increase stepwise but to decrease only to the sleep mode, just like a cascade, from all working frequencies to sleep. The main idea of MCT tends to create more sleep time by keeping an appropriate frequency to handle packets until the buffer is empty. The state diagram is shown in Fig.5(b), and the algorithm is listed in Alg.4.

Algorithm 4 *MCT*, Max-Cascade Threshold

1: **Given** $f(t)=f_i$, $l(t)$; **Output** $f(t+1)$;
2: **if** $l(t) < th_0$ **then**
3:     $f(t+1) = f_0$;
4: **else if** $th_0 \leq l(t) < th_1$ and $f(t) \leq f_1$ **then**
5:     $f(t+1) = f_1$;
6: **else if** $th_1 \leq l(t) < th_2$ and $f(t) \leq f_2$ **then**
7:     $f(t+1) = f_2$;
8:     $\vdots$
9: **else if** $l(t) \geq th_{m-1}$ **then**
10:     $f(t+1) = f_m$;
11: **else**
12:     $f(t+1) = f(t)$
13: **end if**

In both SFT and MCT, the working zone of one frequency can be overlapped with the one of another frequency, i.e., the two thresholds, th_{i-1} and th_i, for the frequency f_i can be the same as the thresholds of other frequency f_j. That will introduce two cases of single threshold and dual threshold to one frequency [23] [24]. They are subsets of our algorithms.

Suppose we evaluate time from 0 to t_1+t_2 for a given traffic. At the beginning, buffer is empty and the router is in sleep mode. After that, packets arrive and accumulate to th_{m-1}, and both SFT and MCT adapt the frequency step by step to f_m in t_1. Then, suppose there is no packet arrive further, and SFT uses another t_2 to switch back to sleep mode. Because MCT processes packets using f_m, the processing time, denoted as s for f_m, is less than t_2. SFT and MCT perform the scaling as the following separately.

$$\sum_{t=0}^{t_1} n(t) \leq \sum_{t=0}^{t_1+t_2} f(t); \sum_{t=0}^{t_1} n(t) \leq \sum_{t=0}^{t_1} f(t) + s*f_m \quad (5)$$

Based on Eq.5, the energy consumption in this scene by SFT and MCT is shown in Eq.6 and Eq.7.

$$\sum_{t=0}^{t_1+t_2} p(f(t)) + 2*m*p(\delta) \quad (6)$$

$$\sum_{t=0}^{t_1} p(f(t)) + s*p(f_m) + (t_2-s)*p(f_0) + (m+1)*p(\delta) \quad (7)$$

The above scene helps to understand the difference of the two methods. Obviously, MCT has longer sleep time and less switching times than SFT. Section 5 will give further comparison based on the results from real data set.

Other algorithms can be designed by building the state diagram similar to SFT and MCT. Essentially, they are all greedy type optimization methods for a NP-hard problem. In our work, we only evaluate the two algorithms.

5. EXPERIMENTS AND DISCUSSIONS

5.1 Experiments Setup

To evaluate the four power-scaling algorithms, we designed a packet-level energy consumption simulator for routers. It accepts collected real traffic in Section 3 with pcap format, and outputs the results. We set two frequency scenarios, one with three frequencies (two working frequencies and a sleep mode) and the other with six frequencies (five working frequencies and a sleep mode).

We use the power percentage in Bolla *et al.*'s survey [1] to estimate the power consumption in a router. The power and heat management, control plane and buffers form the basic power consumption of a router, contributing 51% as an invariable part. The IP lookup, forwarding engines, I/O and switch fabric form the variable part, having 49% as the frequency scaling part. That is, $p(f_0)=0.51$. Other works may find out different percentage in some specific platforms. Similar experiments can be also applied to them.

Linear scaling and quadratical scaling can be both used to estimate the power difference between frequencies. Note that different scaling models may produce different results. In these experiments, the power consumption at different frequencies are measured by linear scaling model. For f_i, its power consumption is shown in Eq. 8.

$$p(f_i) = \frac{f_i}{f_m} * (p(f_m) - p(f_0)) + p(f_0) \qquad (8)$$

Based on the time of each frequency scaling on our prototype, the energy consumption of the cost, $p(f_0)\delta + p(\delta)$, is set to 0.2. The default Δt is 50 times more than a single switching time, $50 * \delta$, and α is set to 4.

5.2 Energy Saving for Three Frequencies

To implement a simplest energy efficient router, three frequencies are required, f_0 as the sleep mode and two working frequencies f_1 and f_2, where $f_0=0$ and $f_1=0.1*f_2$. [1]

Fig. 6(a) presents the time distribution of frequencies under different scaling policies and traffic flows. It shows that MaxLP produces more sleep time than MinLP in the periodical scaling, just as expected. It also shows that MaxLP has less working time in the maximum frequency than MinLP, because there may be a lot of situations that the maximum frequency is invoked by MinLP to process packets but the real occupancy is not that much such as in an average lower bandwidth. In this case, the maximum frequency is working during the rest time of Δt after processing all packets, which actually wastes energy in vain. While SFT and MCT behave similarly except that MCT has more sleep time.

Fig. 6(b) gives the number of frequency switching. MinLP and SFT both have about 10 times more switches than their counterparts. MaxLP and MCT have fewer and similar number of switches because they both accumulate packets.

By using the Eq.1 and the parameters in Section 5.1, the energy consumptions are calculated and compared with the non-scaling routers, as shown in Fig.6(c). As the average bandwidth utilization of home router is very low (4.4%), the router can save more than 47 percent of power no matter which algorithm is used, near to the lower bound, $p(f_0)$ (51%). For 2.5 Gbps and 10 Gbps, MinLP consumes about

[1]We did not choose the case of two frequencies, f_0 and f_1, because it is too simple to get valuable results.

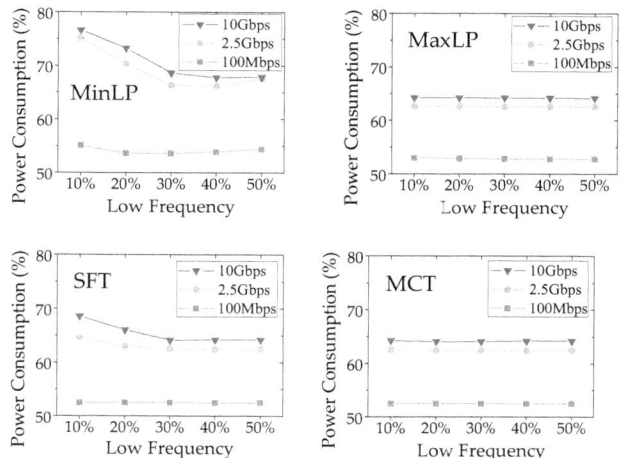

Figure 7: The energy consumption of (a) MinLP, (b) MaxLP, (c) SFT, (d) MCT with different low frequencies, f_1=10%, 20%, 30%, 40% and 50% of f_2.

75% of non-scaling power consumption, while MaxLP, SFT and MCT all achieve around 64% energy efficiency.

The different configurations may influence the results, especially the relationship between f_1 and f_2. Fig.7 presents the energy consumption of four algorithms with different low frequencies, from 10% to 50% stepping 10%. It shows that MaxLP and MCT stay with the same energy efficiency to different low frequencies, while MinLP and SFT like active algorithms may achieve better efficiency with an appropriate lower frequency that has more capacity to handle the average bandwidth. It is obvious for those active algorithms to choose lower and adequate frequency to save more energy.

5.3 Packet Latency and Queue Length

MaxLP and MCT sacrifice packet latency and queue length to achieve better energy efficiency. Fig.8(a) presents the average packet latency in different cases. MinLP has much lower (10%) latency than other methods. SFT, as an active method, has similar latency as other passive algorithms.

Fig.8(b) gives the average buffer length in three frequencies. MinLP also ranks the best, only 2% of others. MaxLP, SFT and MCT have similar results and MCT is slightly better. It is because MinLP will scale to an appropriate frequency in every period to deal with all packets in the buffer.

5.4 Energy Saving for Six Frequencies

Three frequencies gave a basic understanding of our algorithms. How about more frequencies? Here we design such a router with six frequencies, f_0 as the sleep mode and five working frequencies f_1 to f_5, where $f_0=0$, $f_1=0.2*f_5$, and $f_{i+1}=2*f_i$. The power consumption for each frequency can be calculated according to Eq.8.

Similarly, Fig.9 presents three results: the time distribution of different frequencies, the number of frequency switches and power consumption in six frequencies. Referring to Fig.6 with three frequencies, the differences between algorithms remain the same but the absolute gaps are highly reduced. For power consumptions, MinLP still consumes most but only less than 1% higher than others. However, for other three algorithms, MaxLP, SFT and MCT, the en-

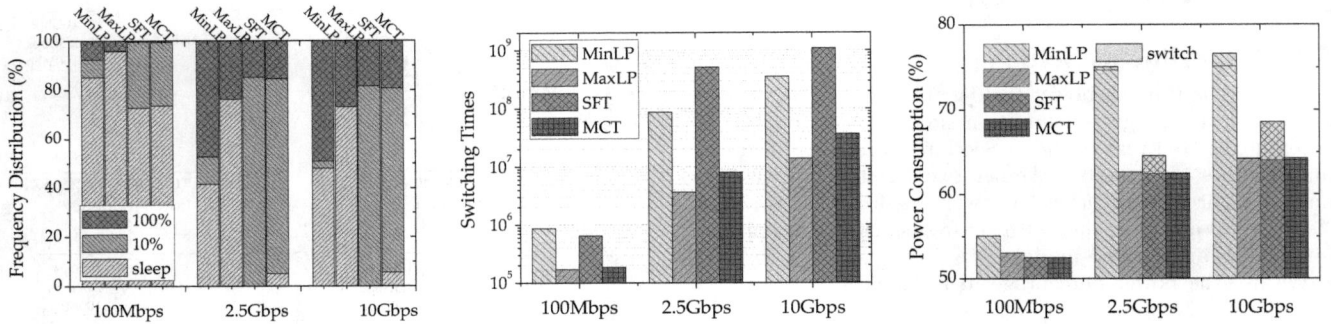

Figure 6: (a) Distribution of different frequencies in time (b) the number of frequency switching for real traces (c) power consumption compared to non-scaling.

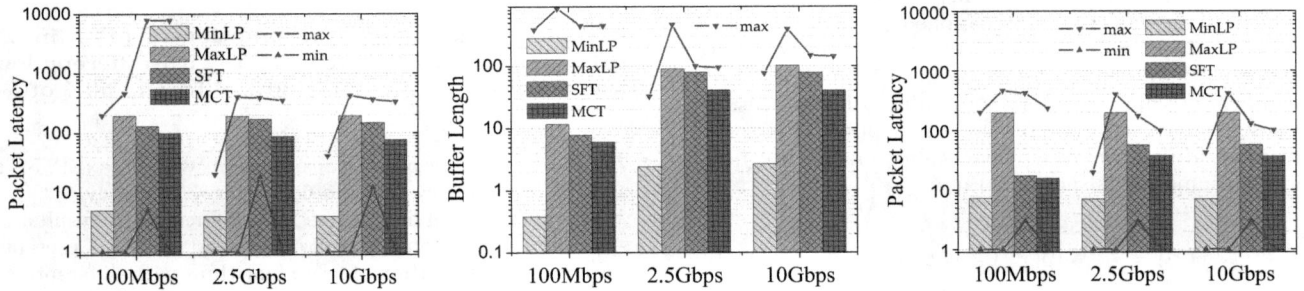

Figure 8: (a) The average packet latency (b) the average buffer length in three frequencies; (c) the average packet latency in six frequencies.

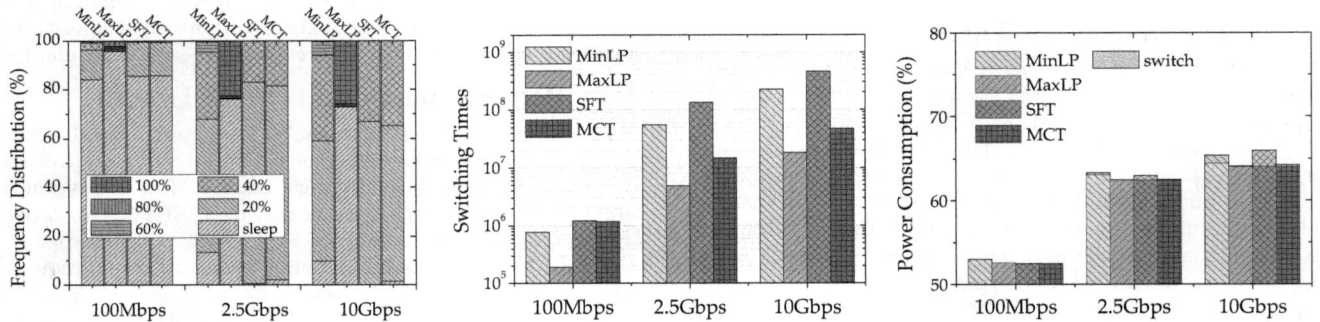

Figure 9: (a) Distribution of different frequencies in time (b) the number of frequency switching for real traces (c) power consumption compared to non-scaling.

ergy efficiency almost remains the same as the one in three frequencies, that is, 53% for 100 Mbps and 63% for 2.5 Gbps and 10 Gbps. It is beyond our intuitive estimation that more frequencies may be much better.

Fig.8(c) shows the average packet latency in six frequencies. Compared to Fig.8(a), the packet latency by SFT and MCT reduced heavily. That means, SFT is sensitive to the number of frequencies. More frequencies can stimulate the beneficial features for them. We omit the buffer length description because it is similar to Fig.8(b).

Now, we draw the conclusions: 1) our algorithms can save about 40% power consumptions for routers in real traces; 2) Both perodical- and threshold-scaling methods, passive and active, are efficient and the differences can be omitted if the energy efficient routers can support five and more stepping frequencies; 3) MaxLP, SFT and MCT can achieve near-optimal results just using two working frequencies and a sleep mode, so that energy efficient router may have very simple architecture; 4) MinLP is also good in general case to save at least 25% energy consumption with less than 10% packet latency and buffer length than other methods.

5.5 Discussions

The default values of parameters are used in the experiments. We discuss the influence of different values in this section to solidify our conclusions.

204

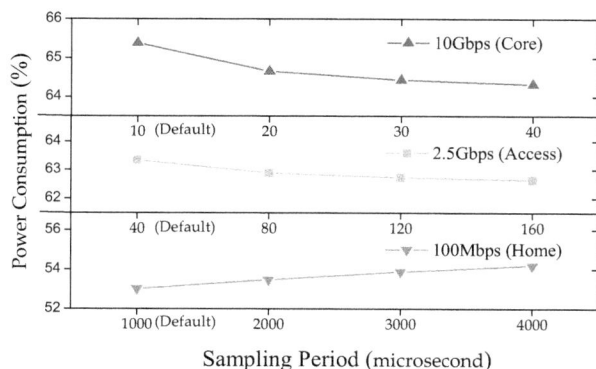

Figure 10: The power consumption variation of different Δt value.

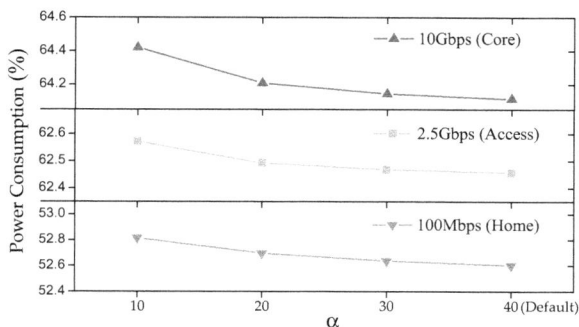

Figure 11: The power consumption variation of different α value.

In the periodical scaling, the time interval, Δt, is set to 50 times of the scaling time, i.e., $\Delta t = 10$. Fig.10 gives the power consumption of different Δt, from 10 to 40, using MinLP in the case of six frequencies. It shows that different Δt may have very limited influence (less than 1%) in energy saving.

The maximum tolerant packet latency is a critical parameter to MaxLP. Fig.11 presents the power consumption of different α, from 40 (default) reduced to $10(\Delta t)$ in the case of six frequencies. It shows that the longer tolerant latency has very limited influence in the energy saving.

6. CONCLUSION

This paper is to design power scaling algorithms for energy efficient routers in the system level. Taking frequency scaling as an example, two design methodologies, periodical- and threshold-scaling, are proposed, as well as the active and passive modes. Then four algorithms, MinLP, MaxLP, SFT, and MCT, are designed in detail. Experiments using three real network traffic, 100 Mbps, 2.5 Gbps and 10 Gbps, were carried out in two scenarios, three and six frequencies, to evaluate those algorithms. Our NetFPGA based prototype provides the critical parameter as well.

We draw conclusions as follows. 1) our algorithms can save about 40% power consumptions for routers in real traces; 2) both periodical- and threshold-scaling methods, passive and active, are efficient and the differences can be omitted if the energy efficient routers can support five and more stepping frequencies; 3) MaxLP, SFT and MCT can achieve near-

optimal results just using two working frequencies and a sleep mode, so that energy efficient router may have very simple architecture; 4) MinLP is also good in general case to save at least 25% energy consumption with less than 10% packet latency and buffer length than other methods.

7. ACKNOWLEDGMENT

The authors would like to thank our collaborators, Dr. Xiaojun Wang, Dr. Martin Coller, in Dublin City University to share their vision. This work is partially supported by the National Natural Science Foundation of China (Grant No. 61272510 and No. 60803002) and the European FP7 ECONET project under No.258454.

8. REFERENCES

[1] Bolla, Raffaele, Roberto Bruschi, Franco Davoli, and Flavio Cucchietti. "Energy efficiency in the future internet: a survey of existing approaches and trends in energy-aware fixed network infrastructures." *Communications Surveys & Tutorials, IEEE* 13, no. 2 (2011): 223-244.

[2] IEEE Std 802.3az: Energy Efficient Ethernet. 2010

[3] ECONET Project: http://www.econet-project.eu. 2012.

[4] Wenliang Fu, Tian Song, "A Frequency Adjustment Architecture for Energy Efficient Router", In Proceedings and Poster Session of the *ACM SIGCOMM*, Helsinki, Finland, Aug.13-17 2012, pp.107-108.

[5] Energy Efficient Router Demo: http://cs.bit.edu.cn/s̃ongtian/eer.html, 2013.

[6] Tian Song, Wenliang Fu, Olga Ormond, Martin Collier, and Xiaojun Wang, "Energy Evaluation of Gigabit Routers towards Energy Efficient Network", In Proceedings of the 20th IEEE International Workshop on Local and Metropolitan Area Networks (LANMAN), May 21-23, 2014, Revo, NV.

[7] NetFPGA Project: http://netfpga.org, 2012.

[8] Bolla, Raffaele, Franco Davoli, Roberto Bruschi, Ken Christensen, Flavio Cucchietti, and Suresh Singh. "The potential impact of green technologies in next-generation wireline networks: Is there room for energy saving optimization?." *Communications Magazine, IEEE* 49, no.8 (2011):80-86.

[9] Tang, J., Mumey, B., Xing, Y., Johnson, A. "On exploiting flow allocation with rate adaptation for green networking." In INFOCOM, 2012 Proceedings IEEE (pp. 1683-1691).

[10] Hu, Chengchen, Chunming Wu, Wei Xiong, Binqiang Wang, Jiangxing Wu, and Ming Jiang. "On the design of green reconfigurable router toward energy efficient Internet." Communications Magazine, IEEE 49, no. 6 (2011): 83-87.

[11] Zhang, Yi, Pulak Chowdhury, Massimo Tornatore, and Biswanath Mukherjee. "Energy efficiency in telecom optical networks." *Communications Surveys & Tutorials, IEEE* 12, no. 4 (2010): 441-458.

[12] Gupta, Maruti, Satyajit Grover, and Suresh Singh. "A feasibility study for power management in LAN switches." , *Proceedings of the 12th IEEE International Conference on Network Protocols*, 2004.

[13] Gupta, Maruti, and Suresh Singh. "Using Low-Power Modes for Energy Conservation in Ethernet LANs." *INFOCOM*. Vol. 7. 2007.

[14] Ananthanarayanan, Ganesh, and Randy H. Katz. "Greening the Switch." In *HotPower*. 2008.

[15] Vishwanath, Arun, Vijay Sivaraman, Zhi Zhao, Craig Russell, and Marina Thottan. "Adapting router buffers for energy efficiency." In Proceedings of the Seventh *COnference on emerging Networking EXperiments and Technologies*, p. 19. ACM, 2011.

[16] Mandviwalla, Malcolm, and Nian-Feng Tzeng. "Energy-efficient scheme for multiprocessor-based router linecards." In *Applications and the Internet. SAINT. International Symposium on*, pp. 8-pp. IEEE, 2006.

[17] Nedevschi, Sergiu, et al. "Reducing Network Energy Consumption via Sleeping and Rate-Adaptation." *NSDI*. Vol. 8. 2008.

[18] The CAIDA UCSD OC48 Internet Traces Dataset, http://www.caida.org /data/passive/passive_oc48_dataset.xml

[19] The CAIDA UCSD Anonymized Internet Traces 2012, http://www.caida. org/data/passive/passive_2012_dataset.xml

[20] Mark C, Balachander K. *Internet Measurement: Infrastructure, Traffic and Applications*. Chichester: John Wiley & Sons Ltd., 2006

[21] Vishwanath, A., Sivaraman, V., Zhao, Z., Russell, C., Thottan, M. "Adapting router buffers for energy efficiency." In *Proceedings of the Seventh COnference on emerging Networking EXperiments and Technologies* (p. 19). ACM, 2011.

[22] Baptiste, Philippe, Marek Chrobak, and Christoph Dĺźrr. "Polynomial-time algorithms for minimum energy scheduling." *ACM Transactions on Algorithms (TALG)* 8.3 (2012): 26.

[23] Gunaratne, Chamara, Kenneth Christensen, Bruce Nordman, and Stephen Suen. "Reducing the energy consumption of Ethernet with adaptive link rate (ALR)." *Computers, IEEE Transactions on* 57, no. 4 (2008): 448-461.

[24] Meng, W., Wang, Y., Hu, C., He, K., Li, J., Liu, B. "Greening the Internet Using Multi-frequency Scaling Scheme." In *Advanced Information Networking and Applications (AINA)*, 2012 IEEE 26th International Conference on (pp. 928-935).

Efficient Software Packet Processing on Heterogeneous and Asymmetric Hardware Architectures

Lazaros Koromilas
FORTH
koromil@ics.forth.gr

Giorgos Vasiliadis
FORTH
gvasil@ics.forth.gr

Ioannis Manousakis
Rutgers University
ioannis.manousakis
@cs.rutgers.edu

Sotiris Ioannidis
FORTH
sotiris@ics.forth.gr

ABSTRACT

Heterogeneous and asymmetric computing systems are composed by a set of different processing units, each with its own unique performance and energy characteristics. Still, the majority of current network packet processing frameworks targets only a single device (the CPU or some accelerator), leaving other processing resources idle. In this paper, we propose an adaptive scheduling approach that supports heterogeneous and asymmetric hardware, tailored for network packet processing applications. Our scheduler is able to respond quickly to dynamic performance fluctuations that occur at real-time, such as traffic bursts, application overloads and system changes. The experimental results show that our system is able to match the peak throughput of a diverse set of packet processing workloads, while consuming up to 3.5x less energy.

Categories and Subject Descriptors

C.2.3 [**Computer-Communication Networks**]: Network Operations; C.1.3 [**Processor Architectures**]: Other Architecture Styles—*heterogeneous (hybrid) systems*

Keywords

Packet processing; packet scheduling; OpenCL; heterogeneous processing

1. INTRODUCTION

The advent of commodity heterogeneous systems (i.e. systems that utilize multiple processor types, typically CPUs and GPUs) has motivated network developers and researchers to exploit alternative architectures, and utilize them in order to build high-performance and scalable network packet

processing systems [19, 22, 23, 32, 40], as well as systems optimized for lower power envelop [29]. Unfortunately, the majority of these approaches often target a single computational *device* [1], such as the multicore CPU or a powerful GPU, leaving other devices idle. Developing an application that can utilize *each* and *every* available device effectively and consistently, across a wide range of diverse applications, is highly challenging.

Heterogeneous, multi-device systems typically offer system designers different optimization opportunities that offer inherent trade-offs between energy consumption and various performance metrics — in our case, forwarding rate and latency. The challenge to fully tap a heterogeneous system, is to effectively map computations to processing devices, and do so as automated as possible. Previous work attempted to solve this problem by developing load-balancing frameworks that automatically partition the workload across the devices [13, 24, 27]. These approaches either assume that all devices provide equal performance [24] or require a series of small execution trials to determine their relative performance [13, 27]. The disadvantage of such approaches is that they have been designed for applications that take as input constant streaming data, and as a consequence, they are slow to adapt when the input data stream varies. This makes them extremely difficult to apply to network infrastructure, where traffic variability [12, 28] and overloads [14] significantly affect the utilization and performance of network applications.

In this paper, we propose an adaptive scheduling approach that exploits highly heterogeneous systems and is tailored for network packet processing applications. Our proposed scheduler is designed to explicitly account for the heterogeneity of *(i)* the hardware, *(ii)* the applications and *(iii)* the incoming traffic. Moreover, the scheduler is able to quickly respond to dynamic performance fluctuations that occur at run-time, such as traffic bursts, application overloads and system changes.

The contributions of our work are:

- We characterize the performance and power consumption of several representative network applications on

---

[1]Hereafter, we use the term device to refer to computational devices, such as CPUs and GPUs, unless explicitly stated otherwise.

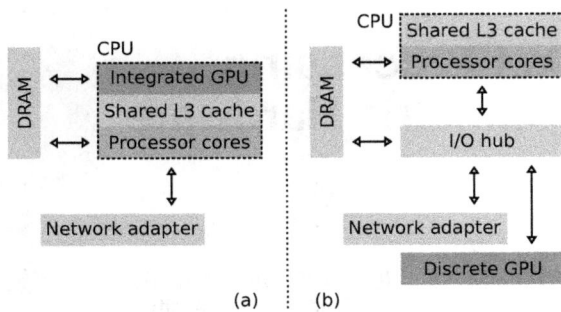

Figure 1: Architectural comparison of packet processing on an (a) integrated and (b) discrete GPU.

heterogeneous, commodity multi-device systems. We show how to combine different devices (i.e. CPUs, integrated GPUs and discrete GPUs) and quantify the problems that arise by their concurrent utilization.

- We show that the performance ranking of different devices has wide variations when executing different classes of network applications. In some cases, a device can be the best fit for one application, and, at the same time, the worst for another.

- Motivated by the previous deficiency, we propose a scheduling algorithm that, given a single application, effectively utilizes the most efficient device (or group of devices) based on the current conditions. Our proposed scheduler is able to respond to dynamic performance fluctuations —such as traffic bursts, application overloads and system changes— and provide consistently good performance.

2. BACKGROUND

Typical commodity hardware architectures offer heterogeneity at three levels: *(i)* at the traditional x86 CPU architecture, *(ii)* at an integrated GPU packed on the same processor die, and *(iii)* at a discrete high-end GPU. All three devices have unique performance and energy characteristics. Overall, the CPU cores are good at handling branch-intensive packet processing workloads, while discrete GPUs tend to operate efficiently in data-parallel workloads. Between those two is the integrated GPU which features high energy efficiency without significantly compromising the processing rate or latency. Typically, the discrete GPU and the CPU communicate over the PCIe bus and they do not share the same physical address space (although this might change in the near future). The integrated GPU on the other hand, shares the LLC cache and the memory controller of the CPU.

2.1 Architectural Comparison

In Figure 1 (right side), we illustrate the packet processing scheme that has been used by approaches that utilize a discrete GPU [22,37–40]. The majority of these approaches perform a total of seven steps (assuming that a packet batch is already in the NICs internal queue): the DMA transaction between the network interface and the main memory, the transfer of the packets to the I/O region which corresponds to the discrete GPU (this operation traditionally

invokes CPU caches, but the cache pollution can be minimized by using *non-temporal* data move instructions) the DMA transaction towards the memory space of the GPU, the actual computational GPU kernel itself and the transfer of the results back to the host memory. All data transfers must operate on fairly large chunks of data, due to the PCIe interconnect inability to handle small data transfers efficiently. The equivalent architecture, using an integrated GPU that is packed on the CPU die, is illustrated on the left side of Figure 1. The advantage of this approach is that the integrated GPU and CPU share the same physical memory address space, which allows in-place data processing. This results to fewer data transfers and hence lower processing latency. This scheme also has lower power consumption, as the absence of the I/O Hub alone saves 20W of energy, when compared to the discrete GPU setup of Figure 1(b).

2.2 Quantitative Comparison

The integrated GPU (such as the HD Graphics 4000 we used in this work) has higher energy efficiency as a computational device, compared to modern processors and GPUs. The reason is threefold. First, integrated GPUs are typically implemented with low-power, 3D transistor manufacturing process. Second, they have a simple internal architecture and no dedicated main memory. Third, they match the computational requirements of applications, in which the main bottleneck is the I/O interface and thus, a discrete GPU would be under-utilized. In Section 3.3.2 we show, in more detail, the energy efficiency of these devices when executing typical network packet processing workloads.

3. SYSTEM SETUP

We will now describe the hardware setup, and our power instrumentation and measurement scheme. Our scheme is capable of accurately measuring the power consumption of various hardware components, such as the CPU and GPU, in real time. We also describe the packet processing applications that we used for this work and show how we parallelized them using OpenCL, to efficiently execute in each of the three processing devices.

3.1 Hardware Platform

Our base system is equipped with one Intel Core i7-3770 Ivy Bridge processor and one NVIDIA GeForce GTX 480 graphics card. The processor contains four CPU cores operating at 3.4GHz, with hyper-threading support, resulting in eight hardware threads, and an integrated HD Graphics 4000 GPU. Overall, our system contains *three* different, heterogeneous, computational devices: one CPU, one integrated GPU and one discrete GPU. The system is equipped with 8GB of dual-channel DDR3-1333 DRAM with 25.6 GB/s throughput. The L3 cache (8MB) and the memory controller are shared across the CPU cores and the integrated GPU. Each CPU core is equipped with 32KB of L1 cache and 256KB of L2 cache. The GTX 480 has 480 cores in 15 multiprocessors and 1280 MB of GDDR5 memory. The HD Graphics 4000 has 16 execution units, a 64-hardware thread dispatcher and a 100 KB texture cache. The maximum estimated performance of this GPU is rated at 294 GFlop/s on the maximum operating frequency of 1150 Mhz [7]. While Intel does not provide it's Thermal Design Power (TDP) limit, we estimate that it is close to 17 Watt. For the whole processor die the TDP is 77 Watt.

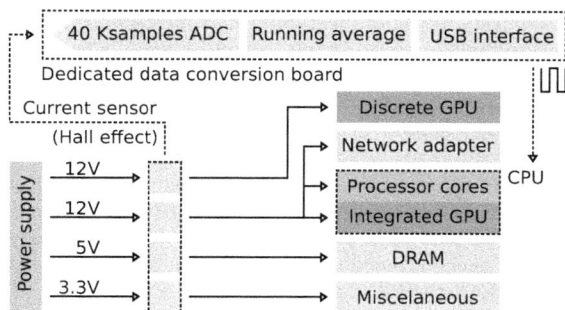

Figure 2: Our power instrumentation scheme. We use four current sensors to monitor (real-time) the consumption of the CPU, GPU, DRAM and miscellaneous motherboard peripherals.

We notice that our hardware platform exposes an interesting design trade-off: even though the on-chip GPU has fewer resources (i.e. hardware threads, execution units, register file) than a high-end discrete graphics card, it is directly connected to the CPU and the main memory via a fast on-chip ring bus, and has much lower power consumption. As we will see in Section 3.3.2, this design is well suited for applications in which the overall performance is limited by the I/O subsystem, and not by the computational capacity.

3.1.1 Power Instrumentation

To accurately measure the power consumption of our hardware system, we have designed the hardware instrumentation scheme shown in Figure 2. Our scheme is capable of high-rate, 1 KHz measurement, and also provides a breakdown of system consumption into four distinct components: Processor, Memory, Network and Discrete GPU.

Specifically, we utilize four high-precision *Hall effect* current sensors to constantly monitor the three ATX power-supply power lines (+12.0a, +12.0b +5.0, +3.3 Volts). The sensors [2], coupled with the interface kit [1], costs less than 110$. The analog sensor values are converted into digital values, and transmitted over a USB interface to a dedicated data logger board. The data logger includes a high-speed analog-to-digital converter (ADC) operating at a frequency of 40 KHz. The output data produced by the ADC are continuously read by a custom firmware running on the board, which also applies a running-average filter and periodically interrupts the processor with a rate of 1 KHz to report the values. A daemon, running in our base server, periodically collects the measurements from the data logger, and makes them available for monitoring and control. We take advantage of the physical layout to achieve a breakdown of the total power consumption: the 12Va line powers the processor, the 12Vb powers the GPU, the 5V line powers the memory, and the 3.3V line powers the rest of the peripherals on the motherboard. The 12Va line also feeds the 10GbE NICs. To calculate their power consumption, we use a utilization-based model.

3.2 Workloads

We implemented four typical packet processing applications, using OpenCL [3], that are typically deployed in network appliances and involve both computational and memory-intensive behavior.

3.2.1 IPv4 Packet Forwarding

An IP packet forwarder is one of the simplest packet processing applications. Its main function is the reception and transmission of network packets from one network interface to another. Before packet transmission, the forwarder checks the integrity of the IP header, drops corrupted packets and rewrites the destination IP address according to the specified configuration. Other functions include decrementing the Time To Live (TTL) field. If the TTL field of an incoming packet is zero, the packet is dropped and an ICMP Time Exceeded message is transmitted to the sender. We implemented the RadixTrie lookup algorithm and used a routing table of 17,000 entries.

3.2.2 Deep Packet Inspection

Deep packet inspection (DPI) is a common operation in network traffic processing applications. It is typically used in traffic classification and shaping tools, as well as in network intrusion detection and prevention systems. We ported a DFA implementation of the Aho-Corasick algorithm [10] for string searching, and used the `content` patterns (about 10,000 fixed strings) of the latest Snort [5] distribution, which we compiled into the same state machine.

3.2.3 Packet Hashing

Packet hashing is used in redundancy elimination and in-network caching systems [9, 11]. Redundancy elimination systems typically maintain a "packet store" and a "fingerprint table" (that maps content fingerprints to packet-store entries). On reception of a new packet, the packet store is updated, and the fingerprint table is checked to determine whether the packet includes a significant fraction of content cached in the packet store; if yes, an encoded version that eliminates this (recently observed) content is transmitted. We have implemented the MD5 algorithm [31], since it has low probability of collisions and is also commonly used for checking data integrity [4] and deduplication [25].

3.2.4 Encryption

Encryption is used by protocols and services, such as SSL, VPN and IPsec, for securing communications by authenticating and encrypting the IP packets of a communication session. We implemented AES-CBC encryption using a different 128-bit key for each connection. This is a representative form of computational-intensive packet processing.

3.3 Packet-processing Parallelization

To execute the packet processing applications uniformly across the different devices of our base system, we implemented them on top of OpenCL 1.1. Our aim was to develop a portable implementation of each application, that can also run efficiently on each device. We used the Intel OpenCL runtime 2.0 for the Core processor family, Intel HD Graphics driver 9.17, as well as the OpenCL implementation that comes with NVIDIA CUDA Toolkit 5.0. Due to space constraints we omit the full details of our implementation, and we only list the most important design aspects and optimizations that we addressed.

Each of our representative applications, is implemented as a different compute kernel. In OpenCL, an instance of a compute kernel is called a *work-item*; multiple work-items are grouped together and form *work-groups*. We followed a thread-per-packet approach, similar to [17, 19, 40], and assigned each work-item to handle (at least) one packet; each work-item reads the packet from the device memory and performs the processing. As different work-groups can be scheduled to run concurrently on different hardware cores, the choice of work-groups number provides an interesting trade-off: a large number of work-groups provides more flexibility in scheduling, but also increases the switching overhead. GPUs contain a significantly faster thread scheduler, thus it is better to spawn a large number of work-groups to hide memory latencies: while a group of threads waits for data fetching, another group can be scheduled for execution. CPUs, on the other hand, perform better when the number of different work-groups is equal to the number of the underlying hardware cores.

When executing compute kernels on the discrete GPU, the first thing to consider is how to transfer the packets to and from the device. Discrete GPUs have a memory space that is physically independent from the host. To execute a task, explicit data transfers between the host and the device are required. The transfers are performed via DMA, hence the host memory region should be page-locked to prevent page swapping during the transfers. Additionally, a data buffer required for the execution of a computing kernel has to be created and associated to a specific *context*; devices from different *platforms* (i.e. heterogeneous) cannot belong to the same context in the general case, and thus, cannot share data directly.[2] To overcome this, we explicitly copied received packets to a separate, page-locked, buffer that has been allocated from the discrete GPU's context and can be transferred safely via DMA. The data transfers and the GPU execution are performed asynchronously, to allow overlap of computation and communication and further improve parallelism. Whenever a batch of packets is transferred and/or processed by the GPU, newly arriving packets are copied to another batch in a pipeline fashion. We notice that different applications require different data transfers across the discrete GPU. For instance, DPI and MD5 do not alter the contents of the packets, hence it is not needed to transfer them back; they are already stored in the host memory. Packets have to be transferred back, when processed by the AES and the IP Forwarder applications, as both applications alter their contents. Still, the IP Packet Forwarder processes and modifies only the packet headers. In order to prevent redundant data transfers, we only transfer the headers of each packet to and from the GTX 480, for the IP Packet Forwarder case; the packet headers are stored separately in sequential header descriptors (128 bytes each), a technique already supported by modern NICs [6]. Nevertheless, these data transfers are unnecessary when the processing is performed by the CPU or the integrated GPU, as both devices have direct access to the host memory. To avoid the extra copies, we explicitly mapped —using the `clEnqueueMapBuffer()` function— the corresponding memory buffers directly to the CPU and the integrated GPU.

Accessing data in the global memory is critical to the performance of all of our representative applications. GPUs require column-major order to enable memory loads to be more effective, the so-called memory coalescing [30]. CPUs require row-major order to preserve the cache locality within each thread. As the impacts of the two patterns are contradictory, we first tried to transpose the whole packets in

GPU memory only, and benefit from memory coalescing. The overall costs, however, pay off only when accessing the memory with small vector types (i.e. `char4`); when using the `int4` type though, the overhead was not amortized by the resulting memory coalescing gains, in none of our representative applications. Besides the GPU gains, the CPU enables the use of SIMD units when using the `int4` type, because the vectorized code is translated to SIMD instructions [33]. To that end, we redesigned the input process and access the packets using `int4` vector types in a row-major order, for both the CPU and the GPU.

Finally, OpenCL provides a memory region, called *local memory*, that is shared by all work-items of a work-group. The local memory is implemented as an on-chip memory on GPUs, which is much faster than the off-chip global memory. As such, GPUs take advantage of local memory to improve performance. By contrast, CPUs do not have a special physical memory designed as local memory. As a result, all memory objects in local memory are mapped into sections of global memory, and will have a negative impact on performance. To overcome this, we explicitly stage data to local memory only when performing computations on the discrete GPU.

3.3.1 Batch Processing

Network packets are placed into batches in the same order they are received. In case two (or more) devices are used simultaneously though, it is possible to be reordered. One solution to prevent packet reordering is to synchronize the devices using a barrier. By doing so, we enforce all the involved devices to execute in a lockstep fashion. Unfortunately, this would reduce the overall performance, as the fast devices will always wait for the slow ones. This can be a major disadvantage in setups where the devices have large computational capacity discrepancies. To overcome this limitation, we first classify incoming packets to flows before creating the batches (by hashing the 5-tuple of each packet), and ensure that packets that belong to the same flow will never be placed in batches that will execute simultaneously to different devices.

Batches are delivered to the corresponding devices, by the CPU core that is responsible to handle the traffic of each network interface. Each device has a different queue —that is allocated within the device's context— where newly arrived batches of packets are inserted.

3.3.2 Performance Characterization

In this section we present the performance achieved by our applications. Specifically, we measure the sustained throughput, latency and power consumption for each of the devices that are available in our base system. We use a synthetic packet trace and a different packet batch size each time. To accurately measure the power spent for each device to process the corresponding batch, we measure the power consumption of *all* the components that are required for the execution. For instance, when we use the GPU for packet processing, the CPU has to collect the necessary packets, transfer them to the device (via DMA), spawn a GPU kernel execution, and transfer the results back to the main memory. Instead, when we use the CPU (or the integrated GPU), we power-off the discrete GPU, as it is not needed. By measuring the power consumption of the right components each time, we can accurately compare different devices.

---

[2]Context sharing is available in the Intel OpenCL implementation [8], but this does not include our discrete GPU.

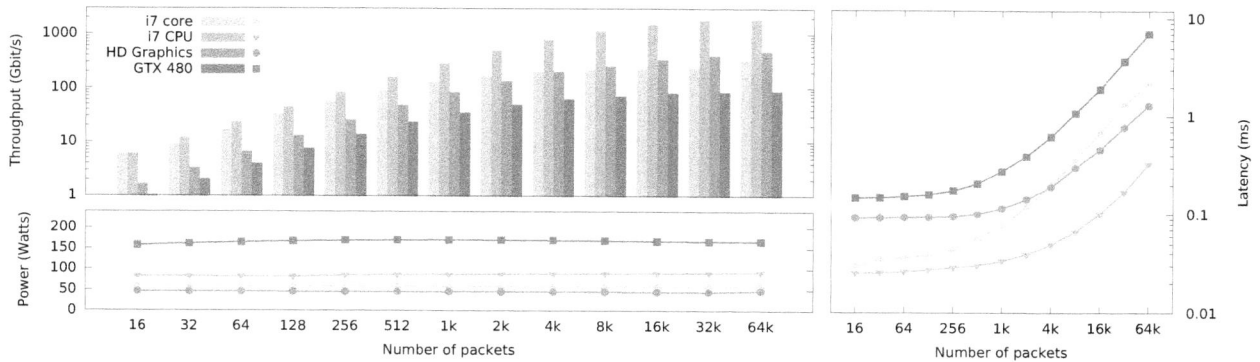

(a) IPv4 Packet Forwarding

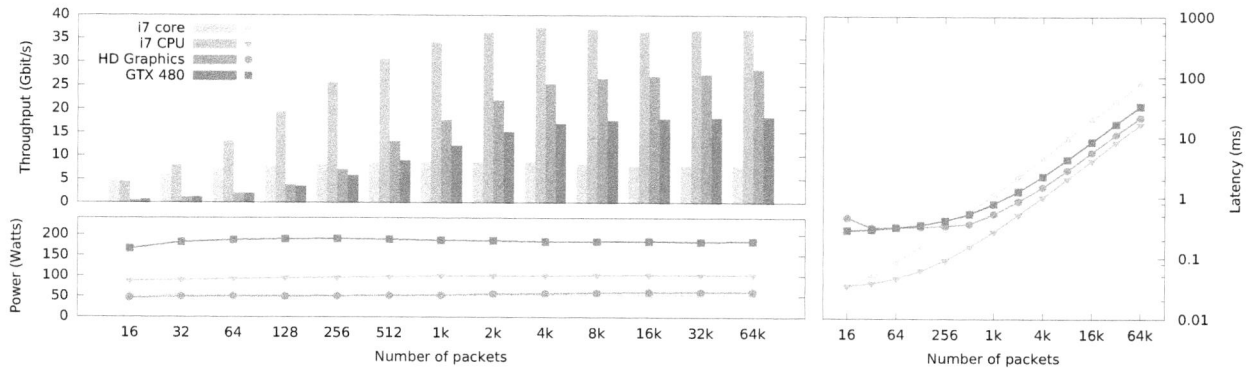

(b) MD5

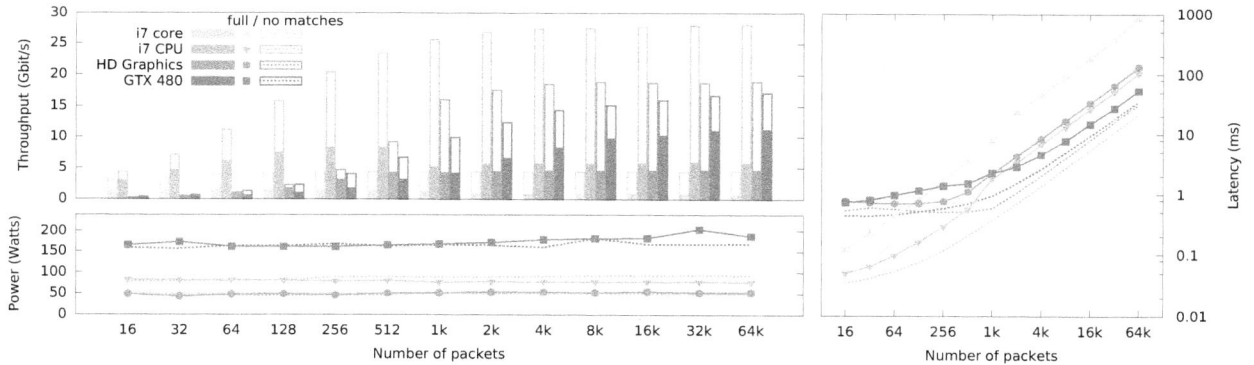

(c) DPI

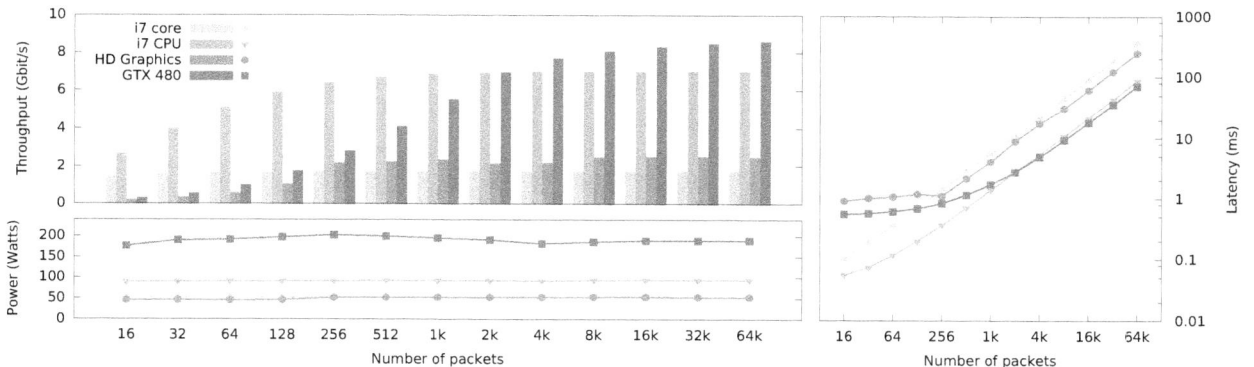

(d) AES-CBC

Figure 3: Throughput, latency and power consumption for (a) IPv4 packet forwarding, (b) MD5 hashing, (c) Deep Packet Inspection, and (d) AES-CBC 128-bit encryption.

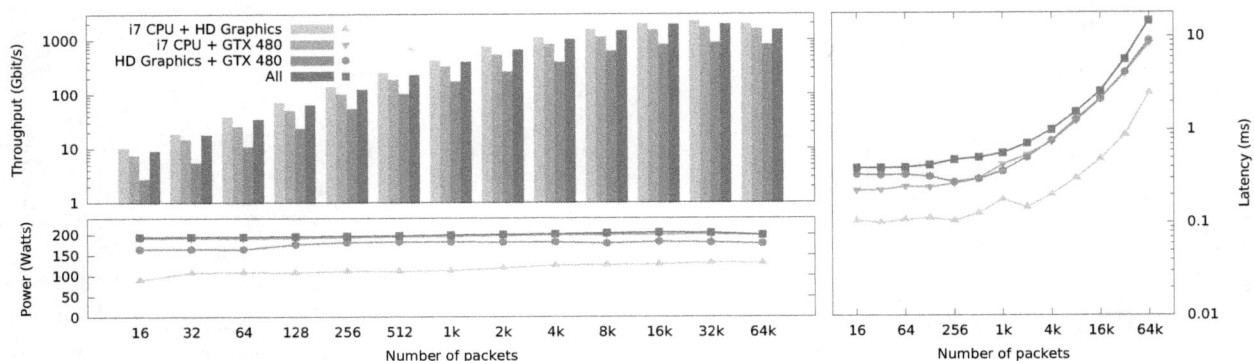

(a) IPv4 Packet Forwarding

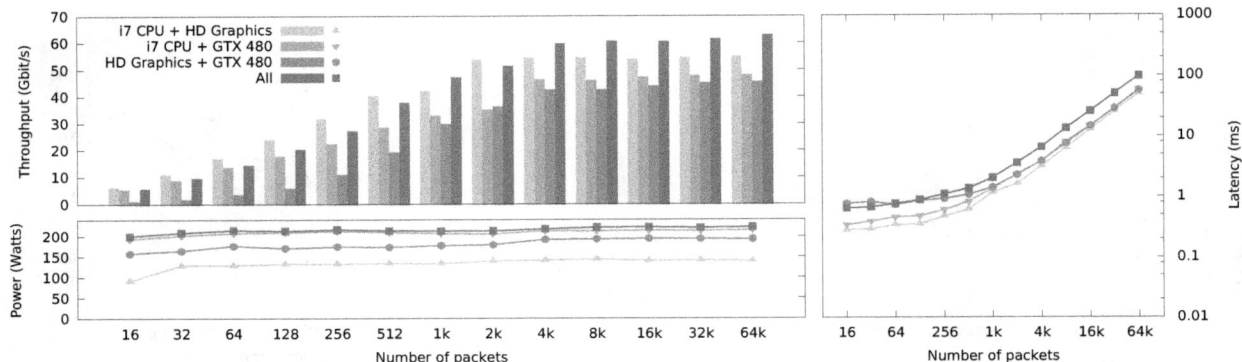

(b) MD5

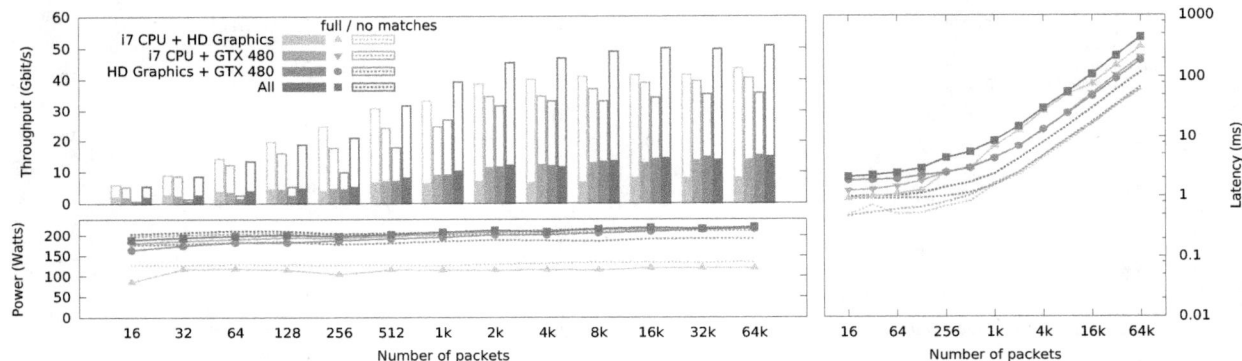

(c) DPI

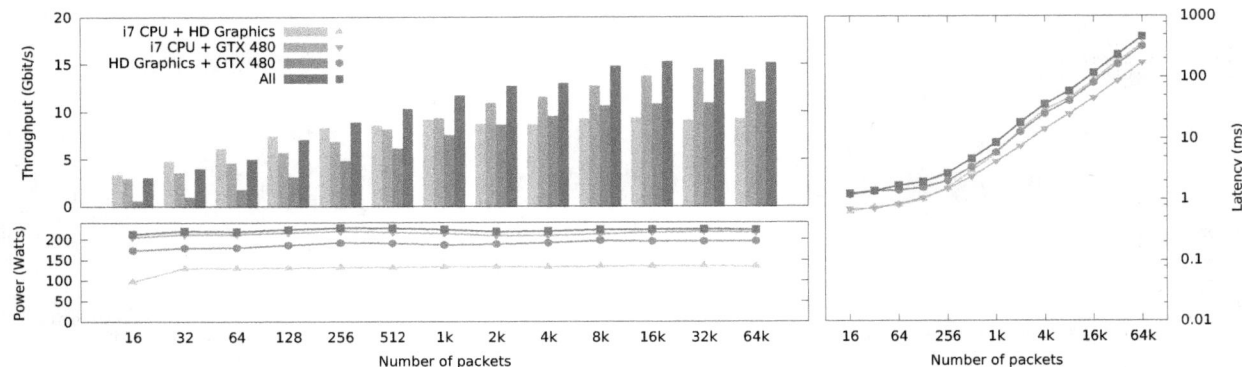

(d) AES-CBC

Figure 4: Throughput, latency and power consumption for (a) IPv4 packet forwarding, (b) MD5 hashing, (c) Deep Packet Inspection, and (d) AES-CBC 128-bit encryption, for combinations of devices.

Figures 3 and 4 summarize the characteristics of each of these types of packet processing during a "solo" run (one device runs the packet-processing workload, while all the other devices are idle) and a "combo" run (more devices contribute to the packet-processing) respectively. In the combo run, the batch of packets needs to be further split into sub-batches, of different size, that will be offloaded to the corresponding devices. We have exhaustively benchmarked all possible combinations of sub-batches for each packet batch and pair of devices. Due to space constraints though, we plot only the best achieved performance for each case. In the case of the i7 processor, we include the results when using a single core only ("i7 core"), as well as all four cores in parallel ("i7 CPU"). Note that in the IPv4 forwarding application, the reported throughput corresponds to the size of full packet data, even though only their headers are processed in separate header buffers, as we described in Section 3.3.

We observe that the throughput always improves when we increase the batch size. However, different applications (as well as the same application on different devices) require a different batch size to reach their maximum throughput. Memory intensive applications (such as the IPv4 router) benefit more from large batch sizes, while computationally intensive applications (i.e. AES) require smaller batch sizes to reach the peak throughput. This is mainly the effect of cache sizes in the memory hierarchy of the specific device. For example, for the DPI in Figure 3(c) we see that a working set larger than 512 packets results in lower overall throughput for the CPU. Increasing the batch size, after the maximum throughput has been reached, results to linear increases in latency (as expected). Furthermore, we can see that the sustained throughput is not consistent across different devices. For example, the discrete GPU seems to be a good choice when performing DPI and AES on large batch of packets. The integrated GPU provides the most energy-efficient solution for all applications (even when using a single CPU-core only), however it cannot surpass the throughput of other devices (except in the case of DPI where it exceeds the discrete GPU's throughput for match-free traffic). The CPU is the best option for latency-aware setups, as it can sustain processing times below 0.1 ms for all applications. In general though, there is not a clear ranking between the devices, not even a single winner. As a matter of fact, some devices can be the best fit for some applications, and at the same time the worst option for another (as observed in the case of AES and IPv4 forwarding when executing on the GTX 480). Besides, we can see that the traffic characteristics can affect the performance of an application significantly. As we can see in Figure 3(c), the performance of DPI has large fluctuations; when there is no match in the input traffic the throughput achieved by all devices is much higher (even four to five times for the CPU) over the case where the matches overwhelm the traffic. The reason behind this is that as the number of pattern matches decreases, the DFA algorithm needs to access only a few different states. These states are stored in the cache memory, hence the overall throughput increases due to the increased cache hit ratio.

When pairing different compute devices, the resulting performance does not yield the aggregate throughput of the individual devices. For example, when executing MD5, the CPU yields 36 Gbit/s and the integrated GPU yields 28 Gbit/s, while when paired together they achieve only 54 Gbit/s. The

reason behind this deviation is two-fold. First, when using devices that are packed in the same processor (i.e. the CPU and the integrated GPU), their computational capacity is capped by the internal power control unit, as they exceed the thermal constraints (TDP) of the processor. Second, they encounter resource interference, as they share the same last level cache. Actually, this is the case for all pair of devices, except in the IP Forwarding case, where the CPU alone reaches the physical limits of the memory bandwidth, hence any extra device does not help to increase the overall throughput. When using all three devices, we can see that the overall throughput is always lesser (between 17% and 22%) than the throughput of the individual devices, as a result of high memory congestion.

3.3.3 Energy efficiency

Figure 5 shows the energy efficiency of each packet processing application, on each computational device. The lines show the Joules that are needed to process one Mbit of data (the lower the better), under different batch size configurations (x-axis). We observe that IPv4 forwarding ends up (for the larger batch sizes) to be the most efficient application when using the i7 CPU or the integrated HD Graphics GPU, and at the same time the worst when utilizing the GTX 480 discrete GPU. We also show the efficiency of forcing the system to use only one of the four i7 cores for comparison purposes. MD5 follows the same pattern, with the gap between the integrated and discrete GPU closing in. For the case of DPI (Deep Packet Inspection) and AES encryption in CBC mode, we can see that all devices converge to about the same efficiency; such large batch sizes, however, negatively affect latency and may be impractical to use for certain scenarios. Smaller batch sizes almost always have a clear winner.

In Figure 6 we see how different combinations of devices perform with respect to energy efficiency. Compared to single-device configurations, the combinations always perform worse, even though they deliver higher aggregate throughput. Among all, the least efficient device combination is the pair of the two GPUs (HD Graphics and GTX 480), especially for small batch sizes where they remain under-utilized. On the other hand, the most efficient combination is the i7 CPU paired with its integrated HD Graphics, which deliver both low consumption and acceptable throughput.

4. EFFICIENCY VIA SCHEDULING

The performance characterization in Figures 3 and 4 indicates that there is not a clear ranking between the benchmarked computational devices. As a consequence of their architectural characteristics, some devices perform better under different metrics, while these metrics may also deviate significantly among different applications. As an example, the GTX 480 achieves the best performance for the AES encryption but the worst performance for the IP forwarding. Additionally, the traffic characteristics can affect the performance achieved by a device. For example, DPI achieves the best performance (28 Gbit/s) on the i7 CPU while there are no matches on the input traffic. On the contrary, the rate falls significantly (at 6 Gbit/s), when the matches overwhelm the traffic (which is half of the performance sustained by a GTX 480).

With these observations in mind, we propose an online scheduler that increases the efficiency of packet processing on such highly heterogeneous systems. Our scheduler explores the parameter space and selects a subset of the available computational devices to handle the incoming traffic for a given kernel. The goal of our method is to minimize: *(i)* energy consumption, and *(ii)* latency, or maximize throughput. Our scheduler consists of two phases. The first phase performs an initial, coarse profiling of each new application. In this phase, the scheduler learns the performance, latency and energy response of each device, in respect to the packet

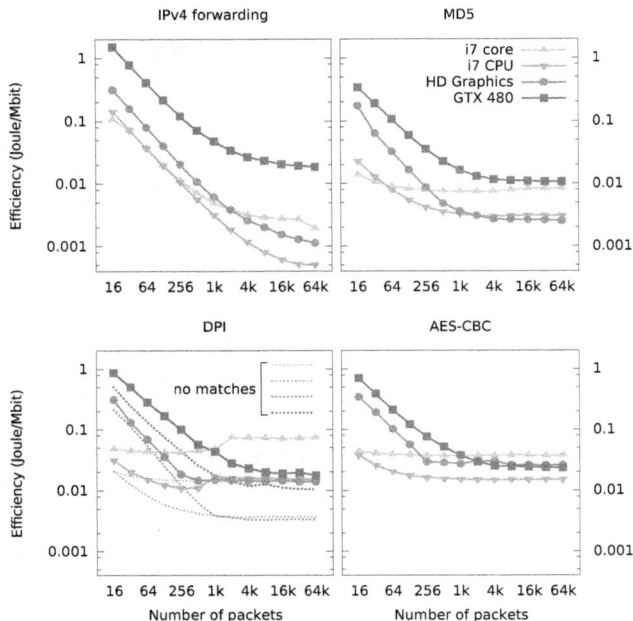

Figure 5: Energy efficiency of different computational devices.

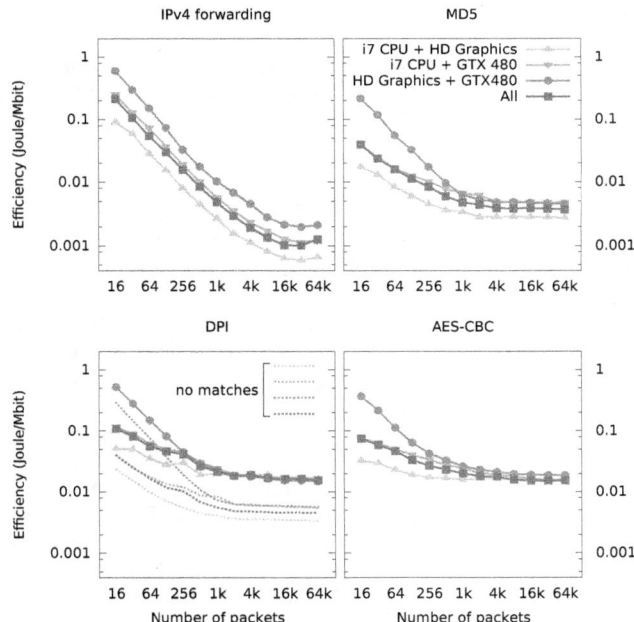

Figure 6: Energy efficiency of different combinations of computational devices.

batching as well as the partitioning of each batch on every device. In the second phase, the scheduler decides the best combination of available devices that meet the desired target (e.g. maximize processing throughput) and keeps track of the incoming traffic in order to adapt the batching and the batch partitioning.

4.1 Initializing the Scheduler

We first discover the best-performing configuration for each device; we then use these per-device configurations to also benchmark the remaining configurations comprised by combinations of devices. For each combination of our parameter space, we measure the sustained throughput, latency and power, and store them to a dictionary; the dictionary will be used at runtime in order to acquire the most suitable configuration. The time needed to compute the whole table requires 90–360 seconds, using a time quantum of 40 ms or a minimum of two samples, whichever comes last, for each configuration.

We use a different binary tree to store each achieved outcome (i.e. throughput, latency, and power) for each configuration. The motivation behind this is to allow throughput-, latency- and energy-aware applications, to find quickly the most appropriate configuration accordingly. At runtime, the corresponding metric (i.e. throughput, latency, and power) is used to acquire the most suitable configuration. The reason we use a binary tree is to allow fast insertions/updates and (more importantly) support both exact and nearest neighbor searches.

Each node in the binary tree holds *all* the configurations that correspond to the requested result. In order to acquire quickly the most efficient configuration, the configurations, within each node, are further ordered using two additional index structures. Specifically we use one index structure for each of the two remaining requirements. We also reverse the value of power and latency, before normalizing them, as they represent less-is-better metrics. The motivation of using three indices is to allow an application to select *(i)* either the configuration that is best for a single requirement, or *(ii)* the configuration that achieves the best outcome for both requirements. As indices we use priority queues as they can return the element with the maximum weight in $O(1)$.

However, requirements (i.e. throughput, latency, and power) are measured with float precision. As such, exact matches will be very rare, at runtime. To overcome this, we can either round to the smallest integral value (e.g. to the nearest multiple of 100 Mbit/s), or implement support for nearest neighbor search queries. By rounding to the smallest integral value we do not guarantee that a given value should be present in the binary tree; we have to explicitly fulfill the values for all missing neighbors. As the updating of the values of all missing neighbors can be quite costly —especially in sparsely populated cases— we implemented the latter solution. Therefore, if we do not have an exact match, we select the immediately nearest (either smaller or greater) match. Since we utilize a binary tree, the selection of the immediately nearest value can be obtained at the same cost. Moreover, in order to prevent from overloading the binary tree, before inserting a new node in the binary tree, we check if it differs with its parent by a threshold δ. If not, we merge them in order to save space. The threshold δ is also used as a parameter of our adaptation algorithm that is described in the next section.

4.2 Online Adaptation Algorithm

The goal of the online adaptation algorithm is to determine quickly and accurately which device (or devices) is more suitable to sustain the current input traffic rate, and to be able to adapt to changes in the traffic characteristics, with as little overhead as possible. Moreover, it allows an application to get the most suitable configuration based on its own needs (i.e. throughput-, latency-, or energy-critical). For example, it would be better for a latency critical application to submit the incoming traffic to more than one devices, while in an energy-critical setup it would be better to use only the most energy efficient device.

Our scheduling algorithm is laid out as follows. We create a queue for each device, and place packet batches in those queues, according to the following iterative algorithm:

1. Measure the current traffic rate. Get the best configuration from the lookup table, using as search key the desired requirement (i.e. latency-, throughput-, or energy-aware). Change to this configuration only if it was measured better than the current one by a factor of λ. Initialize variables α and β.

2. Start creating batches of the specified size. If more than one devices are required, create batches for each device accordingly. The batches are inserted into the queue of the corresponding device(s).

3. Measure the performance achieved by each of the devices for the submitted batch(es). If the sustained performance is similar to the one requested from the lookup table (up to a threshold δ), return to Step 1; otherwise, update the lookup table accordingly, and:

   - If the performance achieved by each device is lower, increase the batch size by a factor of α; set $\beta = \alpha/2$, and go to Step 3.
   - If the performance achieved by each device is higher, decrease the batch size by a factor of β; set $\alpha = \beta/2$, and go to Step 3.

The scheduler gets continually cross-trained and improves as more network traffic is processed across different devices. Moreover, the scheduler can easily adapt to traffic-, system-, or application-changes. Traffic changes (such as traffic bursts) can easily tolerated by our scheduler by quickly switching to the appropriate configuration (Step 1), without requiring to update the scheduler. In contrast, system- and application-changes should update the scheduler: The loop, that starts at the Step 3 of the adaptation algorithm above, finds the best configuration of the given device for the current conditions. After that, the scheduler returns to Step 1, as more appropriate devices might exist to handle the current conditions. The purpose of the λ factor is to avoid alternating among competing configurations and just maintain a "good enough" state.

Therefore, our scheduler can tackle system changes, such as throttling and contention, that may occur more frequently in the i7 Ivy Bridge processor, where multiple computational devices are integrated into a single package and sharing a single memory system and power budget. Application changes, such as in the case of the DPI which has large performance fluctuations according to the current traffic characteristics

are also confronted. To prevent temporal packet loss, in the inter-time that our scheduler needs to adapt to the new conditions, we maintain queues of sufficient size for each device. In Section 5 we show that a few hundred MBs are sufficient to guarantee that no packet loss will occur, during any traffic-, system-, or application-changes.

For the experiments presented in this paper, we set the difference threshold, δ, between the expected and the measured performance to 10%, and the growth and decrease rate, α, β, to 2x; we found that these values provide the best average performance across the set of applications we studied.

4.2.1 Analysis

The complexity of the algorithm, when searching for the configuration of a specific requirement, is $O(logN)$, where N is the total number of configurations. Indeed, the configurations are stored in a binary tree, hence the searching cost is $O(logN)$. As long as the configurations are found, the cost to acquire the most efficient is $O(1)$, because they are stored in a priority queue. Hence, the overall cost to acquire the most efficient configuration for a given requirement, is $O(logN)$. However, our adaptive algorithm requires that the given configuration should be updated, in case the sustained performance differs by a threshold δ. The update cost is equal to the cost required to find the node in the binary tree ($O(logN)$) and the cost to insert it into the priority queue ($O(logN)$), totalling a $2 \times O(logN)$. After the update, the algorithm converges to the batch size that achieves the requested performance, if any (Step 3). This can take up to $log_\alpha M$ steps (or $log_\beta M$ equivalently), where M is the maximum batch size.

5. EVALUATION

We now evaluate the performance of our scheduling algorithm, using the packet processing applications described in Section 3.2. We use an energy-critical policy, i.e. handle all input traffic at the maximum energy efficiency. In Figure 7(a)–(d) we present the applied and achieved throughput, the power consumption and the device selection made by the scheduler, for the four applications under study. For comparison, we illustrate with a dashed line the power consumption when all three devices are used simultaneously. Additionally, we provide the experienced latency with a solid line. Latency variability is a result of the dynamic scheduler decisions for the batching and computational device selection. The input traffic has the same profile for all applications and is comprised of 25% 60-byte TCP packets and 75% 1514-byte TCP packets.

Overall, our scheduler adapts to the highly diverse computational demand among the selected applications, producing dynamic decisions that maintain the maximum energy efficiency during all times. Additionally, it sustains high throughput and avoids excessive latency when possible. Furthermore, our scheduler is able to respond to application specific performance characteristics. For example during DPI (Figure 7(c)), our algorithm detects the requirement for a different configuration at times H and L. H and L introduce packets with a high match rate (in contrast to the low previous match rate), where the target cannot be satisfied without the use of the energy-hungry GTX 480.

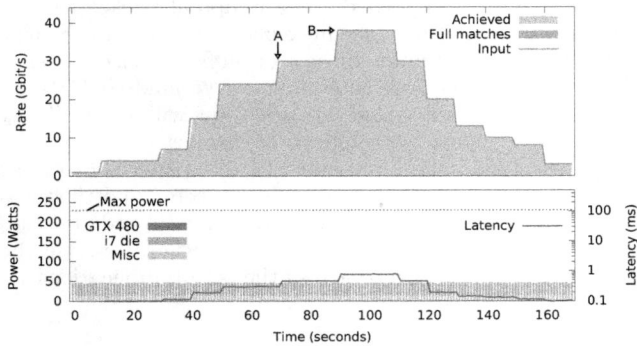

(a) IPv4 Forwarder.

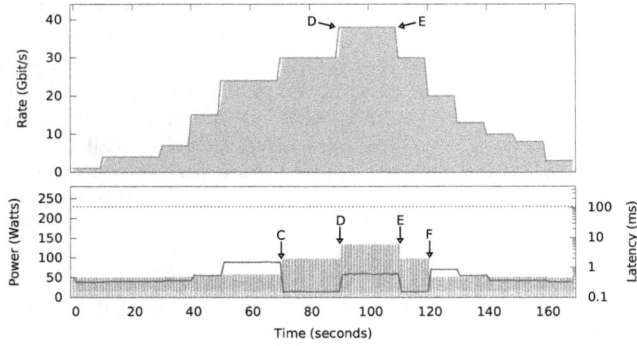

(b) MD5.

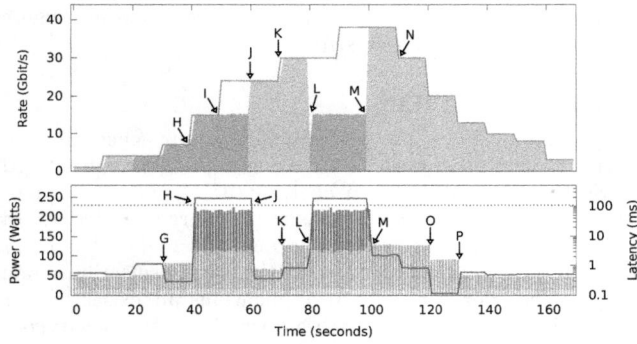

(c) DPI.

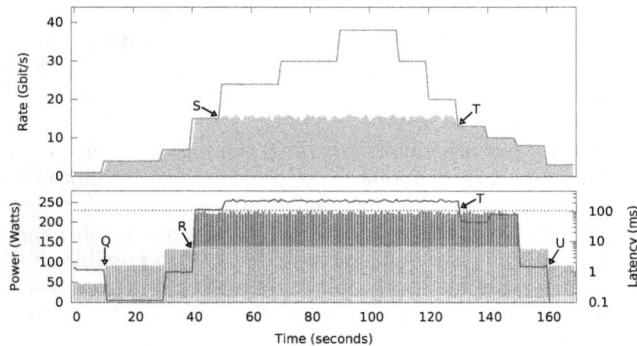

(d) AES-CBC.

Figure 7: Automatic device configuration selection under different conditions. Optimized for maximum energy efficiency.

5.1 Throughput

We observe that our proposed scheduler is able to switch to the configuration that keeps the selected target, under the required computational capacity which is required to process the incoming traffic for each application. However, there are two cases which our architecture does not sustain the input traffic rate: (i) in the DPI application, between I–J as well as L–M, and (ii) in the AES application, between S–T. The reason is that there is not a device, or combination of devices, to handle these cases, as we have already seen in Figures 3 and 4. More specifically, the DFA used by the Aho-Corasick algorithm exhibits strong locality of reference when the traffic does not contain any pattern matches; however when the traffic is overwhelmed by, different, pattern matches that locality of reference no longer holds, degrading the overall throughput. The HD Graphics does not handle more than 5 Gbit/s in any case and the GTX 480 performance is restricted by the data transfer bottleneck.

5.2 Energy Efficiency

Our proposed scheduler consistently switches to the most energy efficient configuration at all rates for each application. The advantage of our approach is more noticeable when the load is fairly low (1–4 Gbit/s) as it switches to the energy-efficient integrated GPU. Especially for the IP forwarding, the integrated GPU is able to cope with the input traffic at all rates, providing a constant 50 W consumption, which is *two* times better over the CPU-only and *more than three* times over the discrete GPU only. Packet hashing switches to the CPU when the rate reaches 30 Gbit/s (at C) and then switches to the CPU-HD Graphics pair (at D) in order to handle the 40 Gbit/s input traffic rate. DPI follows a more composite behavior, as it is affected by both the traffic rate and characteristics (i.e. number of matches). Overall, DPI ends up utilizing the two GPU devices when processing full-matches traffic at rates of 15 Gbit/s or higher (H–J and L–M). Nevertheless, when the matches drop to zero, the CPU is able to cope the input traffic (between J–K and O–P); at rates of 30 Gbit/s or higher the system employs the i7 CPU together with the HD Graphics (K–L and M–N). For all other input rates the CPU or HD Graphics alone can sustain the traffic. At L, we synthetically raise the number of matches that results to a temporal fall to 18.7 Gbit/s, before our scheduler considers to also utilize GTX 480 too. With increased rate, while keeping the number of matches at full ratio, we observe that there is no increase in the sustained rate because there is no better configuration available. AES, which is the most computationally intensive application in our set, ends up using all three devices when the traffic rate exceeds 15 Gbit/s (R–T), and are able to handle up to 15.5 Gbit/s rate.

Overall, our scheduler reaches the maximum consumption in the following cases only: (i) when the traffic rate exceeds 15 Gbit/s for AES, and (ii) when the rate exceeds 15 Gbit/s for DPI, and is overwhelmed with matches. In DPI, interestingly enough, the HD Graphics plus GTX 480 pair is the winner. Overall, our architecture yields an overall energy saving between 3.5 times (IPv4 forwarding) and 30% (AES-CBC) compared to the energy spent when using all three devices.

5.3 Latency

Increasing the batch size results in better sustainable rate at the cost of increased latency, especially for the GTX 480. IPv4 forwarding —executed solely on the HD Graphics— provides a latency that increases linearly with the batch size. However, this is not always the case. For example, in the case of MD5 workload, latency drops significantly in two different time ranges: C–D and E–F. The reason behind this is that the scheduler switches from the HD Graphics to the i7 CPU, in order to handle the increasing traffic rate. Given that the CPU is able handle the requested traffic using a much smaller batch size, results to an extensive latency drop. When the input rate grows further (D–E) though, the HD Graphics is utilized again, together with the CPU. This results to a 3.6 times increase of the measured latency. Similar transitions occur in other workloads as well, e.g. at G and O for DPI, and at Q and U for AES-CBC. We note though that in our experiments we focused primarily on providing a minimum power utilization setup. By using a latency-aware policy, we can obtain much better latency, at the cost of increased power consumption.

5.4 Traditional Performance Metrics

In addition to the previous studied metrics, we measure other significant metrics which are present in the software packet processing domain, namely: packet loss, and reordering. Our algorithm may introduce packet loss by switching to a device too slowly in the face of varying traffic demands. Reordering may be introduced when packets belonging to the same flow are redirected to a different device. Regarding packet loss, our experiments show that our algorithm can react quickly enough to avoid packet drops. We observe that in all cases our proposed scheduler can adapt to changes in less than 300 ms —which is the case where we use the GTX 480 with a batch size of 64K. This roughly results to 1.46 GB of received data (in a 40 GbE network, for a MTU of 1500 bytes), hence a buffer of this size is sufficient to guarantee that no packet loss will occur in the inter-time that our scheduler needs to adapt to the new conditions. We notice however that this is the worst case, in which the input rate goes from zero to 40 Gbit/s and at the same time the algorithm pushes the system to a configuration with the worst latency (300 ms). In our experiments, using a 500 MB buffer was enough.

Finally, we measure packet reordering. In our system, reordering can only occur when traffic is diverted to a new queue. However, as we have described in Section 3.3.1 we ensure that packets with the same 5-tuple will never be placed in batches that will execute simultaneously to different devices. This guarantees that, when using more than one devices, packets of the same flow will always processed by the same device. Indeed, in all our experiments we did not observe any packet reorders.

6. RELATED WORK

Recently, GPUs have provided a substantial performance boost to many individual network-related workloads, including intrusion detection [22,34,37,39,40], cryptography [20,23], and IP routing [19]. In addition, several programmable network traffic processing frameworks have been proposed— such as Snap [36] and GASPP [38]—that manage to simplify the development of GPU-accelerated network traffic processing applications. The main difference with these works is that we focus on building a software network packet processing framework that combines different, heterogeneous, processing devices and quantify the problems that arise with their concurrent utilization. By effectively mapping computations to heterogeneous devices, in an automated way, we provide more efficient execution in terms of throughput, latency and power consumption.

A number of recently proposed load-balancing systems support applications with multiple concurrent kernels [15, 35]. Other approaches rely heavily on manual intervention by the programmer [26]. Approaches to load-balance a single computationanl kernel include [13,24,27]. The simplest approach target homogeneous GPUs and, thus, require no training as they use a fixed work partition [24]. Wang and Ren propose a distribution method on a CPU-GPU heterogeneous system that tries a large number of different work distributions in order to find the most efficient [41]. Other approaches require a series of small execution trials to determine the relative performance [13,27]. The disadvantage of these approaches is that they have been designed for applications that take as input constant streaming data and as a consequence, they adapt very slowly when the input data stream varies. That makes them extremely difficult to be applied to network processing applications in which the heterogeneity of (i) the hardware, (ii) the applications, and (iii) the traffic vastly affect the overall efficiency in terms of performance, latency and power consumption. To that end, our proposed scheduling algorithm has been designed to explicitly account for this.

Furthermore, there is ongoing work on providing performance predictability [16] and fair queueing [18] when running a diverse set of applications that contend for shared hardware resources. There is also work on packet routing [29] that draws power proportional to the traffic load. The main difference with our work, is that they focus solely on homogeneous processing cores; instead we present a system that utilizes efficiently a diverse set of devices.

7. LIMITATIONS

Our scheduler requires live power consumption feedback for each of the available computational devices in the system. Even though such schemes have now become common in commodity, off-the-self, processors (e.g. the *Running Average Power Limit interface* present on latest Intel processor series), they are still in a preliminary stage in current graphics hardware architectures (although we expect this to change in the near future). To overcome the lack of such power estimation in current GPU models, we propose the use of a power model as a substance of real instrumentation [21].

Another notable limitation of our proposed architecture is the lack of optimization capabilities for concurrent running applications. The optimal parallel scheduling of an arbitrary application mixture is a highly challenging problem, mainly due to the unknown interference effects. These effects include but are not limited to: (i) contention for hardware recourses (e.g. shared caches, I/O interconnects, memory controller, etc.), (ii) software resources and (iii) false sharing of cache blocks. To make matters worse, the scheduler complexity grows exponentially with the introduction of multiple applications, as the parameter space should be explored for all possible application combinations. As such, in this work we solely focus on optimizing the performance of a single application that executes on a set of computing devices. As part of our future work we plan to experiment with application multiplexing and investigate the feasibility of a more generic energy-aware scheduler.

8. CONCLUSIONS

In this work we address the problem of improving the efficiency of network packet processing applications on commodity, off-the-self, heterogeneous architectures. Heterogeneous systems can provide substantial performance improvements, but only with appropriately chosen partitioning. Using a static approach can lead to suboptimal performance when the state of traffic, system or application changes. To avoid this, we propose an online adaptive scheduling algorithm, tailored for network packet processing applications, that can (i) respond effectively to relative performance changes, and (ii) significantly improve the energy efficiency of packet processing applications. Our system is able to efficiently utilize the computational capacity of its resources on demand, resulting in energy savings ranging from 30% on heavy workload, up to 3.5 times for lighter loads.

Acknowledgments

This work was supported by the General Secretariat for Research and Technology in Greece with a Research Excellence grant. Lazaros Koromilas and Giorgos Vasiliadis are also with the University of Crete.

9. REFERENCES

[1] 1018_2 - PhidgetInterfaceKit 8/8/8. http://www.phidgets.com/.
[2] 1122_0 - 30 Amp Current Sensor AC/DC. http://www.phidgets.com/.
[3] OpenCL. http://www.khronos.org/opencl/.
[4] OpenSSL Project. http://www.openssl.org/.
[5] The Snort IDS/IPS. http://www.snort.org/.
[6] Intel 82599 10 GbE Controller Datasheet, Revision 2.0, 2009.
[7] Intel HD Graphics DirectX Developer's Guide, 2010.
[8] Intel SDK for OpenCL Applications 2013: Optimization Guide, 2013.
[9] B. Aggarwal, A. Akella, A. Anand, A. Balachandran, P. Chitnis, C. Muthukrishnan, R. Ramjee, and G. Varghese. EndRE: an end-system redundancy elimination service for enterprises. In NSDI, 2010.
[10] A. V. Aho and M. J. Corasick. Efficient string matching: an aid to bibliographic search. Communications of the ACM, 18(6):333–340, 1975.
[11] A. Anand, A. Gupta, A. Akella, S. Seshan, and S. Shenker. Packet caches on routers: the implications of universal redundant traffic elimination. In SIGCOMM, 2008.
[12] T. Benson, A. Anand, A. Akella, and M. Zhang. Understanding Data Center Traffic Characteristics. SIGCOMM CCR, 40(1), 2010.
[13] M. Boyer, K. Skadron, S. Che, and N. Jayasena. Load Balancing in a Changing World: Dealing with Heterogeneity and Performance Variability. In ACM Computing Frontiers, 2013.
[14] S. A. Crosby and D. S. Wallach. Denial of service via algorithmic complexity attacks. In USENIX Security, 2003.
[15] G. F. Diamos and S. Yalamanchili. Harmony: An Execution Model and Runtime for Heterogeneous Many Core Systems. In HPDC, 2008.
[16] M. Dobrescu, K. Argyraki, and S. Ratnasamy. Toward Predictable Performance in Software Packet-Processing Platforms. In NSDI, 2012.
[17] M. Dobrescu, N. Egi, K. Argyraki, B.-G. Chun, K. Fall, G. Iannaccone, A. Knies, M. Manesh, and S. Ratnasamy. RouteBricks: Exploiting Parallelism to Scale Software Routers. In SOSP, 2009.
[18] A. Ghodsi, V. Sekar, M. Zaharia, and I. Stoica. Multi-Resource Fair Queueing for Packet Processing. In SIGCOMM, 2012.
[19] S. Han, K. Jang, K. Park, and S. Moon. PacketShader: a GPU-accelerated software router. In SIGCOMM, 2010.
[20] O. Harrison and J. Waldron. Practical Symmetric Key Cryptography on Modern Graphics Hardware. In USENIX Security, 2008.
[21] S. Hong and H. Kim. An integrated gpu power and performance model. In SIGARCH, 2010.
[22] M. Jamshed, J. Lee, S. Moon, I. Yun, D. Kim, S. Lee, Y. Yi, and K. Park. Kargus: a Highly-scalable Software-based Intrusion Detection System. In CCS, 2012.
[23] K. Jang, S. Han, S. Han, S. Moon, and K. Park. SSLShader: Cheap SSL Acceleration with Commodity Processors. In NSDI, 2011.
[24] J. Kim, H. Kim, J. H. Lee, and J. Lee. Achieving a single compute device image in OpenCL for multiple GPUs. In PPoPP, 2011.
[25] P. Kulkarni, F. Douglis, J. LaVoie, and J. M. Tracey. Redundancy elimination within large collections of files. In USENIX ATC, 2004.
[26] M. D. Linderman, J. D. Collins, H. Wang, and T. H. Meng. Merge: A Programming Model for Heterogeneous Multi-core Systems. In ASPLOS, 2008.
[27] C.-K. Luk, S. Hong, and H. Kim. Qilin: Exploiting Parallelism on Heterogeneous Multiprocessors with Adaptive Mapping. In MICRO, 2009.
[28] G. Maier, A. Feldmann, V. Paxson, and M. Allman. On dominant characteristics of residential broadband internet traffic. In IMC, 2009.
[29] L. Niccolini, G. Iannaccone, S. Ratnasamy, J. Chandrashekar, and L. Rizzo. Building a Power-Proportional Software Router. In USENIX ATC, 2012.
[30] NVIDIA. CUDA C Programming Guide, Version 5.0, 2012.
[31] R. Rivest. The MD5 message-digest algorithm. 1992.
[32] L. Rizzo. netmap: A Novel Framework for Fast Packet I/O. In USENIX ATC, 2012.
[33] J. Shen, J. Fang, H. Sips, and A. L. Varbanescu. Performance Traps in OpenCL for CPUs. In PDP, 2013.
[34] R. Smith, N. Goyal, J. Ormont, K. Sankaralingam, and C. Estan. Evaluating GPUs for Network Packet Signature Matching. In ISPASS, 2009.
[35] E. Sun, D. Schaa, R. Bagley, N. Rubin, and D. Kaeli. Enabling Task-Level Scheduling on Heterogeneous Platforms. In GPGPU, 2012.
[36] W. Sun and R. Ricci. Fast and Flexible: Parallel Packet Processing with GPUs and Click. In ANCS, 2013.
[37] G. Vasiliadis, S. Antonatos, M. Polychronakis, E. P. Markatos, and S. Ioannidis. Gnort: High Performance Network Intrusion Detection Using Graphics Processors. In RAID, 2008.
[38] G. Vasiliadis, L. Koromilas, M. Polychronakis, and S. Ioannidis. GASPP: A GPU-Accelerated Stateful Packet Processing Framework. In USENIX ATC, 2014.
[39] G. Vasiliadis, M. Polychronakis, S. Antonatos, E. P. Markatos, and S. Ioannidis. Regular Expression Matching on Graphics Hardware for Intrusion Detection. In RAID, 2009.
[40] G. Vasiliadis, M. Polychronakis, and S. Ioannidis. MIDeA: a multi-parallel intrusion detection architecture. In CCS, 2011.
[41] G. Wang and X. Ren. Power-efficient work distribution method for cpu-gpu heterogeneous system. In ISPA, 2010.

A Purely Functional Approach to Packet Processing

Nicola Bonelli
University of Pisa
Via G. Caruso 16
56122 Pisa, Italy
nicola@pfq.io

Stefano Giordano
University of Pisa
Via G. Caruso 16
56122 Pisa, Italy
s.giordano@iet.unipi.it

Gregorio Procissi
University of Pisa
Via G. Caruso 16
56122 Pisa, Italy
g.procissi@iet.unipi.it

Luca Abeni
University of Trento
Via Sommarive 5
Povo, Trento, Italy
luca.abeni@unitn.it

ABSTRACT

Today's rapidly evolving network ecosystem, characterized by increasing traffic volumes, service heterogeneity and mutating cyber–threats, calls for new approaches to packet processing to address key issues such as scalability, flexibility, programmability and fast deployment. To this aim, this paper explores a new direction to packet processing by pushing forward functional programming principles in the definition of a "software defined networking" paradigm. This result is achieved by introducing PFQ–Lang, an extensible functional language which can be used to process, analyze and forward packets captured on modern multi–queue NICs (for example, it allows to quickly develop the early stage of monitoring applications). An implementation of PFQ–Lang, embedded into high level programming languages as an eDSL (embedded Domain Specific Language) is also presented. The proposed approach allows an easy development by leveraging the intuitive functional composition and, at the same time, allows to exploit multi–queue NICs and multi–core architectures to process high-speed network traffic. Experimental results are provided to prove that the presented implementation reaches line rate performance on a 10Gb line card. To demonstrate the effectiveness and expressiveness of PFQ–Lang, the paper also presents a few use–cases ranging from forwarding, firewalling and monitoring of real traffic.

Categories and Subject Descriptors

C.2.3 [**Computer-Communication Networks**]: Network Operations—*Network Management, Network Monitoring*; D.1.1 [**Programming Techniques**]: Applicative (Functional) Programming

ANCS'14, October 20–21, 2014, Los Angeles, CA, USA.
Copyright 2014 ACM 978-1-4503-2839-5/14/10 ...$15.00.
http://dx.doi.org/10.1145/2658260.2658269.

Keywords

Software Defined Networking; Functional Programming; Monads; Domain Specific Language; PFQ

1. INTRODUCTION

Network applications in charge of processing huge amounts of data (such as, for example, traffic monitoring applications) are becoming everyday more and more complex due to a broad number of reasons. The volume of traffic crossing the Internet is continuously growing, with recent reports from Cisco [9] forecasting up to 1.3 Zettabytes of network traffic by the end of 2016. The heterogeneity of traffic is rapidly increasing as well, due to the adoption and spreading out of new technologies, protocols and services, bringing new requirements that can hardly be met by traditional systems and applications. Finally, the network scenario itself is changing, with speed of links easily hitting 10+ Gbps and increasing host density in large data centers.

In addition, the central role of the Internet as the key infrastructure driving global social and economic processes, makes it the perfect ecosystem for cyber–threats and network attacks to mutate and become more and more "effective" toward their malicious purposes.

In such a scenario, network nodes – once limited to switches and routers, in charge of very specific operations – see their mission significantly extended and their functions complemented by the adoption of heterogeneous *middleboxes* providing specific services such as intrusion detection systems, firewalls, address translation, etc. However, the appearance of such new devices targeted at very specific functions, brings several drawbacks. At first, middleboxes are typically proprietary and based on closed source software which makes interoperability and management in large–scale multi–vendors scenarios a big issue. In addition, their flexibility and programmability is generally pretty limited, and the programming skills required to actually customize and configure their operations largely exceed those of average network administrators. As a result, device programmability gets significantly impaired and chances for innovation and experimentation reduced.

So far, Openflow [18] is the most effective and convincing answer to the above summarized issues. Its pragmatic approach of proposing an open and stateless programming interface to (closed) inner functions of switching nodes was the key to convince device manufacturers (obviously reluctant to disclose their low level implementation) to expose a virtually vendor–neutral API to enable a reasonable degree of programmability of network devices. As a result, Openflow is today the main platform to develop Software Defined Networking (SDN) solutions.

The ambitious objective of the research presented in this paper is to adopt an analogous (software defined) approach to the development of generic middleboxes whose behavior can be completely "defined" from an open programmable interface equipped with an easy, expressive and robust programming language. The system that we have in mind consists – at low level – of a high performing software platform implementing a wide variety of primitive functions that exposes – at higher level – an interface that can be programmed by a specific functional language.

Why a functional language?

The selection of an adequate programming model for the above introduced system is not of secondary importance. At first glance, the choice of a functional model may look as an unnecessary overkill as it introduces the need to adhere to a strict formalism as opposed to the pretty loose constraints posed by traditional *imperative* languages. Such strict requirements, however, turn out to significantly ease the programming interface, while providing the user code with the typical robustness of functional programming. Indeed, as it will be shown in the rest of the paper, typical packet processing operations will be instantiated by writing *a few lines of code* only, in which the chain of packet processing is represented by the composition of elementary operations. As such operations may be executed in parallel, the *immutability* of data enforced by the functional paradigm prevents possible race conditions. Furthermore, before being executed in the underlying processing engine, the user code is formally verified against the strongly typed language and enforced by the functional model. However, it is worth mentioning that middlebox programmers are not required to know "gory" details of the underlying data–plane implementation as such details are fully hidden behind the set of instructions exposed by the functional language. Obviously, skilled users may still extend the number or modify the behavior of the data–plane primitives included in the system.

The contribution of this work

In practice, the ideal positions expressed so far have been translated in the design and development of an open platform for the development of a generic network middlebox on the Linux platform. To this aim, a functional engine implementing generic data–plane primitives has been integrated on top of PFQ [7], a high–performing packet capturing and distribution platform for Linux. The execution of the actual operations performed in the underlying engine is controlled by programming a functional interface implemented as a Domain Specific Language (DSL). As a result, the device (middelbox) gets its computation machinery decoupled from its (programmable) control logic, hence enabling a software defined approach to packet processing.

The paper is organized in a top–down fashion, by introducing at first the functional model (Section 2) for packet processing and its theoretical foundation rooted in the definition of *monads* (Section 3). Section 4 presents PFQ–Lang, the specific functional language developed to program the middlebox behavior, by giving an overview of the available functions. Section 5 delves into the lower level system im-

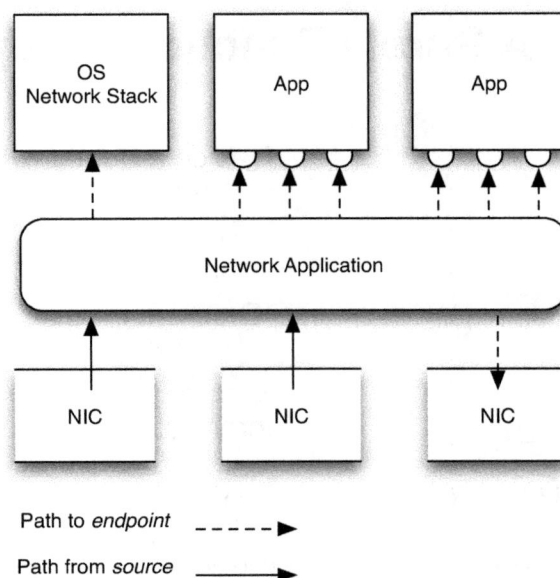

Path to *endpoint* - - - - - ▶

Path from *source* ⎯⎯⎯⎯▶

Figure 1: Logical scheme for network applications

plementation with more details on the system's components. Section 6 presents the performance of the overall system while Section 7 shows a set of simple real use cases, including monitoring applications, firewalls, legacy applications, and so on. Finally, related works (Section 8) and Conclusion end the paper.

2. FUNCTIONAL PACKET PROCESSING

The rationale behind this work comes from the simple intuition that network applications can generally be modelled as a packet processing pipeline composed by a sequence of elementary operations that consume data (packets) and produce computations, i.e. packets associated with actions (e.g. forwarding, storing, filtering, etc.).

In this logical scheme (see Figure 1), packets are retrieved from one or more *sources* (for example, one or more packet queues from a Network Interface Card - NIC), processed through the pipeline and finally delivered to one or more *endpoints*. Possible endpoints can be either network devices to forward packets, or the sockets of other applications in charge of performing additional processing (e.g. second stage applications, GPU accelerated computations, etc.), or the networking stack of the operating system itself for ordinary operations. Along their way to the destination endpoints, packets can be subjected to a wide gamma of operations that may produce different packets (e.g., NAT, TTL decrement), add annotations on the packets themselves (e.g. marking as a result of classification), and select the endpoint(s) for delivery.

More in details, three big classes of operations can be identified within the processing pipeline:

- operations that compute the final endpoints (and their delivery mode) – i.e., the packet *fanout*;

- operations that annotate meta–data on packets (by updating a *state*);

- operations that log data associated with the packet and possibly generate I/O.

From a functional programming point of view, all these operations (that will hereafter be referred to as *actions*) can be modelled by using a new data type `Action P` built around the data type `P` used to represent a packet. The goal of this paper is to model the elementary operations that compose the packet processing pipeline as *pure* functions (that is, functions without side effects) f mapping packets (with domain `P`) into actions (with domain `Action P`):

```
f: P → Action P
```

As previously mentioned, the first class of operations to be modelled is the one that defines the fanout of a packet. The fanout is represented by the endpoints (if any) to which packets are to be delivered, as well as the way this is accomplished.

The elementary fanout operations are:

- `Broadcast`, which delivers copies of the packet to all the endpoints;

- `Deliver class`, which deterministically delivers copies of the packet to a subset of endpoints specified by the `class` parameter;

- `Steer hash`, which *randomly* delivers the packet to a picked endpoint out of all endpoints based on a property of the packet (e.g. symmetric `hash` of the canonical 5–tuple);

- `Dispatch class hash`, which *randomly* delivers the packet to a picked endpoint out of the `class` subset of endpoints based on a property of the packet (e.g. symmetric `hash` of the canonical 5–tuple);

- `Pass`, which passes the packet to the next processing stage without specifying any endpoint;

- `Drop`, which stops the packet processing, and does not deliver it to any endpoint.

The different packet dispatching modes respond to the possible requirements of multi–threaded network applications as well as to the wide heterogeneity of network protocols. In such a framework, the availability of a fine–grained mechanism to handle parallelism among threads and network devices is crucial to take advantage of powerful multi–core architectures.

However, at a first glance, these operations do not seem to be easily modellable as pure functions. For example, the fanout operation `Drop`, which interrupts the processing pipeline, is hard to implement in a purely functional framework. The definition of a new data type constructor `Fanout` helps in addressing this kind of issues.

DEFINITION 2.1. *Let the* **Fanout** *type constructor[1] be:*

---
[1]Notice that the Haskell syntax uses a different construct (**data**) and requires the parameter following the type constructor Fanout to be a *type variable*, hence written as a lowercase letter.

```
TypeDef Fanout P = Drop | Pass P |
                   Broadcast P |
                   Deliver Class P |
                   Steer Hash P |
                   Dispatch Class Hash P
```

where **TypeDef** *is used here to define a new type, while* **Hash** *and* **Class** *are types representing the hash value and the class (i.e. subset of endpoints) used to fully specify the fanout.*

This definition indicates that `Fanout P` is a new data type, parametrized by the `P` data type, and enriched by the aforementioned dispatching modes. In particular, the `Deliver` and `Steer` constructors have additional arguments that specify their behavior: `Deliver` takes a mask of type `Class` that identifies a subset of endpoints, whereas `Steer` takes a value of type `Hash` to select a single endpoint (e.g. through a folding or modulo operation). Finally, `Dispatch` takes two more parameters, one of type `Class` and one of type `Hash`, and combines the `Deliver` and `Steer` fanout.

Along with the newly defined data type, two functions – `unit` and `compose` – can be used to compute a fanout operation (generally called "computation") from a packet and to compose two different functions that associate operations to packets (notice that `compose` is needed because the functions have different domains and codomains). The prototypes of `unit` and `compose` are:

```
unit:    P → Fanout P
compose: (P → Fanout P) x (P → Fanout P) →
         (P → Fanout P)
```

meaning that `unit` maps packets (of type `P`) into computations (of type `Fanout P`), while `compose` maps pair of functions from packets to computations into functions from packets to computations.

DEFINITION 2.2. *The* **unit** *function is defined as:*

```
unit p = Pass p
```

The `compose` function is more difficult to describe, and can be better formulated in terms of a function indicated as "*"* that, given a computation and a function from packets to computations generates a fanout computation:

```
*: Fanout P x (P → Fanout P) → Fanout P
```

Notice that the domain of * is `(Fanout P) x (P → Fanout P)`, which represents the set of possible pairs (computation, function from packets to computations), as the `x` symbol represents the Cartesian product. In the functional programming community, such a function (known as *bind*) is often declared as:

```
*: Fanout P → ((P → Fanout P) → Fanout P)
```

by using the so called "*currying*": a function $f : A \times B \to C$ having two arguments (in the sets A and B) and returning a value in set C is equivalent to a function $f_{curry} : A \to (B \to C)$ having only an argument in set A and returning a function from set B to set C. However, for the sake of simplicity, in this paper we use the simpler notation based on functions with multiple arguments and the Cartesian product.

DEFINITION 2.3. *The $*$ function is defined as:*

```
a * f = case a of
        Drop         → Drop
        Pass p       → f p
        Broadcast p → case f p of
                      Pass p → Broadcast p
                      otherwise → f p
        Deliver c p → case f p of
                      Pass p → Deliver c p
                      otherwise → f p
        Steer h p   → case f p of
                      Pass p → Steer h p
                      otherwise → f p
        Dispatch c h p → case f p of
                      Pass p → Dispatch c h p
                      otherwise → f p
```

According to this definition, $*$ works as follows:

- if a `Drop` operation is combined to any kind of function using $*$, the result is always `Drop`. This means that once a function drops a packet, the following functions in the pipeline are not evaluated, because the final result of the pipeline is `Drop` anyway;

- if a `Pass p` operation is combined to a function, the packet `p` is passed as an input to such a function, which generates the resulting computation;

- if a `Broadcast p`, `Steer h p`, `Dispatch c h p` or `Deliver c p` operation is combined to a function, the function is applied to the packet `p`. The function can select a new operation for the resulting packet, or can simply keep the input operation (if the result of the function is `Pass p`).

Based on $*$, the `compose` function can be defined as

```
(f1 compose f2) p = (f1 p) * f2
```

The presented `Fanout` data type constructor allows to model operations to be performed on packets (broadcast, drop, steer, etc...). However, a real packet processing pipeline has also to perform more complex operations, such as marking a packet, delivery of a packet to a NIC, associating some information with a packet and so forth. This can be achieved by extending the `Fanout` type constructor and adding some notion of *state*, so as to allow the pipeline stages modify such a state. To do this, a more complex data type constructor, named `Action`, has to be defined. The complete `Action` data type constructor, which includes the fanout computations, a state and I/O operations, can be defined by composing `Fanout` to some other data type constructors. The next section elaborates upon the theory behind these data type constructors, proves some relevant properties of the `Fanout` type constructor and refers to known theoretical results to explains how to build `Action` based on simpler constructors.

3. THEORETICAL FOUNDATIONS

The `Fanout` data type constructor equipped with the polymorphic versions of the functions `unit` and $*$ defined in Section 2 represents a construct which is well known in the functional programming community as *monad*. The monad concept originates in *Category Theory* [21] and is defined as a triple composed by a *functor* and two *natural transformations* acting on it.

The mathematical concept of monads has been applied to computer programming by Moggi [19] and adapted to functional programming by Wadler [26, 27]. In this context, a monad is defined as a triple $(M, unit, \star)$, where:

- M is a type constructor;

- *unit* is a function that turns a value from the type a into a computation $M\,a$ that only returns that value:

$$unit : a \longrightarrow M\,a$$

- $\star$ is an operator (also known as *bind*) that applies a function of type $a \longrightarrow M\,b$ to a computation of type $M\,a$:

$$\star : M\,a \times (a \longrightarrow M\,b) \longrightarrow M\,b$$

A monad satisfies the following three fundamentals laws:

1. *Left unit.* For all functions $f : a \longrightarrow M\,b$, and value a of type a:

$$unit\,a \star f = f\,a$$

2. *Right unit.* For all computations m of type $M\,a$:

$$m \star unit = m$$

3. *Associativity.* For all computations m and functions $f : a \longrightarrow M\,b$ and $g : b \longrightarrow M\,c$

$$(m \star f) \star g = m \star (\lambda a.(f\,a \star g))$$

where the notation $\lambda x.y$ denotes a (nameless) function computed on the value x that returns y.

According to the above definition of monad, we need now to prove that the type `Fanout p` introduced in the previous section is indeed a monad, i.e., it satisfies the above monad laws.

THEOREM 3.1. *The parametric type `Fanout P` defined in Definition 2.1 equipped with the `unit` function (Definition 2.2) and the $\star$ operator (Definition 2.3) is a monad.*

PROOF. To prove that the triple $(Fanout, unit, \star)$ is a monad, we need to show that the three monad laws hold.

Left unit. By the definition of $\star$ given in Definition 2.3, it is easy to see that $Pass\,p \star f = f\,p$, $\forall f$.

Right unit. Again, by Definition 2.3, it is easy to verify that $m \star unit\,p = m$ for all possible m.

Associativity. To prove associativity, we need to verify the result of the $\star$ operation for all possible combination of pairs of functions. As we have six possible computations (Drop, Pass, Broadcast, Steer, Dispatch, Deliver), this makes 36 possible combinations. A trivial (but way too verbose to be reported here) direct check easily leads to verify that the associativity property holds. □

As already mentioned, the `Fanout` monad is not sufficient to describe all the possible operations performed on packets and its effects must be combined to the effects of other well known monads, such as the *State monad* (allowing to associate a state to each computation) and the *IO monad* (allowing for computation–driven packet forwarding). The combination [17] of such monads leads to the definition of the more complete `Action` monad that will be used throughout the rest of the paper.

The `compose` function presented in Section 2 operates on pairs of monadic functions. This kind of composition is generally known as *Kleisli composition*. More formally, given two monadic functions $f : a \longrightarrow Mb$ and $g : b \longrightarrow Mc$, the Kleisli composition $\circ$:

$$\circ : (a \longrightarrow Mb) \times (b \longrightarrow Mc) \longrightarrow (a \longrightarrow Mc)$$

of f and g is defined[2] as:

$$(f \circ g)\, x = (fx) \star g \qquad (1)$$

Note that, historically, the triple $(M, unit, \star)$ used to define a monad is known as *Kleisli triple*.

The straightforward abstract consequence is to model the pure functions composing the packet processing pipeline as monadic functions that can be combined together through the Kleisli composition. As a result, application programmers can rely on the functional modelling based on monads with no need to know any details about the underlying implementation. In addition, this approach prevents from irrecoverable errors as the strong type check of common functional languages (for example, consider the Haskell type system) guarantees the semantic correctness of compositions at type–level.

4. THE PFQ–Lang LANGUAGE

As discussed in the previous sections, a packet processing pipeline can be described by composing multiple functions implementing elementary operations. This leads to the definition of a Domain Specific Language (DSL) designed for packet processing (PFQ–Lang).

PFQ–Lang is based on a set of primitive monadic functions implemented in a *functional engine* that represent single stages of the processing pipeline. These primitive functions can be combined by using the Kleisli composition (see Section 3), which was introduced as the `compose` function in Section 2 and indicated with the symbol[3] `>->` in PFQ–Lang.

A PFQ–Lang program can be either a single monadic function or a Kleisli composition of two or more operations, as:

```
c3 =  c1  >->  c2
```

As primitive operations, PFQ–Lang provides a rich set of functions. In addition, since the functional engine is designed to be easily extensible, it allows users to add functions for their specific purposes.

---

[2]An equivalent definition may be given by using λ notation as:
$$f \circ g = \lambda x. fx \star g$$

[3]We could not use the more typical `>=>` symbol as it is already used by Haskell to represent the Kleisli composition.

Like any functional language, PFQ–Lang supports high–order functions (functions that take or return other functions as arguments) and currying, to convert functions that takes multiple arguments into functions that take a single argument, as explained in Section 2.

A special function named `conditional` allows to evaluate two different computations depending on the truth value that a given predicate evaluates to. The syntax of `conditional` is:

```
conditional  predicate  c1  c2
```

where *predicate* is a function that when applied to a given packet, evaluates to a boolean value, and $c1$ and $c2$ are monadic functions. If the predicate evaluates to `true`, then the value of `conditional` is the expression $c1$, otherwise it is the expression $c2$. As shown in the next section, we anticipate that PFQ–Lang provides a rich set of predefined predicates (such as `is_udp`, `is_ip`, etc...).

For simplicity, two additional functions `when` and `unless` are also defined:

```
when    pred c = conditional pred  c  unit
unless  pred c = conditional pred  unit c
```

meaning that `when` computes c if *pred* is `true` or `unit` otherwise, whereas `unless` returns `unit` when *pred* evaluates to `true` or c otherwise.

4.1 Monadic functions

From a semantic point of view, monadic functions are implemented as the combination of the `Fanout` monad with other well-known monads to functional programming community (namely, the so-called *State monad* and the *IO monad*). Remember that a monadic function represents a stage of the pipeline, which takes an argument – a packet – and returns a packet along with an Action (namely, a Fanout operation, a new State and possible I/O side effects). Such functions allow to perform fundamental actions on top of packets, such as filtering, forwarding, steering, classifying, marking, storing, copying, and so forth.

As above discussed, thanks to the currying mechanism, nothing prevents a monadic function from taking additional arguments, provided that they come first in the arguments list.

As a final remark, note that PFQ–Lang does not provide the standard $\star$ (bind) function. Instead, it does provide the Kleisli composition operator, which represents for monads what the functional composition (.) does for simple functions. While, at first sight, this may look odd, it becomes more clear when we consider that the bind function takes a monadic argument (which is a packet along with its context), and that such an argument is not available at the point where the composition is defined. Instead, the Kleisli composition allows to compose a pair of monadic functions into a new monadic function whose effects are chained together. It goes without saying that the bind function (even if it is not exposed by PFQ–Lang) is implemented within the functional engine.

4.2 Non–Monadic Functions

In addition to monadic functions, PFQ–Lang provides a set of functions that take arbitrary arguments (curried from user–space), a packet, and return data. These functions do not specify any action on packets. Instead, they are passed as argument to high–order functions to specify their behavior. Non-monadic functions are roughly divided in the following categories: predicates, combinators, properties and comparators.

Predicates are functions that take a packet and return a boolean value. They are the fundamental building block for high–order functions, like those expressing conditional computations (e.g. conditional, when and unless functions). In addition, predicates can be combined through combinators, which are high–order functions that take one or possibly a pair of predicates and return a new predicate. PFQ–Lang implements combinators by overloading the common boolean operators *not* (!), *or* (||), *and* (&&), and *xor* (xor).

Similarly to predicates, properties are functions that take packets and return values, such as a computed hash, a certain field of a network header or, more in general, a value associated with the packet. Properties can be passed as arguments to comparators, which are predicates that provide a comparison between the outcome of properties and their actual arguments. Examples of comparators are: less (<), less equal (<=), equal (==), not equal (/=), greater (>) and greater equal (>=).

5. IMPLEMENTATION

The proposed packet processing architecture has been implemented in a Linux kernel module, and consists of a functional engine and some user–space bindings (implementing PFQ–Lang) for various programming languages.

The processing functions and the functional engine are implemented in kernel space as close as possible to network device drivers and to the network stack of the Linux kernel. At user–space, bindings for the Haskell language (a pure functional language, which supports monads and their manipulations), for the C++ language, and for the C language (with a slightly awkward, but functionally equivalent, syntax) are provided.

The functional engine has been implemented in the PFQ kernel module [7, 6], a high–performance monitoring framework designed for the Linux operating system.

5.1 The Embedded DSL

To create a programming language for a specific domain, we can either implement a parser along with the related compiler, or exploit the expressiveness of existing languages in order to define a specific *language within the language*. Such a class of languages are known as embedded Domain Specific Languages (eDSL).

PFQ–Lang has been implemented as an eDSL primarily because this choice enables a better integration with general–purpose languages already used for network applications. The eDLS implementations take advantage of the expressiveness of Haskell along with some extensions (e.g., *Generalized Algebraic Datatypes* – GADTs) and of *expression templates* for the C++ language. The lack of expressiveness of the C language has made the implementation of the eDSL more cumbersome. For example, the Kleisli composition is implemented as a traditional function instead of using a custom infix operator.

At the time of writing, PFQ–Lang implements about a hundred functions, and more are expected in the future. As previously mentioned, such functions include: protocol filters, steering functions, conditional functions, or forwarding

functions either to sockets, devices or the kernel stack. Due to space limitation, only a few functions are shown in the paper. The complete reference of the available functions can be accessed at the PFQ–Lang wiki page [2].

As an example of PFQ–Lang expression, a simple function that filters IP packets and dispatches them to a group of endpoints (e.g. sockets) by means of a steering algorithm is described as:

```
composition = ip >-> steer_ip
```

where ip is a filter that drops all the packets but IP ones, and steer_ip is a function that performs a symmetric hash with IP source and destination. Such a composition can be embedded in a Haskell program, associated to a given group of endpoints (identified by the *gid* parameter) and passed to the functional engine in kernel–space (where it is validated and executed on a per–packet basis) with the following command:

```
Q.groupFunction q gid composition
```

where Q is the namespace used for the PFQ and PFQ-Lang symbols, and q is an instance of a PFQ socket type (used as a *handle* to the functional engine).

The C++ version of eDSL uses a slightly modified syntax:

```
q = net::pfq();
...
auto composition = ip >> steer_ip;
q.groupFunction(gid, composition);
```

where, again, q is an object representing a PFQ socket (used to access the functional engine).

The main difference between the PFQ–Lang syntax and the C++ eDSL syntax is in the fact that the Kleisli composition in the C++ eDSL is represented by the >> operator (other differences are the extra parenthesis in the function used to inject the computation into the functional engine, but these are not strictly part of the eDSL). Notice that from now on we will only report examples written in the native PFQ–Lang syntax (which, incidentally, coincides to that of Haskell).

PFQ–Lang implements filters for the most important protocols; to name a few, ip, udp, tcp, icmp, ip6, icmp6, rtp (heuristic) and so forth. In addition, each filter is complemented with a predicate, whose conventional name begins with is_ or has_.

Conditional functions allow to change the behavior of the computation depending on a property of the processed packet, as in the following example:

```
composition = ip >-> when is_tcp
                   forward "eth1"
              >-> steer_flow
```

The function drops all non–IP packets, forwards a copy of TCP packets to eth1, and then dispatches packets to the group of registered PFQ sockets in steering mode. It is worth noticing that since steer_flow works with both TCP and UDP packets, ICMP packets are implicitly dropped by the steering function.

As another example, the following code marks UDP packets with the number 42 (or returns them to the kernel network stack if non–UDP packets), and then dispatches them to PFQ sockets preserving the flow integrity:

```
composition = conditional is_udp
                          mark 42
                          kernel
                          >-> steer_flow
```

The `mark` function is used to mark packets with a value that can be read by subsequent functions through the `has_mark` predicate as well as by user–space applications when packets are received by sockets. This marking mechanism can be used for packet classification.

Finally, it is worth noticing that the whole *Berkeley Packet Filter* machinery can be included into a single monadic function and used in functional compositions.

5.2 The Functional Engine

At the bottom of the system, PFQ [7] retrieves packets from NICs *data sources*. Such packets are then fed into the functional processing pipeline that provides the kernel stage of processing (filtering, classification, steering toward up–stream applications, etc). At the end of the pipeline, PFQ sockets, NICs, or the kernel networking stack can be used as endpoints to feed applications running in user–space, forward packets, or return them to the kernel.

In order to receive packets, user–space applications must register to *socket groups*. Socket groups allow for multiple multi–threaded (or multi–processes) applications to concurrently receive packets from the same set of NICs. As such, each group is served by a specific processing pipeline (instance of functional composition).

The engine evaluates the functional composition specified for an endpoint (or a group of endpoints) on per–packet basis. The number of instances of the functional engine available in a system depends on the number of kernel contexts enabled for capturing packets, that in the Linux kernel corresponds to the number of NAPI threads. A fine grained approach to interrupt affinity allows to select the cores where the functional engines are instantiated.

The functional composition is represented by an abstract syntax tree (AST) of functions and arguments, and it is generated in user–space on the basis of PFQ–Lang expressions. The AST is then represented in terms of a collection of meta information to be transferred to the functional engine (by means of a specific PFQ socket option). Such information includes the actual parameters specified in user–space upon their conversion to a memory layout compliant to the C language.

The eDSL enforces the type level correctness at compile time. In addition, for security reasons, the functional composition is sanity checked at kernel–space to avoid possible kernel panics. In particular, the signature of the various functions along with their argument types are verified, and the presence of loops in the tree is avoided. Subsequently, the descriptors of the various functions undergo a process of transformation through which the abstract tree is converted into a hybrid data structure, equipped with data and pointers to executable functions (see Figure 2). The addresses of various functions are resolved by a run–time linker that uses dynamic symbol–tables. Such tables are populated when either the PFQ kernel module or external modules are loaded. Notice that external modules can add (and remove) on–the–fly new functions to the system (the removal is allowed only when no functional engine is running).

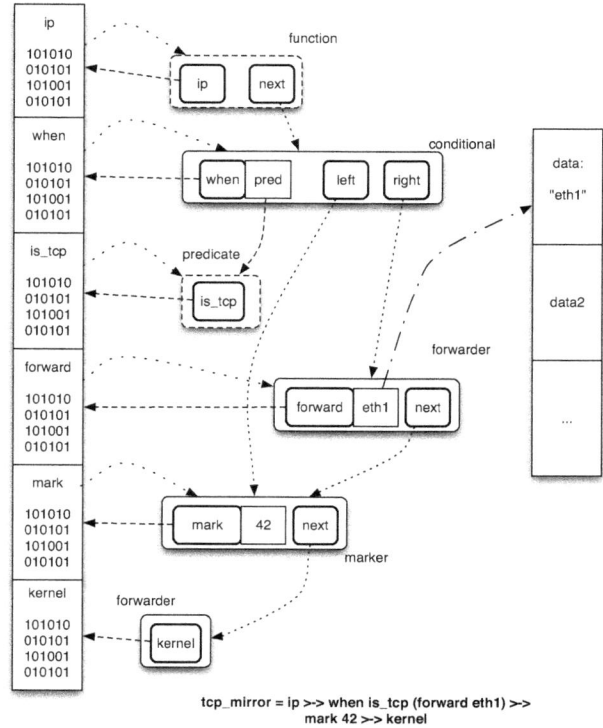

tcp_mirror = ip >-> when is_tcp (forward eth1) >> mark 42 >> kernel

Figure 2: Memory layout of the executable program

The curryfied arguments of such functions are stored in a functional node. For performance reasons, depending on their size (as compared to that of a pointer) either their value or a pointer to a separate chunk of memory is stored in the node. Once the AST is converted into the executable program, the functional composition is transactionally enabled for a specified group of endpoints with a single atomic operation. This enables computations that can be dynamically updated in real–time, for example in response to network events.

The primitive operations implemented in the functional engine are divided into different symbol tables based on their prototypes. Monadic functions take as argument a socket buffer (`sk_buff` for the Linux kernel) and return the `sk_buff` enriched with a context (representing action, state and logs for I/O). Predicates can receive some optional arguments and a `sk_buff` and return a boolean value. Properties return a value associated with the packet. More in general, functions can access the `sk_buff`, some arguments specified by the functional composition in user–space (which are curryfied), possibly additional functions passed as arguments, and a state associated with the packet which is stored in the control buffer of the `sk_buff`. In particular, the control buffer hosts a number of meta information that is used to implement the `Fanout`, the `State` and the `IO` monads used to perform actions on the packet.

Note that the `Action` monad includes the effects of a *State monad*, implementing two different kind of states: volatile and persistent. The volatile one is used to store information related to the current computation and is passed along the chain of functions. Such a state is available to all the functions and to the user–space applications when the packet and its meta–data are passed to the sockets. The volatile state has a scope limited to the composition, it is thread safe and represents a mechanism for classification that can be triggered by in–kernel functions. On the other hand, the persistent state (one per socket, or group of sockets) enables stateful computations (see Section 7.4). Such a state is reset when the computation is associated with a group of endpoints and persists until the group exists, allowing for more complex packet processing. It can be implemented in a purely functional environment by feeding the output state at the end of the pipeline back to the input of the pipeline when the next packet arrives.

As an example, we report the in–kernel function that is executed once the monadic function `l3_proto` is evaluated by the functional engine. The function implements a filter for the layer 3 protocol specified as argument (e.g., `l3_proto 0x800` to filter for IP packets).

```
Action_sk_buff
filter_l3_proto(arguments_t args,
                struct sk_buff *skb)
{
    const u16 type = get_data(u16, args);

    if (eth_hdr(skb)->h_proto ==
    __constant_htons(type))
            return pass(skb);

    return drop(skb);
}
```

The function uses the standard methodology of parsing packets used in the Linux kernel. The return value, instead, specifies a computation by using the functions defined in the **Fanout** monad (i.e. **pass** and **drop**). The type `arguments_t` is an additional argument used to mimicking currying at the kernel level. The function may access to the curryfied arguments by means of the appropriate macro, e.g. `get_data`.

6. PERFORMANCE EVALUATION

The performance of the PFQ–Lang implementation presented in Section 5 has been evaluated through an extensive set of experiments. All the experiments have been performed on a PC equipped with an Intel 82599 10G NIC having 128 hardware queues and based on a 6-core Intel Xeon X5650 running at 2.67GHz. This means that without hyper–threading, the maximum number of parallel instances of the functional engine (processing pipelines) that can be executed simultaneously is 6. Since the more recent release of PFQ does not benefit from hyper–threading, processing pipelines have been tested by varying the number of hardware queues (and therefore the NAPI contexts) from 1 to 6.

The performance has been measured by feeding the PC running PFQ, the functional engine, and the PFQ–Lang coded applications, with packets generated at increasing rates, and measuring the rate of processed packets. The packet length is set to 64 bytes (worst–case).

In the first experiment, the performance of an empty processing pipeline has been measured to have some baseline performance to be used as a reference. This experiment basically measures the PFQ performance in capturing packets and the minimum overhead introduced by the functional engine. Figure 3 shows the results. As it can be noticed, on

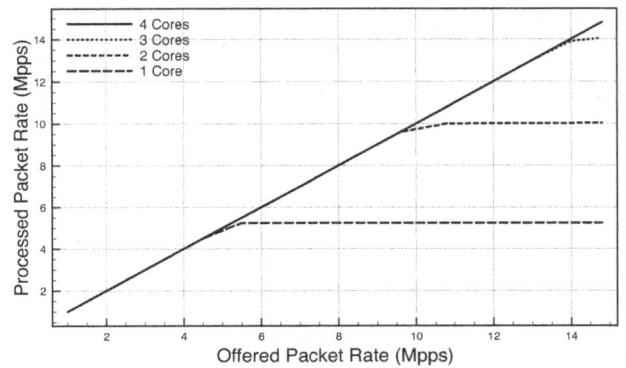

Figure 3: Empty processing pipeline

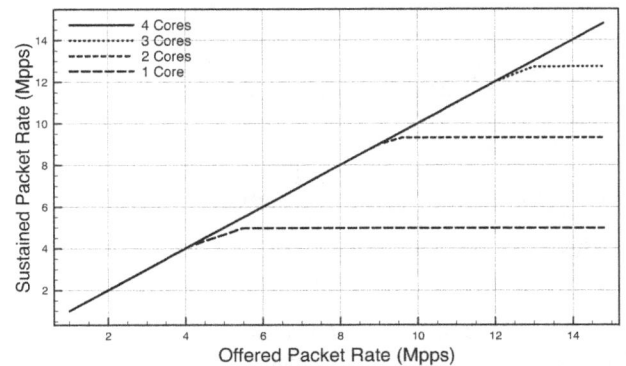

Figure 4: Processing pipeline consisting of a single unit function

the hardware available to us, PFQ is able to capture packets at line rate from a 10Gb Ethernet card by using 4 CPU cores with vanilla drivers (it is worth reminding that this corresponds to around 14.8 Mpps). When 3 CPU cores are used, PFQ can capture up to 14 Mpps. 2 CPU cores can capture up to 10 Mpps, while a single CPU core can reach about 5.5 Mpps.

After measuring the performance of PFQ and an empty computation, the performance of the simplest possible function (a single **unit** action) has been evaluated. The results are reported in Figure 4 and show that introducing a simple action in the pipeline slightly reduces the performance achieved when using 2 CPU cores or 3 CPU cores, while the performance of a single standalone pipeline does not seem to be significantly affected. The functional engine scales (with respect to the number of instances) slightly worse than in the first case, but still scales pretty well.

Then, the performance of the functional engine when executing a more complex computation (including a conditional action and the delivery of packets to user–space) has been evaluated. The function used in this case is

```
(when is_tcp (mark 42)) >-> steer_ip
```

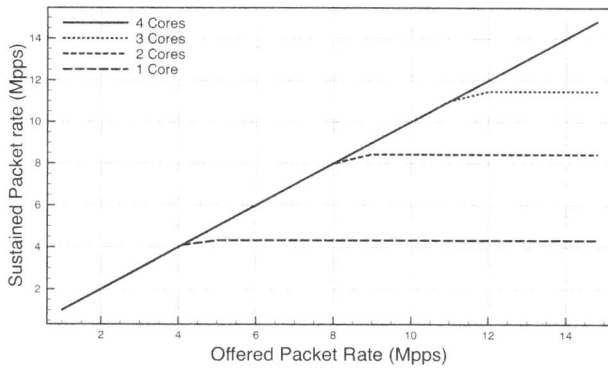

Figure 5: Functional computation: `(when is_tcp (mark 42)) >-> steer_ip`

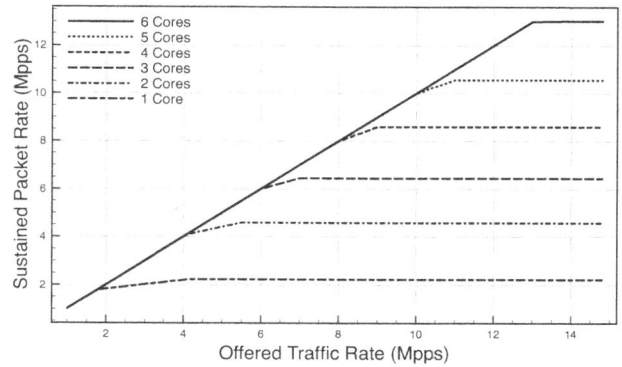

Figure 6: Functional computation: `forward "eth2" >-> drop`

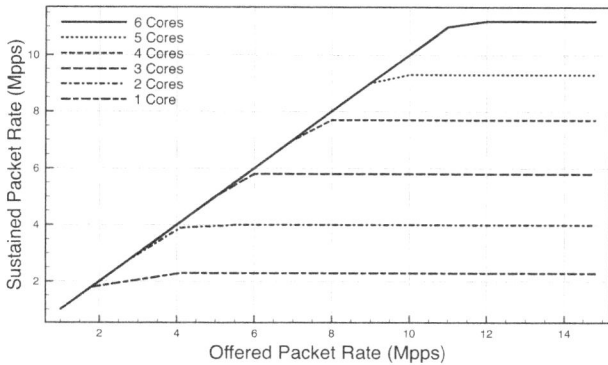

Figure 7: Heavier functional computation: CRC evaluation

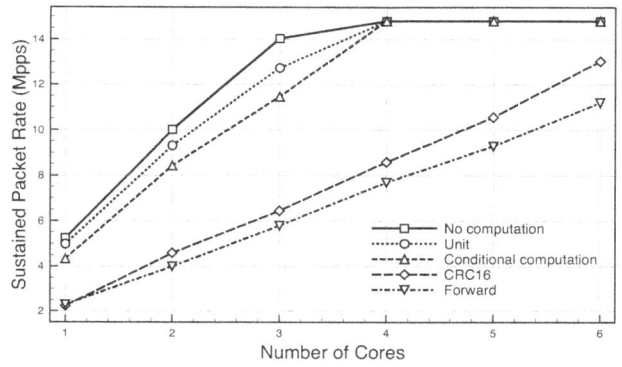

Figure 8: Scalability Overview

which marks the TCP packets with value 42 and then delivers all the packets to user–space by using a steering function. The packet delivery is obtained by calculating a symmetric hash on the IP source and destination addresses, thus forcing packets generated between the same pair of hosts to be always delivered to the same endpoint(s). Figure 5 shows that the engine is again able to process (and deliver to user–space) packets at line rate when using 4 CPU cores. As expected, the performance achieved when using 1, 2, or 3 CPU cores are slightly worse than in the previous cases, indicating that the increased complexity of the computation can affect the number of packets per second that the engine can process.

Figure 6 shows the performance of a computation which performs forwarding to a network device, and then drops all of the packets (hiding them to the kernel). This experiment basically measures the overhead introduced by the I/O monad (the cost of sending a packet), showing that the system can reach a forwarding rate of around 12 Mpps with the hardware available to us.

Notice that, so far, all of the tested computations consumed a very small amount of execution time. In a last experiment, the performance achieved when using a CPU–intensive computation (computing the CRC16 on all of the

bytes of each packet) has been evaluated. The results are reported in Figure 7 and shows that the system still scales linearly with the number of cores and reaches around 13 Mpps processing rate on the hardware available to us.

As a final remark, it is worth noticing that in all of the experiments the performance lines become flat after the peak throughput is reached (in other words, when the maximum "Processed Packet Rate" is reached, increasing the "Offered Traffic Rate" does not decrease the performance). This shows that PFQ and PFQ–Lang work well even in overload conditions. Figure 8 shows the peak throughput measured in the various experiments as a function of the number of used CPU cores, and tells us that the PFQ–Lang/PFQ combination is able to properly scale with the number of cores.

7. USE CASES

This section provides some examples of possible network applications that can be implemented by programming the functional engine. Such examples range from packet forwarding, port mirroring, a load balancer switch, stateless and stateful firewalls, and two simple early–stage processing applications for network monitoring.

7.1 Port mirroring

Since it is possible to use a NIC as one of the endpoints, packets can be easily forwarded to other machines by simply directing them to the proper endpoint. This allows to efficiently implement the data plane of a switching node through a set of pure functions.

The combined use of the *IO monad* [13] and a suitable garbage collector allows the actual forwarding operations to take place at the end of the processing pipeline, even if some intermediate stages might return a different packet. This way, the purely functional "lazy" nature of the pipeline stages is preserved. Furthermore, it turns out that lazy forwarding leads to performance optimization as, the a posteriori knowledge of the number of forwarding operations requested for a packet, always saves one shallow copy of the packet itself.

A mirroring port can then be simply instantiated through the following expression:

```
forward "eth1" >-> kernel
```

where the ports to mirror are specified when the group of sockets (for which the functional composition is specified) is bound to a list of devices.

7.2 Load Balancer

The use of randomized operations easily allow the implementation of a network *load balancer* when endpoints are network devices. To enable this, the application needs to associate NICs to special endpoints (egress sockets) to be used for the fanout. Hence, a very simple flow–based load balancer can be implemented by a single steering function:

```
steer_flow
```

or, in alternative, by any other steering or dispatching functions available from the language.

7.3 Stateless Firewall

A pipeline of purely functional filters can be used to implement a firewall. Filters can drop packets, or set them to be re-injected in the protocol stack (so that they are actually received by the system).

For instance, functional filters can be configured in order to:

- block the packets explicitly recognized by the pipeline. In this case, all the received packets are set by the first stage of the pipeline to be re–injected in the protocol stack, and some of the following stages can explicitly drop the packets to be blocked by the firewall;

```
kernel >-> (when has_port 22 &&
            !(address "131.114.0.0" 16) drop )
```

- block all the packets except for the ones recognized by the pipeline. In this case, by default, packets are not marked in any way (i.e., by the first stage of the pipeline), but are explicitly marked as "re–inject in the protocol stack" when recognized by some filter.

```
when has_port 80 kernel
```

Notice that in this case the firewall is stateless, because packets are received or dropped upon their properties, and not on the basis of previous packets.

7.4 Stateful Firewall

In some cases, a firewall requires a *stateful* approach, in which the doom of a packet is determined by the previous history of the system.

A simple, though very descriptive example, is *port knocking* that can be used to illustrate a stateful in–switch processing chain [5].

Port knocking is a well known method for a host to open a port (say the ssh port 22) on a firewall and consists of sending an ordered sequence of packets to a pre–established number of closed ports (say, 1111, 2222 and 3333). After the complete sequence is correctly received, the firewall opens the port 22 and let packets from that host pass.

A natural way to implement port knocking is to use a state machine, which using a non purely–functional approach can be easily implemented by using a global persistent state that can be modified upon packet arrivals. When using a purely functional processing pipeline, instead, this state machine can be implemented through a state monad. This state is propagated in the pipeline for each processed packet, and the output state is fed back to the input of the pipeline when the next packet arrives, hence implementing a persistent memory.

Naturally, the output value of the pipeline must be stored somewhere in memory in order to be associated with the next packet. If multiple sources are present and feed multiple parallel packet processing pipelines (implemented by threads), this value must be protected from concurrent accesses by using some standard methods.

By using the generic hash table map, the functional code for this application becomes:

```
state3 = (map ip_src) == 3
state2 = (map ip_src) == 2
state1 = (map ip_src) == 1

conditional state3 kernel
  conditional state2  && d_port == 3333
    (set_map ip_src 3) >-> drop
      conditional state1 && d_port == 2222
        (set_map ip_src 2) >-> drop
          conditional d_port == 1111
            (set_map ip_src 1) >-> drop
            (set_map ip_src 0) >-> drop
```

7.5 Monitoring

PFQ–Lang has also been designed for network monitoring. By leveraging the features/performance of PFQ in capturing packets from multiple NICs (or from multiple hardware queues), PFQ–Lang enables the creation of efficient early stages computations for more complex monitoring applications.

PFQ–Lang includes a set of functions specifically designed for packet filtering and steering, covering the most used protocols and heuristics. For instance, an early stage computation suitable for an application that estimates the network parameters of RTP flows (i.e. packet loss, end-to-end delay and jitter) can be instantiated as:

```
conditional is_rtp (class 0 >-> steer_rtp)
               class 1
```

The heuristic `is_rtp` is used to detect VoIP flows even in the absence of RTCP traffic, and `steer_rtp` is the steering function used to dispatch RTP/RTCP packets across the endpoints in use in the class 0 (subset of endpoints of the group for which the composition is specified). Traffic not detected as RTP/RTCP is sent to a subset group of endpoints (class 1) designed to receive packets for other purposes (e.g., debugging).

7.6 Legacy applications

PFQ comes with a full-featured pcap library, enabling legacy applications to benefit from its features. The pcap interface is mapped over the rich PFQ APIs, and when no match is possible – that is when no pcap function is available to wrap PFQ APIs – other mechanisms, such as environment variables, are adopted. As a result, even legacy applications can benefit from PFQ–Lang to create early stages programs for network applications.

Among the predefined steering functions, a very useful one is `steer_net`. Such a function takes a string as network address (IP) along with a prefix (as second argument) to identify a network. The last parameter is a second prefix used to further subnet such a network and to steer the related packets to different endpoints.

```
steer_net "192.168.0.0" 16 24
```

In the reported example, the traffic that belong to the 192.168.0.0/16 network is selected, split into 256 C-classes, and finally steered to the endpoints.

The PFQ pcap interface is extended with an environment variable that allows to launch applications specifying for them the group id of their sockets. Therefore once the above program is specified for a group through a control socket, say group 42, it suffices to launch multiple sessions of the legacy applications and let them see the traffic properly split.

A typical example is that of multiple *snort* sessions:

```
# PFQ_GROUP=42  snort -c /etc/snort.conf \
   -l /var/log/snort1/
# PFQ_GROUP=42  snort -c /etc/snort.conf \
   -l /var/log/snort2/
# PFQ_GROUP=42  snort -c /etc/snort.conf \
   -l /var/log/snort3/
```

8. RELATED WORK

The present work tackles the problem of software defined traffic processing in a purely functional way by the definition of a specific domain language.

A seminal functional approach towards flexible and programmable networks was made by SwitchWare [3]. However, back in 1998, the performance of SwitchWare suffered from the limitations of the underlying Caml lamguage. In the present work, instead, we aim at proving that a functional approach may well reach top class performance, just as close as the ones that can be attained by classic imperative programming.

The adoption of a software defined approach in the monitoring domain has recently emerged as a promising solution and several initial proposals have appeared in the literature. OpenFlow [18] itself has in its more recent releases enriched the type and number of counters exposed to the control plane by introducing some new functions dedicated to monitoring. Still tightly coupled with Openflow, OpenState [5] advocates the introduction of a higher level of control logic within the OpenFlow switch itself to enabling stateful data plane processing by means of extended Finite Automata.

OpenSketch [28] introduces a software defined measurement architecture based on a three-stage computational structure (hashing, filtering, and counting), and on a measurement library to configure the computation pipeline. In the Software Defined Monitoring platform [22], the monitoring hardware is tightly coupled with the control software. While the software performs a detailed application-level monitoring of interesting/suspicious patterns, it configures the hardware to perform a high–speed ordinary NetFlow monitoring of the uninteresting bulk traffic at the same time.

In the past, seminal works on programmable networks have been proposed within the European projects SCAMPI and its follow-up project LOBSTER. Such projects developed a programmable monitoring probe equipped with a Monitoring Application Programming Interface (MAPI) [25] and a dedicated monitoring adapter to allow the development of custom C++ application. CoMo [15] proposes a modular approach based on monitoring plugins, while Prog-ME [29] defines a runtime programmable network flow aggregator that can be configured through an ad–hoc declarative language. RTCmon [12] presents a framework for developing (C++ only) monitoring applications while Coralreef [16] and FLAME [4] grant programmability by means of suitable "hooks" to their C/C++/Perl functions. Recently, Intel has released DPDK [1], a set of libraries and drivers for fast packet processing on multicore architectures for Linux.

Monitoring programmability has also been addressed by Blockmon [14], which introduces the concept of primitive composition on a message passing based architecture. Although providing a remarkable difference with respect to previous solutions, the Blockmon modular structure still proves to be quite strict and requires network programmers to build "nearly" from scratch monitoring applications that must conform to quite rigid templates and configuration layouts. The Blockmon modular principle is borrowed from the Click modular router [20] which is itself a fundamental pillar in the history of device programmability. However, the approach presented in this paper differs from the Click one since it is based on a purely functional language and PFQ–Lang computations are (combinations of) pure functions, while Click configurations are built by connecting elements that can have side effects. Furthermore, the Click approach has recently been complemented to take advantage of GPU computational power in Snap [24].

From a pure traffic measuring point of view, Braun *et al.* [8] present an extensive comparison of available capturing tools with guidelines and possible improvements to reach higher performance. PF_RING [11] uses a memory mapped ring to export packets to user space processes: such a ring can be filled by a regular sniffer or by specially modified drivers, which skip the default kernel processing chain. More recently, PF_RING DNA [10] and Netmap [23] have proposed accelerated solutions with drivers that memory map at user space the ring descriptors of NICs, allowing a single CPU to count 64-bytes-long packets up to 10 Gbps line-speed. PFQ [7], which provides the founding ground of the present work, is a monitoring framework that runs on top of vanilla drivers for any network device and takes full advantage of CPU parallelism and multi–queue network cards.

9. CONCLUSION

This paper presents an attempt towards the definition of a purely functional approach to generic packet processing and network middlebox development. The idea itself is closely related to the philosophy of Software Defined Networking, where data–plane and control–plane are logically decoupled. A functional engine, consisting of a rich set of data–plane primitives for generic packet processing, exposes a programmable interface towards the higher–level user plane. Packet processing is instantiated by composing a number of elementary operations by means of a functional program (written in a domain specific functional language). This way, an initially neutral middlebox gets specialized to the specific operations defined at software (user) level and the behavior of the middlebox nature can be changed as easily as re–programming its functional interface. The overall system prototype is implemented on Linux OS by using PFQ as the underlying packet capturing "arm". Performance evaluation shows results that scale linearly with the amount of offered traffic and the number of cores used in the computations. In addition, a set of possible use cases for everyday experience is presented (namely, a set of functionally different middleboxes) to show the expressiveness of the programming interface as well as the easy reconfigurability of middleboxes themselves.

Acknowledgment

This work was partially supported by the Italian MIUR funded project GreenNet under grant RBFR100QHJ.

10. REFERENCES

[1] DPDK, http://dpdk.org.

[2] PFQ wiki, https://github.com/pfq/pfq/wiki, 2014.

[3] D. S. Alexander et al. The switchware active network architecture. *Network, IEEE*, 12(3):29–36, 1998.

[4] K. Anagnostakis et al. Open packet monitoring on flame: Safety, performance, and applications. In *Active Networks*, volume 2546 of *Lecture Notes in Computer Science*, pages 120–131. Springer, 2002.

[5] G. Bianchi, M. Bonola, A. Capone, and C. Cascone. Openstate: Programming platform-independent stateful openflow applications inside the switch. *SIGCOMM Comput. Commun. Rev.*, 44(2):44–51, Apr. 2014.

[6] N. Bonelli. http://www.pfq.io.

[7] N. Bonelli, A. Di Pietro, S. Giordano, and G. Procissi. On multi—gigabit packet capturing with multi—core commodity hardware. In *Proc. of PAM'2012*, pages 64–73. Springer-Verlag, 2012.

[8] L. Braun et al. Comparing and improving current packet capturing solutions based on commodity hardware. In *IMC '10*, pages 206–217. ACM, 2010.

[9] Cisco Systems. Cisco Visual Networking Index: Forecast and Methodology. "http://www.cisco.com", June 2011.

[10] L. Deri. http://www.ntop.org/products/pf_ring/dna/.

[11] F. Fusco and L. Deri. High speed network traffic analysis with commodity multi-core systems. In *Proc. of IMC '10*, pages 218–224. ACM, 2010.

[12] F. Fusco et al. Enabling high-speed and extensible real-time communications monitoring. In *Proc. of IFIP/IEEE IM'09*, pages 343–350. IEEE Press, 2009.

[13] A. D. Gordon and K. Hammond. Monadic i/o in haskell 1.3. In *Proceedings of the haskell Workshop*, pages 50–69, 1995.

[14] F. Huici et al. Blockmon: a high-performance composable network traffic measurement system. *SIGCOMM Comput. Commun. Rev.*, 42(4):79–80, Aug. 2012.

[15] G. Iannaccone. Fast prototyping of network data mining applications. In *Proc. of PAM 2006*, Adelaide, Australia, 2006.

[16] K. Keys et al. The architecture of coralreef: an internet traffic monitoring software suite. In *Proc. of PAM 2006*, 2001.

[17] S. Liang, P. Hudak, and M. Jones. Monad transformers and modular interpreters. In *Proc. of ACM SIGPLAN-SIGACT*, pages 333–343, 1995.

[18] N. McKeown et al. Openflow: Enabling innovation in campus networks. *SIGCOMM Comput. Commun. Rev.*, 38(2):69–74, Mar. 2008.

[19] E. Moggi. Computational lambda–calculus and monads. In *LICS*, pages 14–23. IEEE Computer Society Press, 1988.

[20] R. Morris, E. Kohler, J. Jannotti, and M. F. Kaashoek. The click modular router. *SIGOPS Oper. Syst. Rev.*, 33(5):217–231, 1999.

[21] B. C. Pierce. *Basic Category Theory for Computer Scientists*. MIT Press, 1991.

[22] V. Pus and L. Kekely. Software defined monitoring: A new approach to network traffic monitoring. In *Proc. of TNC2013*, 2013.

[23] L. Rizzo. Netmap: a novel framework for fast packet i/o. In *Proc. of USENIX ATC'2012*, pages 1–12. USENIX Association, 2012.

[24] W. Sun and R. Ricci. Fast and flexible: Parallel packet processing with gpus and click. In *Proc. of ANCS '13*, pages 25–36, Piscataway, NJ, USA, 2013. IEEE Press.

[25] P. Trimintzios et al. Dimapi: An application programming interface for distributed network monitoring. In *Proc. of IEEE/IFIP NOMS'06*, 2006.

[26] P. Wadler. The essence of functional programming. In *Proc. of ACM SIGPLAN-SIGACT*, pages 1–14, 1992.

[27] P. Wadler. Monads for functional programming. In *Advanced Functional Programming*, volume 925 of *Lecture Notes in Computer Science*, pages 24–52. 1995.

[28] M. Yu, L. Jose, and R. Miao. Software defined traffic measurement with opensketch. In *Proc. of the 10th USENIX Symposium on Networked Systems Design and Implementation (NSDI 13)*, pages 29–42, Lombard, IL, 2013. USENIX.

[29] L. Yuan, C.-N. Chuah, and P. Mohapatra. ProgME: towards programmable network measurement. *SIGCOMM Comput. Commun. Rev.*, 37(4):97–108, 2007.

A Scalable Routing and Admission Control Model in SDN-based Networks

M. Rasih Celenlioglu
Department of Computer Engineering
Gebze Institute of Technology
Gebze, Kocaeli, Turkey
mcelenlioglu@gyte.edu.tr

H. Ali Mantar
Department of Computer Engineering
Gebze Institute of Technology
Gebze, Kocaeli, Turkey
hamantar@gyte.edu.tr

ABSTRACT

In this paper, we propose a scalable routing and admission control model for Software Defined Networks (SDN). We use pre-established multi-path (PMP) model to increase routing scalability and reduce admission control time.

Categories and Subject Descriptors

C.2.1 [**Computer Communication Networks**]: Network Architecture and Design

Keywords

Software defined networking; controller design; QoS routing

1. INTRODUCTION

Recently, the demand for access to the Internet has changed. The Internet is switched to Internet of Services (IoS). The amount of traffic in the Internet has been grown dramatically. Thus, a better network management is required. Software Defined Networking (SDN) [3] has been proposed for efficient and flexible resource management. In SDN, control plane and data plane are separated. Control plane is unified in a logically central entity called controller. It has global network state information and responsible for routing and management of the underlying network. The data plane resides within switches. These switches forward packets based on instructions in their flow tables. Open Networking Foundation (ONF) [3] develops OpenFlow (OF) protocol, which provides signaling between controller and switches.

SDN has several issues to be solved. First of all, controller becomes bottleneck as the network size increases because it is the only entity that makes decisions on behalf of all switches. Secondly, routing itself is a heavy process. Performing routing on behalf of all the switches will be much heavier. Thirdly, since controller is the only decision maker, processing delay must be very low for scalability. Finally, controller is the only entity that is able configure flow tables of switches. When a decision is made, controller updates

ANCS'14, Oct 20–21, 2014, Los Angeles, CA, USA.
ACM 978-1-4503-2839-5/14/10.
http://dx.doi.org/10.1145/2658260.2661770.

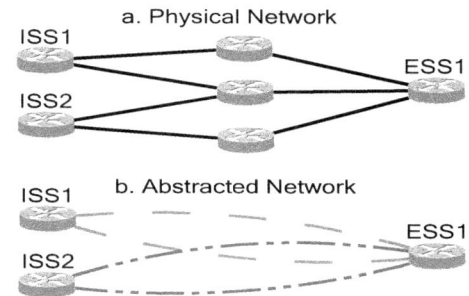

Figure 1: Illustration of physical network (a) and abstracted network with multi-path (b).

flow tables. This produces high volume of signaling traffic between controller and switches. Signaling traffic increases as the number of switches in the network increases.

Most of the SDN related studies in the literature has been made for data center networks. In these studies, incoming requests to data centers are assigned to servers by controller [4] to improve load balancing. For the scalability problems, multiple controllers are used [1]. In [2], we proposed Bandwidth Broker based model for intra and inter-domain networks. However, signaling protocol in that model differs from SDN.

In this paper, we propose a scalable routing and admission control model for SDN-based networks. In our model, complex network is abstracted into a simple network that consists of ingress-egress pairs. Several paths are pre-established (PMP) between each pair. Controller performs routing, admission control, signaling and resource management based on these paths. Network abstraction is made for the ease of network management and resource utilization.

2. SDN-BASED ROUTING AND ADMISSION CONTROL MODEL

We propose a scalable routing and admission control model based on PMPs between each ingress switches (ISS) and egress switches (ESS) as in Figure 1. Core switches between ISS and ESS only perform forwarding. Throughout this work, we assume that paths are pre-defined. Controller performs routing, admission control, signaling and resource management based on these paths.

Figure 2 shows the functional design of controller. Domain topology module handles events related to network topology. Link state database stores up-to-date link state information

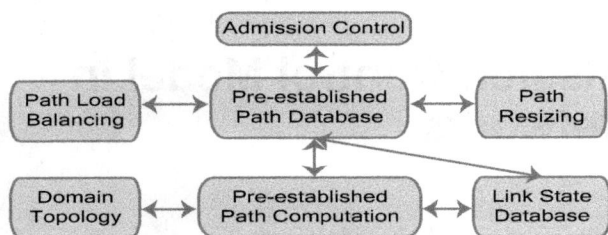

Figure 2: Functional decomposition of controller.

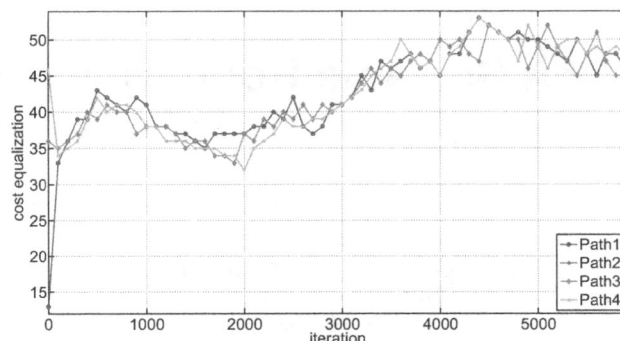

Figure 3: The cost equalization of paths.

similar to OSPF table. PMP computation module establishes several maximally disjoint paths between each ISS-ESS pair (IEP) [5]. The capacity of a path is randomly chosen at the first stage. Path Load Balancing module provides load balancing by shifting flows from one path to another. Controller resizes capacity of paths using Path-Resizing Module based on PMP loads. Controller does not run routing algorithm online. It performs admission control by looking in PMP database. Thus, it makes decisions fast.

Scalable routing and admission control are performed based on PMP between each IEP. Controller does not compute path finding algorithm for each flow request but uses PMPs. These paths are pre-established and can be resized based on aggregated traffic load. Whenever a new flow request is received by an ISS, it informs the controller. Controller finds the corresponding IEP by looking at the destination IP address. Admission control is performed by querying PMP database. If there is enough amount of bandwidth in corresponding IEP, the request is accepted. After acceptance, the flow is assigned to an available path by its IP prefix.

Controller configures core switches at path establishment step or whenever PMPs are changed. These switches take marked packets and perform forwarding based on instructions matching with path-id in their flow table. Controller does not modify core switches for each request. Since signaling occurs only between controller and associated ISS per request, signaling scalability is achieved. Controller performs load balancing between paths of an IEP and path resizing between different IEPs so as to increase resource utilization. For load balancing, since a path consists of links, controller finds link costs by dividing its traffic load by its capacity at first. Then, link with maximum cost becomes path cost. After that, average path cost is computed for a pair. Finally, controller computes the amount of flows to be shifted from congested paths to less congested ones. Controller performs these actions iteratively until the path costs are equalized. In our model, controller reserves certain amount of capacity for each path at the beginning. Only the controller is in charge of updating path capacities. When the traffic load of a PMPs between an IEP exceeds a certain threshold (e.g., 95% of its maximum capacity), controller run path resizing algorithm. The crucial point here is that path resizing process is not triggered based on individual flow requests. It is triggered based on aggregated traffic in PMPs.

We built a simple virtual network as illustrated in Figure 1 using Mininet, Floodlight and and OF v1.0. Realtime network traffic is generated between end points. Static PMPs are created using VLAN. Each VLAN id indicates a single path. Figure 3 depicts that path costs are equalized over time when controller performs load balancing periodically. We compared our model with non-SDN model that does not perform load balancing and resizing. If only one path is highly loaded (over 90 % of its capacity), our model and non-SDN model accepts 57% and 11% of incoming requests respectively. When overall network is highly loaded, our model accepts 40% and non-SDN model accepts 32 % of incoming requests. Finally, we observed that admission control time takes 1 ms in average when non-SDN model varies between 13-26 ms.

3. CONCLUSION

In this work, we propose an SDN-based routing and admission control model. Controller performs admission control based on PMPs. Network abstraction, load balancing and path resizing methods are developed to increase network resource utilization. Signaling scalability is achieved by resizing PMPs based on aggregated traffic in offline.

Acknowledgements

This research was supported by ARGELA and TUBITAK under Grant No. 113E253.

4. REFERENCES

[1] Y. Hu, W. Wang, X. Gong, X. Que, and S. Cheng. Balanceflow: Controller load balancing for openflow networks. In *Cloud Computing and Intelligent Systems (CCIS), 2012 IEEE 2nd International Conference on*, volume 02, pages 780–785, Oct 2012.

[2] H. Mantar, J. Hwang, I. Okumus, and S. Chapin. A scalable model for interbandwidth broker resource reservation and provisioning. *Selected Areas in Communications, IEEE Journal on*, 22(10):2019–2034, Dec 2004.

[3] Open Networking Foundation. [Online]. Available: http://opennetworking.org/.

[4] R. Wang, D. Butnariu, and J. Rexford. Openflow-based server load balancing gone wild. In *Proceedings of the 11th USENIX Conference on Hot Topics in Management of Internet, Cloud, and Enterprise Networks and Services*, Hot-ICE'11, pages 12–12, Berkeley, CA, USA, 2011.

[5] J. Whalen and J. Kenney. Finding maximal link disjoint paths in a multigraph. In *Global Telecommunications Conference, 1990, and Exhibition. 'Communications: Connecting the Future', GLOBECOM '90., IEEE*, pages 470–474 vol.1, Dec 1990.

High Performance Multi-field Packet Classification Using Bucket Filtering and GPU Processing

Cheng-Liang Hsieh
Department of Electrical and Computer
Engineering
Southern Illinois University, Carbondale, IL
hsieh@siu.edu

Ning Weng
Department of Electrical and Computer
Engineering
Southern Illinois University, Carbondale, IL
nweng@uis.edu

ABSTRACT

The literature review shows a trend to arbitrary number of multi-field packet classification is evolved from standard 5-tuple matching to support new applications like OpenFlow switch which processes upto 15 fields [1]. However, arbitrary number of multi-field packet classification becomes a great challenge regarding to performance, memory requirement, and update cost. In this paper, a high performance multi-field packet classification system is designed and implemented using bucket filtering and GPU processing.

Categories and Subject Descriptors

C.2.6 [**Internetworking**]: Routers—*Packet Classification*

General Terms

Design, Performance

Keywords

Packet Classification, GPU

1. INTRODUCTION

Packet classification is a key function to support network applications like firewall, intrusion detection, and differentiated services. In this paper, we design a high performance multi-field packet classification system as Figure 1 with 3 steps: rule sampling, packet pre-match, and final match. The rule set is programmed off-line to generate several lookup tables and sampling positions based on the memory and performance requirement. Similar techniques had been discussed in RFC, modular approach, and [3] but none of them leverages the independence between two sampling spaces. The proposed system exploits two key observations from ClassBench rule set [2]: the independence among bit positions in a rule set and the sparsity of a classification rule set. Our goal is to find out the most significant bit positions from different fields and concatenate them as sampling values for different rules. The rule sampling process create

ANCS'14, October 20–21, 2014, Los Angeles, CA, USA.
ACM 978-1-4503-2839-5/14/10.
http://dx.doi.org/10.1145/2658260.2661768 .

a representative sampling values for rules, breaks the bonds between different rules, and generates a data structure which is easy to update and implement on multi-core platform like GPU for better throughput. The proposed method processes those sampling values to reduce the storage requirement as the pre-match result to improve the processing latency at final match stage. This paper demonstrates a single Nvidia K20C GPU implementation result to show that the proposed solution can achieve about 737 MPPS throughput with 1K rules and 147 MPPS with 100K rules which is about 10 times faster compared to current research on multiple fields [1] but still keep the same memory requirement for 100K rules as 5-tuple HyperCuts solution.

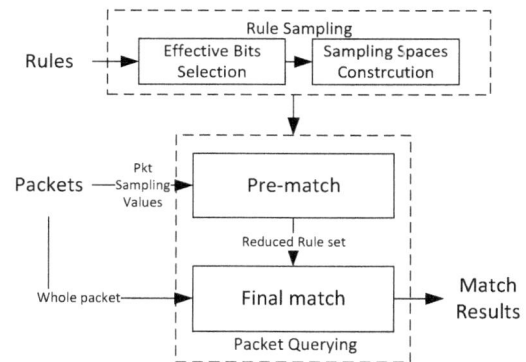

Figure 1: The proposed multiple fields packet classification system.

2. RULE AND PACKET SAMPLING

The proposed solution in this paper produces at least one set of sampling value for each rule. Each set contains a subset index for rule set segmentation and a bucket index to construct a sampling space. A rule set will be divided into several subsets based on the subset index and each subset constructs its own sampling space based on the bucket index. A sampling value is a concatenated value formed by effective bits from different fields. The size of sampling values depends on the rule set character and performance-storage trade-off criteria. An example of rule sampling is shown as Figure 2. Packets are sampled with the same bit positions as the rule sampling process and generates sampling value sets for subset and bucket lookups.

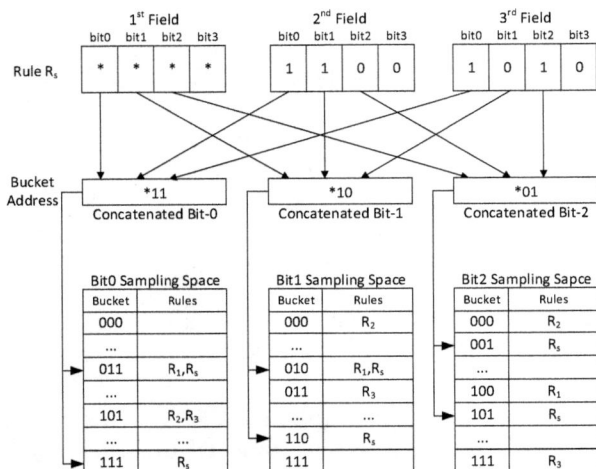

Figure 2: The rule programming and sampling space construction for a 3-field rule, Rs. The concatenation of bit serves as the address of buckets in a sampling space where rules were stored. * is the wildcard and it is expanded to all possible buckets.

2.1 Wildcard ratio

A higher wildcard ratio in a sampling value results in more conflicts on the sampling values from different rules and lower the discretion of the sampling process. The selected bit position should be with lower wildcard ratio compared to other candidates from the same field.

2.2 Dependence index

All bits in the same field have different representative and some of them are identical. The correlation index between different bit positions is used to find out effective bit positions. The correlation between fields also need to be checked to guarantee the independence on all bit positions.

2.2.1 Inter-field correlation

The field-to-field correlation figures out the independence between two fields. To make the sampling values are representative, only those fields with low dependence should be picked to reduce the number of conflicted sampling values for different rules.

2.2.2 Intra-field correlation

The bucketing filtering remove the unrelated rules based the independence between two sampling spaces. The selected bit positions from the same field should have low dependence to each other to guarantee a low conflicts on the sampling values.

2.3 Diversity index

The diversity index of two different bit positions is calculated to detect the distribution of sampling values. With high diversity, sampling values are distribute evenly with more unique sampling values and the lower maximum number of rules in a bucket.

3. BUCKET FILTERING

Rules with same bucket index are kept in the same bucket of a sampling space. Several effective bit positions could be found from the same field in a rule set to create more than one sampling space at the same time. With low dependence index and high diversity index, we can construct sampling spaces with low conflicts on bucket indexes. Bucket filtering leverages the independence between two sampling spaces to reduce the rule candidates significantly as pre-match results by filtering out the common rules in buckets from different sampling spaces. This helps to speed up the final match stage since only few rules need to be checked.

4. EXPERIMENT RESULTS

We conducted experiments on an Intel Xeon E5410 CPU machine with 4GB DDR2 RAM as the main memory and a NVIDIA K20C GPU with 5Gb GDDR5 memory for general computation. The proposed system is implemented with Debian 7.3 64-bit operating system with Cuda 5.5. To create a 15 field rule set and trace file, we follow [2] to generate classical 5-tuple data first and attach additional 10-field data based on [1] for our experiments. For those 10 additional fields, we give 5 fields with wildcard ratio in 0.1 and the rest with wildcard ratio in 0.5. Besides, 4 out of these 10 additional fields are chose based their character to have only few dominated values. All necessary data are assumed to be ready on GPU before the flow classification starts. Table 1 shows the system throughput and memory size regarding to different rule sets with varying number of rules. The proposed solution can achieve about 10 times faster compared to current research on multiple fields flow classification but still keep the memory requirement for 100K rules as 5-tuple solution. Since only significant bits are selected from the rule set, the performance difference between rule sets is small which makes the proposed solution is suitable for different types of rule sets. In the future, we plan to address the performance degradation issue regarding to the rule size.

Table 1: System throughput and memory requirement for different rule sets with 15 fields

RuleSet		Throughput(MPPS)	Memory Size(MB)
ACL1	1K	731.6	256
	10K	468.1	268
	100K	147.2	424
FW1	1K	736.7	258
	10K	483.6	270
	100K	215.2	394
IPC1	1K	737.2	257
	10K	565.1	261
	100K	251.8	328

5. REFERENCES

[1] Y. Qu, S. Zhou, and V. K. Prasanna. Scalable many-field packet classification on multi-core processors. In *SBAC-PAD*, pages 33–40, Porto de Galinhas, Brazil, Oct. 2013.

[2] D. E. Taylor and J. S. Turner. Classbench: A packet classification benchmark. *IEEE/ACM Trans. Netw.*, 15(3):499–511, June 2007.

[3] B. Yang, J. Fong, W. Jiang, Y. Xue, and J. Li. Practical multituple packet classification using dynamic discrete bit selection. *IEEE Trans. Computers*, 63(2):424–434, 2014.

QoS Aware Dynamic Power Scaling Algorithms for Deploying Energy Efficient Routers

Tian Song, Xiangjun Shi, Xiaowei Ma
Beijing Engineering Research Center of Massive Language Information Processing and Cloud Computing Application
School of Computer Science and Technology, Beijing Institute of Technology, Beijing, China, 100081
{songtian, shixiangjun, xwma}@bit.edu.cn

ABSTRACT

Energy efficient routers (EERs) are promising devices to achieve green communications for ISP to save energy and cost. However, deploying this kind of routers may introduce severe accumulated packet delay, especially for high-end optical routers. In this paper, we present three contributions to solve the above issue with dynamically balancing QoS and the energy consumption, while preserve the real deployment simple and flexible. First, we propose a QoS aware power scaling algorithm for single self-motivated EER. Second, we present a QoS aware open-loop deployment method by using a short-term traffic forecast model. This model can assist EERs to adapt their capacities with the information of the incoming network traffic along the traffic path. Third, we propose a QoS aware feedback deployment method for better energy efficiency by building local control systems between two adjacent EER pairs. We evaluate the above algorithms by performing simulations. The results show that our methods are energy efficieny while controlling the packet delay.

Categories and Subject Descriptors

C.2 [**Computer-Communication Networks**]

Keywords

Green network; Energy efficient router; QoS aware

1. INTRODUCTION

In the network infrastructure, routers are the basic devices and widely deployed. So it is promising for ISP to control the operating cost by reducing the energy consumption of those routers. However, this task is very challenging because adapting the processing capacity of routers may result in unstable QoS.

So we introduce a kind of QoS aware EERs which can dynamically adapt the processing capacity, then energy consumption, according to the real network traffics. To evaluate the cost of dynamic scaling of EER, we implemented

ANCS'14, October 20–21, 2014, Los Angeles, CA, USA.
ACM 978-1-4503-2839-5/14/10.
http://dx.doi.org/10.1145/2658260.2661774 .

a 4 Gbps linecard like prototype based on NetFPGA platform. The prototype [1] can dynamically adapt its capacity by scaling frequency to six levels (one sleep mode and five working modes). It works at 125 MHz, and the experiments show that only 160 ns is required to switch frequency.

In this paper, we first presented a power-scaling policy for single EER. Then we focused on deploying multiple EERs to the network easily and flexibly. We proposed and evaluated two methods to guarantee the network QoS by building a lightweight communication between those EERs.

2. POWER SCALING ALGORITHMS IN A SINGLE EER

As the scaling trigger condition, Δt is a fixed time interval of buffer sampling and frequency scalings are based on the results of input buffer occupancy sampling , so we named our method as MinLP (Minimum Latency Periodical).

Given the frequency at time t is $f_i(= f(t))$, with $l(t)$ buffer length. If no scaling occurs, there is no additional cost, the router can process packets in the next Δt time with f_i. If it is need to scale to f_j, there is an period of incapable time δ, the router can only handle packets in the next $(\Delta t - \delta)$ time with f_j. Therefore, the algorithm must balance this tradeoff and adapt frequency to an appropriate capacity level which can deal with all the remaining packets of the current buffer exactly in the next Δt. To determine the frequency of next Δt interval, $f(t + \Delta t)$. MinLP has two steps as follows.

Step 1: Suppose the router has to adapt frequency, and find a minimum (also energy efficient) frequency, f_k, that can process $l(t)$ packets in the next $\Delta t - \delta$ period.

Step 2: Adapt the frequency as follows. If the queue is empty, adapt frequency to f_0. If f_i can process all $l(t)$ packets in Δt, there is no need to scale up the frequency to f_k. Otherwise, the frequency should be scaled to f_k.

3. QOS AWARE DEPLOYMENT METHODS FOR MULTI-EERS

3.1 Open-loop Deployment(OLD)

OLD deploys EERs arbitrarily in the network. Since a single EER adapts its performance and energy in its manner, accumulated packet delays will be introduced by the multiple EERs along the path.

3.2 QoS aware Open-loop Deployment(QaOLD)

As there is no feedback during information transmission between routers, it is difficult to control the accumulated

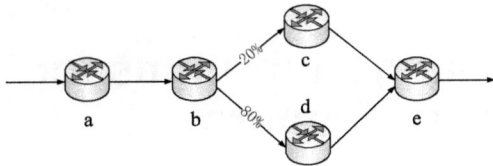

Figure 1: The network topology in our experiment.

packets delay within a limited value. In this scenario, we take use of edge router to scale processing ability independently by MinLP, the follow-up routers must fit their ability to former routers exactly to reach a better energy saving target without bringing in spare packets latency.

Assuming that each router can inform its processing ability and forwarding proportions of output ports to the following up routers in time, thus routers could scale their frequencies to the best values instantly by calculating the sum of their input ports flow rate. When the edge router scaled its process ability, it sends this value and its forwarding proportion to the next router. Once a router received these information, it's triggered to update the input speed value and switch to a suitable ability. Routers should remember the information received from each routers last time as history values, because they may not arrive synchronously.

3.3 QoS aware Feedback Control Deployment(QaFCD)

In this section, we take every two adjacent EER pairs as a feedback system. And not only data packets will be forward between routers, but also some feedforward information. After modulate the frequency, the succeeding EER R_{i+1} will give feedback information of suggestion to the former router R_i. The goal of this method is to achieve a better energy saving effection under the limitation of packet delay by the feedback system of every two EERs' negotiation model.

The feedback method is aiming to assign the delay evenly to each router in the whole data path. Thus, every feedback system has a limited value of packet delay D_{limit}.

In each feedback system, R_{i+1} has kept processing abilities (A_i, A_{i-1}) and the corresponding power consumption (P_i, P_{i-1}) of both R_i and itself. When traffic first arrives, R_i scale its capacity using MinLP. By sampling the queue length of input FIFO, we can know the general situation of traffic flow, and this value is l_i sampled by R_i. The information feedforward from R_i to R_{i+1} includes l_i and current process ability a_{ij} of R_i. Thus, R_{i+1} knows the iFIFO length of R_i and R_{i+1} (l_i and l_{i+1}), and the capacity of R_i (a_{ij}).

$$\begin{aligned} minimize \quad & p_{ij} + p_{(i+1)k} \\ s.t. \quad & l_i/a_{ij} + l_{i+1}/a_{ik} \leq D_{limit} \\ & a_{ij} \in A_i, a_{(i+1)k} \in A_{i+1} \end{aligned} \quad (1)$$

Above all, this method can be triggered every Δt, EERs pass down their information to the next EER. Then, routers run the algorithm according to the following steps.

Step 1: R_{i+1} uses Eq. 1 to calculate the optimal capacity pair of R_i and itself which can maximum the energy saving.

Step 2: Feedback the best value suggestion of capacity just calculated to the former EER.

Step 3: Compare the value which suggested by the succeeding EER to the value of EER calculated itself, chose the bigger one to be the processing ability of the next period.

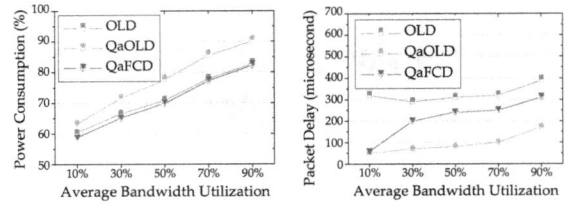

Figure 2: Comparison between OLD, QaOLD and QaFCD (a) power consumption (b) packet delay.

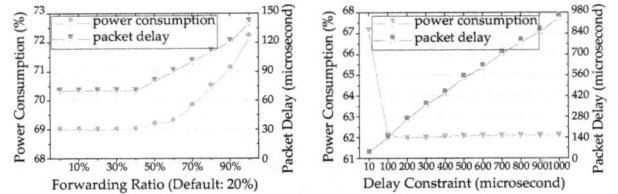

Figure 3: The performance of (a)QaOLD under different actual forwarding ratios (empirical value: 20%) (b)QaFCD under different delay constraints.

4. PERFORMANCE EVALUATION

To evaluate the performance of the algorithms, we set six frequencies for each router, and design the power percentage as $p(f_0)=0.51$ as the sleep mode and five working frequencies f_1 to f_5, where $f_0=0$, $f_1 = 0.2 * f_5$, and $f_{i+1} = 2 * f_i$. So the power consumption for each frequency can be calculated. Besides, we use a designed topology in Fig. 1 as the experiment network, and the default average bandwidth utilization is 30%. In method QaFCD, the default value of constraint packet delay is $160\mu s$. By using a set of generated traffic based on Poisson distribution, we simulated packets delay and energy consumption under different methods.

Fig. 2(a) shows that as the average bandwidth utilization increases, the power consumption of total network will grow, and OLD and QaFCD have lower power consumption, because both of them make routers scale capacity according to their own input buffer. And in Fig. 2(b), by using three methods, the tendency of packet delay increases modestly as the growth of average bandwidth utilization, OLD has the largest accumulated packet delay as our expectation.

Then, we discuss the impact on performance by using various parameter values. The routers in QaOLD have empirical values in forwarding ratio, but if the real traffic can not be forwarded according to the empirical values, the performance is not so good, as shown in Fig. 3(a).

Fig. 3(b) gives the packet delay and power consumption under different delay constraint of QaFCD, the average value of real packet delay increases in a near-liner trend. As the constraint grows to a certain value, the increase of the constraint nearly has no impact to the power consumption.

5. REFERENCES

[1] Fu, Wenliang, and Tian Song. "A frequency adjustment architecture for energy efficient router." *ACM SIGCOMM Computer Communication Review* 42, no. 4 (2012): 107-108.

Network Monitoring Probe Based on Xilinx Zynq

Jan Viktorin, Pavol Korcek, Tomas Fukac, Jan Korenek
Brno University of Technology
Faculty of Information Technology
IT4Innovations Centre of Excellence
Bozetechova 1/2, 612 66
Brno, Czech Republic
{iviktorin, ikorcek, korenek}@fit.vutbr.cz, xfukac00@stud.fit.vutbr.cz

ABSTRACT

To provide reliable network and cloud services, it is necessary to perform precise monitoring and security analysis of cloud, ISP and local networks. Current SOHO (Small Office Home Office) devices have very limited resources and can not provide precise network security monitoring in local networks. Therefore we have designed small and low-power network probe which is able to analyse the network traffic at the application layer. The Xilinx Zynq enables to divide the task between hardware and software efficiently. The FPGA logic provides preprocessing (filtering) of data and the processor performs deep packet inspection to analyse application protocols. Moreover, the probe is ready to offload any time consuming operation (eg. regular expression matching) to the FPGA logic to increase processing speed.

Categories and Subject Descriptors

C.3 [**Special-purpose and application-based systems**]: Real-time and embedded systems

General Terms

Design, Embedded, Networking

Keywords

Zynq; FPGA; Embedded; Networking; Probe

1. INTRODUCTION

Many applications are migrated to the cloud. For reliable cloud services, it is necessary to pay more and more attention to the reliability of the network. It is desirable to monitor and protect not only clouds or ISP networks, but also local networks with end users. The SOHO (Small Office Home Office) routers usually do not provide enough computational power for precise network monitoring and deep packet inspection for security analysis. NetFPGA platform [4] is suitable for network monitoring at multigigabit

ANCS'14, October 20–21, 2014, Los Angeles, CA, USA.
ACM 978-1-4503-2839-5/14/10.
http://dx.doi.org/10.1145/2658260.2661769.

networks, however, the power consumption and size of the complete system (card and a host computer) are not suitable for deployment in SOHO networks.

We have designed a small extendable probe for local networks which can monitor up to four gigabit links. The utilization of the Xilinx Zynq technology enables to perform wire-speed packet capture and filtration in FPGA logic. The ARM processor performs analysis of application protocols with the L7 filter [3] and it can utilize also other standard network monitoring and security tools available in the Linux OS. Moreover, the proposed probe is able to offload any time-critical operation to the FPGA logic. For example the probe can accelerate regular expression matching in the FPGA logic. The utilization of the RSoC Framework [5], a system for rapid prototyping of applications divided between software and hardware, simplifies implementation of the probe and ensures fast communication among the processor system and hardware accelerators.

2. ARCHITECTURE OF THE PROBE

The proposed architecture is designed to take advantage of the tight integration of ARM processor and FPGA logic within a single chip (Xilinx Zynq). The ARM processor runs a Linux OS to support various tools for network security monitoring (tcpdump, L7 filter, Snort IDS [1], etc.). The probe is designed to offload time-critical operations into the FPGA logic. Data are transferred to a custom accelerator through HP or ACP interfaces. As a future work, we plan to accelerate regular expression matching in reconstructed TCP/IP streams in order to speed up L7 protocol analysis.

The architecture is shown in Fig. 1. Packets are captured by Xilinx TEMAC IP core [6] and passed into the Processing Pipeline. The Processing Pipeline extracts metadata from packet headers and then applies filters to the incoming traffic. Every packet is compared to set of IP addresses, IP prefixes, ports and IP flows (src. and dst. IP, src. and dst. port, protocol). The filtering engine leverages the combination of a cuckoo hash engine with a binary search engine to achieve high speed processing together with efficient resource utilization. Its architecture is well scalable up to 100 Gbps [2]. The Processing Pipeline is shared by all four monitoring network interfaces, it is optimized to FPGA resource utilization and provides throughput over 40 Gbps which is more than enough for wire-speed processing on all the 1 Gbps links.

Packets are sent from the Processing Pipeline to the processor system. The probe utilizes the RSoC Framework for fast transfers between FPGA and the processor. We performed measurement of the throughput (see Table 1) to

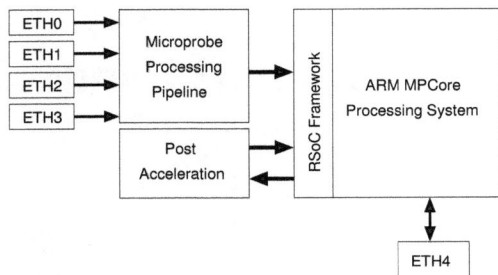

Figure 1: Architecture of the network probe. Processing pipeline and other acceleration cores are in the FPGA logic. Standard network monitoring tools are running on the ARM processor with Linux OS.

assure that the system is able to transfer all the network traffic to the ARM processor without any packet-loss. The software application can read the network traffic by the standard PCAP interface which is very often used in standard network monitoring tools.

3. HW/SW COMMUNICATION

On the Xilinx Zynq platform, The RSoC Framework integrates Xilinx DMA IP core [7]. This DMA IP core implements streaming DMA transfers. It moves data from buffers located in the main memory into the FPGA and vice versa. The transfers are driven autonomously by the DMA IP core based on a descriptor ring shared with an associated driver. The descriptors hold information about buffers' capacities, actual sizes and states (*in progress, completed*).

The raw DMA throughput is high enough to transfer more then 4 Gbps from FPGA to the processor system. However, this requires to avoid copying of buffers between userspace and kernel space and to use large software buffers to avoid overhead of updates of descriptors. The Table 1 shows results of zero-copy transfers with different sizes of software DMA buffers. The DMA IP core takes care of generating AXI bursts (up to 128 B per burst for AXI3 [8] on the Xilinx Zynq) to fill each buffer as specified by its descriptor. However, the DMA IP core does not use the remaining buffer space if a received packet is significantly smaller then the buffer capacity. It simply moves on to use another buffer as specified by the following descriptor.

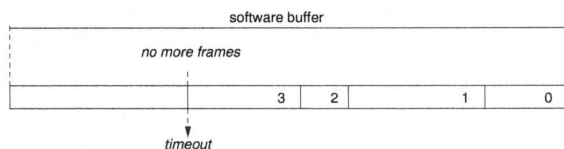

Figure 2: Frames aggregation. Frames are transferred into the software buffer as they are coming. The DMA splits the transfer to AXI bursts. The end of packet mark is masked until the timeout exceeds or the buffer is full enough.

To utilize the buffers efficiently, it is desirable to aggregate sequences of short packets to fill as much of the reserved capacity as possible. For that purpose, we have designed an IP core *Frame Aggregator* that merges many subsequent packets into one long data frame. A timeout for premature

Table 1: Throughput of HW/SW communication

Buffer size (kB)	Throughput (Mb/s)		
	avg	min	max
64	1144	1128	1180
128	1928	1926	1936
256	2924	2852	3016
512	3972	3872	4020
1024	4800	4768	4824

transmit is implemented to solve situation when no more frames are coming for a certain amount of time. The Fig. 2 describes this situation where one long software buffer is filled with packets of different sizes, however, significantly shorter then the total buffer size. This mechanism enables to utilize large buffers for great throughput while transferring even the shortest packets efficiently.

4. CONCLUSION

The paper introduced a small extendable embedded probe for precise monitoring of local networks. The probe is able to monitor up to four gigabit links at wire-speed. The FPGA (Xilinx Zynq) logic is used to accelerate filtering of network traffic. The ARM processor performs application level analysis using L7 filter. Moreover, the processor together with Linux OS enables to use other standard software network security monitoring tools. To achieve high throughput between the ARM processor and FPGA logic, we utilized the RSoC framework with optimized DMA and Linux drivers. Therefore it is possible to accelerate also other time-critical operations in the FPGA logic. For example regular expression matching can be offloaded to the FPGA logic to identify application protocols in reconstructed TCP/IP streams.

Acknowledgment

This work has been partially supported by the IT4Innovations Centre of Excellence project CZ.1.05/1.1.00/02.0070, the grants BUT FIT-S-14-2297 and VG20102015022.

5. REFERENCES

[1] Koziol, J.: *Intrusion Detection with Snort.* Indianapolis, IN, USA: Sams, 2003, ISBN 157870281X.
[2] Kekely Lukas, Zadnik Martin, Matousek Jiri a Korenek Jan: Fast Lookup for Dynamic Packet Filtering in FPGA. In *17th IEEE Symposium on Design and Diagnostics of Electronic Circuits and Systems*, IEEE Computer Society, 2014, ISBN 978-1-4799-4558-0, s. 219–322.
[3] *L7 Filter website.* l7-filter.sourceforge.net.
[4] *NetFPGA website.* netfpga.org.
[5] *RSoC-Framework website.* rsoc-framework.com.
[6] Xilinx. *LogiCORE IP AXI Ethernet v6.0.* Product Guide. October 2, 2013.
[7] Xilinx. *LogiCORE IP AXI DMA v6.03a.* Product Guide. December 18, 2012.
[8] ARM. *AMBA AXI and ACE Protocol Specification AXI3, AXI4, and AXI4-Lite, ACE and ACE-Lite.* http://infocenter.arm.com/help/index.jsp?topic= /com.arm.doc.ihi0022d/index.html.

Network Service Quality Rank: A Network Selection Algorithm for Heterogeneous Wireless Networks

Zeynab Bahrami Bidoni
Department of Computer and Information Systems
Clark Atlanta University
Atlanta, GA
z.bahrami62@gmail.com

Roy George
Department of Computer and Information Systems
Clark Atlanta University
Atlanta, GA
rgeorge@cau.edu

ABSTRACT

High-speed wireless services have achieved remarkable rates of growth in recent years. In order to survive in this competitive market, high levels of service performance are an effective way to improve customer satisfaction and loyalty. This paper aims to identify the best service provider in a heterogeneous wireless network so that we differentiate the quality of service (QoS) and provide a framework for analytical performance evaluation. This problem is considered a ranking problem in Multi-Criteria Decision Making, and so we formulize a novel method to compute collaboration performance utility for each provider. The compromise ranking technique (called VIKOR) is used to aggregate all utility values on alternatives and computes the best level of service among providers. The experimental evaluation results demonstrate the computational efficacy of the solution approaches and derive managerial insights.

General Terms

Heterogeneous Wireless Networks (HWNs), Quality of Service (QoS), Multi-Criteria Decision Making (MCDM).

Keywords

Network Service Quality Rank (NSQR); Correlation Density Rank (CDR); Diversity of Density (DOD).

1. INTRODUCTION

High-speed wireless service has achieved a remarkable market penetration in recent years with numerous service providers. Thus much effort has been concentrated on developing multi-criteria radio access technology (RAT) selection algorithms for heterogeneous wireless networks (HWNs) [1] based on criteria such as bandwidth, maximum data supported, security level provided, battery power consumption etc.

The contributions of this study are as follows: (1) Modeling the suppliers' performance comparison problem as a ranking problem in Multi-Criteria Decision Making (MCDM) [2], (2) Developing an approach to evaluate the probability of non-occurring negative events between two random users, while positively discriminating the events occurring between a user and its significant partners over those with less significant affiliates. (3) Computing the utility and efficiency of collaboration between each pair of alternative resources. Moreover, the tradeoff between criteria can be made by the VIKOR method [3].

ANCS '14, October 20–21, 2014, Los Angeles, CA, USA.
ACM 978-1-4503-2839-5/14/10.
http://dx.doi.org/10.1145/2658260.2661763

2. PROPOSED APPROACH

We consider this issue as a ranking problem in MCDM. Various attributes can be selected as criteria but, here, we focus on negative frequent events which may occur on interaction between users of any pair of device or service providers during a given big enough period of time, and effect on network's collaboration performance. In order to establish the decision matrix, scoring alternatives on criteria needed. So, we should assign to an alternative the performance efficiency value for collaboration with other alternatives. After that, we use VIKOR method which introduces the multi criteria ranking index based on the measure of "closeness" to the "ideal" solution. With the purpose of scoring alternatives on criteria, we proposed a new approach which has three main steps as follows which repeat for all failed type of occurrences:

Step 1: Arranging the failed frequency matrix of the heterogeneous network so that all users from same device or service provider set next to each other to extract sub-frequency matrices related to collaboration between each pairs of potential resource or device types.

Step 2: computing below items for all sub-frequency matrices;

- The Correlation Density Rank (CDR) vector [4] which is customized in this study to compute probability density of given events on homogenous network's users.

  1. Initialize cost distance matrix C.
  $$C[i,j] = \log_{(1-P_{ij}^{ref})}^{(1-\exp(-\gamma f_{ij}))} \tag{1}$$

  (The logarithm of $(1-\exp(-\gamma f_{ij}))$ based on $(1-P_{ij}^{ref})$)

  2. $M \leftarrow$ Normalize matrix C on columns.

  3. For each node n_j ($1 < j < l$) compute inverse of the entropy of related column from matrix M:
  $$ej \leftarrow -\frac{1}{Lnk} \sum_{i=1}^{k} M_{ij} Ln(M_{ij}) \tag{2}$$
  $$\sigma j \leftarrow \frac{1}{e_j} \tag{3}$$

  4. Calculate the density function which results from a Gauss Influence function.
  $$cdr_i \leftarrow \sum_{j=1}^{l} \exp(-\frac{\left(C_{ij}\right)^2}{2\sigma_j^2}) \tag{4}$$

  5. Normalize Correlation Density Rank vector:
  $$CDR_i \leftarrow cdr_i \Big/ \sum_{i=1}^{k} cdr_i \tag{5}$$

  6. Return CDR.

- Unpredictability/ Diversity of Density (DOD) of failed occurrences. We employ the CDR vector as the probability density distribution in Renyi entropy formulate [5].

$$H_{kl}^{e_t} = \frac{1}{1-\alpha} \log_2 \left(\frac{\sum_{i=1}^{N_k} CDR_i^{\alpha}}{\sum_{i=1}^{N_k} CDR_i} \right) \qquad (6)$$

Where $H_{kl}^{e_t}$ the unpredictability of the failed event e_t between users from the network service provider or device type k to l, and N_k is the number of users from service provider or device type number K.

- The estimated probability of non-occurring any failed happening between two random users from given two resource or device types. Considering a Gaussian distribution with below mean and variance parameters, can help us to better understanding about probability distribution of given frequent event through kl cooperation network.

$$\mu_{kl}^{e_t} = \frac{\sum_{i=1}^{N_k} \sum_{j=1}^{N_l} F_{kl}(i,j)}{N_k N_l} \quad , \quad \delta_{kl}^{e_t} = \frac{\mu_{kl}^{e_t}}{H_{kl}^{e_t}} \qquad (7)$$

$$P_{kl}^{e_t} = p(x=0) = \frac{e^{\frac{-(\mu_{kl}^{e_t})^2}{2(\delta_{kl}^{e_t})^2}}}{\delta_{kl}^{e_t} \sqrt{2\pi}} \qquad (8)$$

Step 3: scoring service providers or devices based on their interaction utility and efficiency with other alternatives as criteria, and constructing decision matrix to apply VIKOR method for ranking alternatives' performance. We follow a variant of the sigmoid functions to model the service user's satisfaction. The normalized user satisfaction is modeled as,

$$U_{kl}^{e_t} = \frac{1}{1 + e^{\left(\frac{\left(P_{max}^{e_t} + P_{min}^{e_t}\right)}{2} - P_{kl}^{e_t} \right)}} \qquad (9)$$

Where $U_{kl}^{e_t}$ is the user satisfaction perceived, and $P_{kl}^{e_t}$ is the probability of non-occurring which is computed by Eq. (8), for event e_t in interaction from alternative resource or device type k to l. $P_{min}^{e_t}$ is the minimum and $P_{max}^{e_t}$ is the maximum probability value through all k and l. To compute the efficiency of cooperation between two resource or device type, we proposed Eq. (10) to aggregate utilities of reciprocal interactions per pairs of options.

$$E_{(k,l)}^{e_t} = \frac{1}{1 + \log_{(1-w_x)}^{U_{kl}^{e_t}}} + \frac{1}{1 + \log_{(1-w_y)}^{U_{lk}^{e_t}}} \qquad (10)$$

w_x and w_y are the importance weight of sending and receiving operation, respectively, where their summation is equal to 1.

This research is funded in part by the Army Research Laboratory under Grant No: W911NF-12-2-0067 and Army Research Office under Grant Number W911NF-11-1-0168. Any opinions, findings, conclusions or recommendations expressed here are those of the author(s) and do not necessarily reflect the views of the sponsor.

3. EXPERIMENT

To implement our approach, we consider a synthetic heterogeneous Communication Network with 20 Communication Modules, three alternative devices and two types of failed events during sample time period. Assume a new user wants to enter in this network and should select one of three types of devices. After employing the approach of scoring alternatives based on criteria, the decision matrix constructed is shown on Table 1.

Table 1. Decision matrix resulted by the proposed method

Criteria	Failure occurrence e_1			Failure occurrence e_2		
Sub-criteria	With A	with B	with C	with A	with B	with C
CModule A	0.73	1.80	0.571	1.99	1.85	1.91
CModule B	1.93	1.85	1.67	2	2	1.87
CModule C	0.64	2	1.90	1.89	1.81	2

Table 2. Results of ranking by the VIKOR method

Alternative	CModule A	CModule B	CModule C
Distance to Ideal	0.7439	0.32051	0.5

According to final results of VIKOR (Table 2.), CModule type B is closest one to ideal and then type C and A respectively are in descending orders as expected.

4. CONCLUSIONS

Ranking performance of resources in wireless networks has a broad range of applications such as comparison of resource or device performance in Computer Area, Telecommunication, Electrical, Social, Supply Chains, Financial Networks and etc. We establish the MCDM optimization model for selecting best resource based on their efficiency of collaboration with other alternatives about occurring negative frequencies. The proposed method is composed of three main parts: (1) evaluating the probability of non-happening the negative events between two random users which positively discriminate the events between a user and its important partners over those with less significant affiliates. (2) Computing the utility and efficiency of collaboration between each pair of alternative resources; and, (3) construct the decision matrix and employ the well-known VIKOR method to rank alternative resources. Finally, these algorithms were applied to synthetic Communication network. The results can automatically satisfy the requirements of QoS users preferentially.

5. REFERENCES

[1] Ernst, J. B., Kremer, S. C., & Rodrigues, J. J. (2014). A Survey of QoS/QoE mechanisms in heterogeneous wireless networks. *Physical Communication*.

[2] Triantaphyllou, E. (2000). *Multi-criteria decision making methods a comparative study*. Springer.

[3] Opricovic, S., & Tzeng, G. H. (2004). Compromise solution by MCDM methods: A comparative analysis of VIKOR and TOPSIS. *European Journal of Operational Research*,156(2), 445-455.

[4] Bahrami Bidoni, Z., George, R. (2014). Discovering Community Structure in Dynamic Social Networks using the Correlation Density Rank. *SocialCom, The Sixth ASE International Conference on Social Computing*.

[5] Gonzalez Andino, S. L., et al. (2000). Measuring the complexity of time series: an application to neurophysiological signals. *Human brain mapping* 11(1), 46-57.

Toward Terabyte-scale Caching with SSD in a Named Data Networking Router

Won So, Taejoong Chung, Haowei Yuan, David Oran and Mark Stapp
Cisco Systems, Inc. Cambridge, MA, USA
wonso@acm.org, tjchung@mmlab.snu.ac.kr, hyuan@wustl.edu,
{oran, mjs}@cisco.com

ABSTRACT

Named Data Networking (NDN) routers can cache previously forwarded Data packets, and those can be reused when a matching Interest packet arrives. Unlike traditional IP routers and HTTP caches that exist as separate devices, designing a scalable NDN router is a new challenge because it should perform fast forwarding and massive-scale caching at the same time. This paper proposes a design of an NDN router with unique forwarding and caching mechanisms featuring terabyte-scale caching with solid-state drives (SSD) while still forwarding packets at line speed.

Categories and Subject Descriptors

C.2.1 [**Network Architecture and Design**]: Store and forward networks; C.2.6 [**Internetworking**]: Routers

Keywords

Named data networking, router, packet forwarding, caching

1. INTRODUCTION

Named data networking (NDN) is a networking paradigm that tries to address issues with the current Internet by using *named data* instead of named hosts for the communication model. NDN communication is consumer-driven; a client requests named content via an *Interest* packet, then any node receiving the Interest and having the content satisfies it by responding with a *Data* packet [4]. NDN enables pervasive caching via *Content Store (CS)* subsystem; routers (and any forwarding nodes) in the network can cache previously forwarded Data packets for reuse later when a matching Interest packet arrives.

The Content Store is a part of an NDN router data plane; it is implemented by keeping previously forwarded packets in the packet buffer after transmission. Therefore, the CS size will be limited because it resides in the router memory. For a larger cache that scales up to terabytes, an NDN router must utilize block storage devices. However, accessing block devices in packet forwarding paths could become a serious forwarding performance bottleneck because storage devices tend to be much slower than memory devices in terms

ANCS'14, October 20–21, 2014, Los Angeles, CA, USA.
ACM 978-1-4503-2839-5/14/10.
http://dx.doi.org/10.1145/2658260.2661767.

of bandwidth and latency.

This has not been a problem for traditional IP routers and caches for HTTP or video data because they exist as separate devices. Routers do not involve any block device I/O in forwarding paths, while cache devices just operate at I/O speed. As NDN architecturally integrates caching with forwarding, designing a scalable NDN router is a new challenge because a single device should be able to perform fast forwarding and massive-scale caching at the same time.

In this paper, we propose a design of an NDN router that enables terabyte-scale caching with solid-state drives (SSD), and still forwards packets in a line speed. We first propose a forwarding mechanism that separates block device I/O from forwarding paths by sending packets to a dedicated caching process. We then present a design of this caching process, which minimizes the use of CPU cycles and memory space – so that any available extra resources can be used for forwarding threads running at full throttle – but still maximizes I/O bandwidth utilization and scales up to cache terabytes of packets.

2. DESIGN AND IMPLEMENTATION

In our previous work [3], we demonstrated our NDN software router running on 64-bit Linux which forwards NDN traffic at 20Gbps. We designed and implemented NDN caching with SSDs on top of this software router. The basic design goal is to enable terabyte-scale caching by utilizing large storage devices, but not to affect fast packet forwarding happening on the data plane.

If massive-scale caching is directly implemented as part of Content Store on a data plane, block device I/O becomes a significant forwarding bottleneck due the huge latency and bandwidth difference between DRAM and SSD. For example, DDR3-1600 provides 12800MB/s bandwidth, while SATA3 gives only 600MB/s. Our basic approach is separating slow, long-latency block device I/O from forwarding paths; any packets that require cache read or write operations are forwarded to a *Cache Manager (CM)* process so that forwarding threads are not blocked on I/O.

We introduce additional mechanisms to base NDN forwarding to support integrated SSD caching. The router looks up each Interest packet name in the CS/PIT (Pending Interest Table), as usual. Then the router checks the name against a *Data Plane Filter (DPF)*, a compact filter that quickly determines whether a matching Data packet has been cached on a storage device. If a name matches in the DPF, the Interest packet is forwarded to the CM and it invokes a cache read operation. A Data packet evicted from the in-memory Content Store is forwarded to the CM, unless the packet has a 'no cache' flag set, or a short remaining valid lifetime. A Data packet forwarded to CM invokes a cache write operation.

The only data structure added on the data plane for caching is the Data Plane Filter (DPF). The DPF should have a small memory footprint and spend minimal cycles on lookup in order to minimize its impact on forwarding. In our implementation, we have used a hash table with 32-bit hash keys derived from full-name 64-bit hashes that are already available from CS/PIT lookup.

A key design goal for Cache Manager is to minimize use of CPU cycles and memory space that are shared with forwarding threads – so that any extra available resources can be used for forwarding – while maximizing the bandwidth of block I/O devices. In order to achieve this, we have optimized CM read and write paths by tuning a few Linux I/O[1] options: Vectored I/O (VIO), Linux Asynchronous I/O (AIO), and Direct I/O (DIO).

Vectored I/O (a.k.a. Scatter/Gather I/O) [2] allows the CM to perform I/O using multiple non-contiguous packet buffers with a single system call. It almost gives the same performance benefit as performing a bigger block I/O, without the need for additional memory copy operations. Linux AIO [1] lets a thread issue many parallel I/O operations without invoking another thread, while not blocked on any in-flight I/Os. CM combines these two to improve I/O bandwidth utilization significantly as it performs parallel multiple I/Os with bigger blocks, while saving CPU usage as well.

Lastly, Direct I/O bypasses the OS page cache and initiates I/O directly from user-space buffers to the device [2]. With DIO, our NDN router achieves zero-copy forwarding: no memcpy of a whole packet ever happens throughout the forwarding paths all the way from a NIC to the SSD cache. DIO however is not necessarily the best choice for performance, because a modern OS implements various I/O optimizations through the kernel page cache. From the NDN router design point of view, using DIO is more attractive because the Content Store already works as an in-memory cache for the packets that will be stored into the SSD, hence available memory is better used for the CS.

In the CM, cache requests are processed in a large batch (e.g. 512) of packets. In order to take advantage of VIO for both reads and writes, we exploit an inherent property of the NDN architecture: a big object is split into multiple smaller segments (or Data packets) according to an NDN PDU or link MTU size, and fetched as individual segments. In terms of packet arrival timings, these segments are highly likely to show temporal locality because a consumer who wants a whole object will issue Interest packets naming all segments and receive all segmented Data packets within a short time window.

During CM write processing, all Data packets that belong to the same object are stored into contiguous disk cache locations via a single VIO operation if they arrive within the same batch processing window. During read processing, the CM issues one VIO for cached packets sharing the same object name, once they have been stored into contiguous cache locations. CM maintains an in-memory hash table (HT) for bookkeeping cache locations associated with individual packets. Instead of using full-name hash keys like the CS/PIT, this HT uses object-name hash keys in order to easily combine individual packet read and write requests into vectored I/O operations. Managing stored packets in an object-level granularity also helps with making this in-memory data structure scale up better for caching terabytes of packets, because it uses only a single HT entry per object, not one per packet.

3. PRELIMINARY RESULTS

For experiments, we ran our NDN software router on a Cisco UCS server with two Intel 2.6GHz octa-core Xeon processors. For

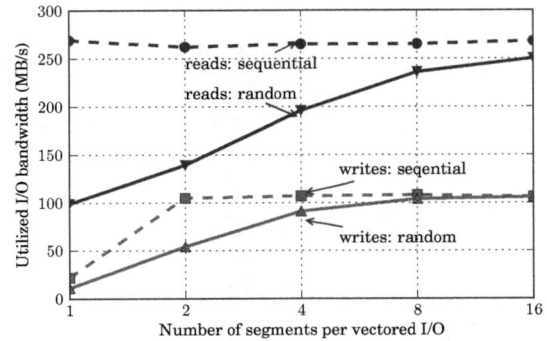

Figure 1: Utilized I/O bandwidth with cache reads and writes

caching, we attached an Intel SATA2 160GB SSD mounted via the *xfs* file system. The total cache size is fixed at 128GB, and every I/O is performed in a 2048-byte unit, the size of a single packet buffer which holds an Ethernet frame plus some metadata. Our experimental dataset used the same set of IRCache traces as our previous work [3], but multiple packet segments were generated from each name to evaluate the effectiveness of vectored I/O. By applying the maximum load to the CM process running on a single core, we measured the average I/O bandwidth utilization of cache reads and writes over 10 runs of 100,000 NDN Interest and Data packets respectively.

Fig. 1 shows utilized I/O bandwidth varying the numbers of segments per VIO (v). The solid lines represent utilization from our experimental workloads where reads and writes happen in random order. The dotted lines represent the maximum utilization that can be achieved with this SSD in a synthetic benchmark where reads and writes are sequential. The performance of writes is less than a half of that of reads in all cases; this is a well-known asymmetric property of SSDs. For both reads and writes, the utilized I/O bandwidth increases as v increases, and gets quite close to its limit eventually: 93% for reads when v=16 and 96% for writes when v=8. This basically demonstrates that our caching mechanism works effectively as it allows utilizing nearly maximum I/O bandwidth of the SSD when NDN object sizes are 32KB or larger.

4. CONCLUSION & FUTURE WORK

In this paper, we proposed the design of an NDN router that features scaleable caching with SSDs while still forwarding packets at line speed. In our design, block device I/Os are separated out from forwarding code paths so that caching does not affect high-speed forwarding. Our Cache Manager processes all cache read and write requests via asynchronous vectored I/Os in order to maximize I/O bandwidth utilization of the SSDs and minimize CPU usage. Our future work includes full experimentation of combined forwarding and caching using more realistic application scenarios, and investigation of various caching polices for ranking the value of Data packets evicted from CS and reducing SSD wear.

5. REFERENCES

[1] D. Ehrenberg. AIOUserGuide.
    http://code.google.com/p/kernel/wiki/AIOUserGuide.
[2] R. Love. *Linux System Programming: Talking Directly to the Kernel and C Library*. O'Reilly Media, Inc., 2007.
[3] W. So, A. Narayanan, and D. Oran. Named data networking on a router: Fast and DoS-resistant forwarding with hash tables. In *Proceedings of the 9th Symposium on Architectures for Networking and Communications Systems*, 2013.
[4] V. Jacobson et al. Networking named content. In *Proceedings of the 5th Conference on Emerging Networking Experiments and Technologies*, 2009.

---

[1] We are aware that utilizing native OS services is suboptimal due to system call overhead. We regard as future work options such as a user-space device driver (like the one we use for NIC I/O).

Spectral Clustering Based Regular Expression Grouping

Zhe Fu[1,2] and Jun Li[2,3]

[1]Department of Automation, Tsinghua University, China
[2]Research Institute of Information Technology, Tsinghua University, China
[3]Tsinghua National Lab for Information Science and Technology, China

fu-z13@mails.tsinghua.edu.cn, junl@tsinghua.edu.cn

ABSTRACT

Regular expression matching has been playing an import role in today's network security systems with deep inspection function. However, compiling a set of regular expressions into one Deterministic Finite Automata (DFA) often leads to state explosion, which means huge or even impractical memory cost. Distributing regular expressions into several groups and building DFAs independently has been proved an efficient solution, but the previous grouping algorithms are either locally optimal or time-consuming. In this work, we proposed a new grouping method based on Spectral Clustering, which defines the *similarity* between regular expressions and then transforms grouping problem to clustering problem. Preliminary experiments illustrate that our grouping algorithm achieves efficient result with much less processing time.

Categories and Subject Descriptors

C.2.0 **[Computer-Communication Networks]**: General – *Security and protection (e.g., firewalls)*

General Terms

Algorithms, Performance, Design, Experimentation.

Keywords

Regular expression matching; deep inspection; DFA; grouping.

1. INTRODUCTION

Nowadays, deep inspection is widely used to identify and filter network traffic. The payload of network packet is examined for virus, spam, intrusions or other criteria which is described as defined signatures. With high flexibility and expressiveness, regular expression matching is playing an important part in network deep inspection systems.

To perform regular expression matching, a set of regular expressions is first compiled to nondeterministic finite automata (NFA), which has less states. However, the space-efficiency of NFA is at the cost of a mass of state transitions to process for each input character. As a result, it is generally necessary to further

Permission to make digital or hard copies of part or all of this work for personal or classroom use is granted without fee provided that copies are not made or distributed for profit or commercial advantage, and that copies bear this notice and the full citation on the first page. Copyrights for third-party components of this work must be honored. For all other uses, contact the owner/author(s).
Copyright is held by the author/owner(s).
ANCS'14, October 20–21, 2014, Los Angeles, CA, USA.
ACM 978-1-4503-2839-5/14/10.
http://dx.doi.org/10.1145/2658260.2661771

convert NFA into DFA, which is deterministic finite automata. DFA only requires precisely one state transition lookup per input character ($O(1)$ time complexity), so DFA is always fast and becomes the prior choice in practical deep inspection systems.

Unfortunately, DFA needs more states and transitions compared to NFA, and in many cases suffers from the state explosion. To achieve fast regular expression matching in practice, varieties of techniques such as DFA compression and hardware acceleration have been proposed. Regular expression grouping [1-4] is a newly proposed method and it is very applicable to parallel computation. In this work, we present a fast and efficient grouping algorithm to address the problem of state explosion of DFA.

2. ALGORITHM

Aiming at distributing a set of regular expressions into several subsets, regular expression grouping can be regarded as a clustering problem. Many sound clustering method have been put forward in machine learning and pattern recognition field. However, one regular expression cannot be considered as a sample point since it has no conventional *similarity* to others.

The basic idea of clustering-based grouping algorithm is to define the *similarity* between regular expressions. If the states number of DFA compiled from regular expression r_i is S_i, and the states number of DFA compiled from regular expression pair r_i and r_j is $S_{i,j}$, then the *similarity* between regular expression r_i and r_j can be defined as follows:

$$Similarity(i, j) = \frac{S_i + S_j}{S_{i,j}} \qquad (1)$$

Larger similarity means that regular expression r_i and r_j are better to be distributed into the same group, where they are less likely to cause the state explosion. To achieve fast and efficient grouping result, we take advantage of the core idea of Spectral Clustering, which is a clustering algorithm based on graph theory and makes use of the similarity relation among sample points to cluster.

Specifically, for a grouping problem of distributing N regular expressions into k groups, the Spectral Clustering based regular expression grouping algorithm has following four steps.

STEP-1: Calculating the similarity matrix

Using definition (1), we can calculate the *similarity* between each two regular expressions of a rule set. In particular, for a rule set with N regular expressions, an N by N adjacent matrix W is generated.

STEP-2: Calculating the unnormalized graph Laplacian matrix L

L is calculated by D – W, where D is a degree matrix.

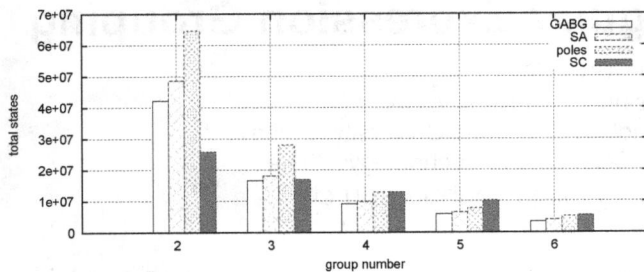
Fig. 1. States number comparison on Snort (120 rules)

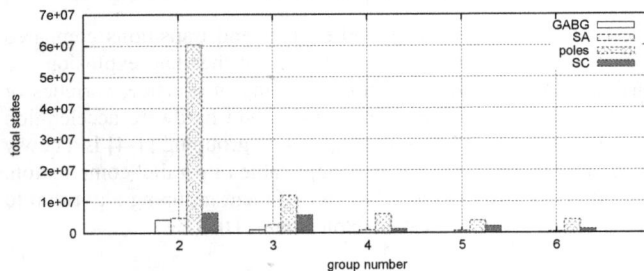
Fig. 2. States number comparison on L7-filter (111 rules)

STEP-3: Building new matrix

k smallest eigenvectors are picked out from matrix L, and then we arrange these k eigenvectors as a N by k matrix.

STEP-4: K-means clustering

Treat each row of the new matrix in *STEP-3* as a vector in k-dimensional space, and use K-means to cluster.

3. EVALUATION

Experiments are conducted on an Intel(R) Xeon(R) E5335 platform (CPU: 2.0GHz, Memory: 4GB, OS: Ubuntu 12.04 64bit). The Regular Expression Processor [5] is used to calculate the number of states of a regular expressions distribution, as the metric of memory consumption. Two rule sets picked from open source software Snort [6] and L7-filter [7] are used.

We implement Simulated Annealing (SA) [2], Poles heuristic (poles) algorithms [2] and Grouping Algorithms Based on Gene (GABG) [4] as comparisons.

In Fig. 1 and Fig. 2, the x axis represents the number of group (which is set to 2~6), and the y axis represents the total DFA number of all groups under each group number. The results show that Spectral Clustering grouping algorithm (SC) outperforms poles but is not as space-efficient as GABG and SA.

However, since both of GABA and SA are heuristic algorithms which need lots of iterations to converge to an optimum solution, it is not quite time-efficient to obtain such a result in a long run time. For the problem of distributing 111 regular expressions into 4 groups with given 50 individuals and 5000 generations in GABG, it takes nearly 2 hours to obtain a final solution. In the

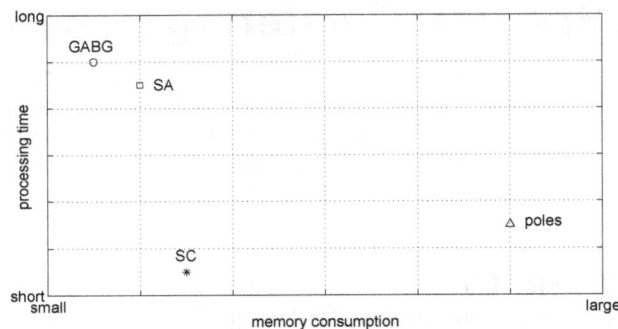
Fig. 3. Time vs. Space

meantime, SC only needs around 5 seconds to finish the matrix decomposition. Figure 3 illustrates the relationship between time-consumption and space-efficiency of each grouping algorithms. As we can see, the Spectral Clustering grouping algorithm is a better trade-off between time and space than other algorithms.

4. CONSLUSION AND FUTURE WORK

In this work, we propose a new regular expression grouping algorithm based on Spectral Clustering, aiming at solving the problem of DFA state explosion. The preliminary experimental results on practical rule set draw the conclusion that Spectral Clustering based regular expression grouping algorithm is a better trade-off between processing time and memory consumption compared to previous methods. Our future work will focus on designing more time and space efficient grouping algorithms. For example, taking the result of SC as a preliminary distribution of regular expressions, which can speed up the convergence of heuristic grouping procedure. Meanwhile more experiments are expected.

5. REFERENCES

[1] F. Yu, Z. Chen, Y. Diao, T. V. Lakshman and R. H. Katz. Fast and Memory-Efficient Regular Expression Matching for Deep Packet Inspection. Proc. of ACM/IEEE ANCS, 2006.

[2] J. Rohrer, K. Atasu, J. V. Lunteren and C. Hagleitne. Memory-Efficient Distribution of Regular Expressions for Fast Deep Packet Inspection. Proc. of the 7th IEEE/ACM international conference on hardware/software codesign and system synthesis, 2009.

[3] R. Antonello, S. Fernandes, A. Santos, et al. Efficient DFA grouping for traffic identification. Proc. of Global Communications Conference (GLOBECOM), 2012.

[4] Z. Fu, K. Wang, L. Cai and J. Li. Intelligent Grouping Algorithms for Regular Expressions in Deep Inspection. Proc. of the 23rd International Conference on Computer Communications and Networks (ICCCN), 2014.

[5] Regular Expression Processor, http://regex.wustl.edu/.

[6] Snort, http://www.snort.org/.

[7] L7-filter, http://l7-filter.clearfoundation.com/.

Change-Point Detection Method on 100 Gb/s Ethernet Interface

Pavel Benáček*   Rudolf B. Blažek*   Tomáš Čejka†   Hana Kubátová*

*Czech Technical University in Prague, Czech Republic, {benacpav,rblazek,hana.kubatova}@fit.cvut.cz

†CESNET, a.l.e., Prague, Czech Republic; cejkat@cesnet.cz

ABSTRACT

This paper deals with hardware acceleration of statistical methods for detection of anomalies on 100 Gb/s Ethernet. The approach is demonstrated by implementing a sequential Non-Parametric Cumulative Sum (NP-CUSUM) procedure. We use high-level synthesis in combination with emerging software defined monitoring (SDM) methodology for rapid development of FPGA-based hardware-accelerated network monitoring applications. The implemented method offloads detection of network attacks and anomalies directly into an FPGA chip. The parallel nature of FPGA allows for simultaneous detection of various kinds of anomalies. Our results show that hardware acceleration of statistical methods using the SDM concept with high-level synthesis from C/C++ is possible and very promising for traffic analysis and anomaly detection in high-speed 100 Gb/s networks.

1. INTRODUCTION

This paper deals with real-time detection of network attacks in ultra high-speed computer networks by dynamically deploying detection methods in a hardware-accelerated monitoring probe with one 100 Gb/s Ethernet port. We use a special programmable FPGA-based card for hardware acceleration of network traffic processing, and Software Defined Monitoring (SDM) as the main implementation methodology [1]. SDM supports advanced monitoring tools as well as aggregation of various statistics, like Cisco NetFlow records, possibly with details like jitter etc.

To illustrate the feasibility of the approach, we have implemented a Change-Point Detection (CPD) method NP-CUSUM [2]. CPD theory is suitable for intrusion detection because network attacks and anomalies appear at unknown points in time and usually are observable as a change of some statistical properties of the network traffic [2]. The NP-CUSUM method is designed to detect the increase of the mean of some characteristic X_n of the observed network traffic. The procedure uses sequential statistic

$$S_n = \max\{0, S_{n-1} + X_n - \hat{\mu} - \varepsilon\hat{\theta}\}, \quad S_0 = 0, \quad (1)$$

ANCS'14, October 20–21, 2014, Los Angeles, CA, USA.
ACM 978-1-4503-2839-5/14/10
http://dx.doi.org/10.1145/2658260.2661773.

where $\hat{\mu}$ is an estimate of the mean of X_n before the attack, $\hat{\theta}$ is an estimate of the mean after the attack started, and ε is a tuning parameter for optimization. The typical optimality criterion in CPD is to minimize the average detection delay (ADD) among all algorithms whose average false alert rate (FAR) is below a prescribed low level. It has been shown in [2] that with optimal value of ε the NP-CUSUM procedure in (1) is asymptotically optimal as FAR decreases.

In our experiments we have chosen for X_n the ratio of SYN and FIN packets of the Transmission Control Protocol (TCP) in a short time window [3]. During "normal" operation of the network we expect the ratio of SYN and FIN packets to be on average close to 1 or at least constant. An abrupt and consistent change of the ratio is suspicious. It can be caused by some sort of attacks (e.g. SYN flood) [3].

2. SOFTWARE DEFINED MONITORING

Our hardware implementation of detection methods in a monitoring probe is based on Software Defined Monitoring methodology [1]. An SDM system consists of firmware for a hardware module, and computer-based software. The two parts are connected via a PCI-Express bus, and tightly coupled for precise control of hardware processing of flows.

The software part of the SDM system consists of monitoring applications and a controller unit. The monitoring applications perform advanced monitoring tasks, such as analysis of application protocols. The controller manages the hardware module by dynamically removing and inserting processing rules (packet actions) into its *State Memory*.

The structure of the SDM hardware module is shown in Fig. 1. Packet actions are specified as processing rules that are stored in the *Rule Memory* and performed by the SDM *Update* block. This block processes packets, manages network flow records, and updates aggregated data records. Packet actions (instructions) from different processing rules are performed in parallel by *"Instr x"* blocks.

Packet protocol headers are extracted in the Header Field Extractor (HFE), and passed to the *Search* block. Together with matching rules from the *Rule Memory*, the packet metadata is then sent to the SDM *Update* block as update requests. Requests are forwarded by the *Instruction Decoder* to the appropriate *"Instr x"* block, based on a routing table. The *Reserve* block controls access to the shared *State Memory* to ensure synchronization between the *"Instr x"* blocks for concurrent processing of update requests. Synchronization is achieved via tags that are assigned to requests before entering the *Update block* and used by the *Merge* block before exporting information to the software module.

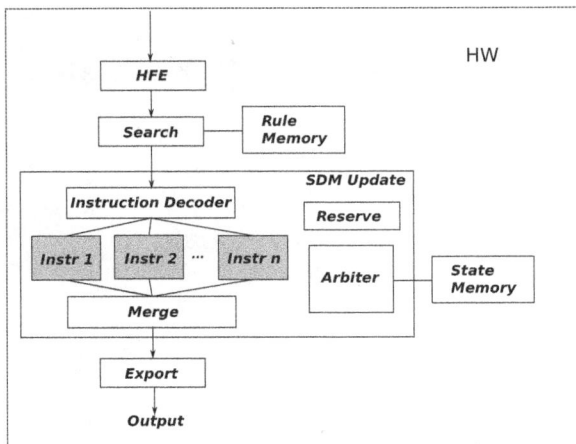

Figure 1: Architecture of the SDM system's hardware component.

Table 1: FPGA resources for the hardware plug-in.

Name	BRAM 18K	DSP48E	FF	LUT
Expression	-	-	0	458
FIFO	-	-	-	-
Instance	-	-	280	252
Memory	-	-	-	-
Multiplexer	-	-	-	1842
Register	-	-	2253	-
ShiftMemory	-	-	0	806
Total	0	0	2533	3358

Table 2: Performance of the CPD hardware plug-in.

Parameter	Fixed-point	Floating-point	Required
Clock period	4.08 ns	16.48 ns	5 ns
Frequency	245 MHz	60.679 MHz	200 MHz
Latency	12	11	-

Table 3: FPGA resources – SDM system & 1 plug-in.

Resource Name	Used Resources [-]	Utilization Percentage
LUTs	47731	13%
Registers	21089	2%
BRAMS	107	11%

3. IMPLEMENTATION

Our implemented CPD block is a hardware plug-in for the SDM system. It corresponds to one of the gray instruction blocks *"Instr x"* of the *Update block* in Fig. 1. For faster implementation and easier debugging of hardware-accelerated methods, we have used high-level synthesis (HLS) and developed the hardware CPD block in C++ instead of a standard hardware design description such as VHDL or Verilog.

We chose fixed-point arithmetic because the range of input values is expected to be limited enough. Compared to floating-point, we can achieve higher frequency, reduce FPGA resource consumption, and speed-up the Initiation Interval (II) for new requests to be accepted in each clock cycle. The floating-point version requires 11 clock cycles.

To integrate the new hardware block into an existing SDM *Update block*, we have to wrap the translated source code of the new block in a VHDL envelope that adapts the behavior of all predefined interface signals. The envelope can be reused in other SDM projects, hence the SDM system acts as a framework for rapid creation of new advanced hardware modules for network monitoring and anomaly detection.

The software component of our SDM-based implementation of the CPD method communicates with an SDM Controller daemon to manage the hardware module. It informs human operators about detection alerts from the hardware module, it manages the detection rules in the hardware module (creation, modification, or deletion), and periodically reports exported detection statistics.

Functionality of the hardware-accelerated implementation of the CPD method was verified using referential software that was written in C for detection in slower networks and for estimation of parameters of the CPD method [4].

4. EVALUATION AND CONCLUSIONS

The implemented NP-CUSUM algorithm was tested on Virtex-7 H580T FPGA platform in an existing 100 Gb/s monitoring probe. Table 1 shows a detailed list of required resources. None of the Block RAMs (BRAM 18K) and DSP48E blocks were used. The number of Look-up tables (LUT) and Flip-Flops (FF) takes less than 1% of the available FPGA resources. Table 2 shows that the fixed-point implementation satisfies the one-cycle Initiation Interval requirement for processing 100 Gb/s network traffic. With synthesis optimization, such as register duplication, all other performance requirements have been met as well. Table 3 lists FPGA resource requirements of the whole synthesized SDM system with one CPD hardware plug-in. About 87% of the resources are still available, therefore it is feasible to include several similar hardware plug-ins for parallel detection of various anomalies without significant latency increase.

In conclusion, our implementation of the NP-CUSUM algorithm demonstrates the feasibility of using SDM and HLS for rapid implementation of hardware-accelerated detection algorithms for 100 Gb/s networks. The hardware design consumes 13% of the resources of the target FPGA platform, and leaves thus space for several similar hardware plug-ins for parallel detection of various kinds of network anomalies. The SDM paradigm allows hardware acceleration of only the most critical parts of the detection algorithm.

5. REFERENCES

[1] L. Kekely, V. Pus, and J. Korenek, "Software defined monitoring of application protocols," in *INFOCOM, 2014 Proceedings IEEE*. IEEE, 2014, pp. 1725–1733.

[2] A. G. Tartakovsky, B. L. Rozovskii, R. Blažek, and H. Kim, "A novel approach to detection of intrusions in computer networks via adaptive sequential and batch-sequential change-point detection methods," *IEEE Transactions on Signal Processing*, vol. 54, no. 9, pp. 3372–3382, 2006.

[3] H. Wang, D. Zhang, and K. Shin, "Detecting SYN flooding attacks," in *INFOCOM 2002. 21st Annual Joint Conference of the IEEE Computer and Communications Societies.*, vol. 3, 2002, pp. 1530–1539.

[4] T. Čejka, "Fast TCP Flood Detector (FTFD)." [Online]. Available: http://ddd.fit.cvut.cz/prj/FTFD

Superspreader Detection System on NetFPGA Platform

Theophilus Wellem[†,‡], Guan-Wei Li, Yu-Kuen Lai
Dept. of Electronic Engineering[†], Dept. of Electrical Engineering
Chung Yuan Christian University, Chung-Li 32023, Taiwan
{g10202604, g10179006, ylai}@cycu.edu.tw
Dept. of Informatics[‡]
Satya Wacana Christian University, Salatiga 50711, Indonesia
theophilus.wellem@staff.uksw.edu

ABSTRACT

We propose a system to detect superspreaders based on combinations of FM sketch, Bloom filter and hash table. It first eliminates sources which are not potential superspreaders, then counts the number of connections to distinct destinations (fan-out) for remaining sources. The proposed system is implemented on NetFPGA platform. Our experiment results show that the system can detect superspreaders with higher fan-out and estimate their fan-outs accurately using small amount of memory.

Categories and Subject Descriptors

C.2.3 [**Network operation**]: Network monitoring

General Terms

Algorithms, Design, Performance

Keywords

Superspreader; Bloom filter; FM sketch; NetFPGA;

1. INTRODUCTION

Detecting sources (or hosts) that have communication with a large number of distinct destinations (also known as superspreader, super source) is an important ingredient for network anomaly detection system. This large number of connections in a short period of time can be an indication of port scan attack, DDoS attack, or worm propagation. Several works using sampling and data streaming algorithm have been proposed to detect superspreaders and estimate the number of distinct destinations they connect to (fan-out) [1, 2, 3, 4]. Most of them utilize the combinations of sampling, hashing, Bloom filter, bitmap counting, and statistical estimation methods to detect and identify the superspreaders. Zhao et al. [2] proposed data streaming algorithm and flow sampling techniques to detect super sources and super destinations. The algorithm uses an online streaming

ANCS'14, October 20–21, 2014, Los Angeles, CA, USA.
ACM 978-1-4503-2839-5/14/10.
http://dx.doi.org/10.1145/2658260.2661766.

module (OSM) and an identity sampling module to process incoming traffic in parallel. The OSM encodes the fan-out information for each source IP and the identity sampling module captures the potential candidate of super sources. An estimation algorithm is used to get the estimated fan-out of these candidates of super source from the OSM. The drawback of this scheme is that, the detectable fan-out value for a source is limited up to 266 ($m \ln m$) due to "saturation" of bitmap array's column. Therefore, the method in [2] can only be used for small fan-out which is impractical as the number of fan-out can be larger than 10,000 in a 60-second measurement interval for high-speed networks.

Kamiyama et al. [3] proposed a superspreader identification using flow sampling. The scheme uses a Bloom filter to check for a new flow, and a hash table to store the source IP address and its flow counter. When the counter value of a source is above a predefined threshold, it is identified as a superspreader. Their scheme uses chaining for hash collision resolution. The length of linked-list is limited to four in order to bound the processing time. However, it is also only work for small fan-out threshold, small number of sources and flows. For higher fan-out, larger number of sources and flows, the memory space needed can be very large.

Motivated by the work in [2] and [3], we propose a superspreader detection system in streaming fashion using a combination of FM sketch, Bloom filter and hash table.

2. DESIGN AND ARCHITECTURE

In general, the number of superspreaders in one measurement interval is usually small compared to regular flows. The main idea of our proposed scheme is to first filter out sources with low fan-out first, and count only the fan-out of potential superspreaders. Therefore, we can save memory space and processing time for counting the fan-out more accurately. Fig. 1 shows the block diagram of the system. The architecture of the superspreader detection system consists of hardware and software parts. The hardware communicates with the host software via NetFPGA register system. All data structures reside in memory. To filter out those sources that are not superspreaders, we use a bitmap data structure. The bitmap data structure is an $m \times n$ bit array of FM sketch. When a packet arrives, the flow ID ($\{s, d\}$) and the source s are hashed to the bitmap. For each row (i.e., source hashed to that row, assuming no collision), we can estimate the number of distinct packets (or distinct destinations) using $\hat{n}_i = \left(\frac{1}{\varphi}\right) 2^{R_i}$, $i = 1, 2, \ldots, m$. [5], where $\varphi = 0.775351$. R_i is the position of leftmost '0' for row i.

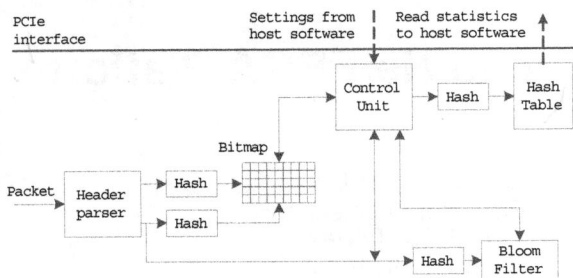

Figure 1: Block diagram of superspreader module

The Bloom filter is adopted to identify a new flow and the hash table maintains fan-out count for each source.

The superspreader detection is executed for each measurement interval. At the beginning of measurement interval, the Bloom filter, bitmap array, and hash table entries are initially set to zero. Upon each packet arrival, the bitmap data structure is updated. After one interval, the R_i value of the bitmap is used as threshold for the subsequent interval. At subsequent interval, when a source s is hashed to row i, the corresponding R_i value will be compared to a predefined threshold, T. If it is less than T then s is filtered out, else the flow ID ($\{s, d\}$) is checked to the Bloom filter. If it is a new flow, it will be added to the Bloom filter, then the source s is hashed to the hash table and its fan-out counter is updated. Currently, no collision resolution is implemented for the hash table. Finally, at the end of measurement interval, the values from hash table are used to report the superspreaders and their corresponding fan-outs.

In this system, we do not sample or save any source IP address to get the superspreader candidates. Instead, we rely on the incoming source IP address of the subsequent measurement interval because superspreaders tend to maintain their connections for a while. This can save memory space especially when implemented on platform with limited hardware resources.

3. EVALUATION

We evaluate our system using traces available from MAWI and CAIDA. The number of distinct sources and distinct $\{s, d\}$ flows in the MAWI trace (15 minutes) are $15,106$ and $48,761$, respectively. The CAIDA trace has $28,744,877$ packets, $440,771$ distinct sources and $1,044,618$ distinct $\{s, d\}$ flows, with duration of 56 seconds. The superspreader is defined as the source whose fan-out is greater than or equal to 50 [3]. The FNR (false negative ratio) is the number of superspreaders being incorrectly not identified divided by the number of actual superspreaders. The FPR (false postive ratio) is number of non-superspreaders being incorrectly identified as superspreaders divided by the number of actual superspreaders. For the results shown in Table 1, the Bloom filter and hash table sizes are 48 KB and 16 KB, respectively. As shown, our results have larger FNR and FPR compared to those presented by Kamiyama *et al.* [3]. The large FPR is due to collisions in the hash table since no collision resolution is implemented.

For the experiment results shown in Table 2, we set the bitmap size to 16384×32-bit (64 KB). The Bloom filter size is varied with three hash functions ($k = 3$). The hash ta-

Table 1: Experiment results

Trace	Kamiyama *et al.* [3]	Proposed	
	NLANR	CAIDA	
Interval	10 secs.	10 secs.	
# of flows	63,638	284,314	
# of sources	16,455	156,172	
# of spreaders	139	271	
Memory (BF+HT)	64 KB	64 KB	512 KB
FNR	0.06	0.21	0.09
FPR	7.5e-4	0.50	0.04

Table 2: Identification and counting accuracy

Trace	BF size	FNR	FPR	Est. error	Total memory
MAWI	32 KB	0.06	0	2.24%	128 KB
CAIDA	256 KB	0.20	0.21	8.75%	768 KB
	512 KB	0.16	0.18	5.17%	1.25 MB

ble has 8192 buckets of each 32-bit counter (32 KB). The total memory size is 128 KB. For CAIDA trace, we increase the total memory size (768 KB and 1.25 MB) to achieve more accurate result since the number of flows and sources per interval are larger. The total memory requirement used in the experiments is fit into memory available on the Net-FPGA board. Compared to the results in [2] and [3], our preliminary result is promising. For MAWI trace (Table 2), it can detect superspreaders and estimate larger fan-out (more than 5000) with average estimation error below 5% using only 128 KB memory.

4. CONCLUSION AND FUTURE WORK

In contrast to previous approach, our system can detect superspreaders with higher fan-out threshold and estimate their fan-outs with average estimation error below 10%. We seek to further optimize the accuracy by applying collision resolution techniques for the hash table. We will also investigate various factors that affect the measurement accuracy, such as measurement interval, threshold, bitmap size, Bloom filter size, and hash table size.

Acknowledgments

This research was funded in part by the National Science Council, Taiwan, under contract number NSC 102-2221-E-033-031, MOST 103-2221-E-033-030, and MOST 103-2632-E-033-001.

5. REFERENCES

[1] S. Venkataraman, D. Song, P. B. Gibbons, and A. Blum. New streaming algorithms for fast detection of superspreaders. In *Proceedings of Network and Distributed System Security Symposium (NDSS'05)*, p. 149–166, 2005.

[2] Q. Zhao, A. Kumar, and J. Xu. Joint data streaming and sampling techniques for detection of super sources and destinations. In *5th ACM SIGCOMM IMC 2005*, p. 77–90, 2005.

[3] N. Kamiyama, T. Mori, and R. Kawahara. Simple and adaptive identification of superspreaders by flow sampling. In *IEEE INFOCOM 2007*, p. 2481–2485, 2007.

[4] X. Guan, P. Wang, and T. Qin. A new data streaming method for locating hosts with large connection degree. In *IEEE GLOBECOM 2009*, p. 1–6, Nov. 2009.

[5] P. Flajolet and G. Martin. Probabilistic counting algorithms for database applications. *Journal of Computer and System Sciences*, 31(2):182–209, Sep. 1985.

On Reducing False Positives of a Bloom Filter in Trie-Based Algorithms

Ju Hyoung Mun
Dept. of Electronics Engineering
Ewha Womans University
Seoul, Korea
jhmun@ewhain.net

Hyesook Lim
Dept. of Electronics Engineering
Ewha Womans University
Seoul, Korea
hlim@ewha.ac.kr

ABSTRACT

Many IP address lookup approaches employ Bloom filters to obtain a high-speed search performance. Especially, the search performance of trie-based algorithms can be significantly improved by adding Bloom filters, because Bloom filters can determine whether a node exists in a trie without accessing the trie. The false positive rate of a Bloom filter must be reduced to enhance the lookup performance. One important characteristic of a trie is that all the ancestors of a node are also stored. The proposed IP lookup algorithm utilizes this characteristic in reducing the false positive rate of a Bloom filter without increasing the Bloom filter size. When a Bloom filter produces a positive result for a node of a trie, we propose to check whether the ancestors of the node are also positives. Because Bloom filters have no false negatives, the negative of the ancestor means that the positive of the node is false. Simulation results show that the false positive rate is reduced up to 67% using the exact same amount of memory. The proposed approach can be applied to other trie-based algorithms employing Bloom filters.

Categories and Subject Descriptors

C.2.6 [**Internetworking**]: Routers

Keywords

IP lookup; Bloom filter; Binary search on levels

1. INTRODUCTION

Classless inter-domain routing (CIDR) architecture makes IP address lookup algorithms perform a task of finding the longest matching prefix with a given input IP address. Finding the longest matching prefix is much more complex than finding an exact matching prefix, and this should be performed in line-speed for every incoming packet [1]. As the Internet grows, the size of routing tables is also growing rapidly. It is an important challenge to develop efficient IP address lookup algorithms working on a large routing table.

ANCS'14, October 20–21, 2014, Los Angeles, CA, USA.
ACM 978-1-4503-2839-5/14/10.
http://dx.doi.org/10.1145/2658260.2661765 .

Many IP address lookup algorithms employ Bloom filters [2, 3]. Adding Bloom filters to trie-based architectures has been proposed recently [3]. Reducing the false positive rate of Bloom filters is a good challenge to enhance the performance of these approaches.

We focus that every node in a trie is stored in trie-based algorithms [4]. This means that all the ancestor nodes of a node are stored in trie-based algorithms. By using this characteristic, we propose a novel algorithm that significantly reduces the false positive. We have verified the proposed approach for the architectures of *the binary search on levels on leaf-pushed trie with a Bloom filter (LBSL-BF)* [3, 5].

2. THE PROPOSED ALGORITHM

It is well known that the size of a Bloom filter should be increased in order to reduce the false positive rate. In this paper, we suggest a different way of reducing the false positive rate. Our proposed method is to use more queries by utilizing the characteristic of a trie; a node cannot exist without ancestor nodes. In performing the binary search on levels in a leaf-pushed trie, every node in valid levels is stored. If a Bloom filter produces a positive for a node in level l, we propose to query level $l-1$, which is an ancestor of the node in level l, to check whether it is also a positive. Because Bloom filters have no false negatives, the negative of the ancestor means that the positive of the level l is false. Assuming that hash indices are chosen independently, the expected false positive rate of our proposed algorithm is $p_f^* = p_{f_L} * p_{f_A}$, where p_{f_L} is the false positive of the current level and p_{f_A} is the false positive rate of the ancestor level.

Building procedure of the proposed algorithm is exactly the same as LBSL-BF. After building a leaf-pushed trie, all nodes in valid levels are stored in a hash table and programmed in a Bloom filter. The search procedure for the proposed algorithm is described in Algorithm 1. In this pseudo-code, one direct ancestor is only queried to verify the positive result of a current level node. However, the decision to check how many ancestor levels can be adaptively made depending on the false positive rate of a level.

The proposed algorithm makes more Bloom filter queries because it checks membership for a node and its ancestor as well in case of a Bloom filter positive in the node. Because the size of a Bloom filter is small enough to fit in an on-chip memory, the time caused by Bloom filter queries can be ignored when compared with the time caused by hash accesses. Furthermore, the proposed algorithm uses exactly the same architecture as the original algorithm.

Routing Data	N	N_T	BF size (KB)	LBSL-BF			The Proposed			
				No. of BF query	P_f	No. of trie accesses	No. of BF query	scaling factor	P_f	No. of trie accesses
Telstra	227223	576370	512	3250168	0.014	3.066	4760774	1.465	0.005	3.016
Grouptlcom	112310	411122	256	2336879	0.036	2.870	3252403	1.392	0.014	2.755
PORT80	170601	299899	256	1586942	0.019	2.623	2127905	1.341	0.007	2.557
MAE-EAST	39464	191757	128	562174	0.023	3.472	939824	1.672	0.015	3.432
MAE-WEST	14553	82156	64	213286	0.022	2.964	304959	1.430	0.011	2.904

Algorithm 1: Search process of the Proposed algorithm

Function *Search (DstAddr)*
  min = minLevel; max = maxLevel;
  while *min ≤ max* **do**
    next = (min+max)/2;
    qBF0 = queryBF(DstAddr, next);
    if *qBF0 is positive* **then**
      qBF1 = queryBF(DstAddr, next-1);
      if *qBF1 is positive* **then**
        node = accessHash(DstAddr, next);
        if *(node == prefix node)* **then**
          return node.info;
        else if *(node == internal node)* **then**
          min = next + 1;
        else
          `// false positive`
          `max = next - 1;`
        end
      else
        `// when qBF1 is negative`
        `max = next - 1;`
      end
    else
      `// when qBF0 is negative`
      `max = next - 1;`
    end
  end
end

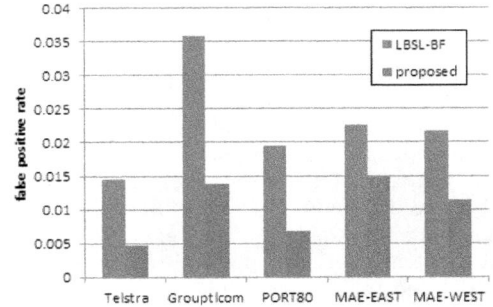

Figure 1: The false positive rate comparison

3. PERFORMANCE EVALUATION

Five actual routing tables [6] are used to compare our proposed algorithm with LBSL-BF. These routing tables have prefixes roughly from 15000 to 227000, and the number of input IP addresses used in the simulation is three times the number of prefixes in each routing table. A 64-bit cyclic redundancy check (CRC) is used to generate hash indices for a Bloom filter and a perfect hashing is assumed for the hash table. The size of the Bloom filter for simulation is chosen based on the basic size $F_s = 2^{\lceil log_2(N_T) \rceil}$, where N_T is the number of stored nodes. The number of hashing indices k for a Bloom filter is chosen according to $k_{opt} = \frac{m}{N_T} \ln 2$, where m is the size of a Bloom filter [2].

Tables 1 shows simulation results comparing our proposed algorithm with LBSL-BF. N is the number of prefixes in each routing table. The number of Bloom filter queries in each algorithm is shown in the table. A scaling factor is the number of queries in our proposed algorithm divided by the number of queries in LBSL-BF. Figures 1 shows comparisons in the false positive rate of both algorithms. The

false positive rates are significantly reduced, up to 67% in our proposed algorithm. As shown in the table, the average number of trie accesses is also reduced.

Our proposed method can be applied to various trie-based algorithms with Bloom filters without changing the architectures of the algorithms.

4. ACKNOWLEDGMENTS

This work was supported by the Mid-Career Researcher Program (2012-005945) under the National Research Foundation of Korea (NRF) grants funded by the Ministry of Education, Science and Technology and by the ITRC support program (NIPA-2013-H0301-13-1002) under the NIPA funded by the Ministry of Knowledge Economy (MKE), Korea.

5. REFERENCES

[1] M. A. Ruiz-Sanchez, E. M. Biersack, and W. Dabbous. Survey and taxonomy of ip address lookup algorithms. *IEEE Networks*, 15(2):8–23, March/April 2001.

[2] S. Dharmapurikar, P. Krishnamurthy, and D. Taylor. Longest prefix matching using bloom filters. *IEEE/ACM Trans. Networking*, 14(2):397–409, February 2006.

[3] H. Lim, K. Lim, N. Lee, and K. Park. On adding bloom filters to longest prefix matching algorithms. *IEEE Trans. Computers*, 63(2):411–423, February 2014.

[4] H. Lim and N. Lee. Survey and proposal on binary search algorithms for longest prefix match. *IEEE Communications Surverys and Tutorials*, 14(3):681–697, Third Quarte 2012.

[5] J. H. Mun, H. Lim, and C. Yim. Binary search on prefix lengths for ip address lookup. *IEEE Communications Letters*, 10(6):492–494, June 2006.

[6] http://www.potaroo.net.

Static Power Reduction in Caches using Deterministic Naps

Oluleye Olorode, Mehrdad Nourani
Department of Electrical Engineering
University of Texas at Dallas
Richardson, TX, 75080, USA
{olorode,nourani}@utdallas.edu

ABSTRACT

We propose a technique that reduces static power consumption in caches with negligible hardware overhead and no performance penalties. Our proposed architecture achieves this by deterministically lowering the power state of cache lines that are guaranteed not to be accessed in the immediate future by exploiting in-flight cache access information. We simulated our architecture using the Simplescalar and Cacti toolsets, and observed up to 92% reduction in static power consumption in SPEC2006 benchmarks with no performance penalties and minimal hardware overhead.

Categories and Subject Descriptors

B.3.2 [**Memory Structures**]: Design Styles—*associative memories, cache memories*; B.5.1 [**Register-Transfer-Level Implementation**]: Design—*memory design*

Keywords

Static Power, Cache, Drowsy Cache, Deterministic Nap

1. INTRODUCTION

Recent advances in processor performance has left memory systems behind [1], leading computer designers to explore different techniques for improving memory system performance. Specifically, processor performance is observed to increase at about 60% annually [2], while memory systems lag significantly behind at about 10% annual improvement. Existing memory systems designed with SRAMs, DRAMs and/or CAMs [3], have not been able to catch up with processor performance either.

System designers therefore turn to memory performance improvements to maintain the computational power of processors. Therefore, a common technique used to boost memory system performance is *caching*, which is achieved by storing recently used data in fast and close memory to the processor unit. These caches lower the memory system miss rate, leading to improved processor speed. As a result, large caches are often employed in memory systems to bridge the memory-processor performance gap, but they increase the area and static power consumed by the processor.

Zhang et al., observed that increased miss rates lead to more power consumption [4], therefore, cache size reduction in an attempt to save power is unacceptable. As a result, system designers have turned to other techniques to reduce the high proportion of the power consumed by caches in memory systems. Some of these techniques include the use of wider cache lines to reduce tag power and area overhead, but this leads to false sharing and fragmentation problems [5]. Phased caches [6] were introduced to reduce the dynamic power consumption, but they suffer from performance loss.

Other techniques include the use of sleep transistors to gate off supply voltage of idle logic blocks [7]. Gated V_{DD}, Dynamic Voltage Scaling (DVS) and the ABC-MT-CMOS circuit techniques were also introduced [8] to reduce static (or leakage) power consumption. Unfortunately, these techniques incur some performance degradation as a result of accesses to cache lines in low power mode.

2. DNAP ARCHITECTURE

In this paper, we propose a deterministic napping (dNap) technique that reduces static energy in caches by leveraging the DVS technique. The *dNap* technique restores full power ahead of accesses to eliminate performance degradation. We also take advantage of the fact that data RAMs do not have to be read in the first cycle of access while the cache lines of the referenced set are being transitioned to full power state. While deterministic napping builds on the idea of delaying data RAM accesses, reads can occur in the cycle after tag RAM query while hit/miss is being determined. This eliminates the need to add an extra pipestage as in Phased caches [6], especially in high performance cache architectures.

Our deterministic napping architecture, is aimed at keeping cache lines that will be used in the immediate future in a full powered state, unlike *drowsy caches* which only begins the power up sequence after DRAM access. This ensures there are no additional latencies incurred when the memory controller attempts to access a referenced cache line. We specifically focus on deterministic naps in the data RAMs only, for two main reasons. Firstly, data RAMs are known to be significantly larger than the tag RAMs, therefore, they contribute a major portion of static energy due to RAMs in memory systems. Secondly, cache accesses are non-deterministic with each access starting with a tag RAM read. Therefore, tag RAMs must always be fully powered to avoid delays due to waking up a *drowsy* tag line.

ANCS'14, October 20–21, 2014, Los Angeles, CA, USA.
ACM 978-1-4503-2839-5/14/10.
http://dx.doi.org/10.1145/2658260.2661764 .

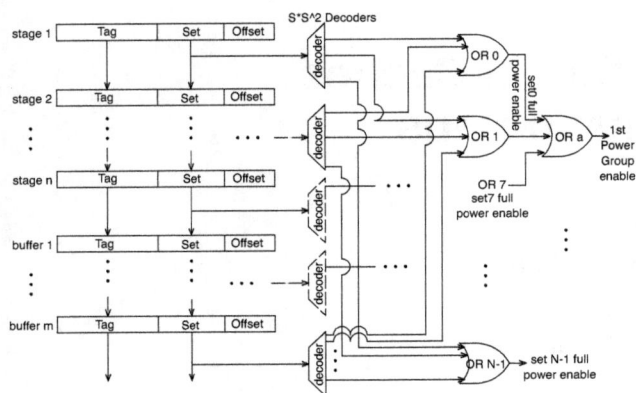

Figure 1: The dNap Power Controller Module

(L1D) cache with 32-byte lines, compared to an equivalently sized conventional cache. This trend was also observed in the instruction and unified level 2 caches. The power savings does not vary much across different associativies, because the number of fully powered cache lines only vary in the first 2 cache pipestages before hit/miss determination.

4. CONCLUSION

Our dNap architecture restores full power to referenced cache lines before access. This eliminates any additional delays due to waking drowsy lines. Only cache lines determined to be accessed in the immediate future are fully powered, while others are put in drowsy mode. As a result, we are able to significantly reduce leakage power with no cache performance degradation and minimal hardware overhead.

5. REFERENCES

[1] David A Patterson and John L Hennessy. *Computer Organization and Design: the Hardware/Software Interface.* Morgan Kaufmann, 2008.

[2] Carlos Carvalho. The Gap between Processor and Memory Speeds. In *Proc. of IEEE International Conference on Control and Automation.* ICCA, 2002.

[3] Hao Wang, Haiquan Zhao, Bill Lin, and Jun Xu. Design and Analysis of a Robust Pipelined Memory System. pages 1–9, 2010.

[4] Youtao Zhang, Jun Yang, and Rajiv Gupta. Frequent Value Locality and Value-centric Data Cache Design. In *ACM SIGOPS Operating Systems Review*, 2000.

[5] Josep Torrellas, H.S. Lam, and John L. Hennessy. False Sharing and Spatial Locality in Multiprocessor Caches. *IEEE Transactions on Computers*, 43(6):651–663, 1994.

[6] Rajesh Kannan Megalingam, K.B. Deepu, Iype P. Joseph, and Vandana Vikram. Phased Set Associative Cache Design for Reduced Power Consumption. In *2nd IEEE International Conference on Computer Science and Information Technology ICCSIT*, 2009.

[7] Michael Powell, Se-Hyun Yang, Babak Falsafi, Kaushik Roy, and T.N. Vijaykumar. Gated-Vdd: A Circuit Technique to Reduce Leakage in Deep-Submicron Cache Memories. In *Proc. of the International Symposium on Low Power Electronics and Design*, 2000.

[8] Heather Hanson, M.S. Hrishikesh, Vikas Agarwal, Stephen W Keckler, and Doug Burger. Static Energy Reduction Techniques for Microprocessor Caches. *IEEE Transactions on Very Large Scale Integration (VLSI) Systems*, 11(3):303–313, 2003.

To achieve the deterministic naps and wake-up proposed in this paper, we use a power controller module, shown in Figure 1 to track in flight cache accesses and deterministically power data RAM lines that will be accessed in the immediate future while keeping all other lines in a low power drowsy state. This is achieved by delaying data RAM access by only 1 or 2 cycles after tag RAM read, thereby ensuring there are no extra latencies incurred on data RAM access.

All outstanding accesses, in all pipe stages and buffers contribute to the overall power ON state of an individual cache line. When way information becomes available, all other ways not scheduled to be accessed are put in drowsy mode if no other member of that set needs the way ON. Figure 1 shows how $S \times 2^S$ decoders are used to determine the accessed sets in different cache stages (where S is bitwidth of the address' "Set" field) and the contribution of each stage to the final power enable of each set. The $log\ N$ of set bits of each stage are decoded to get N-bit wide one hot value, representing the specific set decoded. All bits representing a set across the cache pipe stages and buffers are ORed together to determine which set(s) must be fully powered. For example, OR0 in Figure 1 is used to *OR* all bit-0s of all decoder outputs to control set 0. Fully powered cache lines are retained in the full power state until the request has been completely processed from all pipe stages or buffers.

3. RESULTS

Our experimental results on SPEC2006 benchmarks show up to 92% power savings with our dNap cache architecture. Figure 2 shows the leakage power savings in a 32KB L1 data

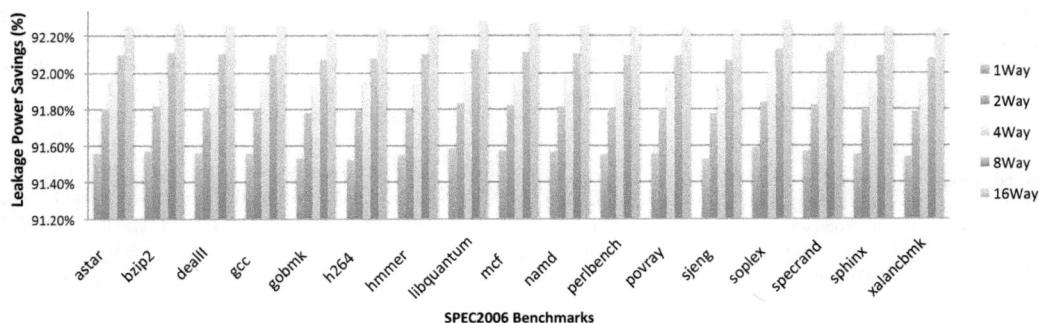

Figure 2: Static Power Savings using dNaps in L1D Cache

Secure and Efficient Key Management Protocol (SEKMP) for Wireless Sensor Networks

Majid Alshammari and Khaled Elleithy
Department of Computer Science and Engineering
University of Bridgeport
Bridgeport, CT 06604
maalsham@my.bridgeport.edu; elleithy@bridgeport.edu

ABSTRACT

Wireless sensor networks (WSNs) are used in the many critical applications, such as, military, health, and civil applications. Sometimes such applications require that the WSNs to be randomly deployed in inaccessible terrains such as a remote territory. As a result, the sensors are left unattended and become a potential target for an adversary. Therefore, we propose a highly Secure and Efficient Key Management Protocol for WSN, called SEKMP. The proposed protocol (SEKMP) adapts a new key management approach by leveraging the advantages of asymmetric cryptography and employs them in a very efficient way for delivering the session key to sensor nodes.

Categories and Subject Descriptors

E.3 [Data Encryption]: Public key cryptosystems; C.2.1 [Computer-Communication Networks]: Network Architecture and Design – *Wireless communication*

Keywords

Wireless sensor networks.

1. INTRODUCTION

Wireless sensor networks (WSN) is a growing area, and today become involved in variety of applications due to the nature of sensors nodes that are small in size and cost effective [1]. WSN in inaccessible terrains is usually left unattended. As a result, they become an easy target for an adversary. In such environments, the major security concern of WSN is the key management protocol. Thus, there are varieties of protocols in literature that utilize one or more of the following schemes: symmetric, asymmetric, or quantum cryptography for addressing the security of key management in WSN. However, the direct application of these schemes is not the best choice when it comes to limited-resource environments such as WSN. With this in mind, we came up with a very Secure and Efficient Key Management Protocol for WSN, called SEKMP. The proposed protocol (SEKMP) adapts a new key management approach by inheriting the advantages of asymmetric cryptography and employs it in very efficient way for delivering the session key to sensor nodes.

Symmetric-based key management protocols are considered more resource-efficient than Asymmetric-based key management. The downsides of these protocols are: 1) maintaining a large number of keys, 2) or dependency on intermediary nodes for the keys distribution. For example, [2] and [3]. Asymmetric-based key management protocols proved to be secure in literature, and thus,

ANCS'14, October 20–21, 2014, Los Angeles, CA, USA
ACM 978-1-4503-2839-5/14/10.
http://dx.doi.org/10.1145/2658260.2661775

they are one of the best protocols for the key distribution. The downside is, the direct application of these protocols in WSN leads to have many keys, and as a result, affecting the protocol performance. For example, in [4] the sink node must maintain n keys with sensor nodes. Where n is the number of nodes.

2. THE PROPOSED PROTOCOL

SEKMP includes three phases: Pre–deployment phase, Key distribution phase, and Key refreshment phase. Table 1 shows the notations used in the proposed protocol.

Table 1. Notations

Notation	Description
N	Number of nodes.
PU_S	Public key used in the sink node.
PR_N	Private key used in each node.
K_S	Session key used to encrypt the communication.
C	Ciphertext.
M	Plaintext.
EK (X)	Function for Encrypting X with K.
DK (X)	Function for Decrypting X with K.

2.1 Pre-deployment phase

In pre-deployment phase, a pair of keys, called public (PU_S) and private (PR_N) key is generated for the WSN. The public key (PU_S) is assigned to the sink node, whereas, the private key (PR_N) is assigned to the sensor nodes. Afterwards, the sink node has the public key (PU_S), and each sensor of the WSN has a copy of the private key (PR_N). Furthermore, building Wireless Sensor Network of N nodes requires two keys only, one for the sink node and the other one for the sensors nodes.

2.2 Key distribution phase

After the sensor nodes have been deployed, the sink node generates a random session key (K_S), and then encrypts the session key by using its key, the public key (PU_S). Then, the sink node broadcasts the following cipher message $C = EPU_S (K_S)$ to its neighbors. These neighbors broadcast the same cipher message to their neighbors if any, in multi-hop fashion until all sensor nodes get the cipher message. Since all the sensor nodes already have the private key (PR_N), they can decrypt the cipher message $C = EPU_S (K_S)$ as, $K_S = DPR_N(C)$. In the end, the entire nodes securely receive the session key (K_S). Figure 1 shows the key distribution phase.

2.3 Key refreshment phase

In the key refreshment phase, the sink node can generate a new session key (K_S) on time-basis (e.g. generating a new session key every 24 hours), or on event-basis, (e.g. generating a new session key whenever a node detects a specific event) based on the desired application, and then securely broadcasts it to the all sensor nodes as it does in the key distribution phase. The key refreshment phase makes the proposed scheme more secure because of its flexibility of generating a new session key at any time and for any reason.

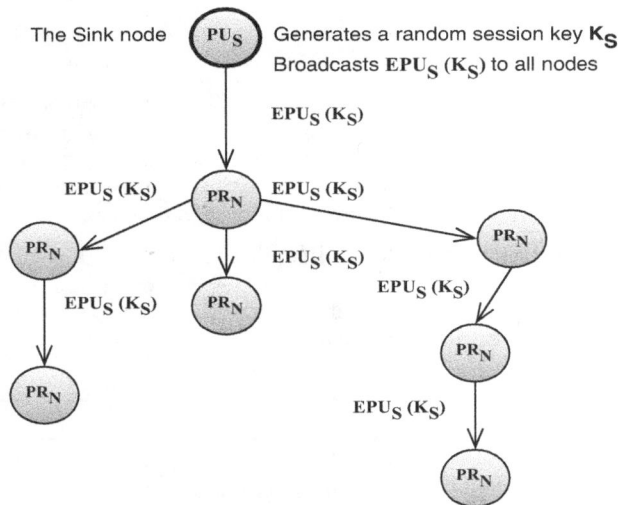

Figure 1. key distribution phase.

3. PROPOSED PROTOCOLS ANALYSIS

3.1 Security analysis
In this section, the security of the proposed protocol (SEKMP) is analyzed and investigated based on the following security services: Confidentiality, Integrity, and Authenticity.

3.1.1 Confidentiality
The proposed protocol (SEKMP) assures the confidentiality of the communication among sensors nodes by using a session key (K_S). This session key is securely delivered by utilizing the asymmetric encryption properties.

3.1.2 Integrity
The integrity is achieved in the proposed protocol by encrypting the traffic by the authorized nodes to prevent data modification. Also, the protocol can employ Message Authentication Codes (MAC) to guarantee that the message has not been altered.

3.1.3 Authentication
This security service is assured by using a pair of keys, called public (PU_S) and private (PR_N) key. Since the sink node is the only node that has the public (PU_S) key, it encrypts the session key (K_S) by the public key and broadcasts it to the sensor nodes. Once the sensor nodes successfully decrypt it by the private key (PR_N), this authenticates the sink node to the sensor nodes in the network and proves that the session key (K_S) is sent by a trusted source.

3.2 Performance analysis
In this section the performance of proposed protocol (SEKMP) is analyzed according to Efficiency, Connectivity, Scalability, and Flexibility.

3.2.1 Efficiency
The efficiency of the proposed protocol (SEKMP) is achieved by using a small number of keys compared to other protocols such as [2], [3], and [4]. It also provides an extremely secure key management protocol in the same time. As a result, SEKMP preserves the energy of the sensors. Table 2, represents the number of keys being used by the sink node/KDC, and each sensor node in SEKMP, [2], [3], and [4].

Table 2. Numbers of keys

Scheme/protocol.	Number of keys in the sink node.	Number of keys in each sensor node.
SEKMP	1	1
[2]	$\sqrt{n}$	$\sqrt{n}$
[3]	$n \times \lfloor n/2 \rfloor$	$n-1$
[4]	n	2

3.2.2 Connectivity
Connectivity of the proposed protocol is considered high because the protocol ensures that each node would receive a session key (K_S) by broadcasting an encrypted message contains that session key.

3.2.3 Scalability
The proposed protocol is able to maintain the security of the wireless sensor as the network expands, and it can be achieved by adding N nodes with an assigned private key (PR_N).

3.2.4 Flexibility
The proposed protocol is flexible due the fact that a node can be added or removed easily; even the sink node can be replaced without affecting the security of WSN. For example, a sink node can be added after it gets assigned with the public key (PU_S). Also with the same approach, a sensor node can be added after it is assigned with the private key (PR_N).

4. CONCLUSIONS
The SEKMP protocol adapts a new key management approach by leveraging the advantages of asymmetric cryptography properties and employs them in a very efficient way for delivering the session key to sensor nodes. We have simulated and compared SEKMP to existing protocols in literature in terms of the number of keys being used. Based on the simulation results, SEKMP is protocol is more efficient than those protocols. Thus, we believe that adapting SEKMP protocol addresses several security challenges of the key management in WSNs.

5. REFERENCES
[1] I. F. Akyildiz and M. C. Vuran, *Wireless sensor networks* vol. 4: John Wiley & Sons, 2010.

[2] H. Chan and A. Perrig, "PIKE: Peer intermediaries for key establishment in sensor networks," in *INFOCOM 2005. 24th Annual Joint Conference of the IEEE Computer and Communications Societies*, 2005, pp. 524-535.

[3] L.-C. Wuu, C.-H. Hung, and C.-M. Chang, "Quorum-based key management scheme in wireless sensor networks," presented at the Proceedings of the 6th International Conference on Ubiquitous Information Management and Communication, Kuala Lumpur, Malaysia, 2012.

[4] Y. Zhang, "The scheme of public key infrastructure for improving wireless sensor networks security," in *Software Engineering and Service Science (ICSESS), 2012 IEEE 3rd International Conference on*, 2012, pp. 527-530.

A Digital PUF-based IP Protection Architecture for Network Embedded Systems

Jason Xin Zheng, Miodrag Potkonjak
Computer Science Department
University of California, Los Angeles (UCLA)
Los Angeles, USA
{jxzheng,miodrag}@cs.ucla.edu

ABSTRACT

In this paper we present an architecture for a secure embedded system that is resilient to tempering and code injection attacks and offers anti-piracy protection for the software and hardware Intellectual Property (IP). We incorporate digital Physical Unclonable Functions (PUFs) in an authentication mechanism at the machine code level. The digital PUFs are used to de-obfuscate, at run time, a firmware that's issued by a central authority with very little performance and resource overhead. Each PUF is unique to the hosting device, and at the same time can be reconfigured with new seeds. The reconfigurable digital PUFs (drPUFs) have much lower risks of side-channel attacks and vastly higher number of usable challenge-response pairs, while retaining the speed and ease to implementation of digital PUFs.

1. INTRODUCTION

Software defined network (SDN) is becoming a new dominant paradigm in the networking systems for two reasons. The first reason is that SDN allows the network equipment maker to deploy systems that can respond to new conditions and traffic patterns. For example, new network features can be supported by uploading a new firmware to the routers. The second reason is that the SDN is inherently resilient against known attacks to the system, as the behavior of the network can be quickly modified to address the system-level mistakes and shortcomings. However, SDN's reprogrammability also presents a new avenue that can be exploited by the attackers. We see increasing needs for securing both the design of the original system to prevent code injection attacks and the mechanisms for the delivering of network hardware and firmware in the context of the SDN.

On the other hand, in the near future, billions more smart devices are becoming connected to the Internet; much of the added intelligence will be in the form of new software Intellectual Properties (IP). In this coming tide of "Internet of Things," parties with commercial interests have great incentives to protect the IPs that they have developed with capital investment and to prevent their smart systems from being wholesale-cloned by competitors.

In this paper we present a secure embedded system architecture that prevents third parties from tempering either the existing or a new firmware being delivered to the system, and from copying the hardware or software designs. The main idea is that while all devices share the same source code, the binaries that are delivered to each device is unique to the device and cannot be run directly by an arbitrary embedded processor. Each device is created with digital Physical Unclonable Functions (PUFs) that is used to translate, at run-time, the unique firmware into the original executable form.

2. DIGITAL RECONFIGURABLE PUF

Physical Unclonable Function (PUF) is a multi-input hardware device that produces difficult-to-predict outputs that are unique to each instantiation of identical devices. PUF is one of the most popular and widely-used hardware security primitives [1]. It is used in a variety of hardware-based security protocols ranging from generation of random numbers to secure storage of privileged information and public key cryptography [4]. However, until recently all PUFs have been analog devices and therefore greatly influenced by operational and environmental conditions and subject to change of their mapping function due to device aging. Very recently, digital PUFs have been developed that eliminate all these drawbacks of analog PUFs. Even more importantly, they are faster, require less energy, and can be easily integrated within conventional digital logic [5].

However, digital PUFs still face certain limitations. Of most importance are potential susceptibility to side-channel attacks and a relatively small number of challenge-response pairs. We address both of these limitations by using multiple Reconfigurable Digital PUFs. While one PUF is in operation mode, other idling PUFs can be continuously updated to prepare for the next activation. Collectively, a set of reconfigurable digital PUFs, by way of run-time reconfiguration, may use an exponential number of seeds to operate without incurring the timing overhead demanded of analog PUFs, and requires a potential attacker to recover all of the seeds in order for a successful attack.

Reconfigurable digital PUF (drPUF) can be used for variety of security, privacy, and trust tasks in many communication and networking applications. For example, drPUF can be used for secure reconfiguration of network elements. It can be also used for trusted data collection by unprotected sensors in sensor networks and the Internet of things.

ANCS'14, October 20–21, 2014, Los Angeles, CA, USA.
ACM 978-1-4503-2839-5/14/10,
http://dx.doi.org/10.1145/2658260.2661776.

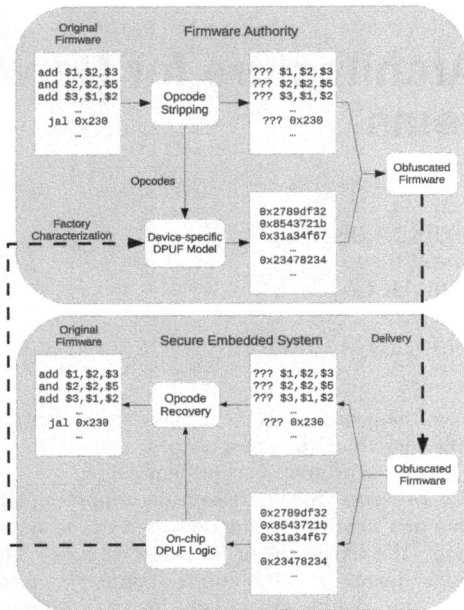

Figure 1: Protection Mechanism

A notable advantage of PUF-based IP protection to crypto-based solutions is that PUFs are truly unique devices. While cryptographic engines can employ unique keys for each device instantiation, once one device is compromised, an attacker can relatively easily make copies of the system by cloning both the hardware and the software components. Cloning PUF-based systems are inherently difficult as the operational secret is embedded in the silicon.

3. PROTECTION MECHANISM

The basic protection mechanism is illustrated in Figure 1. First, the device manufacturer characterizes the digital PUF on each device instance to build a device-specific model for the firmware authority to use. By using the device-specific models, the firmware authority can process the original firmware by stripping away all instruction opcodes and replace them with an obfuscated version that's unique to each device. Finally, when the obfuscated firmware is executed on the intended embedded system, the original instruction opcodes are recovered by using the obfuscated opcodes as challenges to the device's digital PUF logic.

The strength of the obfuscation mainly rests on two points. First, for each opcode, there exists millions of different choices to choose from as the obfuscated opcode. Therefore each occurrence of the same opcode will look completely different from another, making any statistical attack very difficult. Secondly, the on-chip PUF devices are unique physical devices that cannot be easily copied. This has great implications on code-injection attacks; an attacker who successfully attacks one of the devices cannot simply replicate the attack on another device without incurring the same amount of engineering effort for the first attack.

This mechanism is further enhanced by two facts. The first is that multiple digital PUFs are used to obfuscate the firmware. For each instruction, one active PUF is chosen based on a logical combination of the instruction's address.

Benchmark Program	Original Runtime (Seconds)	Modified Runtime (Seconds)	Performance Penalty
FFT	24281.5	25968.25	4.62%
search_lg	8706.5	8888.5	2.09%
search_sm	303.5	311.75	2.72%
bitcount	24331	24331.75	0.00%
basicmath_sm	99091	107023.75	8.01%

Table 1: Performance Penalty for ORPSoc

In addition, while one digital PUF is used for a segment of the firmware, the idling PUFs can be modified by using a different set of initialization seeds. The dynamic transformation of the digital PUFs makes it more difficult for an attacker to collect all the seeds necessary to attack the PUFs.

4. RESULTS

A demonstration and evaluation system is implemented by incorporating real-time instruction de-obfuscation with the OpenRISC Reference Platform System-on-Chip (ORPSoC) project [3]. The implementation targets a Xilinx Spartan-6 FPGA on a Digilent Atlys development board.

We show that the on-line de-obfuscation has low performance overhead by running an embedded benchmark suite based on MiBench [2]. Table 1 shows a comparison of the benchmark results running on the original and modified systems. The effects of the modification are similar to that of a slow instruction memory interface. The performance impacts are well contained within 10% as most of the memory latency is hidden by the instruction cache.

5. CONCLUSIONS

We have presented a novel use of the reconfigurable digital PUFs as instruction-level authentication devices. This mechanism offers temper protection on the firmware and prevents the software and the hardware IP from being copied by third parties with very little performance impact.

6. ACKNOWLEDGMENT

This work was supported by the NSF Award CNS-0958369, Award CNS-1059435, and Award CCF-0926127.

7. REFERENCES

[1] B. Gassend, D. Clarke, M. van Dijk, and S. Devadas. Silicon physical random functions. In *Proceedings of the 9th ACM Conference on Computer and Communications Security*, CCS '02, pages 148–160, New York, NY, USA, 2002. ACM.

[2] M. R. Guthaus et al. MiBench: A free, commercially representative embedded benchmark suite. In *IISWC*, pages 3–14, Dec. 2001.

[3] D. Lampret and J. Baxter. OpenRISC 1200 IP core secification, rev. 0.12, 2011.

[4] M. Potkonjak and V. Goudar. Public physical unclonable functions. *Proceedings of the IEEE*, 102(8):1142–1156, Aug 2014.

[5] T. Xu, J. B. Wendt, and M. Potkonjak. Secure remote sensing and communication using digital pufs. In *ANCS*, pages 1–11, 2014.

PLWAH+: A Bitmap Index Compressing Scheme based on PLWAH

Jiahui Chang, Zhen Chen*,
Wenxun Zheng, Yuhao Wen, Junwei Cao
Research Institute of Information Technology,
Tsinghua University
Tsinghua National Lab for Information Science and
Technologies (TNList), Beijing, China
zhenchen@tsinghua.edu.cn
changjh13@mails.tsinghua.edu.cn

Wen-Liang Huang
China Unicom Groups Labs
China Unicom Groups
Beijing, China
wlhuang@chinaunicom.cn

ABSTRACT
Archiving of the Internet traffic is essential for analyzing network events in the field of network security and network forensics. The bitmap index is widely used to achieve fast searching in archival traffic data requiring a large storage space. As current state-of-art, WAH, PLWAH and COMPAX are proposed for compressing bitmap indexes. In this paper, a new bitmap index compression scheme, named PLWAH+ (Position List Word Aligned Hybrid Plus), is introduced, based on PLWAH. With less storage consumption, PLWAH+ is more suitable for indexing in large-scale and high-speed network traffic.

Categories and Subject Descriptors
E.4 [**Coding and Information Theory**]: Data compaction and compression; C.2.3 [**Network Operations**]: Network monitoring.

Keywords
Internet traffic, bitmap coding, bitmap index, data retrieval, traffic analysis, traffic forensic.

1. INTRODUCTION
Indexing is the core technology underlying answering queries on a large-scale archival data. Bitmap index is designed for quick retrieval of archival Internet traffic data. A bitmap index example is shown in *Table 1*.

Bitmap indexing uses a bit vector to indicate the certain values of the index, which was firstly proposed by P. O'Neil in the design of Model 204 commercial database. [6-7]

Table 1   An example of the Bitmap index

RowID	column	Bitmap			
		=1	=2	=3	=4
1	1	1	0	0	0
2	2	0	1	0	0
3	4	0	0	0	1
4	3	0	0	1	0
5	2	0	1	0	0
6	4	0	0	0	1

ANCS'14, October 20–21, 2014, Los Angeles, CA, USA
ACM 978-1-4503-2839-5/14/10.
http://dx.doi.org/10.1145/2658260.2661777

The technologies used in Bitmap index database includes bitmap indexing [4], bitmap compression and classification. Currently, the state-of-art bitmap index compression algorithms are BBC [1], WAH [3], PLWAH [2], COMPAX [8], SECOPAX [9] etc.

Based on the observation of the result of the WAH performance, this paper improves upon existing work by offering a lossless bitmap compression technique that outperforms PLWAH on both storage and performance perspective. Especially, we propose the PLWAH+ (Position List Word Aligned Hybrid Plus) bitmap compression scheme.

2. PLWAH+ CODING SCHEME
2.1 Definitions for Chunks
In PLWAH+ compression scheme, a bit vector is divided into chunks of 31 bits to ensure they are fit into the L1 cache. At first, we will classify each chunk into different types. Types for a chunk are defined as below:

0-Filled Chunk: If the 31 bits of a chunk are all '0', we call the chunk 0-Filled Chunk.

1-Filled Chunk: If the 31 bits of a chunk are all '1', we call the chunk 1-Filled Chunk.

Literal Chunk: If a chunk cannot be classified into 0-Filled Chunk or 1-Filled Chunk, it is called a Literal Chunk.

Dirty Bit: If only a few bits in a Literal Chunk are different from Filled Chunk, they are all called Dirty Bit. Furthermore, they can be divided into 1-Dirty Bit (1 bit) and 0-Dirty Bit (0 bit).

NI Chunk: If a Chunk is a Literal Chunk with less than 4 Dirty Bit, it is called a NI Chunk. The NI Chunk can be divided into two parts as follows:

NI-0 Chunk: If a Chunk is nearly identical to the '0' sequence with less than 4 1-Dirty Bits, it is called a NI-0 Chunk.

NI-1 Chunk: If a Chunk is nearly identical to the '1' sequence with less than 4 0-Dirty Bits, it is called a NI-1 Chunk.

2.2 Definitions for Codewords
After the categorization of the chunks, we begin to encode the bitmap roughly into the codewords as shown below:

0-Fill: If there are some continuous 0-Filled Chunks, replace them with a 0-Fill codeword which indicates the number of the replaced chunks.

1-Fill: If there are some continuous 1-Filled chunks, replace them with a 1-Fill codeword which indicates the number of the replaced chunks.

Obviously, 0-Fill and 1-Fill are two types of Fill.

Last but not least, we do the ultimate encoding based on rough encoding as shown below:

LF: For a continuous 2-tuple in the sequence, if the first element is a NI Chunk and the second codeword is a Fill, this 2-tuple is encoded into a LF codeword, including NI-0-0-Fill, NI-1-0-Fill, NI-0-1-Fill, and NI-1-1-Fill.

FL: For a continuous-2-tuple in the sequence, if the first element is a Fill and the second codeword is a NI Chunk, this 2-tuple is encoded into a FL codeword, including 0-Fill-NI-0, 0-Fill-NI-1, 1-Fill-NI-0, and 1-Fill-NI-1.

Literal: If a Literal Chunk survives after the encoding procedure with FL and LF, it's called a Literal codeword.

So far, the whole process of PLWAH+ compression has finished. The result is composed of Fill, Literal, LF, and FL codewords.

2.3 Bit-Represented CodeBook

In this section, the final result of every codeword is represented by 4 bytes.

As for Literal, we add a '0' before the 31 bits as a flag for identifying.

And it is easy to find that a Fill word has 23 bits for storing a counter. However, only the lowest byte will be used later in the experiment.

In the FL and LF codewords, the first five bits which represent first dirty bit position can't be zero while, as is shown in *Figure 1*, the second, third and fourth are flexible. So the number of the dirty bits in the NI Chunk is no more than four. The counter of the FL and LF words can be represented within 8 bits, corresponding to the segment of 3,968 (128*31) bit sequence.

The details are shown in *Figure 1*:

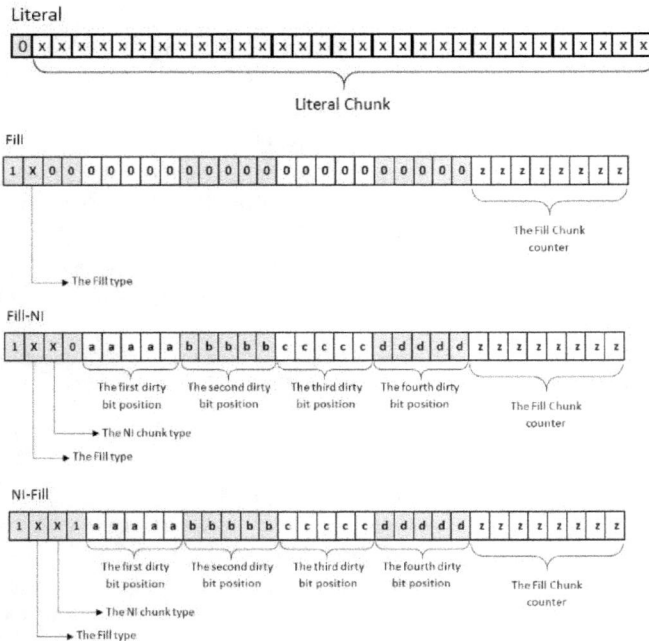

Figure 1 Codebook

3. EXPERIMENT AND RESULTS

In our experiments, the network flow data from CAIDA [5] is parsed using *libpcap* library, and the fields named source IP, source port, destination IP, destination port and protocol ID are extracted from the *pcap* archive, all of which are saved into a plain text file. The row ID of that file is the same as the record ID.

The original data size is 13,581,810 multiplied by 14 bytes, equaling to 47,536,335 Dwords (64 bits). The final compressed files sum up to 20,516,573 Dwords. As shown in *Figure 2*, we can see that the result of PLWAH+ reduces about 3% of the storage comparing to PLWAH and the compression ratio reaches roughly 43% with about 20% reduction of the amount of the literal words.

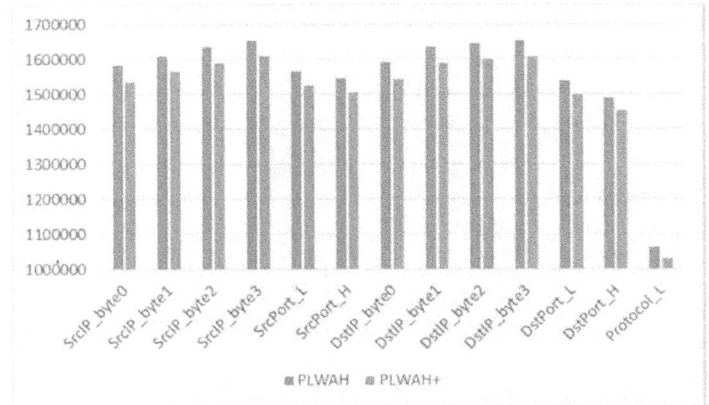

Figure 2 Used storage in Dword (64bits)

4. CONCLUSION

In this paper, we mainly discuss the PLWAH+ which is typical and more suitable for the modern CPU architecture. The concept of the NI-1 chunk and the LF word which are not considered in PLWAH makes PLWAH+ more suitable for indexing in large-scale and high-speed streaming network data.

5. REFERENCES

[1] G. Antoshenkov, Byte-aligned bitmap compression, in: DCC'95, p. 476, 1995.

[2] F. Deli`ege and T. B. Pedersen. Position list word aligned hybrid: optimizing space and performance for compressed bitmaps. EDBT '10, 2010.

[3] Wu, Kesheng, Ekow J. Otoo, and ArieShoshani. "Compressing bitmap indexes for faster search operations." SSDBM'02, pp. 99-108, 2002.

[4] Van Schaik, Sebastiaan et al. "A memory efficient reachability data structure through bit vector compression." ACM SIGMOD' 2011, pp.913-924, 2011.

[5] CAIDA, www.caida.org.

[6] O'Neil, Patrick E. "Model 204 architecture and performance." High Performance Transaction Systems. Springer Berlin Heidelberg, 39-59, 1989.

[7] O'Neil, Patrick, and DallanQuass. "Improved query performance with variant indexes." ACM SIGMOD Record, vol. 26, no. 2, pp. 38-49, 1997.

[8] Fusco, F., Stoecklin, M. P., and Vlachos, M. Net-fli: on-the-fly compression, archiving and indexing of streaming network traffic. Proceedings of the VLDB Endowment, 3(1-2), 1382-1393, 2010.

[9] Yuhao Wen, et al., SECOMPAX A bitmap index compression algorithm, ICCCN HotData'14, Shanghai, China, 2014.

Impact of the End-System and Affinities on the Throughput of High-Speed Flows

Nathan Hanford, Vishal Ahuja,
Matthew K Farrens, and Dipak Ghosal
Department of Computer Science
University of California
Davis, CA
{nhanford, vahuja, mkfarrens,
dghosal}@ucdavis.edu

Mehmet Balman,
Eric Pouyoul, and Brian Tierney
ESnet
Lawrence Berkeley Labs
Berkeley, CA
mbalman@lbl.gov, lomax@es.net,
bltierney@es.net

ABSTRACT

Network throughput is scaling-up to higher data rates while processors are scaling-out to multiple cores. In order to optimize high speed data transfer into multicore end-systems, network adapter offloads and performance tuning have received a great deal of attention. However, much of this attention is focused on how to set the tuning parameters and which offloads to select for higher performance and not why they do (or do not) work. In this study we have attempted to address two issues that impact the data transfer performance. First is the impact of the processor core affinity (or core binding) which determines the choice of which processor core or cores handle certain tasks in a network- or I/O-heavy application running on a multicore end-system. Second issue is the impact of Ethernet pause frames which provides a link layer flow control in addition to the end-to-end flow control provided by TCP. The goal of our research is to delve deeper into why these tuning suggestions and this offload exist, and how they affect the end-to-end performance and efficiency of a single, large TCP flow.

Categories and Subject Descriptors

C.2.2 [**Computer-Communication Networks**]: Network Protocols; C.2.4 [**Distributed Systems**]: Client/server; C.2.5 [**Local and Wide-Area Networks**]: Internet (e.g., TCP/IP); C.2.m [**Miscellaneous**]: Network performance analysis

Keywords

40 Gbps Network, ESnet, Multi-core Affinitization, End-system Performance, high-speed network, Flow Affinity, Application Affinity, RPS, RFS

1. INTRODUCTION

Several physical constraints have contributed to a processing core to hit a clock speed "wall". On the other hand, the data rates in optical fiber networks have continued to increase, with the physical realities of scattering, absorption and dispersion being

ANCS'14, October 20–21, 2014, Los Angeles, CA, USA.
ACM 978-1-4503-2839-5/14/10.
http://dx.doi.org/10.1145/2658260.2661772.

ameliorated by better optics and precision equipment. A similar situation holds for short-range copper networks with better quality conductors and better shielding. TCP is a reliable, connection-oriented protocol which guarantees in-order delivery of data from a sender to a receiver. There is a certain amount of sophistication required to implement the functionalities of the TCP protocol which are all instrumented in the end-system since it is an end-to-end protocol. As a result, most of the efficiencies that improve upon current TCP implementations fall into two categories. First, there are offloads which attempt to push TCP functions at (or along with) the lower layers of the protocol stack (usually hardware, firmware, or drivers) in order to achieve greater efficiency at the transport layer. Second, there are tuning parameters, which place more sophistication at the upper layers (software, systems, and systems management). Within the category of offloads, this work focuses on pause frames interesting. Pause frames in Ethernet support link layer flow control by allowing a receiver to inform the upstream node or router to pause sending data as it requires more time to process data that it has already received.

Within the category of tuning parameters, this work focuses on affinity. Affinity (or core binding) is essentially the decision regarding which resources to use on which processor in a networked multiprocessor system. Message Passing in the Linux network receive process in modern systems principally allows for two possibilities: First, there is interrupt processing (usually with coalescing). In this process, the NIC interrupts the procesor once it has received a certain number of packets. Then, the NIC transmits the packets to the processor through DMA and the NIC driver and the OS kernel continue the protocol processing until the data is ready for the application [2]. Second, there is NIC polling (known in Linux as the New API for networks (NAPI)), where the Kernel polls the NIC to see if there is any network data to receive, and if there is, processes the data up the network stack as mentioned above. In either case, there are two types of affinity: 1) Flow affinity which determines the core that is interrupted to process the network flow and 2) Application affinity which determines the core that executes the application process that receives the network data. Flow affinity is set by modifying the hexadecimal core descriptor in /proc/sys/<irq#>/smp_affinity. Application affinity can be set through taskset or similar tools.

2. EXPERIMENTAL SETUP

There are many valid arguments in favor of various NIC offloads. Furthermore, NIC manufacturers typically offer many tuning suggestions to get the most out of the high-performance hardware. However, light is rarely shed on the empirical rationale for these tuning suggestions and offloads. A valuable resource for tuning parameters obtained from careful experimentation on

ESnet's 100 Gbps testbed is available at http://fasterdata.es.net. ESnet has published a number of papers detailing the experiments that have led to their tuning suggestions. For our experiments, we considered data transfer between two identical 12-core Sandy Bridge host with 40 Gbps NICs connected over the 100 Gbps ESnet testbed. We used iperf3 in zero-copy mode to exhaustively test all 144 combinations of Flow and Application affinity with pause frames on and then off. Finally, we used Oprofile on the receiver to monitor a variety of hardware counters in order to identify the cause of the data transfer performance.

3. SUMMARY OF RESULTS

With pause frames on, we observed packet losses at the upstream router. These losses resulted in TCP congestion control to be invoked which contributed to large throughput variance in the experimental runs. It should be noted that this is a somewhat unusual scenario because of the "quiet" nature of the testbed. Specifically, there was no other traffic through the router and as a result it could dedicate a large buffer to the single flow. However, it still serves as a reminder to avoid setting pause frames on in pause frame enabled routers as they could lead to buffer bloat and potential losses.

Both our current and previous work [3] concluded that there exists three different performance categories corresponding to the following affinitization: 1) Same Socket Same Core (i.e., both Flow and Application affinitized to the same core) reaches a throughput of around 20 Gbps; 2) Different Sockets (thus Different Cores) reaches a throughput of around 28 Gbps; and 3) Same Socket Different Cores reaches a throughput of around 39 Gbps. While changing the OS (from CentOS running a 2.6 kernel to Fedora running a 3.13 kernel) and updating the NIC driver improved the performance, the relative performance for the three affinitization settings remained the same.

Oprofile hardware counter results showed that the main resource consumed was the CPU. This was reflected both in terms of the instructions retired and unhalted clock cycles. When these counters were divided by the amount of data transferred, the efficiency of different affinitizations could be compared. This is shown in Figure 1 for the case with pause frames on. The case where flow and application were affinitized to the same core had by far the worst efficiency measured in terms of CPU-utilization per Gigabyte transferred. Due to the correlation between cache and memory transactions and

Instructions Retired / Throughput (Gbps)

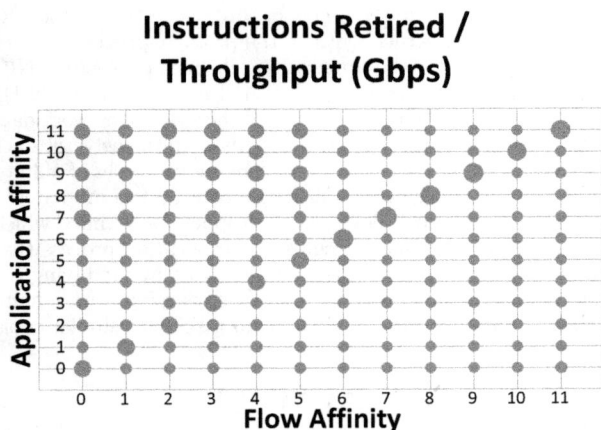

Figure 1: The width of the bubbles represents the amount of instructions retired divided by the throughput in Gbps for each of the 144 tests.

CPU utilization, it appears that the NIC driver could be spinning while waiting for memory. A possible explanation is that using two different cores on the same socket doubles the amount of L1 cache available to the NIC driver and the application in comparison to the case when they are both on affinitized to the same core.

4. CONCLUSION AND FUTURE WORK

One of the most important results of the clock speed wall, (or the "hiatus" of Moore's law) is that the line between intra-system and inter-system communication is rapidly blurring. For one processor core to communicate with another, data must traverse an intra-system (on-chip) network. For large-scale data replication and coherency, data must traverse a WAN. How are these networks meaningfully different? WAN data continues to become less of a limiting factor, and routers and networks are becoming more reliable and more easily reconfigurable. At the same time, intra-system networks are becoming more complex (due to scale-out systems and virtualization), and perhaps less reliable (as energy conservation occasionally demands that parts of a chip could be slowed down, or turned off altogether). When discussing affinitization, it becomes obvious that despite these changes, distance and locality still matter, whether the network is "large" or "small". Therefore, in the future, the most efficient solution may be not only to integrate a NIC onto the processor die [4], but perhaps even integrate the functionality with existing I/O structures, such as the north bridge. However, the feasibility of doing so may be years away.

In the meantime, other NICs and especially, other NIC drivers are being tested in similar ways to see if results are similar, and if generalizations can be made. The relatively recent advancement in NIC drivers that automatically switch between interrupt coalescing and NAPI is also being tested. Finally, results for practical, multi-stream TCP, and UDT GridFTP transfers are being tested along these lines. One future goal could be to implement a lightweight middleware tool that could optimize affinitization on a larger scale, extending the work that has been carried out on Cache Aware Affinitization Daemon [1].

5. ACKNOWLEDGMENTS

This research used resources of the ESnet Testbed, which is supported by the Office of Science of the U.S. Department of Energy under contract DE-AC02-05CH11231. This research was also supported by NSF grant CNS-0917315.

6. REFERENCES

[1] AHUJA, V., FARRENS, M., AND GHOSAL, D. Cache-aware affinitization on commodity multicores for high-speed network flows. In *Proceedings of the eighth ACM/IEEE symposium on Architectures for networking and communications systems* (2012), ACM, pp. 39–48.

[2] BENVENUTI, C. *Understanding Linux Network Internals.* O'Reilly Media, 2005.

[3] HANFORD, N., AHUJA, V., BALMAN, M., FARRENS, M. K., GHOSAL, D., POUYOUL, E., AND TIERNEY, B. Characterizing the impact of end-system affinities on the end-to-end performance of high-speed flows. In *Proceedings of the Third International Workshop on Network-Aware Data Management* (New York, NY, USA, 2013), NDM '13, ACM, pp. 1:1–1:10.

[4] LIAO, G., ZHU, X., AND BHUYAN, L. A new server i/o architecture for high speed networks. In *High Performance Computer Architecture (HPCA), 2011 IEEE 17th International Symposium on* (2011), IEEE, pp. 255–265.

Author Index

www.ingramcontent.com/pod-product-compliance
Lightning Source LLC
Chambersburg PA
CBHW061354210326
41598CB00035B/5984